Cambridge Studies in American Literature and Culture

Landscape and written expression in Revolutionary America

Cambridge Studies in American Literature and Culture

Editor

Albert Gelpi, Stanford University

Advisory Board

Nina Baym, University of Illinois, Champaign–Urbana
Sacvan Bercovitch, Harvard University
Richard Bridgman, University of California, Berkeley
David Levin, University of Virginia
Joel Porte, Harvard University
Mike Weaver, Oxford University

Other books in the series

Robert Zaller: *The Cliffs of Solitude*
Peter Conn: *The Divided Mind*
Patricia Caldwell: *The Puritan Conversion Narrative*
Stephen Fredman: *Poet's Prose*
Charles Altieri: *Self and Sensibility in Contemporary American Poetry*
John McWilliams: *Hawthorne, Melville, and the American Character*
Barton St. Armand: *Emily Dickinson and Her Culture*
Mitchell Robert Breitwieser: *Cotton Mather and Benjamin Franklin*
Albert von Frank: *The Sacred Game*
Beth McKinsey: *Niagara Falls*
Marjorie Perloff: *The Dance of the Intellect*
Albert Gelpi: *Wallace Stevens*
Karen Rowe: *Saint and Singer*
Richard Gray: *Writing the South*
Lawrence Buell: *New England Literary Culture*
Ann Kibbey: *The Interpretation of Material Shapes in Puritanism*
Sacvan Bercovitch and Myra Jehlen: *Ideology and Classic American Literature*
Steven Axelrod and Helen Deese: *Robert Lowell*
Jerome Loving: *Emily Dickinson*
Brenda Murphy: *American Realism and American Drama*
Brook Thomas: *Cross-Examinations of Law and Literature*
Lynn Keller: *Remaking it New*
Paul Giles: *Hart Crane: The Contexts of 'The Bridge'*
David Wyatt: *The Fall into Eden*
George Dekker: *The American Historical Romance*
Lothar Hönninghausen: *William Faulkner*
Tony Tanner: *Scenes of Nature, Signs of Men*

Landscape and written expression in Revolutionary America
The world turned upside down

ROBERT LAWSON-PEEBLES

Department of English, University of Aberdeen

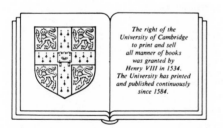

The right of the
University of Cambridge
to print and sell
all manner of books
was granted by
Henry VIII in 1534.
The University has printed
and published continuously
since 1584.

CAMBRIDGE UNIVERSITY PRESS

CAMBRIDGE
NEW YORK   NEW ROCHELLE
MELBOURNE   SYDNEY

Published by the Press Syndicate of the University of Cambridge
The Pitt Building, Trumpington Street, Cambridge CB2 1RP
32 East 57th Street, New York, NY 10022, USA
10 Stamford Road, Oakleigh, Melbourne 3166, Australia

© Cambridge University Press 1988

First published 1988

Printed in Great Britain at
the University Press, Cambridge

British Library cataloguing in publication data

Lawson-Peebles, Robert
Landscape and written expression in
revolutionary America: the world turned
upside down. – (Cambridge studies in
American literature and culture).
1. United States – Civilization – To 1783
2. United States – Civilization – 1783–
1865
I. Title
973.3   E163

Library of Congress cataloguing in publication data

Lawson-Peebles, Robert.
Landscape and written expression in revolutionary America: the
world turned upside down / Robert Lawson-Peebles.
p.   cm. – (Cambridge studies in American literature and
culture)
Bibliography: p.
Includes index
ISBN 0 521 34647 9
1. American literature – Revolutionary period, 1775–1783 – History
and criticism.   2. American literature – 1783–1850 – History and
criticism.   3. Landscape in literature.   4. United States – History –
Revolution, 1775–1783 – Literature and the revolution.   I. Title.
II. Series.
PS195.L35L38   1988   87-18777

ISBN 0 521 34647 9

SE

For my parents

Contents

List of illustrations   *page* ix
Acknowledgements   xi

Prologue   An America of the imagination   1
   Text and terrain   1
   New found land   7
   Unsung hillocks   17

1   The triumph of Redcoatism   22
   The hallucination of displaced terrain   22
   The world turned upside down   29
   An asylum in the wilderness   44
   Innovations and convulsions   57

2   A republic of dreams   63
   Jedidiah Morse and American geography   64
   Noah Webster and American language   73
   Benjamin Rush and American medicine   84

3   Dreary wastes and awful solitude   100
   Crèvecœur's barnyard   100
   Philip Freneau's ruined island   109
   Hugh Henry Brackenridge's cave   122

4   The natural limit of a republic   135
   An uncompounded republick   135
   The flourishing village   143
   A new world of woods   151

5   Thomas Jefferson and the spacious field of imagination   165
        The library on the mountain   165
        The vaunted scene of Europe   170
        The hidden country   175
        The focus of innovation   183
        The dictionary in the garden   188

6   The Lewis and Clark Expedition   196
        Writing the West   196
        A land of plenty   200
        Scenes of visionary enchantment   203
        A certain fatality   213
        The region of fable   222

7   The excursive imagination of Charles Brockden Brown   231
        Various and diffusive reading   232
        The metaphysic wilderness   237
        Scenes of folly, depravity and cunning   243
        Passage into new forms   248
        Confined views   253

Epilogue   The solid ground of Edgar Allan Poe   263

Appendix   The construction and reconstruction of the Lewis and
            Clark Journals   278

Notes   281
List of works consulted   325
Index   371

Illustrations

1 John Trumbull, *The Surrender of Cornwallis* (1824)
  (National Geographic Society Photographer.
  Courtesy, U.S. Capitol Historical Society)   29
2 'A singular species of Monkeys', from *The Scots Magazine*
  (1770)   (Courtesy, Aberdeen University Library)   38
3 William Hogarth, *Hudibras' First Adventure* (1726)
  (Courtesy, Aberdeen University Library)   210
4 Sir Edwin Landseer, *Man Proposes, God Disposes* (1863–64)
  (Courtesy, Royal Holloway and Bedford New College)   210
5 Claude Lorraine, *Landscape with Apollo and the Muses* (1652)
  (Courtesy, National Gallery of Scotland)   232

Acknowledgements

This project has taken more than ten years and has crossed a number of geographical and disciplinary boundaries. It has involved me in many debts. It is a great pleasure to acknowledge them. My one regret is that the book does not adequately reflect all the help and encouragement I have received.

The book has been lucky in its landscapes. It was conceived in the pastoral setting of Sussex University and concluded in the baroque splendour of Schloss Leopoldskron, Salzburg. In the intervening years the work was undertaken at St Catherine's College and Christ Church, Oxford; at Princeton; and at Aberdeen. I thank these institutions for their support and my friends and colleagues for their advice. An early version of chapter 6 appeared in *Over Here* (1982); I was glad of the opportunity to try out some ideas in a more public way.

The groundwork for the project was laid during a fruitful year at Princeton. I am most grateful to the Board of Nominators for recommending me to a Procter Fellowship at that University in 1978/79; and to the Carnegie Trust for funding a return visit in the Summer of 1984. (The Carnegie Trust also paid for the illustrations to this book.) Princeton's Firestone Library has magnificent holdings and a splendid staff. It was a privilege to work there, and at several other institutions. I am indebted to the Hawthorne–Longfellow Library, Bowdoin College; to the libraries of Yale University; to the New York Public Library; the American Philosophical Society; the Library of Congress; the University of Virginia Library; and to the Missouri Historical Society. The visit to the last institution was funded by a Princeton English Department grant kindly arranged by Walton Litz; and while in St Louis I enjoyed the lavish hospitality of Daniel Shea and Washington University.

In the Old World I made extensive use of the Bodleian Library, the

British Library and the National Library of Scotland. All were helpful and efficient; but none more so, I am delighted to say, than the library of my home institution. The Queen Mother Library at Aberdeen is a model of a good university library. The response of its staff to my sometimes odd, occasionally hilarious requests has been consistently constructive, always prompt – indeed, oldworldly in the best sense.

The people who, over the years, have had a hand in the preparation of this book are far too many to name. They are all remembered individually even if they have had to be named collectively. There are a few debts, however, which cannot be dealt with in this way. I am thinking specifically of the Sydnor family of Short Hills, NJ, and of Sally Deutsch and Kim Smith for hospitality and good talk; of Larzer Ziff and Mike Weaver, Peter Conrad and John Whitley, Albert Gelpi and Jay Fliegelman for their encouragement; of Paul Schlicke, at once the kindest and most constructive of critics; and of Marcus Cunliffe who, some fifteen years ago, admitted a nervous, supposedly 'mature' student to Sussex University. He could hardly have anticipated the longstanding burden he was assuming. I hope he does not regret it.

An America of the imagination

The landscape and the language are the same.
And we ourselves are language and are land.

Conrad Aiken[1]

TEXT AND TERRAIN

In outline, the basis of my argument is simple, even obvious. It rests upon a correspondence between the political and cultural republics which form part of that entity we call the United States of America. I want to argue that, just as the political identity of the country was created out of a quarrel with the British administration, so its cultural identity was initiated in a wider quarrel with Old World attitudes towards the New. If elements of the political identity of the Republic are to be found in the Declaration of Independence, with its complaints against George III, then elements of the cultural identity of the Republic may be found, although in a less clearly defined way, in a series of documents which draw upon a quarrel with the Old World and develop that quarrel.

The process of my argument is straightforward, too. Specifically, I am interested in the ways in which the Revolutionary generation wrote about American terrain. I will suggest that the strongly environmentalist roots of the debate between the Old and New Worlds left American writers with a deeply ambivalent endowment. On the one hand, it blessed them with a particularly assertive sense of the relation between nature and culture. On the other hand, it cursed them with a sophisticated means of exploring and expressing the relationship. The endowment was a blessing because it gave them an immediately accessible and unifying way of asserting nationality. It was a curse because the sophistication was European rather than American. It left American writers poorly equipped to understand the ways in which their environment differed from Europe. At its worst, the endowment alienated them from America and drew them back into an identification

1

with Europe. At its best, it indicated the directions which later American writers would develop.

The greater part of my argument proceeds through a series of case-studies. Initially I chose this method because it provided me with a convenient means of organising a large body of material. As the work proceeded two greater advantages became apparent. First, the method allows me to pay due attention to the individuality of each writer and to the development of his career. It permits me to range widely, both temporally and generically. In chapter 2 I look in turn at Jedidiah Morse's geography, Noah Webster's lexicography and Benjamin Rush's medicine. Rush died in 1813. Morse died in 1826, the year which, with its coincidental deaths of Jefferson and John Adams, is normally taken to signal the demise of the Revolutionary generation. Webster died in 1843, his pessimism revealing the largest gap between the initial utopian expectations he shared with his contemporaries, and his distaste at the distended and democratic Republic which had emerged.

Secondly, the case-study method reveals, I hope, that the careers of my chosen figures had a number of common features. Whatever the specific differences between them, they were united in their expectations of the new Republic. Broadly, those expectations were projected in images of an Edenic landscape which were part of their Old World inheritance. When their hopes were not fulfilled, in almost all cases their images of America changed. They now projected a landscape which was malign and unstable. These images, too, had been part of the Old World's gift to the New. When they adopted pejorative images of the terrain, therefore, American writers did not extend their perceptions of their environment. They simply turned them upside down.

My method may initially prompt the complaint that the reader is being forced to sit through the same movie several times. I hope that the complaint will not be justified. The case-studies are intended to be accretive rather than repetitive. The discussion of Morse, Webster and Rush in chapter 2 aims to set the context for chapter 3, which explores the images of American terrain contained in the fictional work of Crèvecœur, Freneau and Brackenridge. The case-studies, furthermore, are set within a historical framework. Chapter 1 discusses the debate over the significance of the New World which preceded and informed the Revolution, and analyses the responses of American writers and the changes in their perceptions of the environment. Chapter 1 therefore provides the setting for the detailed discussions of chapters 2 and 3. Chapter 4 takes up the narrative. If the American writers discussed in earlier chapters were retreating from America, the nation as a whole was advancing further into its embrace. Chapter 4 surveys the tensions which arose over westward expansion, and which were exacerbated by the Louisiana Purchase.

Jefferson was the architect of the document which created the Republic. He was the architect of the Purchase which doubled the size of the Republic. His writings are discussed in chapter 5, an extended case-study which suggests that they present a paradigm of the imperial ordering drives of republican utopianism. Jefferson was not subject to the disillusion which was a feature of the later work of the figures previously discussed. The disillusion is to be found, rather, in the writing of his lieutenant, Meriwether Lewis, who is the subject of chapter 6. The Lewis and Clark Expedition was the tangible expression of Jefferson's imperial vision. Lewis's journals record the failure of republican order, mapped in images similar to those noted earlier. They also show that he went further, beyond disillusion. Most writers conceived American terrain within the terms of the debate initiated in the Old World. As Lewis moved westwards into the Rockies, he moved outside the language of that debate, and into silence. The ordering devices of his prose broke down in the face of a terrain with which they could not cope. That breakdown heralds the first appearance of an important shift away from European environmental attitudes.

Or almost the first. I want to suggest that the breakdown in Lewis's prose was anticipated in the fiction of Charles Brockden Brown. If the work of Jefferson and Lewis collectively provides a paradigm and development of the environmental attitudes of the Revolutionary generation, the work of Brown provides a more clear and concise paradigm, and a firmer development. Brown's work sums up the material I have discussed earlier, and points the way forward. Indeed, if it is possible to talk of an identifiably 'American' culture (always a perilous proceeding), then Brown's 'western' novel *Edgar Huntly* represents the birth of an element of that culture. In chapter 7 I try to show why.

In undertaking this work I have attempted to harness two different but related disciplines. One could be called perceptual geography. The other, for want of a better phrase, is textual analysis. Perceptual geography has a convenient starting point in Carl Sauer's 1925 essay 'The morphology of landscape'. Sauer proposed the marriage of phenomenology and geography when he suggested that elements in a terrain should not be examined in isolation, but in relation to other elements and to the shaping agency of man. Such an examination resulted in what he called 'the cultural landscape'. A number of geographers have developed Sauer's initial thesis to emphasise the role of our preconceptions in the way we look at the terrain. They have shown me that, in the words of James Wreford Watson:

> Geography is made . . . largely in terms of the country we *perceive,* or are *conditioned* to perceive: *the country of the mind.*[2]

I have diverged from the perceptual geographers in one respect. It concerns the change in our beliefs about the environment. As a result of the intellectual currents of which perceptual geography is a part, we now believe, to a surprising extent, that our preconceptions shape what we see. Although I shall be trying to show that this is a fundamental human activity, the Revolutionary generation would not have agreed with me. They were not so cheerfully subjectivist. They thought that the energy flowed in the opposite direction; that the environment shaped human beings. This belief did not stop them from trying to alter the environment. It did mean that terrestrial structures and climatic conditions carried for them a freight of significance that we now tend to dismiss, save in our more doomladen moods. Rolling, sunlit farmland was thus the mark of God's approving smile. A dark, beast-infested wood was evidence of his wrath. I would not want to push too far the distinction between the Revolutionary generation and ourselves, since I would not wish to deny the line which can be drawn from Locke to the phenomenologists, but perhaps I can sum it up by suggesting that, if we live in a world of forms, they lived in a world of meanings.

I cannot, of course, avoid seeing the past through the spectacles of the present. (Henry James's Mrs Wix called her glasses 'straighteners'; would that we all had her moral certitude.) I can however try to acknowledge the refraction by adopting a pedantry that the perceptual geographers may not accept. The word 'landscape' has become so diluted that it is now used interchangeably with other words denoting land. I shall *not* use it in this sense. A variety of words – land, terrain, environment – will be applied to the land as object. 'Landscape' will be limited to mean the land as percept, Watson's 'country of the mind'. Although I am restricting the definition of 'landscape' it will quickly become apparent that it is a flexible term. Sometimes the American landscape is opaque, like Benjamin Rush's Philadelphia miasma; at others it is as invisible as Jefferson's grid. It can be as widespread as Timothy Dwight's globe-encircling empire, or as confined as a Brockden Brown cupboard. The landscape, in short, is as various as the individual mind. At times it almost fits the contours of the land. Sometimes it fits them not at all.

In limiting the definition of 'landscape' I am almost returning the word to one of its earlier meanings: a pictorial representation of scenery.[3] The overwhelming majority of the representations discussed here will however be not on canvas, but in words. In these discussions I place great emphasis on textual analysis, by which I mean close attention to words, their relation to each other and the page on which they appear. Although

I disagree with their ahistorical attitudes, I am obviously indebted, if sometimes in a bemused (perhaps confused) way, to the labours of the New Critics and those who have subsequently supported or belaboured them. I have a particular debt, though, to Benjamin Lee Whorf.

Whorf believed that language is the primary way in which we organise our perceptions of the environment. This belief informs much of his work, but can be found in summary in his essay 'Science and linguistics', published in 1940:

> We dissect nature along lines laid down by our native languages. The categories and types that we isolate from the world of phenomena we do not find there because they stare every observer in the face; on the contrary, the world is presented in a kaleidoscopic flux of impressions which has to be organized by our minds – and this means largely by the linguistic systems in our minds. We cut nature up, organize it into concepts, and ascribe significances as we do, largely because we are parties to an agreement to organize it in this way – an agreement that holds throughout our speech community and is codified in the patterns of our language.

I am more hesitant than Whorf in asserting that language is the key to cognition, but I follow him in thinking that perception and language exist together. Organised into a text, language is a way of seeing, a mode of understanding. In other words, perception is style.

Clearly, Whorf's theories are closely related to those of the perceptual geographers. Indeed, Whorf was working on the language of the Hopi Indians at the time that Sauer was developing his model of the cultural landscape. Both men were influenced by the relativism that was a central element of the developing discipline of cultural anthropology.[4] Which brings me to my second reservation. Once again, a tension exists between the methods I am applying and the texts to which they will be applied. The Revolutionary generation are unlikely to have been impressed by Whorfian linguistics. In their investigations into language they tended to be guided by the belief that it once had a common structure. Genesis 11:1–9 told them that the structure had been shattered by God in retribution for the Tower of Babel. The study of language was therefore a way of retrieving man's lost grace, and of restoring the connection between the Word and the World.[5]

The assumption informing my work is that there is no direct connection between the Word and the World. This presupposes that language, even onomatopoeia, is essentially a displacement of any physical event it may denote. In this sense, the language of terrestrial description is entirely metaphorical. The Word, therefore, acts as a mediator between the Self and the World. Usually it helps us, but sometimes it hinders us in our attempts to express our relationship with the environment. This view of language is perhaps obvious. It is certainly not new. It does, however, provide a fertile way of looking at American texts, as Richard Poirier and Tony Tanner have shown.[6]

It gives me two particular advantages. First, by treating such language as metaphorical I can minimise the distinction which is normally made between factual and fictional writing. I am interested more in the textual description and less in whether or not the phenomenon described has an objective basis. I am not denying that facts are important, and will always indicate the status of the the text analysed. Meriwether Lewis's journals, for instance, were written by a figure whose life and death can be verified from documents. Edgar Huntly is a fiction within a fiction. The Rockies exist. Edgar Huntly's Norwalk cave almost certainly did not. Nevertheless, Lewis's descriptions of the 'real' environment bear some striking resemblances to the fictional Huntly's descriptions of a fictional environment. I hope it will become apparent that such correspondences occur again and again; and that factual and fictional writing are not mutually exclusive modes, but exist in a living dynamic where one assimilates elements of the other.[7]

Secondly, by treating language as metaphor I can emphasise the heroics of the struggle between the text and the terrain. If there is no such thing as an artless language, it follows that descriptions of the environment are never merely empirical. They are strategies which encode the interests and concerns of the writer as well as the physical nature of the terrain, the climate, and so on. As those interests and concerns change, so do the strategies of description. A landscape of optimism can thus be transformed into a landscape of despair. This is particularly the case where the components of the terrain can be rearranged to respond to altered expectations. As I shall explain shortly, the New World is particularly available for this kind of transformation.

So far it seems that the ordering processes of the text are able to perform *any* operation on the terrain. Of course, this is not true. There are at least two instances where the terrain is unlikely to provide material which responds to changing demands. One is where a long tradition of settled values has been attached to it. As I will have nothing to say about this kind of terrain, I can caricature it by suggesting that it is exemplified by rural southern England as it appears in the fiction of Jane Austen. It is the second instance that is relevant to my purposes. This instance is where the terrain eludes the strategies of the text. The most obvious example is unexplored territory. Such territory may contain elements which have hitherto lain outside our conception, and are therefore outside any ordering strategy. Where the first kind of terrain has moved beyond any contention about its status, the second kind has not yet reached the stage where the terms of contention can be created, let alone agreed.

I would like to dwell on this last point for a moment by making a distinction between rhetorical and literal inexpressibility. The rhetoric of inexpressibility is a technique commonly used in the language of love. An example is Shakespeare's Sonnet CIII, 'Alack! what poverty my Muse brings forth'. It is also used in describing terrain that is regarded as spectacular. Several examples will appear in the coming pages. The rhetoric of inexpressibility is a feigning modesty. It announces an inability to describe the subject before proceeding through a farrago of superlatives. Literal inexpressibility is quite different. It is impossible to describe, of course, for it does not exist. But it is possible to describe the moments at which a text fails in the face of literal inexpressibility; and, with much more difficulty, to suggest points at which the text flutters as it approaches it. I will be making some tentative attempts.

From what I have just said it should be apparent that explorers are likely to find themselves on textual as well as terrestrial frontiers. So, too, are the more speculative writers of fictions, their work moving beyond the well-trodden ways of the imagination into areas which perhaps threaten the idea of imagination itself. Two such figures, I will suggest, are the explorer Meriwether Lewis and the novelist Charles Brockden Brown. Both men, in the eloquent words of Friedrich Waismann, groped 'along the borders of the unspeakable, wresting new land from the vast void of the unexpressed'.[8] We shall see what costs the struggle involved, and what achievements resulted.

The problems I have been addressing – the relationship of Word and World, of fact and fiction – will not allow themselves to be solved in this summary fashion. Doubtless the reader will have thought of arguments to complicate or refute the points that I have been making all too briefly and easily. Unfortunately, I have neither the time nor the ability to do more than indicate that these questions exist. Certainly they inform, and will occasionally resurface in, the chapters to come. What I would like to do now is flesh out this rather abstract argument and also set the coming discussion in a broader context by offering a quick sketch of the different attitudes taken to American terrain.

NEW FOUND LAND

Before America existed on the map, it existed in the imagination. There was no room for it elsewhere. Classical maps, developed by the Pythagoreans from their limited knowledge of the Mediterranean, showed a world divided into three land masses – Europe, Africa and Asia – segmented and surrounded by narrow watercourses. Medieval Biblical scholars fitted the knowledge of the Greeks and Romans to their Christian faith. The result was a model of symmetry and order, known as the 'T in O' map. This map reflected the belief that God, using the Latin alphabet, had shaped the earth so that the three continents created a 'T' (terrarum) within the lower half of an 'O' (orbis). The components of this design varied, but often Europe and Africa comprised the quarter-segments below the horizontal of the T. Jerusalem, in accordance with Ezekiel 5:5, was in the centre of the circle, just above the vertical of the T. Asia, because it was not yet explored, was made equal in size to the two other continents, and occupied the upper half of the circle. All that remained was to fill in the detail of existing knowledge. As Ecclesiastes 1:9 asserted:

> The thing that hath been, it *is that* which shall be; and that which i· done *is* that which shall be done; and there is no new *thing* under the sun.

Within the limited earth of the Ancient and Medieval worlds, a small space was left for Paradise. The Greeks called it the Elysian Fields, the place of retirement for heroes after their death. Located at the far edge of the earth, the Elysian Fields were, according to Peter Pindar, 'the isles of the blest' where the flowers gleamed with the gold which the heroes fashioned into bracelets and crowns. Hesiod, too, set the Elysian Fields on distant islands, but he provided his heroes with bounty of a different kind. According to Charles Elton's 1812 translation:

> Them on earth's utmost verge the god assign'd
> A life, a seat, distinct from human kind:
> Beside the deepening whirlpools of the main,
> In those blest isles where Saturn holds his reign,
> Apart from heaven's immortals: calm they share
> A rest unsullied by the clouds of care:
> And yearly thrice with sweet luxuriance crown'd
> Springs the ripe harvest from the teeming ground.

We have here a series of images which will recur in varying contexts in the coming pages. At this point I want to note just two aspects of the poem. The first is that Elysium is not easily attained. It is as far as possible from an unregenerate world where meteorology and melancholy are metaphorically linked; and it is protected by dangerous whirlpools. The second is that, once attained, Elysium provides a natural profusion. It was this profusion, rather than the suspect gold, which appealed to Christian scholars. They transformed Hesiod's Isles into the abandoned Garden of Eden and placed it at the very edge of Asia, away from the sinful western world and, because it must be nearer to Heaven, resembling a nipple on the world's round surface.[9]

There is an old joke, recently retold by Daniel Boorstin, that when Columbus set out he did not know where he was going, when he reached his destination he did not know where he was, and when he returned to

Spain he did not know where he had been. The joke is a slander on a fine navigator and devout Christian. Columbus knew perfectly well where he had been, and his famous First Letter stated it clearly: he had found islands in the Indian Sea. His second and third voyages filled in the detail of his knowledge. Trinidad, he thought, was the much sought-after nipple on the earth's surface because, due to an observational error, he seemed to be closer there to the Pole Star. During his third voyage he finally fitted his 'discoveries' into accepted Christian cosmography. He had found the Terrestrial Paradise, he wrote, because 'all the learned theologians agree that the earthly paradise is in the East', and he had reached 'the end of the East'. Columbus transformed the lands he saw so that they accorded with received Christian opinion. In particular, he shaped them so that they confirmed the traditional concept of Orbis Terrarum, most recently expounded in d'Ailly's *Imago Mundi*, his favourite book.[10]

I have related Columbus's voyages to earlier cosmographies because they illustrate a process which is central to my theme. Explorers and those who follow do not set out without expectations of what they will find. They have usually clear and frequently highly developed ideas about their destination. There is, in other words, no such thing as 'the unknown'. Those who are about to enter an undiscovered area project upon it a collection of images drawn from their personal experience, from the culture of which they are a part, from their reasons for travelling, and from their hopes and fears regarding their destination. On occasion these projections are so strong that they shape the terrain they encounter. This is what happened to Columbus. To his death he persisted in the belief that he had found Asia. The accumulated knowledge of the Classical and Medieval geographers, summed up in d'Ailly's *Imago Mundi*, made the text superior to the terrain. It told Columbus what he would find, and he found it. This is an instance of what could be called the imperialism of the text. Others will appear in due course.

Naturally, this state of affairs could not last. The beliefs of Columbus and the culture to which he belonged had eventually to shift under the pressure of brute American facts. Fortunately, an alternative projection was available. Ever since Plato's *Timaeus*, there had been some speculation about a fourth continent. In 1476 the Florentine geographer Lorenzo Buonincontri revived the idea. Few people believed him; certainly, Columbus did not. It was Amerigo Vespucci who in 1501 sailed westward to test the theory. His conclusion, that the land he had reached was not Asia, was first recorded on maps drawn by the German cosmographer Conrad Waldseemüller in 1507. The Vespucci–Waldseemüller thesis finally gained general approval because it provided a closer relation between image and fact than Columbus's theory.

Waldseemüller named the continent for Vespucci. Appropriately, the name stuck.[11]

In the last paragraph I have been blithely sailing in contentious waters. It follows from what I have been saying that, as America never existed in Columbus's world-view, he did not 'discover' it. Fortunately, this suggestion has been made before, by the Mexican historian Edmundo O'Gorman; and, inevitably, it created a storm. Wilcomb Washburn, for instance, remarked that 'exactly what land Columbus thought he had found makes no difference to the history of the discoveries which he is writing'. What had occurred was a subsequent confusion of 'vocabulary'. In a way, it is a pity that the argument should have raged around the question of priority of landfall, for in talking about confusions of vocabulary Professor Washburn is not too far away from Professor O'Gorman's underlying hypothesis that America emerged from a 'complex, living process of exploration and interpretation'.[12]

I will give a coarsened, simplified version of this hypothesis by presenting two models for interpreting America. The first I shall call the Columbian model. It contains ordering strategies, including the rhetoric of inexpressibility, which stretch back like a lifeline to the Old World. The second is the Vespuccian model. It is seductive because it beckons towards a vocabulary of the New World, but it can also be dangerous because it involves an approach towards literal inexpressibility.

Columbus called his discoveries 'Otro Mundo'. Vespucci described what he saw as 'terra nuoua'. Columbus's description indicates the traditional nature of his thought, whereas Vespucci's asserts novelty. Columbus's 'other world' can be found on Medieval maps; Vespucci's 'new land' cannot. Vespucci's 1501–1502 voyage, moreover, is a benchmark in the empirical method which would soon challenge the authority of received wisdom and abstract calculation. Columbus remarked in 1498 that this land must be Paradise 'because all the learned theologians' say it is. Vespucci, in the letters describing his four voyages, said that he discovered the new lands because he wanted to see for himself.[13]

It is Vespucci's 'new' and not Columbus's 'other' that has usually been associated with America, for the continent became both the result and the symbol of empiricism. Bacon used America as an image of his method. John Donne, in his well-known bawdy 'Elegy XIX: To His Mistress Going to Bed', used America as a metaphor of the freshness of sexual contact. John Locke remarked that 'in the beginning, all the world was America'. Such perceptions, of course, are not confined to Old World writers. Novelty has been invoked in America to the extent that it has become one of the most venerable traditions. It has been used in every conceivable context, and has even been elevated from an adjective to a noun, 'the new'.[14]

The last point suggests that reiterated novelty is a rhetorical strategy of great power, but one that can become self-referential. When it does so, it ceases to relate to the terrain that it supposedly describes. I shall illustrate and develop this by reference to a letter written by Thomas Jefferson to the English scientist Joseph Priestley at an appropriate moment: the beginning of his first term as third President, and near to the opening of the nineteenth century:

> We can no longer say there is nothing new under the sun. For this whole chapter in the history of man is new. The great extent of our republic is new. Its sparse habitation is new.

I have quoted a longer extract from this letter in another context in chapter 5. Here, I will discuss the letter in terms of the rhetorics of novelty and negation, and their relationship to American space.

Jefferson's letter, with its repeated assertions of novelty, clearly falls within the tradition I have just described. (In fact, it goes on to invoke novelty twice more.) It is also in an allied tradition, of negation. According to this tradition, what Europe is, America is not. America must be the New World, because Europe is the Old World. The rhetoric of negation, which is to be found in classical antiquity, took on a new lease of life with the discovery of the New World. Montaigne's 'Of Cannibals', exalting the virtues of a Brazilian tribe by listing a series of absent shortcomings, is a distinguished early example of the form. Shakespeare borrowed it to suggest the qualities of a Utopia in his 'American' play, *The Tempest*. Henry James's 'Epsom, Ascot' passage in his book on Hawthorne is perhaps the best-known and certainly the funniest subsequent example but, as Terence Martin has shown, the form occurs in many contexts in American literature. Here, Jefferson's letter distinguishes the New World from the Old by directly negating the negation of Ecclesiastes.[15]

Jefferson uses the twin rhetorical devices of novelty and negation in connection with references to American space and low population density. There is barely any need for me to say that these references fall within yet another tradition, of amplitude. Whatever the differences between them, both Columbus and Vespucci wrote of the dimensions of the terrain which confronted them. This has continued to be the commonly reported experience of travellers to the New World. Claude Lévi-Strauss speaks for them all when he remarks that the 'impression of enormous size is peculiar to America, and can be felt everywhere, in town and country alike'. And, as we can see from Jefferson's letter, it is not an experience limited to visitors. Indeed, I shall suggest in chapter 1 that amplitude was one of the major justifications for the creation of the Republic. It remains a central component of national identity.

Yet, although Jefferson never overtly shows any awareness of it, sheer space can be a mixed blessing. Claude Lévi-Strauss felt that American amplitude created a 'congenital lack of proportion' between human beings and their environment. If this is so, then American space can produce contradictory responses. On the one hand, it can invite a joyous if unproportionate imaginative dilation. A good example of this is given in an 1844 essay by Emerson, where he talks about the 'wonder' of America:

> Our log-rolling, our stumps and their politics, our fisheries, our Negroes and Indians, our boats and our repudiations, the wrath of rogues and the pusillanimity of honest men, the northern trade, the southern planting, the western clearing, Oregan and Texas, are yet unsung. Yet America is a poem in our eyes; its ample geography dazzles the imagination, and it will not wait long for metres.

I will return shortly to the strongly prospective nature of this passage. For my present purposes the notable aspect of it is the way that it treats America as a physical and imaginative space to be filled with a cornucopia of unrelated images. Detail is rapidly proliferated through a series of short phrases to link the ideas of scale and fecundity. A century later, E. M. Forster felt the same when, at the age of sixty-eight, he made his first visit to the New World. 'America is rather like life', he thought, 'you can usually find in it what you look for'. Then, like Emerson, he produced a rapid list of incongruous images before concluding with a forecast that America 'will probably be interesting, and it is sure to be large'.[16]

On the other hand, America space can be threatening to the imagination. It is not always pleasant to be 'dazzled', and Emerson's clear eye may well have been aware of it. In precisely the same year that Forster emphasised the positive aspects of Emersonian expansiveness, Charles Olson exposed the hint of negation. Beginning his book on Herman Melville, he remarked:

> I take SPACE to be the central fact to man born in America, from Folsom cave to now. I spell it large because it comes large here. Large, and without mercy.

The largeness which excited Forster has troubled many writers. Lévi-Strauss's 'congenital lack of proportion' has prompted some to fear American silence and solitude, while many others have despaired of the New World because it has what Thomas Cole called 'the want of associations such as cling to scenes in the old world'. It is here that Henry James's 'Epsom, Ascot' passage can be contrasted with rather than allied with Jefferson's letter.[17]

Indeed, a number of writers have feared that it is impossible even to write about America. In this view, America not only lacks 'associations', but also eludes the ordering processes of the imagination itself. Henry

Adams devoted his professional life to the creation of models and symbols of order. Yet, near the beginning of his autobiography, that exemplary American *Education*, he speculated about the hated tasks of civilisation which, in 'running order through chaos, direction through space, discipline through freedom', vitally altered or even killed the object which it approached. D. H. Lawrence, safely back in England after his sojourn in the New World, thought that 'the very landscape, in its very beauty, seems a bit devilish and grinning, opposed to us', and asserted that America was 'the doom of our white day'. Claude Lévi-Strauss, on his return home, realised that 'the world I had been looking for disintegrated in my grasp'. Indeed, Tzvetan Todorov has suggested that our attitudes to America have been characterised by the simultaneous recognition and rejection of an alternative to our Eurocentric ordering strategies.[18]

Bryan Jay Wolf has suggested that Romantic texts contain their own negation. The same could, I think, be said of a wider range of texts which purport to describe the American environment. For if American space both encourages and defeats the imagination, it encourages and defeats the linguistic structures through which the imagination expresses itself. The rhetorical strategies of novelty and negation both create the space which allow us to imagine America and raise the question whether or not such imaginings are possible. We have seen the importance of these strategies to American culture. We can now see that they lead nowhere. I do not, of course, wish to suggest by this that America does not exist (although some writers, following Columbus, have wanted to make that suggestion). Everyone but a solipsist will agree that the continent is there, to be looked at, walked over, built upon. But I do wish to say that American culture is marked by an integral instability in the relation of text and terrain.

The rhetorics of novelty and negation, because they are based on a structure of rejection, are ultimately nihilistic. They can offer no positive way in which to construct a relationship between the text and whatever may lie outside it. An illustration of the ultimate end of such rhetoric is given by Melville's 1853 short story 'Bartleby'. The tale is also a good example of Wolf's theory because it reveals a deep cynicism about the value of composition. For Bartleby is a copyist. His work involves him in the mere act of writing, without any external referents. Despite this, he seems initially to 'gorge himself' on documents. Perhaps this leads to a surfeit, because Bartleby begins to refuse his duties. (I say 'perhaps' because, in keeping with its nihilism, the tale offers no explanations.) He does so by adopting the rhetorical structure 'I would prefer not to'. The repeated negations lead him inexorably into the final negation of death. I can think of no better disembodiment of Walter Shandy's robustly mordant little joke, 'when death *is* – we are *not*'.[19]

We can now return to Jefferson's letter. Doubtless Jefferson would strongly have rejected the imputation that his work undermined itself. He believed too firmly in the value of writing. Nevertheless, it may be possible to detect a hesitation in those sentences about the meaning of America. Jefferson does not usually write with this brevity. The four short sentences are notable in that they occur in the middle of a letter couched in a style more typical of his work. A master of English prose, Jefferson normally tends to alternate short, simple and assertive sentences with ones that are long, complex and descriptive. Here, however, as the text approaches the terrain, the sentences become progressively shorter. After the initial rebuttal of Ecclesiastes they are almost identical. Each ends with the adjective 'new' which points both back to the subject of the sentence, and forward into vacuity. It is as if the plentitude of the terrain has seeped out between each closing full stop and the succeeding capital letter, while the last three sentences go into logical loops. The very next sentence marks a return to Jefferson's usual style; but it seems, just for a moment, that his ordering prose will break down. It gives just the hint of a suggestion that the inner ear of the text is infected; that Jefferson, who more than most was responsible for the invention of the Republic which he now leads, will have nothing new to say about America.

This is, of course, speculative. It may, however, give some indication of the way that an ordering strategy can begin to crumble in the face of a terrain for which it may initially seem appropriate but which, finally, it is poorly equipped to describe. I will suggest further examples in the coming pages. It will become apparent, I hope, just how difficult it is to coax language out of a void. Many writers have not even made the attempt. Instead of adopting rhetorical strategies associated with the New World, they continued to employ ones drawn from the Old World. They opted for the Columbian rather than the Vespuccian model. It rewarded them with a cornucopia of images, which they tended to fashion into two conflicting groups. The first contained images of a fertile healthy land of liberty populated by noble savages. The second contained images of a sterile miasmic land of libertinism inhabited by the degenerate.[20]

The first group of images had been used by Columbus himself when he imagined America as the Garden of Eden. The history of such images is too well known to need repetition. I will give just one further example, because it looks back to Hesiod and forward to much of the optimistic imagery I discuss in coming chapters. It is from Michael Drayton's famous 1606 poem, 'To the Virginian Voyage':

> And cheerefully at sea,
> Successe you still intice,
>> To get the pearle and gold,
>> And ours to hold,

Virginia,
Earth's onely paradise.

Where nature hath in store,
Fowle, venison, and fish,
 And the fruitfull'st soyle,
 Without your toyle,
Three harvests more,
All greater then you wish.

The poem is typical of a large amount of optimistic Elizabethan writing about America. Like Hesiod, it suggests that the land is so abundant that it will provide three harvests. There are two essential differences. First, Hesiod's Elysian Fields were not precisely located. Drayton's wonderful landscape is; hence the emphasis on the proper noun 'Virginia', given a line of its own. Nothing can be placed alongside this colony. Secondly, Hesiod's references to the gods have disappeared. There is no need for divine intervention. The land really exists. It is there to be enjoyed by living heroes.

America can apparently provide a physical basis, a toehold in reality which gives an imprimatur to the fantasy. The process may be seen in action in Thomas More's *Utopia*. Published in 1516, it is a good example of the impact of Waldseemüller, for it refers to Vespucci's voyages. But it uses them to suggest a Columbian paradise of sufficient presence to enable More to propose the physical reshaping of London. The result is much more persuasive than Plato's *Republic*. The dreams of Drayton and More, then, are not simply resuscitations of a Hellenic paradise. They move beyond allegory to provide an ideal which is, it seems, potentially real.[21]

The plasticity of the Columbian model is such that images of an American Eden could easily be inverted. This is made apparent by the first of many images we shall see of the world turned upside down. It comes from the 1640 edition of George Sandys' translation of Ovid's *Metamorphoses*. Sandys had been treasurer and director of industry of Jamestown, Virginia, from 1621 to 1625. He seemed to speak with authority therefore when he recorded, in this Old World text, the things he had 'seene in *America*':

Where once was solid land, Seas have I seene;
And solid land, where once deepe Seas have beene.
Shels, far from Seas, like quarries in the ground;
And anchors have on mountaine tops beene found.

If the natural order can be inverted, then America can provide the example *not* to be followed. If it afforded the release for More's *Utopia*, it also enabled the dystopia, of which Bishop Hall's *Mundus Alter et Idem*, published in 1605, is probably the first example. Hall's use of contemporary geographical knowledge is as persuasive as More's, and his purpose is the same: to highlight social problems in England. But he does it by exaggerating them. America is therefore the land of fools and knaves. The terrain is highly fertile, but the fertility only gives rise to gluttony. The title of the 1609 English translation, moreover, adds an irony which would have been available only to the Latin-educated élite. The text was renamed *The Discovery of a New World*. New World? The Latin in fact translates as 'Another World and Yet the Same', which resonates from Ecclesiastes and Columbus, not from Vespucci.[22]

America was large enough to house phenomena much more fearsome than fools and knaves. Pliny's *Natural History* and Mandeville's *Travels* abound with monstrosities. The East had always provided a suitably distant location for such beings. It was understandable, therefore, that Columbus's First Letter reported that 'there are people born with tails' living in 'Avan' (Havana). The discovery that this was not the East simply meant that there was now a fresh soil from which monsters could readily spring. Stories of such beings soon flooded across the Atlantic, to coexist uneasily with images of the Garden. A report of 1597 asserted that headless men would shortly be found in America. George Sandys brought Ovid's story of Hermaphroditus up to date by noting that such creatures 'are most frequent in *Florida*'. A few more tall stories will appear in the coming pages. Here the tall story indicates that Sandys' Ovid has an imperial power similar to Columbus's d'Ailly.[23]

It is clear that the New World did not cease to be the land of the imagination after it became the land of fact. It is the continent from which facts are still taken and elided with fictions to fill out theories – as I have done in presenting two models of interpretation. Yet, underneath all the theory, all the invention, lies the terrain itself, constantly if mutely defying our gaudy schemes. This, I take it, is one of the conclusions of *New-Found-Land*, Tom Stoppard's little celebration for the Bicentennial.[24] The American section of this play within a play (it is surrounded, so to speak, by *Dirty Linen*) opens with an invocation of Donne's 'Elegy XIX'. It begins, therefore, by citing an earlier imaginative engagement with America, and then presents a brilliantly kaleidoscopic torrent of stereotypes as it journeys in a zig-zag fashion across the continent. So far, *New-Found-Land* remains within the Emerson–Forster tradition of imaginative dilation. But as the journey reaches that final frontier, the Pacific, the stereotypes shrivel in the face of the unknown, and the ordering rhetoric moves into a negation, and then stumbles and dies:

> for now beyond the city, beyond America, beyond all, nothing lies before us but an endless expanse of blue, flecked with cheerful whitecaps. With wondering eyes we stare at the Pacific, and all of us look at each other with a wild surmise – silent —

UNSUNG HILLOCKS

I began by saying that the basis of my argument was simple. It is not, however, one which has attracted much support. The attitudes of critics towards the literature of the Revolutionary generation sometimes oscillates between condescension and embarrassment. The period is often dealt with by omission. Figures like Franklin and Crèvecœur are briefly noted in a trajectory which leaps from the Puritans to Irving and Cooper. Even those who write about the period have tended to preface their work with an apology. It is the stepchild of American culture.

There are at least four good reasons for this. The first is that the Revolutionary generation brought the obloquy upon themselves. The grandiloquence with which some of them predicted the rise of America as a cultural power is perfectly understandable, as I shall suggest in the next chapter. Inevitably, it carried in its train disappointment and derision. In 1820 the British clergyman and critic Sydney Smith attacked the Americans as 'this self-adulating race'. His essay has in consequence become notorious; but his fire was drawn by a history of bombast which went back at least fifty years.

The second is that, both at the time and since, circumstances were believed to be unfavourable for the arts. American bombast, it seemed, was predictive but not productive. Late in 1803 the New York Presbyterian clergyman Samuel Miller published *A Brief Retrospect of the Eighteenth Century*. Taking a cool look at American culture, he pointed to many achievements but also listed a number of deficiencies: 'Defective plans and means of instruction in our Seminaries of learning . . . Want of Leisure . . . Want of encouragement to learning' and 'Want of Books'. In particular, American '*love of gain*' promoted what he called 'the Mechanic Arts', but not literature. Despite the boosters, the book market was still dominated by British publications, which tended to be held in higher esteem. Not that Miller approved of every book written in America. Although he liked the work of Charles Brockden Brown, he reproved novels in general as 'frivolous effusions of ignorance and vanity'. Miller was an exponent of Scottish Common Sense Philosophy, which tended to regard fictions as immature and self-indulgent. Today we are more forgiving. Indeed, we look on Scottish Common Sense Philosophy as yet another factor which forced literature towards the margins of American life.[25]

The other two reasons for the neglect of their culture cannot be blamed on the Revolutionary generation. One may be called the Rip Van Winkle Syndrome. Sacvan Bercovitch has shown that the generations who succeeded the Revolutionaries ignored the divisive aspects of the revolt against Britain to create a myth of national unity which drew its power from Puritan teleology. There are other contributing factors to the Rip Van Winkle Syndrome. One aspect of the myth of national unity was the conscious apprenticeship which many writers and artists undertook in Europe. It was Hawthorne, of course, who overtly called England 'Our Old Home', but the attachment, expanded to embrace the entire Old World, prompted many of his contemporaries to find their voices.

Paradoxically, Hawthorne's generation is also the one which declared intellectual independence from Britain. It is Emerson who is the senior member and prime instigator of this movement; and his 1837 Address, 'The American Scholar', which is treated as the cultural equivalent of that document of 1776. We have already seen that the 1844 essay, 'The Poet', repeated the call for American 'metres'. In both these essays and elsewhere Emerson avidly rejected the past, including the American past. Although he attacked some of the elements of American life which had earlier stifled its culture, he had no wish to analyse the sins of his predecessors, or praise their achievements. Even more than Jefferson, he looked resolutely into the future.

Many critics, taking their cue from Emerson, have identified the quarter-century from 1837 as the definitive period in American literature. Although they occasionally nod at earlier writers, the main thrust of their argument plots a ripening process which springs from Emersonian seeds. These gestatory metaphors, I hasten to add, are not mine. They are to be found in the epigraphs of F. O. Matthiessen's classic study, *American Renaissance*, and are developed in his opening sentences. Renaissance, he says, does not imply a rebirth, since nothing had been previously born. Instead, it means the period in which America came 'to its first maturity'. Or, to use my own metaphor, the time when American culture was awakened by the hero's kiss. Towards the close of 'The American Scholar', Emerson told the young men of Harvard:

> in yourself slumbers the whole of Reason; it is for you to know all; it is for you to dare all.

In this tale, Rip Van Winkle's awakening was not accompanied by the penalties of decay and dislocation.[26]

The fourth reason for neglecting Revolutionary culture is the Turner, or Frontier Thesis. In the ninety-odd years since it was first published, the Turner Thesis has probably become the most commonly used means of determining Americanism. It has prompted some striking analyses of American culture, like Richard Slotkin's *Regeneration Through Violence*. But it can give an unduly distorted view of America. Although Turner invoked the entire sweep of American history, his Thesis does not have a universal explanatory force. He identified democracy as 'the most important effect of the frontier'. The Jacksonian era thereby emerges as a particularly dynamic period in American history. The Revolutionary era, with its equivocal attitudes to the frontier and to democracy, does not.

As far as I know, nobody has ever gone to the extent of accusing the Revolutionary generation of unAmerican activities. Yet the Turner Thesis can combine with the Rip Van Winkle Syndrome to persuade critics to focus on the second quarter of the nineteenth century as the breeding-ground of American culture. Matthiessen, for instance, believed that the protagonists of the American Renaissance were united by 'their devotion to the possibilities of democracy'. He was writing at a time when American democracy was again threatened by powerful external forces. It is understandable, then, that he should seize on the Turner Thesis. Unfortunately, the Thesis can also provoke the uncritical into making too easy an equation between Americanism and the wild and woolly. Every bush is shaken in the hope that a barbaric yawper will pop out. As John Jay Chapman remarked, with his characteristic blend of acerbity and acuity:

> It may safely be said that the discovery of Whitman as a poet caused many a hard-thinking Oxford man to sleep quietly at night. America was solved.[27]

I am not so bold as to propose an alternative solution for America, or suggest that the Revolutionary generation can provide it, although they tried hard to do so. I do, however, think that the factors outlined above have in the past led to an inadequate appreciation of their contribution to American culture. Fortunately, this is changing. A number of critics have turned their attention to the Revolutionary period, to good effect. Others have demonstrated that the roots of the American Renaissance reach into the earlier periods in American history. Yet others have anticipated me in revising the Turner Thesis and suggesting that it is the environment, not just the frontier, that is an ingredient of the distinctive flavour of American culture. My debt to them all is clear, even if at times it has led to disagreement.[28]

Our heightened awareness of the importance of the American environment may be powered by the ecological controversies of the last two decades, but it is hardly new. In 1786 an English reviewer of one of the first works of imagination to be published in the Republic revealed a similar awareness when he remarked that:

> A land newly explored, and gradually advancing towards civilization, where the face of nature presents a thousand novel objects to the observer, is certainly more favourable to the descriptive arts and to the efforts of imagination, than these regions where art has exhausted all her powers, 'And scarce a hillock rears its head unsung'.

Earlier in this century William Carlos Williams insisted again and again 'that what has been morally, aesthetically worth while in America has rested upon peculiar and discoverable ground'. *In the American Grain*, his alternative history of America published in 1925, is a particularly forceful plea for us to look afresh at the 'genius of *place*'.[29]

In the American Grain provided the initial impulse for this study. I am not certain that Williams would have cared for the results. They suggest that American culture is a mongrel, vitally changed by the environment, yet bred out of an Old World pedigree. The Revolutionary generation called for a new culture, but expected it to appear in a familiar form which could be compared with its parent, and shown to be superior. The mongrel was (it must be said) too wild and woolly for them, and they tried to stifle it. Even Charles Brockden Brown disavowed his work. Yet all was not lost. I try to suggest in the Epilogue that the mongrel was rescued by Edgar Allan Poe, and has since grown into a lusty if not overly lovable beast. In other words, the factors contributing to the success of American culture were precisely those which were widely regarded as the factors of its failure.

To an extent, they still are regarded as a failure. American literary history has always revealed an uneasy awareness of the uncertain parentage of its subject. On the one hand, Moses Coit Tyler began his *History of American Literature*, published in 1878, by asserting that in the beginning 'a thousand leagues of brine' made no difference to the way people wrote. Seventy years and two world wars had an effect, not only on American political prestige, but also on literary history. The *Literary History of the United States* began its work by countering Tyler with the assertion that the new environment made a world of difference.[30] It will be seen that I try to steer a path between the two views.

Similarly, the nature of the American canon has never been settled. In the last few years pressures for revision have tended to come from two directions. The first could be called documentary. Critics such as Donald Davie and Lawrence Buell have suggested that non-fictional forms such as autobiography and travel narrative form a vital element of American Literature. The second is feminist. Critics like Nina Baym and Jane Tompkins have pointed out that the search for what is specifically American about American literature has a number of misogynist tendencies built into it.[31]

Looking back, I now think that it is unfortunate, although perhaps inevitable, that the texts I have included seem to continue (but do not I hope confirm) the masculine bias of the canon. I take comfort from the belief that my work supports the arguments put forward by both documentary and feminist critics that the canon must be seen in historical context. Returned to history, the writings of the Revolutionary generation reveal their readiness to discuss the principles by which they ran their lives, their culture and their society. Questions which we now regard as settled, if not answered, seemed to them to be open for daily dispute. If my reader leaves this book with some sense of the vigour of those discussions, I shall be satisfied.

1

The triumph of Redcoatism

THE HALLUCINATION OF DISPLACED TERRAIN

People carry their landscapes with them, the way travelers used to cart along their porcelain chamber pots. The stronger their sense of form the more reluctant they are to part with either.

With these arresting remarks, the art critic Harold Rosenberg began an essay that attacked American painters for failing to shrug off the burden of European style. They had, he said, become 'Redcoats' when they should have been 'Coonskins'. The painters he discusses are of no concern here, but the basis of his criticism is central to my theme. I want to suggest in this chapter that people on both sides of the Atlantic and of widely differing opinions shared the same 'sense of form'. That sense of form was derived from an environmental ideology which had become particularly sophisticated and all-embracing in the second half of the eighteenth century. Deeply rooted as it was in European thought, the ideology took little account of the facts of the American terrain. It served to distance Americans from their surroundings.

My argument is a lengthy one, drawing on a variety of texts and contexts. I will begin therefore by outlining it in one particular context, the use of military tactics in America. This allows me to develop my argument in bold, concrete terms. Soldiers invariably express themselves plainly, and their words reveal opinions that are clear-cut. It also helps me to show how widespread was the ideology. Soldiers may be blunt men, but they are not isolated. Their opinions reflect the culture of which they are a part; and the culture I will describe demanded that soldiers and civilians alike remain in camp with their chamber pots, rather than betake themselves to the bushes.

Redcoats and Coonskins: Harold Rosenberg adapts his symbolic

22

opposition from Philip Rahv's 'Paleface and Redskin', but it originates from one of the British defeats during the French and Indian War. The Battle of the Monongahela, or Battle of the Wilderness as it is sometimes (and for my purposes more suitably) called, took place on 9 July 1755. A force of 2,500 British and colonial troops (including a Colonel George Washington) was routed by 250 French Coonskins, so named because of their caps, and 650 Indians. The Redcoats marched in line abreast, and they were easily picked off by their assailants, who hid behind the trees. Some 1,000 British and colonials were killed or wounded (including most of the officers), compared to less than sixty French and Indian casualties. The British commanding General, Edward Braddock, had five horses shot from under him before he was mortally wounded. His dying words apparently were, 'we shall better know how to deal with them another time'.

General Braddock was a stern disciplinarian, a garrison soldier who prized King's Regulations above any appreciation of the American terrain. The tactics he practised had been developed on the open fields of Europe. Observing the concept of limited warfare outlined by Grotius in *De Jure Belli ac Pacis* (1625, translated into English 1654 and 1715) and shortly to be reasserted by Vattel in *Le Droit des gens* (1758, translated into English 1759–1760), highly disciplined armies settled battles by means of set-piece manoeuvres. As he died General Braddock recognised that such practises would not work in the woods of America. The reason is clearly indicated by Harold Rosenberg:

> The Redcoats fall, expecting at any moment to enter upon the true battlefield, the soft rolling greenswards prescribed by the canons of their craft and presupposed by every principle that makes warfare intelligible to the soldier of the eighteenth century.

> The difficulty of the Redcoats was that they were in the wrong place. The dream-world of style always moves ahead of the actual world and overlays it; unless one is of the unblinking wilderness like those Coonskinners behind the trees.

> In honor of the dream-defeated Braddock, I call the hallucination of the displaced terrain, originating in style, Redcoatism. In America it is an experience of the first importance.[1]

Rosenberg's remarks state with admirable concision the thesis I am advancing, and they have a broad application. As we shall see, Redcoatism was not the sole preserve of the Redcoats. Indeed, it predated them. Braddock was not the first to discover that the Indians were unfamiliar with the grammar of European combat. During the Pequot War of 1637 John Underhill, captain of the colony troops at Saybrook, grew tired of Indian raids and decided on a confrontation. We chose, he said,

> to beat up the drum and bid them battle. Marching into a champaign field we displayed our colors; but none would come near us, but standing remotely off did laugh at us for our patience.

Underhill and his disappointed men had to content themselves with 'burning and spoiling the country'.

By choosing a 'champaign field', occupying it and flourishing the flag Underhill and his men showed that they were in the wrong place. They wanted to settle matters with a European battle. No wonder the Indians laughed; they knew nothing about the rules of so-called 'civilised' warfare. In consequence Underhill identified them with the unblinking wilderness. He fell easily into a rhetoric that is, of course, Puritan but would later become more widely used. He described the Indians as 'devil's instruments' and as beasts:

> They run up and down as roaring lions, compassing all corners of the country for a prey, seeking whom they might devour.[2]

Settlers evolved techniques of scouting and woodcraft to deal with Indian raids. The British Army, in contrast, still relied on the drills developed for European war. Rigidly disciplined linear formations created a field of fire intended to thin the serried ranks of opponents. The business was then concluded with a bayonet charge. Accuracy of fire was not needed, and could not be achieved with the standard smoothbore musket. The command 'aim' did not appear in British manuals of tactics.

Evidence has recently been produced to show that, from the 1740s, Redcoats employed irregular tactics whenever they were necessary.[3] This did not stop them from viewing such tactics as 'savage', 'barbaric', and, as the adjective implies, improper. The Redcoats' sense of form, one might say, spoilt their 'aim'. It made them cling to a drill-book that effaced Underhill's experience and contributed to Braddock's defeat. Only after the Battle of the Wilderness did the Army form a company of scouts, Rogers' Rangers, and a regiment of light infantry, the Royal Americans. These formations emphasised marksmanship rather than firepower, mobility rather than discipline, the use of cover rather than linear manoeuvres. Military dispatches frequently identified them with the terrain in which they would fight. Men of the woods, they tended to be dressed not in the distinctive redcoat but in hunting shirts, or in green tunics that provided the most camouflage if issued in the spring, for they faded with the leaves of autumn.[4]

Arboreal light infantry tactics were vindicated in 1763 at the Battle of Bushy Run, where a mixed force of rangers, Royal Americans and Highlanders under the adroit leadership of Colonel Henry Bouquet defeated Indians led by the Ottawa Chief Pontiac. It was a famous victory. An account of Bushy Run and a subsequent Bouquet expedition that ended Pontiac's War was published in Philadelphia by William Smith in 1765. It was reprinted the next year in London by the Royal Geographer and by 1778 had appeared in seven editions in English and French. Anticipating Rosenberg by some two centuries, the account stressed the reason for Braddock's failure and Bouquet's success:

> An European, to be a proper judge of this kind of war, must have lived some time in the vast forests of America; otherwise he will hardly be able to conceive a continuity of woods without end. In spite of his endeavours, his imagination will betray him into an expectation of open and clear grounds, and he will be apt to calculate his manoeuvres accordingly, too much upon the principles of war in Europe.[5]

It seemed that Braddock's lesson had been learnt. But the opening battle of the War of Independence showed how easily the dream-world of military style could obliterate New World experience. Marching from Concord on 19 April 1775, the Redcoats were forced to run a sixteen-mile gauntlet along the road to Boston. The space was too confined for them to execute their textbook manoeuvres; the Yankees sniped at them from every available cover; and the march soon became a rout. Although flanking parties surprised a few Americans, the main British party could only respond, as Underhill's men had done in 1637, by looting and burning. They reached Boston in a wretched condition, having suffered 273 casualties compared with 95 American losses.

Redcoat accounts of Lexington reveal disdain and fear of American tactics. One soldier complained that the rebels 'never would engage us properly', while another told his father that 'we did not fight as you did in *Germany*'. As the colonials would not employ the principles of war in Europe, they were ranked with the wilderness and its inhabitants. 'They did not fight us like a regular army, only like savages, behind trees and stone walls', railed one Redcoat. A second wrote that 'they ran to the woods like devils' when flushed out of their cover. It was a response that would be repeated whenever the Americans adopted irregular tactics. Later in 1775, for instance, William Duff with the 7th Royal Fusiliers in Canada denounced rebel attacks 'under cover of the woods'. He hoped that they would be driven out of the Province by means of 'a body of Canadians and savages', who would doubtless be familiar with such methods.[6]

Yet again the British army went through the painful process of adjusting to American terrain. Greater use was made of light infantry tactics; some regiments adopted the American rifle; and Indians were employed. The adjustments were made reluctantly and as a temporary expedient. Senior officers often regarded new weapons with suspicion.

Light infantry tactics gave junior officers and men too much freedom. It was the use of Indians, however, that caused the greatest controversy. William Duff in Canada saw little distinction between colonial and Indian modes of warfare. Others were less sure. A Hessian officer thought that Indians were not to be trusted 'on account of their inborn bestiality'. Although brave they were undisciplined; in consequence they were officered by Englishmen or Canadians. Even then the Redcoats remained uneasy about the Indians although privately admitting their usefulness.

From the other side of the Atlantic, their employment seemed inexcusable. Both Houses of Parliament debated the topic. In the Lords the Earl of Chatham drew vivid pictures of 'the cannibal savage torturing, murdering, roasting, and eating' his victims, and demanded to know who had

> dared to authorise and associate to our arms the tomahawk and scalping-knife? To call into civilized alliance, the wild and inhuman savage of the woods. . . ?

Britain's 'brethren' in America would never bend to such treatment, and therefore 'Britain must recur to her former means of conquest' if she wished to prevail. She must, in other words, fight a European battle on American soil.[7]

The Commons debate was provoked by Burgoyne's Proclamation. At the beginning of his 1777 Lake Champlain campaign General John Burgoyne had issued a Proclamation intended to overawe the Americans and provide guidelines for his Indian auxiliaries. He ordered the Indians to confine bloodshed to the field of battle, and strictly forbade them from taking scalps, even from the dying. The Proclamation repeats Underhill's mistake, expecting the Indians to abide by European tenets of war. Edmund Burke knew better. In the Commons he spoke with great emotion about Indian atrocities. He then gave a parody of the Proclamation in images which were familiar to anyone who had visited the Royal menagerie at Tower Hill, and which also likened the Indians to the beasts of the wilderness:

> Suppose there was a riot on Tower Hill, what would the Keeper of his Majesty's lions do? Would he not fling open the dens of the wild beasts, and then address them thus? 'My gentle lions, my humane bears, my sentimental wolves, my tender-hearted hyenas, go forth; but I exhort ye, as ye are Christians and members of a civilised society, take care not to hurt man, woman, or child, &c. &c'.

'Gentleman Johnny' Burgoyne has been a laughing-stock ever since.[8]

In later chapters we shall see Burkean aesthetics applied by Americans to their environment. Here, Burke used his flair for comedy to attack a British hallucination about America, but in doing so simply indulged another. While Burgoyne dreamt of America as the battlefields of Blenheim, Burke imagined it as the City of London. A more apposite parody of the Proclamation was written in America by the poet Francis Hopkinson. It treated Indian cruelty almost as a matter of course. The target this time was Burgoyne's pompous language, so flatulent that it made the earth quake:

> The mountains trembled before thee, and the trees of the forest bowed their lofty heads: the vast lakes of the west were chilled at thy presence, and the stupendous cataract of *Niagara* bellowed at thy approach.[9]

The discussion so far has drawn a distinction between European dreams and American reality. Yet the criticisms implied in Hopkinson's images of a plastic terrain could also be levelled at many of his compatriots. Adhering to the same tenets of limited war as their opponents, many Continental officers ignored the lessons of Monongahela, Bushy Run and Lexington, and strove to engage the British Army as their 'brethren' – as if they were on European terrain. Washington emulated British tactics, and General von Steuben tried to instil into the reluctant Continentals the drill-book he had learned as a staff-officer in the army of Frederick the Great. In Britain, Chatham noted the changes with approval. Six months before he rebuked the British Army for adopting 'savage' methods of warfare, he praised the Continental Army for learning the British 'art of war'. The American gentry now had officers fit to lead European armies; they were 'apt scholars'.

Scholars maybe, but not yet masters. The attempt to adopt British tactics had consequences that were almost foreseeable. After Bunker Hill, when the Americans succumbed to the third British bayonet-charge, they seldom won a battle. It is perhaps fortunate that von Steuben, less of a martinet than Braddock, made allowances in his drills for American individualism. If Washington had had an army of Hessian discipline he might well have suffered defeats of greater significance.[10]

The image of war as a debate is hardly a new one, but it is illuminating here. A debate depends upon a series of accords between the adversaries. No matter how divergent the views expressed, the grammar of expression must be the same, otherwise there can be no debate. The War of Independence began with some uncertainty over its grammar. A series of adjustments erased that uncertainty – and ensured that both sides were fighting a European war. The Battle of Yorktown has, in consequence, a greater symbolic function than is normally realised. It may represent the triumph of American resolution after years of adversity; the superb coordination of American and French military might; and the brilliant generalship of George Washington. It also represents the triumph of European style.

Perhaps with Bunker Hill in mind, Washington's orders for the march to Yorktown enjoined his troops

> to place their principle relyance on the Bayonet, that they may prove the Vanity of the Boast which the British make of their particular prowess in deciding Battles with that Weapon.

He hoped that his army would be prompted by 'a generous Emulation'. The subsequent battle must have exceeded his fondest hopes. 'The principles of war in Europe', as the account of Bouquet's Expedition put it, were exemplified by the formal manoeuvres and set-piece confrontations of Yorktown, and particularly by the British surrender. Washington's orders detailing the surrender permitted officers to retain their sidearms, and required the British cavalry to ride to the surrender-field with swords drawn and trumpets sounding. Nothing could have been more magnificent, and nothing more European. Its punctilio and order was reflected in contemporary accounts and was finely caught, albeit through the mist of neoclassicism and four decades, in Colonel John Trumbull's 1824 painting which adorns the Rotunda of the United States Capitol (figure 1).[11] The Americans had travelled a long way from the casually dressed, sharpshooting farmers of Lexington and Concord.

Redcoatism, then, was not confined to the Redcoats. The British and Continental armies conducted the war with greater reference to manuals of military style than to the terrain. The British projected upon the New World a fantasy of Old World warfare. The extent of their attachment to the fantasy is indicated by the terms they applied to methods of warfare more firmly rooted in American terrain, terms such as 'savage' and 'barbaric'. They made no distinction between the various parties that practised New World warfare. Indians were devils, beasts and cannibals. Whites that fought like the Indians were tarred with the same brush. The Continental leaders, not wishing to be tarred, shared the British fantasy with such enthusiasm that they appropriated it, and finally won the war.

More than most, the Revolutionary War abounds with ironies. One of the richest concerns the Earl of Chatham. In the speech which praised American military scholarship he asked the war hawks just what they proposed to conquer. Perhaps it was 'the map of America?' It was all, he concluded, that they would conquer. Pitt was perhaps blinded by the imminent loss of the empire that he, above all, had created. As he should have known, the map of America was the last thing that the British would conquer.[12] In crossing the Atlantic they simply invaded another piece of Europe. It was likewise a hallucinated terrain that the Continental Army defended. Both sides connived in a complex of images that distanced them from the land over which they fought.

The Coonskinners were always closer to the New World. It is

1 John Trumbull, *The Surrender of Cornwallis* (1824)

appropriate therefore that a Frenchman should refute Chatham. A few months after Yorktown one M. de Brentano, aide-de-camp of the French commander, Rochambeau, told John Trevor that:

> no opinion was clearer than that tho' the People of America might be conquered by well disciplined European troops, the Country of America was unconquerable.[13]

Here, in a nutshell, was the element that eluded not just the Redcoats, but both armies on the field at Yorktown. There is a tradition that at the surrender the British bands played a tune entitled 'The World Turned Upside Down'.[14] Doubtless the tune expressed British bitterness at losing this latest but most important battle. The final irony is that it also symbolised, though they did not know it, the attitude of the victors.

THE WORLD TURNED UPSIDE DOWN

Before I turn to the attitudes of Americans to their environment, I want to set them in their European context. The lyric of 'The World Turned Upside Down' provides us with a suitable point of entry. It shows that the military debate in America was part of a wider debate over the nature of the New World itself. The title of the lyric is derived from Acts 17:6, and its images of natural inversion date back to the third century BC and Theocritus' first idyll. From the time of the Reformation and the Peasants' Revolt onwards they are to be found in songs, broadsheets and chapbooks as laments, by reactionaries and revolutionaries alike, over the instability of society. During the English Civil War there were several songs entitled 'The World Turned Upside Down', expressing diverse political and religious opinions. In eighteenth-century Scotland, a Jacobite version mourned the '45. Another, responding promptly to the growing discord between Britain and America, bore the fitting sub-title 'Goody Bull and her Daughter Fell Out'.

The version that relates most clearly to the British experience in America runs as follows:

> If buttercups buzzed after the bee,
> If boats were on land, churches on sea,
> If ponies rode men and grass ate the cows,
> And cats should be chased to holes by the mouse,
> If the mamas sold their babies to the gypsies for half a crown;
> Summer were spring and the t'other way round,
> Then all the world would be upside down.[15]

A complete reversal of the natural order is constructed by collecting images of inversion from a variety of contexts. At the same time, because each image is prefaced by a conditional conjunction, the lyric remains conjectural. As far as the British were concerned, Yorktown transformed the conjecture into reality.

At first sight this seems hyperbolical. It could be argued that a song such as this is unrepresentative and ephemeral. British support for the war was far from universal. Many regarded it as a civil strife provoked by an oppressive government.[16] It could be argued, too, that the song is simply a vehicle for British prejudices and fears, prompted by the condescension with which any metropolitan area regards the provinces, by the paternalism implicit in imperialism, and by a residual dread of a refractory and 'levelling' populace inherited from the English Civil War.[17] The British sense of superiority was, however, both more widespread and deeply rooted. Even those who were sympathetic to the Americans often regarded them as inferiors.

Such a one was John Luttrell, who had visited America as a naval officer before he became Member of Parliament for Stockbridge. Speaking in a Commons debate, Luttrell drew on his 'own personal knowledge of the Americans, their country, and their coasts' to suggest that:

> they will soon cry aloud for the re-establishment of those judicial authorities that have been imprudently overturned, and which are necessary, not only to

> the welfare, but to the very existence of the subject, among the rudest nations of the globe. Sir, I fear, indeed, the Americans at this hour cannot properly be styled the most civilized people in the known world.

He opposed therefore the measures of the Government, which would only alienate. Patient treatment and financial assistance would soon make clear the benefits of colonial subjection. The alternative, he thought, was an inevitable decline into barbarism.[18]

What prompted the thoughtful and knowledgeable to share the beliefs of the prejudiced and fearful? Once again, we are helped by British military attitudes. For years, British soldiers had been openly contemptuous of colonial troops.[19] Their scorn built up a reservoir of American bitterness that burst forth in a postwar recollection by the normally urbane Benjamin Franklin, who remembered a certain General Clarke,

> who had the Folly to say in my hearing . . . that, with a Thousand British grenadiers, he would undertake to go from one end of America to the other, and geld all the Males, partly by force and partly by a little Coaxing. It is plain he took us for a species of Animals very little superior to Brutes. The Parliament too believ'd the stories of another foolish General, I forget his Name, that the Yankeys never *felt bold*. Yankey was understood to be a sort of Yahoo.

Franklin is reporting snobbery, but not pure snobbery. The reference to the Voyage to the Houyhnhnms suggests that military contempt had its roots in a theory of cultural variety that was also the basis of *Gulliver's Travels*. A decade earlier Franklin had retailed remarks that make the point more clearly if less pungently:

> Those who served in America in the last War, know that the Colonists are a dastardly Set of Poltroons; and though they are descended from British Ancesters, they are degenerated to such a Degree, that one born in Britain is equal to twenty Americans.[20]

The belief in the environmental determinants of civilisation is probably as old as civilisation itself. The Greeks posited a close relationship between human and physical nature. Hesiod, in the extract quoted in the Prologue, wrote of 'the clouds of care'. Hippocrates theorised about the relationship. Men in cold climates, he said, tended to be impotent, whilst a variable temperature produced hot-headed people. Hippocratic theory was necessarily limited by the scope of the known world. The discovery of a New World gave it a fresh lease of life. The Renaissance writer Jean Bodin asserted that the climate controlled human abilities and temperaments. Governments should therefore be adapted to take account of human variety. His work was developed by Le Roy, Montaigne and Locke, amongst others; but it was Montesquieu's *Esprit des lois* that made such theories popular. Montesquieu suggested that hot moist climates made people lazy and servile. Free institutions were in consequence more difficult to maintain in such countries as America. The fertility of the American soil, moreover, had not encouraged the aborigines to farm it. They simply hunted the vast numbers of animals and gathered whatever else they needed. In contrast, Montesquieu praised the white colonists who, by their industry, 'have rendered the earth more proper for their abode'. Man, in other words, should not merely live on the surface of the earth, but work it.[21]

The *Esprit des lois* first appeared in 1748 and was translated into English two years later. By 1773 it had gone through ten British editions, published in Edinburgh, Aberdeen and Berwick as well as London. A comic poem which appeared in 1778 gives some indication of its popularity. *The Project* acknowledges Montesquieu, and then begins:

> Since sage philosophers aver,
> That *climate* forms the *character*;
> And prove each nation, tame, or bold,
> Just as its air is hot or cold.

It goes on to suggest that a hot fire should be maintained in the Houses of Parliament, fuelled by such popular tracts as Tom Paine's *Common Sense*. The consequent increase in temperature would replace discord with harmony. Even a gouty Chatham would be softened into agreeing that the war against America was just.[22] With its references to the Revolution and a sly nod at Redcoat censure of Yankees who are not 'bold', *The Project* confirms that much of the British contempt of America may be traced back to the *Esprit des lois*. Of course, Montesquieu could not be blamed for the prostitution of his theories. He never visited America, nor did he need to. Because he used the New World simply as a vehicle to generate an environmentally grounded discussion of primitivism and civilisation, Montesquieu obtained what information he needed from a few travel books.

There is a long distance to travel from Montesquieu's generalised environmental theory to the precisely and forcefully stated British contempt of the very colonial cousins that the Frenchman had exempted from his strictures. British condescension is capable of riding far under its own steam; with help it can encompass the globe. Help came from three related scientific theories which turned Montesquieu's hypotheses into a full-scale and frequently acrimonious debate over the significance of the New World. The first can be briefly outlined and is best illustrated by another anonymous poem, this time published in 1774. *Otaheite* is generally devoted to antipodean scientific exploration, but at points has a more general import:

> Much of their Search through Nature's boundless Reign
> The Sons of Science ask, nor ask in vain . . .

Climes, where the Sun, with unremitting Blaze,
Pours the full Ardour of his fiercest Rays;
Regions of Ice whose deserted Plains,
Inverting Nature's Laws, stern Winter reigns;
Where never Spring with genial Influence rose,
Unbound the Glebe and thaw'd th' eternal Snows,
Patient they trod; nor shunn'd the barb'rous Shore
Where streams the horrid Feast with human Gore.
   Thus toils the Sage whose penetrating View
Dares Nature to her inmost Depths pursue.
He marks how animated Life descends
Progressive, and in Vegetation ends;
Inspects each Series through the great Design,
Each vital Point that fills th' unbounded Line;
Through endless Systems darts his piercing Eye,
And undismay'd attempts Infinity.

The last lines here refer to the Great Chain of Being, the linear hierarchy of nature ascending from the less to the more perfect, from simple organisms to man. The Chain of Being dates back to Plato, and in the age of exploration had come under increasing modification, partly from the plenitude that scientists had discovered in nature, and more seriously by a proto-evolutionary theory of improvement. In *Otaheite* both forms of modification follow an image of natural inversion, but geographically rather than politically or religiously inspired. Antipodal inversion also has its roots in classical antiquity, and is likewise a sign of disquiet. Overall, the poem is celebratory. The scientist, portrayed in ways that echo the images of the sun's sexual energy, attempts to put the natural order to rights. But there are shadows at the edge of the poem's optimism. An element of unease may be detected in the oxymoron 'descends / Progressive', pointed up by the enjambment. It indicates the fear that accompanies any evolutionary theory. If improvement within the natural order is possible, so too is deterioration. Such fears would come into full bloom in the light of Darwinian evolution when Max Nordau proclaimed the need to subdue 'the beast in man'. Here, the beast in man is present in the image of the cannibal who, ever since Montaigne's essay on Brazilian savages, had been used to distinguish primitive man from his supposedly superior civilised cousin. Civilised man discriminated over his dinner. The savage, it seemed, did not; and this placed him further down the Chain of Being, closer to beasts.[23]

We have already seen Indians described as cannibals and beasts. The distinction between civilised and primitive man was eroded by a growing awareness of the physical similarity between humans and beasts such as bears and monkeys, and of the insubstantiality of the rational processes that supposedly set man apart. The erosion was assisted by Montesquieu's environmentalist theory and by scientific interest in the orang-utan. The orang-utan had first been noticed by scientists in the seventeenth century. Edward Tyson, England's leading anatomist, had in 1699 called it 'the Nexus of the Animal and Rational'. Although it appeared to be the missing link, the vital difference between the orang-utan and man, according to Tyson, was that the ape could not speak. For many this was an important distinction. Diderot reports the Cardinal de Polignac addressing an orang-utan in a Paris zoo: 'Parle, et je te baptise.'

A number of writers disagreed with Tyson and Polignac. Chief among them was Lord Monboddo, who asserted in the first volume of his *Origin and Progress of Language*, published in 1773, that language was not natural to man. Monboddo muddied the waters further by pointing out that beasts lower on the Chain of Being did not eat their own kind, and by suggesting that orang-utans were not disqualified from the human species by their silence. After all:

> They are exactly of the human form; walking erect, not upon all-four, like the savages that have been found in Europe; they use sticks for weapons; they live in society; they make huts of branches of trees, and they carry off negroe girls, whom they make slaves of, and use both for work and pleasure.

The amusement with which we treat Monboddo's work today indicates that the questions he raised no longer overtly trouble us, although, particularly with such fantasy figures as Tarzan and King Kong, they can still make us sexually skittish. In the eighteenth century they were of great interest, and America seemed a highly appropriate environment for getting the answers, because of the Indians, because of black slaves, and because of the climate.[24]

The other two scientific theories placed the savage in an appropriate setting. One was geological and can, again, be dealt with briefly. In the Prologue we saw that the Biblical geographers depicted the earth as an immaculate sphere, reflecting the perfection of God's work. As everyone knew, the postlapsarian world was different. God's displeasure with his fallen subjects was revealed in the broken irregular flaws to be seen everywhere on earth. The flood was a central part of the ideology of the Fall, and evidence for it was to be found both in geology and in tales which we now regard as fantastic. George Sandys therefore listed marine fossils, 'Shels', and stories of anchors on mountain tops equally as American proof of the Flood.

That was in 1632. By the end of the century geology had elbowed aside less scientific proofs. This was due in large measure to *Telluris Theoria Sacra*, published in 1681 by the English bishop Thomas Burnet. Burnet brought out an enlarged English edition in 1684, entitled *The Theory of the Earth*. By 1759 it had gone through seven editions, but it was only with the fourth edition of 1719 that it regained the sacramental adjective of the Latin title. For although the book was popular and influential, it was also controversial. It attempted to reconcile the new developments in geology with the old account of the Flood. It suggested that the world had an 'inward composition' resembling an egg. When God cursed mankind the shell broke, allowing the waters beneath to inundate the surface. Mountains provided a constant reminder that we lived on a 'ruin'd Earth', while whirlpools, volcanoes and earthquakes demonstrated that it was now hollow.

As Marjorie Hope Nicolson has shown, Burnet's theory contributed to the growing appreciation of mountains which would lead in due course to Romanticism. It also fostered a more morbid if scientific interest in terrestrial convulsions, the most sustained being Sir William Hamilton's 36-year study of Vesuvius. The Bible had always provided a fertile source for interpreting natural events. Geology now added the weight of its own modern authority. The depiction of storms and earthquakes in *Robinson Crusoe*, published in 1719, is therefore both scientifically credible and theologically significant. Interest in cataclysms was such that, when there were two tremors in London in 1750, the prominent preacher John Wesley quickly sermonised on 'The Cause and Cure of Earthquakes', reminding Christians of the dreadful judgement of a righteous God. The Lisbon earthquake of 1755 provoked a fresh upsurge of scientific analysis and fundamentalist fear, and a pamphlet from Wesley so popular that it quickly went through six editions and greatly vexed Established Churchmen. Lisbon was generally believed to be the epicentre of moral and terrestrial degeneracy. As we shall see, the epicentre was later transferred to America.[25]

The third scientific theory deals more generally with the effects of climate, and relates more closely to Montesquieu. I shall discuss it at much greater length because it referred overtly to the New World, was in part encouraged by the growth of interest about America caused by the French and Indian War, and directly provoked American responses. Its first appearance was in 1749, just one year after the *Esprit des lois*, when Le Comte de Buffon published the first volume of his *Histoire naturelle*. Buffon was already a scientist of international repute. He was a member of the Royal Society of London and the Philosophical Society of Edinburgh, and he numbered lords Chatham and Bute amongst his influential correspondents. After the appearance of the *Histoire naturelle* he became, according to Sainte-Beuve, one of the four most famous men of the century. There were four complete and many more partial editions in English.

Unlike Montesquieu, Buffon discussed America as an entity in itself rather than as a vehicle for a debate on civilisation. Also unlike Montesquieu, he asserted that America had a cold climate, and an unpleasant dampness caused by the profusion of trees and wild vegetation:

In these melancholy regions, Nature remains concealed under her old garments and never exhibits herself in fresh attire; being neither cherished nor cultivated by man, she never opens her fruitful and beneficent womb. Here the Earth never saw her surface adorned with those rich crops, which demonstrate her fecundity and constitute the opulence of polished nations. In this abandoned condition, everything languishes, corrupts, and proves abortive. The air and the earth, overloaded with humid and noxious vapours, are unable either to purify themselves or to profit by the influence of the Sun, who darts in vain his most enlivening rays upon this frigid mass, which is not in a condition to make suitable returns to his ardour. Its powers are limited to the production of moist plants, reptiles, and insects, and can afford nourishment only to cold and feeble animals.

The scarcity of men, therefore, in America, and most of them living like brutes, is the chief cause why the earth remains in a frigid state, and is incapable of producing the active principles of Nature.

The author of *Otaheite*, it seems, had read Buffon. In contrast to the Antipodes, in America the sun's advances get no response and the terrain remains coldly inverted. Buffon extends the blatant imagery of sexual deprivation to the Indians, who have 'been refused the most precious spark of nature's fire', and are consequently below animals on the Chain of Being. His remarks echo Hippocrates, and also Pliny's description of the Esseni on the west bank of the Jordan, who lack 'carnall lust' and who 'keepe companie onely with Date trees'. The Indians are also timid, stupid and lazy. But Buffon, like Montesquieu, drew a clear distinction between them and the colonists. He praised the latter for their efforts to become the masters of nature, and attached utopian expectations to them. When the continent is farmed, the forests cut down and the marshes drained, America 'will become the most fertile, the most wholesome, and the richest in the whole world'.[26]

Unfortunately, the distinction was eroded by writers who were less discriminating than Buffon, and a further element was added to the pejorative imagery of America. From 1749 to 1751 the Swedish scientist Per Kalm, unlike his predecessors, actually visited the Middle Colonies of America. He published his *Travels* in Swedish in 1752. It was translated into German in 1754 and English in 1770. It was an influential book, and the English translation by the well-known linguist and scientist John Reinhold Forster was particularly popular. It was reprinted the following year, and a second edition appeared in 1772, the year that Forster was appointed naturalist on Cook's second voyage.

The *Travels* provides a good example of the hallucination of displaced terrain, for Kalm was so influenced by his reading that he expected to see strange sights in America. Consequently, he believed the tales that he was told. He learned, for instance, of black snakes that chase humans and

rattlesnakes that catch squirrels 'by fascination'. (Kalm was particularly
susceptible to the tall tale; another, on bears, appears in chapter 6 below.)
Yet his work was painstaking and detailed, including thirty pages of
meteorological tables. The result was an air of 'veracity', as one review
put it, that strengthened Kalm's assertion that colonists are afflicted by
Indian degeneration. It was the climate that was at fault:

> The weather is so inconstant here that, when a day is most excessively hot, the
> next is often sensibly cold. This sudden change often happens in one day; and
> few people can suffer these changes without impairing their health ... Several
> distempers prevail here; and they increase every year. Nobody is left
> unattacked by the intermitting fever; and many people are forced to suffer it
> every year, together with other diseases.

The only things that flourish in such an environment are the pests.
Imported animals decline in size, women cease bearing children earlier
than in Europe, people age more rapidly, and colonial troops are inferior
to Europeans.[27] British military condescension, it seemed, was scientifically grounded.

Kalm was placid in comparison with Cornelius de Pauw, whose
Recherches philosophiques sur les Américains was published in two volumes
in 1768–1769. The work created an immediate stir, and by 1774 a further
five French editions had appeared, one of them published in London in
1771. Extensive reviews appeared in British periodicals. The first edition
in English appeared in 1789, and comprised brief selections only, which
were augmented in new editions in 1795 and 1806. The *Recherches* was
therefore widely known in English-speaking countries, although in a
piecemeal fashion. This was perhaps appropriate, for despite its scientific
title, the book was more the work of a controversialist, orchestrating
adverse commentary from a range of sources, including Montesquieu,
Buffon and Kalm:

> At the time of the discovery of America, its climate was unfavorable to most
> quadruped animals, which in fact are one-sixth smaller in the New World than
> their counterparts on the old continent. In particular, the climate was injurious
> to the natives who, to an astonishing degree, were stupified, enervated, and
> vitiated in all parts of their organism.

> The land itself, either bristling with mountain peaks or covered with forests
> and marshlands, presented the aspect of an immense and sterile desert. The first
> adventurers to settle there underwent the horrors of famine or the great
> sufferings of thirst. The Spaniards, from time to time, were forced to eat
> Americans [Indians] and even other Spaniards for lack of nourishment ... The
> first French colonists sent into this hapless world also ended by eating each
> other ...

2 'A singular species of Monkeys', from *The Scots Magazine* (1770). A Caledonian
contribution to the philosophic debate over America, spiced with soft porn.

The surface of the earth, full of putrefaction, was flooded with lizards, snakes, serpents, reptiles, and insects that were monstrous by their size and the power of their poison extracted from the juice of this earth, so barren, so vitiated, so abandoned, where the nutritive sap became sour like milk in the breasts of animals that do not propogate. There, caterpillars, butterflies, centipedes, scarabs, spiders, frogs, and toads were found in gigantic size for their species, and multiplied beyond imagining.

This is an impressive jeremiad, intersected by Biblical references (caterpillars, serpents), verified by pseudo-scientific details (quadrupeds that are 'in fact' one-sixth smaller), and confirmed by the regression of the settlers. No wonder, in a terrain that actively threatens them. Even the mountains 'bristle'. De Pauw presents here a landscape of absolute perversion, a vision of hell.

In descending the Chain of Being, the settlers effectively became Indians. And the Indians? According to de Pauw, they were not only 'fundamentally weak' but were, in fact, orang-utans. This assertion so fascinated *The Scots Magazine* that it interpolated its review of de Pauw with an account of this 'singular species of Monkeys' and added an illustration of an alluringly lissom creature (see figure 2). De Pauw, of course, was not interested in titillation. He arraigned 'a certain pope' who (with more authority if less caution than the Cardinal de Polignac) had decreed that these 'dubious animals' should be recognised as 'true men'. The Pope could do nothing about the malignity of the terrain. Neither could de Pauw; but he could explain it. Earlier, Buffon had suggested that America was a new continent. Not simply had it been discovered more recently, but it had emerged from the Flood more recently than Europe, and hence was in a more primitive condition. De Pauw said that this was not so. Fossil remains showed that there had once been large animals in America; but they had degenerated. What had happened was a second catastrophe, a new flood many centuries after Noah's, a deluge 'of enormous proportions' that accounted for the innumerable rivers, lakes and swamps in America. America was therefore doubly damned, so malignant that it infected Europe. It had done this by means of a virulent syphilitic miasma that infected all who breathed it, humans and animals alike. It had long been believed that syphilis was America's gift to Europe. De Pauw embroidered the belief and like a customs official traced the source of importation. It was a monk that was to blame, a head of the Benedictine Order with the appropriate name of Boil. Boil had sailed with Columbus, and hated him with such poison that he infected Europe and had the navigator excommunicated and imprisoned. 'This great man', concluded de Pauw, 'finding himself prey to the rage of such a vile fanatic, repented for having discovered a new world.'[28]

The French cleric Guillaume, l'Abbé Raynal, was more measured in his treatment of America. His *Philosophical and Political History . . . of the East and West Indies* was first published in 1770, and by 1798 had appeared in thirty-five French editions. The first English translation was of an extract discussing the present American dispute; it appeared in Philadelphia as a pamphlet in 1775. The first complete translation was published in London the following year, and immediately sold out. Three further editions appeared within the next year, and by 1799 fourteen had been published in all, selling more copies than Edward Gibbon's *Decline and Fall of the Roman Empire*. The book served to confirm and promote even further the views of Buffon. Raynal agreed with his predecessor that the American climate was damp and miasmic, the Indians and animals both immature and few in number. 'A rude and unpeopled hemisphere', he concluded, 'denotes a recent world.' Yet, because it was new, America had great potential. Again like Buffon, Raynal praised the colonists. They had 'introduced symmetry' where all before was chaos, clearing the woods and raising farms, draining waters and cutting canals. Eventually, American 'culture, knowledge and population' would lead to a separation from Britain, but at present America was so puny that such a course would be disastrous. In this instance Raynal was forced to agree with de Pauw. America had not yet produced a single good poet or mathematician.[29]

Although the Old World contribution to the debate over America was largely European, the British followed its progress avidly. As we have seen, many of the books were widely reviewed and promptly translated. From the middle of the 1760s references to frightful woods, dreary deserts and a regressive population were to be found in a number of English novels about America. When the Revolution came, any possibility of amelioration was lost. In 1776 a poem entitled *The Genius of Britain, to General Howe* suggested that the rebellion had caused a natural inversion which had transformed the rising British empire into desolation and waste:

> Where her harp contentment strung,
>   Pity's sighs are heard to flow:
> Scenes that loud with rapture rung,
>   Gloom, a wilderness of woe . . .
>
> *Safety* slept in ev'ry field,
>   *Fear* had night's pale empire fled;
> Now, with tyger-crouch conceal'd,
>   *Danger* lurks in ev'ry shade.[30]

Two well-known figures played a prominent role in disseminating the pejorative imagery of America. One was Oliver Goldsmith, whose works were extremely popular and were available in countless editions.

In 1760, through the mouthpiece of a Chinese philosopher, Goldsmith (who had once considered emigrating to America) questioned the overt motives of the French and Indian War. He considered that it was the right to trap fur that was really being contested, and not the right of dominion over a 'cold, desolate, and hideous' country shared by Indians with 'the prowling bear or insidious tyger'. In the same year, Goldsmith also wrote a brief essay on the environmental theories of Montesquieu and Buffon. These two essays are echoed in his poem *The Traveller* (1764), which discusses the variety of European cultures. America is seen as no culture at all but, in a glancing reference to his *A History of England* (also 1764), simply as the hellish stage for Braddock's sad defeat.[31]

Goldsmith's work as a populariser of science enlarged his store of images of America. *A History of the Earth, and Animated Nature*, his compilation published posthumously in 1774 and given one of the longest ever reviews in the *Critical Review*, adds the authority of the European intellectuals to the opinions of the British military when it refers to 'cowardly' Indians who refuse 'to face their enemies in the field, but fall upon them at an advantage'. His descriptions of volcanoes and earthquakes, however, draw entirely on Old World sources like Burnet and the earthquake scares of the 1750s. Buffon and de Pauw provide Goldsmith with material to compare Africa and America, to the disadvantage of the New World. It is a general rule, he suggests, that where men 'are most barbarous and stupid, the brutes are most active and sagacious'. In both continents, therefore, the savages 'suppose monkies to be men'. This adjustment of the Chain of Being is little help to America, which is so infertile that only reptiles flourish, while 'the ant, bear, and the sloth, appear so miserably formed as scarce to have the power of moving and eating'.

The starkest contrast between Old and New Worlds is to be found in Goldsmith's most popular work, *The Deserted Village*, which within two years of first publication in 1770 had gone through seven editions. 'Sweet Auburn', even in its depleted state, is Eden compared with America:

> Far different there from all that charm'd before,
> The various terrors of that horrid shore.
> Those blazing suns that dart a downward ray,
> And fiercely shed intolerable day;
> Those matted woods where birds forget to sing,
> But silent bats in drowsy clusters cling,
> Those poisonous fields with rank luxuriance crowned
> Where the dark scorpion gathers death around;
> Where at each step the stranger fears to wake
> The rattling terrors of the vengeful snake;
> Where crouching tigers wait their hapless prey,

> And savage men more murderous still than they;
> While oft in whirls the mad tornado flies,
> Mingling the ravaged landschape with the skies.[32]

Even the birds are struck dumb by the miasma. Goldsmith here matches de Pauw's vision of hell in images which provided the author of *The Genius of Britain, to General Howe* with much of his inspiration, not only of tigers but also of a natural violence matched by a landscape convulsed by the turbulent weather.

The second British writer to make a major contribution to the debate over America was William Robertson, Principal of Edinburgh University and Historiographer Royal for Scotland. If Goldsmith popularised the pejorative imagery, Robertson gave it his authority as one of Britain's leading intellectuals. His book was well timed. *The History of America* appeared one year after the Declaration of Independence. And, like Goldsmith's, his work was widely read. Within a few weeks of its publication it had, according to Gibbon, 'already become a favourite subject of conversation'. It became Robertson's most popular book, going through thirteen editions by 1817 and being translated into French, German, Spanish and Greek. Robertson did not wholly subscribe to the more outrageous assertions of his European predecessors. He did however believe in the relation between climate and physiology, and therefore he accepted much that had already been written. Like Raynal he thought that the activity of the colonists improved the country:

> The labour and operations of man not only improve and embellish the earth, but render it more wholesome and friendly to life. When any region lies neglected and destitute of cultivation, the air stagnates in the woods, putrid exhalations arise from the waters; the surface of the earth, loaded with rank vegetation, feels not the purifying influence of the sun or of the wind; the malignity of the distempers natural to the climate increases, and new maladies, no less noxious are engendered. Accordingly, all the provinces of America, when first discovered, were found to be remarkably unhealthy.

The colonists had however only improved a few places along the eastern coast of America. The continent had in general been left to the Indians who, 'as rude and indolent as ever, have done nothing to open or improve a country, possessing almost every advantage of situation and climate'. The result was a miasma which not only affected the Indians but also the animals. Robertson agreed with Goldsmith and the European intellectuals that there were a smaller number of species in America than elsewhere and that they were less robust or fierce than their Old World counterparts, although he quibbled over their names. America had no elephants or rhinoceroses, no lions and (despite Goldsmith) no tigers. It had only the puma and the jaguar, which 'possess neither the undaunted courage' of the lion nor 'the ravenous cruelty' of the tiger. And the same causes that checked 'the more noble' animals encouraged the more pestilential:

> As this country is, on the whole, less cultivated, and less peopled, than the other quarters of the earth, the active principle of life wastes its force in productions of this inferior form. The air is often darkened with clouds of insects, and the ground is covered with shocking and noxious reptiles.

Although the *History of America* was apparently more scientific and cautious than de Pauw, it confirmed much of his thesis, including stories about syphilis and toads. It also added one aspect that reflected British colonialism. Goldsmith had drawn on the British military experience in America; Robertson emphasised its consequences. The Treaty of Paris of 1763, concluding the French and Indian War, had more than doubled the territory of British America and consequently changed the British perception of the continent. Words like 'vast' and 'immense' appeared with renewed vigour in the vocabulary of American amplitude, to make the terrain's miasmic qualities all the more pervasive and threatening. Robertson began his *History* by emphasising the extent of the continent, and this initially seemed to endow the terrain with a certain grandeur:

> Nature seems here to have carried on her operations upon a larger scale, and with a bolder hand, and to have distinguished the features of this country by a peculiar magnificence.

Within four pages Robertson began to qualify this appreciation. The climate of the New World was subject to different laws, with results that we have already seen. Grand it may be; but its grandeur only made it all the more difficult to tame.[33]

British military contempt of the New World and its denizens was not, then, simply an expression of ignorance and prejudice. It was grounded in an environmental theory proposed by some of the most respected thinkers and popular authors. The words of the soldiers had a particular authority, although only some of them would have known it. They showed how widely current were the miasmatist theories. A soldier in Boston complained that 'this extensive Continent is all in arms against us'. Hessian officers wrote home about a climate so unhealthy that it stunted the domestic animals and allowed no humans to survive beyond forty — yet it sustained tigers, and rattlesnakes whose very glance was fatal. Major John Bowater in New York cursed 'Columbus and all the discoverers of this Diabolical Country'.[34] When the soldiers spoke they represented the views of the Old World, and with all the more vigour because it was their misfortune to be in the New.

AN ASYLUM IN THE WILDERNESS

Let us turn now to the American response to these European attitudes. Not surprisingly, the environmentalist theories of Montesquieu and his successors caused a festering sore under the American skin that would break out with the slightest provocation. When in 1820, for instance, Sydney Smith reviewed a volume of American statistics, his closing remarks ('Who reads an American book?') caused a furore and placed his name in the American annals of infamy. Perhaps the response took him aback, for he was simply repeating Raynal, and for most of the eleven pages of his review he had been even-handed. His remarks, however, seemed to many Americans yet another example of Old World disdain.[35]

Initially, some writers like Benjamin Franklin had responded to the theories with humour. Franklin had been told, for instance, that American sheep were so wasted that their wool would not make a single pair of socks. That is a lie, he said:

> The very Tails of the American Sheep are so laden with Wool, that each has a Car or Waggon on four little Wheels to support and keep it from trailing on the Ground.

To the report that both whales and cod were to be found in the Upper Lakes of Canada he responded:

> Ignorant people may object that the Upper Lakes are fresh, and that Cod and Whale are Salt-water fish: But let them know, Sir, that Cod, like other Fish, when attacked by their Enemies, fly into any Water where they think they can be safest; that Whales, when they have a Mind to eat Cod, pursue them wherever they fly; and that the grand Leap of the Whale in that Chace up the Fall of Niagara is esteemed by all who have seen it, as one of the finest spectacles in Nature![36]

Franklin was writing in 1765 when it was still possible to be humorous: before he fell out with the British Government, before the publication of the works of de Pauw, Raynal and Robertson, and before the discord between Britain and her American colony had reached the point of rupture. Yet Franklin's caricature illustrates a problem that would afflict American writers for many years (and still occasionally afflicts them). Franklin's sheep and whales (not to mention the poor cod) are figures equally as unAmerican as Kalm's fascinating snakes and de Pauw's gigantic toads. By refuting Old World attacks on America, Franklin assumed an Old World viewpoint. American terrain had been dislocated in the service of a debate that was essentially European.

Very shortly the debate changed quality, but retained the same character. American humour became American rhetoric, and as it did so the dislocation became more insidious. I am not speaking here of the simple denials of European theory, although much useful energy was wasted in making them.[37] I am interested, rather, in the attempts to create a New World culture based upon the environment. They show, I think, that European theory was so potent that it created a hallucination into which Americans ventured, away from the realities of their country. European theory resembled a spider's web. The more that American writers struggled to assert a unique American culture, the more they were trapped in the hallucination of displaced terrain. The Connecticut writer Richard Alsop attacked de Pauw for treating America with such freedom that it was 'as if he had been writing upon the moon and its inhabitants'.[38] The same protest could be made about many of the American responses that I will examine in a moment.

There are two further reasons why the terms of New World culture were set by the Old. The first is well known. Intellectuals on both sides of the Atlantic held the same beliefs about the way that all worlds worked. Benjamin Franklin and George Washington shared with their Old World counterparts the same preoccupations, for instance over the concept of family; and held the same faith that rationality would inevitably reveal the laws of God's nature. The second reason for the identity of New and Old World culture is the theory of its westward movement. Often known as *translatio emperii*, the theory existed (as we saw in the Prologue) as a heliotropic vector before the discovery of America. After the discovery the British reformulated *translatio emperii* as a providential relationship between the terrain and those who settled it. It was an inheritance which was shared, despite all their differences, by the Puritan northern and Cavalier southern colonies.[39]

In the century before the Revolution it was the British, again, who developed the ideology further. Thomas Sprat's *History of the Royal Society* (1667), more usually taken as a harbinger of the Scientific Revolution, is also prophetic of the cultural aspects of the American Revolution when it suggests that the 'next *Increas* of *Manual Arts*' will be located in the New World. It took almost sixty years for Sprat's suggestion to be developed by another Briton. George Berkeley's 'Verses on the Prospect of Planting Arts and Learning in America', suffocated by its too-famous line 'westward the Course of Empire takes its Way', presents a complex of ideas in which civilisation deserts a Europe lost in tyranny and decay for a continent where natural perfection provides a proper setting for cultural advance:

> In happy Climes the Seat of Innocence,
>   Where Nature guides and Virtue rules,
> Where Men shall not impose for Truth and Sense,
>   The Pedantry of Courts and Schools:

> There shall be sung another golden Age,
>   The Rise of Empire and of Arts,
> The Good and Great inspiring epic Rage,
>   The wisest Heads and noblest Hearts.[40]

The fate of Berkeley's poem is significant. It was written in 1726, almost three years before his abortive sojourn in Rhode Island, and remained unpublished until 1752, the year before his death. By this time it had regressed from a radical prospectus, Berkeley's sole serious poetic outing to match his only pragmatic adventure, to a dream swathed in his idealist philosophy. Even as a dream it was too discomforting for Europeans, because the corollary of the rise of the New World was the decline of the Old. With the exception of a few brave spirits like Horace Walpole, most preferred to see their sun arrested over London or Edinburgh. But in the colonies the poem soon began to shine with a providential glow. Nothing promotes cultural identity so much as a threat, and as the conflict with France grew so did the influence of Berkeley's prophecy. It was frequently reprinted in the later 1750s, and the infectiousness of its message can be seen in two disparate documents.[41]

Nathaniel Ames' *Astronomical Diary* was the most popular colonial almanac, with an annual sale of 50–60,000 copies. The edition for 1758 surveys the 'Past State' of America with its ignorant natives, and calls for unity against the French as a prelude to a 'Future State' that hyperbolises Berkeley in pyrotechnic prose:

> The Curious have observ'd, that the Progress of Humane Literature (like the Sun) is from the East to the West; thus it has travelled thro' *Asia* and *Europe*, and now is arrived at the Eastern Shore of *America*. As the Coelestial Light of the Gospel was directed here by the Finger of GOD, it will doubtless, finally drive the long! long! Night of Heathenish Darkness from *America*: – So Arts and Sciences will change the Face of Nature in their Tour from Hence over the Appalachian Mountains to the Western Ocean; and as they march thro' the vast Desert, the Residence of wild Beasts will be broken up, and their obscene Howl cease for ever.

Ames expected the American terrain to bear out his prophecy in two or three centuries.[42]

Ames was a motley figure: an innkeeper, doctor and part-time lawyer. Yet his projection across the centuries and a continent was followed up by a rising member of the theocracy. Ezra Stiles was a grandson of Edward Taylor and had been a tutor at Yale before becoming a Congregationalist pastor. Ames, in the service of his imperial vision, had used the opposing figures of wilderness and promised land that were widely current yet Puritan in origin. The churchman returned the compliment in his 1761 *A Discourse on the Christian Union* by devoting much of it to worldly matters. Stiles insisted on liberty of conscience as an American birthright. It was however grounded not simply in freedom of worship but in 'free and absolute tenure of *land*' (author's emphasis). Stiles' advocacy of real estate went hand in hand with his interest in demography. He drew on Benjamin Franklin's *Observations on the Increase of Mankind* as well as his own statistics to project a population explosion assisted by 'agriculture and rural life'. Berkeley's prophecy, therefore, was happily confirmed by religious belief, scientific observation and fresh air. It only needed 'an honourable peace' to unleash the American drives for progeny and property which would 'cross the continent to the pacific ocean'. Stiles' argument may have been cooler than Ames', but his conclusion warmed up under the authority of Isaiah 35:1, and the licence of a dimensional confusion and an ambiguous main verb:

> We transport ourselves to the distance of 100 years forward, look over this wide spread wilderness, see it blossom like a rose, and behold it planted with churches and temples.[43]

Between them Ames and Stiles illustrate the temper of the time: a growing American sense of imperial power linking scientific prophecy with religious rhetoric and demographic fact to project a westering terrestrial transformation. Indeed, the following years made their prophecies appear conservative. The natural increase of the colonial population was augmented by large numbers of immigrants from the British Isles, lured by a justified belief in economic and social improvement. There was an acceleration, too, in scientific understanding of God's nature, with Americans playing a more significant role. American scientists began to lay the basis of a longlasting love-affair with the public, led by Benjamin Franklin and David Rittenhouse, the Philadelphia clockmaker who in 1767 constructed an accurate orrery. It would be only a matter of time before American science would be transformed into American technology, which would in turn transform 'the Face of Nature'.

Confidence in a colonial future was such that in 1769 an anonymous book predicted the dissolution of Britain. *Private Letters from an American in London to his Friends in America* is set at the close of the next century. The government has been transferred to America. The only people who have not emigrated are 'the scum and refuse' of the land. Decay is apparent everywhere. London, once the hub of a vast empire, is now the site of fallen statues, broken sewers, ruined bridges and buildings. Even the monuments to national glory in Westminster Abbey have been sold off. The portrait of the kingdom was such that the humour of one of the reviewers was severely strained. 'Poor old England', he lamented, 'is represented as quite superannuated.'[44]

Nathaniel Ames died in 1765 and therefore did not live to see the immediate outcome of his prophecy. He would no doubt have shared the delighted amazement of Ezra Stiles, who in 1783 gave an Election Sermon celebrating the growing American empire. Stiles looked forward to expansion westward of such magnitude that America would equal half Europe, and an accompanying population explosion that would exceed the Chinese. He used the recent past to refute the charges that he was being unjustifiably utopian:

> As utopian would it have been to the loyalists, at the battle of Lexington, that in less than eight years the independence and sovereignty of the United States should be acknowledged by four European sovereignties, one of which should be Britain herself. How wonderful the revolutions, the events of Providence! We live in an age of wonders; we have lived an age in a few years; we have seen more wonders accomplished in eight years than are usually unfolded in a century.

From his vantage-point as President of Yale (he was elected to the post in 1778 and would hold it until his death in 1795) Stiles looked out at the new republican culture:

> We shall have a communication with all nations in commerce, manners, and science beyond anything heretofore known in the world . . . all the arts may be transplanted from Europe and Asia, and flourish in America with an augmented lustre, not to mention the augment of the sciences from American inventions and discoveries, of which there have been as capital ones here, the last century, as in all Europe.

Such assertions were common at the time; Ezra Stiles was unusual only in that he made them with greater vigour and certainty. Yet for all Stiles' enthusiasm, his prediction of the new culture reveals that it will include many of the characteristics of the old. The 'communication' that the Republic will have with the world will result in a culture that is 'transplanted'. Thomas Sprat had used the term in its narrow horticultural sense. Stiles adopted a broader interpretation to suit the distended American garden empire, but did not change its root meaning. As he twice remarks, all America will do is to 'augment' what has been achieved in Europe. The only alteration to his earlier prediction and that of the 1769 *Private Letters from an American* is that the government will not now be uprooted from England.[45]

This is nevertheless an important alteration, although as we shall see it was not as indispensible as American patriots pretended. It was, suitably, yet another Briton that added the political element to the rhetoric of cultural transfer. Tom Paine published *Common Sense* when Lexington was a nine-month memory. More than any other document, it focussed American feelings about their continent, and it was extremely popular.

According to one estimate, it sold more than 500,000 copies in 1776, the first year of its publication. Paine's presence in America seemed providential. As a fellow British radical remarked, 'never was a writer better calculated for the meridian under which he wrote'.[46]

And never did a writer more successfully incorporate that meridian into his political argument. Although much of the pamphlet is devoted to a rehearsal of American complaints against the British constitution and aristocratic way of life, through it runs a thread of imagery uniting American terrain with its burgeoning political organisation. An image in the 'Appendix' makes this clear:

> we have every opportunity and every encouragement before us, to form the noblest, purest constitution on the face of the earth. We have it in our power to begin the world over again. A situation, similar to the present, hath not happened since the days of Noah until now. The birth-day of a new world is at hand, and a race of men perhaps as numerous as all Europe contains, are to receive their portion of freedom from the event of a few months.

The image repeated here again and again is of renewal. By asserting that the world can begin again Paine reverses the doomlike interpretation of the legend of Noah and responds to the argument developed in Europe about the age of America. Whatever had happened to America in the past, the moment of renewal will put all to rights. The population explosion that will refute all the theories about degeneration will be caused by the Revolution. Like Ames' and Stiles', Paine's view is prospective; it looks forward to a new dynamic between the terrain and its inhabitants, ordered primarily through its political constitution.

Images such as this are to be found scattered through the whole of *Common Sense*. The youthful America is now in 'the seed time of good habits', a suitably gestatory metaphor rebuffing Kalm and de Pauw. The nation is therefore created at just the right 'time of forming itself into a government'. This vast new world, moreover, provides an 'asylum' for the persecuted of Europe. On arrival they notice an immediate difference:

> In this extensive quarter of the globe, we forget the narrow limits of three hundred and sixty miles (the extent of England) and carry our friendship on a larger scale; we claim brotherhood with eve-European Christian [*sic*], and triumph in the generosity of the sentiment.

The brotherhood is not with the English aristocrats. Americans should shun the easy course, suitably expressed in a metaphor of constriction, of 'getting into holes and corners and talking of reconciliation'.[47]

Images of American amplitude, as we have seen, were common after the Treaty of Paris in 1763. But now Paine was using them in praise of the New World, and contrasting them with images of British confinement.

He would continue to use such images for the rest of his life. In the 'Introduction' to Part 2 of the *Rights of Man* (1792) he made explicit the connection between American terrestrial and political organisation:

> As America was the only spot in the political world, where the principles of universal reformation could begin, so also was it the best in the natural world. An assemblage of circumstances conspired, not only to give birth, but to add gigantic maturity to its principles. The scene which that country presents to the eye of a spectator, has something in it which generates and encourages great ideas. Nature appears to him in magnitude. The mighty objects he beholds, act upon his mind by enlarging it, and he partakes of the greatness he contemplates.

The perspective is from a great height, and there is a clear correlation between that height and the lofty thought that informs American politics.

In another late work, Paine developed the natural scene that presented itself to the eye. No other country, he said, had 'so many openings to happiness' as America:

> the vastness of its extent, the variety of its climate, the fertility of its soil, the yet unexplored treasures of its bowels, the multitude of its rivers, lakes, bays, inlets and other conveniences of navigation offers to these United States one of the richest subjects of cultivation ever presented to any people upon earth.[48]

The earlier reference to Noah in *Common Sense* is here developed into a direct rebuttal of writers like Buffon, de Pauw and Robertson. The great extent of America's water system is not a sign of its damned character, but rather an aid to commerce.

Common Sense transformed the rhetoric of American terrain into politics, and in doing so provided more than a rallying-cry for patriots. Paine's imagery of American political space will appear in the case-studies discussed in the next two chapters. It validated the enthusiasm and shortened time-scale of Ezra Stiles' 1783 prophecy; and can be traced in two texts specifically intended to refute the European intellectuals and attract further settlers to the new agrarian Republic. The first was by John Filson. Little is known about Filson. He was probably born in 1753, and may have served in the Revolution. He was also reputed to have been a schoolmaster but is best known for his one book. Although only one edition of *The Discovery and Settlement of Kentucke* (1784) was issued in America – perhaps because George Washington refused to endorse a second – it was popular abroad, being issued in Paris and Frankfurt in 1785, Nürnberg in 1789 and Leipzig in 1790.

Filson wrote with an eye to a profit. He had moved to Kentucky to speculate in land, and hoped that his book would encourage settlement and thus enhance land values. Perhaps as a result, his book is shot through with the motif of a politically created Eden. America, he said, is a land of promise, flowing with milk and honey:

> where nature makes reparation for having created man; and government, so long prostituted to the most criminal purposes, establishes an asylum in the wilderness for the distressed of mankind.

The rhetoric may be inflated but it is extremely potent, unifying Puritan imagery with the geopolitics of Paine. It is also intersected by practical advice. Detailed instructions are given, for instance, on how to obtain a land title. Indeed, the tension between political rhetoric and practical advice extends to the map included in the book. Technically of high quality and with a wealth of information, it compresses the eastern and western ends of Kentucky thereby emphasising meadowland at the expense of the mountains.[49] Filson's masterstroke, however, was to append an account of the life of Daniel Boone. He portrayed the frontiersman as an innately good man finding happiness in the simple life of nature, although there were moments of danger and discomfort. These would later be developed by James Fenimore Cooper, who with the character of Leatherstocking made the lone figure of the hunter into one of the central motifs of American culture.

In the years immediately following the publication of *Kentucke* it was the supposedly natural relationship between Americans and their environment that caught the imagination. An early example of Filson's influence is Gilbert Imlay's *A Topographical Description of the Western Territory of North America* (1792). Imlay is another shadowy figure in American Letters. Best known perhaps as the sometime lover of Mary Wollstonecraft, Imlay was an adventurer who lived in Paris for a while as agent for the sale of American lands. His *Topographical Description* was first published in London, and it is unlikely that any of it was written in America. Like Filson, Imlay creates generalised Edenic tableaux of America, while relating even more closely the qualities of the land and the characteristics of its inhabitants. American government, he suggests, is as distinctive for its unity, simplicity and efficiency as the American continent is distinguished by its smiling climate and fertile soil. He then universalises the point:

> It naturally struck me that there must be something in climate that debased or elevated the human soul; and that chill penury which a steril country and damp cold climate produces, in accumulating the wants of men, had increased their dependence, which at once saps the first principles of men. I conceived, in the infancy of the world, that men in temperate climates have retained their freedom longest.

Imlay is drawing on Montesquieu to make a comparison, popular in the early years of the United States, with the Mediterranean republics. In contrast, the poor serfs in a feudal and cloud-covered Britain can only be pitied.

Imlay painted America in the most glowing terms:

> Here an eternal verdure reigns, and the brilliant sun of lat. 39°, piercing through the azure heavens, produces, in this prolific soil, an early maturity that is truly astonishing. Flowers full and perfect, as if they had been cultivated by the hand of a florist, with all their captivating odours, and with all the variegated charms that colour and nature can produce, here, in the lap of elegance and beauty, decorate the smiling groves. Soft zephyrs gently breathe on sweets, and the inhaled air gives a voluptuous glow of health and vigour, that seems to ravish the intoxicated senses. The sweet songsters of the forest appear to feel the influence of this genial clime, and, in more soft and modulated tones, warble their tender notes in unison with love and nature. Every thing here gives delight; and, in that mild effulgence which beams around us, we feel a glow of gratitude for that elevation our all-bountiful Creator has bestowed upon us.[50]

It appears that French wine had gone to Imlay's head. His writing here is highly artificial, a farrago of periphrases, superlatives and latinate terms. He appeals to the senses by using sexual imagery and rhythms. In doing so he refutes Buffon and creates an intoxicating Eden that is the antipode of the miasma of de Pauw. At other points in his book Imlay does provide some useful information – the distances between towns along the Mississippi, for instance – but the overall effect is hyperbolical and seems to bear little relation to the realities of American terrain. Imlay simply inverts the assertions of the European intellectuals. Goldsmith's birds were silenced in America; Imlay's birds burst into superior song in the invigorating air.

If it is hard to take Imlay seriously, it is worth recalling that his views were shared by Thomas Jefferson. Before he went to France, Jefferson devoted part of his *Notes on the State of Virginia* to a scholarly and detailed refutation of Buffon. Amongst his many activities in France Jefferson listened to birdsong, and in a letter home he noticed that in the south the song of nightingales:

> is more varied, their tone fuller and stronger here than on the banks of the Seine. It explains to me another circumstance, why there never was a poet North of the Alps, and why there never will be one. A poet is as much the creature of climate as an orange or palm tree. What a bird the nightingale would be in the climates of America!

Jefferson uses Montesquieu for a jocular slap at Goldsmith, yet his remarks would not be out of place in the *Notes*. Underlying the humour is a serious point. Indeed, Jefferson made the point seriously in another letter when he drew a Hippocratic division of northern and southern qualities, and suggested that Pennsylvania was the golden mean.[51] How wise of the Founding Fathers to place the nation's capital in Philadelphia!

Jefferson, Filson and Imlay aimed their books at a European audience. Their arguments were advanced with even greater energy in America. The relation between nature and culture proposed by Ames and Stiles and reaching its mature expression in *Common Sense* was a central tenet of the new Republic, receiving the assent of propagandists and intellectuals, politicians and the public. A poem published anonymously in 1790 encapsulates much of the ideology of the period. Entitled 'The Power of Civilization and Freedom', it talks of savages and the 'furious beast' retiring before spreading harvests and grazing cattle; praises Philadelphia as the paradigm of urban life that will shortly be matched by other towns; sees agriculture transformed by the plough; and then concludes:

> At length, in every other clime oppress'd,
> Virtue asserts her empire in the West;
> Here Genius reigns, by Reason's powerful aid;
> Here flourish agriculture, arts, and trade.
> Here his own soil the happy farmer tills,
> And without dread the great command fulfils.
> Here arts a happier era have commenced;
> Imperial justice is to all dispensed;
> And here religion, honoured by the wise,
> Renders earth pleasant, and insures the skies.
>   *Americans!* proceed in virtue's cause;
> Still honour liberty, restrained by laws;
> Till rage and war shall be to hell consigned,
> And the *West* prove the asylum of mankind.[52]

The pleasures of bucolic owner-occupation are underwritten by a series of guarantees, preeminent among which, and mentioned twice, is 'Virtue'. Virtue enables the release of individual energies (or 'Genius') which, assisted by technology in the form of the plough, are transforming the wilderness into an Edenic empire. The transformation is conducted under the supervision of God, who is portrayed as a benign meteorologist. All these components interlock in the closing image of the asylum. The language of the poem indicates the extent to which it draws on Berkeley and Paine. There is just one crucial difference. Until the closing apostrophe the poem insistently uses the present tense. The asylum is no longer mere prophecy; it is being achieved now. In which case, why is the apostrophe needed? The exhortations to continued vigilance indicate that the environmental ideology contained in the poem has become clichéd. Clichés occur when belief has hardened into dogma; and dogma often fractures into disillusion. I will examine the implications of disillusion for the ideology of the asylum in the next section; and will conclude the present discussion by indicating how widespread were the beliefs contained in 'The Power of Civilization and Freedom'.

Although they expressed themselves in different ways, both an intellectual leader like John Adams and the ordinary Continental soldier believed that 'Virtue' (often treated as synonymous with self-denial) lay at the root of Revolutionary success.[53] The achievement of the soldiers would be continued by the farmers. As Michael Kammen has shown, the plough became a popular agrarian symbol after 1785. It also had an intellectual appeal as a technological symbol. Men of learning agreed that the disorder at present observable in nature could be corrected in accordance with God's laws through the use of machines for land clearance and drainage. It was another sign of Old World decline that, the Netherlands excepted, Europe had tended to alter the terrain merely for ornamental purposes. In contrast, the energies released by the Republic, applied through American technology, would create an enormous yet genuine Garden of Eden in the New World. The intimate connection between political and terrestrial transformation was a widespread and deeply held belief. It may be seen in anonymous, popular occasional poems like 'The Power of Civilization and Freedom'. It also influenced writings as diverse as William Currie's account of the climates and diseases of the United States, and the developing political analyses of the writer and diplomat Joel Barlow.[54]

The new republicans had a vision of the environment that expressed a coherent set of beliefs drawn from the realms of politics, morality, religion and science. That vision, they believed, was distinctive and novel, derived from the special circumstances in which they found themselves. It was, in fact, an engaged response to European theories about the terrain. This is made particularly clear by Thomas Bond's 1782 *Anniversary Oration* before the American Philosophical Society. Dr Bond, who taught at the University of Pennsylvania, drew on Hippocrates as well as modern science to suggest that 'the frequent Changes in the sensible Qualities of the Air' not only protected Americans against 'epidemical Diseases' but made them tougher and more independent. Evidence of this was originally provided by the Indians, who were 'stout, hardy, brave, virtuous, healthy, and remarkably long-lived'. They led a temperate life under a mild government. The recent war proved that the climate had similarly affected the colonials. Had the British government been aware of this, they would have realised the impossibility of enslaving 'a People thus destined by the God of Nature, to be great, wise and free'.

Bond's remarks depend on the identity of what he called 'the natural and moral World', and he took it to extraordinary lengths. 'Storms, Thundergusts and Earthquakes', he said, were necessary 'to correct the Air' and provide a salubrious variety in the frame of nature. Likewise, 'Convulsions have been found necessary to restore the lost Balances of Government and Liberty.' The most glorious convulsion in the history of man had just come to a close.[55] Bond believed his *Oration* to be an empirical explanation of the natural success of the new Republic. On the contrary, it is deeply rooted in Old World theory. Bond agrees with Kalm about the climate and with Goldsmith about earthquakes. He agrees with de Pauw that the settlers have taken on Indian qualities. Having accepted their premises, he reverses their conclusions and those of Buffon, Raynal and Robertson. At the same time he inverts the beliefs of Burnet, Defoe and Wesley that terrestrial cataclysms are God's punishment for moral turpitude. In his enthusiasm for the new Republic, Bond turned Old World science and religion on its head.

Bond's *Oration* perhaps represents the frontier of republican environmental enthusiasm. But similar if more judicious remarks may be found in a series of state histories published over the next thirty years. Jefferson's *Notes on the State of Virginia*, first published in 1785, is the most accomplished and best known. It has already been mentioned and will be discussed further in chapters 4 and 5. The first to appear after the Revolution was Jeremy Belknap's *History of New Hampshire*. The first volume was published in 1784, and a second edition came out in 1813. Like Bond's *Oration*, the *History* projects a providential relationship between politics, science and the terrain. It closes with a vision of the agrarian nation. Yet even as he attends closely to the local scene, Belknap looks over his shoulder. He addresses himself directly to the 'European philosophers', particularly William Robertson, when he asserts that uncleared land:

> is so far from being an object of dread, that there are no people more vigorous and robust than those who labour on the new plantations . . . the air of our forest is remarkably pure. The tall and luxuriant growth which an European might call 'rank vegetation', not only indicates strength and fertility of soil; but conduces to absorb noxious vapours.

Americans, as they transformed the land, would do well to retain 'rank vegetation'. Nature would do their work for them.[56]

According to Samuel Williams in *The Natural and Civil History of Vermont* (first edition 1794; second edition 1809) the same could be said for his state. Indeed, the magnitude of Vermont forests, together with 'the total want of sandy deserts, and barren places' indicated a vigour in the climate unequalled in any other part of the globe. Here again, the text was aimed at European theories, as the Preface makes clear:

> And while the ministers of kings were looking into their laws and records, to decide what should be the rights of men in the colonies, nature was establishing a system of freedom in America, which they could neither comprehend, or discern. The American Revolution explained the business to the world, and served to confirm what nature and society had before produced.

These two sentences, framed around an allusion to Tom Paine's newly published book and drawing on Berkeleian rhetoric, provides the standard contrast between the retrospective restrictions of European monarchies and the prospect of a natural American society. The images, however, reflect the Old-Worldliness of the debate. The image of the monarchical Old World is precise and vivid, while that of the New is vague and opaque.

Books on other states reveal similar attitudes. David Ramsay's 1796 *Sketch of the Soil, Climate, Weather and Diseases of South-Carolina* suggests that his home state provides a happy medium between the tropics and the colder latitudes. Jefferson's Pennsylvanian golden mean, it seems, is more broadly based. Also like Jefferson, and like James Sullivan's *History of the District of Maine* (1795), Ramsay suggested that the terrain and the climate were improving under the influence of cultivation. In South Carolina, earthquakes had been so few and so slight that they had never been recorded; and now hurricanes were decreasing in number. It was apparent that Goldsmith's view of America was becoming more incorrect with the passage of the years.[57]

In his attempts to disprove the European miasmatists, Ramsay was probably drawing on the work of the North Carolinian Hugh Williamson. In 1770 Williamson presented a paper before the American Philosophical Society which strove to substantiate one of Buffon's favourable hypotheses. Cultivation of the Middle Colonies, he asserted, had indeed made the climate more temperate and healthy. The settlers, it seemed, could transform the wilderness, and also refute Per Kalm, whose book had just appeared in English. The events of the next forty years politicised Williamson's work. In his 1811 *Observations on the Climate in Different Parts of America* and 1812 *History of North Carolina*, Williamson attacked 'writers of great celebrity' like Buffon and Robertson. He accepted Montesquieu's climatic theory, but also drew upon Tom Paine when he suggested that the climate and 'the face or form of the country' would create 'the character of the American nations'. His conclusion agreed with Gilbert Imlay:

> The proper nursery of genius, learning, industry and the liberal arts, is a temperate climate, in a country that is diversified by hills, enjoying a clear atmosphere. The reader will be pleased to consider, whether there is any part of the old continent, in which these circumstances occur, in so extensive a degree, as they do in America, at least in North America.

America, it seemed, was specially favoured.[58]

Leo Marx has suggested that Americans 'transferred the ancient pastoral dream of human possibilities from its conventional literary context to an actual political context'.[59] They did so however in a way which pulled them towards Europe and away from the facts of the American continent. Even the writers who attended closely to those facts shaped them so that they answered European criticisms, and in doing so they collaborated in a dream-world. The most dreamy of Americas, only distantly connected to the real terrain, had been created by John Filson and Gilbert Imlay. Their asylum could have been any asylum, their wilderness any wilderness. To a greater or lesser extent, all the texts so far examined contained anaesthetic elements. Like the soldiers, the writers had ejected the Redcoats, but had adopted Redcoatism. By engaging in intellectual conflict with the Old World, they had constructed a landscape which owed many of its contours to their adversaries. It was in consequence fragile, vulnerable, and easily inverted. In the last part of this chapter we shall see a further group of inversions, but this time of the ideal landscape. They, too, were constructed out of Old World images, and they moved even more firmly into Redcoatism, accepting not only the terms of the debate but now agreeing with the Redcoats that the world had been turned unpleasantly upside down.

INNOVATIONS AND CONVULSIONS

There is no need to detail the many and well-known troubles that afflicted the new Republic – although two incidents, the Illuminati Scare and the Whiskey Rebellion, will be discussed in the next two chapters. If 'Virtue' seemed to be the key of Revolutionary success its antonym, 'Corruption', was used to characterise post-Revolutionary failings. 'Corruption' appeared to be a hydra infinitely more dangerous than Kalm's fascinating snakes. It seemed to poison all aspects of republican life. It was detected in the political and financial problems of the Confederation and in the rise of what was pejoratively called 'faction'. It was supposed to be at the root of the linguistic violence with which opponents assaulted each other, and to be the cause of the physical violence which occasionally broke out. Pre-Revolutionary mob action, it was discovered, did not abate with the new regime. 'Corruption' played a central role in the later thought of John Adams, and could be heard issuing from the lips of anyone confused by the uncertain times. There seemed to be much evidence to indicate the fatal sickness of the infant Republic. Past republics had not endured for long, and the cyclical theory of history seemed to demand the demise of this one. Tom Paine had imagined America as Noah's Ark; before the end of the century others imagined it as the Tower of Babel.[60]

Corruption went hand-in-hand with conspiracy. Gordon Wood has shown that the widespread fears of conspiracy arose less from paranoia and more from a theory of individual responsibility that could not cope with rapidly diffusing political movements. The republicans saw a close relationship between personal morals and political change.[61] They also saw a close relationship between personal morals and environmental change. We have already seen Thomas Bond equating 'the natural and moral World' and celebrating 'Convulsions'. Bond died in 1784; like Nathaniel Ames he did not have to modify his beliefs. In the charged atmosphere of *fin-de-siècle* America Presbyterian leaders produced a quite different view of the way the world worked:

> when formidable innovations and convulsions in Europe threaten destruction to morals and religion; when scenes of devastation and bloodshed, unexampled in the history of modern nations, have convulsed the world; and when our country is threatened with similar calamities, insensibility in us would be stupidity; silence would be criminal. The watchmen on Zion's walls are bound by their commission to sound a general alarm, at the approach of danger. We therefore desire to direct your awakened attention, towards that bursting stream, which threatens to sweep before it the religious principles, institutions, and morals of our people.[62]

Bond's bracing republican world has undergone another revolution. The imagery here is of natural disaster, of violent terrestrial disorder that threatens the state, conceived as a Christian city. The correlation of social and political disorder and a mutable landscape is confirmed in an image of the Flood that draws its power from Burnet's *Theory of the Earth*.

Such fears were often voiced during this period. They characterise, for instance, Washington's 1796 Farewell Address. And, as the Presbyterian leaders indicated, the fears could be traced to Europe – in particular, to the French Revolution. Initially, most Americans saw the French Revolution as an extension to Europe of the American republican experiment. Tom Paine explained his involvement as follows:

> After the Revolution of America was established I ventured into new scenes of difficulties to extend the principles which the Revolution had produced.

The French, for their part, used the American Revolution as a model. There were among the French reformers those who wished to adopt the British constitution, but they were outnumbered by the enthusiastic 'Américanistes'. The French Revolution, therefore, seemed to provide evidence that Europe was beginning to catch what one writer, in an optimistic disease metaphor, called 'the seraphic contagion' of liberty. Paine's terrestrial transformation would become global. As a 1790 poem 'On the American and French Revolutions' put it, 'Science, triumphant, moulds the world anew.'[63]

As it developed, however, the French Revolution began to appear to many American conservatives as a frightful perversion of their own Revolution. It was Edmund Burke's 1790 *Reflections on the Revolution in France*, describing a systematic plan by the French intelligentsia to destroy Christianity, that sounded the first warning note. Burke's allegations seemed to be confirmed by the militant deism of Tom Paine's response, *The Rights of Man*, and by his subsequent *The Age of Reason*, both of which were widely read in America. The activities of Edmond Genêt, the first Minister from the French Republic to the United States, did nothing to dispel conservative unease. Citizen Genêt arrived in April 1793 to a general welcome, but he quickly alienated American opinion by a series of acts apparently aimed at American national integrity. Without consulting his hosts, he enlisted Americans for French privateers and for a mercenary army to attack Spanish and British possessions on the American continent. He was recalled in 1794 at the request of the American government, but he left behind him a number of societies aimed at fostering sympathy for the French cause.

Disillusion with the French Revolution was increased by the execution of Louis XVI and the Reign of Terror, by the outbreak of the Franco-British War and by the XYZ Affair, the revelation that the French had attempted to extort bribes from American ambassadors. Recent history was now reinterpreted so that the 1778 French intervention in the War of Independence took its place alongside the French and Indian War as another Gallic attempt at continental domination. After Yorktown the French, it was believed, had adopted subversive tactics. Conservatives reviled any pro-French organisations, and the term 'Jacobin', originally indicating a founder of the French Revolution, was now applied to any troublemaker.[64]

A number of French intellectuals tried to distinguish the French and American Revolutions and explain the upheavals in France. Writing to Jefferson in 1790, Madame d'Houdetot suggested that:

> The characteristic diffirence [sic] between your revolution, and ours, is that having nothing to destroy, you had nothing to injure, and labouring for a people, few in number, uncorrupted, and extended over a large tract of country, you have avoided all the inconveniences of a situation, contrary in every respect. Every step in your revolution was perhaps the effect of virtue, while ours are often faults, and sometimes crimes.

This is carefully argued. Madame d'Houdetot panders to American self-esteem by invoking 'virtue' and places in another context the link between space and politics made by Tom Paine in *Common Sense*. Yet if the Americans had been able to achieve a revolution easily because there was nothing to replace – and the noblewoman showed her awareness of this in the double use of the negative – it also meant that there was everything to achieve. As Americans were painfully aware, their culture was young and therefore both innocent and vulnerable. In its plastic condition it could easily be transformed by foreign influences.[65]

Cultural transformation meant terrestrial transformation. The link between political activity and environmental change can be seen, for instance, in *The Political Green-House, for the Year 1798*, a verse satire written by Richard Alsop and other Connecticut Wits. In part the poem is an attack on the 'Jacobinic band' that wishes to destroy 'this happy land'. France provides a warning of the chaos wrought by radicals:

> Across the Atlantic wing your way,
> And Gallia's wretched land survey.
> There the foul breath of every crime,
> Contaminates th' extended clime . . .
> There the rich soil neglected lies,
> No harvest meets the wandering eyes,
> Commerce reclines her drooping head,
> And Industry the land has fled.
> Where Justice rears her awful seat,
> The blockhead, and the villain meet,
> While Law astonish'd quits the place,
> And blushing Virtue hides her face.

Paine had looked across the Atlantic and depicted Europe as a confined space. Here that space is stretched and a number of key images injected to present France as a perversion of American terrain. The portrayal of France closes, and the poem returns home with a warning that echoes the pious ending of Robert Burns's evocation of Scottish rural simplicity, 'The Cotter's Saturday Night':

> In scenes like these, let those who dare
> *E'en wish* this peaceful land to share,
> Change their dark purpose ere too late,
> Or else prepare to meet their fate.[66]

The sword-rattling indulged by Richard Alsop and his friends seemed to others to provide no protection against the insidious influence of France. The gloomiest projections of the future came from the Federalist leader Fisher Ames. He described France as an 'open hell' and saw the face of American nature transformed by its spell into the antipode of the utopia predicted by Nathaniel Ames, his father:

> A mob-government, like a West India hurricane, instantly strews the fruitful earth with promiscuous ruins, and turns the sky yellow with pestilence. Men inhale a vapor like the sirocco, and die in the open air for want of respiration . . . It is not doing justice to licentiousness to compare it to a wind which ravages the surface of the earth; it is an earthquake that loosens its foundations, burying in an hour the accumulated wealth and wisdom of ages. Those who, after the

calamity, would reconstruct the edifice of public liberty, will be scarcely able to find the model of the artificers, or even the ruins. Mountains have split and filled the fertile valley, covering them with rocks and gravel; rivers have changed their beds; populous towns have sunk, leaving only frightful chasms, out of which are creeping the remnant of living wretches, the monuments and victims of despair. This is no exaggerated description.

Britons like Edward Gibbon described the French Revolution in similar metaphors. Britain was directly menaced by French forces, but the Eden in the New World was being turned upside down by French influence. Ames expresses his greater sense of fear by denying that his description is metaphoric. Having set up the terms of the comparison, he tries to escape from them, overtly at two points and elsewhere by resourceful use of parallelism, counterpoint and phonology. The denial of metaphor is also achieved by using the European pejorative accounts of America. Ames' warning harks back to Burnet and Goldsmith; and his description resembles de Pauw's, particularly when he goes on to describe American Jacobins – Alsop's blockheads and villains – in animalistic terms. They are salamanders who 'breathe only in fire' and toads who 'suck no aliment from the earth but its poisons'.[67] This is the landscape of nightmare, but seen in daylight and without the protection of the Atlantic Ocean.

The landscape of Fisher Ames is sketched with great vigour, but it is hardly new. It unites three traditions of terrestrial description: the wilderness of the Puritans, the cataclysms of the geologists and evangelists, and the miasma of the European intellectuals. Neither is this particular confluence of images new. It is to be found a decade or two earlier in the bitter poetry of the American tories, as they were called. The loyalists paid dearly for their devotion to the British Crown. Many of them were hounded and imprisoned during the Revolution, and many chose to leave at its conclusion. Like some of the patriots they experienced at first hand the ease with which civilisation reverted to savagery. But they did not forget it, and the experience is reflected in the rancour of their writings.

No loyalist was more rancorous than Jonathan Odell. His verse plots a path similar to that of *The Genius of Britain, to General Howe*. According to Odell, before the Revolution America was developing in the way that Nathaniel Ames and Ezra Stiles had predicted, sustained by an umbilical cord from Britannia:

> The shoots of Science rich and fair,
> Transplanted from thy fostering Isle,
> And by the Genius nurtur'd there,
> Shall teach the Wilderness to smile.

That cord was cut by the Revolution, and the Eden is turned into a hell, here evoked in remarkable images that combine a charge of Gothic horror with references to geology, and to two of the beasts that still were daily threats to American farmers:

> They come, they come! – convulsive heaves the ground,
> Earth opens – lo! they pour, they swarm around;
> About me throng unnumber'd hideous shapes,
> Infernal wolves, and bears, and hounds, and apes.

A particular target for Odell's ire was Benjamin Franklin, whom he attacked in a doggerel piece not for being the principal rebel spokesman in the Old World, but for being a scientist who debased his talents:

> Let Candor, then, write on his Urn –
>   Here lies the renowned Inventor,
> Whose flame to the Skies ought to burn,
>   But, inverted, descends to the Center![68]

The Federalists may not have agreed with the loyalists that Franklin was responsible for inverting their world. But they accepted their predecessors' view that America had become a mutable and hellish land where beasts and beastlike men held sway. When their dream turned sour, they saw in their disappointment a dystopian landscape that was essentially European. It was inevitable that this should happen, because their American utopia had also been essentially European. Although they now saw its other face, the coin remained the same. This brings me back to the opening section of this chapter. The structure of the military debate in America – a series of accords over the natue of the discord – is therefore a microcosm of the larger conflict. Radical and conservative Americans alike constructed a landscape that was Old-Worldly in its origin, scope and detail.

The next two chapters will attempt to work out the implications of this landscape by looking at the careers of six diverse figures. Chapter 2 is devoted to three men – Jedidiah Morse, Noah Webster and Benjamin Rush – whose work is usually regarded as outside the realm of imaginative literature. Chapter 3 examines another trio – Crèvecœur, Freneau and Hugh Henry Brackenridge – more commonly discussed by literary critics. This division is for convenience only. It will I hope become apparent that all six men had a vision of American terrain which transcends the boundaries between fact and fiction that have sub-sequently been laid. Despite all their differences, they had two things in common. All six believed that they were assisting at the birth of a New World culture. All six revealed that they were collaborating in the triumph of Redcoatism.

2

A republic of dreams

In this chapter I will focus on the careers of three prominent Revolutionary intellectuals: Jedidiah Morse, Noah Webster and Benjamin Rush. Webster is famous as the creator of the *Dictionary* and, in an age of Founding Fathers, Morse has been called 'the Father of American Geography' and Rush 'the Father of American Psychiatry'. Posterity has done all three men a disservice by restricting their paternity. Like other eighteenth-century virtuosi each of them had wide-ranging interests. Morse, for the majority of his adult life, combined the twin occupations of geographer and minister. Webster and Morse proposed to collaborate on a geography. Between 1797 and 1813 almost one third of Webster's written work was on epidemiology, and for fifteen years he corresponded with Rush on medical matters. Rush was a brilliant teacher, an educational theorist, and an Abolitionist. All three men had strong views on religion and politics which deeply influenced their professional work; and all three believed devoutly that it was their duty to create an American utopia. Merle Curti rightly identifies them as leading proponents of a republican culture.[1]

The three men were also united in their belief that the War had simply produced the conditions congenial to the creation of a republican culture. Benjamin Rush spoke for them all when in 1787 he published remarks which he had made privately the year before:

> There is nothing more common, than to confound the terms of *the American Revolution* with those of *the late American war*. The American war is over: but this is far from being the case with the American Revolution. On the contrary, nothing but the first act of the great drama is closed.

He wished to create an American empire founded 'in *knowledge* as well as virtue'. It was the task of Revolutionary leaders 'to prepare the principles, morals, and manners' of the citizens so that they conformed with republican principles.[2]

Rush anticipated by some twenty-eight years the famous maxim of John Adams, made in a letter to Jedidiah Morse, that the Revolution was achieved 'in the minds and hearts of the people' rather than in military conflict.[3] It is ironical that in the intervening period Morse, Webster and Rush had developed a considerably darker view of those minds and hearts. Of course, their increasing pessimism was in part the companion of their increasing age. But it was also demanded by the environmental ideology that they shared with those discussed in the preceding chapter. The careers of Morse, Webster and Rush, in all their diversity, reveal a number of striking similarities because of the way they viewed their surroundings. Their revolutionary work began in a republic of great expectations. It ended with their attempts to escape from a landscape of nightmare.

JEDIDIAH MORSE AND AMERICAN GEOGRAPHY

In the Prologue I suggested that geography is no more an 'objective' discipline than any other; it involves the shaping imagination of the perceiver. The work of Jedidiah Morse is a case in point. Like the state 'histories' described in the last chapter, the work of Morse and other American geographers was impelled by nationalism. Immediately after the Revolution there was everything for the nation to achieve. No national geographies existed, and most descriptions of America were published in Britain. The nearest approach to an American geography had been Robert Rogers' *Concise Account of America*, but as that had been published in 1765 and in Britain, it was hardly suitable for the new Republic. Jedidiah Morse was disturbed to find, as a newly graduated schoolteacher, that there were no truly American geographies available. He therefore published his own primer, *Geography Made Easy*, in 1784. It was an immediate success, and he was encouraged to produce a more substantial work. It was, he emphasised, a patriotic duty. The Preface to the first edition of his *American Geography*, published in 1789, asserted that his work was:

> calculated early to impress the minds of American youth with the idea of the superior importance of their country, as well as to attach them to its interest.[4]

Geographies were also instruments of religious conviction. A number of geographers were ministers of religion, and even their lay colleagues tended to regard geography as a moral activity. Elijah Parish, a Congregationalist minister who collaborated with Morse on a *History of New England* (1804), wrote in his own *A New System of Modern Geography* (1810) that:

> Though geography is an earthly subject, it has been justly denominated 'a heavenly study'. It includes many of those subjects which enlarge the mind, and improve the heart, which give just views to Providence, and of human nature.

Before graduating from Yale, Jedidiah Morse had been strongly influenced by its President, Ezra Stiles, and he determined 'to promote the highest Interests of Mankind' by becoming a minister. His work as a schoolteacher was simply a stopgap while preparing for the ministry, and for the greater part of his life he combined the occupations of geography and the church.[5]

Morse's two professions were profoundly intertwined: he believed that geography was a Christian pursuit, and was uneasy about collaborating with geographers whose devotion was suspect. Accused on one occasion of plagiarism, he asserted that the charges were:

> weapons of warfare fabricated to wound an advocate of the orthodox faith, and through him, to wound the cause which he advocated.

Morse's geography was coloured not only by his Christian beliefs, but also by a tendency, which he shared with Noah Webster, to hope that the new nation would become a larger New England. As a minister and as a Yankee he could not approve of the Southern way of life; hence his description of Williamsburg, Virginia:

> Every thing in Williamsburg appears dull, forsaken and melancholy – no trade – no amusements, but the infamous one of gambling – no industry, and very little appearance of religion.

We have here an example of the negative catalogue which I discussed in the Prologue. In Morse's version, the climax confirms all that has gone before. It is only to be expected that such a Godless place would lack the other amenities of civilised life.[6]

The description of Williamsburg naturally offended many in the South, and drew from the Virginia Senator St George Tucker a stinging rebuke:

> 'Heavens, what a picture!' A few more touches of the reverend Geographer's pen would have exhibited to us Sodom, or Gomorrah, on the eve of eternal wrath.

The furore eventually made Morse withdraw other offending remarks, but he stood by his judgement on the observance of the Sabbath in Williamsburg, revealing an intransigence that would make more secular practitioners uneasy. One of the most distinguished European geographers, the German, Christoph Ebeling, was forced to arbitrate in the dispute over 'Godless' Williamsburg, and for a while severed relations with Morse because of the dispute over plagiarism.[7]

In 1794, ten years after the publication of his first book, Morse wrote a letter on the nature of his work:

> I am as sensible as any person, of the defects of my work – but I have the comfort to know that I have done my best – I have meant well – & endeavoured to do good – I have travelled an unbeaten path – have had everything to collect *de Novo* – my sources of intelligence have not in all instances, been accurate – many have failed – and much remains to be done – the field before me is extensive – & I sometimes contemplate it with a misgiving heart.

He talks of his indifferent health and of the burdens of his pastoral work, and then continues:

> Under all these Circumstances, to undertake a description of an unexplored, or but *partially* explored Country, rising into importance with unexampled rapidity, – & to attempt, in successive Editions, of a Universal Geography, to keep pace with the progress of things, in this age of discoveries, improvements, Changes, & revolutions, – are objects from which I shrink, when I think of their difficulty and magnitude – But I am forgetting myself. I hope you will forgive my *frankness*.[8]

As Morse admits, the letter is revealing, particularly as it initiates a long if spasmodic correspondence with Christoph Ebeling. I will spend a little time looking at its implications.

The letter indicates Morse's method. He assembled the information for his geographies almost entirely by correspondence. The process was intensely factual. He remarked in the Preface to his 1789 *Geography* that Europeans 'have too often suffered fancy to supply the place of facts'. His task would be to correct their speculations, and to this he was highly suited. Data-gathering was much more congenial to him than metaphysics. He would circulate questionnaires to the 'respectable' intellectuals of his acquaintance and make extensive use of other books – thus giving rise to that charge of plagiarism. Morse was a collator, not an innovator. As he remarked to Jeremy Belknap in a letter defending his forthcoming *Geography*:

> The nature of the work will not admit of much originality. The book must derive its merit, (if it has any) from the accuracy and judgment with which it is *compiled*, rather than from the genius with which it is *composed*.[9]

Morse ignored a warning that Belknap had administered two years earlier:

> To be a true Geographer, it is necessary to be a traveller. To depend on distant and accidental information is not safe, and there is a material difference between describing a place that we have seen and one that we have not seen.

To rely on other people, Belknap concluded, is merely to acquire their prejudices.[10] Such warnings were in vain; Morse made only one trip primarily for his *Geography*. Late in 1786 he arranged a temporary pastorate in Midway, Georgia. His journey was notable more for his meetings with intellectuals than for his fieldwork. Among others, Morse saw John Witherspoon, the President of Princeton, and Benjamin Franklin, both of whom approved his plans for a *Geography*. His notes on the terrain tended to be casual. Subsequent journeys were made primarily for missionary purposes. At the beginning of that 1794 letter to Christoph Ebeling, Morse asserted that a geographer is obliged to describe places that he would never see. But he never really made much effort to see. In consequence, his geographies are barely visual. The first edition of the *Geography* contained only two maps; and Morse's prose is spare, confined largely to facts and figures with the occasional evaluative comment such as that made about Williamsburg.

In his 1789 *Geography* and in the 1794 letter Morse said that he was travelling 'an unbeaten path'. The path did not take him to the frontier. Despite his fear that his books would have difficulty assimilating a rapidly changing United States, he made little effort to keep himself informed. His knowledge of the frontier was extremely limited. He relied on Jonathan Carver's outdated and incorrect *Travels*, and was criticised by two acquaintances (the zoologist Samuel Latham Mitchill and the politician Oliver Wolcott) for following its errors. Scanty treatment of the frontier was, however, a necessary corollary of a design which became increasingly extensive from edition to edition. The second American edition of the *Geography*, published in 1793, now included a second volume covering the Eastern hemisphere. Suitably entitled *The American Universal Geography*, it had become encyclopaedic in nature, deliberately intended to replace the English geographies of which there had been so many patriotic complaints. He included sketches of Europe, Asia and Africa and, much to the annoyance of Jeremy Belknap, even an account of the insanity of George III.[11]

The path that did not lead to the frontier led instead to Britain. Morse's *Geographies* were deeply indebted to British models. The questionnaire, the major technique for obtaining information for the early *Geographies*, had been initiated by Robert Boyle, the founder of the Royal Society, in 1665. Boyle's 'General Heads for a Natural History of a Countrey', with its questions marshalling in logical order the information to be gathered, provided a model for scientists for the next two centuries. British geographies in the eighteenth century followed Boyle in describing the political boundaries and physical face of the terrain before turning to its human features. Typical of such organisation was William Guthrie's 1771 *Geographical Grammar*, which Morse aimed to supplant but simply transplanted. The first five editions of Morse's *Geography* adhered closely to Guthrie's organisation. Perhaps he followed Ezra Stiles' enthusiasm for *translatio emperii* too slavishly.[12]

By dividing the country according to its political organisation Morse followed the dictates of Tom Paine's geopolitical rhetoric – and the British geographers. Christoph Ebeling told him of the new German methods, which included the division of a country according to its natural contours, such as mountains and rivers. Ebeling also said that Morse could only keep abreast of geographical research if he learned German. Morse paid no attention. He was less interested in the physical face of the country than in attempting to impose a political unity upon it. He called his 1784 *Geography Made Easy* a 'system', a term which, as we shall see, was used by other writers, and which indicates his desire to order and unify the country he was describing. He welcomed the 1787 Constitution because he believed that it would give the United States 'a fixed character', and in his 1789 *Geography* he looked forward to a time when linguistic, social, political and religious differences would be 'lost in the general and honourable name of AMERICANS'. At times, it seemed that his work would achieve its desired end. One well-wisher praised Morse's *Geography* for 'cementing the Union of the states, by making them not only acquainted but pleased with one another'.[13]

Yet there is little pleasure in that 1794 letter to Ebeling. Its brief, breathless phrases, punctuated by commas and dashes, seem to anticipate both Jefferson's letter to Joseph Priestley and the night thoughts of Emily Dickinson. Morse has to bring them to a halt by admitting that he is losing control, an extraordinary revelation in a letter to a stranger. The overall tone of the letter is fearful. The metaphors of unbeaten paths in extensive fields indicate agoraphobia rather than open-minded enquiry; and the remainder of the letter shows Morse shrinking from the task of writing a geography of a country which persistently changes. The changes are, of course, largely political. Morse created his own problems by attempting to apply a British model of political geography to American terrain. As Ebeling pointed out, German methods avoided the problem of accounting for political change by simply ignoring it. Rightly or wrongly, the British geographies presupposed a political stability that did not exist in America in the 1790s, as we saw in the last chapter. America had not been 'fixed' by the documents which announced its political identity.

Morse was greatly affected and his work as a geographer altered by two political events that to him seemed to be connected: the French Revolution and the Illuminati Scare. Initially, he had welcomed the Revolution, and for several years he believed that its aims were good. Of the forty-nine pages on France in the 1793 *Geography* he devoted twenty-one to the events of the Revolution. His Fast Day Sermon of February 1795 excused deism as a natural reaction against Catholicism, and suggested that the excesses of the Reign of Terror stemmed from the magnitude of the undertaking. So far, it seemed that Morse was following his mentor Ezra Stiles, who died in May 1795 with his approval of the French Revolution unshaken. But already Morse had begun to harbour private doubts. In that 1794 letter to Christoph Ebeling Morse voiced at length his concern over 'the convulsions in Europe'. While he approved the French cause he shuddered over the enormity of its effects. In particular, he feared 'the introduction of French principles into America'.[14]

French 'principles', and their attendant geological metaphor 'convulsions', had already been imported by Citizen Genêt. Morse, who had been alarmed by Genêt's intentions, found them confirmed by the visit of Le Comte de Volney, the philosopher and politician whose later book on America would be promptly translated by Charles Brockden Brown. In December 1798 Morse took notes of conversations between acquaintances of his and Volney. The Frenchman had apparently 'expressed himself greatly gratified at the rapid progress of the principles of the french Revolution'. Soon most of Europe would 'put christianity behind their back'.[15] America, no doubt, would shortly follow.

Compared with the French Revolution, the Illuminati Scare was a storm in a teacup. No blood was spilt, no governments toppled, no countries convulsed. The Illuminati were members of a brotherhood of learning that had been formed in 1776 with the aim of fostering internationalism, moral perfectionism, and freedom from all religious and political authority. They were innocuous, powerless, and had ceased to exist by 1787. Despite this – or perhaps because of this – they were widely feared. A number of books hinted darkly at blood rites and other nefarious deeds, and linked the work of the Illuminati with the excesses of the French Revolution. One book, by an Edinburgh professor named John Robison and entitled *Proofs of a Conspiracy against all the Religions and Governments of Europe*, treated the Illuminati as one of the principal clandestine organisations devoted to spreading anarchy and irreligion. It was widely read at the time. Within a year of its first appearance in the autumn of 1797 it had gone through five editions, published in London, Edinburgh, Dublin, New York and Philadelphia. It still is read by those who fear conspiracies against America, and is presently published by the John Birch Society, which regards the Illuminati as a precurser of Communism.[16]

Like the word 'fascist' today, 'Illuminatus' had towards the end of the eighteenth century become a general term of political derogation. By 1799 it had been used against Jedidiah Morse himself. This is perhaps fitting, for no-one had done more than Morse to kick up dust about the Illuminati. He had read Robison's *Proofs of a Conspiracy* in April 1798, and he was greatly agitated by it. They were, to be sure, apprehensive times.

John Adams, now the second President and worried about the deteriorating relations between the United States and France, spoke in March 1798 about the nation's critical position and the need for repentance. He proclaimed a Fast Day for 9 May. This presented Morse with his opportunity to attack the Illuminati. In his scare-mongering Fast Day Sermon he talked at length about the 'present danger'; and he embroidered on Robison's book, blaming the Illuminati for starting the French Revolution and fomenting the present troubles with France, and asserting that there were several Illuminati Societies in America with members in high places.[17]

In this and two subsequent sermons about the Illuminati Morse disturbed a nest of hornets which buzzed around him for the next year or so. On the one hand, he received a number of letters of support. John Rodgers, the popular and respected Presbyterian leader who had many friends in high places, including Benjamin Rush, agreed with Morse that Robison's *Proofs* was 'a most important & valuable book' that only 'infidels & warm democrats' would try to discredit. On the other hand, many who were hardly infidels and warm democrats felt that the burden of proof rested upon Morse. 'If this conspiracy be a fact', wrote the Rev. Abiel Abbott, 'well may we tremble for the ark & city of God.' He asked Morse to substantiate his allegations. Morse wrote to Christoph Ebeling asking for the facts he needed. The German geographer could not help him. Although European politics were by now so threatening that he felt it was too dangerous even to write about them, Ebeling completely exonerated the Illuminati, who were now in any case defunct. Morse, disappointed but unrepentant, replied that Robison's book, even if it did have errors of fact, was correct in substance. And in a letter to Timothy Dwight, who had succeeded Ezra Stiles as President of Yale, he suggested that Ebeling was probably friendly to the principles of revolution in Europe even if he was 'no Jacobin or Illuminee'.[18]

By the spring of 1801 it was the election of Thomas Jefferson as third President that was causing controversy. Morse himself regarded it as the source of fresh 'convulsions'.[19] Lacking any substance, the Illuminati Scare had run its course. In its three-year existence it anticipated in a number of ways the supposed 'Red Menace' of the early 1950s: the constant sense of threat; the charges of conspiracy in high places; purportedly factual assertions which could not be substantiated; and suspicions that those who did not assist the witch-hunt were fellow-travellers of the conspiracy. I do not wish to suggest by this that Jedidiah Morse was reincarnated as Joseph McCarthy, despite the coincidence of initials. Morse was both a more isolated and a more substantial man. He was isolated because he was distrusted both by the conservatives for his international correspondence with foreign liberals, and by the liberals for his religious conservatism. He was more substantial because of his earnest attempts to create an American geography. Unfortunately, his joint professions of geographer and minister rendered him particularly vulnerable to fears of subversion. Seeing American terrain in Christian terms, it was easy for him to imagine a nightmare vision of the serpent abroad in Eden.

This is made particularly clear in his 1798 Thanksgiving Day Sermon, published when the Illuminati Scare was at its height. The United States, he said, was 'situated in the *climate* of freedom, between the extremes of heat and cold'. This golden mean (which, ironically, coincided with the view of his enemy Jefferson) was in Morse's view guaranteed by the Christian faith. But the religio-climatic balance was delicate and susceptible to '*foreign intrigue*', which attacked the Christian Republic like a virus, causing widespread dissipation. The devil was abroad in America; his work was to be seen everywhere, and did not cease with the Illuminati Scare. It was even to be found in foreign geographies of America. As Morse remarked in the Preface to his 1812 *Geography*, such books provided further evidence of 'sinister motives'.[20]

As the years passed Morse shrank further and further from the American terrain, transforming his books into self-referential micro-cosms which bore little relation to 'the ever changing state of the world' that he once again lamented in the Preface to his 1812 *Geography*. Morse's attitude to his work is revealed by the failure of the proposed collaboration with Noah Webster. In September 1793 Webster had agreed to assist in the preparation of a gazetteer. Much ink was used in discussing the method of compiling information. They would divide the states between them, verifying their facts with friends or other 'respectable' persons, and also by means of circular letters. The collaboration ended early in 1797 because of the time it was taking Webster to assemble his material. Morse pressed on alone, and the *Gazetteer* was published later in the same year. Morse was able to continue with his work because it was becoming less and less innovative. Each new edition of the *Geography* became more commonplace with Morse's increasing reliance on published sources. He discontinued the questionnaire and in the 1812 edition he relied entirely on his past work and the travel journals of others.[21]

The 1812 edition revealed other changes. Previous editions had used Guthrie's *Geographical Grammar* as the model. The 1812 edition used the method of the Scottish geographer John Pinkerton. Pinkerton emphasised more strongly than Guthrie the Christian aspects of geography. Morse, following him, described each region under the headings of 'Historical Geography', those elements of the terrain which 'are dependent on the instrumentality of man for their existence and character'; and 'Natural Geography', including those elements 'which owe either their character or existence immediately to the AUTHOR OF NATURE'. The movement of Morse's *Geographies* away from the American terrain that they were supposed to describe even led him to adopt a new generic name for the United States. In his 1789 *Geography* he had been content with the name 'Americans' for his countrymen. By 1810 he had changed his mind. Samuel Latham Mitchill had in 1803 written to Noah Webster seeking support for the name 'Fredonia':

> There is scarcely anything for which we are suffering more, in our public and national capacity, than for want of a 'name'. Without it we cannot be completely national, nor properly express national feelings, concerns, relations of any kind.[22]

Mitchill found his most enthusiastic supporter not in Webster but in Morse. Morse's 1810 *Gazetteer* used the term, under which 'is comprehended the whole territory now under the government of the United States'. Morse depicted the territory in a wash of generalities. Fredonia, he said:

> is estimated to contain nearly 2,000,000 square miles, which is four fifths as many as are contained in all Europe. It is about twice the size of the Chinese empire, and, if we except Russia, it is by far the largest territory on earth, whose inhabitants live under the same general government. The Missisippi [*sic*] river divides *Fredonia* nearly in its centre, leaving 1,000,000 square miles E of it, in the present United States, and nearly the same number of square miles W of it. The vale, if it may be so called, between the Allegany and Shining [Rocky] Mountains, which is intersected by the Missisippi, and watered by its numerous and large eastern and western branches, contains nearly a million and a half square miles, and may be reckoned among the finest portions of the globe . . . Its mountains, lakes, and rivers, are all upon a large scale. Its climate and soil are adapted to almost all the variety of productions which the earth affords . . . The *Fredonians* . . . are a people collected from almost every nation on earth, and their posterity.

The celebration of size and unity here is verified by echoes of the myth of Noah, by the Edenic imagery associated with the interior, and by the providential symmetry of the continent. The concept of geographical symmetry had been adapted from the beliefs of the Biblical geographers. It asserted that vestiges of prelapsarian perfection could be found in America. It was no accident, many people thought, that the continent was bisected by an enormous river, and that parallel ranges of mountains ran down each coastline. We shall encounter aspects of geographical symmetry when looking at the work of Philip Freneau and Thomas Jefferson. Here, all elements add up to a potent dream of America. But it is little more than a dream, often at odds with the information that was available both from texts and travellers. More and more details of the

American interior were being published; and Morse himself had interviewed Sergeant John Ordway, a member of the Lewis and Clark Expedition to the Pacific. He chose to ignore such information. The later editions of his *Gazetteer* and *Geography* barely reflect the growing experience of the West.[23]

Morse tried to turn America into 'Fredonia', the Christian Republic. In this respect his compatriots ignored him and by 1820 Fredonia had disappeared, its memorial a scattering of place-names and its resurrection celebrated, suitably, in the 1933 Marx Brothers' satire of politics and patriotism, *Duck Soup*. Yet when Morse died in 1826 he was still trying to create his ideal republic. Disappointed by the recalcitrance of his countrymen, he passed the labours of Christian geography to one of his sons and set out instead on a mission to convert the Indians. His plans 'for the rescue of these outcasts' were curtailed by ill-health, and he turned instead to an activity for which he was more fitted, compilation. His last work was the *Annals of the American Revolution*, published in 1824. At least the past seemed susceptible to the order that he so fervently desired.[24]

NOAH WEBSTER AND AMERICAN LANGUAGE

It was John Witherspoon, the Scottish minister who emigrated to assume the Presidency of Princeton, who in 1781 coined the term 'Americanism'. Americanisms had existed in everything but name almost as long as the British in America. The British had, after all, to develop new ways to describe their new experiences across the Atlantic. Now they had to be identified with a title; for it was with the growth of the debate over the significance of the New World that American adaptations and neologisms became the subject of British scorn. Even Witherspoon, a signatory to the Declaration of Independence and as patriotic as anyone, was forced to agree that, compared with their British counterparts, the speech of the educated in America was riddled with 'errors in grammar, improprieties and vulgarisms', and he wrote several essays in an attempt to correct those errors.[25]

Many Americans were sanguine about the future of their language. John Adams was one of many who related it to their political system when he suggested that Congress should create the first Academy to regulate and refine the English language:

> The constitutions of all the States in the Union are so democratical that eloquence will become the instrument for recommending men to their fellow citizens, and the principal means of advancement through the various ranks and offices of society.

He left it to others like Hugh Henry Brackenridge later to consider the problems that 'eloquence' could involve. Adams hoped that America would become the most important nation to advance the language. Some enthusiasts, indeed, went further. A rumour circulated that Congress was considering the abolition of English in the United States, and substituting Hebrew or Greek. The whole debate was supposedly brought to a close by one Congressman's suggestion that 'it would be more convenient for us to keep the language as it was, and make the English speak Greek'. The story is apocryphal, but its persistence showed what an attraction it had for members of the newly emergent and apparently omnipotent state.[26]

Among the intellectuals of the new Republic none expressed a deeper concern for the future of the language, and none related it so closely to America's political and cultural future, than Noah Webster. The hopes that Jedidiah Morse nursed for American geography were echoed by Webster in relation to American language. Webster was born in 1758 and, after some service in the Revolutionary Army, he graduated from Yale and for a brief period was a schoolmaster and lawyer. In 1783 he became one of the Republic's first professional authors with the publication of Part 1 of his *Grammatical Institute of the English Language*, later known as *The American Speller*. The book became extremely popular, selling some seventy-five to eighty million copies. It was the major primer for American schools until replaced by the McGuffey *Reader* in the middle of the nineteenth century. Unfortunately, due to poor business ability and an absence of copyright laws, Webster profited little from the sales of his book.

Undeterred, Webster went on to produce the dictionaries for which he is now best remembered. In 1806 he published *The Compendious Dictionary of the English Language*, a smallish work containing a number of Americanisms. The next twenty years were spent working on his *American Dictionary of the English Language* which, with its 70,000 entries, was at that time by far the largest dictionary ever published. On his death in 1843 the *Dictionary* was taken over by G. and C. Merriam, who have published it ever since. Lexicography was, however, only part of Webster's activities. His work on geography and epidemiology has already been mentioned; he also published books and articles on history, literature, meteorology and politics.[27]

At the beginning of his first book, the 1783 *Speller*, Webster announced the programme to which he would adhere for the rest of his life. It was 'to render the acquisition of our language easy and the pronunciation accurate and uniform'. He swept aside possible objections by using the common American assertion that a new political situation demanded linguistic innovation. Then followed the statement which made him famous and which, as it contains the germ of ideas he would develop later, will be quoted at some length:

The author wishes to promote the honour and prosperity of the confederated republics of America; and chearfully throws his mite into the common treasure of patriotic exertions. This country must in some future time, be as distinguished by the superiority of her literary improvements, as she is already by the liberality of her civil and ecclesiastical constitutions. Europe is grown old in folly, corruption and tyranny – in that country laws are perverted, manners are licentious, literature is declining and human nature debased. For America in her infancy to adopt the present maxims of the old world, would be to stamp the wrinkles of decrepid old age upon the bloom of youth and to plant the seeds of decay in a vigorous constitution. American glory begins to dawn at a favourable period, and under flattering circumstances. We have the experience of the whole world before our eyes; but to receive indiscriminately the maxims of government, the manners and the literary taste of Europe and make them the ground on which to build our systems in America, must soon convince us that a durable and stately edifice can never be erected upon the mouldering pillars of antiquity. It is the business of *Americans* to select the wisdom of all nations, as the basis of her constitutions, – to avoid their errours, – to prevent the introduction of foreign vices and corruptions and check the career of her own, – to promote virtue and patriotism, – to embellish and improve the sciences, – to diffuse an uniformity and purity of *language*, to add superiour dignity to this infant empire and to human nature.

The opening statement of overt nationalism is the characteristic for which Webster is best remembered. It is perhaps a reflection upon his financial interest that his patriotism is expressed in a metaphor of money. He campaigned constantly for the establishment of copyright laws, and he was always prepared to ring the Liberty Bell to announce his latest project in the hope that the mite thrown into the common treasury would yield a good return. But if Webster tended to elide personal and national fortunes, there is no doubting the vehemence of his patriotism and its abiding nature. In a letter written before the publication of his first book, he asserted that literature was a bulwark against tyranny, and that America must therefore be 'as famous for *arts* as for *arms*'. Fifty years later, whatever reservations he now privately held, he still publicly asserted that his work was nationalistic. One of his last books, the 1833 bowdlerisation of the Bible, was published because, he said, Americans had too long been subservient to the language of the King James Bible. If they wished to preserve their national language and identity, they must use their own Bible.[28]

For many years Webster vigorously expressed a great distaste of European, and particularly of British, cultural dominance. British literary styles, he thought, were not worth following. Expressions of a declining aristocratic culture, they were mere 'fashion'. How could Americans pay homage to something so worthless? 'Posterity' would find it incredible:

> that a nation of heroes, who have conquered armies, and raised an empire, should not have the spirit to say – *we will wear our clothes as we please*.[29]

In attempting to enlist the support of his fellow-countrymen Webster used the device of appealing to the common-sense of the common man. The passage quoted from the *Speller* asserts that the Republic's treasure is common; that is, both ordinary and belonging to all. The result was that, despite later repudiations of his early radicalism, the mud of the common man stuck to him. When he published his first *Dictionary* in 1806, many people wondered if he had too easily admitted 'vulgarisms' into his work. Such worries were groundless. The new entries in the *Dictionary* were prompted solely by Webster's linguistic nationalism.

The American quality most celebrated by Webster was novelty, the condition of American terrain deplored by Buffon and Raynal, and celebrated by Paine and Jefferson. It was the basis of Webster's defence for introducing Americanisms into his *Dictionaries*; and in the passage from the 1783 *Speller* inspires the organic metaphors of childhood and youth, growth and change. The impact of novelty in America also prompted Webster into one of his occasional theoretical excursions, in this instance in his 1789 *Dissertations on the English Language*:

> a new country, new associations of people, new combinations of ideas in arts and science, and some intercourse with tribes wholly unknown in Europe, will introduce new words in the American tongue.

The liveliness of his prose at this time reflects his amazement at recent events. Like Ezra Stiles in his 1783 Election Sermon, Webster believes that he has lived through 'an aera of wonders'.[30]

It is the political system that enables such change. In that passage from the 1783 *Speller* Webster uses 'constitution' in the double sense of political organisation and bodily health. The second flows from the first. The sources of novelty identified in the 1789 *Dissertations* are overwhelmingly 'associations . . . combinations . . . some intercourse' – social relations, in other words, which are controlled through the political process. Of the two resources available to distinguish the New World from the Old – geography and politics, land and liberty, free access to terrain and free access to government – Webster chose politics. In this he was again following Paine, who showed that the right political system transformed the terrain. Unfortunately, Webster's politics became less optimistic with the passing years, and therefore his landscape, like Jedidiah Morse's, grew more foreboding.

Webster used organic metaphors such as 'constitution' to attack a Europe which he regarded as far gone in decay; and in so doing he beat European intellectuals with their own sticks. England, he thought, had enjoyed an Augustan period stretching from the Elizabethans to

Addison, and closing with the death of George II. This was a convenient time-span, enabling Webster to explain the source of American genius (as he would have to if he accepted the notion of *translatio emperii*) while pinpointing the moment of divergence between the two countries. With the accession of George III Britain had set into a decline which America had avoided by quarantining herself from the 'seeds of decay', a widely used metaphor whose initial oddness is explained by the epidemiology of the time, as we shall see when examining the work of Benjamin Rush. According to Webster's scheme, American culture had grasped the torch of knowledge at the point where British culture had dropped it and fallen back, exhausted. The scheme also gave Webster a personal advantage. The age of George III was the age of the English philologists and grammarians. At the beginning of each new *Grammar* Webster claimed that the work of Johnson, Lowth and other English competitors was conservative and erroneous, whereas his own work was radical, correct and new.[31]

The empiricism celebrated in the quotation from the 1783 *Speller* is also repeated in later works. The 1789 *Dissertations*, for instance, is dedicated to Benjamin Franklin, who 'in his philosophical researches . . . has been guided by experiment, and sought for *practical truths*'. In a 1796 letter to Le Comte de Volney Webster asserted, as Jedidiah Morse had done, that 'all our useful knowledge is derived from *facts*'. He commended Volney for his practical method. Certainly, in relation to all his interests, Webster was an avid collector of facts; but he tended, particularly in linguistics, to fit those facts to a ready-made theory.[32] His celebration of organicism, moreover, was of a limited form that moved from flux into fixity. He rejoiced that the post-Revolutionary period was one of great plasticity because he wished to mould it to his own pattern. The thrust of the quotation from the 1783 *Speller* is thus from the flexibility of youth into the 'uniformity and purity' of his own Websterian Augustan period; hence the architectural metaphor of Augustan aesthetics, the 'durable and stately edifice'.

The movement from flux to fixity is important both for Webster's politics and for his theory of language. It is well known that Webster's politics became more conservative, particularly after his conversion from deism to evangelicism in 1808. But elements of conservatism had always been present in his thought. In the fourth sketch of his 1785 *Sketches of American Policy* Webster proposed a strong Federal government founded firmly on a basis of law and order. This sketch is at odds with the first three, which advocate democracy and a Rousseauesque contract theory of government; an inconsistency which Webster later corrected by rejecting the first three and reaffirming the fourth. In 1797 he sent a copy of the work to Jedidiah Morse, adding that it was now 'a little too Democratic'. And in his 1802 *Miscellaneous Papers* he attacked 'the democratic spirit', suitably in organic imagery, as 'a violent disease, incident to free states'.[33]

The tendency to conservatism in Webster's thought was accentuated by the unsettled condition of America, discussed in the last chapter. He began to fear ordinary people, and wrote to Benjamin Rush that they were ignorant, prejudiced and easily swayed. They should be denied suffrage until they were forty-five years old. Like Jedidiah Morse, many of Webster's fears were brought into focus by the French Revolution. At first, in common with most Americans, he had welcomed the Revolution; but gradually he changed his view – as a poem, dated 1790 and addressed to the Spirit of France, indicates:

> Go, tell your country, she is still
> Heaven's care; and happy, *if she will.*
> But all must first their station fix,
> Nor craze their skulls with politics;
> His proper calling each pursue,
> And thus his worth and wisdom shew.[34]

The Spirit of France must at the time have been steeped in lofty idealism, for she paid no attention to this doggerel.

In August 1793, shortly after Edmond Genêt had arrived in America, Webster met him at a dinner in New York. Initially well-disposed to the French Minister, Webster was soon enraged by his supercilious behaviour and remarks about the British influence in America, to the extent that the lexicographer shortly afterwards swore several affidavits recording the meeting. The onset of the Reign of Terror only served to confirm his belief that France was not in 'Heaven's care'. In consequence he moved to a conservative pessimism that deepened as the years went by. In a manuscript fragment dated 1833 he recalled wondering in 1793 and 1794 if it were Washington or Genêt that governed the United States; and concluded that now, forty years after, the revolutionary leaders would be deeply depressed at the change in 'republican institutions'. In a letter four years later Webster lamented that he could 'see no end to our disorders'.[35]

Webster makes great use of the term 'disorder'. It indicates the antithesis of the state of order that he desires for the country, and he uses it in many contexts. He wrote of the Philadelphia yellow fever epidemics as disorders, and in a late pamphlet asserted that 'popular errors, proceeding from a misunderstanding of words, are among the *efficient causes of our political disorders*'. He reacted to disorder in two ways. The first was to surrender to it. His writing is occasionally marked by the intense fear that accompanied such a surrender. It is revealed in a landscape created out of malevolent, bestial images.

An example of this may be found in a newspaper article reflecting on the use of the guillotine during the Reign of Terror:

> Is man a tyger, a savage, restrained only by laws and a little education, but let loose from these, delighting in war, in death and all the horrid deeds of savage ferocity . . . inflamed by passion, what is he but a beast of prey? A more ingenious animal, indeed; for the beast has the teeth, the horns, and he poisonous sting that nature gave him to destroy his adversary; but man has improved upon the works of nature and *invented* numberless weapons of destruction.

Much later Webster wrote in a letter that the only escape might be a reclusive existence, confined within the smallest space possible:

> I would, if necessary, become a troglodyte and live in a cave in winter, rather than be under the tyranny of our desperate rulers . . . We deserve all our public evils. We are a degenerate and wicked people.[36]

More often Webster reacted to disorder with strenuous attempts to restore order. If misunderstood words gave rise to political disorder then he would counteract it by operating on language. He asserted that 'nothing should be permitted in the language, which tends to impair reverence for the sacred order', a statement which anticipates by some 150 years the Newspeak philologist in *1984*. Webster, it can be seen, was one of the most thoroughgoing authoritarians of his day. A browse through any edition of his *Speller* will show his 'Lesson of easy Words, to teach children to read and to know their Duty' presenting his readers with a stark choice of obedience or a violent disfigurement:

> The eye that mock-eth at his fa-ther, and scorn-eth to o-bey his mo-ther, the ra-vens of the val-ley shall pick it out, and the young ea-gle shall eat it.

This horrific vision extends beyond the individual images. One critic has noted that the fables in the *Speller* are of pain and death in a landscape of treacherous forests, thorns and brambles. The narratives concern flight, hiding and pursuit, entrapment and capture.[37] The alternatives are clear: accept republican duty through an ordering language, or capitulate like a Loyalist to a frightful landscape stalked by ravening beasts.

Webster's attempts to order America through language were doomed to failure because he regarded language as a political instrument for shaping his country. This is made clear in another excursion into theory, this time in 1828:

> Language is the expression of ideas; and if the people of one country cannot preserve an identity of ideas, they cannot retain an identity of language. Now an identity of ideas depends materially upon a sameness of things or objects with which the people . . . are conversant. But in no two portions of the earth, remote from each other, can such identity be found. Even physical objects must

> be different. But the principal differences between the people of this country
> and all others, arise from different forms of government, different laws,
> institutions and customs.[38]

Two underlying theories may, I think, be deduced from this passage.
Significantly, neither of them takes account of the particular nature of
American terrain. They are also initially incompatible. The first is a
universalist philosophy of language. The second is a politically inspired
belief in American uniqueness. I shall deal with them in order.

Webster uses linguistics to modify Montesquieu's theory of cultural
difference. The theory of language on which he draws is, as I suggested in
the Prologue, the accepted one of the time. It still remains potent. Based
on a Cartesian division of man and world, it asserts that language is
transparent, a mere medium. Thus, if people see the same object or have
the same idea, they will express themselves in the same way. This declares
in effect that the underlying structure of language is universal;
dissimilarities between human tongues are essentially superficial. The
universalist philosophy of language is supported in Christian teaching by
the story of the Tower of Babel. Etymology is in consequence regarded
as an attempt to achieve a mystic unity, to reconstruct the wholeness that
man once enjoyed before he incurred the displeasure of God.[39]

Webster spent much of his later life on etymology. He emphasised the
importance of the discipline in his *Observations on Language*; and he told
Jedidiah Morse that etymology threw 'a flood of light' not only on
language but also on history. He had a special table constructed on which
were placed dictionaries of many different languages, and he would
move from one dictionary to another, tracing derivations of words.
Unfortunately his work was largely frustrated because of his poor
scholarship. He tried to learn many languages but mastered few. His
poor command of German, for instance, led him to commit a howler. He
tried to justify the usage 'them horses' by asserting that 'in dem Himmel'
was correctly translated as 'in them heavens'. He was unaware that the
German preposition 'in' when used in a context of position or rest
required the dative case. Like Jedidiah Morse, his ignorance of German
also led him to overlook modern German research, in this instance on the
Indo-European roots of Western languages. He was, however, aware of
the work of Sir William Jones, and attacked it because it suggested a
difference between Arabic and Sanskrit. The languages were derived
from the same root, he said; they must be, because the unity of mankind
was scriptural truth, and if mankind was once unified, so also was
language. Webster's fears of a republican Babel led him, like most of his
American opponents, into a long and committed study of language, in
his case in an attempt to devise a unitary system which he could impose
on his country.[40]

The Preface to the *American Dictionary* also reaffirms Webster's belief that it is America's political structure that essentially distinguishes it from Europe. Although he was aware, like Montesquieu, that 'no two portions of the earth' were the same, and that this gave rise to a different vocabulary, he believed that this difference was less significant than America's political character. In consequence Webster was not being superficially chauvinistic in expressing linguistic and national identity. The structures of his political and linguistic thought were closely intertwined, and both were authoritarian. As he demanded a strong central government, so he tried to find a strong centralised language; as he sought to prescribe action by law, so he sought to regularise language by rules; and as he saw internal order as essential to the American polity, so he saw a clear internal structure as essential to American language. He bent his efforts therefore not towards discovering the reasons for linguistic difference, but towards classifying and regularising that difference. It is at this point that Webster's authoritarianism engages with his universalism. Both are expressions of his desire to place the American language in a strait-jacket. Webster was a system-builder and not, as was once suggested, 'a kind of intellectual frontiersman, as fertile of ideas as the frontiersman is fertile of more material resources'.[41]

Webster later admitted that he 'rejected innovation', and in his 1789 *Dissertations on the English Language* he plotted the path he had been treading and would continue to tread for the rest of his life:

> An attempt to fix a standard on the practice of any particular class of people is highly absurd: As a friend of mine once observed, it is like fixing a light on a floating island. It is an attempt to *fix* that which is in itself *variable* . . . If a standard cannot therefore be fixed on a local and variable custom, on what shall it be fixed? If the most eminent speakers are not to direct our practice, where shall we look for a guide? The answer is extremely easy; the *rules of the language itself*, and the *general practice of the nation*, constitute propriety in speaking.[42]

The process of this argument, as with the argument of the quotation from the 1783 *Speller* given earlier, moves from flux into fixity, from the simile of the 'floating island' to the enumeration of rules. It is an irony, as it was in the 1790 poem addressed to France, that Webster should use as the lynch-pin of his argument that most ubiquitous and plastic of American verbs, 'to fix'.

It is worth considering further the two structuring processes which, according to Webster, should 'fix' the standard of language. The first, 'the rules of the language itself', was the familiar eighteenth-century linguistic principle of analogy. Words and phrases were considered not by reference to their own usage but in terms of their similarity to other words and phrases within the same language, or within another language in the same group.[43] We shall come across another context for analogical thinking when we look at the work of Benjamin Rush. The second rule is less clear and is probably another example of Webster's authoritarianism. 'The general practice of the nation' may well be the one most related to his own ideas of propriety. Americans would therefore be dismissing a set of 'eminent speakers', the English gentry, in favour of a Yankee pedagogue.

From the very beginning but increasingly as he grew older, Webster sought linguistic regularity and order, propriety and purity. To an extent, that search led him to assert Americanism, particularly with regard to his orthographical proposals. Like his countrymen Benjamin Franklin, James Carrol and Jonathan Fisher he experimented with changes in the alphabet and in conventional spelling. Such changes would have the advantage of laying the basis of a unique American speech and an indigenous printing industry. But the emphasis was on purity; and this allied him with the Englishmen that he affected to despise, for purity and fixity were basic tenets of the English grammarians.[44] The emphasis also cut him off from his fellow Americans, who continued to indulge a linguistic inventiveness against which he thundered Johnson-like but in vain.

Indeed, in later years Webster forsook his belief that linguistic uniformity with Britain was impossible and unacceptable. Despite his assertions that his works differed from those of the English philologists, the gap between them had not been wide, and it was narrowed by his interest in etymology. By 1824 Webster was advocating linguistic identity with Britain, and he spent the two years 1824 and 1825 in Europe and England while preparing his *American Dictionary*. He cut a sorry figure at this time. He attempted to meet Oxbridge dons, but his letter to Oxford was ignored, and he met only one philologist in Cambridge, spending much of his time there in idleness. Suitably, the manuscript of the *American Dictionary* was completed in England, in January 1825. In 1841 he sent a copy of the new edition of the *Dictionary* to England to be presented to Queen Victoria. In the accompanying letter he expressed the hope that the gift 'may furnish evidence that the genuine descendants of English ancesters, born on the west of the Atlantic, have not forgotten either the land or the language of their fathers'. A covering letter from his English agent told Lord Melbourne that Webster regarded 'our common language [as] one of the ties that bind the two Nations together'.[45]

It is in the tradition of the prodigal son that Noah Webster, the arch-nationalist, should complete his *American Dictionary* in England and present a copy to Queen Victoria. As Edgar Allan Poe remarked in 1849, Webster had tried to become more English than the English. His desertion to the enemy was prefigured by the Loyalist imagery of a world turned upside down. Like Jedidiah Morse he had moved away from the American terrain. While Morse regarded his America as 'Fredonia' Webster thought of it, in a flourish of geographical legerdemain, as the west coast of the Atlantic. Because he saw a correlation between politics and language, and because he tried to order both by authoritarian methods, he had isolated himself from his own people and allied himself with those he initially despised. Americans paid lip-service to his rules and little more. Their linguistic innovations reflected a need to come to grips with the environment rather than the dicta of a distant grammarian.

Thomas Jefferson seemed to have a clearer idea of the natural roots of American language. He was offered, but refused, the Presidency of the American Academy of Language and Belles Lettres. When he learned that, despite his refusal, he had been elected an honorary member, he wrote:

> There are so many differences between us & England of soil, climate, culture, productions, laws, religion & government, that we must be left far behind the march of circumstances were we to hold ourselves rigorously to their standard . . . judicious neology can alone give strength & copiousness to language and enable it to be the vehicle of new ideas.

There are similarities here with Webster's theory of language. Jefferson regards language as a vehicle of ideas. Like the earlier Webster, he also asserts a distinction between the American and English languages, grounded in a concept of novelty.

In Jefferson's list of the other determinants of the distinction, natural influences (soil, climate) come first and regulatory influences (laws, religion, government) last. Webster thought that politics was the most important factor in American culture. Jefferson thinks that geography is the most important factor, and in this context he believes that language must take on new shapes to accord with 'the march of circumstances', a suitably mobile metaphor. In consequence, as we shall see, Jefferson insisted that the Lewis and Clark Expedition should keep records naming and describing the natural phenomena they encountered as they crossed America. The Lewis and Clark Journals are replete with neologisms, and their writers have, with some justice, been called 'linguistic pioneers'.[46] Webster, despite his initial celebration of novelty and empiricism, conceived the relationship of language and environment in the opposite direction from Jefferson. He thought that the institutional, regulatory determinants were most important and the natural determinants least. Webster tried to shape the environment to accord with the language. In consequence his rules petrified and he alienated himself from the nation that he affected to lead.

BENJAMIN RUSH AND AMERICAN MEDICINE

As Michel Foucault and Susan Sontag have shown, medicine is no more an objective science than geography or linguistics. Health and illness are as much a component of the human landscape as are natural objects. The structure of eighteenth-century medicine resembled that of geography and linguistics in its belief in the unity of creation, with a mechanical universe sympathetically conceived and harmoniously governed by a superior Being. The study of God's works was therefore a duty for all scientists; and Noah Webster's work in epidemiology was, like his work in linguistics, aimed at uncovering the unity and stability of the cosmos. Similarly, Benjamin Rush praised the astronomer David Rittenhouse for displaying 'the beauty and harmony of the universe' that necessarily resulted from 'unity and system in the plans of the great creator of all things'.[47]

Rush was born in 1745. He studied at Princeton and at Edinburgh, the most prestigious centre for medicine. Returning to America shortly before the Revolution, he became a member of the Continental Congress, a signatory to the Declaration of Independence, and Surgeon General in the Revolutionary Army. He believed that the struggle against Britain would 'fix the constitution of America forever'. But his progress, and America's, was not easy or without cost. An independent-minded man, he criticised Washington too freely, and had to resign from the Army. His letter of resignation talked of the War as 'a dreary wilderness', but he remained optimistic, likening the struggles of the Americans to those of the Jews in search of the Promised Land.[48]

Once the War had been successfully concluded, Rush felt that the Promised Land could be imminent:

> Here everything is in a plastic state. Here the benefactor of mankind may realize all his schemes for promoting human happiness. Human nature here (unsubdued by tyranny of European habits and customs) yields to reason, justice and common sense.

The closing reference to *Common Sense* is deliberate. Rush knew Tom Paine and advised him on the composition of the pamphlet. He claimed, indeed, to have suggested the title. Certainly, both men had an intense enthusiasm for the Revolution, an enthusiasm revealed in this letter in the repeated use of the adverb 'here'.[49]

Rush had a similar onset of enthusiasm five years later, when the ratification of the Constitution apparently bonded the states into a tightly knit union. He regarded the Federal Procession in Philadelphia as one of the highpoints in his life; and he communicated his jubilation in a letter written immediately afterwards:

> The torpid resources of our country already discover signs of life and motion. We are no longer the scoff of our enemies. The reign of violence is over. Justice has descended from heaven to dwell in our land.

America, it seemed, would become the land of divine reason.

These two letters, written at propitious moments in the nation's history, indicate Rush's beliefs. Like Berkeley and Paine and (following them) Morse, Webster and a host of others, Rush subscribed to the theory of *translatio emperii*. Europe, of course, was lost in tyranny and decay. In contrast, the 'plastic', unformed character of America that others would later lament made it in Rush's eyes at this moment the only country in the world that could be aligned with the rational harmony of God's system. Without going as far as his colleague Thomas Bond, Rush believed that Americans had emerged from the Revolution a healthier people, and that Philadelphia would become the natural home of science and medicine. There were problems, including a Revolutionary disease called 'Anarchia'. But the Constitution would cure this; hence the 'signs of life and motion' mentioned in the second letter. A further alignment was taking place. Once it had been completed America would become a paradise.[50]

As the last paragraph suggests, a paradise is also a medical utopia. Health is the inevitable outcome of the paradisal harmony between human beings and their environment. We have already seen evidence of medical utopianism in the state histories and in the work of Imlay and Webster as well as Thomas Bond. Ever since the Declaration of Independence, Life – with Liberty and the Pursuit of Happiness – had been regarded as an essential right of republicans; and doctors, naturally, would interpret Life in terms of health and longevity. They would also, like Noah Webster, see a 'constitution' as a document with medical as well as political consequences. America's most distinguished doctor, Benjamin Rush, turned the University of Pennsylvania (where he held a series of chairs) into the leading medical school in the new nation. He seemed ideally placed to turn the nation itself into a medical utopia. As he once remarked, science seemed to have caught the spirit of the revolutionary age.[51]

Americans were, of course, hardly the first to subscribe to a medical utopia. The origins of medical utopianism are Old Worldly, and old. They may be traced back to the Hippocratic treatise 'Airs, Waters, Places'. As I pointed out in the last chapter, 'Airs, Waters, Places' is the origin of the belief in the environmental determinants of both the physical and moral qualities of human beings. In the succeeding twenty-one centuries this belief had changed in two ways. Firstly, the doctrine of the four humours had been developed into a complex theory of environmental and temperamental stimuli and physiological responses.

The doctrine long remained potent. It was finally destroyed by the discovery of micro-organisms. The last printing of 'Airs, Waters, Places' for medical rather than historical purposes took place in 1874.[52]

Although some Enlightenment physicians were sceptical about Hippocratic theory, they accepted its underlying environmentalism, and developed it in a second way. The environment would now be observed and plotted with precision, by means of records and calculations. And, since calculation implies control, this was the development that led to medical utopianism. It was an English doctor, Thomas Sydenham, who was largely responsible for the growth of precision in medicine. Sydenham (1624–1689) acknowledged a debt to Hippocrates, but stiffened it with Baconian empiricism. Believing that 'numerous errors . . . spring from hypothesis', he insisted repeatedly on 'close and faithful observation'. In doing so he consciously emulated the botanists, who emphasised that order in classification could only be achieved through 'exactness of description'.[53]

Sydenham's doctrines were accepted by many American intellectuals, including Noah Webster. No one followed the English doctor more ardently than Benjamin Rush; he must have been delighted when David Ramsay hailed him as 'the American Sydenham'. Rush named his home after his transatlantic predecessor, and in 1809 published an American edition of his works. He thought that Sydenham had transformed medicine's 'apparent darkness and confusion into light and order', and he followed many of his methods and diagnoses. Yet Rush had a number of reservations about Sydenham's work. Two are relevant here. Sydenham, like Hippocrates, believed in the healing powers of nature. Rush attacked both men for this. Nature, he believed, was not to be trusted, for 'millions have perished by her hands in all ages and countries'. Instead, Rush thought that he must operate on nature to achieve the desired result. He subscribed wholeheartedly to the expectation that America would be transformed by the application of science. He believed, as he once said in a letter, that man must subdue the earth. And where better to subdue it than in the New World, where the earth's plasticity seemed to make it a willing partner to the process?

Secondly, Rush had reservations about Sydenham's empiricism. Facts, he thought, must be connected by a theory; and Sydenham overtly rejected theory. Rush insisted time and again on the need for 'principles' and, fond of composing epitaphs, asked that his tombstone be adorned solely with the words, 'I was an advocate of principles in medicine.' Without them the physician was reduced 'to a level with the cook and the nurse, who administer to the appetites and weakness of sick people'. He also rejected Sydenham's method of following the classification processes of botanists. Diseases, he believed, could mutate in a way that defied classification. This did not mean that he was a pluralist, for he thought that the essential unity of God's universe prevailed over all mutations. Rejecting some of the theories he had learnt in Edinburgh, Rush developed a theory that all fevers had the same root cause, and that one supreme fever would drive out all the others. The major means of diagnosis, suitably, was the 'principle' of analogy. Whenever confronted by a problem Rush would retire to the library and hunt up a comparison.[54]

The charm of Rush's belief in the essential unity of disease was that there was no means of testing it empirically. Even if there was, he would not have accepted it. It is odd nowadays to see an American subscribing to dogmatism; odder still to see him accusing an Englishman of excessive pragmatism. It indicates the way that Rush, in common with a number of Revolutionary intellectuals, viewed their environment. America's apparent novelty and plasticity encouraged her intellectual leaders to play the role of designer. Men of interests as various and attitudes as different as Thomas Jefferson and Noah Webster tended to see their country as an inchoate mass awaiting their forming plans. The lined walls of the library provided the fortress from which America would be ordered. In chapter 5 I shall suggest that Jefferson's empiricism was at the service of a rage for order. I have already suggested that Webster's empiricism was superficial, and did little more than serve his need to create a system.

Webster's system of language and Rush's system of medicine were both built upon the analogical method. We have seen Webster using such terms as 'constitution' and 'disorder' to indicate a relationship between health and politics. Rush returned the compliment when in a lecture first delivered in 1798 he referred directly to Webster's theories, adding that the 'connexion between morals and philology ... is not more intimate and necessary, than the connexion of morals and medicine'. He concluded that 'physical and moral evil began together'. The intimate and necessary connection between morals and medicine affected all areas of life and all aspects of human psychology. In 1786 he read a paper to the American Philosophical Society on 'the Influence of Physical Causes upon the Moral Faculty', showing that habits of work and diet had a profound effect. One of the first and most virulent advocates of temperance in America, he once drew a thermometer relating physical and moral breakdown by showing the effects of distilled liquor. They included anarchy and apoplexy; idleness and 'ideotism'; murder and melancholy; and swearing and swollen legs.[55]

Rush's analogical method was firmly grounded in the environmentalism he had inherited from Hippocrates and Sydenham, but it had a particularly American dimension. The primary physical influence on the moral faculty was climate. He agreed with Gilbert Imlay and Thomas Jefferson that America was singularly blessed. While the November fog and rain of Britain led to an increase of 'the worst species of murder', the vernal American sun inculcated 'gentleness and benevolence'. He also agreed with Jefferson that, of the American states, Pennsylvania seemed endowed with all the advantages. Or almost all; for the relation of environment and morals would remain inert unless activated by a third analogical domain, that of politics. As Rush remarked in a letter to Jefferson, 'I have often been struck by the analogy of things in the natural, moral, and political world.'[56] Here again we can see the influence of Paine's providential geopolitics. If physical and moral evil began together, then the American polity would make them cease together.

After the Revolution Rush set about creating what he called his 'Republic of Medicine'. It was primarily agricultural. He encouraged immigrants to work on the soil, and advised a newly formed newspaper to have as its principal object the advancement of agriculture. In a long letter which anticipates by more than a century the Frontier Theory of Frederick Jackson Turner, Rush saw the process of settlement relating to three stages of civilisation. The first, pioneer, stage made the frontiers-man resemble an Indian. The second, settlement, stage diluted Indian manners. The third stage completed the process of civilisation, and on it he lavished his fertile imagination:

> The human imagination can hardly conceive a picture more agreeable than the sight of a family, depressed by poverty in an old settlement, removing to a new country and there creating new sources for independence and affluence by converting woods into meadows and fields, causing forest trees to yield to orchards, weeds to regular gardens, and beasts of prey to useful domestic animals. To this picture of human happiness there can be but one addition; and that is, the same family carrying with them and preserving in their new settlement a sense of the obligations of religion and the blessings of a wise, just, and vigorous government.[57]

Such a landscape, pictorially framed and pivoting around a series of conversions from wilderness to pastoral, achieved perfection in Rush's image of a frontier education. In the middle of the 1780s he was very active in educational projects. He thought that education should be compulsory, and had produced a plan for a Federal University in which natural philosophy and philology would be central disciplines. He was also instrumental in founding Dickinson College at Carlisle, 140 miles west of Philadelphia. A 1784 letter describes the College; and projects, in ecstatic apostrophe, an ideal landscape:

> Happy County of Cumberland and highly favored Village of Carlisle! your hills (once responsive only to the yells of savages and beasts of prey) shall ere

long awaken our young philosophers from their slumbers to trace the planets
in their courses. And thou, Canedoginet, whose streams have flowed so long
unnoticed and unsung, on thy banks shall our youth first feel the raptures of
poetic fire! *There* he shall learn, by praising thy silver streams winding along
the variegated country, to celebrate the praises of those friends to God and man
who by their wisdom, valor, or piety have devoted themselves to the best
interests of mankind.

This picture, ending like the last in an image of rational Christianity,
draws on Puritan imagery to show nature as the spur not only for a future
breed of Rittenhouses but also for the poets who will honour this perfect
land and its leaders. Rush was widely read in poetry from Virgil to
Thomson, and believed in the close relationship between a pastoral
landscape and the production of literature. The transformation of the
frontier would therefore result in American poets who would challenge
their European predecessors and refute Raynal. There remained just one
element to complete the landscape of the Christian Republic, and Rush
added it sixteen years later. In another letter to Jefferson he wrote that
distinguished leaders were best remembered by naming places after
them. In this way the terrain would become both a memorial to the
history of the country and a constant reminder of past virtue.[58] In
chapter 6 we shall see this suggestion carried into effect.

The best farmers achieved the necessary pastoral balance between
nature and culture. Rush praised the German settlers in Pennsylvania for
their 'industry', and attacked the Irish for their indolence. The 'marks' of
the Irish presence were houses without windows, broken fences, lean
cattle, standing pools of water and forests of dead timber. It was apparent
that they were insufficiently 'cultured'. On the other hand, it was a
mistake to clear the land completely. Although Rush agreed with Hugh
Williamson and the European intellectuals that cultivation made a land
salubrious he also believed, with David Ramsay and Jeremy Belknap,
that 'rank vegetation' absorbed 'noxious vapours':

> It is only in proportion as these new countries are cleared of their woods that
> they become sickly, in consequence probably of a more free passage being
> opened for the propagation of exhalations from the rivers.

It followed that completely cleared land was dangerous. Rush rebuked
the British army for cutting all the wood for fuel when they occupied
Philadelphia. Basing his anti-British sentiments on medical fact, he added
that the incidence of fever in the city was now five times greater than
before the War.[59]

Philadelphia was not simply a sink of disease. Rush also regarded it,
like other cities, as a sink of iniquity. In a further letter to Jefferson, the
prophet of agrarianism, he agreed that disease would diminish the

influence of the cities. Quoting from William Cowper to the effect that God made the country but man made the cities, he added:

> I consider them in the same light that I do abscesses on the human body, viz., as reservoirs of all the impurities of a community.

William Cobbett, who (as we shall shortly see) was a sworn enemy of Rush, would later use his opponent's figure to better-known effect when he called London 'this monstrous WEN'.[60]

For a while it seemed to Rush that his model of a salubrious Christian Republic would come to pass. In a 1789 letter to John Adams he noted that 'political passions produce fewer diseases in a republic than a monarchy', and that faction in America seemed in decline. Ten months later he concluded a long letter providing 'Information to Europeans Who Are Disposed to Migrate to the United States' with the comment that 'the present is the age of reason and action in America' – a conclusion similar to Tom Paine's but based on quite different religious premisses. Indeed, his views seemed to be gaining so much ground that in 1792 he looked forward optimistically to an ordered and happy society in which 'supernatural prophecies are fulfilled by natural means'. Nothing, however, could exceed his ecstasy at witnessing the 1788 Federal Procession, not simply because it celebrated unity or was sanctified by beautiful weather, but because it was marked by the consumption only of 'Federal liquors', beer and cider. He was so delighted at the sobriety of the Federal Procession that he suggested a monument commemorating the event at William Hamilton's Bush Hill estate, where the Procession concluded.[61]

Within five years Rush's optimistic expectations were dashed. It was in part the excesses of the French Revolution that caused him, in company with many of his countrymen, to abandon his utopianism. He later told John Adams that in 1792 he had despaired both of the Revolution and of 'the visionary ideas of the perfectionists'. Yet these were only the most perceptible symptoms of a more general malaise. I use such terms advisedly, for it was and still is common to think of society in images of sickness. Susan Sontag has alerted us to the ways in which illness can be used as a metaphor, and has suggested that the French Revolution marks the beginning of disease metaphors reflecting conservative despair. In the last chapter, indeed, we saw the optimistic image of republican 'contagion' transformed by Fisher Ames into a fearsome vision of a pestilential and ravaged landscape. Similar if less striking metaphors may be found in other conservative writings of the time. Oliver Wolcott, in a letter to Jedidiah Morse, called the French Revolution a 'mental epidemic'. Joseph Lathrop, a Massachusetts clergyman, referred to political faction generally as 'a distempered state of the body'.[62]

Benjamin Rush's medical theories and analogical method took him beyond metaphor. Fisher Ames had created images of terrestrial disorder, and had then attempted to deny that they were figurative. Rush did not need to go to that trouble, for in August 1793, the year after he had abandoned his utopianism and just over three months after he had deplored the execution of Louis XVI, the first of an annual series of yellow fever epidemics broke out in his home town of Philadelphia. He thought that there was nothing coincidental about the outbreaks. Yellow fever had first appeared on the American continent in 1693, after the beginning of the first French and Indian War, and had recurred periodically until 1762, just as the last French and Indian War ended. Then it was absent for thirty years, its return following hard on the heels of the start of the Franco-British War, with its consequent unrest in the Caribbean, and a slave revolt in Santo Domingo (now Haiti). As he wrote to a friend at Aberdeen University after the first outbreak had subsided, war and pestilence and the horrors of the French Revolution all seemed to be consequences of God's malediction.[63]

In 1793 the fever was confined to Philadelphia, but from 1794 until 1805 it broke out repeatedly in most major cities and many smaller towns on the eastern seaboard. Today, we know that the greatly increased movement of soldiers and sailors in the West Indian and American seaports would have assisted the outbreaks. We know about micro-organisms, and know too that the carrier of yellow fever is the *aedes aegyptii* mosquito, first identified in 1902. Eighteenth-century doctors could only guess at these things, and other reasons seemed more persuasive. Rush and his friends thought that the connection between disease and political disturbance was indisputable. In September 1798 Rush wrote to a New York minister that the greater malignancy of the epidemic that year reflected 'a bitter and unchristian spirit' that now divided American citizens. Three weeks later John Rodgers told Jedidiah Morse (in another letter congratulating Morse on his defence of John Robison) that the 'public Mind' was too concerned with the physical causes of the disease. If people were 'properly attentive to its *Moral* Causes' they would realise that 'the Judgments of God are indeed abroad in the Land'.[64]

The belief that disease is divine retribution for moral turpitude is as old as the myths of Agamemnon and Oedipus and as new as the AIDS scare. Similarly, the maxim that 'cleanliness is next to Godliness' existed in other forms long before John Wesley coined it around 1788. More than a century earlier Francis Bacon and George Herbert had made similar remarks, and Benjamin Rush noted in 1786 that the cleanliness prescribed by Jewish law had been adopted by medical officers as a military method of instilling virtue in the ranks. The belief in disease as a political as well as a moral scourge may be a consequence of the Age of Revolutions. Perhaps the French Revolution, Susan Sontag's benchmark of change in images of disease, also enlarged its retributive nature – although others before the French had indulged in naughty politics. Certainly, the connection had become well established by the nineteenth century. In England, for instance, conservative Christians regarded the 1831 and 1866 cholera epidemics as evidence of God's displeasure at Reform agitation.[65]

The disillusion that Rush felt would doubtless have been exacerbated by his New World ideology. After all, disease would be a natural concomitant of Old World decay. But now it was visiting a youthful nation which he had hoped to shape. Both Jedidiah Morse and Noah Webster had despaired at the recalcitrance of their countrymen and their environment. Rush's environment was more than simply unyielding. It underwent a terrifying metamorphosis; and Rush's attitude to his country and countrymen changed accordingly. The Philadelphia plagues eventually proved to him that his Republic of Medicine was no more than a specious hope.

The havoc caused by the 1793 plague was recorded by the publisher Matthew Carey in a vivid and meticulous account which was widely read. The epidemic lasted for more than three months. At its height more than 100 people died each day. The death-rate only began to decline with the advent of colder weather in mid October. Various antidotes were tried such as garlic, vinegar and tobacco. The city authorities even discharged gunpowder from a cannon that was dragged around the streets. Nothing seemed to have any effect, and the death-toll mounted until around 10% of the city's population of 42,500 had died. A comparative figure of Philadelphia deaths today would be 166,500.

As America's leading town and the seat of government, Philadelphia was the supposed centre of republican harmony and virtue. In fact, the city was nervous and divided, principally because of the impending transfer of government to Washington, and the arrival of numbers of the poor seeking employment and political refugees seeking asylum. The facade of order was quickly destroyed by the onset of the epidemic, and by a number of rumours: that Blacks were poisoning the water; that hundreds of corpses were being flung into mass graves; that the French were marching on the town. None of the usual services operated in a city noted, since Benjamin Franklin, for its public concern. Business languished. People fled the town. Families split up. The sick were shunned, in part because of their sinister appearance. With yellow skin and faces black with blood, they looked diabolic, conforming to the popular image of radical incendiaries. And everywhere the marks of the plague were apparent: in the streets of the capital, empty now save for the corpses and the carts bearing them off to graveyards that resembled ploughed fields; and in the stench of death, the all too tangible proof of the constant, malignant presence of the miasma.

The symbol and heart of the disorder was Bush Hill, the estate that Rush had celebrated just five years previously as the site of republican sobriety. The house had been converted into an isolation hospital. Matthew Carey remarked that it was so badly run by 'a profligate, abandoned set of nurses and attendants' that it became 'a great human slaughter-house, where numerous victims were immolated at the altar of riot and intemperance'. The sick preferred to die in the streets. Carey's words here, with their faint allusion to cannibalism, hint at the fears of 'the beast in man' discussed in the last chapter. These fears would not have been lost on Benjamin Rush. We have seen that he had constructed a ladder of civilisation, with the Germans superior to the Irish. At the bottom of the ladder were the Indians. Although initially, like Thomas Bond, Rush believed that the Indians exhibited the vigour of American natural life, he soon changed his mind. He decided that they were mere animals and an easy prey to all the vices, particularly that of intemperance, which was a species of madness. At worst, an Indian was 'half a beast, and half a devil'.

Bush Hill showed how precarious was the white man's place on the ladder. The attendants at the hospital resembled the Indians, and proved the truth of Rush's thermometer, providing appalling evidence of the connection between moral and physical breakdown. Unfortunately, the isolation hospital was not an isolated instance of the connection. It seemed as if all Philadelphia had regressed to the first stage of civilisation in Rush's Frontier Theory. Other commentators remarked on the facility with which people were 'demoralized' – a term invented by Webster to describe the effect of the French Revolution, and later used by Rush. Matthew Carey retailed a number of 'frightful scenes' of inhumanity. The plague turned people into monsters. Charles Brockden Brown, who was acquainted with and influenced by Rush, set his novel *Arthur Mervyn* in Philadelphia during the epidemic. It was later recommended by Carey as an accurate account of 'the horrors of the period', and gives abundant evidence of moral breakdown. I will deal with the novel and its role in Brown's career in chapter 7.[66]

There were, basically, two opposing theories about the cause of the disease, contagionist and environmentalist. The contagionists believed that the disease was communicated by contact with an infected person. They held that yellow fever was not natural to America and had, therefore, been imported by foreign sources. They pointed to the number of foreigners in Philadelphia in 1793: refugees from Santo Domingo, sailors from Genêt's privateers, and a number of French exiles who seemed more interested in creating their own ghetto than in learning English and integrating with their hosts. In general the contagionists were more influential, and they succeeded in introducing a series of quarantine laws that grew more severe as the epidemics continued. In contrast, the environmentalists held that quarantine was worse than useless. It had no effect against the disease and diverted attention away from city planning, sanitation and housing reform.[67]

At first sight the environmentalists were more liberal than the contagionists. They did not make the nativist connection between the disease and foreign visitors. They believed instead that the disease floated in the atmosphere, seeds of pollution that one simply, and fatally, inhaled. The now inappropriately used word 'malaria', a result of Horace Walpole's Italian journey, remains a monument to their influence, which persisted well into the nineteenth century. The beliefs of the environmentalists can be traced back to the Flood, as amplified by Burnet's *Theory of the Earth*; hence two 1832 letters from a Dr Ennalls Martin to Noah Webster. After the Deluge, said Dr Martin, the earth had become 'a vehicle of corruption, and the cause of disease'. 'Internal fires' not only caused volcanoes and earthquakes, but also gave rise to 'unwholesome vapours and other emanations from the bowels of the earth'.[68]

It was this that made the environmentalists ultimately more conservative than the contagionists. Although they devoted much effort to recording the relation of climate and disease, they subsided into pessimism once the consequent controls had proved ineffective. They reverted to the belief in original sin, their efforts hopeless against an environment that was damned, all-pervasive, and inescapable. Richard Alsop's *Political Green-House*, written just after the 1798 epidemic, gives a good indication of the terrors of the environmentalist view:

> Where'er the *yellow* Fiend draws nigh,
> He fills with death the tainted sky,
> The city wraps in midnight gloom,
> And marks whole myriads for the tomb. . .
>
> No rules by which the wisest live,
> No aid that Med'cine knows to give,
> When Pestilence burst dreadful forth,
> Can save the fated sons of Earth.[69]

Ennalls Martin's anthropomorphic phrase, 'bowels of the earth', came from Rush's edition of Sydenham, for they believed that the 'effluvia' of the earth were the sources of disease. Rush had already accused the British of opening Philadelphia to miasmata by cutting down the trees. Now, the arrival of the 1793 epidemic seemed to confirm his fears. He hurried to locate the origin of the effluvium. It was, he believed, a consignment of rotting coffee which had been dumped on the Philadelphia wharf. A half century later his diagnosis was still influential. Another distinguished Philadelphia physician, Alfred Stillé, maintained in 1848 that a rotting cargo could be a source of disease. He would perhaps have agreed with Rush's long-term remedy, drainage and cultivation. It is doubtful that he would have accepted the immediate cure.[70]

Rush's remedy was severe and highly controversial. It involved copious purging and bloodletting. Just as he believed in a supreme fever, so he believed in one supreme antidote. This is best illustrated by an anecdote, widespread at the time, of a visit to the Philadelphia suburb of Kensington. Rush was surrounded by a crowd of several hundred people pleading for help. He stood in his curricle and addressed them:

> 'I treat my patients successfully by bloodletting, and copious purging with calomel and jalap . . . and I advise you, my good friends, to use the same remedies'
> 'What', said a voice from the crowd, 'bleed and purge every one?'
> 'Yes', said the doctor, 'bleed and purge all Kensington! – Drive on, Ben'.[71]

Rush became the hero of the 1793 epidemic. Because he immediately and universally applied his remedy, it seemed as if he would chase the disease from the capital. This was the highpoint of his career, and he devoted much of his later life to dealing with its consequences. He promoted his remedy with the fervour of a devout republican Christian. Bloodletting, he asserted, was not appropriate in Britain but conformed rather with the American climate and 'state of society'. He even went to the extent of suggesting in 1796 that his remedy was the fulfilment of Biblical prophecy, and compared it to the invention of printing. Believing that he would be instrumental in creating the Kingdom of Heaven on earth, Rush echoed the millennial language of Noah Webster and Ezra Stiles:

> The present is an eventful aera in human affairs. Our world appears to be on the eve of a great and universal revolution . . . in favour of human happiness. I believe in the rapid approach of a new order of things, from the coincidence of the present events with the predictions contained in the Old and New Testaments. . . To this delightful change . . . there exists but one natural obstacle: and that is the plague.[72]

Rush had suffered from one of his occasional relapses of utopianism. Unfortunately, as that closing qualification indicates, his remedy was not working. Some three weeks after the 1793 plague had broken out he wrote to his wife that it was spreading alarmingly, mocking medicine. Two weeks later, despite his constant claims that his cure was working wonders, the plague seemed more pervasive than ever. He wrote again to his wife:

> Every room in our house is infected, and my body is full of it. My breath and
> perspiration smell so strongly of it that a lady with more truth than delicacy
> complained to me of it a few days ago. My eyes are tinged of a yellow color.
> This is not peculiar to myself. It is universal in the city.

He later noted in his own account of the outbreak that, from this time
onwards, 'the atmosphere in every street was loaded with contagion'. It
even seemed to stick to one's clothing. There was no end to their
afflictions. Dead animals, abandoned by their owners, littered the streets
and enhanced 'the impurity of the air'. And, in a remark as prophetic as it
was unwitting, he added that 'Moschetoes (the usual attendants of a
sickly autumn) were uncommonly numerous'.[73]

By mid November 1793 the epidemic was over; but next summer it
returned, and it continued to return, year after year, with horrible
regularity and increasing virulence. There seemed to be little that Rush
could do. The 1805 edition of his essay on bloodletting contained no
reference to his earlier millennial expectations. Yet he still believed
firmly in his cure. He was so dogmatic about it that he caused a great
controversy among his Philadelphia colleagues. Many physicians were
more circumspect than he. Unlike Rush, a French doctor named Devèze
followed Hippocrates and Sydenham in believing that 'Nature is the first
Physician'. Devèze was a pragmatist, and he obliquely attacked Rush's *a
priori* rigidity:

> Being in the habit of seeing the diseased, and to observe nature, can alone guide
> the practitioner, and render medicine a really useful science; but any one who,
> seduced by the brilliancy of a system, will force nature by the rules of the
> method he has adopted, he, I say, is a scourge more fatal to the human kind than
> the plague itself would be.[74]

Perhaps Devèze was being oblique because, like Rush, he was an
environmentalist. William Currie was less circumspect. He had already
published an extensive proof of the salubrity of America and, therefore,
he was a leading contagionist. He compared Rush to the bloody Dr
Sangrado of Le Sage's *Gil Blas* and claimed that Rush would rather let
patients die than change his opinion. Many others attacked Rush. Philip
Freneau, whose work will be examined in the next chapter, wrote several
poems against him. The collective vituperation was such that Rush told
his wife that he was 'publicly accused at every corner of having murdered
the greatest part of the citizens who have died of the present disorder'. He
wished to leave Philadelphia for good.[75]

Rush's other opponents were mild compared with William Cobbett.
The English journalist's nose for controversy did not desert him in his
first period of asylum in America. During the 1797 epidemic he used
every device to attack Rush, calling him 'Doctor Sangrado' and other less

flattering names, blaming him for the death of Washington, and even composing mock advertisements:

> Wanted, by a physician, an entire new set of patients, his old ones having given him the slip; also a slower method of dispatching them than that of phlebotomy, the celerity of which does not give time *for making out a bill.*

Eventually Rush was pushed into legal action, and in 1799 was awarded £5,000 against Cobbett, who took his usual course of fleeing the country.[76]

Each year the return of the epidemic was accompanied by the outbreak of the controversy, with a bad effect on Rush's practice. He responded to such goads by applying his therapy more vigorously than ever. But this, and his environmentalist beliefs, took their toll. It seemed at times that he was coming close to collapse, could even be going mad. One Philadelphian reported that during the height of the 1797 epidemic Rush acted 'like a Man escaped from Bedlam', telling people to fly, for it was hazardous to breathe the air. Even a friend remarked that Rush's mind 'was greatly clouded'. Rush now believed that there was a conspiracy against him, and wrote that his remedy was opposed because he was a Republican and a signatory to the Declaration of Independence.[77]

Rush's last years were marked by unrelieved gloom. Responding in 1810 to an election which gave him further evidence of the deteriorated 'morals and liberties' of his country, he composed an epitaph to the United States very different from the jubilant one written after the Federal Procession:

> Here lie interred
> the liberties of the United States.
> They were purchased with much treasure and blood, and
> by uncommon exertions of talents and virtues. Their dis-
> solution was brought on by the cheapness of suffrage in
> some of the states, by a funding system which begat banks
> and lotteries and land speculations, and by the removal of
> Congress to the city of Washington, a place so unfriendly
> to health, society, and instructing intercourse, and so cal-
> culated to foster party and malignant passions, that wise
> and good men considered a seat in it as a kind of banish-
> ment, in consequence of which the government fell into
> the hands of the young and ignorant and needy part of
> the community, and hence the loss of the respect and
> obedience due to laws and hence one of the causes of
> the downfall of the last and only free country in the world.

Here again he made explicit the connection between miasmic terrain and misgovernment. Misuse of politics through the suffrage, and land through speculation, were both symbolised by Washington, the city that nobody wanted, drained from a marsh alongside the Potomac River. From the removal of Congress to this swamp Rush was able to construct a closely reasoned argument for the further decline of government.[78]

Yet, even with an apparently clear diagnosis of his country's ills, Rush had not been able to minister to it. He had not been able to save his home Federal city of Philadelphia, or the state which he had once regarded as peculiarly blessed. From 1793 onwards the epidemics seemed to surround him wih a miasma which was only exceeded in its malignancy by the medical and political odium that he attracted. The result, he wrote to John Rodgers, was that 'since the year 1793 I have lived in Philadelphia as in a foreign country'. The map of America had failed him, and now it was the Bible that provided 'the only correct map of the human heart'. When war broke out again – this time in 1812 against the British – he considered it a just punishment for a reprobate country.[79]

Benjamin Rush had spoken for Jedidiah Morse and Noah Webster in 1787 when he suggested that the Constitution would create the political and geographical conditions which would bring forth a cultural revolution. Now he seemed to speak for them again. The 'great drama' had produced a number of unpleasant surprises. All three lamented the changes that their country had undergone. Its plasticity, which initially they celebrated, had not adapted to their systems but had led (in their view) to a perversion. We have seen that Morse and Webster tended to respond to the perversion in two ways. One was to imagine America as a malign and savage landscape. The other was to withdraw to a hallucinated terrain, called either Fredonia or the west coast of the Atlantic.

Benjamin Rush, too, tended to respond in these ways, as can be seen in a letter written in 1806 to John Adams. It had by this time become apparent that the 'Happy County of Cumberland' would not become reality. Rush's first reaction was to project his disappointment in images of a beast-infested landscape:

> All systems of political order and happiness seem of late years to have disappointed their founders and advocates. Civilization, science, and commerce have long ago failed in their attempts to improve the condition of mankind, and even liberty itself, from which more was expected than from all other human means, has lately appeared to be insufficient for that purpose. If we fly from the lion of despotism, the bear of anarchy meets us, or if we retire from both and lean our hand upon the wall of our domestic sanctuary, the recollection of past or the dread of future evils bites us like a serpent.

He immediately followed this by adopting the second tactic, withdrawing into a poetic evocation of a generalised, Edenic terrain:

Oh! for a lodge in some vast wilderness!
Some boundless contiguity of shade,
Where rumor of oppression and deceit,
Of unsuccessful and successful war,
Might never reach me more.

Like Jedidiah Morse and Noah Webster, Rush wishes to abscond into an aboriginal existence. He expresses that wish in images of the arboreal amplitude of America which, I suggested in chapter 1, were adapted from British sources. This one, however, is not an adaptation. It is a direct quotation from William Cowper's *The Task*. Rush had earlier used the English poet to attack the cities as sinks of moral and physical disorder. Now he used him to escape entirely from a United States disunited and damned by pestilence and war.[80]

Rush's Republic of Medicine had proved illusory. With hindsight, it seems clear that it was bound to fail, just as Morse's republican Geography and Webster's republican Language had failed. All three men had adopted Old World theories and imposed them on the New World, believing in the transformative powers of American geopolitics. But the providential relation between politics and geography disappeared; and the transplanted seeds had mutated in ways that were unforeseen and undesired. In consequence, all three men rejected their country and retreated into the arms of the Redcoats, realising in their despair that the republic for which they had nurtured so many hopes had been no more than a Republic of Dreams.

3

Dreary wastes and awful solitude

The preceding chapter described the attempts of three leading intellectuals to create a Revolutionary culture. It suggested that their work in different spheres was united by a concern for order; and that their failure was inevitable because their sense of order was deeply indebted to the Old World. Their failure, moreover, revealed a further unity. It was expressed in images of a malign and disordered landscape populated by fearsome beasts and savage, depraved men. Here again, those images drew heavily upon Old World sources.

My discussion so far has, perhaps, been necessarily rather schematic. In this chapter therefore I have two purposes. First, I want to demonstrate that the fictional environments created by Crèvecœur, Freneau and Brackenridge are closely related to those which appear in the non-fictional work of Morse, Webster and Rush. Secondly, it will I hope become apparent that, working from an identity of interest, my three chosen writers began to dwell on the implications of Redcoatism, implications which receive their first sophisticated consideration in the fiction of Charles Brockden Brown.

CRÈVECŒUR'S BARNYARD

J. Hector St John de Crèvecœur was invalided out of the French army in Canada in 1759. He became a naturalised citizen of New York, married, and in 1769 bought Pine Hill, in New York's Orange County. A seven-year idyll as a successful farmer was brought to an abrupt end by the Revolution. As an aristocrat and a Tory sympathiser Crèvecœur was subjected to mounting suspicion from the surrounding Patriot farmers. He decided that it would be a suitable time to return to France to ensure that his French estate would pass to his children. But in New York he was suspected by the British of being a Patriot and was imprisoned for three months, during which time his health suffered badly, perhaps permanently. Through the efforts of some friends he was released and, after a nervous breakdown, sailed for England. In London in May 1781 he sold the manuscript of his *Letters from an American Farmer* that had occupied him from time to time at Pine Hill.

The publication of the *Letters* in 1782 was immediately successful. A second edition appeared in London the next year, quickly followed by editions in Dublin and Belfast. It was then translated into French, Dutch and German and was published in Leipzig, Leyden, Paris and Maestricht. Crèvecœur was lucky with his timing. Coming at the close of hostilities between Britain and America and with the apparent success of the American experiment, the book was regarded as an opportune and essential contribution to the debate on the significance of the New World. For more than a decade it provided Europeans with their major primer on America. Then its popularity waned, not to be revived until the twentieth century when its invocation of Americanism seemingly explained the country's rise to world power.[1]

Then, as now, many commentators focussed on Letter III, 'What Is An American?' There are a number of reasons. The Letter echoes a number of the prominent contributors to the transatlantic debate. It repeats the praise bestowed on the colonists by l'Abbé Raynal (the dedicatee of the *Letters*) for introducing 'symmetry' to America. It rephrases Tom Paine's assertion that the extended terrain releases ambitions cramped in Britain, but in images that are both more concrete and less controversial:

> An European, when he first arrives, seems limited in his intentions, as well as in his views; but he very suddenly alters his scale; two hundred miles formerly appeared a great distance, it is now but a trifle; he no sooner breathes our air than he forms schemes and embarks in designs he never would have thought of in his own country. There the plenitude of society confines many useful ideas and often extinguishes the most laudable schemes, which here ripen into maturity. Thus Europeans become Americans.

The concrete imagery is matched by interviews with a frontier farmer and with 'Andrew the Hebridean', the latter ending with a detailed valuation of Andrew's property. The text seems therefore to provide irrefutable evidence for the agrarian dream. George Washington noted that although the picture painted by Crèvecœur was 'in some instances embellished with rather too flattering circumstances', it seemed to be founded on fact.[2]

Letter III reaffirms the theory of *translatio emperii*. The Americans are 'the western pilgrims' who will complete 'the great circle' of imperial culture. It also lists other elements since regarded as central to Americanism: the love of newness; the idea of the melting-pot; and most of all a wholeness and wholesomeness apparently derived from the propinquity of man and nature. The intense environmentalism of the *Letters* draws upon Locke, is reminiscent of the work of Ezra Stiles, and develops the theories of Sprat and Berkeley by means of images of men as plants, metamorphosed by the terrain:

> in Europe they were as so many useless plants, wanting vegetative mould and refreshing showers; they withered, and were mowed down by want, hunger, and war; but now by the power of transplantation, like all other plants they have taken root and flourished!

Crèvecœur creates a potent mixture, called by one critic 'the most enthusiastic and fullest statement of agrarian nationalism'.[3]

Yet there are limits to the agrarianism of the *Letters*. Despite the rhetoric of expansion, the landscape of the farmer is a limited one. In Letter III the environmentalism is, first of all, contained within Montesquieu's theory of the relation of climate and character:

> Whoever traverses the continent must easily observe those strong differences, which will grow more evident in time. The inhabitants of Canada, Massachusetts, the middle provinces, the southern ones, will be as different as their climates; their only points of unity will be those of religion and language.
>
> (p. 73)

This theory is developed in two alternative models of society. The farmer looks briefly at fishermen, and concludes that the 'boisterous element', the sea, has made them industrious but also selfish and litigious. The criticisms of fishermen are, however, mild compared with those of frontiersmen. A similitude between the human and natural worlds is again invoked, but this time to show that in the woods, 'beyond the reach of government', white men degenerate until they are inferior to the Indians. They become 'no better than carnivorous animals of a superior rank' such as wolves, bears and foxes (pp. 71–73, 76–77).

In consequence nature and culture exist in tension. The wilderness and wild behaviour is restrained by a man-made system, a lesson taught in *Robinson Crusoe* but now applied to the wide American continent. Appropriately, the sentence which introduces the natural similes begins in a cluster of phrases about rational organisation:

> Everything has tended to regenerate them: new laws, a new mode of living, a new social system; here they are become men: in Europe they were as so many useless plants. . .

That organisation, moreover, is colonial. The farmer is deliberately portrayed as the simplest of men existing under the mildest government. He holds to Jefferson's belief that the best government is that which governs least; and it is easy for him to do so, for it is exercised locally but 'ratified and confirmed by the crown'. Society and nature are therefore predicated on a notion of George III and God as absentee mechanics. This is made clear in a vivid and significant image in Letter II:

> the law is to us precisely what I am in my barnyard, a bridle and a check to prevent the strong and greedy from oppressing the timid and weak.

It follows that the farmer's landscape is not only limited but fragile. If men are like plants, they need careful tending. Take away the farmer, or God, or George III, and they wither or are eaten up. This is, he thinks, precisely what happens when the Revolution breaks out.[4]

The *Letters*, then, displays a sunny Americanism within strictly circumscribed limits. While Crèvecœur, like Filson and Imlay, aimed at presenting his American experience to a European audience, his experience was markedly different from theirs. Filson and Imlay project a generalised and widespread image of an Edenic America in answer to the European miasmatist theories. Crèvecœur, too, conjures up a potential Eden, founded in a vision of a middle landscape balanced between the decadent, overdeveloped city and the rude, underdeveloped frontier. But the Eden is confined and the balance is uneasy. When it is disturbed, the landscape opens out into a vista of terror. Crèvecœur realises the fears implicit in the theory of the Great Chain of Being by suggesting that the frontier imposes a moral degeneracy on its inhabitants. He anticipates by four years the first stage of Benjamin Rush's frontier theory, and would indeed go on to develop his own version of the theory in his last book, the 1801 *Voyage dans la haute Pensylvanie et dans New York*. Like Morse, Webster and Rush he believes that bestiality can be held in check only by the imposition of order; and he foretells their dismay when that order collapses. The ambivalence of Crèvecœur's experience and the acuteness of his analysis of America is conveyed in a text that is more sophisticated than any so far discussed. In recent years it has become apparent that the *Letters* is much more than a simple statement of American agrarianism. It has increasingly been regarded as a complex fiction which manipulates personae and carefully arranges the individual letters to convey an experience that, finally, is far from simple or sunny.[5]

The hints of potential disorder that are almost hidden in letters II and III are brought to the surface and examined in subsequent letters. Letters IV to VIII deal at length with the seafaring community of Nantucket. The fishermen are seen as healthy and industrious, but they are so engrossed with their trade that they have failed to improve their farming. The farmer indicates his disapproval in a paragraph full of conditional sentences and with an image of transplantation which resonates from Letter III:

> There are many useful improvements which might have meliorated their soil;
> there are many trees which if transplanted here would have thriven extremely
> well and would have served to shelter as well as decorate the favourite spots
> they have so carefully nurtured. The red cedar, the locust, the buttonwood, I
> am persuaded, would have grown here rapidly and to a great size, with many
> others . . . they might raise, if they would, an immense quantity of buckwheat.
>
> (p. 161)

The fishermen have, in a way, reverted to an earlier form of civilisation. They are the seaborne equivalent of the hunter. They live off their territory rather than develop it; and the result is apparent in their treatment of the land.

The air of disapproval becomes terror when the farmer sees the fishermen's natural element:

> The ever-raging ocean was all that presented itself to the view . . . it irresistibly
> attracted my whole attention: my eyes were involuntarily directed to the
> horizontal line of that watery surface, which is ever in motion and ever
> threatening destruction to these shores. My ears were stunned with the roar of
> its waves rolling one over the other, as if impelled by a superior force to
> overwhelm the spot on which I stood. My nostrils involuntarily inhaled the
> saline vapours which arose from the dispersed particles of the foaming billows
> or from the weeds scattered on the shores . . . who is the landman that can
> behold without affright so singular an element, which by its impetuosity seems
> to be the destroyer of this poor planet, yet at particular times accumulates the
> scattered fragments and produces islands and continents fit for men to dwell
> on!
>
> (p. 163)

The farmer's feelings anticipate the agoraphobia of Jedidiah Morse's 1794 letter to Christoph Ebeling; and they are exacerbated by images quite different from those of the expansive Americanism of Letter III. Letter III had drawn on *Common Sense*; and *Common Sense*, in its turn, had employed the myth of Noah to celebrate the renewal of mankind. But here in Letter VIII the imagery derives from the natural forces used by God to threaten Noah with destruction. Discomfort and fear are suggested both by the open plateau, extending to the horizon, and the instable and fragmenting immediate surroundings. The farmer's disorientation is conveyed in a counterpoint of individual impotence, emphasised by the double use of the adverb 'involuntarily', and the enveloping turmoil. This is the very reverse of the image of the farmer in his barnyard.[6]

It is in Letter IX, on Charles Town and slavery, however, that the farmer's fear becomes uncontrollable. Ironically, the farmer is here in his own element; in a region, moreover, noted for its healthy climate and fertile soil (pp. 166–167). But Carolina is a slave colony and, wandering through a wood, the farmer comes upon a black who has been suspended in a cage from a tree for two days. The scene is described in horrific detail:

the birds had already picked out his eyes; his cheek-bones were bare; his arms had been attacked in several places; and his body seemed covered with a multitude of wounds. From the edges of the hollow sockets and from the lacerations with which he was disfigured, the blood slowly dropped and tinged the ground beneath. No sooner were the birds flown than swarms of insects covered the whole body of this unfortunate wretch, eager to feed on his mangled flesh and to drink his blood. I found myself suddenly arrested by the power of affright and terror; my nerves were convulsed; I trembled; I stood motionless, involuntarily contemplating the fate of this Negro in all its dismal latitude. (p. 178)

This episode is the inverse of the parable of the king-bird and the bees in Letter II. There, the farmer had acted to resolve the conflict, killing the bird and laying the 171 bees from his craw out in the sun to dry. This image of potency closed with the farmer seeing himself as the lawgiver in the barnyard. Here, in a series of statements of impotency connected with the Nantucket episode by that adverb 'involuntarily', the farmer is seen as inferior to nature. The birds and insects now collaborate to dismember the Black. Even the earth drinks his blood. There is nothing the farmer can do.

This episode also shows the farmer that his environmentalist theory must be further qualified. Compared to the 'frigid sterility' of the arctic and antarctic, or 'the parched lands of the torrid zone, replete with sulphureous exhalations', this is Eden. But it is still the scene of barbarity. Imlay is refuted even before he put pen to paper. The farmer now believes that:

famine, diseases, elementary convulsions, human feuds, dissensions, etc., are the produce of every climate; each climate produces, besides, vices and miseries peculiar to its latitude. (p. 175)

The farmer, like Noah Webster and Benjamin Rush, treats natural diseases and human feuds alike as perversions of order. The geographical use of the term 'latitude' here prepares for its more figurative use in describing the Black. It suggests that there is something evil in both terrain and man, something finally alien to intellection and order.

Letter IX looks forward to the natural violence of snakes and hummingbirds in Letter X, and particularly to the human violence of the Revolution in Letter XII. These last two Letters are, however, intersected by one final paradigm of order. Letter XI recounts the visit by the Russian Iwan Al-z to the Quaker botanist John Bartram. Bartram, who (as we shall see in chapter 6) was not above leading other foreign visitors up the garden path, is here on his best behaviour, keen to demonstrate his achievements:

We went to his favourite bank; he showed me the principles and method on which it was erected, and we walked over the grounds which had been already

> drained. The whole store of Nature's kind luxuriance seemed to have been exhausted on these beautiful meadows; he made me count the amazing number of cattle and horses now feeding on solid bottoms, which but a few years before had been covered with water. Thence we rambled through his fields, where the right-angular fences, the heaps of pitched stones, the flourishing clover, announced the best husbandry, as well as the most assiduous attention. His cows were then returning home, deep-bellied, short-legged, having udders ready to burst, seeking with seeming toil to be delivered from the great exuberance they contained; he next showed me his orchard, formerly planted on a barren sandy soil, but long since converted into one of the richest spots in that vicinage.   (p. 192)

Inspired by Linnaeus, the new techniques of drainage, and a love for rectangular order, Bartram has transformed watery and barren wildernesses (the natural environments of fishermen and frontiersmen respectively) into an Edenic terrain. The Blacks are happy and free; the local Quaker community provides a model of democratic religious tolerance. This is, moreover, a middle landscape. Crèvecœur, who knew Bartram, alters the details of his family life so that he resembles the French aristocrat and demonstrates the happy coexistence of nature and culture. In Letter XI Bartram has gained a French father, a coat of arms in the hall and an Eolian Harp in the bedroom. His residence now anticipates the sophisticated log cabins of Cooper's frontier literati. Iwan, of course, is suitably enthusiastic. He adopts the farmer's earlier natural metaphors when he says that he regards 'the present Americans as the seed of future nations', and his visit ends on an upbeat. He later recalls it as 'the golden days of my riper years'. Significantly, Bartram is less sanguine; he is a wiser farmer, unimpressed by natural imagery. Tyranny, he suggests, can exist in any part of the globe, old or new.[7]

Bartram's hint is prophetic. American technology cannot, it seems, hold anarchy at bay, and in Letter XII the horror and immobility become all-pervasive. Previously the disorders had been limited to the sea, the non-domestic natural world, and the Southern slave-holding society. These were, after all, no barnyards. For all their horror, they could to an extent be isolated as outside the farmer's control. Drains and square fields are, however, poor protection against the violence which in Letter III had been depicted as a European disorder but which in Letter XII stains the farmer's happy valley with blood. It is now the turn of New World plants to wither. The farmer's collapse is total, and the image in which the collapse is seen provides a comment on John Bartram's architectural husbandry and a prophecy for the new Republic:

> I resemble, methinks, one of the stones of a ruined arch, still retaining that pristine form which anciently fitted the place I occupied, but the centre is tumbled down.   (p. 211)

Similarly, the form of the Letters has collapsed. The epistolary mode that previously provided a flexible but nevertheless firm control over the text is now abandoned in favour of an open-ended lament.

Letter XII erupts with a hysteria which both reflects the internecine aspects of the Revolution and anticipates the work of Charles Brockden Brown. In place of the cosy but restricted vistas of the valley we are now confronted with the panoramas of terror. Man is subject to 'the dark wheel of fortune' and spends sleepless nights with 'imagination furrowed by the keen chisel of every passion'. The images now are of a landscape populated only by wild beasts. The barnyard, without its lawgiver, has become bestial. The farmer asks if he must 'be shunned like a rattlesnake, or be pointed at like a bear?' Anticipating Noah Webster's response to the Reign of Terror, the farmer even regards animals as morally superior. The lions of Africa, he says, would not require so many victims to slake their appetite as are claimed by the Revolution (pp. 205–207).

In the face of such terror, the farmer now attempts to create a new model of society located on the frontier, the area he had previously eschewed as beyond the ordering control of government. In yet another anticipation, this time of Benjamin Rush's 1806 letter to John Adams, the farmer longs for an asylum beyond the supposed advantages of civilisation. He now sees the Indians in conventionally sentimental terms as 'the immediate children' of nature from whom the whites have degenerated. He prays to God that in his Indian village:

> our ancient virtues and our industry may not be totally lost and that as a reward for the great toils we have made on this new land, we may be restored to our ancient tranquillity and enabled to fill it with successive generations which will thank thee for the ample subsistence thou hast given them.

The contrast between traditional values and their fate in a new land could not be clearer.[8]

The experience so carefully shaped throughout most of the *Letters* can be seen in much starker form in the *Sketches of Eighteenth-Century America*. The manuscript of the *Sketches* was discovered in France in 1923 and was first published two years later. The first chapter opens in an attitude of admiration of American nature which is transformed in the second paragraph to praise of husbandry. The rigour of the winter means that the farmer 'has to provide food and shelter for so many animals, on the preservation of which the husbandman's welfare entirely depends'. But this bucolic barnyard image of interdependence soon starts to disintegrate. In chapter 4, 'Various Rural Subjects', cold weather is regarded in terms of severe frosts which can appear even in summer and destroy crops. Indian corn is seen as the most profitable crop but also the one 'most subject to accidents from seasons, insects, birds and animals'.

Families which live on the most fertile ground are seen in poverty because no market exists for their produce. In such a situation 'they were inferior to the Indians' (pp. 232, 291, 319).

The stage is now set for the opening of the Revolution. The French-Canadians are presented as free under the monarchy and 'happier than the citizens of Boston, perpetually brawling about liberty without knowing what it was'. George Washington is seen early in his career as a perfidious murderer. In chapter 8, 'On the Susquehanna', a picturesque tour that might have appealed to Coleridge ends with a vision of demagoguery which shows the superiority of Indian wisdom. The final paragraph of the chapter sees the Revolution as a 'poison' which has caused 'intestine divisions', and which is also like 'an epidemy of the mind'. Crèvecœur's similes resemble Rush's theory of disease. The Revolution is a supreme fever which 'swallow'd up every inferior contest' and leaves its victims with 'that languor, that internal weakness, that suspension of industry, and the total destruction of their noble beginning' (pp. 338, 340–341, 379–380).

The distresses of the Revolution are developed in the next three chapters, the slaughter and plunder that it generates leaving the country's farms devastated. Noah Webster's reaction to the Reign of Terror is even more clearly foreshadowed with the remark that man seems to adopt the ferocity of the tiger but not its restraint. Man seems to shed blood for pleasure, not out of need. The text closes with six closet dramas depicting the mean, hypocritical behaviour of a community under the Revolutionary government. Ironically called 'Landscapes', they are 'the works of neither Salvator Rosa nor Claude Lorrain'. Unlike the landscaping of America in the earlier chapters, these scenes portray the pettiness and vulgarity of American behaviour which, because of the Revolution, is 'now transmuted into a wide extended surface on which new and deceiving perspectives are represented'. Paine's spatial imagery is now the butt of sarcasm. The perspective does not reveal 'the soaring eagle' but rather its filthy nest. The dramas close with four 'copper plates' depicting executions, wounded men and despairing women, and finally a scene of bestiality. A stallion rushes from the woods and mounts a mare. The mare's owners try to beat off the stallion, but in vain. The farmer can no longer protect his barnyard, and the result is a threat that is both sexual and economic. From references to the grand or beautiful landscapes of Rosa and Lorrain to a mere copper-plate of equine rape: the framework of 'Landscapes' represents in miniature the depressing decline of America resulting, in Crèvecœur's view, from the Revolution.[9]

Crèvecœur's two texts reflected his experience as a quietist in unsettled times. They were prophetic not only of the experience of Morse, Webster and Rush, but also of the remainder of Crèvecœur's life. When, in 1783 at the conclusion of the Revolution, he returned to New York as French Consul, he discovered that his wife was dead, his house had been destroyed and his children had vanished. Once again his American experience drove him close to insanity. He found his children and returned to France in 1790 only to live uneasily through the Reign of Terror. He died in 1813, having spent two-thirds of his life in extremity. By that time the popularity in Europe of the *Letters* was declining. It had never been popular in America. The first American edition, brought out finally in 1793 by Matthew Carey, was a failure. We do not know why. Perhaps it was because of Crèvecœur's politics. Or perhaps it was because, by 1793, Americans no longer wanted to read about the sorrows of the Revolution. They had post-Revolutionary sorrows enough to contend with, and those sorrows would be portrayed by two of their own writers, Philip Freneau and Hugh Henry Brackenridge.

PHILIP FRENEAU'S RUINED ISLAND

Freneau and Brackenridge were classmates at Princeton. They were also friends and literary collaborators. The best known of their joint works is 'The Rising Glory of America', originally written for the Princeton Commencement Exercises of 1771, and read by Brackenridge. The poem looks forward to a time when the American empire will triumph over 'Mere dreary wastes and awful solitude', and when 'no dangerous tree with deadly fruit' or 'tempting serpent' will threaten this new Paradise. The poem had a long career but, as we shall see, a varied one. In its 1809 edition, the poem concludes:

> No thistle here, nor thorn, nor briar shall spring,
> Earth's curse before: the lion and the lamb
> In mutual friendship linked, shall browse the shrub,
> And timorous deer with softened tygers stray
> O'er mead, or lofty hill, or grassy plain;
> Another Jordan's stream shall glide along,
> And Siloah's brook in circling eddies flow:
> Groves shall adorn their verdant banks, on which
> The happy people, free from toils and death,
> Shall find secure repose. No fierce disease,
> No fevers, slow consumption, ghastly plague,
> (Fate's ancient ministers) again proclaim
> Perpetual war with man: fair fruits shall bloom,
> Fair to the eye, and sweeter to the taste;
> Nature's loud storms be hushed, and seas no more
> Rage hostile to mankind – and, worse than all,
> The fiercer passions of the human breast
> Shall kindle up to deeds of death no more,

But all subside in universal peace ————
——————————————— Such days the world,
And such AMERICA at last shall have
When ages, yet to come, have run their round,
And future years of bliss alone remain.[10]

There are many echoes here: of the King James Bible, of Milton, and of Drayton's 'To the Virginian Voyage'. They combine to produce Edenic images of peace and plenty in a landscape of greensward and orchards, free from disease and dissent.

'The Rising Glory of America' generally is in the tradition of *translatio emperii*. Freneau was familiar with Berkeley's poem, the central text of the tradition, and printed it as an epigraph to his translation of the Abbé Robin's *New Travels Through North-America*. Yet, in its 1809 version, 'The Rising Glory' could hardly be called an unqualified celebration of the American empire. In the first place, the landscape is generalised. In part it is described in clichés, and in part defined by negation which, as we have already seen, is a much-used strategy in American literature. Secondly, it is only after the enormous pause of the caesura that the landscape is given a geographical location – the world. The succeeding conjunction and the phrase 'at last' suggests that Freneau's continent will not become an Eden until everywhere else has achieved that blissful condition. This is a novel interpretation of *translatio emperii*, particularly for an American.

Freneau did not always feel this way. He persistently tinkered with his poems, and 'The Rising Glory' is no exception. The 1771 Commencement version, published in Philadelphia in 1772, quite reasonably depicted a rising glory within the British Empire. In 1775 Freneau removed the British references. Yet in his 1786 *Poems, Written Chiefly During the Late War* and his 1795 *Poems on Several Occasions* he still dated the poem 1771. He may have done this because of its climactic lines. In the 1772, 1786 and 1795 versions they were:

Such days the world
And such, America, *thou first* shall have. . .

In the 1809 version Freneau altered the phrase I have underlined, and now dated the poem 1775. The new date suggested that it was a Revolutionary poem, and this perhaps comported with the assertive capitalisation of the proper noun. But what had the Revolution achieved? Clearly, Freneau had abandoned his hope for an early American millennium.[11]

The unease suggested by the textual history of 'The Rising Glory of America' is to be found in an earlier collaboration with Brackenridge. *Father Bombo's Pilgrimage to Mecca*, produced in the autumn of 1770, is probably the first novel written in America. Without the restraints of a solemn Commencement, the two young men produced much coarser material, a lively squib full of undergraduate humour. *Father Bombo*, like 'The Rising Glory', derives from European forms. Generally, it apes the vogue of English orientalism following the translation of *Arabian Nights*. Specifically, its derivation reveals a polylinguistic intertextuality that would have delighted Jorge Luis Borges. Its title and overall structure is almost certainly taken from Samuel Johnson's first book, the *Voyage to Abyssinia*, his 1735 translation of Joachim Le Grand's 1728 French version of the Portuguese manuscript of the travels of Father Jeronimo Lobo. Again like 'The Rising Glory,' *Father Bombo* does its best to shun America. In the first chapter Bombo is expelled from Princeton for plagiarising Lucian (a crime his authors winked at in their own cases). His journey takes him to New York City, where he creates mayhem by plundering the High Table at the rival King's College (now Columbia). Then he travels eastwards. Of course, this is required by the form of the text. But Bombo's is no simple journey. He goes to Mecca via Ireland, Scotland, London and Rome. He returns to Philadelphia in the penultimate chapter only to retire immediately to his chambers in Princeton and thereafter to a retreat on Long Island. Bombo, it seems, is reluctant to have anything to do with the New World.[12]

Eighteenth-century poets frequently used the rhetorical device of retreat. Yet Father Bombo's progress anticipated Philip Freneau's. Much of Freneau's career was spent retreating from America. He was raised on the eastern seaboard, and his furthest venture westwards was to the Maryland woods, where for a brief period he joined Brackenridge in schoolteaching. Otherwise, his life was spent clinging to the East, living in New York, Philadelphia and New Jersey, or sailing the Atlantic. He published his first independent book of poems in 1772, when he was twenty. The major poem in the collection was the 438-line title piece, 'The American Village', which continues the theme announced in 'The Rising Glory of America'.

Once again, the text is derivative. Freneau draws much of his theme and imagery from Goldsmith's *The Deserted Village*. We saw in chapter 1 that Goldsmith depicted America as a ravaged landscape with 'savage men', 'crouching tigers' and 'matted woods'. Freneau accepts this imagery, but transforms it into the basis for a redemptive movement in which the chaos of nature will become fruit trees and wheat harvests. He draws a clear distinction between England and America. England, like the classical republics, is far gone in the decay of luxury and idleness. Here, Freneau's attitude is no different from that of Paine, Filson and Imlay. But his view of America is. Unlike the others, he regrets that the primitive terrain must be shaped by American activity. He is therefore caught in a dilemma where he simultaneously accepts yet is dismayed by the rising glory of American empire. This becomes clear in the following lines:

> But envious time conspiring with the sea,
> Wash'd all its landscapes, and its groves away.
> Its trees declining, stretch'd upon the sand,
> No more their shadows throw across the land.
> Its vines no more their clust'ring beauty show,
> Nor sturdy oaks embrace the mountain's brow.
> Bare lands alone now overwhelm the coast,
> Lost in its grandeur, and its beauty lost.
>
>   Thus, tho' my fav'rite isle to ruin gone,
> Inspires my sorrow, and demands my moan;
> Yet this wide land its place can well supply
> With landscapes, hills and grassy mountains high.[13]

The narrator's ideal landscape is an island, a primitive yet perfect Eden where educated man is essentially an interloper. Yet it is doomed. An image of the Flood transforms it into a wilderness, anticipating the westward movement of land clearance across America which would be regretted by Benjamin Rush as medically unwise. The new stanza, signalled by the opening adverb, marks a hairpin-bend in the narrator's thought and presents a consolation in the nature of an afterthought.

Like Crèvecœur, Freneau had read *Robinson Crusoe* closely, and he tended to operate in Defoe's two constrasting landscapes: the precise, controllable detail of an island and the vast but generalised vistas of larger land masses. These landscapes seemed to blind Freneau to his immediate environment. Even when he was in the Maryland woods he could not describe his surroundings. In a letter to another Princeton classmate, James Madison (later to be fourth President), Freneau accounted for his experience in terms of a generalised Pastoral:

> Deep to the woods, I sing a Shepherds care,
> Deep to the woods, Cyllenius calls me there.
> The last retreat of Love and Verse I go –
> Verse made me mad at first and – will keep me so.[14]

Although Freneau claimed that the woods were to be his Muse, he did his best to ignore them. 'The Power of Fancy', first published in 1786, uses Joseph Warton's ode 'To Fancy' as its model, but its scope is much wider. The progress of poetry is seen to move, like Bombo, eastwards; and it more firmly reverses *translatio emperii*. We travel to the Hebrides, the home of Ossian; then to Rome and Greece and 'over Ganges' streams' until:

Farther, farther in the east,
Till it almost meets the west,
Let us wandering both be lost
On Taitis sea-beat coast,
Bear me from that distant strand,
Over ocean, over land,
To California's golden shore —
Fancy, stop, and rove no more.[15]

Signalled by another heavy caesura, poetry does not quite circle the globe. There is a significant gap in its ranging arc. It ignores the entire American continent, a strange omission in a man with an apparent poetic investment in America's rising glory.

Freneau turned his back on America. Again like Bombo, he went to sea. Although he remarked in a 1775 poem, 'MacSwiggen', that the scenes of the western world 'conspire / To raise a poet's fancy and his fire', he preferred to leave America, 'this disast'rous shore', to the arguments of theologians and lawyers, transporting himself to 'a safe retirement from all human kind'. Again, he conceived that retirement in terms of a limited landscape:

In distant isles some happier scene I'll choose,
And court in softer shades the unwilling Muse.

The poem prophesied Freneau's career. In 1776, just as the Revolution was becoming a reality, Freneau left home. This was the first of a number of departures, for he spent much of the years 1776–1780, 1784–1790 and 1802–1807 at sea. Although he once wrote that 'the world is undone by looking at things at a distance', that is precisely what he would do.[16]

In 1776 it seemed that he had found his ideal limited terrain. The Isle of Santa Cruz appeared to be a 'Blessed Isle'. Initially it provided him with a perfect pastoral retreat, and he described it with convincing detail in 'The Beauties of Santa Cruz':

The smooth white cedar, here, delights the eye,
The bay-tree, with its aromatic green,
The sea-side grapes, sweet natives of the sand,
And pulse, of various kinds, on trees are seen.
Here mingled vines their downward shadows cast,
Here, cluster'd grapes from loaded boughs depend,
Their leaves no frosts, their fruits no cold winds blast,
But, rear'd by suns, to time alone they bend.

In an 'Account of the Island of Santa Cruz' that served as a preface to the first version of the poem in Brackenridge's *United States Magazine* in 1779, Freneau called the place 'inexpressibly beautiful'. He employs here the rhetoric of inexpressibility I discussed in the Prologue. From Virgil

onwards writers had protested their inability to do justice to their subject
– and had then made the attempt. Ironically, Freneau's essay in rhetoric
will miscarry and the island will turn into a hell, for its plantations were
worked by slaves.

Like Crèvecœur, Freneau reacted with intense horror to slavery, and
particularly to the punishments that it involved. Santa Cruz had been the
scene of a slave revolt in 1733, and in consequence stringent laws were
formulated which regulated every minute of the slave's existence and
which imposed pitiless punishments on transgressors. A runaway slave,
for instance, would have a leg amputated. In his 'Account' of the island
Freneau's response to slavery transformed the paradisal landscape:

> It casts a shade over the native charms of the country; it blots out the beauties of
> the eternal Spring which Providence has there ordained to reign, and amidst all
> the profusion of bounties which nature has scattered, the brightness of the
> heaven, the mildness of the air, and the luxuriancy of the vegetable kingdom, it
> leaves me melancholy and disconsolate. . . And thus the earth, which were it
> not for the lust of pride and dominion, might be an earthly paradise, is, by the
> ambition and overbearing nature of mankind, rendered an eternal scene of
> desolation, woe and horror; the weak goes to the wall, while the strong
> prevails; and after an ambitious phrenzy has turned the world upside down, we
> are contented with a narrow spot.

The natural order has been upset, and the result here is a contraction of
landscape that, just three years after *Common Sense*, makes the New
World resemble the Old. Freneau anticipates at this point the fear of
earthly perversion to be experienced by his enemies, the British, at the
Yorktown surrender.

The poem, having assembled an account of earth's 'onely paradise' in
Draytonesque detail, abandons it as soon as a Black figure appears, bent
with pain and toil, in the landscape. Now Freneau curses the slave ship
that brought the toiler here, and wishes it shipwrecked – a particularly
intense feeling for one who spent much of his life at sea. In a clear echo of
the disintegration of landscape depicted in Goldsmith's *The Deserted
Village*, the island is torn and shredded by storms:

> Wild were the skies, affrighted nature groan'd,
> As though approach'd her last decisive day,
> Skies blaz'd around, and billowing winds had nigh
> Dislodg'd these cliffs, and tore yon' hills away.

The image of the Flood in 'The American Village' is repeated here, and
the result is, again, a land stripped of its beautiful features and
transformed, like Crèvecœur's sea, into 'endless plains [which] deject the
wearied eye'.[17]

The result was projected back upon the 'disast'rous shore' of America.

Two poems published in 1779 reveal the extent of Freneau's horror. The first, 'George the Third's Soliloquy', looks at the Revolution not from the point of view of a Patriot, but rather from that of the unfortunate monarch. In consequence the war is seen the way Crèvecœur saw it, as an internecine struggle, with George III sending gangs of cut-throats and jailbirds to quell what is described as a slave rebellion. The terrors of George's images are further realised in 'The House of Night', a poem which (as F. O. Matthiessen recognised) anticipates Poe. The poem begins with the poet wandering at midnight in the woods of Chesapeake Bay. It is spring, but the scene is hardly springlike:

> And from the woods the late resounding note
> Issued of the loquacious *Whip-poor-will*,
> Hoarse, howling dogs, and nightly roving wolves
> Clamour'd from far off clifts invisible.
>
> Rude, from the wide extended Chesapeke,
> I heard the winds the dashing waves assail,
> And saw from far, by pictur'd fancy form'd,
> The black ship travelling through the noisy gale.

In part, the poem's landscape is reminiscent of Crèvecœur's letters VIII and XII. The first stanza here also echoes Crusoe's horrific Pyrenean encounter with wolves. But this is hardly the final test before reaching the Promised Land. The narrator sees light from the upper windows of 'a noble dome, rais'd fair and high', and finds Death awaiting him there instead of the expected 'mirth and hospitality'. The conversation that ensues is brought to an abrupt end by a tempest:

> Lights in the air like burning stars were hurl'd
> Dogs howled, heaven mutter'd, and the tempest blew,
> The red half-moon peep'd from behind a cloud
> As if in dread the amazing scene to view.

In consequence the grove surrounding the house lies 'in wild confusion'. The poem closes on a generalised note of death and terrestrial instability:

> Hills sink to plains, and man returns to dust,
> That dust supports a reptile or a flower;
> Each changeful atom by some other nurs'd
> Takes some new form, to perish in an hour.

The only paradise, the final stanza asserts, is (like Hesiod's) the one to be found after death.[18]

In the following year Freneau's 'pictured fancy' was turned into horrific reality. Apparently, on 25 May 1780 he was aboard the privateer 'Aurora' when it was captured by the British frigate 'Iris'. He was herded with more than 100 other prisoners between decks, where the intense heat and overpowering smell turned the place into a hell. Then he was placed with 300 others in the prison-ship 'Scorpion', where again he was suffocated by the heat and stench. The prisoners were fed beef crawling with vermin. Miscreants were badly beaten by Hessian guards. Others died after staggering the confined space in the throes of disease. Freneau himself caught a fever, and eventually was released on 12 July 1780, turned in those short weeks into a grey cadaver of a man. On the basis of this experience Freneau wrote his most bitter poem, 'The British Prison Ship'. The ship is seen as a perversion, a mere hulk that lacks masts and sails. It is better to meet death in battle than to endure a living death, a slow wasting punctuated only by the groans of those that are dying all around. Now, unlike 'The House of Night', death is not seen in terms of paradise. Hesiod's 'clouds of care' have become all-enveloping:

> Death has no charms – his realms dejected lie
> In the dull climate of a clouded sky.[19]

Freneau's despair, however, reaches its peak in a poem first published in 1785 and reprinted a decade later under the title 'The Hurricane'. The poem begins with the image of a man safe on shore before his 'evening fire', and then moves through a series of images of 'the dark abyss' of the storm-tossed ocean. The second half of the poem continues:

> But what a strange, uncoasted strand
> Is that, where fate permits no day –
> No charts have we to mark that land,
> No compass to direct that way –
> What pilot shall explore that realm,
> What new COLUMBUS take the helm!
>
> While death and darkness both surround,
> And tempests rage with lawless power,
> Of friendship's voice I hear no sound,
> No comfort in this dreadful hour –
> What friendship can in tempests be,
> What comforts on this troubled sea?
>
> The barque, accustom'd to obey,
> No more the trembling pilots guide.
> Alone she gropes her trackless way,
> While mountains burst on either side –
> Thus, skill and science both must fall;
> And ruin is the lot of all.

The imagery here resembles Crèvecœur's Letter VIII. The metaphor of mountains generalises the seascape and threatens the safe landsman of the first stanza. There is portrayed here an eternal darkness as a setting for an actively violent, collapsing landscape from which there is no escape through death, and no help through companionship, seamanship or science. Freneau has here taken to its hellish ultimate a number of themes and images adumbrated in his earlier poetry and sharpened by his experiences on Santa Cruz and in the 'Scorpion'. These lines point towards a nihilism that rejects any meaning in American terrain. It would have been better had Columbus not sailed.[20]

A short story, published in 1788 and ironically entitled 'Light, Summer Reading', fills in the picture. The narrator accompanies an unnamed man 'in a white linen coat' to a walled garden stocked with a vast array of elegant and exotic flora and fauna. In the garden sits 'the once admirable Marcia', who has been rejected in love and whose imagination is now 'disordered'. The man in the white coat suggests that:

> we are all more or less affected with idiotism at times. Do not fogs and clouds produce a heaviness and melancholy temper in the mind which nothing but the clear beams of the great luminary can dissipate.

Besides, he later adds, the imagination can transform 'every thing that happens in real life to the more agreeable landscapes of an inchanted and fictitious country'. As the references to fog and 'idiotism' suggest, the man in the white coat is a parody of Benjamin Rush. Freneau would later attack Rush in three poems about 'Doctor Sangrado'. Here he shows how illusory is the doctor's environmentalist optimism and faith in the power of the imagination. Marcia dies in the sunlit garden. Death stalks the landscape, whether it is 'real' or fictitious.[21]

Yet, even while he was writing these accounts of personal or terrestrial collapse, Freneau continued to celebrate the 'Rising Empire'. He helped to edit the *Freeman's Journal* in 1781–1782, and one of his official duties was to provide an accolade for Washington when the victorious General was feted in Philadelphia on 2 January 1782:

> Illustrious hero, may you live to see
> These new republics, powerful, great, and free;
> Peace, heaven born peace, o'er spacious regions spread,
> While discord, sinking, veils her ghastly head.[22]

Freneau's spread-eagle imperialism was developed just one week later with an essay that occupied most of the front page of the *Freeman's Journal*. In that essay America is regarded as a vessel of natural perfection waiting to be filled with inhabitants. It is folly for Britain to rule America, for Britain is:

> a little island situated on the extremities of the ocean, encumbered with rugged mountains, barren heaths, and useless broken lands; a spot whose strength is merely artificial.

Freneau now accepts without reserve the contrast developed in *Common Sense* between the limited perspectives of Europe and the wide vistas of America. He banishes Britain to the chilly margins of the globe, and fills its centre (and his page) with a vision of a 'vast and fertile' American continent that is 'naturally invincible'. It is the land beyond the Appalachians that endows America with most of its promise:

> after passage of a ridge of lofty mountains lying on the eastern frontiers of these republics a new region opens, of inexpressible beauty and fertility. The lands are there of a quality far superior to those situated in the neighbourhood of the sea coast; the trees of the forest are stately and tall, the meadows and pastures, spacious, supporting vast herds of the native animals of the country, which own no master, nor expect their sustenance from the hands of men. The climate . . . is moderate and agreeable; there the rivers no longer bend their course eastward to the atlantic, but inclining to the west and south, and moving with a gentle current through the channels that nature has opened fall at length into that grand repository of a thousand streams, the far-famed Missisippi [*sic*], who from a source unknown collecting his remotest waters, rolls forward through the frozen regions of the north, and stretching his extended arms to the east and west, embraces those savage groves, as yet uninvestigated by the traveller, unsung by the poet, or unmeasured by the chain of the geometrician; till uniting with the Ohio and turning due south, receives afterwards the Missori [*sic*] and a hundred others, this prince of rivers, in comparison of whom the Nile is but a Rivulet and the Danube a mere ditch, hurries with his immense flood of waters to the Mexican Sea, laving the shores of many fertile countries in his passage, inhabited by savage nations as yet almost unknown, and without a name.[23]

I have quoted this passage at some length because it anticipates Morse's description of 'Fredonia' and shows Freneau hard at work to create an imperial portrait which contrasts starkly with his nihilism. The rhetoric of inexpressibility that had formerly been used to describe the Island of Santa Cruz is now applied to the whole North American continent. This time, however, there are no slaves to impair the exercise. A wide range of devices are employed in a suitably enormous sentence. The open spaces of the continent are composed into a pastoral landscape by the use of such terms as 'meadows'. A Draytonesque fertility suggests that the animals need no tending, but simply await the attention of the hunters. The sonorous cadences of the clauses reach a climax with the description of the Mississippi. The river is a giant personified and seen in embrace with a continent that, at the very beginning of the essay, had been described as feminine. The river's benevolence and vitality is brought vividly to mind by the phonological qualities of the verbs 'laves' and 'rolls'. The river, moreover, is the major link in a whole chain of rivers which provides easy transit across the continent and proves that 'nature does nothing in vain'. The whole scene is bathed in a golden glow; the continent dances attendance on her surveyors and poets.

A poem probably written in the middle of the 1780s highlights the division between Freneau's nihilist landscapes of collapse and his optimistic imperialism. *The Miscellaneous Works* of 1788 opened with 'The Pictures of Columbus, the Genoese'. Unlike the despairing image of Columbus in 'The Hurricane', the navigator here faces trackless wastes with a confidence based on his knowledge of geographical symmetry. The first 'Picture' is titled 'COLUMBUS *making* MAPS', and is supported by a footnote claiming cartography as 'his original profession'. The poem begins:

> As o'er his charts Columbus ran,
> Such disproportion he survey'd,
> He thought he saw in art's mean plan
> Blunders that Nature never made;
> The *land* in one poor corner plac'd,
> And all beside, a swelling waste –!
> 'It can't be so', Columbus said;

This particular view of the globe, once again placing Europe at the margin, determines Columbus to go in search of the 'gay, painted picture of the mind', despite the interdict of the Inquisition and the disdain of Ferdinand's advisers and scholars. He is 'confirm'd in [his] design', finds the land where 'God and nature reign', and despite being jailed when he returns takes comfort in the 'golden fancy' which projects:

> When empires rise where lonely forests grew,
> Where Freedom shall her generous plans pursue.[24]

The antithesis between a constricting Old World and an expansive America, depicted in the *Freeman's Journal* essay, is here developed in the opposing images of the cramped jail and Columbus's vaulting imagination. The absolute certainty of the navigator in the opening stanza is vindicated by his subsequent experience, and his prediction of an American future is implicitly verified by the imperial ideology of the poem. 'Pictures of Columbus' runs completely counter to 'Light, Summer Reading', which was published in the very same volume. The poem asserts an absolute relation between the landscape of the imagination and the real terrain that the short story aims to undermine.

The radical disjunction between Freneau's despairing and his imperial landscapes began to disappear with his marriage in 1790 and a growing belief in deism. A God of nature and reason was, he believed, best expressed in science; hence a poem published in 1809 and entitled 'Science, Favourable to Virtue':

> The lovely philanthropic scheme
> (Great image of the power supreme,)
> On growth of science must depend;
> With this all human duties end.

Science and nature are unified through technology. Like Joel Barlow and Thomas Jefferson, Freneau often saw roads and canals as the tangible expression of American imperialism. In his poem on the Great Western Canal he celebrated an achievement so great that even the Great Wall of China was dwarfed:

> To make the purpose all complete,
> Before they bid *two oceans* meet,
> Before the task is finished all,
> What rocks must yield, what forests fall?

> *Three years* elapsed, behold it done!
> A work from Nature's *chaos* won;
> By hearts of oak and hands of toil
> The Spade inverts the rugged soil
> A work, that may remain secure
> While suns exist and Moons endure.[25]

Before the building of the Canal the land was occupied only by tigers and Mohawks. Now the aboriginal chaos has been transformed into the scene of busy commerce by a capitalised (and capitalist) spade. The transformation is no longer the source of regret, and the soil is turned upside down not in an image of perversion but rather in one of jubilation, for it is done in the service of the Passage to India originally conceived by Columbus.

Freneau now abandoned his fear of trackless wastes, and with it any attempt to come to grips with the less pleasant implications of American terrain. He adopted instead a faith in frames, maps, plans and systems – influenced, perhaps, by his association with Jefferson.[26] Freneau set out to systematise America and renew his Commencement pledge in a huge poem, *The Rising Empire*, a grand design nationalistic in purpose and intended for a large audience. The opening poem, 'A Philosophical Sketch of America', first published in 1790 and reprinted in the 1795 and 1809 volumes with the new title 'On American Antiquity', clearly intends in its subject matter and titling to answer the European miasmatists. It conceives America as a vast continent including every kind of climate and yet uniformly fertile, teeming with life. Its vast scheme begins with the Flood reshaping the continent, sees the Indians simply as an earlier form of civilisation which superseded the bear and the panther, and which will in its turn give way to an agrarian civilisation. The fragment ends in a moment of fertile optimism: 'Their harvests ripen, and their gardens grow'. The 'pathless woods' are giving way to the hand of man.

The poem was never completed, but the six fragments that exist in addition to the 'Philosophical Sketch' indicate that, just as Columbus the mapmaker had seen that America fitted within a divine scheme, so Freneau the poet wished to show that the United States would carry the scheme to completion. The poems were to be organised by state in a north–south sequence, and each would contain descriptions of the state's terrain and products, its towns and the character of its inhabitants. It would be, therefore, a version not only of the state histories but also of Jedidiah Morse's *American Geography*, suitably arranged into couplets. The perspective was maplike, from a great height:

> Spread with stupendous hills, far from the main
> Fair Pennsylvania holds her golden reign,
> In fertile fields her wheaten harvest grows,
> Charg'd with its freights her favorite Delaware flows[27]

Poetry moving towards the status of geography, *The Rising Empire* was conceived in the tradition of Drayton's *Poly-Olbion*, but on a much more ambitious scale to accord with the larger terrain. Although the poem was perhaps too ambitious, Freneau showed the nature of his scheme in a number of later and more modest poems. Two in particular illustrate the last phase of his vision of America. The first was published in the 1809 collection and has a title, the significance of which would not be lost on his fellow Americans: 'Reflections on the Constitution; or Frame of Nature'. Although its Americanism is thereafter tacit, its scheme follows that of the 'Philosophical Sketch', starting with an image of the creation of the earth and proceeding to justify the imperial image this time by means of Newtonian physics:

> THOU, nature's self art nature's God
> Through all expansion spread abroad,
> Existing in the eternal scheme,
> Vast, undivided, and supreme.
>
> Here beauty, order, power, behold
> Exact, all-perfect, uncontrouled;
> All in its proper place arranged,
> Immortal, endless, and unchanged.[28]

The perspective of the second poem is very different; its purpose is the same. Published in 1822, ten years before his death, the 'Ode Written on a Remote Perspective View of Princeton College' returns Freneau to his *alma mater*, but at a distance. Occasioned by the installation of a telescope on the highest hill near Freneau's home, the poem begins with an excursion up the hill. Viewing the college through the telescope, the poet recalls Princeton life under its President, the '*Caledonian* Sage' Witherspoon, gives a snapshot history of the Revolution, and ends on a note of adoration of 'the sacred Spire'. United States history, Freneau's biography, and the cultural life of the nation are thus tr..med within thirteen stanzas and closed with a benediction. American space is there too, a vast scheme contained and ordered by science and the poet in an image suitably derived from Pope:

> Among the rest, but far remote,
> We *Princeton's* summit scan,
> And verdent plains which there denote
> The energies of man:
> By aid of art's *Perspective Glass*,
> O'er many a woody vale we pass;
> The *glass* attracts, and brings more near
> What first, to naked vision here,
> Seem'd a chaotic mass.
>
> And there we trace, from far displayed,
> The muses favorite seat,
> And groves, within whose bowery shade
> The Sons of science meet.
> *Devotion* to her altars calls
> In plainly decorated halls –
> Those walls engage the *Athenian* muse
> Where Science, still, her course pursues –
> Those venerated walls![29]

Like Father Bombo fifty-two years earlier, Philip Freneau now sought retreat in a confined spot. His withdrawal from America was complete.

HUGH HENRY BRACKENRIDGE'S CAVE

Brackenridge met Freneau at Princeton after a boyhood on the Pennsylvania frontier. After graduation, he taught in a village with the suitable name of Back Creek, Maryland. Freneau joined him briefly. Brackenridge returned to Princeton to take an MA, and then became a chaplain in the Continental army. The literary ambitions which he exhibited in 'The Rising Glory of America' were developed in two plays about incidents in the War. In 1778 he moved to Philadelphia and, like many of his contemporaries, showed growing concern for the creation of a republican culture. Brackenridge's contribution was to publish the *United States Magazine* in January 1779. His 'Preface' to the first issue indicates his happiness with the apparently growing public interest in literature:

For what is man without taste and the acquirements of genius? An Ouran-Outan with the human shape and the soul of a beast.

It was the language of our enemies at the commencement of the debate between America and what is called the mother country, that in righteous judgment for our wickedness, it would be well to leave us to that independency which we seemed to affect, and to suffer us to sink down to so many Ouran-Outans of the wood, lost to the light of science which, from the other side of the Atlantic, had just begun to break upon us. They have been made to see, and even to confess the vanity of this kind of *auguration*.

The bitterness against Britain reflects Brackenridge's concern by being expressed in cultural rather than military terms. The pattern of images in which that bitterness is displayed is revealing. The dark woods, the home of the beasts and the site of Brackenridge's boyhood, are contrasted to the light of science and culture. It is only such light that distinguishes man from the beast. The distinction, and the image-pattern, pivots around the two references to that animal whose humanity had been discussed by Edward Tyson and Lord Monboddo. Far from the woods of America, European intellectuals could speculate on the Chain of Being. Here, however, Brackenridge reveals raw emotion, because in the woods the connection between the bestial and the human was no speculation. He had experienced the instability of frontier conditions following Braddock's defeat in 1755, and a frightened awareness of the beast lurking beneath the veneer of civilisation would inform his writing for the rest of his life.[30]

The *United States Magazine* was published throughout 1779, with contributions from Brackenridge and Freneau. From January until July the magazine carried instalments of Brackenridge's second piece of prose fiction, 'The Cave of Vanhest'. (The first had been *Father Bombo*.) Despite his scorn of 'that romantic kind of writing which fills every mountain with a hermitage', the narrator gets lost in the New Jersey woods and is relieved to discover 'a kind of gothic building in the bosom of the mountain'. The cave is occupied by a philosopher, his wife and two charming daughters, and an orang-utan in the shape of a dwarfish servant called Bernardus, or Nardy. The cave resembles Iwan Al-z's description of John Bartram's home, and anticipates Fenimore Cooper's frontier comforts. It is hung with chintz, carpeted from Persia, and furnished with mahogany, silver and the finest china. Of course, it overflows with books.

The conversations which garnish the narrator's stay with the hermit largely concern the Revolution. Brackenridge had already attacked the British as savage cannibals, and here he pulls no punches about the horrors of war. He depicts a headless body buried so hastily that one foot remains exposed. A symbolic opposition emerges between such misuses of the soil and the Edenic existence of the hermit's family. The latter has Draytonesque overtones:

> Plumbs shaken from the tree; peaches gathered from an orchard on the brow of the hill above; apples at the same time; vegetables from the garden; dried fish; milk, cheese, butter were upon the board.

Everything, it seems, is in perfect order, and the tale closes with the hermit's account of his love for three Muses: Miss Urany (the Muse of astronomy), Miss Theology, and Miss Law ('a grave and comely lady, a little pitted with the small pox'). There are hints of potential disorder in this apparently self-sufficient microcosm of American culture. Nardy, initially portrayed as a potential Caliban, sprains his ankle and the visitor has to tend for him. But the tale is possibly incomplete, and such hints remain underdeveloped. Was Brackenridge intending a disquisition on feet? We will never know.[31]

Unfortunately, 'The Cave of Vanhest' and Freneau's poems did not attract the expected audience, and in a year the magazine had to close. In view of the hopes that Brackenridge pinned on it, it is not surprising that he ended on a bitter note. He blamed the War and inflation of republican currency for the magazine's failure; but he also blamed the ignoramuses of the Republic:

> the people who inhabit the region of stupidity, and cannot bear to have the tranquillity of their repose disturbed by the villainous jargon of a book.

He hoped that the magazine would be merely 'suspended' until better times, when once again it would take its place in 'the commonwealth of letters'.[32] In the meantime, he followed the hermit's love for Miss Law, overlooked her disfigurement, and was admitted to Philadelphia bar in 1780. The next year he moved to the frontier village of Pittsburgh. He lived there until 1801, when he moved to Carlisle, Pennsylvania.

In moving to the frontier Brackenridge tried to realise the belief in republican culture embodied in 'The Cave of Vanhest'. He quickly became aware that life on the frontier was not unalloyed pleasure. Pittsburgh, he discovered, was the capital of the region of stupidity. It was noted for its disorder and was the scene of regular street fights and tavern brawls. As an ambitious newcomer Brackenridge soon created a number of enemies, whom he later dismissed as orang-utans, baboons and (adopting Gulliver's description of the Yahoos) as 'a thousand monkeys leaping and chattering amongst the trees, and incommoding the Caravan by the fall of excrement'.[33] Yet despite all this he identified with his new home, and shared western views of the American East as overly European, aristocratic and unaware of the special problems confronting the frontier. The West did not receive enough Federal protection from Indian depredations, and it was hard hit by Federal excise laws. Spain held the navigation rights on the Mississippi and obstructed exports. The farmers consequently converted their excess grain into whisky but found that, in addition to expensive transport costs eastwards, they had to bear an excise tax. The result was a series of disturbances culminating in the Whiskey Rebellion of 1794.

Brackenridge regarded the excise tax as part of an evil system of national debt. Inflation had already been one of the causes contributing to the demise of his magazine. Now he saw that a paper currency funded by a national debt favoured the East to the detriment of the West. Most of the government's creditors lived in the East, and the interest on their securities was paid partly by the excise tax. Therefore money flowed eastwards with the whisky. In addition, Brackenridge thought that paper credit was not 'real'. There was nothing solid or respectable about it compared with landed property and the image of the virtuous farmer. Here Brackenridge followed other liberal thinkers who drew their ideas from the British Country Party earlier in the century. The rise of paper credit in Britain and the resultant speculation had created many new fortunes. The Country Party, based firmly on the squirearchy, suggested that the *nouveaux riches* were not attached to the country's interest, for after all they had no stake in the country's land. Now, the same process seemed to be happening in America; and it may have caused the demise of the *United States Magazine*.[34]

Brackenridge sympathised with the farmers. In 1785 he defended twelve rioters accused of attacking an excise collector. Seven years later he published two articles attacking the excise law in Freneau's *National Gazette*. In the first he deplored the government's failure to protect western farmers and disparaged their support for paper credit which, using an environmental image that would have pleased Benjamin Rush, he saw as having:

> brought a great evil, fortunes rising like exhalations from the earth by other means than common industry.

In the second he portrayed the westerners as oppressed but virtuous 'hewers of wood and drawers of water', honest if sometimes misled. He thought that if they were relieved of the burdens they would transform into reality the image of peace and plenty that had graced 'The Cave of Vanhest'. The West, he believed, would be 'a glorious garden to cultivate, and the fairest blossoms will bloom and the richest fruit grow there for the benefit of this government'.[35]

The East paid no heed, and the excise disturbances were kindled into a full-scale rebellion. In view of his past history Brackenridge seemed the natural choice to mediate between the government and the rebels. But he regarded the distinction as a dubious one, and wrote a lengthy account of his involvement. It presents vivid evidence of a man caught between two evils. On the one hand, the government was not listening to the farmers' genuine grievances. On the other hand, the situation was out of control. At one point Brackenridge, while marching on Pittsburgh with the rebels, depicts a sleepless night spent worrying about his position. The prose both recalls Crèvecœur's unease and looks forward to Brockden Brown's breathless self-examination. Brackenridge worries that Secretary of the Treasury Hamilton, angered by the opposition to the excise law, 'will be inclined to sanguinary counsels'. If anything, the farmers' thirst for blood is even greater. Brackenridge imagines a pitched battle between government troops and farmers:

> They may defend the passes of the mountains; they are warlike, accustomed to the use of arms, capable of hunger and fatigue, and can lie in the water like badgers. They are enthusiastic to madness, and the effect of this is beyond calculation. . . These were my reveries as I lay, with my head upon a saddle, on the flooring of a cabin.

Already an exciseman's house has been burned and looted. It seems that a full-scale revolution is about to break out:

> Let no man suppose that I coveted revolution. I had seen the evils of one already, the American; and I had read the evils of another, the French. My imagination presented the evils of the last strongly to my view and brought them so close to probable experience at home that, during the whole period of the insurrection, I could scarcely bear to cast my eye on a paragraph of French news.

Previously, Brackenridge had supported the French Revolution and had even joked about the execution of Louis XVI. Now, images of Jacobin bloodshed had changed his mind.[36]

Eventually, Brackenridge successfully negotiated a settlement and obtained an amnesty for the ringleaders. Yet the image of the Rebellion was not erased from his mind. The farmers were, after all, elevated by republican ideology to be the natural legatees of virtue. The Whiskey Rebellion, together with Shays's Rebellion of 1786–1787 and Fries's Rebellion of 1798, showed that they could riot against the Republic if sufficiently motivated by self-interest. Brackenridge's attitude to the West and its inhabitants altered. The change, in the first place, linked him with Crèvecœur. Both were thinking, peaceful men caught in a situation beyond their control. There is a similarity between Brackenridge's midnight fears, lying awake with his head on a saddle, and Crèvecœur's Letter XII, presenting the harrowed imagination of the frightened farmer. Secondly, the Rebellion confirmed fears of demagoguery that had worried Brackenridge for some time. Those fears allied him with easterners such as Webster and Morse who were otherwise his political opponents. Brackenridge was driven to qualify the Edenic image of the West projected in 'The Cave of Vanhest' and seen as a potentiality in his 1792 articles.

Such qualifications are clearly expressed in Brackenridge's longest fiction, the work for which he is best remembered, *Modern Chivalry*. Published serially between 1792 and 1815 and amounting to more than 800 pages, it has for many years been regarded as a sprawling, at times incoherent, picaresque novel. In recent years, however, a number of critics have shown that it has a tightly controlled satirical form and a sophisticated, experimental narrative stance. *Modern Chivalry* draws upon Old World models and yet reveals an awareness of the implications of writing in the cultural vacuum of a new republic and a newly settled territory. Unlike the entirely derivative *Father Bombo*, it can be regarded as the first truly American novel, anticipating the more sustained achievement of Charles Brockden Brown and initiating the cavalcade of American fiction that will include such masterpieces as *Huckleberry Finn* and *Catch-22*.[37]

Modern Chivalry portrays the adventures of one Captain Farrago, a man not unlike the hermit of Vanhest. Farrago is a model of the rural gentry, gifted yet naturally modest. With his combination of intellectual vigour, classical learning and rhetorical power he is intended to be a natural leader. Yet he puts public service before personal advancement, and his religious devotion before both. The novel opens as Farrago sets out on a trip along the frontier:

> the idea had come in to his head, to saddle an old horse that he had, and ride about the world a little, with his man Teague at his heels, to see how things were going on here and there, and to observe human nature.

The similarity with *Don Quixote* is immediately apparent, and has been discussed by a number of critics. Yet Farrago is different from Quixote in one vital respect. He has been instructed rather than deluded by his reading, as the next sentence indicates:

> it is a mistake to suppose, that a man cannot learn man by reading him in a corner, as well as on the widest space of transaction.

This sentence is important for another reason. It reveals that Brackenridge, like all satirists, sees a fundamental uniformity in human nature. At times, he shows that he is quite aware of the theories of cultural relativity made popular by Montesquieu. He is also, when necessary, willing to use the spatial imagery of *Common Sense* to attack the British. Farrago rebukes a haughty English ostler and adds a scatological dimension that is Brackenridge's own. The entire British isles, he remarks, 'would be little more than a urinal to one of our Patagonians in South America'. But here, at the very beginning of the novel, Brackenridge reverses Paine's spatial opposition to suggest that all the differences endowed by culture and environment are merely superficial.[38]

Unfortunately Farrago, although a knowledgeable man, is not without his own delusions. Like the novel in which he is a character, he has a didactic intention. He moves therefore out of his corner, out of his cave, and into the wide spaces of the Republic to communicate what he has learnt. He discovers that the Republic already regards itself as adequately instructed. It is confirmed as the region of stupidity. It is, moreover, money rather than learning that leads to status. As a result, rogues are to be found everywhere. They seem to concentrate in Philadelphia, supposedly the centre of republican wisdom, but seen as a circus for placemen: 'fat swabs, that guzzle wine, and smoke segars' (p. 105). A comparison is drawn between the flimsy paper credit and the flimsy pretensions of the office-seekers who seem to be as worthless as the stuff of which their fortunes are made. The criticism is, however, extended to the rituals of élite groups. Farrago mocks presidential levees, and pokes fun at the induction ceremonies of the American Philosophical Society. He has a clear eye for humbug, whether it comes from those at the top, or those trying to get there. And, underpinning Farrago's attacks on the pretensions of American society is the novelist's awareness that all societies may come to naught. During his travels Farrago visits a cave quite unlike the one occupied by the hermit of Vanhest. It contains the petrified remains of a race of giants (pp. 276–277). Even a civilisation of Patagonian proportions may perish.[39]

Farrago is dogged by his servant, Teague O'Regan, justifiably called the first in a long line of American confidence tricksters. The figure of Teague represents the culmination of genteel fears about bribery and vote-seeking that had been growing in the years around the Revolution. Such fears had emerged already in plays like Robert Munford's 1770 *The Candidates*, in which a politician worries about the fate of his constituency 'when coxcombs and jockies can impose themselves upon it for men of learning'.[40] But now, in what is apparently an unchecked democracy, the confidence trickster is the perfect operator, for he is able to shape the world to accord with the wishes of the electorate. Farrago, the man of learning, is isolated and outpointed at every turn by O'Regan. Endowed with grandiose social ambition and the protean ability to achieve it, Teague presents himself as a clergyman, Greek scholar, philosopher, senator, and Indian treaty-maker. He is enormously successful with businessmen, voters and women alike. Everyone, it seems, wants to know 'Major' O'Regan – for Teague promotes himself above his master although, as Farrago remarks, 'he is about as much a Major as my horse' (p. 229).

Intertwined with Brackenridge's attack on demagoguery and deception is one against brutality and bestiality. The fears of Caliban submerged in Nardy, the servant in 'The Cave of Vanhest', and surfacing briefly in the 1792 reference to frontiersmen as 'badgers', reappear at loose in *Modern Chivalry*, unchecked. In part, such fears are expressed in the erosion of the line between sanity and madness. Visiting a bedlam, Farrago wonders if there is any difference between the inmates and those outside (p. 387). His meditation develops the questioning stance taken by Freneau in 'Light, Summer Reading' and moves toward the complex psychological theories of Charles Brockden Brown. More centrally for my purposes, the fears of the Caliban in man are expressed in another, related erosion, this time of the line between humanity and bestiality. Shortly after Farrago emerges from the cave containing the petrified Indians, he sees some Indian engravings and recalls that it is 'abstract pleasures, which feed the imagination' that distinguish man from the beast. American society, it is now clear, places little stock in the pleasures of the imagination (pp. 280–281). There is, therefore, no way of distinguishing man from the supposedly lower animals. The dread of an instable, savage landscape already seen in the work of Morse, Webster, Rush, Crèvecœur and Freneau emerges with greater clarity in *Modern Chivalry*. The opposition between light and dark images in the 'Preface' to the *United States Magazine* has now disappeared.[41]

This is particularly apparent in an episode that is at once the most comic and the most portentous in the book, and which brings to bear Brackenridge's experience in the Whiskey Rebellion. Teague is appointed an excise officer, but when he tries to collect the taxes he is tarred and feathered by a mob. He is thus robbed not only of all his false identities, but also of his human identities. The tar and feathers give him 'the appearance of a wild fowl of the forest' (p. 305). The comic fate of Teague extends over two chapters, and is the richer because it is divided by a discussion of Paine's *Rights of Man*. The servant is left to wander and has to climb a beech tree to escape the attention of wolves who might mistake him for prey; only to attract the attention of a pair of hunters, who debate his species:

> At first they took him for a bear; but seeing the feathers, it was decided that he must be of the fowl kind. Nevertheless his face and form, which appeared to be human, made him a monster in creation, or at least a new species of animal, never before known in these woods. (p. 317)

He is caged and taken to Philadelphia where he is brought to trial to determine 'whether this creature is of the brutal or the human kind' (p. 323). In Philadelphia he also receives a visit from members of the American Philosophical Society, who go through the same enquiry as the hunters, but in a learned language that reflects the philosophic debate over the fauna of America:

> If this animal is to be referred to the quadruped, or beast kind, it would most naturally be classed with the Ouran Outang, or Wild Man of Africa: If with the bird kind, we shall be totally at a loss to assign the genus. For though it has a head and face not unlike the ouzel, or the grey owl, yet in the body it has no resemblance. Nevertheless we should certainly give it a place amongst fouls, were it not that it has ribs instead of the lamina . . . also, because we have reason to think it has an epiglottis, from the articulation of its sounds, by which it has come to imitate our speech, with a pronunciation not unlike that kind of brogue, which we remark in some of the west country Irish.
>
> (pp. 319–320)

It seems that the British were right; that man in America has regressed to the orang-utan. The members of the American Philosophical Society are also right, for the creature does speak Irish. O'Regan, as his name suggests, is an Irish rogue: ill-dressed, when he is dressed; often called a bog-trotter, when his identity is certain; redheaded and sporting an Irish accent. Brackenridge had earlier written some sections of *Father Bombo* in Irish vernacular, and had also experimented with poetry in Scots. Now his skill with vernacular was being used in the service of a widespread prejudice against the Irish. Teague is just one of a number of ill-favoured, thick-tongued, seditious Hibernian Jacobins to be found in the literature of the period.[42]

Brackenridge's racist attitudes were similar to Benjamin Rush's. Like Rush, he distinguished the different races in America according to their apparent appetite for the graces of civilisation. His most racist remarks are therefore reserved for the Indians. Although he had some interest in Indian art and respected Indian stoicism in the face of white oppression, he had none of the sentimental primitivism which marked Crèvecœur's Letter XII and which was espoused by John Bartram's son William and such foreign writers as Chateaubriand. As a boy Brackenridge had witnessed the terrors of Indian warfare, and in 1783 he published a captivity narrative as a vehicle for an argument for property rights based on use. Indians had no entitlement to land because they merely hunted over it. They were, moreover, beasts. In the well-known opening sentence of his 'observations' Brackenridge referred to them as 'the animals, vulgarly called Indians'.[43]

In *Modern Chivalry*, Brackenridge used the Indians to make more explicit the connection he saw between demagoguery and bestiality.

Compared with his other impersonations, Teague has an easy task when he is an Indian Treaty-maker:

> Indian speeches are nearly all alike. You have only to talk of burying hatchets under large trees, kindling fires, brightening chains; with a demand, at the latter end, of blankets for the backside, and rum to get drunk with.
>
> (p.57)

If you make a treaty with an Indian, why not with a bear or wolf? Similarly, if you open the franchise to ordinary people, why not to leopards and bears?

> If pards and bears are to be admitted to appear, or officiate in any department or representative capacity, it ought to be at the bar, where noise may be better tolerated, and growling may pass for ability.   (pp. 658–659)

Brackenridge suggests that a continuum exists between the wilder human antics and those of the beasts. Whites and Indians can be difficult when drunk. Therefore one had better avoid trading whisky with an animal, because 'a drunk wolf, or bear, would be a dangerous animal' (p. 62).

In a disordered world, then, the separate spheres of the mad and the sane, of whites, Indians and beasts collapse into each other. Captain Farrago suggests early in the text that the only way to maintain a supposedly proper distance is through force. To illustrate his argument he draws on the two realms that Brackenridge had used in his 'Preface' to the *United States Magazine*: the Newtonian physics which Freneau would use to illustrate Design and Rush to explain environmentalism; and the animal world, where 'the weaker is always subject to the strong' (p. 134). The problem with democracy, in Brackenridge's view, is that it partakes of the animal realm, not that of Newtonian physics. Democracy turned the world upside down, and it would have to be righted by force.

Many adventures later Captain Farrago, now governor of the state, ponders the nature of government. He decides that it consists of three expressions of force different only in detail from the three Muses beloved by the hermit of Vanhest. They are religion, language and law. Farrago suggests that 'the *priest* is an adjunct of fear, because he holds out the horror of what is to come, or is invisible' (p. 558, Brackenridge's emphasis). Language, too, is seen as a means of control. Like Noah Webster, Brackenridge had come to the conclusion that 'a reversion of the order of things' involves an affront to language (p. 14). 'You are mistaken if you think your Irish will pass for Hebrew', Farrago tells Teague early in their travels (p. 39). But it does, for in a democracy it seems that little education is necessary. Confusions of station are synonymous with linguistic confusions. What is needed is rigour. As Farrago remarks:

> a bear is a real bear, a sheep is a sheep; and there is no commixture of name, where there is a difference of nature. (p. 75)

It is appropriate, therefore, that Brackenridge should introduce *Modern Chivalry* with an oblique reference to Webster:

> It has been a question for some time past, what would be the best means to fix the English language. Some have thought of Dictionaries, others of Institutes, for that purpose. (p. 3)

Brackenridge ironically claims that he intends his work to be an exemplar of style, 'not in the least regarding the matter of the work' (p. 3). This 'book without thought', he hopes, will become 'a kind of classic of the English language' (p. 77). The idea of an empty classic, like the form of the picaresque, is of course immediately derived from that other comic epic, *Tom Jones*. 'The excellence of the mental entertainment consists less in the subject, than in the author's skill in well dressing it up', the narrator asserted in the very first chapter of Fielding's novel. The difference between *Tom Jones* and *Modern Chivalry* lies in the extent of the joke, of the comic gap between assertion and demonstration. The narrator's opening comment in Fielding's text is at odds with the tightly, symmetrically structured plot, and with the marital resolution which became such a feature of the English novel. In contrast, there is a real fear of vacuity in *Modern Chivalry*. Perhaps the disorder is simply a mask for no order at all. This fear is, I think, consonant with the inconclusive nature of the novel. Although it is true that when Brackenridge died in 1816 he had in mind further adventures for Farrago and O'Regan, the structure of the whole text is reiterative rather than purposive. The line from *Modern Chivalry* to *Huckleberry Finn* and *Catch-22* is, I think, a clear one.[44]

Finally, the most effective method of control is the law. It is the lawyer who embodies the functions of both the priest and the lexicographer, enforcing morality in the visible world and employing linguistic rigour in doing so. Brackenridge spent much of his later life in the law, and in 1799 he was appointed a justice of the Pennsylvania Supreme Court. Towards the end of his life he published *Law Miscellanies*, in which (amongst other things) he tried to distinguish Pennsylvania law from its English parent. He regarded the book as evidence of his separation from 'the brutal world' and as a contribution to the American cause during the second Anglo-American War. To Brackenridge the law was truly American and truly applicable to the frontier. He used it to order his environment in the way that Freneau, a few years later, would use the perspective glass to order the terrain around their beloved Princeton.[45]

In their attitudes to the law Judge Brackenridge and Governor Farrago are united. It is appropriate, therefore, that Farrago, towards the end of *Modern Chivalry*, should use the supreme source of American law against another Teague, an 'orator' who suggests that:

> Having cleared the ground of the British, along wid you, we are entitled to the raising of a cabin on the spot; you may call it a constitution, or what you please. But all we want is a bit of ground to set potatoes and plant cabbage, with the free use of the shilelah into the bargain, as we had it in our country.

To which the Governor replies:

> That being the case . . . the constitution that you have, will answer every purpose. It is for securing you in your possessions; and the free use of the shilelah subordinate to no law but that of the country, that the constitution has been framed. But for the constitution and the laws, what would you differ from the racoons and opossums of the woods? It is this which makes all the *difference that we find between man and beast.*   (p. 755)

Brackenridge saw the Constitution as a means of framing nature, of creating order in an environment which all too easily dissolved into disorder. It is a document like the Constitution, or *Modern Chivalry* for that matter, which distinguishes a man from an orang-utan, and which turns a region of stupidity into a republic. Yet, as we have seen, Brackenridge could never escape the uneasy feeling that the orang-utans were waiting at the edge of the woods to deny the difference, to tear the document to shreds. A document seems a poor defence against a beast on a dark night.

In this and the two preceding chapters I have tried to show that the Revolutionary intellectuals asserted a landscape constructed out of materials adapted from the Old World they all despised. When those materials proved to be inadequate to describe the New World they retreated. The retreat took them between the confining walls of a library or behind a 'perspective glass'. In three instances – Webster, Crèvecœur and Freneau – it took them for a period physically out of the country. In all cases, the retreat threw them intellectually further into the embrace of the Old World, with a consequent increment of unhappiness, for in retreating they adopted the pejorative images of the New World which they associated with their enemies.

Brackenridge's work was also constructed out of Old World materials. After all, the references to orang-utans derive from a European philosophic debate and not from the American environment. However, Brackenridge did his best to understand his frontier home. In consequence, although he retreated from his environment, principally by means of legal documents, the retreat is not so marked. His writings show more clearly images that appear fleetingly in the work of the others; images of a threatening, frequently mutable landscape stalked by beasts and beastlike men. These images and the underlying fear of vacuity will emerge with greater clarity in the fiction of Charles Brockden Brown and will be established by Edgar Allan Poe as a central theme of American culture. The nature of the achievement of Brown and Poe will, however, only be fully apparent after a further examination of the implications of republican terrain. In the next chapter, therefore, I will outline the various attitudes to the extent of the Republic, and its expansion under the guiding hand of Thomas Jefferson. In chapter 5 I will discuss the amplitude of Jefferson's thinking, and in chapter 6 examine its application in the form of the Lewis and Clark Expedition.

4

The natural limit of a republic

In this chapter I want to survey the tensions that arose over the expansion of the Republic. If the nation's intellectuals were retreating eastwards, the nation itself was advancing westwards. I suggested in chapter 1 that the imperial ideology became popular during and after the French and Indian War. Following the conclusion of the Revolutionary War the ideology moved from the realm of dreams into that of possibility. In consequence it was questioned in two ways. First, it conflicted with an equally received but quite contradictory republican theory. After a brief further survey of the roots of the imperial ideology I will discuss this conflict in the context of the debate over the admission of new states to the Union. The second conflict relates to the first, but is less theoretical. Frontier facts did not lend themselves to an optimistic view of imperialism. I will examine the work of Timothy Dwight to illustrate the demise of the imperial ideology in a shocked awareness of frontier savagism. The worries troubling Dwight in Vermont became more widespread with the question of expansion beyond the Mississippi. In the final part of this chapter I will look at the debate over the Louisiana Purchase.

AN UNCOMPOUNDED REPUBLICK

Until the French and Indian War, the question of western migration had not been prominent in British attitudes to America. Whenever it was raised, the discussion tended to be in terms of restriction. The political economist Sir William Petty, for instance, remarked that a dispersed populace was less defensible and more costly to govern than one compressed into a small area. Indeed, he advocated the settlement of Ireland rather than America. His suggestion came to nothing. Not only did the Government fail to encourage migration across the Irish Sea; it also failed to persuade the Irish to stay at home, with results that we have seen comically portrayed in the last chapter.

Petty's ideas seemed all the more valid in 1763 when the Treaty of Paris gave Britain control of all North America east of the Mississippi. To the more thoughtful observers this great acquisition was no prize. Even before the Treaty was signed Oliver Goldsmith noted that:

> It is in the politic as in the human constitution; if the limbs grow too large for the body, their size, instead of improving, will diminish the vigour of the whole.

When Goldsmith died in 1774 he still believed (and now with even more cause) that an extensive dominion was a mistake. He was not alone. Some commentators even suggested that France had ceded Canada to Britain deliberately to destroy her. The new territory should be managed with care.[1]

The British Government took the business of management seriously. In 1763 it decided to limit western expansion. In his draft of 5 May to Petty's great-grandson Lord Shelburne (at that time President of the Board of Trade), Lord Egremont showed that he had done some political arithmetic:

> It might ... be necessary to fix upon some Line for a Western Boundary to our ancient provinces, beyond which our People should not at present be permitted to settle, hence as their Numbers increased, they would emigrate to Nova Scotia, or to the Provinces on the Southern Frontier, where they would be usefull to their Mother Country, instead of planting themselves in the Heart of America, out of reach of Government.

It was much easier for the British to trade with a colonial people massed along the eastern seaboard, and much easier to provide there the supports and controls of government. In the heart of America they might soon begin making their own goods, and might more easily become disaffected.

The proposal, shorn of its reasoning, was included in the Royal Proclamation of 7 October, and remained official British policy. However, despite colonial discontent, British fears by and large were unfounded. At the time of the Revolution, the line of white settlement had advanced barely more than 300 miles from the Atlantic coast. With the exception of certain parts of Virginia and Pennsylvania, the frontier was marked by the Appalachian Mountains. In 1783, of almost two and a half million citizens of the new United States, only some 56,000 lived west of the Mountains. As one historian of the American frontier has remarked, at the end of the Revolution the typical westerner was red rather than white.[2]

But not for long, if the Revolutionary generation had its way. The image of America's 'Rising Glory' discussed in earlier chapters was not mere rhetoric, although predicated on a sense of wonder and projected across a vast territory. Two examples will suffice to show how pervasive and persuasive was the belief in the expansive republican Garden. The first is from an early work of Noah Webster. He spoke for many when, in his 1785 *Sketches of American Policy*, he worked out in some detail the benefits of westward movement. Looking with distaste at the unhealthy 'flat lands' of the Southern states with their slave systems, he looked forward to migration to the mountains of 'the back parts'. Men would naturally be drawn there, he thought, by the salubrity of the air, and under its benign influence they would become hardy and independent.

Webster then theorised on the dispersion of population, and reversed British opinions. A limited and populous territory, he believed, led to overspecialisation of employment. Americans, in constrast, were forced to become jacks-of-all-trades:

> In countries thinly inhabited, or where people live principally by agriculture, as in America, every man is in some measure an artist – he makes a variety of utensils . . . he is a husbandman in summer and a mechanic in winter – he travels about the country – he converses with a variety of professions – he reads public papers – he has access to a parish library and thus becomes acquainted with history and politics, and every man in New England is a theologian. This will always be the case in America, so long as their [*sic*] is a vast tract of fertile land to be cultivated, which will occasion emigrations from the states already settled. Knowledge is diffused and genius roused by the very situation of America.

This charming rural view of America, grounded in imperial rhetoric but substantiated by a detailed environmental theory, reflects Webster's Connecticut background. The view of the husbandman as literate mechanic contracts from a general to a New England image with the reference to the parish library, and is clinched by the joking afterthought about theology. The next sentence broadens the argument and the spatial reference once again, thereby turning all America into a large New England. As we shall see shortly, problems would develop about the assumptions underlying the process of this argument; but there can be no doubting how widely it was believed, or how persuasive was its detail.[3]

Cheerfully interlocking with the imperial ideology was an agrarian aesthetic, as may be seen in the following extract from a diary:

> Tues. 3rd . . . The Ohio River of all that I ever saw is the most beautiful stream. It flows in a deep and gentle current, is from 1/2 to 3/4 of a mile in width; it is confined in high banks, which it seldom if ever overflows. The adjoining hills are lofty, from whence a charming view of the river and low lands presents itself to view. How delightful will be the scene, when these banks shall be covered with towns, these hills with houses, and this noble stream with the rich

produce of these fertile and fruitful countries. We rode down the river 3 or 4 miles to the south of Bull Skin creek, then left the river and pursued a northwardly route thro a rich and beautiful country. The land, after leaving the river, lies high and is very level. The trees, which are mostly red and white oak, are the tallest and most beautiful timber I ever beheld. The soil appears deep, clear of stone and wild pea-vine in abundance. It was very pleasant to see the deer skipping over the bushes and the face of the country clad in a livery of green.[4]

This is taken from the journal kept by the Reverend James Smith during a tour of the 'Northwest Territory' in the autumn of 1797. Although it was written twelve eventful years after Webster's *Sketches* by a Virginian, slave-owning, Methodist minister, it further fills out the imperial ideology sketched by the Connecticut Yankee.

The aesthetic comes, of course, directly from the Old World. It is well known that in the eighteenth century England was the centre of landscape gardening and the focus of attention for foreign naturalists and botanical illustrators. Writers such as Addison and Pope, critics like Lord Kames and Horace Walpole, and painters such as Reynolds and Hogarth had led a revolt against the symmetrical tyrannies of French style. The result was a union of nature and culture best summed up by Walpole's admiring sentence about William Kent: 'He leaped the fence, and saw that all nature was a garden.'[5] In America, it seemed, the garden aesthetic could be applied with ease. The language of the extract from the Reverend Smith's journal oscillates between a journalist's factuality and a future vision of an agrarian and commercial republic. What could be a description of an English garden easily falls into place on the Northwest Frontier. The pastoral vision is therefore at one with a clear-eyed assessment of the area's suitability for settlement. The river does not flood here; the land is stone-free and fertile. The agrarian aesthetic does not merely glaze the land with 'a livery of green'. It is borne out in hard fact.

Although Northerner and Southerner joined in an optimistic belief in a United States widespread across the continent, their optimism was undermined by the received political wisdom of the time. Americans could perhaps dismiss Sir William Petty as a British tyrant. They could not so easily dismiss Montesquieu. The French sage had, after all, frequently been invoked against Tory repression. Unfortunately, Montesquieu was quite clear about the extent of a republic. In *The Spirit of Laws* he had asserted that 'it is natural to a republic to have only a small territory; otherwise it cannot long subsist'. It lacked the administrative apparatus to govern a large territory. Because a republic did not possess the unifying symbol of a monarch, it was suited only to small geographical units with essentially homogeneous populations.

Montesquieu's republican theory, therefore, coalesced with his speculations about the climatic determinants of character.[6]

Montesquieu's influence was apparent in the debates over the admission of new states to the Union. In the years immediately following the Revolution a number of people feared that the interests of the East and the West were inimical. Echoing Lord Egremont, they wished to curb western migration. Rufus King, the representative to the Continental Congress for Massachusetts, summed up such feelings when he remarked that:

> every Citizen of the Atlantic States, who emigrates to the westward of the Allegany is a total loss to our confederacy. Nature has severed the two countries by a vast and extensive chain of mountains, interest and convenience will keep them separate, and the feeble policy of our disjointed Government will not be able to unite them.[7]

When the 1787 Constitutional Convention met to reunite the Government, such questions naturally had their place. Gouverneur Morris, the wealthy New Yorker, believed with Montesquieu that republicanism was suitable only for certain kinds of people, and worried that the westerners were not among them:

> The Busy haunts of men not the remote wilderness, was the proper school of political Talents. If the Western people get the power into their hands they will ruin the Atlantic interests. The Back members are always most averse to the best measures.

Although he looked forward to the formation of new states, he worried that they would be too influential.

The more liberal Virginian George Mason spoke on behalf of equal rights for the new states although he, too, was uneasy about the drift westward:

> If it were possible by just means to prevent emigrations to the Western Country, it might be a good policy. But go the people will as they find it for their interest, and the best policy is to treat them with that equality which will make them friends not enemies.

The 'extent and fertility' of the soil was such that the westerners would in time 'be both more numerous and more wealthy than their Atlantic brethren', Mason added, with perhaps a nod at Morris.[8]

The debate continued in the press while the Constitution was before the states for ratification. Tench Coxe, the Philadelphian politician and economist, expressed a view starkly at odds with Rufus King's. 'The various parts of the North American continent', he said, 'are formed by nature for the most intimate union.' He saw a network of rivers and canals creating a symbiotic relation between the states, the needs of one being supplied by the produce of another. It was James Madison, however, who addressed himself directly to Montesquieu in one of *The Federalist* essays. The Princeton classmate of Brackenridge and Freneau noted that Montesquieu was a Frenchman living in a monarchy, and had consequently confused two non-monarchical organisations that were, in fact, quite different in character. Montesquieu was really writing about democracies. The United States was a republic. Once again, the appeal was to nature:

> in a democracy the people meet and exercise the government in person; in a republic, they assemble and administer it by their representatives and agents. A democracy, consequently, will be confined to a small spot. A republic may be extended over a large region. . . As the natural limit of a democracy is that distance from the central point which will just permit the most remote citizens to assemble as often as their public functions demand, and will include no greater number than can join in those functions; so the natural limit of a republic is that distance from the centre which will barely allow the representatives to meet as often as may be necessary for the administration of public affairs.[9]

Madison's optimistic correction of Montesquieu was immediately answered by his opponent James Winthrop. With blistering scorn Winthrop showed that Madison was quibbling over a question of definition. It was the spirit of Montesquieu's laws rather than their letter that was important:

> Large and consolidated empires may indeed dazzle the eyes of a distant speculator with their splendour, but if examined more nearly are always found to be full of misery. The reason is obvious. In large states the same principles of legislation will not apply to all the parts. The inhabitants of warmer climates are more dissolute in their manners, and less industrious, than in colder countries. A degree of severity is, therefore, necessary with one which would cramp the spirit of the other. . . The idea of an uncompounded republick, on an average one thousand miles in length, and eight hundred in breadth, and containing six millions of white inhabitants all reduced to the same standard of morals, of habits, and of laws, is in itself an absurdity, and contrary to the whole experience of mankind.

It was impossible to unify the laws of Massachusetts and Georgia. Madison had been blinded by the imperial ideology and, perhaps, by a greed for gold.[10]

Benjamin Rush wrote a number of articles warmly supporting the Constitution, but even he was uneasy about the size of the United States. In that 'Address' looking forward to a cultural revolution he remarked that 'there is but one path that can lead the united states to destruction, and that is their extent of territory'. He then repeated fears voiced by the British at the end of the French and Indian War: 'It was probably to effect this that Great Britain ceded us so much waste land.' He concluded that only one new state should be settled at a time. Within three years he had buried – or disguised – his fears. In a lengthy piece intended for European immigrants he asserted, with an aquatic metaphor quite different from those used by Crèvecœur and Freneau, that 'the free and extensive territories of the United States' would create 'an ocean of additional happiness' for people who migrated there.

Privately, Rush continued to be apprehensive about frontier settlement. The Indians, he thought, provided an instructive example. He refuted a theory that western earthworks were evidence of a defunct civilisation. He thought instead 'that they are the works of the ancestors of our Indians'. They showed therefore that the Indians had degenerated. He then speculated on the effect of the environment:

> The extent of our country, and the facility of substance by fishing and hunting and the spontaneous fruits of the earth, would naturally accelerate the progress of the descendants of the first settlers of our country to the savage state.

Ever since Joseph Hall, pessimists had worried that a people of plenty might degenerate. The Puritans had seen Indians as beasts and devils, and had feared that whites might adopt their ways. Here, Rush unites the pessimistic and Puritan views to suggest a fate for mankind in its way as foreboding as Brackenridge's image of the petrified Patagonians. Perhaps the Old World intellectuals were right; perhaps, in frontier conditions, whites could descend the Chain of Being. Rush's Frontier Theory would thus wither at its first stage.

Nor was he alone in these apprehensions. Benjamin Smith Barton, for instance, prefaced an enquiry into the origins of the Indians by suggesting that his researches taught:

> a mortifying truth, that nations may relapse into rudeness again; all their proud monuments crumbled into dust, and themselves, now savages, subjects of contemplation among civilized nations and philosophers.[11]

Immigrants, clearly, would have to guard carefully against the seductions of the western soil if they wanted to achieve the wealth envisaged by George Mason rather than the dissolution deplored by James Winthrop.

The size, present or potential, of the United States, and the character of its inhabitants, dramatised therefore the fears of men of differing political persuasions. What was the natural limit of a republic? Was there any way of checking the credentials of migrants? How could clashing interests be reconciled? An anonymous French Government memoir summed up the problems by setting them within an environmental context:

> Nature has traced the future revolutions of North America. All the territory of the United States from the sea to the Mississippi is cut from North to South by long ranges of mountains which enclose the sources of an infinity of rivers,

some of which flow toward the Mississippi, and others toward the sea. The eastern part is populated, the western hardly at all. The climates of the two areas present as many differences as those to be found in the interests of the inhabitants. Some will direct all their activities toward New Orleans, which will be their only outlet; others toward the established towns on the Atlantic coast.

Rivalry was therefore inevitable.[12] Basing his reasoning on Montesquieu, the memorialist had done some hard, and largely accurate, thinking. It appeared that a slight touch would make the United States fly apart, so varied were its component parts.

Such questions continued to concern the Republic's intellectuals because they were not merely theoretical. In chapter 1 I described some of the problems confronting the new nation. A few were created by outsiders such as Citizen Genêt. The French memoir quoted above was addressed to Genêt shortly before he took up his post as Minister to the United States. As we have seen, he heeded its advice and caused much alarm. Most of the problems, however, arose from internal threats. There is no need for me to detail here the factional strife that split the United States in the early years of its existence. Washington's second term as President was in part solicited because it was felt that, like a monarch, he might be able to keep the Union alive. Yet a cursory glance at post-Revolutionary history shows that even the most illustrious figurehead could not have dispelled the pains that afflicted the growing nation.

There are, however, two particular problems that are relevant to my theme. The first concerns what Brackenridge might have called 'backwoods orators'. The closed circle of republican intellectuals was disrupted by a number of duplicitous demagogues, many of them former Revolutionary heroes. Ethan Allen, for instance, had in 1775 captured Fort Ticonderoga with that arch-traitor in American history, Benedict Arnold. Within a few years he seemed to be following Arnold's example. In the 1780s he claimed that Vermont was an independent state, separate both from the United States and from Britain. When Congress in 1782 refused to recognise Vermont, Allen opened negotiations with the British to return his home to its original owners.

Another character cast in the Allen mould was Matthew Lyon, known to his enemies as 'Hibernian Mat, the Beast of Vermont'. It would be wrong, however, to think that Vermont held a monopoly in demagoguery. George Rogers Clark hailed from Virginia. He became famous for his exploits against the British in the Old Northwest, but his reputation was later besmirched by his eagerness to serve the French. Genêt appointed him a General in l'Armée du Mississippi, charged with the capture of Louisiana from the Spanish. The scheme failed when Genêt was recalled. Men like Allen, Lyon and Clark appeared as paragons of virtue alongside General James Wilkinson. Sometimes known as Bombastes Furioso, Wilkinson's army career was punctuated by rows and by charges of peculation. As Governor of Louisiana Territory in 1805–1806 he implicated Aaron Burr in a scheme to separate the western lands from the United States. He eventually decided that more was to be gained from betraying Burr to President Jefferson.[13]

A second problem confronting the Republic was related to the first. From the intellectuals' point of view, the backwoods orators always seemed able to rouse a dissolute, violent mob to prosecute their nefarious designs. We have seen Hugh Henry Brackenridge's vivid portrayal of such a mob. The Revolution had already provided abundant evidence that the fears hinted at in Crèvecœur's Letter III and coming to fruition in Letter XII were quite justified. In the right circumstances, whites could be just as savage as the Indians in their modes of warfare. The frontier seemed to provide a permanent setting for such behaviour, to the extent that the clichéd collocation 'frontier violence' has frequently been identified as a central theme in American culture.[14]

Rent by faction and sedition, divided by topography and animosity, the United States seemed to many to be a fragile, even artificial, construction. The theories of Montesquieu seemed so apposite that they mocked the very name of the United States. Little wonder that concerned men like Samuel Mitchill and Jedidiah Morse sought an alternative name. The imperial ideology seemed badly flawed; and although the debate was conducted in places like Paris and Philadelphia, it was not simply a theory. Safe at their desks, American intellectuals tried to minimise the divisions threatening the Republic. When they travelled to the frontier, they were confronted with evidence suggesting that their compatriots had relapsed into rudeness, and that Montesquieu was right after all. The conflict between the imperial ideology and frontier reality troubled them greatly.[15] The conflict, and the consequent unease, is revealed by the work of Timothy Dwight.

THE FLOURISHING VILLAGE

Timothy Dwight, born in 1752, was successively a student, tutor and President of Yale, retaining the last appointment until his death in 1817. He was also a prominent Calvinist pastor, an acquaintance of Noah Webster and Jedidiah Morse, and became an opponent of Thomas Jefferson. Yet he joined Jefferson in his initial enthusiasm for the future of America. His 'Valedictory Address' of July 1776 asserted that the great fact of the United States was its diversity, contained within a unified country. His poetry, however, soon revealed a monolithic model of society. A long poem published in 1794, *Greenfield Hill*, contains Dwight's image of his ideal America in its second part, suitably entitled 'The Flourishing Village'. It begins:

> Fair Verna! loveliest village of the west;
> Of every joy, and every charm, possess'd;
> How pleas'd amid thy varied walks I rove,
> Sweet, cheerful walks of innocence, and love,
> 5   And o'er thy smiling prospects cast my eyes,
> And see the seats of peace, and pleasure, rise,
> And hear the voice of Industry resound,
> And mark the smile of Competence, around!
> Hail, happy village! O'er thy cheerful lawns,
> 10   With earliest beauty, spring delighted dawns;
> The northward sun begins his vernal smile;
> The spring-bird carols o'er the cressy rill:
> The shower, that patters in the ruffled stream,
> The ploughboy's voice, that chides the lingering team,
> 15   The bee, industrious, with his busy song,
> The woodman's axe, the distant groves among,
> The waggon, rattling down the rugged steep,
> The light wind, lulling every care to sleep.

The echo of Goldsmith's *The Deserted Village* is clearest in the first line, and continues through the rest of the stanza. Lines 10 to 12 emphasise that the season is earliest spring, and with this construction of the natural cycle Dwight is able easily to contain the less cheerful times of the year. The poem bursts with a life and joy that is built upon 'Industry', and rewarded by 'Competence'. Lines 14 to 18 show man and the terrain in happy collaboration. The ploughboy's voice, bee's song and the less melodic sounds of the axe and the wagon blend with the breeze into a seductive harmony.[16]

The adjective in the title indicates, however, that Dwight's poem will use Goldsmith's to assert difference rather than similarity. While the English poet diverges at the end of his first stanza into the despair that will inform the rest of his poem ('These were thy charms – but all these charms are fled'), the American continues with the hymn of praise. The political ideology that accounts for the difference is soon revealed, in lines typical of the freehold agrarianism of the time:

> No griping landlord here alarms the door,
> To halve, for rent, the poor man's little store.
> No haughty owner drives the humble swain
> To some far refuge from his dread domain;
> Nor wastes, upon his robe of useless pride,
> The wealth, which shivering thousands want beside;

Nor in one palace sinks a hundred cots;
Nor in one manor drowns a thousand lots;   (ll. 81–88, p. 399)

This is an Eden, recast by means of the geopolitics of Tom Paine into an expansive version of the Puritan typology of mission. The Eden, in the first place, contains a Black, singing and whistling as he works (ll. 193–196, pp. 402–403). Dwight at this point in the poem differs from Freneau in 'The Beauties of Santa Cruz', because the Black is a servant, not a slave; he 'takes his portion of the common good' (l. 212, p. 403).[17]

Suddenly the poem changes. The Black reminds Dwight of slavery, and at once the landscape is changed into 'one wide, frigid zone' (l. 216, p. 403). A generalised lament about slavery reaches a climax and, like Crèvecœur's Letter IX, becomes closely focussed with an account of a tortured slave. The landscape now becomes a terrifying instrument of God's displeasure:

Ask not, why earthquakes rock that fateful land;
Fires waste the city; ocean whelms the strand;
Why the fierce whirlwind, with electric sway,
Springs from the storm, and fastens on his prey,
Shakes heaven, rends earth, upheaves the cumbrous wave,
And with destruction's besom fills the grave:
Why dark disease roams swift her nightly round,
Knocks at each door, and wakes the gasping sound.
                                          (ll. 329–336, pp. 406–407)

Natural disaster is here presented in images of a mutable landscape, a ravening beast and a personified, stalking disease. In a manner similar to Benjamin Rush and Fisher Ames (and, before them, Burnet and Goldsmith), Dwight equates moral evil not merely with the physical distresses of the slave, but with a more general distress, environmentally determined. The disease and the whirlwind have become tangible.

But this is a diversion. There is an equally sudden change back to the image of a church bathed in sunlight (l. 345). Dwight resumes his approving inspection of the village, and draws towards a close with another expansion, this time into imperial imagery:

All hail, thou western world! by heaven design'd
Th' example bright, to renovate mankind.
Soon shall thy sons across the mainland roam;
And claim, on far Pacific shores, their home . . .
Where marshes teem'd with death, shall meads unfold;
Untrodden cliffs resign their stores of gold;
The dance refin'd on Albion's margin move,
And her lone bowers rehearse the tale of love.
Where slept perennial night, shall science rise,
And new-born Oxfords cheer the evening skies;

> Miltonic strains the Mexic hills prolong,
> And Louis murmur to Sicilian song.   (ll. 707–710, 729–736, p. 418)

The theme of renovation, made so popular by Paine, is here combined with a Berkeleian progress of Empire that is traced from England across America to the Pacific, its course replacing Indian tribes with white men and finally even waking China from her 'long torpor'. The poem ends in an image of a world-encircling Eden, with all nations joining in 'one great bond the house of Adam'.

That house, of course, is modelled on Dwight's flourishing village. *Greenfield Hill* is named from the promontory overlooking Greenfield, Dwight's Connecticut home from 1783 to 1795. Like Noah Webster in his 1785 *Sketches* Dwight perceives a potential America – and ultimately the whole world – as Connecticut writ large. His imagination has created a continental landscape full of villages where rustic simplicity combines with learning, where ploughboys' voices provide an enlivening descant to more sober Miltonic strains. The imperial scheme tames the rising Napoleon, irons out differences of climate and character, sanitises the terrain and even flattens mountains. As Dwight remarks in Part 7 of the sequence:

> In these contrasted climes, how chang'd the scene,
> Where happiness expands, in living green!
> Through the whole realm, behold convenient farms
> Fed by small herds, and gay with cultur'd charms.
> (Part 7, ll. 215–218, p. 513)

Dwight has here expanded the garden imagery of his Southern clerical counterpart, James Smith, so that it spreads abroad across the continent.

In 1795 Dwight became President of Yale and moved from Greenfield. In the next year he began to undertake horseback tours in the college vacations. The journals of his tours were published posthumously in 1821. The *Travels* reveals further elements of Dwight's acquaintance with eighteenth-century landscape aesthetics, in particular the writings of Edmund Burke and William Gilpin. We have already met Burke as a statesman. Earlier in his career, in the middle of the 1750s when earthquake-fever was at its height, Burke published *A Philosophical Enquiry into the Origin of Our Ideas of the Sublime and Beautiful*. Gilpin, an English vicar and schoolteacher, was famous for his *Essay on Prints*, first published in 1768, and particularly for his five volumes of 'Picturesque Tours', the first of which appeared in 1782.

Through Burke, Gilpin, and a number of other writers, Italian painters had a great impact on methods of environmental description. The work of Claude Lorrain and Salvator Rosa was particularly well known, largely by means of copies and engravings. Their names will recur in later chapters. Claude, together with his contemporary Gaspar Poussin, came to represent nature in its benign, noble moods. Claude's landscapes, suffused with gentle Italian sun, were easily transformed into the pastoralism of the Beautiful. Rosa, in his personal life as well as in his paintings, symbolised the Sublime, which was much more dramatic. William Gilpin summed up eighteenth-century attitudes to Rosa when he remarked that the painter's 'romantic ideas in landscape' were derived from 'the rocky and desolate scenes, in which he was accustomed to take refuge'. Although Rosa painted a variety of canvasses, including figures and history paintings (which he valued most highly), he became famous for landscapes made up of rough limestone cliffs and rocky débris, supporting shattered trees and rent by rushing streams. The prototype of the Rosa painting was supposedly that of a sole small figure silhouetted against a stormy sky, with jagged trees and crumbling ruins crowding in on him, and suitable *memento mori* to hand in the form of a repulsive wreckage including human and animal skulls. Once again Horace Walpole provided *le mot juste*, this time in a letter about his 1739 Alpine journey: 'Precipices, mountains, torrents, wolves, rumblings, Salvator Rosa'.

Claude and Rosa were constantly contrasted. One writer talked of 'the mild and beaming skies of Claude Lorrain; and the rude and tangled precipices of Salvator Rosa'. Occasionally, Poussin was brought in for the sake of variety; hence Thomson's 'Castle of Indolence':

> Whate'er Lorraine light-touched with softening hue,
> Or savage Rosa dashed, or learned Poussin drew.

Or, as a traveller to the English Lake District remarked, Claude was Windermere, Poussin was Ullswater – and Rosa was Keswick. Between them, Burke and Gilpin developed the contrast into a sophisticated and popular means of describing the terrain. Burke's *Enquiry* established that the two major terrestrial forms were associated with emotional states. Gilpin permitted people to apply Burkean emotions to their surroundings by means of books describing his tours, and by means of the term 'Picturesque', which came to be defined as 'variety' and therefore allowed Burkean terminology to be mixed, much as a painter mixes colours on his palette. Indeed, Gilpin encouraged his followers to manipulate the terrain. In part this was done through the use of a 'Claude-glass', a darkened mirror with convex edges which not only reversed the scene viewed but softened its contrasts and limits. In part it was achieved linguistically, descriptions of the scene rearranging its elements in the service of a felicitous composition.[18]

While Goldsmith provided the inspiration for *Greenfield Hill*, Burke and Gilpin were the sources of Dwight's *Travels*. His indebtedness to the two Englishmen, and behind them the Italian painters, is to be found throughout the text, but particularly in the following passages on the Connecticut Valley:

> The valley of the Amonoosuc is scooped with uncommon beauty, the surface bending with a graceful, inverted arch from the river to the summit of the mountains, by which it is bounded on the north. This range, called the Peaks, presents to the eye at Lancaster two conical summits; the handsomest, and most regular, which I have ever met with. The Little Moosehillock, which separates this valley from the great bason, is a magnificent ridge. Its whole length is in full view for twenty miles. Its summits are finely figured, and richly diversified. The bason is a vast ellipsis, comprising the townships of Durand and Jefferson, and several other extensive tracts; and is watered through its whole length by Israel's River. The mountains of Littleton protrude their bold and lofty promontories into its south-western border; and the White Mountains bound it upon the south-east with a grandeur indescribable.[19]

This passage deploys many of the techniques that Dwight had learnt from Gilpin. The scene is viewed from a sufficient distance to allow Dwight's long sentences to blend the vocabulary of the Beautiful ('graceful', 'regular') with that of the Sublime ('magnificent', 'grandeur'). In particular, Dwight makes extensive use of architectural terms, which convey a sense of command over the scene and indicate that the statement of inexpressibility is simply a hyperbole employed to bring the paragraph to a fitting climax and close. The happy choice of name for the river seems to place an appropriate benediction over the whole scene.

The terrain is not yet perfect, but within a couple of sentences Dwight's shaping prose, now drawing on Burkean psychology, easily becomes prophecy:

> In so vast an expansion the eye perceives a prevalence of forest, which it regrets; and instinctively demands a wider extent of smiling scenes, and a more general establishment of the cheerful haunts of man. This temporary defect, from a long acquaintance with objects of this nature, and a perfect knowledge, from experience, of the rapid progress of cultivation, I easily overlook; and am, of course, transported in imagination to that period, in which, at a little distance, the hills, and plains, and valleys around me will be stripped of the forests, which now majestically, and even gloomily, overshadow them; and be measured out into farms, enlivened with all the beauties of cultivation . . . The meadow will glow with verdure, and sparkle with the enamel of flowers. Flocks and herds will frolic over the pasture, and fields will wave with harvests of gold.
>
> (Vol. II, pp. 128–129)

As the Sublime is displaced by the Beautiful, the architectural imagery modulates into a painterly imagery which is alive with colour. Like James Smith on the Ohio River, Dwight has transformed the terrain into a landscape of bucolic pleasure. The transformation that he performs with words is, of course, in reality achieved through work. The use of the verb 'measure' is significant. In the first place it reflects the activity of the surveyor in mapping the terrain prior to its transformation. Secondly, it reflects the activity of Dwight himself, for in part the purpose of his travelling is statistical. It is aimed at correcting the errors of the Philosophes. In answer to Buffon, Dwight (like Jefferson in his *Notes on the State of Virginia*) prints a comparison of the weights of animals in the Old and New Worlds:

	Europe	Vermont	
The bear	153 lbs	456 lbs	
Wolf	69	92	
Porcupine	2	16	
Beaver	18	63	(Vol. I, p. 25)

The statistics are also part of the process of transforming the terrain, for in writing about it in such detail Dwight is preparing the way for the farmers that must follow. The *Travels*, then, is not a text written lightly, an idle Picturesque tour. It is a document of commitment, aimed at bringing into effect the imperial image at the close of 'The Flourishing Village'.[20]

So far so good. But in his travels Dwight encountered elements of the frontier which would not fit into his monolithic scheme of empire. In comparison with the order of Massachusetts, where the process of settlement proceeded in an orderly fashion because 'a regular state of society was introduced at a very early period' (Vol. II, p. 449), Vermont is anarchic. Dwight hopes that there will be a smoothing of the frontier, and he describes its process in a manner reminiscent of Benjamin Rush. Vermont, however, seems frozen in the first stage of settlement feared by Crèvecœur. The government has not matured but has spontaneously erupted, with the result that the state is run by Teaguish demagogues, 'the restless, bold, ambitious, cunning, talkative, and those who are skilled in land-jobbing' (Vol. II, p. 450). Ethan Allan appears as the paradigm of the demagogue. Allen, says Dwight, was interested only in his own advancement, willing to sell himself to the highest bidder like a piece of property. He was, furthermore, a deist like Tom Paine, notorious in his country for the pretentious *Reason the Only Oracle of Man* (Vol. II, pp. 387–389).

The infidelity, brutality and coarseness of Allen and his Green Mountain Boys are consonant with the terrain from which they take their name:

> the rude and desolate aspect of the mountains, the huge, misshapen rocks, the precipices, beyond description barren and dreary, awaken emotions verging towards melancholy, and mild and elevated conceptions. Curiosity grows

naturally out of astonishment, and inquiry of course succeeds wonder. Why, the mind instinctively asks, were these huge piles of ruin thus heaped together? What end could Creative Wisdom propose in forming such masses of solid rock, and accumulating such collections of bleak and barren mountains, unfit for habitation, and apparently useless to man?   (Vol. II, p. 411)

The structure of this passage resembles the one describing the Connecticut Valley. It moves from the natural scene, to the impressions created in the mind of the perceiver, to the moral conclusion. This time, however, it is hardly the Garden that is prophesied. Rather, the prose draws on the 'elevated conceptions' of the Burkean Sublime and, behind it, the fears of cataclysm heightened by Burnet's *Theory of the Earth*.

Indeed, Dwight goes one step further. While the earthquake in 'The Flourishing Village' had been a retribution so just and obvious that no question was necessary ('Ask not, why . . .'), here there are no answers. There seems to be no evidence of 'Design' in the Green Mountains. Everything is out of shape, ruined without the sense of departed order normally associated with ruins, as in Crèvecœur's Letter XII. The prose cannot codify the view; it is 'beyond description barren and dreary'. Even those Puritan adjectives of distaste fail to cope with the scene. The assertion of inexpressibility is here not used as the climax to an exercise in rhetoric, but rather turns into a series of worried questions. Deformity of terrain is such that it threatens the form of the description, the Old World structures of the text. The unanswered questions indicate that the Green Mountains have tested Burkean aesthetics to their breaking point, if not beyond. Burkean aesthetics, it is true, are highly instable. As Thomas Weiskel and Bryan Jay Wolf have shown, the Sublime can easily become sublimated. But here the Sublime is not instable. It is inadequate. What seemed to oppress Dwight in the Green Mountains was not sublimation, but breakdown. We have here, I believe, an example of the distinction between rhetorical and literal inexpressibility which I discussed in the Prologue. The distinction will occur again, particularly in chapter 6.[21]

The Green Mountains presented Dwight, then, with a vivid apprehension of the frontier. The fact that it was so close to Yale discomforted him. If such disorder could be present in New England's back yard what hope did the distant West have? He might be able to regard the West as a safety-valve to draw off the 'restless', but on the other hand it was much farther away from the parish libraries and the Miltonic strains. Montesquieu, it seemed, was right. The West was now only acceptable to Dwight if it did not become part of the United States. His fears increased when Jefferson was elected President in 1800, for Jefferson represented those levelling and deist principles that Dwight had seen in Ethan Allen. Dwight had already, in his 1798 Sermon *The Duty of Americans, at the Present Crisis*, followed Jedidiah Morse in attacking the

Illuminati and the French Revolution. Now, he joined Morse in publishing a conservative newspaper, *The Palladium*, which attacked the supposedly 'French' principles of Jefferson and his Republican Party. Dwight's last years were spent, like Webster and Morse, with a growing sense of identity with Britain. The Green Mountains and Ethan Allen caused him to abandon his imperial ideology.

A NEW WORLD OF WOODS

Others began to share Dwight's fears about the frontier when in 1803 they learned of the impending Louisiana Purchase. The Purchase presented Congress and country with the problem of the frontier in a particularly acute form. In the first place the territory was so much larger than the Green Mountains of Vermont, and so much further away from the controlling influence of the eastern metropolitan centres. Secondly, the territory provided a precise focus to the debate over expansion. The 1787 debate had speculated in general terms about the admission of new states to the Union. In contrast, if Congress approved the Louisiana Purchase, it would transform immediately and for ever the composition of the Union.

Thirdly, and ironically, the problem was exacerbated because so little was known about the trans-Mississippi West. It was therefore possible at will to project upon the territory imperial or fearful images. Legend or hearsay spiked the little information that had been gathered by the expeditions edging into the West. For instance, no one could agree on the height or extent of the Rocky Mountains. It was known only that they existed. Imlay's *Topographical Description* of 1793 referred to them as ridges of hills separating the Pacific from the Mississippi. They were not 'so high or so rugged' as the Alleghany Mountains. Little more was known about them a decade later. Jedidiah Morse's *New and Elegant General Atlas*, published in 1804 to accompany his *American Universal Geography*, contained two maps showing the Rockies. One of them displayed an unbroken continental divide; the other revealed several breaks through the mountain range which could, perhaps, enable a passage to the Pacific.[22]

The uncertainty that enshrouded the Rockies also covered the rest of the western territory. Charles Brockden Brown spoke for all when he said that 'there are vast regions of which no nations know anything . . . there is no certainty whether it be land or sea, mountain or plain'. Even Jefferson, who had made himself expert on western America and who would engineer the Purchase, was forced to admit that he knew little about what he was buying. In a letter of August 1803 to Senator John Breckinridge of Kentucky he remarked that 'our information as to the country is very incomplete'. He was no further forward when on 14 November 1803 he submitted to Congress his 'Description of Louisiana'. He had, indeed, become less certain of his information. In the letter to Breckinridge he had asserted that the boundaries of Louisiana were 'not admitting question'. In the 'Description' he was forced to admit that even they were 'involved in some obscurity'.[23]

Jefferson had assembled the fullest information possible, but it was woefully inadequate. In some instances he knew only that there were settlements which 'are separated from each other by immense and trackless deserts'. Unable to distinguish between fact and the factitious, Jefferson dutifully relayed to Congress tales of numerous Indian tribes, a soil too fertile for trees and, some 1,000 miles up the Missouri, a mountain of salt 180 miles long and 45 wide. His opponents pounced gleefully upon such material. The New York *Evening Post* wondered why the President had not reported 'an immense lake of molasses' and 'an extensive vale of hasty pudding, stretching as far as the eye could reach'.[24] Of course, Jefferson's opponents made no allowance for the problems confronting him. Although he was probably the best informed man on western America, much of his information was unreliable. He therefore selected material which conformed with a mental map of the West which he shared with many Americans. It was a complex map, comprising a series of interlocking images which can be simplified into three main areas: the Garden, the miasmatist debate, and the Northwest Passage.

Jefferson shared with men such as Noah Webster and James Smith the belief that America was a Garden. That belief was confirmed by the most respected books on western America available to Jefferson in his extensive library. In the next chapter I will discuss at some length Jefferson's library. Here I will confine myself to just one text, Thomas Hutchins's *Louisiana and West-Florida*, published in 1784. Hutchins, born in New Jersey, was for over twenty years an officer in the British army. He had served in the Royal Americans during the French and Indian War and had drawn the maps for William Smith's account of Bouquet's Expedition. Sympathetic to the Revolution, Hutchins had resigned his commission in 1780, and just over a year later was appointed Geographer General of the United States. He was in charge of land surveys from 1784 until his death in 1789.

Like Tom Paine, Hutchins saw the Revolution as a chance for mankind to start afresh, and he regarded Montesquieu's strictures about the size of a republic as appropriate only to the decaying Old World. Such attitudes meshed with his view of the West, on which he was an acknowledged expert. To an extent his *Louisiana and West-Florida* was a handbook, for it was full of detailed information about the lands adjacent to the Mississippi. But accompanying the information was a vision of the West as a Garden. Hutchins was enthusiastic about the climate and fertility of Louisiana, and he waxed lyrical about its big river. He asserted that 'whatever is rich or rare in the most desirable climates of Europe, seems natural to such a degree on the Mississippi'. Other explorers provided corroborating evidence. Indeed, as one went west, it seemed that the natural world became magnified. One French traveller, Louis Vilemont, noted that:

> Each step which one takes from East to West, the size of all kinds of objects increases ten fold in volume. It seems that nature has made this corner of the terrestrial globe the most favorite of its immense sphere. The products which one discovers there in proportion as one goes into the interior are more majestic, more beautiful than elsewhere.[25]

If the West was big and beautiful, it must also be venerable. Jefferson, along with many other intellectuals, sought information about the West's Indian and animal life to refute the miasmatist theories of the Europeans. He was entirely more sanguine about the Indians than the Benjamins Barton and Rush. In his *Notes on the State of Virginia*, prepared between 1780 and 1784, he defended the Indians against charges of degeneracy, and even suggested that they were an older race than the aborigines of Asia. Some thirty years later he gave evidence of his continued interest by summing up, in a letter to John Adams, the various theories of their origin. For instance, Benjamin Barton thought that they had migrated from Asia, as did Rush. James Adair, an Irish trader, had an altogether more striking theory. In 1775 he published a book suggesting that the Indians were descendants of the Ten Lost tribes of Israel.

As Jefferson was well aware, such theories dated back to the sixteenth century. Indeed, one of the oldest theories was that the Indians were descendants of a Welsh expedition led by Prince Madoc which discovered America in AD 1170. Initially used by the Elizabethans as a gambit against Spanish claims to the New World, the myth of Madoc was revived in the early 1740s. It was however with the growing interest in America that it took its place in the 1770s as part of the philosophical debate over America. A summary of the tale appeared in 1770 in *The Scots Magazine*. In 1771 John Reinhold Forster, who the year before had translated Kalm's *Travels*, now published his translation of further *Travels*, by Jean Bossu, a French Captain of Marines. He questioned Bossu's suggestion that the Welsh influence could be traced in Indian languages. This did not deter Lord Monboddo, who duly reported the myth in his enquiry into the *Origin and Progress of Language*.

The myth of Madoc spread to America. John Filson sought evidence of the Welsh language; and in 1795 a Welshman, John Evans, went up the

Missouri in search of his compatriots. The leader of the expedition, the Scots explorer James MacKay, also instructed Evans to find the route from the Upper Missouri to the Pacific. Both quests were fruitless, but Evans's documents came into Jefferson's hands, and would later influence the Lewis and Clark Expedition. The story of the Welsh Indians still exists, and is still unproved.[26]

In Jefferson's view the Indians were noble. So too were the American beasts. In both instances Jefferson was combating European scientific theory. Buffon had castigated Indians and beasts alike as small and degenerate. Like many less wise men, Buffon thought that big was beautiful. He called the elephant the most respectable animal in the world save man. It was reasonable, then, that Jefferson should search for the American elephant. And if the continent could not provide an elephant, then any mammoth would do. Other intellectuals like Hugh Williamson, John Bartram and Charles Willson Peale were also deeply interested, and numbers of people went off on mammoth-hunts. Unfortunately, only bones were ever found, amongst others by someone who wrote to the *Royal American Magazine* in 1774, and by James Smith during his 1775 voyage along the Ohio River.[27]

Few Americans matched Jefferson's interest in mammoths. In 1781 he asked George Rogers Clark to obtain the front teeth from some remains found on the Ohio. Clark took time out from his intrigues to oblige the former Governor of Virginia. His letter to Jefferson shows the frontiersman wrestling stoutly with science and syntax. He could not locate any front teeth, and suggested that the beast was 'by no means as Carnivorious as many suppose'. All he had been able to find was 'a large thigh Bone that dont please me being broke'. Clark promised to get Jefferson some more bones from the West, yet discovered that even in the cause of science he could become enmeshed in controversy. Others had dared to criticise 'what they are pleasd to call Quixotic Scheams'. The flourish closing his letter was doubtless more polite than the verbal response he must have given to his critics:

> I shall recommend it to them to learn a little more of the Geografy of their own Cuntry and its true Interests before they presume to Speak so frely for the future.

In his *Notes on the State of Virginia* Jefferson developed his attack on Buffon, in part by printing (as Timothy Dwight would do in his *Travels*) comparative tables of European and American quadrupeds, demonstrating the greater weight of American beasts. Heading the lists was an entry for the mammoth, left blank. The subsequent years provided him with more information about it. In 1796 he received a box of bones unearthed in western Virginia. They were leg bones bearing the closest resemblance to those of the African lion, but three times larger. Jefferson wondered if the animal could be seven feet high and weigh 2,000 lbs. He called it the megalonyx, and when he published his analysis of the discovery in the *Transactions of the American Philosophical Society* he suggested that:

> In the present interior of our continent there is surely space and range enough
> for elephants and lions, if in that climate they could subsist; and for mammoths
> and megalonyxs who may subsist there. Our entire ignorance of the immense
> country to the West and North-West, and its contents, does not authorise us to
> say what it does not contain.

He had already made a similar defence of the blank entry for the mammoth in the *Notes*. Here the ungainly double negative conveniently opens the West for explorers to fill in the blank. The results were unsatisfactory until 1807. In that year Jefferson asked William Clark, the younger brother of George Rogers Clark, to supervise the excavation of a find at the Falls of the Ohio. (Clark had just returned from the Expedition which will be discussed in chapter 6.) Some 300 bones were collected and shipped to Jefferson. They were laid out in one of the larger rooms of the White House, surely one of the most unusual employments of the President's official residence.[28]

Late in his life Jefferson's old friend, Benjamin Rush, speculated further about the origins of the Indians and mammoths. Perhaps, he thought, the Indians had migrated from Asia across a land bridge, and on elephants of one sex. American elephants, of course, had become extinct; but the notion of the land bridge certainly had not. It was one aspect of the idea of the Northwest Passage, which had been in the minds of explorers before Columbus. The history of the Northwest Passage has been well documented. I want to emphasise here, however, how well the idea fitted with the other elements of the Jeffersonian mental map of the West, and how appropriate it was therefore that Americans should take over the old European imperial and commercial image of the Passage to India.[29]

Henry Nash Smith has called Jefferson 'the intellectual father of the American advance to the Pacific'. There were also many uncles and one grandfather, Benjamin Franklin. The anonymous French memoir of 1792, once again, tells us why. It had talked of a land divided by ridges running from north to south. It also talked of rivers flowing from east to west. American optimism joined these rivers to provide an easy passage across the continent. Interest in a water route was such that otherwise hard-headed men were fooled by hoaxes. Benjamin Franklin, himself a master of the hoax, wrote a defence of a 'Letter from Admiral Bartholomew de Fonte', which described a voyage made in 1640 from the Pacific to the Atlantic entirely by water.

The de Fonte letter made a flattering distinction between America and

Asia. In the neighbourhood of what would later be called the Bering Strait, the letter remarked that the Asian mountains were 'ruinous, cleft, & broken, cover'd with perpetual Snows', while those on the opposite American coast were covered 'with fruitful Earth or Mould, and therefore are decked from the Foot to the very Top of them, with thick and very fine Trees'. This deft piece of terrestrial legerdemain duped Franklin, who in 1762 wrote a long letter to a friend in the British Royal Society describing the land in Edenic terms and concluding:

> That though there may probably be no practicable Passage for Ships, there is nevertheless such a Passage for Boats as De Fonte found & has describ'd; & That the Country upon that Passage is for the most part habitable, & would produce all the Necessaries of Life.[30]

A number of explorers attempted to find the Passage, but simply added to the store of tall tales. I have already mentioned James MacKay and John Evans. Jonathan Carver, a former colonial militia officer, tried to find the Passage by way of the Mississippi and Lake Superior, and in 1778 published an account of his journey. It became extremely popular. Although he had not found the Passage or seen the Rockies, Carver suggested that the mountains were divided by a tract of level ground, by which it was possible to reach the Pacific. Another explorer, Jean-Baptiste Truteau, agreed with James MacKay that the Missouri River could provide the sought-after Passage. But the route across the Rockies apparently lay much further to the north. In 1793 the fur-trader Alexander Mackenzie led a party from Canada to the Pacific. His *Voyages from Montreal . . . to the Frozen and Pacific Oceans*, published in 1801, earned him a knighthood and widespread interest. He reported immense resources of fur and fish. And, much to everyone's excitement, he had walked across the Rockies. He had found a portage of 817 paces across a slight ridge that separated navigable waters flowing into different oceans.[31]

So the Northwest Passage existed – but only for Mackenzie and the British in Canada. Little was known about the Rockies further to the south. The few available facts, therefore, were consistently wrapped in hopeful theory. That is why the de Fonte letter had fooled Franklin. Jefferson had inherited Franklin's images of the West, and much of Franklin's ignorance. Despite all his efforts he had little hard evidence to hand, but rather an array of very attractive circumstantial or hearsay material. It was open to him to believe what he wanted to believe. Not that Jefferson was simply a dreamer. He was, after all, a pragmatic politician (the claims of his enemies notwithstanding) and it is doubtful that his pipe-dreams about the West would have prompted him into vigorous and immediate action, had it not been for the transfer of Louisiana from Spain to France.

Until 1801 the major issue over Louisiana that concerned the Federal government had been the free navigation of the Mississippi and the transit of goods at New Orleans, thereby enabling the produce of the interior to reach the Atlantic. Spanish obstruction had already indirectly caused the Whiskey Rebellion of 1794; and in 1795 the American Minister to Britain was despatched to Spain to negotiate a treaty which, among other things, gave the westerners the free access they desired. Their relief was short-lived. On 1 October 1800 Spain secretly ceded Louisiana to France by the Treaty of San Ildefonso. When in May 1801 Jefferson learned of the cession he was immediately alarmed. It was one thing to have a feeble and inefficient Spanish administration on one's western doorstep; Napoleonic France was a different matter. In one letter he suggested that the United States would be forced to ally itself with Britain as soon as France assumed its rights in New Orleans. Jefferson therefore instructed his Minister in Paris, Robert Livingston, to negotiate an irrevocable guarantee of free navigation. The results of that negotiation, culminating in the transfer of the whole of Louisiana Territory to the United States on 20 December 1803, are too well known to require repetition.[32]

Jefferson was lucky that Napoleon's eyes were elsewhere, for French accounts of the territory had consistently emphasised the importance of the area. (I have already referred to the anonymous memoir of 1792 and the Vilemont letter of 1802 and will discuss another, earlier text in the next chapter.) The British concurred; they, too, were interested in Louisiana as a stepping-stone to Canada. Jefferson was aware of these attitudes and, together with his images of the West, they informed the 'Description of Louisiana' that he now submitted to Congress, and the Purchase that he urged upon it. Congress, however, was divided. Enthusiasm for the potentiality of the immense territory was tempered by an awareness of the immense problems involved in administering it.

Opinion against the Purchase was concentrated amongst the New England Federalists, but they were not alone. It was a Delaware Senator, Samuel White, who voiced the fears of many during the debate on the creation of stock to fund the Purchase. He regarded American possession of New Orleans and free navigation of the Mississippi as essential. His view on the purchase of the entire territory was quite different:

> But as to Louisiana, this new, immense, unbounded world, if it should ever be incorporated into this Union, which I have no idea can be done but by altering the Constitution, I believe it will be the greatest curse that could at present befall us.

Almost everyone, no matter their political persuasion, was aware of one especial danger. Louisiana, he said, would be settled by:

> the very population that would otherwise occupy part of our present territory. Thus our citizens will be removed to the immense distance of two or three thousand miles from the capital of the Union, where they will scarcely ever feel the rays of the General Government; their affections will become alienated; they will gradually begin to view us as strangers; they will form other commercial connexions; and our interests will become distinct.

Clearly, Samuel White was raising questions that Madison had tried to answer some sixteen years earlier.

At one point there had been, continued Senator White, a scheme mooted by Jefferson for removing the Indians to the west bank of the Mississippi, thereby 'making the fertile regions of Louisiana a howling wilderness, never to be trodden by the foot of civilized man'. This scheme was 'impracticable and chimerical'. Everyone 'acquainted with the adventurous, roving, and enterprising temper of our people, and with the manner in which our Western country has been settled', knew that it would be impossible to 'restrain' them. He would, therefore, prefer to give the territory to France or Spain than see a single United States citizen settle on it.[33]

Unlike Paine and Jefferson, Senator White is afraid of novelty. He also reveals here a constellation of fears held by many politicians. Like the debates on the Constitution, these fears reflected the thinking of Montesquieu. The territory would be too large and too varied to govern effectively. White reveals fears, too, about the kind of people who would migrate to the new territory. Although the terms he applies to them are superficially approving, they also suggest an instability which is confirmed by their potential alienation from the Federal Government and its benign sunshine. It is only a step, therefore, to a distaste of frontier folk like that expressed by Timothy Dwight and shared by many.

A number of politicians took that step. Some thought that only the restless and lawless would migrate to Louisiana; others that the people already living there, notably the French and Spanish, would destroy the essentially Anglo-Saxon nature of the polity. Even those in favour of the Purchase recognised that it would have to be governed in an authoritarian manner. It was common to regard the inhabitants as children who had yet to mature sufficiently to merit the fruits of liberty. As the enabling legislation was passing through Congress, Jefferson was planning a government in which the people had no voice at all.

The Louisiana environment, too, held its terrors. Representative Thomas Griffin of Virginia, for instance, worried about 'the influence of climate upon our citizens who should migrate thither' (8 Cong., 1 Sess., Col. 443). Jonathan Dayton of New Jersey went further. He suggested that the dews of Louisiana were so damp and the sun so fierce that white men could not work the land. The right of slavery would in consequence be essential. John Smith responded that the slaves would become so numerous that they would endanger the government, a problem that his home state, Ohio, had avoided. Moreover, the land was so full of swamps that it would provide an easy refuge for escaped slaves. For Smith as for several other senators, the spectre of the Santo Domingo insurrection loomed over the issue of slavery.

Many Northern politicians regarded the Louisiana Purchase as a device to spread the influence of the supposedly democratic politics of Jefferson and his fellow-Southerners. Senator William Plumer of New Hampshire thought that the Purchase would 'destroy at once the weight and importance of the Eastern States, and compel them to establish a separate independent Empire'. Timothy Pickering, who had been Secretary of State under Washington and Adams, also believed that the Union would end, and advocated a Northern confederacy instead. But these fears were not confined to the Federalist Northeast. Thomas Griffin of Virginia agreed with his fellow-Representative Roger Griswold of Connecticut that the new territory would create a political imbalance (8 Cong., 1 Sess., Cols. 441–443).

Such worries did not end with the Purchase. During the debate in February 1811 on the admission of Louisiana to statehood, Senator Josiah Quincy of Massachusetts asserted that if Louisiana became a state, he would regard the Union as 'virtually dissolved'. He drew a clear distinction, as Dwight did in his *Travels*, between the imperial image and the sordid reality. His love of the Union was 'rooted' in his attachment to his 'native soil'. If Louisiana were admitted his attachment, he said (continuing his horticultural metaphor), would 'be trampled under foot by foreigners'. The purity of the Constitution would be impaired. It was designed for citizens of the United States, not for 'those wild men of the Missouri'.

The Constitution could not, moreover, 'be strained to leap over all the wilderness of the West'. Quincy dwelt upon the image of horrific infinity:

> We are about to cross the Mississippi. The Missouri and Red Rivers are but roads on which our imagination travels to new lands and new States to be raised and admitted . . . into this Union, among undiscovered lands, in the west.

He concluded that 'there is no limit to men's imaginations, on this subject, short of California and the Columbia River' (11 Cong., 3 Sess., Cols. 524–542). Quincy's imagery here is remarkably similar to Jefferson's, as we shall see in the next chapter. But whereas Jefferson used such images as a springboard for his optimism, Quincy recoiled in horror. His revulsion was in vain, as the more pragmatic Gouverneur Morris had realised eight years earlier. Morris regarded any attempt to limit the Republic, no matter how prudent, as 'Utopian'. He thought it inevitable 'that all North America must at length be annexed to us'. Yet this was not the limit to Morris's prescience. 'Happy, indeed', he added, 'if the lust for dominion stop there.'[34]

The arguments raised in Congress against the Purchase reflected conservative opinion in the country. The *Columbian Centinel*, a Boston Federalist newspaper, ran a series of articles by 'Fabricius' attacking the Purchase. 'Fabricius' modified Montesquieu when he remarked that 'a pure republic cannot . . . subsist in a very small territory, nor be long preserved from the most incurable extremes of degeneracy in one that is too widely extended'. His other arguments were more partisan. The Purchase, he said, was Jefferson's method of getting votes for 'imperial *Virginia*'. There could be no other reason for buying 'a great waste, a wilderness unpeopled with any beings except wolves and wandering Indians'. Louisiana would destroy the 'balance in the Union', and would 'drain' away people who should otherwise be engaged in bettering husbandry or manufactures in the East. The distant territory would also attract 'renegadoes, and outlaws, and fugitives'. The spectre of Ethan Allen and the Green Mountain boys seemed to loom over 'Fabricius' when he asked, in words that forty years previously would have been issuing from British mouths, 'will not these new mountaineer states claim power, and resist taxes?'[35]

We have already seen Richard Alsop attacking the Jacobins. For several years he satirised Jefferson, particularly over his images of the West. Alsop laughed at the supposed fertility of Louisiana, at its Welsh Indians and salt mountains. His most pointed barbs were directed at the Virginian's interest in the mammoth:

> At random here the Mammoth browses,
> As large as common meeting-houses;
> Snakes reach the size of saw-mill logs,
> And rats and mice as large as dogs;
> Musquetoes weigh as much as crows
> And man to such a giant grows,
> So long, so wide, that at a meal,
> He'll eat a loin of Mammoth veal.

For Fisher Ames the Purchase was no laughing matter. Indeed, his brother accused him of writing the 'Fabricius' articles. Certainly, in his private letters Fisher Ames reviled this latest crime of Jefferson. In 1799 he had written of the French Revolution in images of a diseased and cataclysmic landscape. Now he regarded the former French territory as so frightening that it was no landscape at all. The Mississippi acted as a boundary which, in confining the United States, also defined it. In contrast, by adding an unmeasured world beyond that river, we rush like a comet into infinite space. In our wild career, we may jostle some other world out of its orbit, but we shall, in every event, quench the light of our own.

Ames anticipated one of Samuel White's objections to the Purchase. He also, if unwittingly, echoed Gouverneur Morris's shocked response to the French Revolution. While in Paris in 1790 Morris had noted in his diary that 'here conjecture may wander through unbounded space'. Ames' spatial imagery is all the more terrifying because it is attempting to describe unbounded space, rather than acting as a metaphor for the imagination.[36]

Not all Federalists agreed with 'Fabricius'. On the other hand, opposition to the Purchase was not confined to the Federalist Northeast. We have already seen the New York *Evening Post* make short work of Jefferson's 'Description of Louisiana'. Other voices were raised in protest as far south as Mississippi. The Washington *National Intelligencer*, strongly supportive of Jefferson, reprinted a letter from 'Watty Watersnake of Possum Town' to the *Mississippi Herald* which called New Orleans a 'little, paltry island' upon 'a downright swamp', and dismissed Louisiana as 'an absolute barren that nobody knows the bounds of'.

Andrew Ellicott, the mathematician and surveyor, knew the bounds of Louisiana as well as anyone. He had surveyed the boundary between the United States and Louisiana when it was still apparently in the hands of Spain. Ellicott's *Journal* of the survey was published as the debate over the Purchase was proceeding, and he took the opportunity to voice his opinion. The immediate sale of lands west of the Mississippi would, he said, depress the market and scatter the citizens too widely. Like 'Fabricius' he worried that the new lands would be a natural home for fugitives from the law, and like Benjamin Rush in 1787 he thought that the frontier forced settlers to degenerate from bravery into ferocity.

The Marques de Casa Yrujo, the Spanish Minister to the United States, agreed. A friend of Jefferson and married to the daughter of Thomas McKean (the Republican Governor of Pennsylvania), he was nevertheless furious at the purchase of what had so recently been Spain's. Yet his opposition to the Purchase also showed some concern for his wife's country. His report home repeated the fears of dissolution first raised by the British after the 1763 Treaty of Paris and echoed, once again, by Benjamin Rush:

> it is a kind of madness, with only five millions of people already scattered over so extensive a surface, to add a new world of woods to the actual possessions.[37]

Those against the Purchase were vociferous, but they were in the minority. Despairing geographers like Elijah Parish and Jedidiah Morse would later, on the slimmest evidence, create the myth of the 'Great American Desert', but they could not stop the westering instinct of a restless people. Ordinary citizens, even in the Northeast, subscribed to images of the West which agreed with Jefferson, and accorded with the imperial imagery of Dwight's *Greenfield Hill* rather than the despair of his *Travels*. They anticipated that Louisiana would become uniformly fertile, with vast herds of game grazing under smiling skies; and looked forward to the time when Samuel White's sovereign sun would beam over the new land. An anonymous poem, for instance, looked westward to a Louisiana yet to be settled by Americans:

> Towards the desart turn our anxious eys,
> To see 'mong forest statelier cities rise;
> Where the wild beast now holds his gloomy den,
> To see shine forth the blessed abodes of men.
>
> The rich luxuriance of a teeming soil,
> Rewards with affluence the farmer's toil,
> All nature round him breathes a rich perfume,
> His harvest ripens and his orchards bloom.

The opposition of images is now familiar to us. The empty terrain of Puritan distaste − 'desart' being used here in the sense of deserted − presided over by beasts, is transformed by American activity into a salubrious, even aromatic, republic.[38]

Many people admired the cosmetics of imperialism, and for many reasons. An American physician named Paul Alliot had been practising in Louisiana while it was a French possession. Among the illnesses he claimed he could cure were deafness, epilepsy, dropsy, 'venereal diseases, even the most inveterate, without mercury . . . suppression of the monthly courses', and loss of milk. Despite (or perhaps because of) his work, he was imprisoned in New Orleans and deported to France. After his release and return to New York he wrote a lengthy memoir to Jefferson about the new territory. (He also advertised his services.) The 'vast forests' of Louisiana, he said, teemed with game. Buffalo and bears were enormous and delicious to eat. St Louis was 'one of the best places on the globe'. But the territory was plagued by 'atrocious acts of injustice that are dictated by ambition and corruption'. The change of political master would, however, transform the terrain:

> that vast dying land is about to receive that health-giving balm which will entirely heal the leprosy which had been gnawing it for so long a time.[39]

Men of more secure reputation agreed with Alliot, and said so in a flurry of pamphlets. One of the most optimistic was by David Ramsay. Ramsay spent his time in the South Carolina legislature rather than in prison, and wrote medical and political history rather than self-advertisement.

Nevertheless, his *Oration on the Cession of Louisiana* shares Alliot's enthusiasm and recalls both Thomas Bond's 1782 *Anniversary Oration* and Ezra Stiles' 1783 Election Sermon. Less than thirty years ago, said Ramsay, Americans had been British subjects; now American soil had been doubled. Its huge rivers, waterfalls and forests, and the western mammoth showed that America was indisputably bigger and better than any other part of the globe. Yet Ramsay did not merely celebrate America as an answer to the strictures of Buffon, for it had pleased God to create in the New World 'a corresponding exalted state of man'. This bloated version of Paine's geopolitics could easily be inflated further. Louisiana was therefore 'a heaven sent boon', bringing 'the most desirable portion of our continent under the operation of the best constitution in the world'.

The Virginia Senator St George Tucker had earlier corrected Jedidiah Morse's criticism of Williamsburg. As one might expect, he shared David Ramsay's Southern enthusiasm for the Purchase, and in doing so gave a further puff to the imperial balloon. He suggested that Spanish West Florida should be added to Louisiana and the joint territories hurried to statehood. The benefits of the American political system should be delayed as little as possible.[40] Congress, after a brief but intense debate, acceded. The legislation enabling the Purchase was passed by both Houses of Congress with comfortable majorities early in November 1803.

The acquisition of Louisiana more than doubled the territory of the United States at a stroke.[41] In a sense, the conservatives were right. The composition of their nation was altered forever. Gradually, its identity would change from an Atlantic to a continental state. The architect of the transformation had been Jefferson. With great finesse he had engineered the Purchase from Napoleon. Senator John Breckinridge summed up the President's achievement when he remarked during the debate that:

> to acquire an empire of perhaps half the extent of the one we possessed from the most powerful and warlike nation on earth, without bloodshed, without the oppressing of a single individual, without in the least embarrassing the ordinary operations of your finances, and all this through the peaceful forms of negotiation, and in despite too of the opposition of a considerable proportion of the community, is an achievement of which the archives . . . cannot furnish a parallel.　　　　　　　　　　(8 Cong., 1 Sess., Col. 60)

Senator Breckinridge had underestimated by one half the extent of the Purchase. Had his opponents known of its true size, doubtless their fears would have increased commensurately. Jefferson, of course, was not troubled by doubts. When he wrote to Breckinridge before the legislation had been submitted to Congress, he used a domestic image to convey his sense of the importance of the Purchase:

> It is the case of a guardian, investing the money of his ward in purchasing an important adjacent territory; and saying to him when of age, I did this for your good.

In that letter, Jefferson used a similar image to reject the strictures of Montesquieu. 'We have seldom', he said, 'seen neighborhood produce affection among nations.' There was no reason why people in contiguous regions should naturally think alike.

Jefferson's imagery may be seen in an ironic light. Many of his neighbours in Congress felt little affection for him. During the course of the debate over the Purchase they, and many of their sympathisers in what Breckinridge had called 'the community', had been forced to confront a fear that only a few like Dwight had earlier experienced. They saw the Purchase in terms akin to Dwight's Green Mountains: a disordered terrain occupied by disordered people, a new world of woods which should forever be kept apart from the rational but limited Christian Republic.

In spite of their objections, the United States had acquired a land which, as one informed commentator remarked, was 'the region of fable', apparently inhabited by westering watercourses, mammoths, Welsh Indians and a ferocious fertility. Jefferson happily regarded it as an enlargement of his agrarian Republic. In the letter to Breckinridge he envisaged 'range after range' of farms spreading across the terrain, just like the landscape of *Greenfield Hill*. Jefferson had executed an imperial ideology which was rooted in an aesthetic proposed by *Greenfield Hill* and to be found throughout Jefferson's writings. I have suggested that Jefferson was a practical politician. His interest in the Republic as a political entity however was always subject to his passion for the republic of letters. In the next chapter I will try to place the Louisiana Purchase in the context of Jefferson's developing literary and spatial imagination.[42]

5

Thomas Jefferson and the spacious field of imagination

In 1771 Thomas Jefferson was asked by Robert Skipwith, his future brother-in-law, for recommendations for a library 'worth about 30 lib. sterl'. Skipwith's parsimony was thwarted by the enthusiasm of the 28-year-old philosopher. Jefferson provided a select list of some 147 titles costing, he believed, £107/10/-. He told Skipwith to buy a few books now, completing his library as funds permitted. In the meantime he was invited to Monticello, Jefferson's newly built home in the Blue Ridge Mountains of Virginia:

> Come to the new Rowanty, from which you may reach your hand to a library formed on a more extensive plan. Separated from each other but a few paces, the possessions of each would be open to the other.[1]

The way in which the invitation is framed is particularly relevant to this chapter. It indicates a close relationship between the text and the terrain, between Jefferson's library and its surroundings: Virginia and, ultimately, America. In the following discussion I will explore the relation between text and terrain in Jefferson's thinking. I want to focus on his declining belief in the function of the imagination. I will do this, first, by emphasising the value he placed on the written word as a mode of order; secondly, by showing how his visit to Europe helped him to order his imagination; and thirdly, by illustrating how he applied that ordering function to American terrain.

Rowandiz was the mountain of the world, the Arcadian Olympus, the pivot on which heaven rested. Jefferson's 'little mountain' may have been of more modest size than Olympus, but the letter to Skipwith indicates his sense of the prospect it commanded. Its eminence was noted by le Chevalier (later Marquis) de Chastellux when he visited his friend's home. Owning 'fairly extensive lands in the neighborhood', Jefferson could have chosen to live anywhere. It was only proper that he picked this site, for:

> Nature so contrived it, that a Sage and a man of taste should find on his own estate the spot where he might best study and enjoy Her.

As its name suggested, the house was 'in an Italian style' and thus 'quite tasteful, although not however without some faults'. Yet Jefferson was to be praised because he was the first American who had 'consulted the Fine Arts to know how he should shelter himself from the weather'.[2]

The elevated aspect of Monticello did not please everyone. When, a decade and a half later, le Duc de la Rochefoucault-Liancourt visited Monticello, he had mixed feelings about it. On the one hand, he saw that its 'great elevation' provided it with the purest air and hence exempted it from 'the pestilential effluvia' which afflicted baser sites. On the other hand, he found the view troubling. The 'immensity of prospect it enjoys is . . . too vast', he wrote, accustomed perhaps to the limited hedgerow vistas of France. At Monticello, he felt that the balance between nature and culture had not yet been perfected:

> The aid of fancy is, however, required to complete the enjoyment of this magnificent view; and she must picture to us those plains and mountains such as population and culture will render them in greater or smaller number of years. The disproportion existing between the cultivated lands and those which are still covered with forests as ancient as the globe, is at present much too great.

Even when the forests 'shall have been done away', the prospect would still be incomplete; it needed a broad river 'to render it completely beautiful'.[3]

Unlike his aristocratic French visitors, Jefferson felt no reservations about his chosen site. He became ecstatic about it in one of the few love letters that remain, the well-known 'Dialogue of Head and Heart' to Maria Cosway, wife of the Royal Academician Richard Cosway and herself a reputable painter:

> our own dear Monticello, where has nature spread so rich a mantle under the eye? mountains, forests, rocks, rivers. With what majesty do we there ride above the storms! How sublime to look down into the workhouse of nature, to see her clouds, hail, snow, rain, thunder, all fabricated at our feet! And the glorious Sun, when rising as if out of a distant water, just gilding the tops of the mountains, and giving life to all nature![4]

Jefferson's 'fancy', assisted by the sun, has provided the water that la Rochefoucault-Liancourt missed. Of particular interest, however, is the position of Jefferson in his mountain home. If Monticello is Olympus, then he is Zeus. The exclamation marks and clustered nouns indicate

Jefferson's excitement at his godlike position. Whereas la Rochefoucault-Liancourt suffered from agoraphobia at Monticello, Jefferson gloried in its elevation. He seems here to supervise rather than endure the varied weather conditions, for they are apparently constructed beneath him. The passage is closed (paradoxically) in an image of renewal, the rising sun that seems to respond to his fiat, enlivening the scene around him.

In the pages that follow we shall often see Jefferson looking down on America, as if from a great height, and imposing order upon it. This is less presumptuous than it seems. Jefferson shared the beliefs of men like Rush, Freneau, Dwight and others discussed earlier that the new Republic provided the political and economic tools that would allow control of the climate and hence would transform the terrain into an Eden. There were just two differences between Jefferson and his contemporaries. The first was the greater ease with which Virginia would be transformed. Indeed, human intervention was almost unnecessary. Even before the Revolution had changed everything, an anonymous writer had remarked that:

> Spots are here frequently found that possess every picturesque beauty which in England our nobility are so emulous to create in their parks.[5]

Secondly, Jefferson was distinguished even from his fellow Virginians by his fondness for heights. The commanding positions of Monticello and the Virginia Capitol at Richmond (which he also designed) were unusual. Encouraged by the country's many waterways, his compatriots built along river-banks. If Jefferson consulted the fine arts, they consulted the environment.

This is not to say that Jefferson ignored the environment; rather, he wished to understand and control it, and the aerial view was a favourite means to that end. His 'Hints to Americans Travelling in Europe' show how important the view, and books, were to his thinking:

> Buy beforehand the map of the country you are going into. On arriving at a town, the first thing is to buy the plan of the town, and the book noting its curiosities. Walk round the ramparts when there are any. Go to the top of a steeple to have a view of the town and its environs.

His collection of town plans, his part in the design of Washington, and – late in his life – his supervision of the construction of the University of Virginia by telescope from Monticello, provide further evidence of his interest in the aerial view.[6]

The extent of that ordering vision is suggested by the letter Jefferson wrote to Joseph Priestley. Jefferson had just become third President, and he was overjoyed at having survived the long and acrimonious debates that had accompanied the election:

> As the storm is now subsiding, and the horizon becoming serene, it is pleasant to consider the phenomenon with attention. We can no longer say there is nothing new under the sun. For this whole chapter in the history of man is new. The great extent of our republic is new. Its sparse habitation is new. The mighty wave of public opinion which has rolled over it is new. But the most pleasing novelty is, its so quickly subsiding over such an extent of surface to its true level again.

The Union, he concluded, was now much stronger than it had been before the election. I quoted this letter in the Prologue to draw attention to its invocation of novelty, and its references to American space and emptiness. More germane to my argument here are the climatic and water images, which follow the pattern of that earlier letter to Maria Cosway about Monticello. Storms give way to serenity. Yet here the image is applied to an entire republican space which Jefferson would double within three years by means of the Louisiana Purchase. In a more attenuated form, Jefferson used similar imagery in his Inaugural Address just seventeen days earlier, and of that Address Henry Adams remarked that 'the republic which Jefferson believed himself to be founding or securing in 1801 was an enlarged Virginia'.[7]

Stormy disorder giving way to sunny order, expressed spatially: this is a process that Jefferson believed could be changed from image into reality. It would be done through the medium of the written word. I suggested earlier that Jefferson was more liberal than Noah Webster in his attitudes to language. He believed, unlike the Yankee whom he regarded as 'a mere pedagogue', that the differences between England and America could only be properly reflected in a 'judicious neology'. He was interested like Webster in philology, writing an *Essay on the Anglo-Saxon Language*; but his interest was aimed at enriching rather than restricting the language. He believed it would be inevitably enlarged by a growing population in an extensive country.[8]

Yet Jefferson was not an advocate of linguistic anarchy, any more than he believed in political or geographical anarchy. Neology would be 'judicious', a term reflecting his legal training, and would be contained within ordering sentences and ordering texts. In a letter to Webster disputing the lexicographer's politics, Jefferson asserted that 'no republic is more real than the republic of letters' (4 December 1790; Boyd, xviii, 132). The terrestrial Republic would become real as it was ordered through writing. It is appropriate therefore that Jefferson's earliest public documents include a project for making navigable the neighbouring Rivanna River and a bill for the maintenance of Virginian roads and bridges (Boyd, i, 87–90). Highways, whether on land or water, are the impress of organised society upon terrain. Jefferson made his impression through a pen which enabled that organisation. His interest in highways was lifelong; and, as we shall see, he frequently used images of highways to organise the scene he was describing.[9]

No pen was more active. The 75,000 letters that he may have written are only a fragment of his work. He documented everything. His rage for written order was such that Fawn Brodie called it 'compulsive'. Certainly, he saw the closest connection between the businesses of writing and living, as is revealed by two letters written some fifty-five years apart. When in 1770 a fire destroyed his mother's house at Shadwell and almost all the family records and correspondence, he lamented the loss at some length. 'I am utterly destitute', he wrote. All his papers were gone and 'like the baseless fabric of a vision, Leave not a trace behind' (Boyd, I, 34–35). The opposition between the solidity of paper and the evanescence of the imagination is central to my later discussion, and is here hyperbolically conveyed in an allusion to Prospero's 'vext' assertion of the transience of 'the great globe itself'. Again, in 1825, when his newly-married granddaughter lost her luggage at sea, Jefferson condoled with her in a manner which echoes his Shadwell loss:

> The documents of your childhood, your letters, correspondencies, notes, books, &c, &c, all gone! And your life cut in two, as it were, and a new one to begin, without the records of the former.

An action unrecorded, it seemed, was worthless.[10]

Jefferson's Farm and Garden Books are good examples of the range and extent of his records. The Farm Book begins in January 1774, when he was thirty-one, and ends one month before his death on 4 July 1826. The Garden Book was started in 1766 and continued until the autumn of 1824. In it he recorded the dates that flowers bloomed and their heights; kept details of crop rotation; maintained continuous records of the temperature four times daily (from 1 July 1776 for over forty years); even computed how much more quickly ground could be excavated using a one-wheel rather than a two-wheel barrow. Jefferson was similarly active in book-collecting, building three collections during the course of his life and making extensive recommendations, to his University of Virginia as well as to Skipwith.[11]

The 1771 letter to Robert Skipwith, then, indicates a particularly intimate relation between Jefferson's library and the lands that it overlooked. If the lands were at present empty the shelves and document presses of the library would rapidly overflow. His collecting and recording may have been compulsive but, as Julian Boyd remarked, it was without a hint of 'bibliolatry' (Boyd, I, ix). Every book, every paper was intended for use. In all they amounted to a model of his vast Republic.

THE VAUNTED SCENE OF EUROPE

The components of Jefferson's model were derived from Europe. Although he always asserted that America must remain separate from the Old World, he was afflicted by the problems confronting any book-collector. The first printing press was installed in North America in 1638, but until well into the nineteenth century most books had to be imported. As Jefferson had the best library in America (the universities notwithstanding) the problem of dependence for him was acute. Throughout his life he was forced to obtain most of his books from the continent he avowedly despised. It was, he complained, even impossible to buy American history in America.[12]

Of course, he took more than books from Europe. The 1771 list for Skipwith and the remarks of Chastellux indicate how deeply Jefferson was read in European politics, history, science, religion, law and literature. He visited France in 1784 to assist Franklin and Adams in drawing up commercial treaties, and remained there from 1785 to 1789 as US Minister. While he was in France he made one of his periodic denunciations of the Old World. Responding to an enquiry from a young American, he advised against a European education. An American abroad, he said, 'loses in his knowledge, in his morals, in his health, in his habits, and in his happiness' (letter 15 October 1785; Boyd, VIII, 637). Yet Europe provided Jefferson with gains rather than losses, particularly in his knowledge. (We know little of what Europe accomplished for his morals, although Fawn Brodie does her best with very slim evidence.) Building on his reading, Jefferson became during his five years in France the most cosmopolitan of the Revolutionary leaders, more cosmopolitan even than Benjamin Franklin.

While he was US Minister Jefferson undertook three tours. In 1786 he visited England; the following year he toured France and Italy; and just before his return to America he visited Holland and the Rhineland. His travels were made ostensibly for utilitarian reasons. He went to England to assist with commercial treaties, and he toured Europe to look at its agriculture. But he took time off to look at 'the vaunted scene of Europe', as he once described it to Charles Bellini (letter 30 September 1785; Boyd, VIII, 568), and in doing so he developed ways of seeing that had been book-learned. In England he made a tour of some well-known gardens – to see, perhaps, how English creations matched up to Virginia's natural beauty. As his 'Memorandum' of the tour indicates, his selection of the gardens to be visited and his evaluation of them was guided by Thomas Whately's *Observations on Modern Gardening* (1770):

> While his descriptions, in point of style, are models of perfect elegance and classical correctness, they are as remarkable for their exactness. I always walked

over the gardens with his book in my hand, examined with attention the particular spots he described, found them so justly characterized by him as to be easily recognized, and saw with wonder, that his fine imagination had never been able to seduce him from the truth.[13]

We see here a relationship between the book and the surrounding terrain that expresses precisely the intention announced in that letter to Skipwith. Whately had worked from the terrain to the text. Jefferson reverses the process and expresses his admiration of the consonance of the two. Here is no baseless fabric. Whately combined vision and style to chart the scene precisely, and he had held his 'fine imagination' in check in doing so. That long second sentence of praise, clause building upon clause, would resonate through Jefferson's later work.

Jefferson was particularly sympathetic to garden aesthetics. In 1771 he had recommended to Skipwith *The Spectator* and *The Tatler*, the works of Pope, Kames' *Elements of Criticism* and Hogarth's *Analysis of Beauty*. The *Analysis of Beauty* (1753) treated nature as a continuous process that should be fractured as little as possible by human artifice and proposed the serpentine line as a means of accommodating one to the other. Kames' *Elements of Criticism* (1762) asserted that:

> a straight walk has an air of stiffness and confinement: and at any rate is less agreeable than a winding or waving walk; for in surveying the beauties of an ornamented field, we love to roam from place to place at freedom.

These remarks would inevitably strike a chord in 'a savage from the mountains of America', as Jefferson jocularly referred to himself in that letter to Bellini (Boyd, VIII, 568); and he happily applied them to the gardens he saw. 'This straight walk has an ill effect', he remarked of Caversham; whereas at Esher Place he noted that 'clumps of trees' were finely balanced to produce 'a most lovely mixture of concave and convex'.[14]

Jefferson's visit to Italy enabled him to apply an aesthetic that was wilder than and yet related to the English garden. He wrote to Maria Cosway of his Italian experience:

> You conclude, Madam, from my long silence that I am gone to the other world. Nothing else would have prevented my writing to you so long. I have not thought of you the less. But I took a peep only into Elysium. I entered it at one door, and came out at another, having seen, as I past, only Turin, Milan, and Genoa ... Why were you not with me? So many enchanting scenes which only wanted your pencil to consecrate them to fame. Whenever you go to Italy you must pass at the Col de Tende. You may go in your chariot in full trot from Nice to Turin, as if there were no mountain. But have your pallet and pencil ready: for you will be sure to stop in the passage, at the chateau de Saorgio. Imagine to yourself, madam, a castle and a village hanging to a cloud in front.

On one hand a mountain cloven through to let pass a gurgling stream; on the other a river, over which is thrown a magnificent bridge; the whole formed into a bason, its sides shagged with rocks, olive trees, vines, herds, &c. I insist on your painting it.   (1 July 1787; Boyd, XI, 519–520)

The jocularly loving opening is simply a prelude to an exercise in the Picturesque. Jefferson had praised Whately's exactness of description. Here, in a different context, he made his own attempt. The result is creditable. Jefferson uses natural phenomena to structure the scene, thus indicating their power. The view is divided between the mountain and the river, and set within a basin. Against the starkness of the setting, evidences of human occupation seem mere accretions. The castle and the village hang to a cloud, suggesting their transience; detritus obstructs the farms which hug the sides of the basin; and Jefferson employs a vivid adverb, 'shagged'.

Yet the scene is framed and intersected by the Grand Tour. Immediately before the presentation of the Gorge of Saorge (as it is now euphoniously called, for it is now in Southeast France), Jefferson places Maria Cosway in a fast-moving coach, ready to stop her headlong journey only to record such a scene. Her sketching is described in religious terms; it is a consecration. Suitably, Jefferson's own record breaks down – '&c' is hardly a term of Whateleian exactitude – to repeat her superior ability. The bridge links the two images of Maria painting, just as it links the road from Nice to Turin 'as if there were no mountain'. The forceful natural scene is contained within a graceful yet orderly architecture. This may be Elysium – and here Jefferson is returning to its Mediterranean source the term popularly applied to the New World – but to see it you enter at one door, and exit at another.[15]

Exemplifying his advice to American travellers, Jefferson used three guidebooks to help him see Italy.[16] They performed the same function as Whately in England and as the image of Maria Cosway painting at Saorge. In each case the text, verbal or visual, mediated between Jefferson and the terrain. It was in recording nature that he was particularly assisted by Europe. He eschewed European morals and politics but adored European art. 'Were I to proceed to tell you how much I enjoy their architecture, sculpture, painting, music, I should want words', he wrote to Bellini; 'It is in these arts that they shine' (Boyd, VIII, 569). This oxymoronic statement, coming from 'an American savage', indicates the force of his admiration, suitably by using the rhetoric of inexpressibility.

Jefferson's protest may be more than rhetoric. Given the depth of his attachment to the act of writing, there may be a frisson of fear in the face of the inexpressible, and a concomitant relief in the recovery. In my discussion of the letter to Priestley in the Prologue, I suggested that its descriptive strategies verged on breakdown. It seems, here, as if his fine description of the Gorge of Saorge would break down, but it is saved by the image of Maria Cosway the painter. On the tour of Germany a similar hesitation occurs, with a similar extrication. Of the gardens, climbing in terraces up the mountain behind the castle at Heidelberg, he says:

> The situation is romantic and pleasing beyond expression. It is on a great scale much like the situation of Petrarch's chateau at Vaucluse on a small one.[17]

The movement out of language is arrested here by the image of the great poet and the question of 'scale'.

Jefferson's European tour deepened his cultural debt to the Old World. When he wrote to Governor Rutledge with advice for his son's Grand Tour, Jefferson said that it would be so improving that the boy would 'return home charged, like a bee, with the honey gathered on it' (17 July 1788; Boyd, XIII, 375). With Jefferson the honey flowed over. He returned to America in 1789 with over fifty cases of luggage and eighty-six packing cases of books and furniture. European culture, moreover, made available to him a more sophisticated way of relating the text to the terrain, the library to the Blue Ridge Mountains. European painting was especially helpful to him because indigenous American painting was almost non-existent. American painters of talent like Benjamin West and John Singleton Copley made their careers in Europe. The New World was forced to recruit painters from Europe, and they spent their time painting portraits or family mansions. Engraving began to appear in American magazines in the later years of the eighteenth century, but it was not until well into the nineteenth that indigenous painters and engravers began to specialise in landscapes.[18]

Italian painters like Claude and Rosa, and the aesthetics constructed upon them, supplied what Americans did not. Jefferson was, of course, familiar with Burke's *Enquiry*; he recommended it to Skipwith in 1771. He rejected the more mystical, gothic elements of Burke's thought, but in his earlier years responded to the grandeurs of the Sublime. He may in general have found Kames' *Elements of Criticism* more congenial; it is included not only in Skipwith's list but in the later catalogue of his library (Sowerby, V, 41). Perhaps this was because Kames placed the Beautiful and the Sublime in an English garden. Gardening, said Kames:

> beside the emotions of beauty by means of regularity, order, proportion, colour and utility, can raise emotions of grandeur, of sweetness, of gaiety, melancholy, wildness, and even of surprise or wonder.

It was commonplace to relate gardening and painting, but Kames agreed with Whately who thought that gardening was 'superior to landskip painting, as a reality to a representation', a sentiment that would have had the approval of the pragmatic Jefferson.[19]

In Jefferson's library there were a number of the most important texts on painting. He owned Jonathan Richardson's *An Essay on the Theory of Painting* (1715), Walpole's *Aedes Walpoliana* (1752), and William Gilpin's *An Essay on Prints*, and listed them under 'Gardening – Painting – Sculpture' alongside Whately's *Observations on Modern Gardening*. Each of these books spoke of the differing virtues of the Italian painters.[20] In addition, Jefferson listed paintings that he wished to acquire, particularly after he discovered that copies or prints could be had quite cheaply. He owned a Poussin; his list of paintings of 1782 show his interest in Rosa; and he possessed paintings by Peale and Zoffany which clearly reveal Rosa's wild influence. In later years his drawing room, said his friend William Wirt, was 'hung thick' with paintings, an observation confirmed by lists left at his death.[21]

Jefferson was distinguished for the extent of his interest in painting, but other Virginians shared it, if to a lesser degree. George Washington, for instance, owned several landscape prints in the style of Claude, while William Carter took the Rosa cult to the extent of owning John Vanderlyn's sketch of Rosa's Roman Garden. As in England, the names of the Italian painters became signs invoking the Sublime and the Beautiful. When Chastellux and Timothy Dwight each visited the Catskills they called Rosa and Poussin to their aid, just as Jefferson had enlisted Maria Cosway at Saorge. Jefferson was more able in landscape description than Dwight or Chastellux and yet he shared their fatal disability. Faced with a terrain that taxed his ability with words, he would appeal to an ordering function, whether it was the code word of a painter's name or the concept of 'scale'. As William Wirt remarked with unconscious irony in praise of Jefferson's wide-ranging Monticello conversations:

> There seemed to be no longer any *terra incognita* of the human understanding: for, what the visitor had thought so, he now found reduced to a familiar garden walk.[22]

Jefferson's training in European aesthetics made his escape from *terra incognita* all the more sophisticated and assured, but it was an escape nevertheless, and in the next chapter we shall see it tragically consummated in the face of a terrain that was beyond those aesthetics. First, however, I will examine Jefferson's denial of the function of the imagination, and then trace that denial through three facets of his interest in American terrain: his *Notes on the State of Virginia*, the Land Ordinances, and his sponsorship of exploration.

THE HIDDEN COUNTRY

In his youth Jefferson wrote a little poetry. One poem that remains creates a landscape:

> Shores there are, bless'd shores for us remain,
> And favor'd isles with golden fruitage crown's [*sic*]
> Where tufted flow'rets paint the verdant plain,
> Where ev'ry breeze shall med'cine every wound.
> There the stern tyrant that embitters life,
> Shall vainly suppliant, spread his asking hand;
> There shall we view the billow's raging strife,
> Aid the kind breast, and waft his boat to land.[23]

Entitled 'Inscription for an African Slave', the poem is an early example of Jefferson's worries about the relation of liberty and slavery. (He was, of course, a slaveowner.) It is set in a landscape that is familiar: a Hesiodic blessed isle, a medical utopia that anticipates the opening stanzas of Freneau's 'Beauties of Santa Cruz'. The poem also anticipates the process of imagery seen in the 1786 letter to Maria Cosway and the 1801 letter to Joseph Priestley. The 'billow's raging strife' gives way to the calm of the 'favor'd isles'. The view, once again, is from above, with Jefferson as a godlike painter, touching in the detail of the island, pointing out the conflicts surrounding the tyrant and bringing him safely ashore. Suitably, the poem ends on the location of liberty and the object of Jefferson's interest, the land.

In the same year as that poem, Jefferson recommended the library to Skipwith. The list comprised 147 titles, divided into eight categories. By far the largest category was 'Fine Arts'. It contained some seventy-six titles including plays by Shakespeare, Dryden, Vanbrugh and Congreve; poetry by Chaucer, Milton, Pope, Thomson and Ossian; and novels by Smollett, Richardson and Sterne. In the accompanying letter Jefferson moralised about the uses of fiction:

> We never reflect whether the story we read be truth or fiction. If the painting be lively, and a tolerable picture of nature, we are thrown into a reverie, from which if we awaken it is the fault of the writer . . . We neither know nor care whether Lawrence Sterne really went to France, whether he was there accosted by the poor Franciscan, at first rebuked him unkindly, and then gave him a peace offering; or whether the whole be not a fiction. In either case we are equally sorrowful at the rebuke, and secretly resolve *we* will never do so . . . Considering history as a moral exercise, her lessons would be too infrequent if confined to real life . . . We are therefore wisely framed to be as warmly interested for a fictitious as for a real personage. The spacious field of imagination is thus laid open to our use, and lessons may be formed to illustrate and carry home to the mind every moral rule of life.   (Boyd, I, 77)

The defence of fiction is a commonplace of the time. The imagery indicates Jefferson's interests: he desires 'a tolerable picture of [human] nature' and sees imagination as an 'open' and 'spacious field' to provide lessons which then can be 'carried home'. Jefferson's pictorially imaginative landscape is broad and detailed, and clearly regarded as superior to the confinements of real life. It provides early evidence that he was not narrow and provincial. Unfortunately, it is a position that he would reject.

In Jefferson's later libraries the proportion of imaginative literature shrank drastically. Of the five volumes of Sowerby's *Catalogue* a mere 153 pages describe his entire collection of imaginative works. Poetry emerges relatively unscathed: Milton, Pope and Thomson are still represented. Freneau has been added. Shakespeare and Dryden, Vanbrugh and Congreve are still there. It is in fiction that his library has dwindled most. Of the fiction of Smollett and Richardson only *Roderick Random* remains. The rest, a heterogeneous collection under the pejorative classification 'Romance: Tales – Fables', now rubs shoulders with Chaucer, Dante, Ossian and a survivor, Sterne, in two editions. Brackenridge's *Modern Chivalry* and Brockden Brown's *Wieland* are among the few additions; the authors gave them to Jefferson. Drayton's 'tour' of England, *Poly-Olbion* is now classified safely under 'Didactic'. The Romantic poets, Wordsworth, Coleridge and Byron, are not represented. Jefferson didn't care for them (Sowerby, IV, 410–562).

Two letters confirm the constriction of Jefferson's 'spacious field of imagination'. The first, written in 1801, tells a clerical correspondent that he is unable to comment on the notion of transmigration of souls. 'When I was young I was fond of the speculations which seemed to promise some insight into that hidden country', he concluded, but he remained in ignorance. The second letter shows more precisely the area of Jefferson's imaginative contraction. In 1818 he wrote a letter on female education. Drawing, he suggests, is 'useful'. (Perhaps he remembered Maria Cosway and what he had learned from the Italian painters.) Reading fiction is harmful; it 'infects the mind' and 'reason and fact, plain and unadorned, are rejected'. The result is 'a bloated imagination'.

Jefferson's revised opinion accorded with the dicta of Scottish Common Sense Philosophy. Fiction-reading now leads not to a positive spatial expansion but rather to something that is indulgent, inflated, unnatural. Jefferson now constructed a more and more rigorous test for art. Its basis was Horace's *Utile dulce*, repeated in Hogarth's *Analysis of Beauty*. 'In nature's machines', said Hogarth, 'how wonderfully do we see beauty and use go hand in hand!' In an 1814 letter Jefferson followed the Horace–Hogarth dictum when he asserted 'that nature has constituted *utility* to man, the standard and test of virtue'. What he called 'the fancy', whether it was addressed by visible forms such as terrain, dress or architecture, or by imagery and metre in literature, was 'taste, a faculty entirely distinct from the moral one'.[24]

The disappearance of 'the hidden country' from Jefferson's thought is implicit in his *Notes on the State of Virginia*, which is now most remembered for its descriptions of the passage of the Potomac River through the Blue Ridge Mountains, and of the Natural Bridge. In his 'Dialogue of Head and Heart', sent to Maria Cosway between the publication of the French and the corrected English editions of the *Notes*, Jefferson had recommended the Potomac and the Natural Bridge along with the Niagara Falls as 'subjects worthy of immortality to render her pencil immortal' (Boyd, x, 447; the remark occurs just before the description of Monticello quoted near the beginning of this chapter). The description of the Potomac is too long and too well known to warrant full quotation here.[25] I will restrict myself, therefore, to the sentences which open and close the passage:

> The passage of the Patowmac through the Blue ridge is perhaps one of the most stupendous scenes in nature. You stand on a very high point of land. On your right comes up the Shenandoah, having ranged along the foot of the mountain an hundred miles to seek a vent. On your left approaches the Patowmac, in quest of a passage also. In the moment of their junction they rush together against the mountain, rend it asunder, and pass off to the sea.

Jefferson then writes of the scene hurrying 'our senses into the opinion' that during the Creation the mountains were formed before the rivers flowed, an opinion confirmed by the 'piles of rock on each hand'. He continues by contrasting a 'small catch of smooth blue horizon' in the distance to 'the riot and tumult roaring around'. It is this 'true contrast' between horizon and 'fore-ground' that allows a resolution. The calm of the skyline enables an escape from such natural violence:

> Here the eye ultimately composes itself; and that way too the road happens actually to lead. You cross the Patowmac above the junction, pass along its side through the base of the mountain for three miles, its terrible precipices hanging in fragments over you, and within about 20 miles reach Frederic town and the fine country around that. This scene is worth a voyage across the Atlantic. Yet here, as in the neighbourhood of the natural bridge, are people who have passed their lives within half a dozen miles, and have never been to survey these monuments of a war between rivers and mountains, which must have shaken the earth itself to its center.

The passage performs a number of functions. As the reference to the Atlantic indicates, it is intended for European consumption. Indeed, earlier in the Query Jefferson castigates European geographers for misnaming the mountains. The speculation about the formation of the terrain owes much to Burnet's *Theory of the Earth*. Jefferson owned a copy of the 1684 edition, the first in English.[26] Jefferson's friend Charles Thomson, Secretary of the Continental Congress, added the further suggestion that there may once have existed a lake whose banks were fractured by a 'convulsion'. Jefferson provided Thomson's remarks as an Appendix to the *Notes* (Peden, 197–199).

The major attribute of the passage – and this is why it is well-known – is its painterly quality; hence the references to the horizon and foreground. It is a sustained example of Picturesque description without any of the hesitations that marked Jefferson's attempts to write about Saorge and Heidelberg. Any misgivings have been overcome by careful control, first of all in the narrative presentation. The passage is set in the present tense and, with one exception, in the second person plural. The consequence is to place the reader in the scene with the narrator directing him. The directions are implicit for the majority of the passage, but they are clearly signalled by imperatives near the opening and close ('You stand . . . You cross') and by the sole shift into first person plural ('our senses'). The narrator situates the various elements of the scene ('On your right . . . On your left') for the reader in a way that is similar to the Saorge letter. (Indeed, in a more attenuated way, it anticipates 'Kindred Spirits', Asher Durand's 1849 painting of Thomas Cole and William Cullen Bryant in a similarly Picturesque Hudson River scene.) But where the Saorge letter hesitated, this description carries confidently on. The eye 'composes' itself – a verb deftly indicating both control and calm – optimistically on the horizon. It is moreover not a baseless optimism, for the road goes that way too. The narrator as controller is thus endorsed by a reference to the mark of organised society in which Jefferson was so interested. Further controls are inserted in the naming and placing of the town, and by the references to the indifferent population. A credulous European is recommended to make a special journey to view the scene; the locals prefer to continue the ordinary business of life.

Not simply in its painterly devices, but in its syntax, imagery (as in previously discussed examples, storm gives way to calm) and social setting, this passage controls a scene of great natural wildness and violence. Other writers believed that it was appropriate to feel oppressed when looking at similar scenes. Not Jefferson; he deliberately landscapes it into a social occasion. In the other well-known passage, on the Natural Bridge, he tames the terrain with similar methods. Once again, the passage need not be quoted in its entirety.[27] After two introductory sentences, which place the Bridge on a hill and assert its Sublimity, Jefferson provides a series of analyses. He measures the fissure that is capped by the Bridge; talks of the earth, trees and rocks; and suggests that 'the arch approaches the Semi-elliptical form'. After this exercise in surveying, geology and architecture Jefferson goes to the top and peeps into the abyss:

> Looking down from this height about a minute, gave me a violent head ach [*sic*]. If the view from the top be painful and intolerable, that from below is delightful in an equal extreme. It is impossible for the emotions arising from the sublime, to be felt beyond what they are here: so beautiful an arch, so light, and springing as it were up to heaven, the rapture of the spectator is really indescribable! The fissure continuing narrow, deep and streight for a considerable distance above and below the bridge, opens a short but very pleasing view of the North mountain on one side, and Blue Ridge on the other, at the distance each of them about five miles. This bridge is in the county of Rockbridge, to which it has given name, and affords a public and commodious passage over a valley, which cannot be crossed elsewhere for a considerable distance. The stream passing under it is called Cedar creek. It is a water of James river, and sufficient in the driest seasons to turn a grist-mill, though its fountain is not more than two miles above.

Garry Wills has provided an illuminating analysis of the whole passage, but omitted the final three sentences quoted above. Wills compared Jefferson's description with that of his friend le Chevalier de Chastellux, and concluded that both men had been influenced by Burnet and Burke. The major difference between the two descriptions was that, whereas Chastellux (as befits a travel journalist) provided a natural description first, following it with aesthetic reaction and scientific analysis, Jefferson bracketed natural description between science and aesthetics. Wills' analysis supports the discussion put forward here, and can be taken further. The final three sentences add other controlling mechanisms to those of science and art. Like the preceding passage on the Blue Ridge, they place a natural scene in a social context, partly by naming and partly by indicating the social uses of the terrain. The Natural Bridge is a short-cut; the stream beneath provides water-power.[28]

There are, at first sight, indications of fragility in the passage. Jefferson confesses to a headache, and at one point the passage appears to be on the verge of breakdown. But this is a false fragility. Garry Wills has shown that headaches were a common display of sensibility in such scenery.[29] Indeed, it may in part account for la Rochefoucault-Liancourt's unease at Monticello. Furthermore, it is the 'rapture of the spectator' rather than the scene itself, the psychological explanation of the European Sublime rather than the objective American terrain, that this time is 'indescribable'. Jefferson contains the scene with considerable elegance within his prose.

Indeed, he was feeling so much power at this point that, like William Gilpin, he rearranged the terrain to accord with his display of sensibility.

The mountain is not visible from the bottom of the fissure. Jefferson himself later realised this. In a manuscript note interleaved in his copy of the *Notes* and dated 16 August 1817 he apologised for 'an error of recollection'. The description was written, he said, several years after he had visited the Bridge. He now provided a correct description:

> This painful sensation is relieved by a short but pleasing view of the Blue ridge along the fissure downwards, and upwards by that of the Short hills, which, with the Purgatory mountain is a divergence from the North ridge; and, descending then to the valley below, the sensation becomes delightful in the extreme.

The original sentence of spectatorial emotion follows next, and then the revision continues:

> The fissure continues deep and narrow and, following the margin of the stream upwards about three eights of a mile you arrive at a limestone cavern, less remarkable, however, for height and extent than those before described. Its entrance into the hill is but a few feet above the bed of the stream. This bridge is in the county. . .   (Peden, 263–264, 25)

The 1817 revision makes the description accord with the terrain. Jefferson's sensations, however, remain unaltered. The indescribable rapture is still there, with a new landscape tailored around it. Indeed, Jefferson takes the opportunity to introduce extra controls over the terrain. It is plastered with more names, the second person plural is introduced, and further measurement and analysis is provided in a segment previously confined to aesthetic response. In addition, Jefferson asserted another textual control outside the leaves of his own book. The trip to the Natural Bridge that caused the revision to his copy of the *Notes* was undertaken in the company of l'Abbé Correa, the Portuguese botanist and geologist, and Francis Walker Gilmer, Jefferson's former law pupil and close friend. Jefferson persuaded Gilmer to describe the terrain from a purely scientific viewpoint. The consequent paper was read to the American Philosophical Society in 1816 and published in its *Transactions* two years later. Gracefully acknowledging Jefferson's influence, it nevertheless concentrates on geological description and a hypothesis about the origin of the phenomenon.[30]

Certainly, Jefferson responded to the Sublime; but his response was directed through a text. Before Jefferson and Chastellux visited the Natural Bridge they sat up overnight reading extracts from that counterfeit bard of the Sublime, Ossian. It was as if they needed to prepare themselves for the terrain by undergoing a nocturnal rite of passage with an appropriate text. Similar remarks could be made about the *Notes*. The descriptions of the Potomac and the Natural Bridge are not outcrops of Romanticism in the stony soil of Enlightenment

Rationalism, but rather carefully prepared and controlled landscape essays. As Robert Ferguson has shown, Jefferson took immense care over his own text. His formal models were legal and scientific. The *Notes* rearranges but otherwise follows closely the list of enquiries sent by François Barbé de Marbois, Secretary to the French Minister to the United States, even to the extent of a negative response to Query III (Peden, 17). Marbois' list itself follows, with a number of variations, Robert Boyle's 'General Heads for a Natural History of a Countrey'. Like Jedidiah Morse's geographies, then, Jefferson's *Notes* owes its formal structure to European models. It celebrates Virginia, and by extension America, but it does so in European terms.[31]

This is perhaps best illustrated by the figure of David Rittenhouse. In a passage attacking Buffon and Raynal, Jefferson presents Franklin and Rittenhouse as examples of scientists of world rank. Suitably, they would both precede Jefferson as presidents of the American Philosophical Society. Of Rittenhouse Jefferson remarked:

> We have supposed Mr. Rittenhouse second to no astronomer living; that in genius he must be the first, because he is self-taught. As an artist he has exhibited as great a proof of mechanical genius as the world has ever produced. He has not indeed made a world; but he has by imitation approached nearer its Maker than any man who has lived from the creation to this day. (Peden, 64)

With this reference to Rittenhouse's orrery, Jefferson signals his belief in design and order. The principal architects of a mechanistic universe were, of course, Newton and Locke. The revolution in perception (in optics and of objects) ushered in by Newton's 1687 *Principia* were supplemented by Locke's materialist philosophy. Newton, Locke and Bacon were the three Europeans that Jefferson admired most, the gods of his empiricist pantheon. Locke had said that 'in the beginning, all the world was America'.[32] Jefferson set out to prove empirically that America had matured to the extent that it could now equal and exceed the best that Europe could produce; hence his praise of Rittenhouse, and hence a text that is full of statistics about America.

The *Notes* starts, as Boyle had recommended, with a map and a series of boundary definitions. There follows a compendium of facts about the face of Virginia – its topography (of which the Potomac and the Natural Bridge are prominent parts), flora and fauna – and about its population and productions. In doing so Jefferson uses the binomial taxonomy of Linnaeus, listing Virginia's plants and birds both by their popular and Linnaean names. He attempts to refute Buffon in those comparative tables of European and American quadrupeds. He cannot refute Montesquieu, for he recognises that the combination of a warm climate and slavery has debilitated the Southern whites.[33] Jefferson, therefore, had produced a detailed cultural anthropology of his home state, which surpassed the accounts of their home states by his contemporaries Hugh Williamson, David Ramsay, Jeremy Belknap and Samuel Williams. But in doing so he produced a text that was, even more firmly than theirs, European in form, in content, and in aesthetics. Virginia had been rigorously ordered and presented for European inspection. It was appropriate that the first editions were published in Paris and London.

One aspect of the text's form remains to be noticed. The Queries start with scientific measurement (the boundaries), move through a description of the country (queries II–XII) to a discussion of the Constitution, laws and institutions (queries XIII–XXII), concluding with a list of 'Histories, Memorials, and State-Papers' (Query XXIII). Marbois' queries were reshuffled to give the text a tripartite structure, similar to that of the description of the Natural Bridge, but with institutional control replacing aesthetic response. The greatest relocation of Marbois' queries – his No. 4 becoming Jefferson's No. 23 – takes institutional control one step further, so that the text ends in a library, with a catalogue. It is as if that upper room in Monticello has expanded imperially to engulf the whole of Viriginia.

Since the text lists the contents of the library, it contains the library, and with it the whole of the state. This dilation stretches the text too far. It is marked by hesitations which, unlike those at Saorge and Heidelberg, go far beyond a rhetorical posture to reveal deepseated fears of its inadequacy. The 'Advertisement' for the London edition apologises for treating its subjects 'imperfectly' (Peden, 2). One particular imperfection was the description of the Natural Bridge. Another turned out to be the description of the Blue Ridge. When le Comte de Volney visited America he visited Jefferson and saw the Blue Ridge. In 1803 Volney published an account of America derived largely from his trip. (It was translated by Charles Brockden Brown, and will be discussed in chapter 7.) Jefferson possessed a copy and complained that Volney's description was incorrect. Yet the Virginian had to admit that 'the same scene may excite very different sensations in different spectators, according to their different sensibilities'.[34]

The hesitations over natural description became more marked with the references to the library and the text. Jefferson prefaced the library catalogue of Query XXIII with a particular apology: 'It is far from being either complete or correct.' A New York bookseller issued a more complete edition for all the states from 1792 to 1794 (Peden, 178–179, 296). But if the errors and omissions in the library could be repaired, those in the text could not. For some time Jefferson pondered a second edition of the *Notes*, but in 1814 abandoned the idea. He told an interested publisher that 'a new copy' of it 'was no more to be entertained'. He concluded:

> The work itself indeed is nothing more than the measure of a shadow, never stationary, but lengthening as the sun advances, and to be taken anew from hour to hour. It must remain, therefore, for some other hand to sketch its appearance at another epoch, to furnish another element for calculating the course and motion of this member of our federal system.[35]

The images here are enlightening. He sees Virginia as a terrestrial body in a planetary system. Unfortunately, his text is not an orrery. Indeed, the Notes' very title suggests the text's provisional nature. Jefferson's complaint recalls Jedidiah Morse's lament that his geographies could not keep pace with 'the ever changing state of the world', but is all the more vivid for the use of the natural image. The shadow moves; the text is condemned to stasis. What had worked in an English garden would not in an American state.

Jefferson's attempt at an imperial text had failed because it was too limited for his purpose – limited temporally because of the rapid social and political changes in America, and spatially by the boundaries of Virginia. At times, indeed, the text had broken through the boundaries. Jefferson was forced, for instance, to move outside Virginia to refute Buffon. He had confined his imaginative appreciation of wild terrain within a scientific and social framework, and then placed the framework within other constraints, rather like a nest of Chinese boxes. The whole construction was small, rigid and closed. He sought one that was large, extensible and open; and he found it in the grid. Unfortunately the grid, even more than the text, denied the function of the imagination and retreated from the American terrain.

THE FOCUS OF INNOVATION

There is little that is new about the grid. The Romans used the square *centuria*, or hundred (measuring about 2,340 feet per side) for surveying. The Dutch, too, had used the grid pattern in surveying reclaimable land.[36] America was like the Dutch polders writ large: a huge new land without any of the distinguishing marks of civilisation. Lewis Evans's aquatic metaphor anticipates Crèvecœur and appropriately describes the indiscriminate American terrain that almost defies the 'analysis' to his 1755 *General Map of the British Colonies in America*:

> Here are no Churches, Towers, Houses or peaked Mountains to be seen from afar, no means of obtaining the Bearings or Distances of Places, but from the Compass, and actual Mensuration with the Chain. The Mountains are almost all so many Ridges with even Tops, and nearly of a Height. To look from these Hills into the lower Lands, is but, as it were, into an Ocean of Woods, swelled and deprest here and there by little Inequalities, not to be distinguished, one part from another, any more than the waves of a real Ocean.

America seemed therefore to be all the more suited to the grid, and many of the colonial settlement plans used it. The grid appears in grants of colonies and townships, and in instructions to governors. In 1669 John Locke, then unofficial Secretary to the Carolina Company (of which his patron Shaftesbury was a leading proprietor), proposed that the land should be laid out in squares of 10,000 acres apiece, with progressive settlement preceded by survey in squares bounded by North–South, East–West lines. If America represented the world in its infancy, then the philosopher would try to ensure that it matured between rational lines. The Carolinian Surveyor-General did not agree. Good tracts of land did not occur in square shapes and settlers would not heed the orderly pattern. The same fate befell William Penn's plans for Pennsylvania. When he arrived in America in 1682 Penn laid out Philadelphia on the checkerboard pattern used by Sir Christopher Wren for London after the Great Fire of 1666. But what worked in a limited European urban area failed in the sprawling American wilderness. A similar scheme for the whole grant was outstripped by Penn's colonists. Lumberjacks, traders, land scouts and settlers preceded the tardy surveyors, and their tracks followed the Indian line of least resistance to the terrain.[37]

Nevertheless, the idea of the grid persisted. The immediate predecessor for Jefferson's plans was contained in the *Historical Account of Bouquet's Expedition Against the Ohio Indians*. The book proposed a system of forts and settlements in Indian country formed of squares of 640 acres. Following the Roman fighting square, it suggested that the rectangular form of settlement provided the best method of defence. As we saw in chapter 1, the Redcoats ignored to their cost the military advice the book contained. Jefferson, on the other hand, heeded a planning system paradoxically related to the thin red line so fatal to the British in America. Marcus Cunliffe has called the grid 'a geometry of expansion'.[38] It could also be called the impress of Redcoatism across the continent.

In 1784, before he went to France, Jefferson submitted to Congress two linked plans to deal with unoccupied western territory. The first derived in part from his 1776 draft Constitution for Virginia. Entitled 'A Plan of Government for the Western Territory', it divided an area stretching northward almost from the Gulf Coast to the Canadian border (latitudes 31° to 47°) and westward from a line of longitude drawn through the Great Kanawha River and the Falls of the Ohio (in what is now West Virginia) to another line of longitude drawn through the mouth of the Mississippi. This huge rectangle was then divided into fourteen smaller ones, which were the putative new territories of the Union. The Plan provided for democratic self-government of the territories, which would eventually become states with full membership rights in Congress. It also gave complex classically rooted names to those territories already ceded to the Federal Government; names such as Cherronesus and Metropotamia (now parts of Michigan, Indiana and Ohio), Assenisipia and Polypotamia (parts of Illinois, Indiana, Kentucky and Tennessee). Sensibly, Congress discarded the names, and the Plan became law on 23 April 1784.[39]

The second plan arose initially from the cession of some Virginian land to Congress on 1 March 1784. Jefferson was appointed to head a committee to dispose of the lands by means of a land office. The resultant proposal, 'An Ordinance establishing a Land Office for the United States', was submitted to Congress on 30 April 1784. The proposed Ordinance did not become law, but major parts of it survived in the first Federal land law, the 1785 Land Ordinance. The 1785 Ordinance provided for survey prior to sale, the survey being conducted by means of orientation to the cardinal points of the compass and rectilinear subdivision. Under the supervision of the Geographer of the United States, each territory would be divided into townships six miles square and numbered from south to north. The Ordinance made particular provision for detailed mapping of the territories:

> whereon shall be noted by the surveyor, at their proper distances, all mines, salt-springs, salt-licks and mill-seats, that shall come to his knowledge, and all water-courses, mountains and other remarkable and permanent things, over and near which such lines shall pass.

One section in each township was set aside for a public school.[40]

The 1784 Ordinance was superseded by the Northwest Ordinance of 1787. Although it owed its immediate origin to a group of land speculators and was not drafted by Jefferson (who was still in France), the Northwest Ordinance was based on Jefferson's work. It provided for the government of the territories and their eventual admission into the Union. Article 3, in ringing Jeffersonian phrases, insisted that:

> Religion, morality, and knowledge, being necessary to good government and the happiness of mankind, schools and the means of education shall forever be encouraged.

Article 5 furnished a grid for division of the territories. As a whole, the Ordinance set a precedent for their orderly rectilinear division and administration. It was the grid turned into Manifest Destiny. Together, the 1785 and 1787 Ordinances provided a matrix for western America.[41]

There are two major drawbacks to the grid. The first is that it assumes that the world is flat. Its parallels and meridians, based as they are on the Mercator system, provide a method of dividing the terrain that is correct only at the equator. The rectangles become less and less accurate as they approach the poles. The second drawback was more germane to the immediate settlement of the western territories. The grid makes no allowances for the idiosyncrasies of the terrain. The 1785 Ordinance provided for the mapping of natural objects, but the grid simply marched over them. They were items to be noted within the system rather than means of orientation. In Jefferson's 1784 Plan, one territory (No. 7, Saratoga) was completely bisected by the broad Ohio River, while another (No. 5, Metropotamia) was denied any access to Lake Michigan.

The Puritans tended to think in terms of enclosing frames, such as boundary walls. Their method of surveying, however, was pragmatic, operating by 'meets and bounds', the natural features of the terrain. Here is another paradox, for the grid was the Virginian's homage to the rigidities of Puritan thought without the benefit of pragmatic flexibility. It paid no attention to the natural features of the terrain, and gave rise to a number of objections. Timothy Pickering, who would later be disturbed about the Louisiana Purchase, pointed out the inaccuracy which would arise from the grid. A number of surveyors also raised their voices. One, Richard Spaight from North Carolina, asserted that the grid was 'formal and hitherto unheard of'. His second criticism was incorrect; but the first indicated in one word the vice-like grip that the grid placed on the terrain. Another surveyor, who was also President of the United States, remarked that:

> the lands are of so versitile a nature, that to the end of time they will not, by those who are acquainted therewith, be purchased either in Townships or by square miles.

Yet Washington had already been forced to admit that time was against the surveyor. After returning from a western trip, he wrote:

> The spirit of emigration is great, people have got impatient, and tho' you cannot stop the road, it is yet in your power to mark the way; a little while and you will not be able to do either.[42]

The benefits of the grid were that the lots could be easily mapped, transferred and exchanged. The 'meets and bounds' method required detailed description of the terrain. The grid method required simple description by cartographic lines and points, and an identifying number.

In view of the provenance of Jefferson's system, it was entirely appropriate that the supervisor of the base point and westward 'Geographer's Line' from which the American grid would begin, was Thomas Hutchins. Hutchins had already published 'Topographical Descriptions' of Virginia, Pennsylvania, Maryland, North Carolina and Louisiana, and may well have been responsible for proposing the rectangular form of settlement in the account of Bouquet's Expedition. Like Pickering, he was perfectly aware of the problems of using the grid as a method of survey, and told the President of Congress so. Nevertheless, he conducted the survey, cutting a swathe through America with a corps of axemen and four Commissioners, one of whom was David Rittenhouse, another appropriate choice. He marked a boundary between Pennsylvania and Virginia through the forests of the Alleghany Plateau by 'cutting a wide vista over all the principal hills . . . and by falling or deadening a line of trees'. The boundary was aligned by means of a 'Transit Instrument', a meridional device set up on successive ridge-tops and oriented at night by observations of the Pole Star. Existing trails were ignored.[43]

It is possible to see here a relationship with Philip Freneau's later poetry. Freneau rejected his fear of trackless wastes by pinning his faith on plans and systems. He celebrated the spade in 'The Great Western Canal' and the telescope in the Princeton 'Ode'. Both instruments placed order where all before was 'chaotic mess'. Here, it was the axe that was carving a pattern out of the wilderness, directed by another optical instrument. There was one vital difference. Freneau's celebration was after the event. Jefferson's initial report had given rise to an Ordinance that had in turn shaped a landscape. Jefferson's report and the Ordinance moved in two directions: onto the library shelf and out into the surrounding terrain. Whereas Jefferson's *Notes* was too rigid and small to encompass America, the proposal for the grid did it with ease.

Hutchins's base line pointed west, both literally and symbolically. Several of the men who worked for him laid out the rest of the Ohio country, and the remainder of the continent followed, territory by territory. The result has been called 'the greatest land-measurement project in world history', and its effect can be seen everywhere in America, in field layouts, city grids and road patterns, as well as on the political map of the country. The grid has also deeply influenced aspects of modern visual art. A line may be drawn from the ideal landscape of the Ordinances to that of Piet Mondrian. Mondrian's terrestrial distillations took him from the Dutch polders to Manhattan, where his grid-paintings achieved their natural locus and final form. Alfred Hitchcock's comedy thriller *North by Northwest* begins where Mondrian finishes. The grid, badly skewed, directs the title sequence and is then transformed into a Manhattan skyscraper. This is just the first of a series of transformations. The gridlines of roads, fields and crops become the alleys along which the hero runs for his life. The heads of the presidents sculpted into Mount Rushmore become the site of a slippery and dangerous ballet. The icons of terrestrial order are easily inverted.[44]

With good reason Thomas Hutchins, down in the woods, was still uncertain of the wisdom of the survey. He could see the sense of the grid for large divisions, but suggested that subdivisions should follow natural features like rivers.[45] From the comfortable distance of Paris, Jefferson could only see the benefits of the grid. When he read a copy of the 1785 Ordinance, he regarded it as an improvement on his Plan (Boyd, viii, 445). A number of his mathematical innovations failed to become law. Division by the hundred (100 square miles, the origin of the old English term) and measurement by the nautical mile (the length of a minute of latitude) had never been adopted. The grid, and the contemporaneous proposal for decimal coinage, had both been accepted. In a letter written after his Plan had been laid before Congress, Jefferson asserted that 'this is surely an age of innovation, and America the focus of it!' (Boyd, vii, 205–206). He had been dissatisfied with the *Notes*, but here, faced with such a successful expression of rationality, he could only express delight.

In Europe Jefferson rejected the French formal garden in favour of the English creation of a 'natural' terrain; yet in the grid he had created a continental example of French formality and confinement. Certainly, one could not imagine him applying a Hogarthian serpentine line to the American terrain – although it would have eventuated, say, in more interesting Nebraskan roads. He followed, instead, the practical Kames, who thought that whereas in a garden a straight walk was stiff and confining, outside the garden 'a straight road is the most agreeable, because it shortens the journey'. But the grid's imposition of Euclidean two-dimensional order was so all encompassing that it made Thomas Hutchins hesitate, and has since incurred the wrath of ecologists. One, indeed, regards it as an early landmark in the history of topophobia, a method of organising perception that ignores the land.[46] The French formal garden, furthermore, is intended to be a spectacle of spatial harmony and order, predicated on simplicity and symmetry. It is meant to be viewed as a unity, from a height. These virtues would certainly have appealed to Jefferson and, ever since the building of Monticello, he was used to heights. (An English garden, in contrast, is meant to be viewed from Hutchins's level.) But the height from which Jefferson would have had to imagine the American grid was so great (far greater than Monticello) as to render the land itself faceless, a mere floor over which would be laid a cross-hatched carpet. America, in a word, would be invisible; and that invisibility was made all the greater when Congress removed Jefferson's clumsy if vivid names from the new territories.

THE DICTIONARY IN THE GARDEN

There is nothing to suggest that Jefferson was aware of the problem of invisibility; and yet, at the time that he became interested in the grid, he also took steps to obtain more detailed descriptions of the terrain. Jefferson became a sponsor of exploration, and it was this that pulled him back down to the height of Monticello. It would also, perhaps, place some figures on the carpet. Unfortunately, Jefferson's first four attempts at sponsorship proved inauspicious. The first, a proposal to seek the Northwest Passage, was declined by George Rogers Clark. The second was undertaken by John Ledyard, a year older than Clark but much less famous.

The story of John Ledyard provides both a lunatic by-way in the usually serious history of exploration, and a striking contrast to Jefferson's fifth, successful sponsorship. When he was in Paris, Jefferson was approached by Ledyard with a project for exploring the West. Ledyard's credentials seemed sound. He had been a member of James Cook's third voyage, and when in 1783 he had returned to his home state of Connecticut he had published an account of it. Jefferson had a copy of the book in his library (Sowerby, III, 148). Ledyard wrote of the contiguity of the Asian and American continents, although he doubted the existence of a Northwest Passage. When he presented himself to Jefferson it was therefore as an expert. Yet with hindsight his project appears frivolous. He proposed to explore America in the reverse direction, walking from Paris to the Bering Strait through Russia and Siberia, catching a boat across the Strait, and then concluding his eastward journey across America. Freneau's 'fancy' had failed at California; Ledyard would resolutely walk on to the east coast. His equipment consisted of two dogs, a hatchet, and an Indian pipe. The dogs would serve as companions and hunters; the hatchet would be useful as an all-purpose tool; and the pipe would proclaim his peaceful intentions. He had no money, and believed that he needed none. He would rely on the hospitality of his hosts; and in this way, as he wrote to Jefferson, he would 'be kicked round the world'.[47]

Jefferson thought that Ledyard had 'ingenuity and information [but] too much imagination'. Despite his reservations, however, he gave the explorer his blessing and a passport. Unfortunately, neither cut any ice with the Empress of Russia. Ledyard got as far as Irkutsk, some 2,600 miles east of Moscow. His rambling journal includes some astute ethnographical speculations, and some remarks on furs and fossils. At Irkutsk he was arrested, kicked back across Siberia, and released at the Polish border. He died exploring the Nile in 1789, and in his death captured the popular attention which had eluded him in life.[48]

The next two attempts would be much less imaginative, much more scientific. In 1792, Jefferson and some other members of the American Philosophical Society tried to raise money to send the Philadelphia botanist Moses Marshall up the Missouri. The next year a similar consortium instructed the French botanist André Michaux 'to find the shortest & most convenient route of communication between the U.S. &

the Pacific Ocean'. He was also asked to make notes of the face of the country through which he travelled. Both proposed expeditions failed, the latter because Michaux (like George Rogers Clark) became involved with Citizen Genêt.[49]

Ten years elapsed before the fifth expedition sponsored by Jefferson. It would be led by Meriwether Lewis, who moved from a career as an army paymaster and recruiting officer to become Jefferson's secretary shortly after Jefferson's election to the Presidency. It appears that Jefferson particularly requested Lewis's services to help in reshaping and reducing the US Army.[50] Lewis lived as a member of Jefferson's household from 1 April 1801 until 20 June 1803, when he took command of the expedition to cross the continent to the Pacific. Jefferson's prior knowledge of Lewis was slight. The two men were distantly related and were neighbours in Virginia, but the President's only previous contact with Lewis was when Jefferson had been contemplating yet another western expedition. Lewis heard about it and volunteered. Jefferson turned him down; not surprisingly, since Lewis was just eighteen at the time. Now, in 1803, he seemed to be the right choice to lead the expedition.

Unlike the Ledyard expedition, this one would be a model of careful preparation. 'Imagination' would be kept to a minimum. All the resources that Jefferson could muster were placed at its service. In addition to a vast array of food, arms, clothing, and presents for the Indians, the expedition carried instruments for measuring and observation, vaccine to inoculate the Indians against smallpox, a model vocabulary for collecting and comparing Indian languages, the first friction matches (specially invented for them), and an airgun. The gun, a recent innovation powered by a canister of compressed air, had a phenomenal range and accuracy, far better than the ordinary rifles of the day. It was taken to impress the Indians, and was highly successful.[51] The expedition, then, represented the last word in scientific modernity. All the latest knowledge in weaponry, navigation, astronomy, medicine, botany and biology was lavished on it. Its philosophy so infected Lewis that he invented a collapsible boat, constructed out of iron rods and intended to be covered with hides. He wrote a long letter to Jefferson about it, specifying its size, weight and capabilities. He called it 'The Experiment' (Jackson, 1, 39–40). Its fate will be mentioned in the next chapter.

Jefferson appointed as co-commander of the expedition William Clark, the younger brother of George Rogers Clark. Clark was also a soldier, but with much greater frontier experience than Lewis. Clark had taken part in various military patrols between 1789 and 1795, and had kept journals of them. He had experienced combat, had dealt with the Spanish who still occupied parts of Louisiana, and was a superb cartographer. He was also a close friend of Lewis, and an ideal confederate. They jointly commanded a party of three sergeants and twenty-eight other ranks, together with a support group of sixteen that would accompany them as far as Fort Mandan, where the Missouri bends westwards in what is now North Dakota. There could not have been a starker contrast to Ledyard's hatchet, Indian pipe, and two dogs.

Lewis was, in Jefferson's words, 'not regularly educated', but he possessed 'a great mass of accurate observation on all the subjects of nature'. So the President sent him to the University of Pennsylvania, at that time the best centre for the natural sciences, to achieve some regularity. Lewis met Benjamin Smith Barton, the naturalist; Caspar Wistar, Professor of anatomy; and Benjamin Rush. In addition, for the twenty-seven months that he was Jefferson's secretary, Lewis had access to his library. The library was particularly strong in texts on America. When he went to Europe, Jefferson took great pains to amass geographies and travellers' accounts of his country. Jefferson possessed the works, amongst others, of Per Kalm, William Smith, Thomas Hutchins, James Cook, John Ledyard, Jonathan Carver, Alexander Mackenzie, Chastellux and la Rochefoucault-Liancourt.[52]

The books in Jefferson's library presented the most complete picture of the western parts of America available at the time, and as new material arrived Jefferson took care to pass it on to Lewis. Some books, indeed, were so important that Lewis and Clark carried them on the expedition. One was by a French engineer, Antoine Le Page du Pratz, who had been in Louisiana from 1718 to 1734. During that time he had travelled up the Lower Mississippi and supervised a French post among the Natchez Indians. He listened to their tales, and from these and his own limited experience he wrote *The History of Louisiana*. It was first published in French in 1758. British interest in Louisiana caused by the Treaty of Paris prompted English editions in 1763 and 1774. Another edition appeared in 1804, by which time the book had become one of the standard texts on western America. Jefferson had a copy of the 1763 edition, and Lewis borrowed the 1774 edition from Benjamin Smith Barton, returning it to him at the conclusion of the expedition.[53]

There were three reasons why *The History of Louisiana* was so important to Jefferson and Lewis. The first was that, in a chapter on the Indians, it included an account by one of them, Moncacht-Apé, of a journey towards the Pacific:

> We continued our journey along the Missouri for nine days, and then we marched directly northwards for five days more, when we came to the Fine River, which runs westwards in a direction contrary to that of the Missouri... I again embarked on the Fine River... till I arrived at the nation that is but one day's journey from the Great Water on the west.

The previous chapter discussed the attempts to discover the Northwest Passage. The Indians, ever ready to please when not to scalp, happily told travellers of an easy route across the Rockies. As early as 1623 George Sandys wrote home to England that 'a general report of the Indians' confirmed that the mountains were 'not past four days iourny above the falls, they two days over, & rivers on the other sid [side] there into [the Pacific] of no great length'. There seemed to be too much evidence not to believe in a short portage to the Pacific. Jefferson did; and he told Congress so in his proposal for the expedition in January 1803.[54] So did Lewis — for this is why he built the collapsible boat.

Secondly, Le Page du Pratz's *History* supported the belief that the Rockies consisted of a single mountain-range running from north to south. Du Pratz's remarks accorded with the concept of geographical symmetry which we have already seen informing the work of Jedidiah Morse and Philip Freneau. It was commonly known that parallel ranges of mountains ran down each coastline. Jefferson and Lewis both lived in the range that ran down the east coast. It is therefore understandable that they imagined the Rockies in terms of the Blue Ridge Mountains of Virginia, a series of beautiful rolling wooded hills. Indeed, the de Fonte manuscript which Benjamin Franklin had championed had described the Rockies in terms exactly like the Blue Ridge. Perhaps the hoaxer was a Virginian.[55]

The third reason for the importance, and indeed the popularity, of du Pratz's *History* is best illustrated by another quotation, this time apparently from the Frenchman's own observation:

> we travelled over a charming country, which might justly furnish our painters of the finest imagination with genuine notions of landskips. Mine, I own, was highly delighted with the sight of fine plains, diversified with very extensive and highly delightful meadows. The plains were intermixed with thickets, planted by the hand of Nature herself; and interspersed with hills, runing off in gentle declivities, and with valleys, thick set, and adorned with woods, which serve for a retreat to the most timorous animals, as the thickets screen the buffaloes from the abundant dews of the country.

> I longed much to kill a buffalo with my own hand; I therefore told my people my intention to kill one of the first herd we should meet; nor did a day pass, in which we did not see several herds; the least of which exceeded a hundred and thirty or a hundred and fifty in number.[56]

The imagery is of course the familiar one of America as the Garden. The first sentence signals that those following will provide a painterly landscape. The terms employed emphasise calmness, order, beauty and fertility. They also emphasise the importance of the observer, who is shaping everything he sees. We have here a landscape such as would be painted by Claude and Poussin; but their use of 'imagination' would here be hardly necessary, for this land, like Drayton's Virginia, really exists – witness the precise numbers of buffalo which lend an air of factuality to the scene. The vision of western America is therefore conveyed in terms that would be both aesthetically familiar and factually convincing to Jefferson. It is a vision, moreover, that interlocks convincingly with the supposed facts provided by Moncacht-Apé, for the vision of the Garden related to the theory of geographical symmetry, which in turn related to the belief in the short portage.

Lewis and Clark carried other books with them: books on astronomical observation, tables for finding longitude and latitude, and a book on minerology. They took two botanical texts, one by Benjamin Smith Barton, the other an explication of the Linnaean system. They also took a dictionary, possibly a four-volume compendium with the following portentous title:

> *A New and Complete Dictionary of Arts and Science, comprehending all the branches of useful knowledge, with accurate descriptions as well of the various machines, instruments, tools, figures and schemes necessary for illustrating them, as of the classes, kinds, preparations, and uses of natural productions, whether animals, vegetables, minerals, fossils, or fluids.* (London, 1753; 2nd edn. 1764)

Classes, kinds, preparations and uses of natural productions; the calm phrases of the dictionary title almost mask its intent. The dictionary was concerned with classifying first and identifying usage last. In doing so it reversed the priorities of the medieval textbook, which was concerned with medicinal or magical characteristics, and hardly at all with classification. The dictionary was of course the child of the Enlightenment; it aimed at organising the world within a text. Linnaean classification, seeing the world from a botanical garden, was just one element of the encyclopaedist programme.[57]

When William Kent leaped the fence he eroded the distinction between the garden and the natural terrain. Jefferson's excursion beyond his own garden, to be conducted through his amanuensis, seemed in contrast bent on applying formal patterns to western America. It was the grid over again. It was also more than that. In the first place it was, in this instance literally, a distension of the imperial library. Lewis's training in that Monticello room and at the University of Pennsylvania was being exported in the form of books that would be carried into the unknown. His expertise would enable him to apply the text to the terrain and, through its medium, landscape the terrain so that it accorded with accepted knowledge. Before Jefferson sent Lewis to Caspar Wistar, he wrote a letter to Penn's Professor of Anatomy which indicated his intentions. Lewis's 'great mass of accurate observation' was such:

that he will readily seize whatever is new in the country he passes thro, and give us accounts of new things only: and he has qualified himself for fixing the longitude and latitude of the different points in the line he will go over. I have thought it would be useful to confine his attention to those objects only on which information is most deficient and most desireable: and therefore would thank you to make a note on paper of those which occur to you as most desireable for him to attend to.[58]

There is a deep if unconscious irony in the letter. On the one hand, it is another example of Jefferson's constant search for novelty. On 4 April 1787, for instance, Jefferson had written to Chastellux that his journey to Paris had been 'a continued feast of new objects, and new ideas' (Boyd, XI, 261). Perhaps he imagined that Lewis's progress would provide a similarly leisurely repast. On the other hand, the verbs in the letter to Wistar move in the opposite direction, towards constriction rather than expansion. Lewis is already qualified to 'fix' the terrain, a usage Noah Webster would have approved; Wistar's assistance will further 'confine' his attention to it. Thus equipped, Lewis will 'readily seize' what is new as he pursues his 'line' across the terrain. These are words which savour of imperialism and the grid. In terms of the polarity suggested in the Prologue, Jefferson wanted Lewis to be a Columbus, not a Vespucci.

Secondly, as the letter to Wistar indicates, the Lewis and Clark Expedition would improve on the grid, because it would provide all the detail that the grid lacked. It would fill in the figures in the carpet. Jefferson attached paramount importance to the records of the Expedition. In addition to supervising Lewis's training, he issued detailed instructions to control the activities of the Expedition. The instructions were modelled on James Mackay's directive to John Evans for his journey to the Pacific, and on two of Jefferson's documents: the 1784 draft for the Land Ordinance, and his directive to André Michaux.[59] In a formal memoir some 2,200 words long, Jefferson instructed Lewis to seek the short portage across the Rockies. Beginning at the mouth of the Missouri, Lewis was to 'fix by observation [align with the compass] such natural marks and characters of a durable kind'. Jefferson then laid particular stress on the process of recording:

> Your observations are to be taken with great pains and accuracy, to be entered distinctly & intelligibly for others as well as yourself, to comprehend all the elements necessary, with the aid of the usual tables, to fix the latitude and longitude of the places at which they were taken, and are to be rendered to the war-office, for the purpose of having the calculations made concurrently by proper persons within the U.S. Several copies of these as well as your other notes should be made at leisure times, & put into the care of the most trust-worthy of your attendants, to guard, by multiplying them, against the accidental losses to which they will be exposed. A further guard would be that

one of these copies be on the paper of the birch, as less liable to injury from
damp than common paper.

There followed a list of the phenomena to be recorded: the climate, the
face of the country, its flora and fauna, and the Indians. The memoir gave
instructions on the favourable treatment of the Indians. It suggested that
Indians or traders be employed to send back to Jefferson 'at seasonable
intervals, a copy of your journal, notes and observations, of every kind'.
On arrival at the Pacific Lewis was to obtain information about the fur
trade and 'send two of your trusty people back by sea . . . with a copy of
your notes'. The remainder of the party should also return later by sea, if
a ship was available, or return by land, making further observations.
Open letters of credit were provided to discharge all expenses.[60]

The memoir indicates Jefferson's intense concern over the maintenance and care of records. Lewis was instructed to prepare throughout
the Expedition a full and accurate account of the terrain, and to call on the
assistance of his party to do so. He and Clark were *required* to keep
journals, and the other ranks were *requested* to do so if they could write.
The memoir recalls Jefferson's distress over the Shadwell loss, and
anticipates the grieving letter to his granddaughter. It attempts to
provide a framework on which Lewis would erect a structure more
extensive and more complete than the *Notes on the State of Virginia*.
Jefferson was asking Lewis to do in reverse what he had done with
Whateley's *Observations* in an English garden. The memoir, together
with the books the Expedition would carry, would transfer the text onto
the terrain, and the terrain would be transferred back again into the text
by the journals – for Jefferson intended to have them published. If Lewis
heeded the injunctions of the memoir and the books, the consonance
between text and terrain would be perfect. Lewis, with Jefferson behind
him, would have charted 'the spacious field', and without being seduced
from the truth by a 'fine imagination'. The next chapter will show what
actually happened.

6

The Lewis and Clark Expedition

And I saw a new heaven and a new earth: for the first heaven and the first earth are passed away . . . And he that sitteth on the throne said, Behold, I make all things new. And he saith, Write: for these words are faithful and true.

(Revelations 21: 1, 5)

WRITING THE WEST

After a winter of preparation, the Lewis and Clark Expedition left St Louis on 14 May 1804, helped by 'a jintle brease' and the cheers of the populace on the banks, and secure in the general knowledge of what lay ahead of them.[1] That knowledge included the popular ideology of the West sketched in chapter 4; a West which was not only vast but uniformly fertile, inhabited by Indians of Asian or Welsh origin, and by huge and venerable quadrupeds. It awaited the transforming power of the American farmer. Jefferson endorsed the popular view. In his first Inaugural Address he had deftly attempted to salve the wounds of his opponents by reminding them that all Americans, of whatever political persuasion, possessed 'a chosen country, with room enough for our descendants to the thousandth and thousandth generation . . .'[2] By great political dexterity, Jefferson had now doubled the chosen country. It would contain the mammoth and unknown Indian tribes – hence the model vocabulary that the Expedition carried.

Of course, Lewis and Clark shared the Jeffersonian view of the West, and attached great importance to the Expedition. At one point Lewis explicitly compared it to the expeditions of Columbus and Captain Cook (Codex D, p.5; Thwaites, I, 284). Indeed, his sense of identification with Columbus was so strong that, on his first foray into undiscovered territory, he believed he had heard a nightingale. Although the nightingale is not native to America, Columbus fulfilled his desires by hearing them there. The bird has a special place in western cultural history. Ever since Lucian populated his Elysian Fields with nightingales, they have provided the plaintive anthems of the pastoral spirit, celebrated by poets as various as Anne Bradstreet and John Keats. Le Page du Pratz perpetuated the myth of their presence in America by

supposedly hearing one in Louisiana. Oliver Goldsmith had denied that
any bird could sing in the woods of the New World. Jefferson, in
contrast, had listened to the nightingale on the Seine and the Languedoc
Canal, and had asserted that America would improve its song. Now,
Lewis believed that his mentor would not have to go to the trouble of
importing it. Three weeks after leaving St Louis, Lewis named
Nightingale Creek after 'a Bird of that discription which sang for us all
last night, and is the first of the Kind I ever heard'.[3]

It is perhaps cavalier to compare Lewis to Columbus on the basis of
misheard birdsong. It indicates, however, how deeply conscious he was
of the significance of the Expedition. Lewis and Clark were far from
cavalier about their duties, particularly with regard to their journals.
They wrote field notes wherever and whenever they could, transferring
them to and developing them in a notebook journal which was carefully
sealed in a tin when complete. At times the Expedition was halted so that
journal entries could be made. As one of the sergeants remarked on one
occasion, 'Continued Hear as the Capts is not Don there Riting'
(Thwaites, VII, 21). In addition to the two 'Capts', seven other members
of the Expedition kept journals. Three of the nine journals have been lost.
One lasts just five months; its writer, Sergeant Floyd, died from
appendicitis, the only casualty amongst members of the Expedition. The
other five, with one important exception which will be discussed later,
covered the whole period of the Expedition. The amount of material is
considerable. It occupies some 5,000 pages of printed text, a tribute to the
explorers' assiduity in carrying out Jefferson's injunction.

In the early stages of the Expedition it is clear that the two leaders were
also taking care to develop a proper format for their journals. Lewis had
many examples available to him, in Jefferson's library and elsewhere.
Travel narratives were particularly popular in the eighteenth and
nineteenth centuries and publishers gladly supplied the market, to the
extent that one American reviewer was driven to complain that almost
anybody who:

> happens once in his life to wander from the precincts of his own native village,
> thinks it his duty to enlighten the publick with a narrative of his adventures.

As the market became deluged by the dilettante, men of science insisted
more and more on a rigorous record of objective detail. The model
provided by Boyle's 'General Heads for a Natural History of a
Countrey', already discussed, was supplemented by Count Leopold
Berchtold's *Essay to Direct and Extend the Inquiries of Patriotic Travellers*
(1789). Berchtold provided classifications under which information
should be categorised, and insisted that descriptions should be committed
to paper on the spot to ensure accuracy.[4]

There were two major formats available to Lewis and Clark, the sequential and the topical. Sequential form was generally regarded as essential to the travel account; but this did not always enable a scientific approach, for scientific hypotheses are rarely compatible with the repetitively quotidian nature of the journal. Lewis and Clark therefore developed a form which maintained a daily narrative whilst inserting descriptions and speculations at appropriate points, often as reflections at the end of the day. In doing so they had a number of models. The first was the *Historical Account of Bouquet's Expedition*, discussed in chapter 1. The body of that text was set in simple diary form, giving precise details of the distances covered, with references to particular features of the terrain traversed. Thomas Hutchins, who had been involved in the publication of the *Historical Account*, had himself written a journal in this form during an earlier expedition, and would develop it in later books. Andrew Ellicott, too, had written in this format.

A somewhat different model was provided by Jonathan Carver's *Travels*, the most popular publication of the time by an American explorer. It contains lengthy descriptions and even Indian speeches (rendered verbatim) inserted into the journal. Yet a third model was supplied by Alexander Mackenzie's *Voyages from Montreal*, with a lengthy topical essay preceding a journal similar in form to that of *Bouquet's Expedition*. Ironically, both Carver's and Mackenzie's texts were developed for publication in London, the latter ghostwritten by William Combe from a debtor's prison. To compound the irony, Combe would later become famous for Doctor Syntax, his parodies of William Gilpin's Picturesque travelling. *Bouquet's Expedition*, and the texts by Hutchins, Ellicott, Carver and 'Mackenzie' were available in Jefferson's library, giving Lewis and Clark practical guidance in carrying out the President's instructions.[5]

Doubtless the most important model was provided by Clark himself. In his journals of his army expeditions between 1789 and 1795 Clark had ample opportunity to develop a brief yet detailed method of recording the topography. A typical example is from his journal of General Charles Scott's expedition, written on 27 May 1791:

> Marched 22 Miles to day and crossed a fork of White River Seventy yards wide Beautifull flat gravelly Bottom, the land generally very rich and level Interupted by very bad Swamps and Ponds. Intervales of High Rich level land fine streams, richly timbered, Flat excellent Meadow lands on all those streams, Much Wind and Hard rain this afternoon.[6]

A linear narrative runs the risk of too great an emphasis on autobiography; it tends to construct a drama out of the daily life of the journalist. In contrast, the topical approach flattens the personality of the journalist in favour of an objective account of the environment. This can be seen happening in this example of Clark's writing. His linear narrative is a mere framework into which is packed a topographical account. The suppression of personality even extends to the omission of the subject in the first sentence. Clark is attempting to push his writing as close as possible to the face of the country.

When Lewis left Pittsburgh on 30 August 1803 to travel down the Ohio River towards St Louis and the final preparations for the Expedition, he immediately adopted Clark's method of journalising. The entry for the third day provides a good example:

> Septr 2ed Set out at sunrise 2 miles 1/2 to a riffle got out and pulled the boat over it with some difficulty – 9 Oclock reched Logtown riffle unloaded and with much difficulty got over detain[ed] 4 hours. The hills on either side of the ohio are from 3 to 400 feet which runing parallel to each other keep the general course of the river, at the distance of about two miles while the river pursuing a serpentine course between them alternately washes their bases. – thus leaving fine bottom land between itself and the hills in large boddys, and freequently in the form of simecicles or the larger segment of a circle or horseshoe form. The weather is extreemly dry but there was some appearance of rain this morning which seems now to have blown over.[7]

The general format is the same as Clark's, down to the suppression of the subject, but Lewis demonstrates his greater education. His syntax is more complex, and whereas Clark tends to confine himself to direct description, Lewis uses terms derived from geometry (parallel, 'simecicle', segment) and painting (serpentine, washes). Jefferson's training made a strong impact.

Lewis continued this particular form of journalising until he left the Ohio River and started to ascend the Mississippi on 20 November. At this point, as he moved into a terrain less familiar to travellers, he appended to each journal entry a table comprising the course, the time taken, estimated distances and brief 'references' to the nature and quality of the terrain. The narrative section often included sextant readings and even sketches of the shapes of islands and sand bars. When Clark temporarily assumed command of the Expedition at Louisville he continued the journal in precisely the same format. This format was adopted by both commanders when the party left St Louis the next spring. There was just one slight alteration. On completing his second notebook, Clark wrote on the inside rear cover: 'after this I will put the Course Destance & refferences of each day first and remks after' (Thwaites, I, 139).

Lewis and Clark, then, placed the greatest importance on their journals and took immense care to evolve a form which would accurately reflect the terrain. They intended not only to traverse the undiscovered country to the Pacific, but to provide a model account of it for their philosopher-President. They planned to spend the winter of 1804–1805 at Fort Mandan. The following spring they would travel to the Pacific, leaving the support group to return to St Louis. They intended to return to Mandan by the winter of 1805–1806, or sail to the United States by one of the vessels that called on the Pacific Coast.

A LAND OF PLENTY

As the Expedition travelled up the Missouri in the spring and summer of 1804 the terrain provided ample evidence that Louisiana was a Garden. The journalists talked of 'delightfull' prospects, beautiful plains and fine grassland abounding with game and fruit of every description. They saw elk, rabbit, antelope, geese, birds, 'butifull' goats, 'very gentle' deer and huge herds of buffalo. They found plum orchards and 'an amence Site of Grapes' (Thwaites, 1, 38, 150, 158; Quaife, 96, 124). The land seemed also to be a medical utopia, of the kind that Benjamin Rush had failed to engineer in the East. The air was 'pure and helthy' and Clark noted that:

> It is worthey of observation to mention that our Party has been much healthier on the Voyage than parties of the same number is in any other Situation.
>
> (Thwaites, 1, 99, 85–86)

This was, moreover, the abode of the mammoth and of an ancient civilisation. On the top of a bluff they found the petrified backbone of a fish forty-five feet long. Clark spent some time measuring, drawing and describing 'antient fortifications'; and noted that, according to the French interpreters, 'a great number of those antient works are in Defferent parts of the Countrey' (Thwaites, 1, 135–137, 193). Their beliefs were so deeply rooted that, in very different circumstances, they thought they had proved another myth of the West. As Sergeant Whitehouse remarked:

> we take these Savages to be the Welch Indians if their be any Such from the Language.

They were the Flatheads. Henry Marie Brackenridge, the son of the lawyer–novelist and in 1811 one of the first educated men to follow Lewis and Clark up the Missouri, roundly asserted that Welsh Indians did not exist. Yet he added that there was much evidence of an ancient civilisation.[8]

Suitably, the images of the Garden reached a peak on the twenty-eighth anniversary of the founding of the Republic. After a day spent traversing extensive prairies and a clear lake containing 'great quantities of fish and Gees & Goslings' they camped (wrote Sergeant Ordway) in:

> one of the most beautiful places I ever saw in my life, open and beautifully Diversified with hills and vallies all presenting themselves to the River.

They named the creek in which they camped 'Creek Independence'. The connection between the Republic and Jefferson's 'chosen country' could not have been clearer (Thwaites, I, 66–67; Quaife, 92).

The republican Garden easily assimilated any adversities. Relations with the Indians were sometimes unhappy; the treacherous current and soft banks of the Missouri caused trouble; snakes and mosquitoes were aggravating. But almost all problems were absorbed, even the death of Sergeant Floyd, apparently from appendicitis:

> We Set out under a gentle breeze from the S.E. and proceeded on verry well – Serjeant Floyd as bad as he can be no pulse & nothing will Stay a moment on his Stomach or bowels – Passed two Islands on the S.S. and at the first Bluff on the S.S. Serjt. Floyd Died with a great deal of Composure, before his death he Said to me, 'I am Going away' I want you to write' me a letter' – We buried him on the top of the bluff 1/2 Mile below a Small river to which we Gave his name . . . after paying all the honor to our Decesed brother we Camped in the Mouth of *floyds* river about 30 yards wide, a butifull evening.
>
> (Codex B, p. 13; Thwaites, I, 114–115)

Clark's journal entry indicates that Floyd's death is not only contained within the images of the Garden but also within the processes of measurement and naming practised by Jefferson in his description of the Natural Bridge and conveyed to the two leaders in his Memoir. This is a natural Garden, but it is being controlled by a text.

There was one slight but significant exception. Private George Shannon lost his way while exercising the horses. He exhausted his food and ammunition, and lived for twelve days on grapes and a rabbit he killed by using a piece of hard wood as a bullet. He rediscovered the Expedition after an absence of sixteen days, causing Clark to reflect on the importance of American technology, even in the Garden:

> thus a man had like to have Starved in a land of plenty for the want of Bullitts or Something to kill his meat.   (Thwaites, I, 145)

Fields of grapes are pleasant to see and sample, but provide poor sustenance. The episode of the erring Shannon was potentially more threatening to the Expedition because it showed the inadequacy of *any* preparation. It forced Clark to moralise. In contrast, the techniques available to Clark allowed him to describe the death of Floyd with dignity, but without any sense of danger. Other potential threats were handled in a similar fashion. Some Indians pointed out a hill that they shunned because it was inhabited by 'Deavels . . . in human form with remarkable large heads' whose arrows could kill at long distance. So (as one critic has noted) the explorers climbed it and measured it.[9] They also arrived at an ecological explanation of the diabolism. Wind drove insects to shelter on the mound, and birds (supposedly the sign of devils) followed the insects. The explorers classified the birds, and then used the mound for sightseeing.

Naming was frequently used to convey order. After a disagreement with the Teton Sioux which culminated in a show of force, Clark commemorated the occasion: 'I call this Island bad humered Island as we were in a bad humer' (Thwaites, I, 164–165). Dismal Swamp and the Isle of Caution (now safely called Plum Island) quietened similar moments of unease. The explorers also took up Benjamin Rush's suggestion (in a letter to Jefferson, already discussed) that the glory of the Republic should be imposed upon the terrain. In consequence the names of many of the Republic's leaders adorned the topography of the West. Their names remain. Those of republican qualities fared less well; Philanthropy River subsequently became Stinking Water, and Wisdom River sank to Big Hole. With the flora and fauna the process of naming was less easy. The explorers used a variety of techniques. Plants and animals that seemed familiar were given the names of their eastern counterparts. They adopted names from the French and various Indian languages. They invented words by means of combinations, such as 'prairie-dog'. Applying some 2,000 names, they assimilated the new by adapting it to the old.[10]

The journey up the Missouri to Fort Mandan, then, confirmed the optimistic image suggested in Le Page du Pratz's *History of Louisiana* and demanded by the explorers' imperial ideology. An extract from Lewis's journal of 17 September, as the party were nearing Fort Mandan, illustrates the Edenic vision of the young American ex-secretary and its similarity to the ageing text of the Frenchman:

> the shortness and virdu[r]e of the grass gave the plain the appearance throughout its whole extent of beatiful bowling-green in fine order . . . the surrounding country had been birnt about a month before and young grass had now sprung up to hight of 4 Inches presenting the live green of the spring to the West a high range of hills, strech across the country from N. to S and appeared distant about 20 miles; they are not very extensive as I could plainly observe their rise and termination no rock appeard on them and the sides were covered with virdu[r]e similar to that of the plains this senery already rich pleasing and beatiful was still farther hightened by immence herds of Buffaloe deer Elk and Antelopes which we saw in every direction feeding on the hills and plains. I do not think I exagerate when I estimate the number of Buffaloe which could be comprehended at one view to amount to 3000.
>
> (Codex Ba, pp. 4–6; Thwaites, I, 152–153)

Lewis's observations here resemble those of du Pratz's *History of Louisiana*, and the composition is reminiscent of Claude's paintings. The perspective is from a high vantage-point. It starts with the immediate surroundings, moves to the horizon, and then fills in the detail of animal life. The prospect easily takes on the image of the Garden. Young grass has sprung up so quickly and abundantly to replace burnt patches that, although it is autumn, the area seems to have the youthful vitality of spring. The buffalo are far more numerous than du Pratz suggested. He saw several herds of 150 animals; Lewis sees 3,000. Du Pratz, it seems, was too conservative. Perhaps Moncacht-Apé's account of the five-day portage would be conservative, too; perhaps the passage to the Pacific would prove easy.

The initial stages of the Expedition satisfied Lewis's highest hopes and seemed to justify Jefferson's purchase of Louisiana. During the long winter months at Mandan Lewis took much time and trouble over a lengthy 'Summary View of Rivers and Creeks' which feed into the Missouri. The 'Summary View' follows the form of 'Rivers', Query II of Jefferson's *Notes on the State of Virginia* (Peden, 5–16). Lewis, like Jefferson, provides a list of the rivers, starting with their names and giving details of their navigability, accompanied by a commentary on the quality of the terrain (Thwaites, VI, 29–55). Like the methods of measuring and naming, and his painterly description of the terrain around the Missouri, Lewis is here assimilating his view of the West to a familiar eastern landscape. He was now aware that the Rockies were a chain of mountains with multiple ridges rather than a single ridge. But this presented no challenge to his image of them, because he was familiar with the path of the Potomac and Shenandoah Rivers through the ranges of the Blue Ridge, not least from Jefferson's description in the *Notes*. What the Potomac could do, so could the Missouri.

He believed that the northern branch of the Missouri was:

> navigable to [the] foot of [a] chain of high mountains, being the ridge which divides the waters of the Atlantic from those of the Pacific ocean. the Indians assert that they can pass in half a day from the foot of this mountain on its East side to a large river which washes its Western base.   (Thwaites, VI, 55)

Those complaisant Indians again! They had told white men from George Sandys onwards what they wanted to hear about the Northwest Passage. At Fort Mandan it seemed to Lewis that his optimism had been justified. It looked as if Moncacht-Apé's account of the five-day portage was too pessimistic. That second sentence also indicates Lewis's belief in the symmetry of the rivers; it was so easy to imagine the far side of the mountain in terms of the near side. And these beliefs, in the short portage and the symmetrical terrain, interlocked with the Garden landscape that Lewis had so lovingly constructed.

SCENES OF VISIONARY ENCHANTMENT

The Expedition set off again on 7 April 1805. Lewis's optimism was so great that it overcame his unease on entering *terra incognita*:

we were now about to penetrate a country at least two thousand miles in
width, on which the foot of civillized man had never trodden: the good or evil
it had in store for us was for experiment yet to determine . . . however, as the
state of mind in which we are, generally gives the colouring to events, when
the immagination is suffered to wander into futurity, the picture which now
presented itself to me was a most pleasing one. enterta[in]ing as I do, the most
confident hope of succeeding in a voyage which had formed a da[r]ling project
of mine for the last ten years [*of my life* crossed out], I could but esteem this
moment of my departure as among the most happy of my life.

(Codex B, p. 5; Thwaites, I, 285)

The 'picture' before him was of his 'little fleet', two large pirogues and six
small canoes. It is in this journal entry that Lewis makes the explicit
comparison with Columbus and Cook. He also uses the phrase 'darling
project', used by Mackenzie about his own crossing to the Pacific.[11]
Clearly, Lewis continues to yoke his vision of the West to the literature of
exploration available to him in Jefferson's library. There is one aspect of
Lewis's painterly prose, however, that casts a shadow forward to the days
ahead. He was making greater use of the first person singular and
employing the one faculty that Jefferson had suppressed in himself and,
through the rigour of his instructions, had tried to suppress in Lewis.
Jefferson had disapproved of Ledyard's 'immagination'. Now Lewis was
using his imagination to 'colour' the path before him. His empiricism
was cheerfully anticipatory; but 'experiment' would determine other
than he hoped. Unpleasant events lay ahead, and these would colour his
state of mind.

At first, however, Lewis's hopes seemed to be realised. Images of the
Garden continued. On 12 April he wrote about the fertility of the soil and
projected it onto the sources of the Missouri. He even noted an evergreen
plant that 'would make very handsome edgings to the borders and walks
of a garden' (Thwaites, I, 298–299). The others shared the vision, but
with less delicacy. Sergeant Ordway, always utilitarian, noted on 18
April that 'the Game is gitting pleantyier every day' (Quaife, 198). Then
the explorers began to note a decline in the game, and sterile soil.
Wooded countryside was replaced by prickly pear, which was pretty
now it was in full bloom but shredded the men's feet whenever they went
ashore. The frequent rapids in the river and its swift current caused great
difficulty. They progressed only by pulling the pirogues from the banks;
but the banks were soft and often fell into the river, making the tow a
difficult, slow and dangerous process. It was an experience which
impressed later explorers greatly. Prince Maximilian of Wied during his
1832 expedition, and the ornithologist Audubon in 1843, commented on
the terrifying vision of the Missouri breaking up the banks and carrying
off trees. It seemed to them like a life–and–death conflict.[12]

In these circumstances, Lewis's mood began to change. On 26 May he climbed a hill and saw the Rockies for the first time. But his feelings were mixed:

> these points of the Rocky Mountains were covered with snow and the sun shone on it in such manner as to give me the most plain and satisfactory view. while I viewed these mountains I felt a secret pleasure in finding myself so near the head of the heretofore conceived boundless Missouri; but when I reflected on the difficulties which this snowey barrier would most probably throw in my way to the Pacific, and the sufferings and hardships of myself and party in thim, it in some measure counterballanced the joy I had felt in the first moments in which I gazed on them; but as I have always held it a crime to anticipate evils I will believe it a good comfortable road untill I am compelled to believe differently.   (Codex E, p. 9; Thwaites, II, 79)

Lewis is here as much interested in his imagination as in the scene before him. Unlike his earlier reporting style, he is now indulging the personal pronoun. The structure of his sentences also indicates his mixed feelings; the prose is punctuated by conditional hairpins, 'while . . . but . . . but'. For he can see that the mountains are 'broken'. This is the first indication that the Rockies are not like the Blue Ridge; the first sign that the concept of geographical symmetry is faulty. Jefferson had used a highway to confirm the optimism of his far-flung horizon when writing of the passage of the Potomac through the Blue Ridge. Now, the 'road' of Jefferson's imperial scheme is crossed by a 'barrier'.

There now appeared sights quite different from any that had been seen before. The river cliffs in the area now known as the Breaks of the Missouri are made of soft limestone and have been sculpted by wind and water into strange shapes. When he saw them Lewis wrote that they 'exhibit a most romantic appearance'; and he devoted some 800 words to them. Here is an extract:

> The water . . . has trickled down the soft sand clifts and woarn it into a thousand grotesque figures, which with the help of a little immagination and an oblique view at a distance, are made to represent eligant ranges of lofty freestone buildings, having their parapets well stocked with statuary; collumns of various sculpture both grooved and plain, are also seen supporting long galleries in front of those buildings; in other places on a much nearer approach and with the help of less immagination we see the remains or ruins of eligant buildings; some collumns standing and almost entire with their pedestals and capitals; others retaining their pedestals but deprived by time or accedent of their capitals, some lying prostrate an broken othe[r]s in the form of vast pyramids . . . As we passed on it seemed as if those seens of visionary inchantment would never have and [an] end.
> (Codex E, pp. 24–25; Thwaites, II, 100–101)

Grotesque figures, visionary enchantment: Lewis's prose has moved a

long way away from the calm orderly scenes of the Garden that he owed
to Claude. First, with its extensive use of architectural terminology, this
passage owes its imagery to the architectural texts on Jefferson's shelves.
Particularly, it derives from the several books of engravings that
Jefferson owned of Roman and French ruins and monuments, especially
a book on the engravings of Piranesi. As a result of renewed interest in
classical antiquity, it had become commonplace in the eighteenth
century to compare broken geological structures to architectural ruins.
Here at the Missouri Breaks the appearance of a dead city gave Lewis's
prose a melancholic feeling, aided at one point by the personification of
the landscape ('lying prostrate an broken') and generally by its
endlessness.[13]

Secondly, Lewis's landscape vision here owes something to Burnet's
Theory of the Earth, which he would have found on Jefferson's shelves.
Burnet's belief that mountains had resulted from a cataclysm is reflected
here in an imagery of devastation that will shortly reappear in a
heightened form. Thirdly, Lewis also obtains his imagery from Salvator
Rosa. Rosa's broken landscapes, with their solitary figures and *memento
mori*, not only gave Lewis a syntax with which to describe the Missouri
Breaks, but also encouraged his budding imagination. Claude's paintings, and the landscape that Lewis derived from them, emphasised
calmness and order. The viewer looked down on the scene and arranged
it. In contrast, Rosa's paintings prompted a landscape which loomed over
an introspective figure. In the description of the Missouri Breaks, Lewis
refers to his 'immagination' twice, and it is an imagination that is turning
sour. A few days previously, one of the boats was almost lost in a squall.
Lewis wrote about the event with 'the utmost trepidation and horror'
(Codex D, p. 125; Thwaites, II, 34). And now, on the same day that he
saw the Missouri Breaks, the tow-rope of the same boat parted and it
nearly sank. Lewis wrote:

> I fear her evil gennii will play so many pranks with her that she will go to the
> bottomm some of these days.   (Codex D, p. 23; Thwaites, II, 100)

Nine months earlier he had calmly dealt with Indian superstition by
scaling the Devil Mound and using it to give him a Claudian landscape.
Now he was starting to refer to the forces of nature as if they were
directed by some malign power.

Occasionally the Garden reappeared, and Lewis gladly responded to
it. A northern tributary of the Missouri was found to be fertile and
abounding in 'anamals of the fur kind'. Lewis wrote of it as:

> one of the most beatifully picteresque countries that I ever beheld, through the
> wide expance of which, innumerable herds of living anamals are seen, its
> borders garnished with one continued garden of roses, while its lofty and open

forrests are the habitation of miriads of the feathered tribes who salute the ear of
the passing traveler with their wild and simple, yet s[w]eet and cheerfull
melody. (Thwaites, II, 131)

He seems now to be writing under pressure. The introduction of the
code-word 'picteresque' signals a jaded travelogue replete with latinisms,
fatigued phrases, and a sub-Popeian periphrasis. The inflation of Lewis's
language is counterpointed against the reduction of his party to 'the
passing traveler'.

Lewis was heartened when one aspect of Indian lore proved correct.
They had been told that near the source of the Missouri there were some
great falls and on 13 June Lewis, leading an advance party, found them.
He was delighted; now perhaps they would find the short portage. They
did not. The Great Falls proved such an obstacle that it took them from
21 June until 14 July to climb round them. The men's feet were shredded
by cactus, their eyes were tormented by thick clouds of mosquitoes, and
they were assailed by a freak storm. Clark's phlegmatic weather diary
provides a detailed account:

> At 1 P M a black cloud which arose in the S.W. came on accompanied with a
> high wind and violent thunder and Lightning; a great quantity of Hail also fell
> during this storm which lasted about two hours and a half the hail which was
> generally about the size of pigions eggs and not unlike them in form, covered
> the ground to one inch and a half. for about 20 minutes during this Storm hail
> fell of an inno[r]mous size driven with violence almost incredible, when they
> struck the ground they would rebound to the hight of 10 to 12 feet and pass 20
> or 30 before they touched again . . . Capt. Lewis weighed one of these hail
> Stones which weighted 3 ozs and measured 7 Inches in Secumfrance; they were
> generally round & perfectly Solid. I am Convinced if one of those had Struck a
> man on naiked head [it] would certainly [have] fractured his Skull.
>
> (Thwaites, VI, 193)

The party hid under canoes and 'Sundery articles', and even then they
were badly bruised. Several bled freely and 'complained verry much',
according to Sergeant Ordway (Quaife, 239). The detachment led by
Clark was also overtaken by a flash flood and narrowly escaped
drowning. The rain, reported Sergeant Ordway, 'fell like one voley of
water falling from the heavens' (Quaife, 240).

There is no doubting the veracity of Clark's account of the storm. The
narrative is spattered with facts and is verified by the less detailed
accounts of the others. Yet, as Ordway's phrase suggests, the storm also
seemed, in circumstances already adverse, like a visitation from heaven.
In Virginia the occasionally unpleasant weather had increased Jefferson's
godlike feeling as he saw it 'fabricated at our feet'. Here, at the Great Falls,
the explorers were beneath, subject to weather conditions far worse than
any experienced in the East. It is worth recalling, too, that from Exodus

to Revelations, hail is an expression of God's wrath. References to hail occur some twenty times in the Bible of which the following is unusual only in that it is accompanied by storms and earthquakes:

> And great hail, *every stone* about the weight of a talent, cometh down out of heaven upon men: and men blasphemed god because of the plague of the hail; for the plague thereof is exceeding great.   (Revelations 16:18–21)

The Garden, the expression of God's pleasure, had turned into its opposite, a disordered hell not unlike the hell imagined by Burnet and Goldsmith, and realised in Rush's plague-ridden Philadelphia.

Even the animals, hitherto the source of food and scientific enquiry, changed. On one night a buffalo ran amok through the party's camp. Lewis's Newfoundland dog 'Scannon' deflected it so that it did little material damage; but everyone was aware that the incident could have been fatal. There were many other incidents with rattlesnakes and cougars as well as buffalo. Lewis, returning to camp one night, was attacked in quick succession by a cougar and three buffalo. With his imagination at full stretch he wrote that:

> It now seemed to me that all the beasts of the neighbourhood had made a League to distroy me . . . the succession of curious adventures wore the impression on my mind of inchantment.
>
> (Codex E, pp. 79–80; Thwaites, II, 158)

The animals, of course, preyed on each other. Lewis noted that buffalo now appeared 'attended by their shepperds the wolves', who picked off the slow and the maimed (Thwaites, II, 113). This image of the perversion of Pastoral was poor preparation for the next sight to greet them. The explorers were affronted by the stench of death and the sight of hundreds of mangled carcasses at the foot of a precipice. Buffalo had been stampeded there by Indians, or had simply been pushed over by the herd. Their remains, noted Lewis:

> afford fine amusement for the bear wolves and birds of prey; this may be one reason and I think not a bad one either that the bear are so tenatious of their right of soil in this neighbourhood.   (Thwaites, II, 93, 167)

Here was a gruesome wreckage far in excess of anything that Rosa could cram into his canvas. It was a sight that the explorers saw several times.

Lewis's remarks also indicate the relationship that he and his party had towards the bear. If bears have 'right of soil' they are proprietors of the land that the Expedition has come to claim. One of the Sergeants, Patrick Gass, confirmed this attitude a few days later:

> In the evening, most of the corps crossed over to an island, to attack and rout its monarch, a large brown bear, that held possession and seemed to defy all that

would attempt to besiege him there. Our troops, however, stormed the place, gave no quarter, and its commander fell.[14]

In the bestiary of Western Europe the bear has a modest place. Although Ursa Major gave it an elevated role in Greek mythology, the bear had declined by the time of the Renaissance to the status of a side-show. Evidence of this is to be found in Shakespeare's stage-direction in *The Winter's Tale*, 'Exit, pursued by a bear'. It is to be found, too, in the comic Hudibrastic combat between Friday and the bear in *Robinson Crusoe*. That encounter makes an immediate contrast with ensuing, horrific meeting with wolves in the Pyrenees. In nineteenth-century Britain the bear was still being subjected to the indignity of being shaved, dressed and exhibited as 'the pig-faced lady'. However, after the Lewis and Clark Expedition some attitudes did change. In Landseer's frightening painting 'Man Proposes, God Disposes' (1863–1864) two polar bears, cousins to the grizzly, mockingly despoil the remains of a successor to Lewis and Clark, Sir John Franklin's ill-fated search for the Northwest Passage in 1845–1848. But such potency is only achieved in foreign parts. Landseer uses an eerie green light to emphasise the alien nature of the Arctic setting (see figures 3 and 4).[15]

In non-western culture the bear had not degenerated. Indeed, in some societies bear rituals still exist.[16] Some awareness of Indian myths and rituals may be responsible for the hybrid nature of eighteenth-century white writings about the American bear. In this example the image of the animal floats uneasily between fearsome potency and black comedy:

> BEARS are very numerous higher up in the country, and do much mischief. Mr *Bartram* told me, that when a bear catches a cow, he kills her in the following manner: he bites a hole into the hide and blows with all his power into it, till the animal swells excessively, and dies; for the air expands greatly between the flesh and the hide.

Per Kalm was in general unimpressed by the British Middle Colonies. Here he seems to have been led astray by an American tall tale, much to the disgust of his British translator, John Reinhold Forster. 'This has all the appearance of a vulgar error', snorted the footnote; 'the most judicious travellers' assert that American bears are herbivorous. One of those judicious travellers may have been Le Page du Pratz, who talks of bears turned lazy, fat and herbivorous by the lush terrain. Yet du Pratz's text reveals an instability similar to Kalm's. On the one hand he tells of a wounded bear squeezing its assailant to death. On the other he depicts bears as tubby comedians wrestling each other for pails of milk put out by Louisianan tricksters.[17]

The books by Kalm and du Pratz were available on Jefferson's shelves. If Lewis had read Kalm's tale, it would not have impressed him. He had

3 William Hogarth, *Hudibras' First Adventure* (1726), is an example of the popular conception of the bear before Lewis and Clark encountered the grizzly. Samuel Butler's quixotic Hudibras routs a poor bear in mock-heroic combat.

4 Sir Edwin Landseer, *Man Proposes, God Disposes* (1863–64), reflects a new view of the bear after Lewis and Clark. One polar bear shreds a sail, while its mate gnaws at a human rib-cage.

never seen a bear blow up a cow. But he had read du Pratz and taken an edition with him on the Expedition. He was, therefore, contemptuous of Indian accounts of the Northwestern grizzly. It had first been encountered by a white man in 1691. Mackenzie, on his journey to the Pacific, recorded that he had seen 'two grisly and hideous bears'. But little was known about the grizzly's abilities. Lewis, in another example of the projection of eastern images onto the West, assumed that the eastern black bear and the grizzly were similar. They are disturbingly different. The black bear is five or six feet long and weighs from 200 to 500 lb. when fully grown. It can be dangerous, but is tameable and often seen (by such as Shakespeare) in zoos and circuses. Its Latin generic title is a neutral *Ursus Americanus*. The grizzly, in contrast, can be seven to nine feet long and can weigh 900 lb. when fully grown. One example was believed to weigh 1,800 lb. The grizzly can be unpredictable and highly dangerous, a lethal fighting machine that can run at thirty m.p.h. A live grizzly cub was later sent to Charles Willson Peale for his museum at Philosophical Hall, Philadelphia. It quickly grew up, broke out of its cage one night, and stalked the cellar of Philosophical Hall, much to the terror of the Peale family. The next morning it was shot. Since then the grizzly has normally only been seen stuffed. Its Latin generic title is *Ursus Horribilis* or *Ursus Horribilis Horribilis*, depending perhaps on the experience of the namer.[18]

Shortly after leaving Fort Mandan the party met their first grizzlies, but the bears only ran away. Lewis looked forward to having some fun with them:

> I expect these gentlemen will give us some amusement sho[r]tly as they soon begin now to coppolate. (Thwaites, II, 4)

Lewis's oleaginous interest in the bears' sexual habits, and his smiling reference to them as gentlemen, soon changed. One of the first grizzlies he shot turned round and pursued him for seventy to eighty yards. Lewis escaped because the bear was too badly wounded to run at thirty m.p.h. There were many subsequent instances of bears, wounded several times and spouting blood in all directions, still attacking their assailants. Lewis now treated the bears seriously. He took up much space in his journals describing encounters with them and distinguishing the grizzly from the black bear (Codex D, pp. 67, 85; Thwaites, I, 350–351, 372).

One incident was recorded by Lewis in great detail. Private Bratton had shot a grizzly but failed to kill it. He reported back to Lewis:

> I immediately turned out with seven of the party in quest of this monster, we at length found his trale and persued him about a mile by the blood . . . we finally found him concealed in some very thick brush and shot him through the skull with two balls . . . we now found that Bratton had shot him through the center

of the lungs, notwithstanding which he had pursued him near half a mile and had returned more than double that distance and with his tallons had prepared himself a bed in the earth of about 2 feet deep and five long and was perfectly alive when we found him which could not have been less than 2 hours after he received the wound; these bear being *so hard to die* reather intimedates us all; I must confess I do not like the gentlemen and had reather fight two Indians than one bear [my emphasis].   (Codex D, pp. 117–118; Thwaites, II, 24–25)

After many incidents such as this, Sergeant Gass concluded that grizzlies 'will attack a man at any opportunity'. The attitude towards them had changed from condescension to fear. On one occasion when a grizzly 'declined the combat', Lewis found 'this curious adventure . . . misterious and unaccountable'. It was clear that they were not herbivorous. They were, indeed, an unsought mammoth, and the publication of Gass's journal marks a new respect for the bear in American culture. Henry Marie Brackenridge remarked in 1811 that:

The African lion, or the tyger of Bengal, are not more terrible or fierce. He is the enemy of man; and literally thirsts for human blood. So far from shunning, he seldom fails to attack; and even to *hunt* him . . . The Indians complain that some of their best warriors, have fallen victims to this animal. Lewis and Clark's men, on several occasions, narrowly escaped from their attacks. The Grizzly bear is sufficient to disprove, the idle theories of Buffon or Raynal, as to the impotency of the NEW WORLD in the production of animals.[19]

Here was a refutation of Old World theories that Americans could well have done without.

The grizzly had been transformed from the hunted to the hunter; but one much more dangerous and apparently designing than the stray buffalo or cougar. It had appeared on the terrain just as Lewis's landscape was becoming overcast and malevolent. The bodily configuration and occasional upright stance of bears can make them appear as a para-human embodiment of evil. Lewis, in his account of the wounded grizzly, turns the species for the second time into human beings. But this time, as is indicated by the wondering phrases piled one on the other by conjunctions, he describes them without a trace of humour. They are gentlemen; and gentlemen that are 'hard to die'. This unusual phrase will occur again.

The difficulties of the party continued. It seemed now that scientific ingenuity was failing, as Clark had feared when Private Shannon lost his way. The vaccine planned to transform Indian health had proved useless; and the 'Experiment', the collapsible craft which Lewis had proudly and possessively called 'my boat', would not float. The skins covering it split and parted. 'To make any further experiments in our present situation seemed to me madness', Lewis wrote bitterly (Thwaites, II, 169, 218).

The sentence symbolises the collapse of Enlightenment order in an environment with which it is not equipped to cope. Their predicament worsened as they crossed the Divide. They had to endure the storms that continued to rage around the Rockies. Their surroundings provided no food or water. They had to live off some of their horses, melted snow, and a dreadful concoction they brought with them called 'portable soup'. It was not until 21 September that they found a river large enough to take them to the Pacific, which they eventually reached in November 1805.

A CERTAIN FATALITY

The Lewis and Clark Expedition was the first to cross the continent. But, outstanding as its achievement had been in terms of planning, execution and sheer endurance, it had failed to realise its objectives. Only parts of Louisiana had answered the dream of the Garden. The short portage had proved to be a myth. Moncacht-Apé had said five days. It had taken them two months to get from the Falls of the Missouri to the upper reaches of the Columbia. In such adversity the introspection and fear, already noted in Lewis's writing, increased. The following example is from his journal for 19 July:

> whe[ne]ver we get a view of the lofty summits of the mountains the snow presents itself, altho' we are almost suffocated in this confined valley with heat. the pine cedar and balsum fir grow on the mountains in irregular assemb[l]ages or spots mostly high up on their sides and summits. this evening we entered much the most remarkable clifts that we have yet seen. these clifts rise from the waters edge on either side perpendicularly to the hight of 1200 feet. every object here wears a dark and gloomy aspect. the tow[er]ing and projecting rocks in many places seem ready to tumble on us. the river appears to have forced its way through this immence body of solid rock for the distance of 5 3/4 Miles and where it makes its exit below has thrown on either side vast collumns of rocks mountains high . . . from the singular appearance of this place I called it the *gates of the rocky mountains*.   (Codex F, pp. 10–11; Thwaites, II, 248)

The place bears that name today, and the terrain is very impressive. More important for my argument, however, is Lewis's attitude towards it, for it reveals his state of mind. There is no sense here that Lewis's writing is shaping the terrain. It is, rather, simply responding to it. All the power is vested in the dark and gloomy scene that looms over him. The verbs he uses – suffocate, tumble, force, throw – tend to be associated with violent natural forces and not with his ordering power as an observer. In this Rosan landscape the solitary figure has become very small indeed.

There is a European literary source for Lewis's language here which adds a further dimension:

> Hence, in old dusky time, a deluge came:
> When the deep-cleft disparting orb, that arched
> The central waters round, impetuous rushed
> With universal burst into the gulf,
> And o'er the high-piled hills of fractured earth
> Wide-dashed the waves in undulation vast,
> Till, from the centre to the streaming clouds,
> A shoreless ocean tumbled round the globe.

This passage reveals a similar violence with its jagged phrases and sharp, doom-laden alliterated 'd's and 't's reaching a climax with the plosive 'b' of 'burst'. Its tumultuous nature is derived, as Marjorie Hope Nicolson has noted, from Thomas Burnet's cataclysmic view of the Flood, when the waters beneath the earth's surface burst through to ruin the symmetry of the world. The passage is from Thomson's *Seasons*, a work that was very popular in America. Jefferson had two editions in his library. It expresses what Thomson called 'vindictive' nature; it is the language of eternal damnation, the complete opposite of the language of the Garden that Lewis had earlier used.[20] Lewis's sense of calm and order has vanished. At this time he often feels hemmed in by the mountains and frequently gets depressed. He fears losing his way and aborting the expedition. He sees 'our trio of pests' – mosquitoes, gnats and prickly pear – as 'equal to any three curses that ever poor Egypt laiboured under', a remark that reinforces the imagery of the hailstones as God's wrath. One night he stays out alone (a spiritual confrontation in the wilderness?), returning to find the party very uneasy about him.[21]

In these circumstances Lewis's language itself begins to waver. On 13 June he had already put on record his sense of despair at the growing inadequacy of his writing. He had that day seen the Great Falls of the Missouri for the first time, and after some 1,000 words of description he gave up:

> After wrighting this imperfect discription I again viewed the falls and was so much disgusted with the imperfect idea which it conveyed of the scene that I determined to draw my pen across it and begin agin, but then reflected that I could not perhaps succeed better than pening the first impressions of the mind; I wished for the pencil of Salvator Rosa or the pen of Thompson, that I might be enabled to give to the enlightened world some just idea of this truly magnificent and sublimely grand object, which has from the commencement of time been concealed from the view of civilized man; but this was fruitless and vain.   (Codex E, p. 70; Thwaites, II, 149–150)

The rhetorical self-deprecation and subsequent appeal to Rosa and Thomson was commonplace amongst educated men when confronted by such terrain. It was a code invoking the Sublime. We have seen similar invocations by Jefferson, Dwight and Chastellux. At the Great Falls there was one crucial difference, however, for the Falls had 'from the commencement of time been concealed from the view of civilized man'. Thomson, and his successors the Romantic poets, had developed a subtle and strong method of expressing the relationship between man and the more rugged parts of the world; but they were writing about a terrain made safe by familiarity. Ever since Hannibal it had been known that the Alps could be crossed. In Europe Jefferson was writing about a terrain made familiar by the Grand Tour, and in America Dwight and Chastellux were writing about a terrain *rediscovered* by the leisured traveller.[22] The terror that such writers occasionally expressed was therefore something of an indulgence, an emotion encrusting the terrain rather than instilled by it.

Occasionally, the more sensitive Old World writers revealed an awareness of the conventions upon which rested their ability to write about rough terrain. John Ruskin expressed this most clearly when peering down a ravine in Switzerland. How would such a scene appear, he wondered, 'in some aboriginal forest of the New Continent?' Then he saw that:

> The flowers in an instant lost their light, the river its music; the hills became oppressively desolate; a heaviness in the boughs of the darkened forest showed how much of their former power had been dependent upon a life which was not theirs.

Similarly, Coleridge's poem 'Frost at Midnight' shows a keen awareness that the beauty of 'mountain crags' depends on evidences of human presence. In contrast, Wordsworth was less resolute when approaching the edge of such conventions. In *The Prelude* he imagines 'Indian cabins over the fresh lawns' in the Chartreuse, but hesitates at the 'soulless image' of Mont Blanc, and then gladly diverts his eye to the so-called 'realities' of reapers, maidens, and 'cottages by beds of flowers'. He reveals here, as he does throughout his poetry, the importance of what Thomas Cole called 'associations' in making sense of the environment.[23]

The Rockies presented a challenge precisely because they were bereft of 'associations'. Lewis was in *terra incognita* and, repeating at the Great Falls the remarks he had made when leaving Mandan on 7 April, he was acutely aware of it. The experience was straining a language of natural description that had been developed in the Old World and adopted by the New. It was, primarily, a language of tourism. Lewis was not a tourist. He was an explorer with a committed vision of western America. He ran through the gamut of devices of aesthetic tourism. In addition to appealing to Rosa and Thomson he wished he had included a camera obscura in the Expedition's equipment. The camera obscura is Gilpin's Claude-glass. It performed a function similar to Freneau's 'perspective glass' and was a standard item in the baggage of the Picturesque tourist. Jefferson had several at Monticello. Lewis even tried making a pencil sketch of the Falls. Clark found it in his effects after his death (Jackson, II, 490).

None of the devices worked. The Rockies, and the West generally, defied all attempts at description. They would continue to test writers and painters for the rest of the century. Prince Maximilian of Wied hired a Swiss illustrator, Karl Bodmer, for his 1832 expedition up the Missouri. Like Jefferson, he demanded an exact record of the scene. Bodmer was as faithful and assiduous as Lewis but he, too, was forced to abandon Old World pictorial conventions as he went west. It was a disquieting and disorienting experience which he repudiated when he was safely back in Europe. Albert Bierstadt, lacking Bodmer's sensitivity, simply used his European training to paint over the Rockies, transforming them into Gothic cathedrals. Frederic Remington was more alive to the problems presented by the Rockies when he remarked in 1895 that the Golden Gate Pass was:

> utterly beyond the pen or brush of any man. Paint cannot touch it, and words are wasted.[24]

Lewis had become painfully aware that his words were wasted. He was moving beyond the use of inexpressibility as a rhetorical figure towards a genuine awareness of the fissure between old words and a New World. I have suggested that writers like Morse, Rush and Brackenridge recoiled in fear from images of a savage, instable landscape. The work of Crèvecœur, Dwight and Jefferson, too, revealed moments of hesitation which were more than just rhetoric. None of them was under the pressure faced by Lewis, enjoined to describe a land that was beyond existing descriptive strategies. Lewis was now not merely on a physical frontier; he was on a linguistic frontier.

The strain that the Rockies placed on Lewis's language gave rise to one moment of comedy. He could not decide whether the Great Falls were Beautiful or Sublime. Eventually he decided to hedge his bets. One waterfall was '*pleasingly beautifull*'; while the other was '*sublimely grand*' (Codex E, p. 74; Thwaites, II, 154; Lewis's emphases). But in general the tone was dark; the Sublime and the Beautiful were equally inadequate for this oppressive terrain. At one point Lewis, in fateful words, reminded himself of Jefferson's memoir and forced himself ahead of the party so that he might rest the sooner:

> to accomplish some wrightings which I conceived from the nature of my instructions necessary lest any accedent should befall me.
>
> (Thwaites, II, 322–323)

The accident that befalls him is not of a physical nature. Lewis's depression is such that he is incapable of responding to a change in the Expedition's fortunes. They meet the Shoshone Indians, who would eventually guide them across the Divide. Lewis orders 'the fiddle to be played and the party danced very merily'; but he sits to one side, his mood at odds with the 'prevailing mirth'. Then, after two more sentences full of foreboding about his Expedition, he writes the following:

> I had nothing but a little parched corn to eat
> this evining.
> This morning Capt. C. and party
>
> (Codex Fb pp. 25–26; Thwaites, III, 43)

And there the record stops, in mid sentence and despite the express instructions of Jefferson, Lewis's Commander-in-Chief.

With the exception of three short periods, Lewis leaves the entire burden of recording to his co-commander. He does not record the 'most intolerable road' through the Rockies, with the party 'hourly complaining of their retched situation' (Clark; Thwaites, III, 63, 45). He writes nothing of the dangerous canoe journey down the Columbia River, or of the high winds and bad weather at the fort on the Pacific. The accounts that exist for the period 27 August to 31 December 1805 are provided by Clark and three of the soldiers. When Lewis does start writing again, he is both literally and metaphorically turning over a new leaf. His next entry starts a new notebook on 1 January 1806; but the celebration is an empty one, for he simply looks forward to 1 January 1807.[25]

Lewis was not, then, as Jefferson had thought, qualified to 'seize' the new country and 'give us accounts of new things only'. Indeed, it was precisely Jefferson's training that disqualified him. The gap between the lessons taught in the East and their application in the West was too great. None of the other four journalists stopped writing. They were men of a much lower level of education and, ironically, that made them more suitable than Lewis for Jefferson's purpose. The best educated was Clark, but instead of spending the two years before the Expedition in Jefferson's library, he spent them travelling up and down the United States frontier, writing his own rough-hewn prose and drawing maps. Lewis, formed by Jefferson especially to render the terrain into a text, was not a man of maps or of rough-hewn prose. But it was Clark who was closer to the terrain. Unable to retreat from it into a world of words, Clark paradoxically provided more material for the dictionary.[26] Lewis could evade neologism by escaping into a broader vocabulary, into euphemism and circumlocution. Lewis had made himself the fool of words and those words covered him until, on a heath so blasted that they could withstand the strain no longer, they fell away leaving him naked and paralysed.

In a world turned upside down, threatened by malign elements and animals that seemed to express the wrath of God, deserted by his orderly and ordering prose, Lewis withered and began to die. One of the first signs was a changed attitude towards the Indians. Jefferson had insisted that the Expedition maintain friendly relations with the aborigines. The first indication that Lewis was disobeying Jefferson in this regard, too, came when he saw the near-starving Shoshone, their rescuers, eating the raw guts of a deer. Watching with disgust 'the blood runing from the corners of their mouths', Lewis concluded that:

> I really did not untill now think that human nature ever presented itself in a shape so nearly allyed to the brute creation.   (Thwaites, II, 355)

Hugh Henry Brackenridge on the Pennsylvania frontier had allied the Indians with 'pards and bears'. Now Lewis does the same and the result, in the words of a student of Lewis's attitude to the Indians, is 'almost pathological'.[27] Before he reached the Rockies, Lewis had been motivated by Jefferson's scientific curiosity towards them. Now he classes them with bears, and treats them with the same fear and distrust. During their enforced stay on the Pacific, the Expedition had of necessity to deal with the Indians. Lewis tried to ensure that the relationship was unhappy, warning his men against 'the treachery of the aborigenes of America' and on one occasion beating an Indian for theft – the first time that such punishment had been meted out (Thwaites, IV, 89, 308).

Before he reached the Rockies, Lewis had been an extraordinarily successful young man. In 1799 he had been an ensign in the Army. In 1801 he became the President's private secretary. In 1803 he led the first expedition to explore the acquisition that had doubled the territory of the United States. Even by American standards this was phenomenal progress. But from the Rockies onwards Lewis's life was marked by failure. The party's return journey to St Louis was notable less for natural hazards than for its leader's mistakes. After it recrossed the Rockies the party temporarily divided. Clark's exploration of the Yellowstone River was entirely successful. In stark contrast, Lewis's journey to the northernmost boundary of the new Territory came close to disaster. A series of misjudgements led to a fight with some Indians. Two were killed, the only bloodshed during the entire Expedition, and Lewis's detachment fled from the area. Just before he was reunited with Clark he was shot ignominiously in the buttocks by one of his own men, in error. Thereafter he again desisted from 'wrighting', this time for the remainder of the Expedition (Thwaites, V, 243). They arrived at St Louis on 23 September 1806. Through no fault of their own they were several months late and many people had given them up for lost.

When he had passed the Great Falls on the return journey, Lewis recorded an incident in which one of his men, McNeal, was treed by a bear. Eventually the bear got bored and wandered off. The soldier returned late but unharmed, and Lewis concluded:

> these bear are a most tremenduous animal; it seems that the hand of providence has been most wonderfully in our favor with rispect to them, or some of us would long since have fallen a sacrifice to their farosity. there seems to be a sertain fatality attatched to the neighbourhood of these falls, for there is always a chapter of accedents prepared for us during our residence at them.
>
> (Thwaites, v, 204)

The images of the Falls, where his language had faltered, and the bears that had pursued him, would remain as harbingers of ill-omen. Although Lewis was feted on his return to the East, and appointed Governor of Upper Louisiana Territory with the rank of general, his misfortunes continued. He was a poor administrator. He was quickly at loggerheads with the Secretary of the Territory and could cope neither with the Territory's finances nor with the constant wrangling of frontier politics. He failed to keep in touch with his old friends, in particular with his powerful mentor, Jefferson. Most of all, he failed to publish his journals.

Jefferson regarded the journals as 'the fruits of the expedition undertaken at such expense of money and risk of valuable lives' (Jackson, II, 612). Intended to broadcast the Jeffersonian imperial vision to 'the Republic of Letters', they would also consummate a relationship between text and terrain conceived with Whately's *Observations* in an English garden. But Jefferson waited for the consummation in vain. In August 1809 he wrote to Lewis about the journals once again. Everyone was impatient for them, he said; he had promised their publication so often to his fellow philosophers that he had become 'almost bankrupt in their eyes' (Jackson, II, 458). The complaint was too late to have any effect. Within two months Lewis was dead, and his publishers wrote to Jefferson:

> Govr. Lewis never furnished us with a line of the M.S. nor indeed could we ever hear any thing from him respecting it tho frequent applications to that effect were made to him.   (Jackson, II, 469)

The details of Lewis's death are fragmentary and the subject of much debate. In the autumn of 1809 he had to return from the Territorial capital, St Louis, to Washington to explain the Territory's disordered finances. At sunset on 10 October he had reached a rough hostel on the Natchez Trace (a Tennessee wilderness trail) with the quaint name of Grinder's Stand. (A 'stand' is a hostel, and the proprietor was Robert Grinder.) Grinder was not there, but his wife agreed to give Lewis a room for the night. During the course of the evening, however, she became alarmed at her guest's agitated conduct. Her alarm increased later that night when she heard shots from the cabin where Lewis lay alone.

After the final shot Lewis staggered out of his cabin and over to hers. She was so scared by now that she locked herself in and refused to answer his pleas for help. With two wounds in his skull and more perhaps in his side, Lewis spent the rest of the night in agony and without assistance. At dawn, his Black servant told Mrs Grinder that Lewis was again trying to kill himself. At last she went to his aid. She found that, in addition to the gunshot wounds, there were lacerations on either his throat or his wrists. Lewis begged her to take his gun and kill him. She refused, and later that morning of 11 October 1809 he expired without her help.

This account of Lewis's death has been taken from the evidence of Mrs Grinder and the servants, given to an Indian agent the next day and confirmed some twenty months later by the ornithologist Alexander Wilson.[28] There may have been an inquest, but no records survive. The evidence is therefore uncorroborated. It is possible that Lewis was murdered. The Natchez Trace was a dangerous road, the regular haunt of bandits. When Lewis's body was prepared for burial, only twenty-five cents were found. He had been carrying at least 100 dollars in cash and cheques. The money was never found although, of course, it may have been taken from his body after death. There is a strong folk tradition that he was murdered, but it is hearsay only.

Lewis apparently had a tendency to hypochondria, and on the journey towards the Natchez Trace he had been unwell and taking a wide variety of medicines. At Fort Pickering (now Memphis) he had been both drunk and suicidal, and the captain of the Fort had been obliged to keep a strict watch on him. When Jefferson in Washington and the Territorial Officials in St Louis learned of his death, they accepted that it was suicide. A few months later a magazine report suggested that it was public indifference to his Expedition that had 'operated strongly on his mind'.[29] In 1813 Jefferson, writing a biographical sketch of Lewis at the request of the eventual editor of the journals, asserted that the Lewis family suffered from 'sensible depressions of mind'. The constant exertions required during the Expedition had suspended, said Jefferson, 'these distressing affections' which the explorer had inherited, but the return to sedentary occupations had 'redoubled' them, leading to 'the deed which plunged his friends into affliction and deprived his country of one of her most valued citizens' (Jackson, II, 592).

Jefferson conveniently explains Lewis's death while exempting the Expedition as a cause. Yet, if the President was aware of the inherited trait, why did he risk Lewis on such an important venture? Perhaps it was Jefferson's bugbear 'imagination' that, beyond the limits of the ordered Republic, had run out of control and caused a change in Lewis that resulted in failure and death. This suggests that exploration involves more than physical hardship for those that undertake it. It challenges and may disorientate habitual patterns of thought and behaviour. John Ledyard, Lewis's predecessor in Jefferson's affections and western ambitions, died on the Nile of an overdose of vitriol, or 'of rage'. That rage first became apparent in Siberia. John Evans, the Welshman who had gone up the Missouri in search of his Indian compatriots, 'deranged himself' with drink and died in May 1799.[30] Is exploration so dangerous, a movement beyond the physical frontier also taking some explorers beyond a psychological frontier, so that the emptiness of the terrain drains away the resources of the self? These speculations will recur. In Lewis's case, they can only be reconstructions after the event, just as Jefferson was reconstructing a life four years after its close. They provide no more than clues to the cause of the events on the night of 10 October 1809.

There is one detail of Mrs Grinder's story, however, that is worth attention. In Alexander Wilson's report, published in 1811, Mrs Grinder and her servants had at daybreak entered the barn where Lewis was lying. He was badly wounded, and:

> He begged that they would take his rifle and blow out his brains, and he would give them all the money he had in his trunk. He often said, 'I am no coward; but I am *so* strong, *so hard to die*'.

Here Wilson underlines precisely the same phrase that Lewis used in his manuscript journal of 11 May 1805 (unpublished until 1904) when describing the bears. They had been 'gentlemen' who were 'so hard to die'.[31] Now Lewis applied the phrase to himself, just as he had applied the gun to himself. He had despatched the grizzly with two bullets through the skull; and now he had shot himself twice in the same place. But the wounds that were sufficient to finish off 'this monster' had been insufficient for him. Two bullets in the skull gave him a lingering and painful death, the final and saddest failure of a series of failures that had afflicted him ever since he had seen the Rockies.

It seems from the evidence altogether possible that Lewis, riding through rough Tennessee country and anticipating an unpleasant time in Washington, may have recalled those disappointing and frightening events in the West in the summer of 1805. The terrifying image that could have been provoked by the recollection, an image of malign nature that had driven him beyond language, may have caused him to shed his blood on the Natchez Trace. The coincidence of words and wounds suggests that Jefferson was wrong. It was precisely the Expedition that could have caused 'sensible depressions of mind'. Jefferson had intended to bring back the West to the East in the ordered phrases of a text. Instead, the West had invaded the East in images of disorder – and the most disordered, most dangerous image was of the bear.

THE REGION OF FABLE

After Lewis's death Clark took over responsibility for the journals, appointing as editor first Nicholas Biddle and then (when Biddle was elected to the Pennsylvania state legislature) Paul Allen, who also wrote a biography of Charles Brockden Brown. But the journals were so disorganised that their publication was delayed (much to Jefferson's displeasure) until 1814, five years after Lewis's death and eight after the return of the Expedition.

In the absence of the 'official' journals, the vacuum was filled by several inferior texts which tended to perpetuate an imagery of the West previously apparent in the divisions over the Louisiana Purchase discussed in chapter 4. Those divisions, indeed, were rekindled by the events immediately following the return of the Expedition. As soon as he had arrived in St Louis, Lewis sent Jefferson a letter which discussed at length the fur trade that would be assisted by the 'passage across the continent'. Although Lewis called the Rockies 'that formidable snowey barrier' and talked of a long and difficult portage, he asserted:

> with confidence that we have discovered the most practicable rout which dose exist across the continent.   (Jackson, I, 320–323)

Otherwise, Lewis said nothing about the nature of the terrain crossed. He was writing what Jefferson wanted to hear.

Jefferson, in his Second Annual Message to Congress on 2 December 1806, emphasised the positive aspects of Lewis's letter to him:

> The expedition of Messrs. Lewis & Clarke, for exploring the river Missouri, and the best communication from that to the Pacific ocean, has had all the success which could have been expected. They have traced the Missouri nearly to its source, descended the Columbia to the Pacific ocean, ascertained with accuracy the geography of that interesting communication across our continent, learnt the character of the country, of its commerce and inhabitants. [Clark's name was frequently misspelt.]   (Jackson, I, 352)

The empty last clause of the first sentence indicates the disingenuousness of the Message. By this time Jefferson would have learned more of the problems confronting the Expedition and of the varied terrain of the West. Indeed, a draft of his Second Message refers to the two-and-a-half year gap between the departure from and the return to St Louis, and also mentions 'the high mountains' that divide the Missouri and the Columbia (Jackson, I, 352). He chose to omit these remarks.

The alert newspaper reader must have noticed that Jefferson's Second Annual Message gave a view of the West somewhat at odds with the one appearing in the press. The source of the newspaper reports, once again, was Lewis. At the same time that he wrote to Jefferson he drafted a letter for Clark to send to one of his brothers. This letter said nothing about the fur trade, and instead gave a brief narrative of the journey, emphasising the difficulties in crossing the Rockies (Jackson, 1, 325–335). The letter appeared in newspapers from Kentucky to Washington.

Kindling for a new controversy over the West was therefore available immediately after the return of the Expedition. It was ignited by a celebratory dinner held for Lewis in Washington on 14 January 1807. The poet Joel Barlow had the previous day written to Jefferson suggesting that he change the name of the Columbia River to the Lewis; and he wrote a poem, read out at the dinner and subsequently published, which enlarged on his admiration for the explorer. Barlow's imperial enthusiasm joined the Lewis River to the Potomac, Ohio and Missouri in an image of geographical symmetry:

> These four brother floods, like a garland of flowers
> Shall entwine all our states in a hand,
> Conform and confederate their wide spreading powers,
> And their wealth and their wisdom expand.

Together the rivers would create a Garden. The ultimate responsibility for this, the refrain asserted, was borne not by a deity but by Meriwether Lewis:

> Then hear the loud voice of the nation proclaim,
> And all ages resound the decree:
> *Let our Occident stream bear the young hero's name,*
> *Who taught him his path to the sea.*[32]

Such hyperbole deserved and quickly received a response. John Quincy Adams had earlier been so opposed to the Louisiana Purchase that the whole subject gave him sleepless nights. Now, in a poem published anonymously, he attacked one of the first results of the Purchase. Leaving Lewis to tell of his 'heroick' toils, Adams listed the things that had not been discovered. Once again, it was the mammoth that was the focus of attention:

> He never with a Mammoth met,
> However you may wonder;
> Nor even with a Mammoth's bone,
> Above the ground or under –
> And, spite of all the pains he took
> The animal to track, sir,
> He never could o'ertake the hog
> With navel on his back, sir.
> And from the day his course began,
> Till even it was ended,
> He never found an Indian tribe

> From Welchmen straight descended:
> Nor, much as of Philosophers
> The fancies it might tickle;
> To season his adventures, met
> A Mountain, sous'd in pickle.

Adams's scorn of the fables of the West came to a peak with his attack on Jefferson's mountain of salt. But his greatest fury was reserved for Barlow, whom he regarded as an acolyte of Tom Paine. Paine and Barlow had not been able to pervert by deeds the principles of 1776 and 1787. It seemed that they were now trying to pervert them in an orgy of renaming. Adams was, in consequence, sceptical of such neologisms as 'prairie-dog' (the animal was not new – it was a skunk); he was bemused about changing the name of the United States to Fredonia; and he was furious about Barlow's suggestion for the Columbia:

> True – Tom and Joel now, no more
> Can overturn a nation;
> And work, by butchery and blood,
> A great regeneration; –
> Yet, still we can turn inside out
> Old Nature's Constitution,
> And bring a Babel back of *names* –
> Huzza! for REVOLUTION![33]

The poem echoes both British distress at a world turned upside down (here, inside out) and Noah Webster's fears of a Babel. But the 'revolution' of naming will achieve nothing. As Joseph Hall had suggested two centuries earlier, the world will remain the same. A wilderness renamed is still a wilderness.

A subsequent expedition seemed to confirm John Quincy Adams's belief that the West was not worth the Purchase. In 1806–1807 Zebulon Pike led a party up the Osage, Kansas and Arkansas Valleys towards the Rockies, and reported on his return that there were vast plains 'on which not a speck of vegetable matter existed'. But he drew comfort from this, in phrases which recall Montesquieu and the conservative objections to the Purchase. The great advantage of 'these immense prairies' was:

> The restriction of our population to some certain limits, and thereby a continu-
> ation of the union. Our citizens being so prone to rambling and extending
> themselves, on the frontiers, will, through necessity, be constrained to limit
> their extent on the west, to the borders of the Missouri and Mississippi, while
> they leave the prairies incapable of cultivation to the wandering and
> uncivilized aborigines of the country.[34]

With the notable exception of Lewis, the members of the earlier Expedition made haste to get into print. By the close of 1806 privates

Robert Frazier and Joseph Whitehouse had taken steps to have their journals published. Sergeant Ordway was sent to Jedidiah Morse for advice on the publication of his; eventually Lewis and Clark bought it for 150 dollars. However, the only explorer to publish his journals before the 1814 'official' edition was Sergeant Patrick Gass. Gass collaborated with a Pittsburgh bookseller, David McKeehan, and the result appeared in June 1807. It quickly went through seven editions, in Pittsburgh, Philadelphia, London and Paris.[35]

Little is known of David McKeehan. It seems likely, however, that his collaboration with Gass was undertaken for political as well as commercial reasons. There are some indications that McKeehan did not like Jefferson or his former secretary. One was a response to a letter Lewis published in *The National Intelligencer*. Having heard that 'there were several unauthorised and probably some spurious publications now preparing for the press', Lewis warned the public that only one soldier, Frazier, had been given permission to publish, and that his account would be unscientific. He gave notice of the publication within the year of his own journals. This drew a lengthy and vitriolic letter from McKeehan in which he accused Lewis of interference and extortion. McKeehan, it may be thought, was simply protecting his interests; but his attack far exceeded sound commercial practice for a publisher of one of Lewis's sergeants. He mocked the size and cost of the Expedition; attacked Barlow's poem; accused Jefferson's administration of despotism; drew attention to the unfortunate fight with the Indians; and closed with the scurrilous image of Lewis deliberately baring his buttocks to obtain an 'honourable' wound that would 'excite the curiosity and compassion of some favorite widow Wadman'.[36] Sterne, Jefferson's favourite novelist, was here being used against his lieutenant.

Another indication of McKeehan's hatred is given by a footnote in Gass's text which congratulates an Indian chief for refusing a Jefferson medal: 'he was the wisest Indian on the Missouri' (Gass, 307). The text of the journal itself, as edited by McKeehan, provides further evidence. It slyly hints at the promiscuity of the Expedition with willing squaws before concentrating on 'more useful information', which indicates that the West is hardly a Garden. There are references to 'beautiful' plains but these are offset by interminable 'scenes of barrenness and desolation' and 'the most dismal country' ever beheld, which is also the home of bloodthirsty grizzlies. The simple sequential nature of the account, moreover, serves to emphasise the time taken and difficulties encountered by the Expedition in crossing 'the dismal and horrible mountains'. Over one half of the text deals with this aspect of the Expedition. It is the Gass journal that notes 'desert' conditions which would shortly be developed by Pike and Brackenridge and would eventually turn into the myth of the 'Great American Desert'. The imagery of 'this howling wilderness' provided by Gass, then, is also at odds with Jefferson's Second Message.[37]

A quite different impression was conveyed by the next so-called *Travels of Lewis and Clarke*. Between 1809 and 1813 a number of texts were published under this title. They conflate published letters from Lewis and Clark, and Jefferson's Message to Congress, with material drawn from Jonathan Carver's *Three Years Travels* (of 1766–1768), Alexander Mackenzie's *Voyages from Montreal* (in 1789 and 1793), and Patrick Gass. Jonathan Carver's remarks about the Mississippi terrain are moved westward towards the Rockies, a textual construction of a landscape quite different from Jefferson's intentions. The account of the Missouri ranks it:

> among the greatest rivers. It is an object of astonishment to the whole world. The uniformed man admires its rapidity, its lengthy course, salubrity of its waters, and is astonished at its colour, while the reflecting mind admires the innumerable riches scattered on its banks, and foreseeing the future, behold [sic] already this rival of the Nile flowing thro' countries as fertile, as populous, and as extensive as those of Egypt.

> A traveller, however intelligent he may be, can give but a faint idea of the innumerable riches accumulated on its banks.[38]

To back up his repeated claim to 'innumerable riches', the 'traveller' then lists qualities of this new Egypt quite different from those suffered by Lewis. The 'natural prairies' are so fertile that they produce in the first year of tillage 'a considerable crop' with little labour. Amongst the innumerable natural products of the terrain is 'a certain and prompt cure for venereal disease'. The stones of the Missouri can be polished into fine jewels. The minerals to be found on its banks include iron, lead, coal and the finest salt. There is a clay that equals Chinese porcelain and a plaster that eclipses Paris. According to the Indians there is tin, copper, silver and gold. The fur trade is enormous. The only flaw in the Garden is one mountain. Separating the headwaters of the Missouri and Columbia, its land is 'cold and very steril, except in pasturage only'.

The spurious editions, in the words of one reviewer, 'pillaged and dislocated' materials from diverse sources. Indeed, the 'dislocation' was terrestrial as well as textual. The spurious editions created a fiction, perpetuating a Jeffersonian image of the West that preceded the Lewis and Clark Expedition. The interior, said one:

> now only inhabited by the tawney sons of the forest, and the howling beasts of prey, will be converted into the residence of the hardy votaries of agriculture, who will turn these sterile wildernesses into rich, cultivated, and verdant fields.

This image of the West was supported by the composite structure of the text. Whereas Gass's bare sequential narrative had emphasised the perils of the Expedition, the spurious editions tended towards a topical format which would underplay any adversity, had their compilers known of it. The spurious *Travels* were, in effect, promotional accounts. As one published in 1813 and bearing the name William Fisher remarked, 'the great object of our expedition was to aid *Commerce* and *Population*'.[39]

The 'official' account of the Expedition, known as the Biddle edition after its major editor, was based on the original journals. Nicholas Biddle worked hard to prepare them for publication, questioning some of the explorers and reading a good deal about the Indians. He assigned the scientific material to Benjamin Smith Barton, but Barton died with the projected addendum still in progress. It never appeared. The remainder, which Jefferson called (with a hint of contempt) 'the mere journal', was reworked, according to Biddle, into a 'succinct and circumstantial narrative'.[40] In doing so he smoothed away not only the rough edges of the journalists' style but also some of the adverse imagery of the West. He does not neglect to mention 'desert and barren' country (Biddle, 1, 303), but spends much more time on the Garden. Whereas Gass, in the second week of July 1804, simply restricts himself to the comment 'handsom prairie' (Gass, 23), Biddle provides a full, literary treatment:

> From the top of the highest mound a delightful prospect presented itself – the level and extensive meadows watered by the Nemehaw, and enlivened by the few trees and shrubs skirting the borders of the river and its tributary streams – the lowland of the Missouri covered with undulating grass, nearly five feet high, gradually rising into a second plain, where rich weeds and flowers are interspersed with copses of the Osage plum; further back are seen small groves of trees; an abundance of grapes; the wild cherry of the Missouri, resembling our own, but larger, and growing on a small bush; and the chokecherry, which we observed for the first time. Some of the grapes gathered to-day are nearly ripe.   (Biddle, 1, 62–63)

Biddle's piled-up clauses and painterly terms have transformed the West into the Picturesque tourism of the East. Biddle had never been further west than the Susquehanna River; it was, therefore, easy for him to turn the land into a landscape. As the penultimate line quoted indicates, Biddle uses the first person plural in the narrative. This has three effects. The first is to present a particularly authoritative view of the Expedition; the second is to elide differences in the individual journals; and the third is to paint over Lewis's forebodings. Lewis's account of the Great Falls is followed closely, but the appeal to Rosa and Thomson is omitted. Biddle the Philadelphia writer is quite capable of providing his own description. The Rockies become 'a beautiful view' (Biddle, 1, 337).

The difficulties in crossing the divide are muted, as is Lewis's animosity towards the Indians and the sheer boredom of the enforced stay on the Pacific. There is now no gap in Lewis's journal, and the bears are mere bears.

Biddle follows the encounter between Lewis and the bear discussed earlier, but concludes it as follows:

> The wonderful power of life which these animals possess render them dreadful; their very track in the mud or sand, which we have sometimes found eleven inches long and seven and a quarter wide, exclusive of the talons, is alarming; and we had rather encounter two Indians than meet a single brown bear.
>
> (Biddle, 1, 285)

Biddle's alterations of Lewis's prose effectively tame the bear. He emphasises accuracy of observation: it is a brown bear, and the size of its tracks (exclusive of the talons) is given precisely. He replaces Lewis's vividly direct verb 'fight' with the abstract latinate 'encounter'; and the bears are animals, not 'gentlemen'. The result is not foreboding but urbane.

The reviews of the Biddle edition perpetuated the divided responses to the West already apparent in the texts discussed. The Philadelphia *Analectic Magazine*, on the one hand, emphasised the Edenic aspects of the terrain described in Biddle's account: the abundance of game and timber, and the Picturesque nature of the Great Falls. On the other hand, the *Western Gleaner* retailed at length the perils involved in crossing the Rockies and the terrors of that 'sanguinary monster', the bear. 'Though provided with every thing that could ensure the success of the expedition', lamented the reviewer, 'they soon found how numberless are the difficulties and dangers to be overcome at every step in such an attempt.' The terrain west of the Divide is so broken that it will forever be 'unfit for an extensive inland navigation'. Far from providing a cure for venereal disease, the environment causes it. It also causes early deaths, and early decay of teeth. Clearly, the *Gleaner's* reviewer was well read in Old World books. Yet, this starkly different image of the West may also have arisen from the *Gleaner's* closer contact with the terrain; it was published in Pittsburgh. It certainly derived from political animosity. The *Gleaner* used the naming of rivers as a vehicle for a jibe at Jefferson. The Philosophy River was 'a scanty and insignificant rivulet'; surely this inadequate distribution of compliments would hardly 'gratify the wishes or the pretensions of the illustrious personage to whom they are addressed'.[41]

The Lewis and Clark Expedition, then, did little to disturb the established images of the West. Even its promoter, Jefferson, ignored the facts that were staring him in the face. In a manuscript entry in his copy of the *Notes on the State of Virginia*, Jefferson remarked that the Blue Ridge Mountains were not, as he had previously thought, the highest in America. That honour belonged to the White Mountains of New Hampshire, which were 4,885 feet above sea level. Of the Rockies' 14,000 feet Jefferson said nothing. Similarly, although Jedidiah Morse met Sergeant Ordway in 1807, his subsequent geographies barely reflected the encounter. The third, 1810, edition of his *American Gazetteer* remarks that Louisiana 'in general is unknown', and refers the reader to the information gathered in the second, 1804, edition when 'the region was a topic of general conversation'. The Rockies are described simply as 'lofty'.[42]

If the men who should have been the best-informed about the West could make such an oversight it is little wonder that others followed suit. Zadoc Cramer's *The Navigator*, intended principally as a practical guide to the Ohio River, was generally regarded as the most accurate and well-informed source on the West. First published in 1801, it had by 1824 gone through twelve editions. Information from the Lewis and Clark Expedition first began to appear in the sixth edition of 1808. The seventh edition talks a little about barren land around the Rockies and the ferocity of the bears. The tenth (1818) and twelfth (1824) editions, appearing after Biddle's *History*, expand somewhat on the desolation of the mountains. Yet the overall image of the West conveyed by *The Navigator* is still of 'the most fertile soil on earth'. The opening sentence of the tenth edition's 'Abridgment of Lewis and Clark's Expedition' remarks that:

> Before the cession of Louisiana to the United States, this was the region of fable. Fancy peopled it, and a thousand miraculous tales were related. The mammoth, that wonder of the creation, it was thought might be there, and Welsh Indians, with remnants of the Jewish tribes.

The same edition solemnly retails information of the salt mountain, 180 miles long and 45 miles wide, included by Jefferson in his 'Description of Louisiana' of November 1803 and mocked by John Quincy Adams. It was imperialism rather than accuracy that shaped *The Navigator's* view of the West. The opening sentence of each edition asserted that:

> No country perhaps in the world is better watered with limpid and navigable waters than the United States of America, and no people better deserve these advantages, or are better calculated to make proper use of them, than her industrious and adventurous citizens.[43]

The West continued to be the region of fable. Despite the accurate information that should have been available, it remained a screen on which were projected the hopes and hates of Americans.

Yet the Lewis and Clark Expedition had not been entirely futile. It added to the growing body of American mythology; a mythology which, while helping to create a sense of American identity, occasionally obscures the failure of the Expedition to achieve its object. The journals also initiated a tradition of Western writing. James Fenimore Cooper used the Biddle edition when preparing *The Prairie*, and a number of later novelists have drawn on Biddle or the *Original Journals*.[44]

The Biddle edition also made a deep impact on Edgar Allan Poe. In the Epilogue I will suggest that Poe transformed its parboiled material into one of the important themes of American culture. In doing so he also drew upon the work of Charles Brockden Brown. It is to Brown that the next chapter is devoted. By means of a survey of the entire span of Brown's writing career, I will try to show that his work encapsulates the achievements and the failures of Revolutionary environmentalism. The achievements, in fact, led directly to the failures. As Poe would later realise, the careers of Meriwether Lewis and Charles Brockden Brown ran in parallel. It was fortunate for Brown that his venture into American terrain was in the realm of fiction.

7

The excursive imagination of Charles Brockden Brown

Oft has the towering pride
Of Rome or Athens, fill'd my eager eye!
The dome that rear'd aloft, repos'd in air
Sublime as heavens high arch, in tranquil state,
Majestic, as a slumbering deity.

The scene (figure 5) is bathed in soft Italian light. The sacred swans create bright, reflected scintillas on the dark and gently winding river. Deer are watering by the river and, in the middle distance where it emerges into the sunlight, two men are fishing. To the right of centre the sun-god muses, prompted from the opposite bank by the nine sisters. Climbing into the left of the frame are flights of steps leading the eye and a votary to Parnassus, majestically surrounded by protecting trees. The broad blue sky and soft rolling land converge in a washed haze of horizon broken only by Mount Soracte, looking rather like an extinct volcano. The painting, by means of carefully placed elements related through a series of planes, constructs a peaceful landscape in which gods and men, flora and fauna, nature and culture coexist in tranquillity. The landscape is so potent that, almost a century and a half later and on a different continent, a young man recreates it in verse. The painting is Claude's 1652 'Landscape with Apollo and the Muses'. The poem, later called 'Devotion', was written in 1794 by Charles Brockden Brown, in Philadelphia.[1]

Brown would never visit the Old World; nor would he see this particular painting in its original state. Yet the components of 'Landscape with Apollo and the Muses' appear in other Claude paintings; and copies or engravings were widely available, particularly after the publication in 1777 of Richard Earlom's fine etchings of *Liber Veritatis*, Claude's pictorial catalogue of his work. These provided Brown with enough material to transcend temporal and spatial boundaries, and place an Old World aesthetic in a New World setting. Brown's reading was extensive, his imagination voracious. Although his physical journeys were limited to the eastern seaboard, his mental travels extended beyond America, even at times into and above the earth. They took him to the most

5 Claude Lorrain, *Landscape with Apollo and the Muses* (1652)

extensive vistas and the most cramped confines. In the following pages I
will discuss Brown's spatial imagination and the changes that it
underwent. I will try to show his initial infatuation with European
aesthetics; the gradual movement in his fiction towards an appreciation
of American terrain unmediated by those aesthetics; and a shocked
withdrawal, out of fiction and back towards Europe. I also want to
suggest that Brown was a man of his time, sharing many of the beliefs of
his contemporaries. Indeed, his career highlights as well as summarises
much of the discussion in earlier chapters. Occasionally, Brown even
anticipates changing attitudes towards the American continent. At its
finest, his fiction provided his peers with an omen about the gap between
their perceptions of the terrain and its reality. It is unfortunate that few, at
the time, paid any heed.[2]

VARIOUS AND DIFFUSIVE READING

Brown's earliest extant manuscripts demonstrate the sheer geographical
range as well as the constantly shifting passions of his imagination. The
importance of that faculty to him is illustrated by a letter written in 1792,

while the 21-year-old was still studying what he called, with deep hatred, 'the rubbish of the law':

> O my friend! How miserable should I be were I not rescued from the tedious or distressful present, by the aid of excursive imagination.[3]

He seems to have followed the advice of Fielding's Parson Adams, who thought that reading provided 'the only way of travelling by which any knowledge is to be acquired'. Brown's excursive imagination took him to many parts of the globe, away from 'insipid reality'. Another letter, written in Philadelphia, provides an example of the detailed creations of a man who never visited London:

> I have taken decent lodgings in Oxford Street. I banquet every morning on French rolls and Coffee, but spend the time between sunrise and breakfast, generally in traversing the fields around Islington and Chelsea. I spend the morning at Debrets, in talking with literary men, and reading new publications, or at a Coffee-house, over a newspaper or in writing anonymous remarks for the London Chronicle, on the reigning topics of conversation.

Last summer was apparently spent in Staffordshire and Wales; this one will include a visit to Westmoreland or Durham.[4] Other letters talk of Italy, or are written as from 'Cuilli', in Rousseau's Pays du Vaud, Switzerland. In Switzerland it is not only the landscape that enchants him. He tells of his marriage with 'beautious Jacquilette'. Fortunately for his real romances, Brown quickly kills off his fictitious bride. 'Death snatched from me the object of my vows', he writes, lost in a 'bewildering melancholy.'[5]

Imaginary voyages usually fade after childhood. These letters are from a man in his twenties who will shortly become a leading literary figure in Philadelphia and New York. They oscillate between fancy and reality. One page describes a walk with his fictional wife in Le Pays du Vaud. The next is headed 'Vine Street, Philadelphia' and moans about his 'present situation'. In one letter he asks why imagination should not 'supply the place of reality'. In another, during a trip to Connecticut, he is drawn away from Le Pays du Vaud to a Claudian depiction of the local scene:

> I am certain however that the lake of Geneva washes no shores more luxuriantly beautiful than those of Connecticut River, than Middletown and its environs, nor is a witness to scenes of greater happiness or more abundant fertility.[6]

The letters, too, provide exercises in a Rosa-inspired depiction of more gloomy psychological states. Several talk of suicide, and one places Brown on a precipice, where he addresses the 'Angel of destruction':

> How dreadful how desirable thy presence! What mingled terrors and delight accompany thy steps! Forbear to push me farther. I have gotten, I tell you, on

> the very edge. I overlook the precipice. What a turbulent and stormy sea!
> Darkness sits upon it. Shall I leap? Spring this second? NO. I will stay till I am
> irresistibly impelled. Yes – I will spend the night upon the virge of this jutting
> promontory.

Letters such as this, with their vivid present-tense account of the minutiae of mental torture, worried his friends greatly. They also prepared for the psychological description which would distinguish his novels; and made that preparation, moreover, in terms of a landscape. The landscape at present reveals the commonplaces of the Gothic and is reminiscent of the turbulence occasionally apparent in the work of Crèvecœur and Freneau, but Brown will develop it into a profound meditation on the nature of American terrain.[7]

Brown's early letters, indeed, indicate his dissatisfaction with the fictions he had read. Responding to a tale told by a friend, he saw in it further evidence that fact exceeded the fictions that had so far been created:

> I never met with in books, what I do not believe frequently to be discoverable
> in nature. Richardsons fictions have, I doubt not, been, a thousand times
> paralleled or exceeded by realities.

He set out to develop a fictional form which would be able to grasp those facts. His first known fiction, the 'Story of Cooke', probably written in 1788, concerns an Irish drunkard and not only gives further evidence of contemporary American prejudice against the race but initiates Brown's method of using a stranger to disturb a settled community.[8]

'The Story of Julius', dated 1792, is framed by the narrator, seated at his writing-desk overlooking the confluence of the Delaware and Schuylkill Rivers and commanding a broad prospect. From this vantage-point his imagination and his landscape expand. Julius's story is set near Keswick, a site known for its Picturesque terrain and hence a suitable one to improve on Richardson:

> There is no country in Great Britain, or perhaps in Europe that abounds with
> more magnificent and beautiful scenery amid rural grandeur and elegance than
> this part of Cumberland and the Neighbouring districts of Westmoreland, and
> none, in which the manners are more worthy of Philosophical observation. I
> had read but few accounts and those slender and imperfect of either the country
> or of the Inhabitants. But I was then possessed of a map of the northern
> provinces wonderfully extensive, accurate, and picturesque, and my fancy had
> long brooded on the scanty materials with which my various and diffusive
> reading had furnished me, with the utmost ardour and intensiveness. I longed
> to reduce the vague but brilliant images, which had amused my visionary
> hours, into some form and order.[9]

Clearly, Brown's 'various and diffusive' reading has been similar to

Jefferson's, but his response moves in the opposite direction.[10] In chapter 5 I suggested that Jefferson chose to limit his imagination. Here, and in subsequent fictions, Brown would allow his to roam. The map leads here to an exercise of 'fancy', but one which will be 'reduced' to a form. Brown will not suppress his imagination, but try rather to order it within a fiction. The rein is free, but it is a rein nevertheless.

Two fragments of 1797 show that Brown was beginning to yoke his wandering imagination to American terrain. 'Sky-Walk, or The Man Unknown to Himself, an American Tale' was apparently completed at the very end of the year. An extract was published in *The Weekly Magazine* in March 1798; the remainder was never published and has disappeared. The title suggests the relation, already noticed, between space and psychological states, and asserts its nationality. Brown's preface to the extract remarks that 'to the story-telling moralist the United States is a new and untrodden field', a sentiment which echoes the optimism of the English reviewer of *Poems on Several Occasions* rather than the sceptical fears of Jedidiah Morse. Apparently, the major site of 'Sky-Walk' was to be the wild terrain in the Norwalk area of Connecticut which Brown may well have seen during the visit described in the 1792 letter. He would deal with that area fully in *Edgar Huntly*. Unfortunately, the only allusions in the extant fragment of 'Sky-Walk' are to Bordeaux and Dublin.[11]

The other fragment of 1797 does, however, deal with the New World. Entitled 'Signior Adini', it consists largely of a conversation between a stranger of that name and Mr Ellen, a Pennsylvania gentleman-farmer. The landscape is constructed so that a contrast is made between the Old and New Worlds. A summer-house:

> was erected on the verge of an abrupt descent, whose bottom was laved by the river. The opposite bank, which for some miles was uniformly towering and steep, fell away when it came in from off this promontory, as if it were on purpose to allow us the spectacle of the setting sun, and a limited but charming prospect of corn fields and meadow.

The prose coyly reveals that the comparison is deliberate. The contours of the land around the river and the siting of the summer-house resemble the Claude landscape that opened this chapter. As his name suggests, the stranger is Italian, and when he is not talking he spends much time looking anxiously into the West. In part the prospect is a 'limited but charming' one that resembles Dwight's *Greenfield Hill*, but Adini has Jefferson's broad imperialism more in mind when he frowns into the setting sun.

The comparison is developed in conversation. Using 'lieutenant Robert's chart of the discoveries of Cook', Adini and the Ellen family talk about the empty spaces of the Pacific. One of the topics of conversation is the concept of geographical symmetry. We have seen it appearing several times in the work of the Revolutionary generation. Freneau, for instance, described it as the impulse driving the navigator westward in 'Pictures of Columbus'. Adini asserts that geographical symmetry does indeed exist. Ignorant people believe that the Pacific is 'a realm of barren and inhospitable turbulence, populous only in the mute and scaly kind'. After this wordy dismissal Adini claims that, as is demanded by 'analogy', the Pacific is occupied by land – Thomas More's 'Eutopia'. But it is a utopia that has degenerated. Shortly after this comment the fragment breaks off; Adini's remarks are not developed. It seems clear, however, that Brown intended to make an ironic contrast between the congenial if restricted local prospect, and the attractively rational but apparently fallacious planning of imperialism.[12]

Brown's early letters and fictions, then, demonstrate the spatial nature of his imagination. At times his landscapes resemble Rosa's wild, threatening canvasses. Occasionally they look like an adaptation of Claude's peaceful classical scenes to the demands of the agrarian Republic – 'Adini and the Muses by the Schuylkill', perhaps. At yet other times it is a map or an abstract geographical concept which provides the imagery. Brown's landscapes are varied and derived from many sources; and he placed them at the service of his major interest, the relation of terrain to psychology.

His thinking on psychology is complex and has been the subject of much attention.[13] It can perhaps best be summed up by a quotation from the 'Memoirs of Stephen Calvert', a fiction that Brown began after the publication of his first complete novel, *Wieland*. Like so many others, 'Stephen Calvert' was never completed. This is a pity, for it presents at one point the core of this thought:

> The constitution of man is compounded and modified with endless variety. The wisest and soberest of human beings is, in some respects, a madman; that is, he acts against his better reason; and his feet stand still, or go south, when every motive is busy in impelling him north.[14]

The first sentence opens with the noun which would immediately alert most Americans, but ends in dubiety. There is nothing certain about man's 'constitution'; it is at the mercy of complexity and mutation, two notions that are central to Brown's fiction. The long second sentence says the same thing in three different ways: the second clause clarifies the first, whilst the third restates the proposition in the suitably clear and simple image of two cardinal points of the compass.

The subject described by the image is far from simple. The sense of wonder at man's motivation seems to give Brown's prose at this point a

Romantic colour. But this is not the overall tone of Brown's mature fiction. The main thrust of Romanticism is towards a synthesis of the individual and nature that elevates both. A superficial mechanistic ordering of the world is rejected in favour of a more profound if impalpable order. The thrust of Brown's mature fiction involves the same rejection, but then proceeds in the opposite direction. There is no sense of final order in the work that Brown wrote between 1797 and 1800. Certainly, he aims at plotting as well as he can 'the constitution of man'. Yet he has a nihilistic awareness that there is no organic relation between the creative mind and the physical universe – that, finally, there is nothing to plot. Morse Peckham called such an attitude 'Negative Romanticism'.[15] It is as if Coleridge's fire has gone out, or as if Ruskin's ravine is in the New World.

THE METAPHYSIC WILDERNESS

The fate of the Old World in the New is first fully expressed in *Wieland*, published in September 1798 and Brown's best-known novel. The underlying nihilism in his thought is apparent on the first page. Clara Wieland, the narrator, states it clearly in the third paragraph, suitably in storm imagery:

> I address no supplication to the Deity. The power that governs the course of human affairs has chosen his path. The decree that ascertained the condition of my life, admits of no recal. No doubt it squares with the maxims of eternal equity. That is neither to be questioned nor denied by me. It suffices that the past is exempt from mutation. The storm that tore up our happiness, and changed into dreariness and desert the blooming scene of our existence, is lulled into grim repose; but not until the victim was transfixed and mangled; till every obstacle was dissipated by its rage; till every remnant of good was wrested from our grasp and exterminated. (*W*, 5–6)

Of course, the complaint against God is not maintained. By the close of the tale it seems that a 'double-tongued deceiver' (*W*, 244) is to blame. Carwin – surely the first character in or out of fiction to attempt a seduction by means of ventriloquism – admits to Clara that he had filled her mind 'with faith in shadows and confidence in dreams' (*W*, 211). The irony is that Clara is duped by the false sense-impressions derived from ventriloquism, while she ignores the genuine warnings of her brother's murderous tendencies because they come to her in a dream.[16]

Clara's dreams perpetuate the storm imagery. The lull of 'grim repose' is broken yet again in her dream in the closing chapter. Her imagination becomes 'a theatre of uproar and confusion', another storm against which she fleetingly sees all the male protagonists. The storm enveloping them is nothing compared to the one into which she is now plunged, her terror being conveyed in images of a horrific mutable landscape:

> Sometimes I was swallowed up by whirlpools, or caught up in the air by half-seen and gigantic forms, and thrown upon pointed rocks, or cast among the billows. Sometimes gleams of light were shot into a dark abyss, on the verge of which I was standing, and enabled me to discover, for a moment, its enormous depth and hideous precipices. Anon, I was transported to some ridge of Aetna, and made a terrified spectator of its fiery torrents and its pillars of smoke.
>
> (*W*, 236)

Once again, the dream proves to be a warning. Clara's chamber is on fire. The imagery of the warning, however, is not specifically American. Precipices are commonplace in the Gothic. We have seen in earlier chapters how frequently images of climatic or terrestrial instability are to be found. Indeed, the final 'transport' here is to the Sicilian volcano which, ever since Hesiod, has been used to indicate natural or moral instability.[17]

If Brown tends to tread well-beaten paths of imagery, they often lead him into novel situations. I would like to demonstrate this by reference to his friendship with Elihu Hubbard Smith, and to one of Brown's most often used images – namely those of paths which, like Jefferson and Lewis, he frequently employed. One such image is to be found in that third paragraph of Clara's narrative. Another is in the text's epigraph:

> From Virtue's blissful paths away
> The double-tongued are sure to stray;
> Good is a forth-right journey still,
> And mazy paths lead but to ill.
>
> (*W*, 1)

This reads like a threadbare *Pilgrim's Progress*. In fact, the poem imitates another written in 1788 and sent by one Mason Fitch Cogswell to Smith, who doubtless showed it to Brown.[18]

Smith and Brown became friends around 1791, and the two men may have worked together on the first anthology of American poetry, *American Poems, Selected and Original*, published in 1793. Smith had studied at Greenfield Academy with Timothy Dwight and at Philadelphia under Benjamin Rush, and he followed with equal fervour the professions of medicine and letters. It was therefore entirely appropriate that he should write the dedicatory 'Epistle' to the first American edition of Erasmus Darwin's *The Botanic Garden*. Darwin had produced translations of Linnaeus in 1783 and 1787. In 1789 and 1791 he published *The Botanic Garden*, a two-part poem setting the sage of Uppsala to rhyming couplets. The book was so popular that by 1806 it had gone through one Irish and six English editions, and had been translated into French, Portuguese and Italian. Smith's 'Epistle' to the 1798 American edition rings with enthusiasm. Darwin's poem, he says, is not only 'read with rapture, studied with delight' on the East Coast. It will help to civilise all corners of the far-flung American continent, even

> where Oregan foams along the West,
> And seeks the fond Pacific's tranquil breast,
> With kindred spirits strike the sacred lyre,
> And bid the nations listen and admire.[19]

Brown shared many of Smith's enthusiasms. He delighted in the Newtonian order imparted by Linnaeus's classification system, and probably became familiar with it through Darwin's work. The influence is apparent in Brown's early images of paths. In one of the 1792 letters he had walked a blissful path with his arm around 'Jacquilette', expounding Newton to her. By 1794, though, the image has become more complex. Newton has a less delightful function in 'Devotion', the poem which opened this chapter. Brown now proceeds under 'Newtonian banners' to wage war with 'Ignorance and Prejudice'. He marches 'in the footsteps of Linnean guide' and is:

> by the clue
> Spun by Upsalian hands, conducted safe
> Through pleasant paths: And long has been the march
> And weary through the thorny tracts that lead
> To nothing in the metaphysic wilderness.

The first half of this could have been written by Smith, or Mason Fitch Cogswell for that matter. It anticipates the task of Meriwether Lewis, destined to carry Linnaeus into the West. The caesura in the third line, however, signals a diversion from Smith and Cogswell. It portends the difficulties that would confront Lewis a decade later, and the concerns of Brown's four major novels. For, by 1798, the paths of *Wieland* have become 'mazy', less available to Linnaean analysis. It is not Linnaean order that has spread, but rather the 'metaphysic wilderness', appearing in storm imagery and destroying the landscape.[20]

Suitably, the confrontation between the Old World and the New occurs on a path which leads to the precipice overlooking the Schuylkill River and surmounted by a temple built by Clara's father. The prospect is similar to the one constructed in 'Signior Adini', and the landscape bears a strong resemblance to the Claude painting at the beginning of this chapter:

> The view before it [the precipice] consisted of a transparent current, fluctuating and rippling in a rocky channel, and bounded by a rising scene of cornfields and orchards. The edifice was slight and airy. It was no more than a circular area, twelve feet in diameter . . . edged by twelve Tuscan columns, and covered by an undulating dome. (*W*, 11)

This is where the solemn Wieland Senior addresses his Deity. It is later the site of a more fashionable gathering of the younger generation, graced with a harpsichord and a bust of Cicero. It is, it seems, the perfect New World setting of Old World tranquillity. All that is needed to complete the scene is the presence of Apollo.[21]

Yet, as early as the second chapter, the landscape changes. One evening Wieland Senior, gloomier than usual, ascends the path to the temple. His anxious wife, forbidden to accompany him, stares at the precipice. Anticipating the transformation to come, her worries rearrange the terrain:

> She strained her sight to get a view of the dome, and of the path that led to it. The first painted itself with sufficient distinctness on her fancy, but was indistinguishable by the eye from the rocky mass on which it was seated. The second could be imperfectly seen; but her husband had passed, or had taken a different direction . . . An half hour passed away in this state of suspence. Her eyes were fixed upon the rock; suddenly it was illuminated.   (*W*, 16)

Her husband has been fatally wounded by an inexplicable visitation, a spontaneous combustion, an enlightenment beyond the normal bounds of the term. The Claudian setting, too, has been transformed. An *auto-da-fé* has nothing Apollonian about it; it is outside the aesthetic that informs such landscapes. It comes from the 'metaphysic wilderness'.

The death of Wieland Senior presages the derangement of Wieland Junior. This time the visitation is even more clearly related to the American soil – for Wieland Junior becomes an American farmer:

> It was determined that his profession should be agriculture. His fortune exempted him from the necessity of personal labour. The task to be performed by him was nothing more than superintendance. The skill that was demanded by this was merely theoretical, and was furnished by casual inspection, or by closet study.   (*W*, 21)

Wieland Junior here resembles Jefferson. According to La Roche-foucault-Liancourt, Jefferson was a poor farmer because he relied excessively upon books.[22] Brown does not pursue the possible comparison. Instead, he concentrates on the young man's religious conversion. It takes place in a moment of 'irradiation' related to his father's spontaneous combustion (*W*, 167). The result is that he kills his wife and children.

As Clara remarked in the third paragraph of the text, 'the blooming scene [is] changed into dreariness and desert'. Brown reverses the normal process of land-transformation anticipated so hopefully by many of the figures examined in earlier chapters. Furthermore, a Europeanised setting on the Schuylkill is constructed only to be destroyed in two inexplicable visitations. Brown, it can be seen, is moving away both from the imperial ideology of many of his contemporaries, and from the enthusiasms of his own juvenilia. He still has a long way to go. His examination of the meaning of American terrain is brief and tends to remain at the level of assertion, as is suggested by the novel's subtitle, *An American Tale*. Brown has not yet fully demonstrated the relation between his 'excursive imagination' and the land in which he lives. It is appropriate, therefore, that Clara should conclude her narrative in 'the ancient world' (*W*, 237), the scene of Brown's youthful imaginary voyages.

On Christmas Day, 1798, Brown sent a copy of *Wieland* to Jefferson, expressing the hope that he would find time to open this mere work of 'imagination & invention'. The covering letter has hitherto been taken as evidence of Brown's admiration of the Vice-President. The gift may not, however, be without malice. The Jeffersonian elements in the text's landscape are viewed in an ironic if not destructive light, as is the temple which bears a resemblance to Monticello. Furthermore, the solicitations in the covering letter are measured.[23] Jefferson sent a late, brief and non-committal response. Although the book remained in his library, there is no evidence that he read it. Doubtless he would have regarded the visitation of the temple and the destruction of two American farmers by fire as further evidence of the 'bloated imagination'. In any event, he did not sell the book to Congress (Sowerby, IV, 466).

While he was writing to Jefferson, Brown was working on another fiction. This became his second published novel, *Ormond*. American terrain appears only fleetingly; the novel is concerned partly with the rights of women. Like *Wieland*, it also addresses itself to the disjunction between appearance and reality.[24] Brown takes the opportunity to attack the 'discipline' of physiognomy. The narrative uses mock-scientific jargon to assert that the heroine, Constantia Dudley, 'delighted to investigate the human countenance, and treasured up numberless conclusions as to the coincidence between mental and external qualities' (*O*, 77). In consequence, Constantia is helpless before the appearances assumed by confidence-tricksters.

Constantia derives her interest in visible objects from her father. It is with Stephen Dudley that Brown develops his views about the Picturesque. Like Benjamin West and John Singleton Copley, Dudley spent much time in Europe. He trained with Henry Fuseli (presumably in London) and lived in Italy, where he studied 'the Augustan and Medicean monuments'. The death of his father forced him to take over the family apothecary business, but his European training made him contemptuous of such drudgery. It also makes him believe that he has a superior understanding:

> The habits of a painter eminently tended to vivify and make exact her father's conceptions and delineations of visible objects. The sphere of his youthful observation comprised more ingredients of the picturesque, than any other sphere. The most precious materials of the moral history of mankind, are

> derived from the revolutions of Italy. Italian features and landscape, constitute the chosen field of the artist. No one had more carefully explored this field than Mr. Dudley.

This 'chosen field of the artist' provides no guidance to moral behaviour in the New World. Dudley employs a plausible young man, Craig, who embezzles his money. Penniless, Dudley turns to drink; then his wife dies and he goes blind. He can no longer exercise that faculty on which he placed, to his cost, so much reliance. He is even more helpless than he was as a gullible chemist, condemned as he now is to 'eternal dark'.[25]

Into the lives of Constantia and her stricken father comes Ormond, compared with whom Craig is an amateur. Ormond is a protean fiend whose 'projects' are 'diffused over an ample space', so ample indeed that, in one flight of fancy, he threatens to measure the lunar mountains 'by travelling to the top of them', thereby becoming the sky-walker that Brown had abandoned two years before (*O*, 116, 255). In general, however, he confines his attention to the West. Ormond has allied himself 'with schemers and reasoners, who aimed at the new-modelling of the world'. On their behalf he spends six years on expeditions to the unexplored parts of the globe, and seems to have fixed 'on the shore of an *Austral* continent, or in the heart of desert America' as a suitable site for their work (*O*, 252, Brown's emphasis). Brown here develops the hints of the 'Signior Adini' fragment by reference to the Illuminati. Like Jedidiah Morse, Brown and his circle were alarmed by the revelation of apparent secret societies in America, and Ormond is the third Brown villain to be a member of the Illuminati. Ludloe and Carwin, in the *Memoirs of Carwin* (the unfinished sequel to *Wieland*) had been members of the utopian sect. Ormond's utopia, it seems, was intended as the successor to the experiment which, according to Adini, Thomas More had created in the Pacific. Open American space is apparently easily perverted by European schemes.[26]

Brown's agoraphobia and his new-found dislike of the Picturesque coalesce near the close of the novel. Stephen Dudley has been murdered by Craig, just as he was proposing to end his days in Italy. Constantia has retired to the country-house she has inherited in New Jersey. It contains a study 'illuminated by a spacious window, through which a landscape of uncommon amplitude and beauty was presented to the view' (*O*, 268). The view so 'illuminated' faces, of course, westward. One evening Constantia is there as the sun sets and:

> her eyes rested for a moment on the variegated hues, which were poured out upon the western sky, and upon the scene of intermingled waters, copses and fields. The view comprized a part of the road which led to this dwelling. It was partially and distantly seen, and the passage of horses or men, was betokened chiefly by the dust which was raised by their footsteps.

> A token of this kind now caught her attention. It fixed her eye, chiefly by the picturesque effect produced by interposing obscurity between her and the splendours which the sun had left. Presently, she gained a faint view of a man and horse. (*O*, 269)

It is Ormond. He arranged the death of Dudley; he has killed Craig, Dudley's murderer; and now he has come to rape Constantia.

The set-piece looks forward to the work of Hawthorne and James. In particular, the way that the pictured setting comes to life – a man emerging, as it were, from the canvas – anticipates the 'Strether by the River' sequence in James's *The Ambassadors*. The careful placement of key terms indicates Brown's interest. Constantia is seated in a room and a position similar to Mrs. Wieland's before the disaster overtook her husband, and her vision is similarly obscured. Burke had noted in his investigations into the Sublime that 'to make any thing very terrible, obscurity seems in general to be necessary'.[27] Brown uses the theory to good effect. The result, here, is another attack on the Picturesque. Just as the aesthetic had earlier blinded her father, first figuratively and then literally, now it leads to Constantia's eyes becoming 'fixed'. The view is the same setting sun that had fascinated and worried Adini. One of the components of the picture, indeed creating its Sublime obscurity, is the man who had earlier led her by dissimulation into 'untried paths', who had gone West for the Illuminati, and who now comes out of the West and the sun for his 'prize' (*O*, 253, 285). Fortunately, Constantia has a penknife to hand, and she kills Ormond. Like Clara Wieland, she retreats to a Europe of established paths and not (as her father had wished) to a Europe of the Picturesque.

The landscapes in *Ormond* appear briefly but to great effect. They confirm the trend in Brown's earlier fictions and decisively reject political utopianism and European landscape aesthetics. Although at the end of the novel Constantia retreats to Europe, Brown does not on this occasion follow her. Neither, at this point, does his imagination move westward; for *Ormond* also indicates a rejection of the 'untried paths' that will later be explored in *Edgar Huntly*. There is, in consequence, only one direction that Brown's excursive imagination can take. His next novel, *Arthur Mervyn*, contains his most complete examination of the immediate environment.

SCENES OF FOLLY, DEPRAVITY AND CUNNING

Brown no longer needs to assert that he is writing 'An American Tale' in *Arthur Mervyn*. The novel's credentials are immediately demonstrated by its subtitle, *Memoirs of the Year 1793*, and confirmed by the first sentence (*AM*, 5). It is, of course, Philadelphia during the first year of the yellow fever that killed so many and marked forever the life and career of Benjamin Rush. It is likely that Brown was in his home town during some of the plague months. Certainly, the 1794 letter which included the poem 'Devotion' shows that he was also working on this tale. Yet, however mature the novel may have been in 1794, it must have been crucially affected by two events some four years later. In 1798 Brown caught yellow fever in New York. He was cured by Elihu Hubbard Smith. Then Smith himself caught the disease from a fellow doctor, and died.

If a brief eulogy by Richard Alsop is anything to go by, Smith's friends were deeply distraught. Certainly, the death of his close friend and physician had a strong effect on Brown, for he now published his fictional settings of the unpleasant experience.[28] *Ormond* briefly deals with the plague, but it is *Arthur Mervyn* that is justly renowned for its description of the illness that Brown had initially encountered in 1793. This is not the moment to discuss the plague as such, or the complex narrative method of *Arthur Mervyn*, although both will have their place. Rather, what follows is an account of the various terrains that confront the eponymous hero in his Fieldingesque progress.[29] It will show Brown's growing interest in a mutable landscape.

Arthur Mervyn's childhood environment is simple enough: his patrimony is 100 acres, a small farm in Chester County, outside Philadelphia. The evocation of the pastoral is, however, immediately cancelled by his father's remarriage to Betty Lawrence, 'a wild girl from the pine forests of New Jersey' (*AM*, 18). This invasion from the woods makes Arthur an 'alien' in his own home, and he decides to seek 'asylum' in Philadelphia. This echo of the ideology of migration from the Old World to the New is confirmed by a specific reference to the removal of Arthur's father from Scotland to America (*AM*, 21). The hero's own journey down 'this unwonted path' to the city is directed by the formula of the picaresque; he is easily gulled out of his money and arrives penniless in the city (*AM*, 25–27). It is accompanied, too, by a contraction of the landscape. The restriction of horizon that naturally occurs in an urban area is increased by the onset of darkness. The extent of Arthur's vision is marked by street lamps.

Arthur's vision is cramped even further. He is tricked into a yard where the buildings loom over him and where the darkness allows him 'to see nothing but outlines'; then into a house; then into a bedroom. Suddenly realising he is alone in alien territory and fearing the return of the owner, Arthur hides in a cupboard, where he is in 'utter darkness' and without 'the privilege of upright deportment' (*AM*, 42, 38). The contraction of landscape could not be more complete: from the open vistas of the Pastoral to the confines of a cupboard in which his position is both foetal and simian. Nothing more opposed to the ideology of migration could be imagined, and nothing better illustrates the disjunction of appearance and reality. Crouching in the cupboard, Arthur can only guess at the events outside. He is screened from reality just as a mask screens the intentions of a confidence trickster. Much later, in the second part of the novel, Arthur asserts that people must draw conclusions from what is 'exposed to their view'; not to do so would prove them 'brutish' (*AM*, 341). Within the first four chapters of the novel he has graphically and comically disproved his assertion.

Less comic events await Arthur. He catches yellow fever and is taken to a hospital that is based on Mathew Carey's description of Bush Hill.[30] In a manner that recalls Benjamin Rush's miasmic view of a plague-ridden environment, the narrative makes the scene tangibly horrific:

> The atmosphere was loaded with mortal stenches. A vapour, suffocating and malignant, scarcely allowed me to breathe. No suitable receptacle was provided for the evacuations produced by medicine or disease. My nearest neighbour was struggling with death, and my bed, casually extended, was moist with the detestable matter which had flowed from his stomach.

The plague, furthermore, is treated as both a cause and a metaphor of spiritual corruption. The next sentence signals a shift from natural to moral infirmity:

> You will scarcely believe that, in this scene of horrors, the sounds of laughter should be overheard. While the upper rooms of this building, are filled with the sick and the dying, the lower apartments are the scene of carrousals and mirth. The wretches who are hired, at enormous wages, to tend the sick and convey away the dead, neglect their duty and consume the cordials, which are provided for the patients, in debauchery and riot.
>
> A female visage, bloated with malignity and drunkenness, occasionally looked in. Dying eyes were cast upon her, invoking the boon, perhaps, of a drop of cold water, or her assistance to change a posture which compelled him to behold the ghastly writhings or deathful *smile* of his neighbour.
>
> (*AM*, 173)

Inevitably, the living are occasionally encoffined as dead, a mistake that Poe would turn into a motif.

The narrative here has great impact. The shift from past to present tense and the evocation of all the sense-impressions combine to make the scene as vivid as possible. The description concentrates, in a manner that anticipates Dickens, on parts of the body – a visage, eyes and, in the next paragraph, 'rude hands' – to heighten the counterpoint between physical and moral illness. The mirth of the attendants seems unnatural alongside the rictus of death that is emphasised shortly afterwards. Brown's metaphor, however, is more extensive; for he shows the plague destroying 'all the sentiments of nature'. Husbands desert wives, parents forsake children, a fearful populace flees into the country and, in an echo of 'The Memoirs of Stephen Calvert', a deranged few are hurried by 'their misguided steps' into the very danger they are trying to escape (*AM*, 129). In this instance like Benjamin Rush, Brown sees a correlation between the plague and the iniquities of urban life; for the moral chaos engendered by the yellow fever is only an extreme version of everyday life in Philadelphia, with its lies, deceit and chicanery. The City of Brotherly Love, it is clear, is no asylum.[31]

In these circumstances Arthur wishes to return to the country, to which, ironically, he has now transferred the label of 'asylum'. After further adventures he reaches his goal. He meets a Quaker farmer in a 'buck-wheat field and measuring, as it seemed, the harvest that was now nearly ripe', and obtains employment (*AM*, 118, 123). The simple pastoral beauty of the scene is completed when Arthur falls in love with the farmer's daughter. Then he has to return to the city on an errand. He catches the fever, and meets Dr Stevens, the benevolent physician whose narration of the meeting opens the novel. The narrative cycle is thus complete, and what is now called Part 1 of the novel ends.

Part 1 of *Arthur Mervyn* is formally complete. Thematically a number of loose ends are left, doubtless because Brown was contemplating a second part. The Preface to Part 1 informs the reader that the adventures brought to a close here 'are necessarily connnected' with subsequent events which 'may hereafter be published' (*AM*, 3). They were indeed published, but some fourteen to eighteen months later, in the late summer of 1800. Critics have tended to regard the second part as a disappointing sequel. Norman Grabo, for instance, concludes that although the two parts are philosophically sympathetic, the second part is in the nature of an afterthought. On the other hand, Emory Elliott has shown that Part 2, by contradicting Arthur's story in Part 1, now makes him an unreliable narrator.[32] Hints that are given in Part 1 – for instance, in the extensive use of verbs of appearance – now emerge into a fully developed critique of Arthur, revealing him not as a Fieldingesque innocent but rather as a complex and duplicitous character.

In addition, the simple country–city opposition of Part 1 disappears in Part 2. In Part 1 Arthur, ill with the fever, tells Dr Stevens that he regards 'the trade of the plowman [as] friendly to health, liberty and pleasure' (*AM*, 11). These Jeffersonian remarks, so close to the famous triad of the Declaration, anticipate his return to the Quaker family whom he has only temporarily left. In Part 2 Arthur goes back to the farm. A changed scene awaits him:

> The road was miry and dark, and my journey proved to be more tedious and
> fatiguing than I expected. At length, just as the evening closed, the well-known
> habitation appeared in view. Since my departure, winter had visited the world,
> and the aspect of nature was desolate and dreary. All around this house was
> vacant, negligent, forlorn.

Arthur compares it with 'the luxuriance and vivacity' that had greeted
his first arrival at the farm (*AM*, 271–272). Heralded by the visual
obscurity that we have come to expect at key moments, Arthur has come
upon a transformed scene. As the echo of Goldsmith suggests, the farm
has been deserted – not for the superior attractions of the city, but because
of the plague from the city. The farmer died of fever, whereon 'his
servants fled from the house, and the neighbours refused to approach it'
(*AM*, 276). Moral frailty exists in a pastoral setting, too.

Now Arthur's attitudes change. At first, although he admits that the
'excursions' of his 'fancy' sometimes went beyond what he could expect,
they were usually limited to his proper 'field':

> All I wanted for the basis of my gaudiest and most dazzling structures, was an
> hundred acres of plough-land and meadow. Here my spirit of improvement,
> my zeal to invent and apply new maxims of household luxury and
> convenience, new modes and instruments of tillage, new arts connected with
> orchard, garden and cornfield, were supplied with abundant scope.
>
> (*AM*, 291)

In Part 1 the Jeffersonian agrarianism had been limited to fairly simple
assertion. Now Jefferson himself is parodied in direct references to such
interests of his as the dumb waiter, the mould-board plough, and
experiments with European plants. The hint that Arthur is not being
quite candid here is confirmed within two pages when he has 'a
revolution in [his] mind'. Although on his first visit to the city he had met
only 'scenes of folly, depravity and cunning', his attitude is now less
'gloomy'. He has become interested in 'manners, professions and social
institutions' (*AM*, 293). In consequence he rejects the farmer's daughter
and returns to Philadelphia, where he eventually marries a wealthy
Jewish widow, named Fielding.

What has prompted Brown to abandon the Pastoral? There have been
suggestions that at this time Brown was moving rightwards from
Jeffersonian agrarianism towards Federalism. Certainly, it is possible that
his views polarised at a time of great 'faction'. The months during which
Part 2 of *Arthur Mervyn* was being prepared for publication saw
extraordinary party rivalry, with Jefferson finally being elected President in February 1801 after thirty-five ballots in Congress.[33] However,
this does not seem fully persuasive. I have suggested that Brown may

have disliked Jefferson for several years; yet distaste for a man does not usually lead, even in a person of great passion such as Brown, to rejection of a whole way of life. The answer, perhaps, is provided by *Edgar Huntly*, the novel that Brown published between parts 1 and 2 of *Arthur Mervyn*. *Edgar Huntly* was Brown's 'excursion' to the woods from which Arthur's stepmother, Betty Lawrence, had issued. As its 'Preface' boldly announced, the novel would go west, and in doing so would develop the materials of 'Sky-Walk' and ignore the warnings of 'Signior Adini' and *Ormond*. The experience would take Brown's imagination further into American terrain than ever before.

PASSAGE INTO NEW FORMS

Edgar Huntly has rightly been related to a variety of sources, European and American. The Indian Captivity Narrative, the Gothic, the Picturesque, and contemporary thinking (by Erasmus Darwin and Benjamin Rush) on the nature of the unconscious, have all been traced in the novel. It is perhaps best remembered for its use of the double, anticipating Poe's better-known exercises in the genre.[34] The device of doubling is relevant to this discussion, because it leads the eponymous hero into the wilderness. The significance of the first meeting between Edgar and Clithero Edny (who, like Cooke, is Irish) is signalled, as usual, by:

> the obscurity in which external objects were wrapped, and which, conse-
> quently, did not draw my attention from the images of fancy.

In this state Edgar makes his way through an area which, although 'trackless and intricate', is familiar to him, until he comes upon Clithero, digging and sobbing (*EH*, 9).

Edgar's suspicion that Clithero has murdered a close friend has been discussed by many critics, as has the relationship between mental conflict and the rough terrain into which Edgar follows the servant.[35] It is worth noticing, however, that until he follows Clithero, Edgar is on the civilised side of the frontier. He is 'on the verge of Norwalk', but the area is known to him (*EH*, 9). Clithero leads him beyond the verge, into a fantastic terrain. Because the area is of soft limestone, it 'abounds in rifts and cavities' (*EH*, 22). We have already encountered this terrain: it is the landscape of Rosa, the landscape of the Gothic, and would become part of the mythology of the West. Lewis would meet an example at the Breaks of the Missouri.[36] Here, Brown is fusing a European aesthetic with an American locality.

Therefore, although this is a wilderness area, it is easily contained within conventional imagery. Edgar refers to it as 'romantic' (*EH*, 22). Edgar, moreover, has a companion. When Clithero set off Edgar 'resolved to tread, as closely as possible, in his footsteps' (*EH*, 18). Clithero, then, is acting as a pathfinder into another area which, at first sight, is 'trackless'. This is emphasised ironically when Clithero disappears and Edgar sets out to find him. Edgar repeats the process of his first encounter with the servant. At first he passes through a 'sterile region' which 'admits neither of plough or spade', but with which he is nevertheless familiar. Until Clithero had led him from such 'customary paths', he had often rambled across this area, only to end 'in the prospect of limits that could not be overleaped'. Now he goes on and his path becomes 'more intricate and more difficult'. Eventually he has to creep along a narrow ledge overlooking a gulf. It leads into a fissure which is the site of an impressive waterfall (*EH*, 95–97, 101).

At last, it seems that he is in *terra incognita*:

> A sort of sanctity and awe environed it, owing to the consciousness of absolute and utter loneliness. It was probable that human feet had never before gained this recess, that human eyes had never been fixed upon these gushing waters. . . Since the birth of this continent, I was probably the first who had deviated thus remotely from the customary paths of men.

Edgar anticipates Ruskin when he looked into a Swiss ravine and imagined it to be Canada. The irony is that this sensation is immediately shown to be specious. Looking at the 'phantastic shapes, and endless irregularities' of the scene, Edgar sees a face. It is Clithero; but a transformed Clithero. As one critic has remarked, the servant has reverted to the savage state.[37] His clothing is scanty and ragged; his hair is long and matted. He has regressed in the manner feared by Hugh Henry Brackenridge: from the despised Irish to the detested Indian. Then he disappears, and Edgar vows to return another day in an attempt to recall him 'into better paths' (*EH*, 103, 110). Edgar's next visit to the site of Clithero's disappearance is less fortunate. In place of the servant he meets a cougar, which he calls a 'savage'. (Brown provides a footnote which nods at Buffon: the cougar is smaller than the tiger, but 'equally formidable to man'.) It leaps at him across the ravine, but misses its footing and falls to its death. Chastened, Edgar resolves to bring with him on further journeys to 'this darksome maze' a tomahawk, the weapon associated (particularly after Burgoyne's 'Proclamation') with savagism (*EH*, 124, 126, 128).

This lucky escape, and the change in terminology from 'path' to 'maze' are, however, no preparation for what is to come. Neither is the tomahawk, at first, of any help. At the beginning of chapter 16 Edgar wakes in complete darkness. So too does the reader, for there is a complete break in the narrative flow.[38] The reader's disorientation thus matches Edgar's, and the narrative pace is decelerated so that every movement of Edgar's fearful imagination is charted:

> I emerged from oblivion by degrees so slow and so faint, that their succession cannot be marked. When enabled at length to attend to the information which my senses afforded, I was concious, for a time, of nothing but existence. It was unaccompanied with lassitude or pain, but I felt disinclined to stretch my limbs, or raise my eye-lids. My thoughts were wildering and mazy, and though consciousness were present, it was disconnected with the loco-motive or voluntary power.   (*EH*, 159)

Edgar has been sleepwalking in the wilderness and has fallen into a pit. But the reader has to guess the former, and is not told the latter for another three pages. The concentration required of the reader, and conveyed by the narrative, is intense. The narrative pattern, indeed, looks forward to the dislocations and interior monologues of modern fiction. The paragraph quoted is also prophetic in other ways. Attention is directed to the primal, absolutely uncivilised essence of life: 'nothing but existence'. This last word is emphasised by its position at the end of the short main clause and at the centre of the paragraph. Brown is here describing a psychological state later defined by Emily Dickinson's poem 'After Great Pain'. He is doing it with a proto-Jamesian syntactical structure, the slow reachings of consciousness plotted by the slowly moving prose and the pinpoints of revelation suitably realised at the end of the sentence. 'Existence', therefore, is held in suspension by the reversal of main and subsidiary clauses. Meaning and structure combine to convey a terrifyingly nihilistic image which is further stressed by the momentary landscaping of consciousness, 'wildering and mazy', and the otherwise chillingly detached language.

The remainder of the chapter graphically portrays Edgar's 'Hour of Lead' and charts his gradual reorientation. He opens his eyes, but as he is 'wrapt' in 'impenetrable' darkness, he thinks that (like Stephen Dudley) he may be blind. He tries to explore his surroundings, but they are 'vast and irregular' and the blackness prevents him from 'comparing directions and distances'. The standard method of orientation used by explorers such as Lewis is therefore not available to him. He sits down and his landscape immediately contracts. He imagines he is in a dungeon, or has been buried alive. His state is now 'full of tumult and confusion'; he is unable even to gauge the passage of time. It is a living death that both recalls the hospital-scene in *Arthur Mervyn* and looks forward to much of the work of Poe (*EH*, 160–162).

Eventually the darkness changes. He sees two obscure flames. They are the eyes of a panther. With a good luck which Fenimore Cooper, with a stronger sense of probability than of understanding, would later call impossible, Edgar has his tomahawk to hand.[39] He kills the animal he once again calls 'a savage', drinks its blood and eats its 'reeking fibres' (*EH*, 166–167). It is at this point that hints given earlier in the text coalesce. The brutalised appearance of Clithero, the shift in landscape terminology from paths to mazes, the references to animals as savages and the use, specifically, of the tomahawk all presage the necessary degradation of Edgar. Previously, Clithero had acted as a pathfinder, pushing back the wilderness. Now Edgar has outstripped him, and the motif of doubling falls away to reveal the supposedly superior man in an attitude of bestiality. Grovelling on the ground with the agony brought on by the meal, the wretched man epitomises the demoralisation feared by Webster and Rush; and embodies the horrific images held at the margins of the work of Freneau, Dwight and others discussed earlier, adumbrated by Brackenridge, and realised to his cost by Meriwether Lewis. He represents an absolute rejection of the sentimental savagism occasionally indulged by Revolutionary writers. At the mercy of a mutable terrain and reduced to an animal condition, Edgar provides the antipode of the republican ideology. With this character, in this setting, Brown has brought into focus the deepest fears of the political owners of the New World – fears that America would not be the Old World renewed, but rather turned upside down.

Chapter 16 of *Edgar Huntly*, then, both summarises Revolutionary unease and anticipates, in subject and form, more modern American literature. It is, I think, the most important chapter written by Brown, possibly by any Revolutionary writer; but it does not mark the end of Edgar's demoralisation.[40] He escapes from the pit and meets a band of Indians with a captive white girl. Brown now employs the more lurid elements of the Captivity Narrative; Edgar kills five Indians and rescues the girl. Here again, Brown moves beyond formula, for Edgar kills one of the Indians solely in retribution, not out of necessity. Suitably, the Indian is portrayed in animal images, for Edgar treats him as he had treated the cougar, as a 'savage'. The horror is heightened by Edgar's inadequacy as a marksman. He possesses only negative savagism, not the survival skills of the Coonskinners (*EH*, 199–203).[41]

In another context at the close of the novel, but with imagery that echoes his earlier attitude to the frontier, Edgar sums up his experiences:

> Few, perhaps, among mankind have undergone vicissitudes of peril and wonder equal to mine. The miracles of poetry, the transitions of enchantment, are beggarly and mean compared with those which I had experienced: Passage into new forms, overleaping the bars of time and space, reversal of the laws of inanimate and intelligent existence had been mine to perform and to witness.
>
> (*EH*, 239)

Before his fall into the pit, Edgar had been confined within 'limits that could not be overleaped' (*EH*, 97). Now he has gone beyond them. Once again, a comparison with Meriwether Lewis is enlightening. Lewis's path to the West had been relatively comfortable until he saw the Rockies for the first time, when he remarked that his 'way' was crossed by a 'barrier'. Soon after he saw the Missouri Breaks, which he talked of as an 'inchantment' (Thwaites, II, 79, 101). When he crossed the 'barrier', the transition was such that he passed out of form, and ceased writing his journal. We have seen Brown's imagined frontier experience stretching the form of his work beyond the Captivity Narrative and beyond the normal linear flow of the tale so that it anticipates more modern narratives.

Presumably because it was imagined rather than experienced, the frontier does not utterly fracture the form. Instead, it leaves an indelible mark reflected in the musings of Brown's amanuensis, Edgar:

> Possibly, the period will arrive when I shall look back without agony on the perils I have undergone. That period is still distant. Solitude and sleep are now no more than the signals to summon up a tribe of ugly phantoms. Famine, and blindness, and death, and savage enemies, never fail to be conjured up by the silence and darkness of the night. I cannot dissipate them by any efforts of reason ... My heart droops when I mark the decline of the sun, and I never sleep but with a candle burning at my pillow. If, by any chance, I should awake and find myself immersed in darkness, I know not what act of desperation I might be suddenly impelled to commit.   (*EH*, 158)

Adini had looked nervously at the western sky; Ormond had come out of he setting sun to rape Constantia; now, for Edgar, it recalls his wilderness experience, and he is changed, perhaps forever.

It is possible to argue that it changed Brown, too. In the 'Preface' to *Edgar Huntly*, pleased with the reception given to Part 1 of *Arthur Mervyn*, he had been assertive about the proper materials for an American 'moral painter':

> Puerile superstition and exploded manners; Gothic castles and chimeras, are the materials usually employed for this end. The incidents of Indian hostility, and the perils of the western wilderness, are far more suitable.   (*EH*, 3)

The materials were not only suitable; they were popular. *Edgar Huntly* was his only novel to go into a second edition in his lifetime. Yet Brown never again dealt with the West in fiction. As we have seen, Part 2 of *Arthur Mervyn* specifically rejects the agrarian dream and denigrates Jefferson, its leading proponent. It also links and questions the future of America and the future of literature. The closing two chapters of *Arthur Mervyn* suggest that marriage is preferable to writing. They anticipate Brown's own nuptials and his unease over the role of fiction. Ironically, Arthur's attack on the 'impertinent loquacity' of books (*AM*, 427) brings him close to Jefferson's fears for the 'bloated imagination' that they can cause. Quite unlike Jefferson, he also rejects America. In rapid succession and like Clara Wieland before him, Arthur abjures both the pen and his home country. He plans to go east to Europe with Mrs. Fielding once he 'has been made the happiest of men' (*AM*, 445–446).

CONFINED VIEWS

The formulaic ending of *Arthur Mervyn* signals a major shift in Brown's fiction, regressing back to Richardson and involving an even greater rejection of specifically American materials. Brown published just two more novels, *Clara Howard* in the summer of 1801 and *Jane Talbot* by the end of that year.[42] They both concern the moral adjustments which have to be made to convert a young man into a suitable groom. In each case the fellow has to go west before the heroine recognises his suitability. In *Clara Howard* the young man, Philip Stanley, his condition 'forlorn and dreary', plans to execute a childhood dream to find the Northwest Passage. He imagines his journey in terms of the received geographical wisdom of the time. He will sail down the Ohio and Mississippi Rivers and ascend the Missouri to its source. He will then, he says, 'drag my bark over mountains and rocks' until the sources of the rivers to the Pacific are found. After reaching the great ocean he may well go to China or sail down the Pacific coast. Clara Howard, responding to this dream, oscillates between indignation and worry. The 'forests and wilds' are inimical to 'the charms of nature' (clearly, human nature), 'the attractions of science', and the demands of familial duty. How can he desert all the joys and duties of civilisation? Clara's remarks are effective; Philip gets no further than Wilmington, Delaware.

Jane Talbot develops the theme in a more serious and sustained fashion. This time the young man, Henry Colden, is an atheist, a rationalist, and an apparent opponent of marriage. The heroine reproves him for his views. He is 'wandering in a maze of passions and doubts; devoured by fantastic repinings and vague regrets'. The imagery here, a pale shadow of the imagery of earlier novels, is intended to recall Colden to 'the joys and energies of religion', the 'foundation' and 'guide' that he needs. Like Philip Stanley he decides to travel. But he is much more practical. He sails to Japan via the Horn. Japan, although a 'new world', is a civilised world, not savage like the American West. From Japan he travels to Hamburg, where he awakens from his 'dreams of doubt and misery' and now believes in 'his Divine Parent and Judge'. Jane, meanwhile, has gained an interest in maps, and follows his journeys avidly. She fears that he may go:

> to the end of the world; where even a letter cannot find him; into unwholesome climates; through dangerous elements; among savages . . .

Her fears are not realised. Henry Colden returns to domestic bliss.[43]

Brown's movement away from *Edgar Huntly* is contained within the spatial elements of his last published novel. As before, the image of the maze indicates confusion, but it is not a confusion to be explored. Jane's images of the West both accord with her image of Colden's rationalism and confirm the strictures of Old World writers. The West is dangerous, not only because of the savages but also because of the climate. Colden, furthermore, seems to have agreed with her. For, like Freneau's 'fancy', although in the reverse direction, he omits America entirely from his itinerary. Here there are no dreams of the Northwest Passage, but rather a circumnavigation that resembles the civilised Grand Tour of earlier decades.

The West, furthermore, is beyond that mark of civilised contact, the letter. It is also beyond the form of the text, for both *Clara Howard* and *Jane Talbot* are artless epistolary novels. If Meriwether Lewis passed beyond the journal in the Rockies, Henry Colden would pass outside the novel there. Once again, Brown seems to be anticipating the problems that would afflict Lewis four years later. The West is not merely dangerous; it is, in these contexts, incommunicable. We have seen the effect of the West upon Lewis. Here, the effect upon Brown is a retreat to an epistolary mode that by 1801 had been jaded for some time. Brown's engagement with the West in *Edgar Huntly* had been accompanied by an adventurousness in form. The retreat back to the East and a growing conservatism is accompanied by a formal timidity. The epistolary novel, moreover, imposes immediate spatial limits. In *Edgar Huntly* the hero, and Brown with him, had overleaped 'the bars of time and space' (*EH*, 239). Now, writer and heroine confined themselves to the closet where the letters are written.

Nor are there any epistemological problems raised by the closet. The letter-writers do not see themselves as trapped. Whereas the novels published in 1798 and 1799 had been confessional, the later novels reflect an accessible social interaction. (The earlier novels, it is true, have epistolary elements in them, but these are no more than springboards to a greater formal complexity.) Finally, the heroine of *Jane Talbot* points the direction of Brown's future interests. She likes to pore over maps and read travel narratives. Her travelling, in other words, is vicarious. Of course, Brown's travelling had nearly always been vicarious; but with *Jane Talbot* he is reverting to a form of imaginative travelling that he had last used in 'The Story of Julius', a form which is vast in its scope but which involves little contact with American terrain. This will be the kind of imaginative excursion that Brown will take in his later writings, and it is on this that the discussion will close.

It is well known that the last decade of Brown's life was marked by a growing conservatism, perhaps accentuated by his marriage and involvement in a trading venture with his brothers. In contrast to his earlier fiction, and the professed views of Thomas Jefferson, Brown now found that there was nothing new under the sun.[44] Of course, the change did not take place overnight. The earlier part of this chapter indicated that he may in his youth have been less approving of Jefferson than has previously been recognised. Furthermore, in 1798 and 1799, when he was writing his most adventurous fictions, he also published two pieces which contained the seeds of his later thinking. The first appeared in *The Weekly Magazine* in August 1798. It was a two-part article entitled 'Facts and Calculations Representing the Population and Territory of the United States of America'. The contents conform with the dryness of the title: they consist of a turgid collection of figures, projecting the value of American lands up to 1834 and the number of citizens up to 1956. The exercise in prediction leads to the conclusion that by the middle of the twentieth century America will have eight times the population of Europe in 1798. Brown's optimism is however balanced by a final phrase that seems to contain a threat in its confident future tense. 'Among this number', he asserts, 'there will prevail a similitude of language, government, and manners.'[45]

Although Brown's thought is not noted for its consistency, 'Facts and Calculations' indicates an authoritarian strain which is confirmed by a short story he published in *The Monthly Magazine* in May 1799. Entitled 'Thessalonica: A Roman Story', it details the mayhem that can result from a small infraction of the rules. A Roman tries to enter a stadium by a gate reserved for Senators. His passage is barred, and the ensuing scuffle escalates into a riot which presages the decline of Rome 'and the return of the human species to their original barbarity'. The narrator, a Senator, feels oppressed by the burden of his task:

> to count up the victims, to describe the various circumstances of their death, is a task to which I am unequal. Language sinks under the enormity and complication of these ills. I was a witness and partaker; the images exist in my imagination as vividly as when they were presented to my senses; my blood is still chilled, my dreams are still agonized by dire remembrance; but my eloquence is too feeble to impart to others the conceptions of my own mind.

The intensity of feeling places the Senator alongside narrators like Clara Wieland and Edgar Huntly. But there is one important difference. The Senator finds language inadequate for his purpose. Other narrators had hesitated before their task, and had then gone boldly on. Here the narration ends in a linguistic doubt that mirrors the narrator's cultural despair. The fear of language 'sinking' anticipates both Jane Talbot's fears for Henry Colden and the actual fate of Meriwether Lewis. The political message of 'Thessalonica', however, prescribes an antidote. If the American Republic is not to follow its Roman predecessor into extinction, it must confine its citizens within strict rules.[46]

I discussed the interrelation of Noah Webster's politics and linguistics in chapter 2. A similar authoritarianism marks the last years of Charles Brockden Brown. When he died in 1810 he was only thirty-nine years old. Yet the distance that he had travelled in his imaginative excursions brought him quickly to the same conclusions as the ageing lexicographer. Brown now sought a form that would convey his authoritarian vision. It involved a movement away from fiction. Indeed, in 1803 he specifically rejected his former 'exertions'. This did not involve however a complete rejection of fiction as a form, but rather a movement towards a particular form of fiction, the historical. R.W.B. Lewis identified *Arthur Mervyn* as initiating a movement which would take the hero out of time and into space. Anticipated by 'Thessalonica', Brown's fiction after *Jane Talbot* moved in the opposite direction, most substantially in the 'History of the Carrils'. Nine or ten fragments, comprising some 100,000 words, remain of a large work accounting for the Carril family from Roman times until 1810. But even more time was spent editing magazines, translating, and writing political pamphlets.[47]

Brown, in short, had become the member of the literary establishment that he had imagined in the 1792 letter supposedly written from 'The Cocoa Tree, Pall Mall'. Now, he no longer needed to travel imaginatively to such exotic places. Indeed, he even seemed to regret travelling in his own country. In 'A Jaunt to Rockaway, in Long-Island', a short, far from jaunty essay published in October 1803, Brown regrets that he ever went on the trip. There seems to be little that is worth recording. The linguistic deprivation bemoaned by the Senator in 'Thessalonica' is recalled here, but in very different circumstances. Brown would clearly much rather stay in the editor's study than expose himself 'to an hundredth part of the perils which beset the heels of a Ledyard or a Parke'.[48]

Brown's voluntary confinement carried with it an imaginative withdrawal from American terrain. He adopted an elevated prospect paradoxically similar to that of his opponent Thomas Jefferson. Brown's description of America in 1807 is a case in point:

> The plane of the continent above the thirtieth degree of latitude, and below forty-fifth, is diversified by two ridges of mountains, one of which descends from the north-east, two or three hundred miles from the coast of the Atlantic ocean, while the other approaches from the north-west, nearly the same distance from the western margin of the continent. Between these ridges lies an enormous valley, the sides of which are washed by a vast number of great rivers.[49]

The description resembles Freneau's *Freeman's Journal* essay and Jedidiah Morse's 'Fredonia'. It is contained within compass points and meridians, and reflects a belief in symmetrical geography. There is no evidence that he expects the description to be altered by the Lewis and Clark Expedition, although he had earlier shown great interest in it.[50] Again like Morse and many easterners, Brown's image of the West will not be disturbed by any conflicting reports.

The continent was no longer observed for its relation to psychology, but seen simply as a field for the imperial ideology. Brown expressed the ideology in two of the fragments from the 'History of the Carrils', published in 1805. Entitled 'A Specimen of Agricultural Improvement' and 'Specimen of Political Improvement', they provide a model of agricultural administration. Sir Arthur Carril resumes his estate in Scotland and dismisses an inefficient manager. The prospect is not promising:

> Much of it was continually wet, and many hollows and low places were filled with stagnant water. The exhalations from these bogs and pools, in a warmer climate, would be fertile sources of bilious and pestilential fevers. As it was, obstinate agues were extremely prevalent in spring and autumn.

> This circumstance considerably increased the natural asperity of the climate, and rendered it not only more uncomfortable and unwholesome to man, but also more ungenial to the soil.

Brown here reflects the received environmentalist wisdom of the time, enhanced by his experience of the Philadelphia plagues. It makes the achievement of Sir Arthur all the more notable. He discovers a fertile subsoil in some areas, and creates small farms of the kind admired by Timothy Dwight, with:

> neat and substantial dwellings and barns, the fields . . . completely hedged, or fenced, or ditched, and tenants admitted, under strict conditions as to the mode and objects of their cultivation.

Less fertile areas are drained, planted with trees, and turned over to pasturage. In consequence, the whole estate 'has been converted into a smiling and busy scene of cultivation', with an accompanying increase in population – and revenue for Sir Arthur.[51]

Brown now applied the model to America. It was effected in part by means of a translation of Volney's *A View of the Soil and Climate of the United States of America*. The book resulted from the Frenchman's extended visit to America from 1795 to 1798. It is likely that Brown met Volney while he was in Philadelphia.[52] In any event, Brown published his translation in 1804, taking the opportunity to correct a number of errors and add some extensive footnotes which reflect his view of America. In particular, Brown once again uses his experience of the Philadelphia plague to correct Volney's theories. Like Rush, he links physical and moral disease. Those most subject to the plague are 'the most poor and the least thrifty'. He also shares Rush's view that alcohol is a prime source of disease and 'the great curse of the country'. It is the duty of government to regulate 'the passions' and discipline 'the manners' of the people. Brown, like Dwight, has little sympathy with the wildness of the westerners; neither is he now much interested in the Indians. They provide an example to be shunned rather than a means of measuring the savagism of the whites. In a footnote which reflects the mercantile business that he entered with his brothers in 1800, he wishes the Indians off the face of the earth. The Indians are 'hastening to oblivion', and Volney's interest in them would bring a smile to the face of 'the busy merchant, artizan, or farmer'.[53]

Brown's purpose is not simply to expose the faults in Volney's text. His main aim is to bring before the American public a textual method of ordering America. Volney's book is not a travelogue, but rather a detailed analysis of American terrain. Brown recognises that, although a number of detailed accounts of particular states have been written – he doubtless has in mind, amongst others, books by Jefferson, Williamson and Belknap – Volney's is the first to attempt the whole Republic. It is, he asserts, 'the best and the most complete that has hitherto appeared'.[54] The Frenchman has achieved much during his stay in America. Brown, from the vantage point of his editor's desk in America's cultural (if no longer political) capital, clearly hoped to achieve much more. In part the process of ordering America would be prosecuted through his magazines. From 1803 onwards they included a higher and higher proportion of factual material, confirming the penchant for statistics revealed in the 1798 article on American land and population. Brown's drive toward factuality, evident also in his shift towards historical fiction, reached a climax with the publication of *The American Register, or General Repository of History, Politics and Science*. It was published biannually from November 1807 until Brown's death and, as its title suggests, was simply a compendium, providing a digest of contemporary American and European events, lists of publications in the Old and New Worlds, scientific and cultural information, and a calendar of American and foreign state papers.

Despite all their personal and political differences, Timothy Dwight and Thomas Jefferson had concluded their business with America in the library. The list of state papers at the end of *Notes on the State of Virginia* and the intense factuality of much of *Travels in New-England and New-York* were attempts to transform the land by cataloguing it. Brown differed from Dwight and Jefferson only in exceeding their pedantry, his *American Register* being an attempt to place between boards everything that was known about America and its relations with the rest of the world. The catalogue would later be revitalised in the work of Emerson and Whitman. Here it symbolises the death of Brown's imaginative engagement with the New World. This is, I think, highlighted by reference again to the two models of interpretation sketched in the Prologue. In *Edgar Huntly* Brown had resembled Vespucci, seeing America in terms of its novelty. In *The American Register* he resembled Columbus, relating the terrain to the pages of a book.

Nor did he stop there. Brown's political pamphlets, suitably more assertive, pursued the imperial ideology further. The 1803 *Address . . . on the Cession of Louisiana to the French* was largely made up of a fictional French document extolling their newly acquired territory and dismissing the Americans as 'pedlars and shop-keepers'. Brown's talent with fiction was here employed in an attempt to goad Congress into wresting Louisiana from the French. In the essay enclosing the fake document, Brown proclaimed that the time was now ripe to colonise the territory. Anticipating the later rhetoric of Manifest Destiny, he asserted that 'America is *ours* . . . and therefore Louisiana is ours'. Americans were waiting upon the command of Congress to 'rise as one man, and STRIKE!'[55] The theme was continued in another pamphlet published in 1803, entitled *Monroe's Embassy* and concerned with Mississippi navigation. Sharing Jefferson's growing unease over the French ownership of Louisiana, Brown asserted that the 'unbounded territory' of the West was waiting 'to be claimed by us'.

Brown's next pamphlet, however, published four years later and called *The British Treaty*, introduced a note of caution to his growing spread-eagle imperialism. More concerned over trading rights than westward movement Brown, for once, confirmed the shopkeeper mentality of which the fictional French counsellor had accused the Americans in the 1803 *Address*. The Government's westward ambitions, he said, had made them overlook the fact that American independence was really founded upon trade. Congress was giving away commercial rights in exchange for land. They had 'set their fancies to work in stretching the boundary north and west', far beyond the needs of the Republic's population. Brown took the opportunity to attack Jefferson. The President was 'a weak visionary, timorous and irresolute', quite good with telescopes but unfitted for leadership. As evidence of Jefferson's failure, Brown repeated the jibe that the President believed in a mountain of salt in Louisiana.

The 1807 *British Treaty* continued Brown's opposition to Jefferson but otherwise was out of keeping with his imperial ideology. That ideology was reasserted in the 1809 *Address . . . on the Utility and Justice of Restrictions upon Foreign Commerce*. Once again, he saw America as a 'level and fertile' continent awaiting the territorial expansion that, 'barring deluges . . . and pestilences. . . *must* happen'. In an echo of his 1798 article, he asserted that America 'is occupied by one language; one people; one mode of government; one system of salutary laws'. The 'unpeopled waste' would disappear and the whole continent would be united under one ordering system.[56]

All this while, Brown was working on a geography which would provide the most thoroughgoing order to the American continent. In 1807 he issued a 'Prospectus' for a two-volume work suitably entitled a *System of Geography*. The title reflected Brown's desire for a unified continent, and resonated from Jedidiah Morse's description of his own first geographical publication, the 1784 *Geography Made Easy*. Morse, indeed, was the only geographer for whom Brown had any praise. The rest simply presented 'medleys' of little usefulness. His own proposed work, in contrast, would provide a complete account of the physical and political nature of America and the eastern hemisphere. Brown then continued in terms which link his early letters with his last work:

> When the surface of the earth is delineated as fully as the materials in our possession admit, we may make excursions, in almost any direction, over the world of man and nature. In these excursions, however, the present writer will confine his views to that relation in which soils, minerals, plants, and the lower animals bear to the well being and subsistence of men. With respect to mankind immediately, his inquiries will almost entirely resolve themselves into what may be called statistical.

Fifteen packed years after the 1792 letter discussed near the beginning of this chapter, Brown revived the image of the excursion, but this time with a vital difference. He had learned from *Edgar Huntly* the costs that would be incurred by an overly excursive imagination. Now it would be 'confined' to statistics. In an 1804 article he had suggested that 'the state of this part of the world' should be obtainable at a glance from a statistical table.[57] Now, in 1807, he was proposing to provide an exhaustive tabulation of America. It would not include any attempts to relate terrain to human psychology.

The wilderness which had enticed him to 'overleap' the limits was now relegated to an object for Picturesque analysis. In *Ormond* (1799) Brown had attacked the Picturesque; he made it the direct cause of Stephen Dudley's poverty and blindness. Just over a year later he changed his mind. An article first published in 1800 and sufficiently favoured to be reprinted in 1804 indicates Brown's return to the original source of his interest in landscape:

> Much may be done . . . by solitary efforts to analize the scene before us, and nothing can be done without such efforts. It is likewise of great use to examine the works in this kind of celebrated painters; but it is an advantage scarcely to be hoped for by us who stay on this side of the ocean. Books are of the most use.

Included in a list of recommendations are the works of Gilpin and:

> books for little other purpose than to deduce the application of the principles of this kind of beauty, and to furnish out such a set of pictures, *in words*, as Verney, Claude, and Salvator exhibited on canvas.[58]

Brown's imaginative excursion into America was over. In the last decade of his life he tended to restrict his description of the New World to quantitative matters, relying on the European masters for such pastime activities as the Picturesque. He would no longer allow the less pleasant aspects of American terrain to upset him. In another article on the Picturesque, published in 1806, he remarked that 'visions of fancy' provide leisurely enjoyment. They recreate 'exquisite scenes'. The dangerous parts of the world now had no place in his scheme of things. In 1798 a dream-image of Aetna had warned Clara Wieland of a fire in her room. In 1805 such blemishes on the face of the earth had no function in Brown's imperial vision of an American Garden. In an article on volcanoes published in that year, Brown asserted:

> Happily for us in the United States, we are exempted from the evils which are inseparable from a volcano. For the sake of this security, we shall readily dispense with the gratifications which the fancy might receive from the spectacle, and which, like all other pleasures of that kind, would grow stale with repetition.[59]

Mount Soracte would never erupt in Brown's scheme. It would continue to remain a quiet embellishment to the horizon.

Brown, then, is not only the United States' first professional novelist. His was a representative life, and his career highlights many of the themes of earlier chapters. The fictions he published between 1798 and 1799 contain the most thoroughgoing attempt to escape from Redcoatism, the European canons of style that were laid over the American terrain. In those fictions Brown realised, more than any other writer save Meriwether Lewis, the implications of Eurocentric writing. They are implications that Edgar Allan Poe, building on the work of both the novelist and the explorer, would develop into the first full consideration of the meaning of American space. I will examine Poe's work in the Epilogue, and suggest that Brown's imaginative excursions, like Lewis's actual explorations, were not conducted in vain.

Yet they had their costs. Brown retreated to the position adopted by most of his contemporaries, a position in which the land would be confined within a system derived from Europe. Inevitably, it led to despair. Webster, Morse, Rush and many of the others lived long enough to reap the bitter harvest of that despair. Brown was still hoping to systematise the land when he died in 1810. His manuscript *System of Geography* was lost; only the 'Prospectus' remains. Once again, it seemed, the wilderness had the last word.

The solid ground of Edgar Allan Poe

It seems to me that a major theme (or constellation of themes) in American culture is the mutability of the environment, the fear of regression among the inhabitants, and the instable relation between the text and the terrain it is supposed to describe and systematise. I emphasise that this is *not* the only American theme. In a culture so diverse and complex no single theme could possibly take precedence. It is clear, however, that the world (and the word) turned upside down has intrigued or afflicted a number of writers. Their work, I suggest, finds its origin in the Revolutionary generation.

The world turned upside down may be found in many shapes and forms. It is 'the Power of Blackness' identified by Harry Levin. It is the 'sense of the radical disjunction between words and things' plotted in Stephen Fender's analysis of the rhetoric of the California Trail, and in Tony Tanner's study of fiction written a century later. It enforces a dialectic in modern poetry between, say, the work of W. D. Snodgrass, which struggles to create objective correlatives for personal feelings in the environment; and the work of the confessional poets, which shuns the struggle and closes the door on external reality. It is to be found in the fruitless proliferation of words to encompass space in *On the Road*. It directs the images of escape from a limited and limiting text when Huck Finn lights out for the territory, or when Yossarian paddles away from the confining and discordant island of Pianosa in search of (Sw)Eden. It symbolises white oppression in Toni Morrison's *Sula*. It informs the ideas of an imposed order in the poetry of Eliot, Stevens and Olson, and the fears of a nocturnal disorder contained within Richard Wilbur's urban and urbane 'After the Last Bulletins'.

The landscapes of this theme loom austerely in many of Willa Cather's novels, and infiltrate the body of Gary Snyder's poetry. They may be

found everywhere in the imaginary Republic. Of course, they occur in
the West; for instance, at the Rocky Mountain resort of Stephen King's
The Shining, with its savagely mobile topiary. They also occur in the
South, as in James Dickey's *Deliverance*, where a hunting party (led by
Lewis Medlock, a reincarnation of Meriwether Lewis?) slides into
bestiality in a backwoods shortly to be washed away by a man-made
lake. *Deliverance* begins with a map of the area which will disappear. The
landscapes of human duplicity are beyond mapping in the Montana
of Francis Scott Key Fitzgerald's 'The Diamond as Big as the Ritz'; and in
the Chesapeake Bay (the 'birthplace of white America') of John Barth's
Sabbatical, which aptly gives the absent landmarks the names Key Island
and Poe Cove. The list of literary examples could go on; and the
discussion could then be extended to examine the terrible beauty of
Georgia O'Keeffe's desert paintings and the Sublime of Mark Rothko,
his work so ambitiously expansive that it burst the two-dimensional
confines of the canvas to find its ultimate form in the Houston Chapel.[1]

But this is not my purpose here. I wish to close my discussion of the
world turned upside down by examining the theme in the work of Edgar
Allan Poe, for it was Poe who firmly established the tradition upon
which so many others have drawn. This last remark, I am aware, flies in
the face of a critical tradition which asserts that Poe's landscapes are too
confined within the cranium to relate to American terrain. One strand of
this tradition can be summarised by remarks made in 1926 by Joseph
Wood Krutch, who said that for Poe 'the American scene was non-
existent', and that his works 'have no place in the American literary
tradition'. The other strand is represented by the French writers and
critics who have assiduously recomposed Poe, sometimes as a saint,
sometimes as a structuralist, and sometimes as a successor to Franklin, a
buckskin genius. Perhaps they had their predecessors' coonskin experience in mind.[2]

I believe that this critical tradition does a disservice to Poe by isolating
him from his context. I am not the first to think this. Writing just one
year before Krutch, William Carlos Williams expressed a similar view of
Poe very firmly when he said:

> He was the first to realize that the hard, sardonic, truculent mass of the New
> World, hot, angry – was, in fact, not a thing to paint over, to smear, to destroy
> – for it WOULD not be destroyed, it was too powerful – it smiled!. . .
>
> Americans have never recognized themselves. How can they? It is impossible
> until someone invent the ORIGINAL terms. As long as we are content to be called
> by somebody else's terms, we are incapable of being anything but our own
> dupes.

Thus Poe must suffer by his own originality. Invent that which is new . . . and there's none to know what you have done. It is because there's no *name*. This is the cause of Poe's lack of recognition. . . Here Poe emerges – in no sense the bizarre, isolate writer, the curious literary figure. On the contrary, in him American literature is anchored, in him alone, on solid ground.[3]

In his superbly direct and succinct way, Williams states here the thesis that I have been labouring in the preceding pages. I disagree with him in just one important respect. He treated Poe's work as a beginning rather than as a summation. In his assertive fashion Williams was claiming more for Poe than he deserved; and this may have caused the awkward metaphor. One does not anchor in solid ground, but rather in a sea-bed. But if we go beyond Williams and seek Poe's antecedents, the metaphor (despite the highly mobile landscape created by Poe) becomes crystalline. For Poe's work is deeply rooted in Revolutionary American culture. Poe is the writer who transforms the earlier failures into success. The final pages of this study will attempt to demonstrate this by examining a limited selection of Poe's work – principally *The Narrative of Arthur Gordon Pym* – in the context firstly of Charles Brockden Brown; secondly of *Symzonia*, a quasi-scientific utopian fantasy; and finally of the Biddle edition of the journals of Lewis and Clark.

Poe believed that the finest American novelists were Nathaniel Hawthorne and Charles Brockden Brown. His indebtedness to Brown has been fairly clearly established.[4] The theme of the double in *Edgar Huntly* is to be found in 'The Fall of the House of Usher', and most fully in 'William Wilson' (both 1839). Images of confined space and mutable landscapes, dealt with in most of Brown's fictions of 1798–1799 but most fully in *Edgar Huntly*, are to be found in much of Poe's work, from the contracting pit of 'The Pit and the Pendulum' (1843) to the multicoloured, irregular apartments of 'The Masque of the Red Death' (1842), their curtains perpetually in motion. Poe uses the plague in 'King Pest' (1835) and, of course, in 'The Masque of the Red Death'. And his tales drip with the blood and malevolence of savagism. 'The Tell-Tale Heart' (1843), 'The Cask of Amontillado' (1846) and 'Hop-Frog' (1849) are just three examples of Poe's abattoir sensibility.

Doubling, savagism and mutable geography are all to be found in Poe's only full-length novel, *The Narrative of Arthur Gordon Pym of Nantucket*, published in 1837 and 1838. I do not intend to give here a full analysis of the novel. It has already been discussed extensively and with great insight in those linked contexts of mystic penetration, adventure and hieroglyphics. Rather, I shall confine myself to sketching an analysis of those aspects of *Pym* that are germane to my thesis. With regard to doubling, Harold Beaver has already shown the close relationship between the eponymous hero and his friend Augustus Barnard, the man who smuggles him aboard the whaler. Professor Beaver plots the parallelism between Pym, confined in the hold, and Barnard above decks. He shows the end of the relationship when Pym leaves his hiding-place and replaces Barnard in his affections with Dirk Peters, a misshapen half-breed.[5]

Peters, with his huge head and bowed arms, also resembles Bracken-ridge's orang-utans. Tyson had regarded the orang-utan as the nexus between the animal and the rational. As such it would naturally interest Poe, who was fascinated with the idea of the littoral, physiological and geographical as well as psychological. In 'The Murders in the Rue Morgue' (1841) the orang-utan has been endowed with a voice, although one devoid of all 'intelligible syllabification'. If the Cardinal de Polignac had admitted it to the Christian Church, perhaps it would not have committed the brutal murder.[6] In *Pym*, the beastlike figure of Peters has a less speculative function. He serves to prepare Pym and the reader for the scenes of savagism which lie ahead. There is one difference between the savagism of *Edgar Huntly* and that of *Pym*. Huntly seemed more savage than the Indians, a view perhaps reflecting Brown's Philadelphia Quaker upbringing. Poe, who regarded himself as a Southern gentleman and supported the slave system of his home state of Virginia, projected much of the savagism of *Pym* onto the Blacks of the strange South Sea island of Tsalal. Initially the natives befriend the ship's company, but their perfidy becomes apparent when they lure the whites into a gorge and create a landslide, killing all but Pym and Peters.

There are, nevertheless, two linked echoes in *Pym* of the savagism of *Edgar Huntly*. The first occurs when Pym, cramped in the hold of the whaler, falls into a stupefied sleep. He dreams that a monster has pinned him to the ground. He wakes up slowly, his disorientation similar to that of Edgar in the pit. He discovers that the monster is another (and this time animal) double, the dog, his 'inseparable companion' for whom he has 'an affection far more ardent than common'. Somehow the dog has crept aboard, and now he shares Pym's captivity. The similarity with the panther incident in *Edgar Huntly* is heightened by the dog's name, Tiger, and the ambivalent relationship he has with Pym, despite their mutual affection. The first appearance of Tiger as the monster in the dream presages (in a fashion similar to Clara Wieland's dreams) his transform-ation into a monster by his confined and ravenous condition. He is now a tiger in behaviour as well as name. When next Pym emerges from a delirium, Tiger leaps at his throat. His despair giving him strength, Pym escapes only by trapping the dog in blankets and barricading himself in another area of the hold (pp. 66–67, 77–78).

The second echo of the savagism of *Edgar Huntly* is the incident of cannibalism. This is prefigured by the terrible sight of the plague ship. At the bowsprit as it approaches is a sailor, apparently smiling and gesticulating. As the ship passes, Pym and his three shipmates see that the movements are created by a seagull which is feeding off the sailor. The gull has already eaten the sailor's eyes and lips, creating the dreadful smile. Now it is eating his intestines, and as the ships pass the gull tosses 'a portion of clotted and liverlike substance' onto the whaler. Pym and Augustus momentarily think of devouring the meat, but quickly throw it overboard. Two days later the men are less squeamish. They draw lots and one of them, Parker, is eaten by the others. Parker's sacrifice is anticipated by one of Pym's delirious moments, when he imagines that Parker is Tiger the dog. When they draw lots, Pym feels an intense antagonism towards Parker. 'All the fierceness of the tiger', admits Pym, 'possessed my bosom.' Although earlier in the plot Pym had been able to separate himself from Tiger, it is apparent here that he has assumed the ferocious qualities of his sagacious dog. In the right circumstances both dog and man can be tigerish. Here, Pym is as keen to eat the man he had confused with Tiger, as Edgar Huntly was to eat the panther (pp. 130–133, 125, 145).

Echoes of *Edgar Huntly* may also be found in the mutable geography of *Pym*. The dark hold of the whaler, with its 'innumerable narrow passages' and poorly stowed and therefore shifting cargo presents to the confused sense-perceptions of Pym the same fluid space that the pit did to Edgar. The spatial mutations of the hold are to be found in the terrestrial landscape, too. On their journey southward on the 'Jane Guy', Pym records details of earlier explorations and notes that a number of islands, presumably volcanic, have now disappeared. The island of Tsalal is made mutable by the natives, who cause the landslide killing the sailors. Pym records the event with a reference to the Flood. It seems to him:

> that the whole foundations of the solid globe were suddenly rent asunder, and that the day of universal dissolution was at hand.

When he eventually escapes from the near-suffocation of his 'tomb', he finds that the gorge is now filled with 'the chaotic ruins' of a vast quantity of earth and stone, an echo of the language of Burnet's *Theory of the Earth* (pp. 61, 175, 207, 211).

The most mutable area of all, of course, is the sea. Crèvecœur's Letter VIII (which uses Pym's hometown, Nantucket, as its setting) and Freneau's 'The Hurricane' had already depicted horrifically mutable seascapes. Poe adds an increment of horror when the whaler, dismasted and out of control, becomes 'a mere log, rolling about at the mercy of every wave'. In this predicament, with 'huge seas' roaring 'in every direction around us and above us' and inverting the environment, Pym's mind also undergoes a revolution. He has a waking dream of a pleasant yet mobile landscape. Green trees and waving meadows of ripe grain pass before his mind's eye. In all this, he recalls, '*motion* was a prominent idea' (pp. 123–124, Poe's emphasis). He sees an endless succession of mobile objects. Nothing is stationary. Then he imagines he is back in the hold, with Tiger alongside him. The mobility of terrain and imagination comes to a climax in the closing paragraphs of the text, when Pym is rushing 'with a hideous velocity' towards the cataract and is afflicted by 'a chaos of flitting and indistinct images'. The penultimate sentence sees Pym entering the void. Such space is beyond imagination, and beyond description. The text breaks off, to be taken up by the 'editor', who notes that the final two or three chapters of the narrative have been lost (p. 238–240).

Edwin Fussell has suggested that *Pym* was one of a number of texts in which Poe projected a western landscape upon the South Seas. The foregoing analysis confirms this, for the American frontier of *Edgar Huntly* has been transformed into a strange new frontier where earth and sea seem to be interchangeable. *Pym*, therefore, dislocates America. In doing so it draws upon an earlier fiction, *Symzonia*, published in 1820 by John Cleves Symmes (1780–1829). His uncle, also named John Cleves Symmes (1742–1814), had been the founder of the Miami Purchase, a vast area north of the Ohio River settled under the provisions of the 1785 Land Ordinance. Unfortunately, the expansive enthusiasms of the older Symmes outstripped the precision of his surveyors. He sold land beyond the limits of his patent, was ruined and ended his days an embittered man. His nephew took steps to avoid such disappointments by setting his Eden beyond the United States – beyond, in fact, the surface of the earth.[7]

Like Meriwether Lewis, the younger Symmes had both an army commission and a vivid imagination. However, his wish to become an explorer remained chairborn. In the circumstances perhaps it was fortunate, for he believed that the earth was 'hollow and habitable within', and that access to the inside could be obtained at the poles. Symmes's 'theory of concentric spheres' also indicates that he had probably read Burnet's *Theory of the Earth*, for it resembles the English bishop's image of the earth as an egg. The 'Sectional View of the Earth' given as a frontispiece to *Symzonia* closely corresponds to Burnet's sectional view. Symmes first broadcast his theory in 1818, announcing to the world that, if adventurous explorers could break through the icebound polar rim, they would find a warm and fertile land where life would flourish.

Two years later Symmes published his novel under the potently American pseudonym of Captain Adam Seaborn. Perhaps infected by the senior Symmes's ill-fortune, Seaborn decides to leave the United

States because of its 'want of scope'. He sails beyond the Antarctic Circle, and at the pole enters the interior of the earth, where he discovers the perfect democratic republic. It is governed by men who resemble Jefferson's natural aristocracy and occupied by people who are automatically virtuous. This is a racial as well as a rational republic, for only the fairest people live there. The landscape is fair, too, a model of pastoral perfection. Seaborn talks of 'a succession of well-cultivated meadows' of fertile soil in a permanently temperate zone, with 'gently rolling hills' and a picturesque horizon resembling the Claude painting I discussed in chapter 7. There is 'a lofty mountain, which in the distance reared its majestic head above the clouds'.[8]

If today Symmes's work appears to provide an odd terminus for the Edenic vision that has so often appeared in this study, it must be remembered that the true nature of the polar regions was not established until the Amundsen and Scott Expeditions of 1911–1912. Symmes was taken seriously by many of his contemporaries, particularly by one Jeremiah Reynolds, who publicised his theory with great fervour. The Russian government offered Symmes a place on an expedition to Siberia, and eventually his theory received enough support in America to persuade Congress to fund their own expedition. One of the supporters, of course, was Edgar Allan Poe.

Poe was deeply read in accounts of exploration, but contemptuous of many of them. A review of a new edition of *Robinson Crusoe* tells why:

> Alas! the days of desolate islands are no more! . . . Wo, henceforward, to the Defoe who shall prate to us of 'undiscovered bournes'. There is positively not a square inch of new ground for any future Selkirk. Neither in the Indian, in the Pacific, nor in the Atlantic, has he a shadow of hope. The Southern Ocean has been incontinently ransacked, and in the North – Scoresby, Franklin, Parry, Ross, Ross & Co. have been little better than so many salt water Paul Prys.

Impatient, even afraid of the unknown, the explorers of the polar regions struggled to tame it by applying the aesthetic dicta of the known. Their published journals reveal accounts of polar terrain in terms of the Sublime and the Picturesque. In stark contrast, Poe was interested (like Charles Brockden Brown before him) in such regions precisely because they prompted an imaginative expansion into the unknown.[9]

Many people sneered at what they called 'Symmes's hole' or, with a little more elegance, 'holes in the poles'. Poe was fascinated by Symmes's theory, I suggest, precisely because *Symzonia* brought *Robinson Crusoe* up to date. It provided an imaginative account about one of the few places as yet unviolated by the salt water Paul Prys. There is ample evidence of his fascination. He spoke of the theory in his magazine articles, and made references to it in two of his early stories. The 1833

'MS. Found in a Bottle' ends when the narrator's vessel plunges into a whirlpool at the South Pole. Poe may have obtained the idea of the whirlpool directly from Burnet's *Theory of the Earth*, which suggests that whirlpools are 'Subterranean out-lets' providing entry to the inner chasms; or perhaps he had read Elton's translation of Hesiod. In the 1835 'Unparalleled Adventure of one Hans Pfaall' Poe this time takes the adventurer to the North Pole in a balloon, en route for the moon. When he crosses over the pole, Pfaall sees that it is concave, with a sharply defined centre.[10]

'Hans Pfaall', perhaps, took Symmes's theory to its lunatic extreme. *Pym*, as the similarity of names suggests, provides the most sustained example of Poe's serious interest in it. There are many references to Symmes and his theory, and some passages written by Reynolds are included wholesale in the novel.[11] However, Poe is too sophisticated to limit himself to simple plagiarism. *Symzonia* is, after all, a model of the hallucination of displaced terrain that I discussed earlier. It provides a politics of pastoralism which had been a driving force for the new Republic but which, as it clearly no longer applies to America, has to be dislocated and projected upon new territory. *Symzonia* is therefore available for ironic treatment; and Poe achieves the irony in two ways, by inversion and by omission.

The Tsalalians are a perfect counterpoint to the Symzonians. Their perfidy resembles the machinations of Brown's confidence tricksters. There is nothing open or rational about them; they are the embodiment of self-serving evil. And they are perfectly, horrifically black. Even their teeth are black. It is natural, therefore, that the Tsalalian hostage who accompanies Pym and Peters on the final journey southward should die of fright as the canoe approaches the cataract. Had he lived, the landscape he entered would be for him the world turned upside down (or, rather, outside-in), an absolute perversion in its pastoralism, rationality, and the whiteness of its inhabitants. The second irony, of course, is that the narrative places the reader in the same position as the Tsalalian. Pym and Peters may, perhaps, reach Symzonia. The narrative dies at the cataract. We are never able to judge if Symmes's terrain, like the terrain of the Revolutionary ideologues, is mere hallucination.

Poe, then, makes extensive and adroit use of *Symzonia*. In doing so he makes no distinction between fact and fiction, for he freely combines passages pillaged from Symmes with those taken from factual sources. These include the narratives of Captains James Cook and Benjamin Morrell; a compendium entitled *The Mariner's Chronicle*; and the Biddle edition of the journals of Lewis and Clark. Two articles in the *Southern Literary Messenger* for January 1837 reveal Poe's interest in Lewis and Clark. The first, a review of Washington Irving's *Astoria*, shows his familiarity with the Expedition and its place in western exploration. The second shows why he is interested. In a review of Reynold's *Address on the Subject of a Surveying and Exploring Expedition to the Pacific Ocean and South Seas*, Poe extensively quotes his discussion of 'the appalling weight of responsibility' which rests on the shoulders of explorers. Reynolds regarded Jefferson's instructions to Lewis as a model for all exploration journals. Indeed, he asserts that, among all the records of Jefferson's genius, it is second only to the Declaration of Independence. The sheer 'range' of the instructions provide no finer evidence of 'the extended views and mental grasp of this distinguished philosopher'.

Poe's review and quotations from Reynolds's *Address* clarify the nature of his interest in the West. Like the polar regions, the West provides a space available for imaginative endeavour. But space, in Charles Olson's words, is large and without mercy. Most writers fail to live up to its inexorable demands. Poe thought, for instance, that *The Columbiad* (1807), Joel Barlow's essay at an American epic, had revealed no more than his 'perseverance'. Even worse, attempts to use the West as the proving-ground of American antiquity were often merely ludicrous. George Jones's *Ancient America* (1845), yet another account of the Israelite–Indian succession, gave rise to one of Poe's most vituperative reviews. The polar regions seemed to fare no better. As we have seen, Poe believed that the journals of earlier polar exploration had revealed their writers as pusillanimous Paul Prys. In contrast, the scope of Jefferson's instructions might prompt polar writing of an altogether more monumental scale and execution. Such a journal would befit the grandeur of this final frontier, which Reynolds described as 'that point where all meridians terminate . . . the axis of the earth itself!'[12]

One can only speculate on the effect that the original journals of Lewis and Clark would have had on Poe. Certainly, the 1814 Biddle edition made a deep impression on him, even though it dissipated some of the darker elements of the journals. It is a source for five tales, written over a period of ten years. Together with Irving's *Astoria*, the Biddle edition is used most extensively in 'The Journal of Julius Rodman' (1840), where it undergoes relatively minor but playful alterations. Poe claims that Rodman crossed the Rockies in 1792, some thirteen years before Lewis and Clark. This provides another Poe irony, suggesting that the Biddle edition plagiarises Rodman's journal, instead of the other way round. There is a similarity of event and of landscape. The accounts of the Indians and the animals follow those of the Biddle edition; but the Edenic landscape is superior:

> I strolled to some distance to the southward, and was enchanted with the voluptuous beauty of the country. The prairies exceeded in beauty anything told in the tales of the Arabian Nights.

The members of the Rodman Expedition resemble those of Lewis and Clark. There is a Black servant based on Clark's slave York; a Newfoundland dog like Lewis's Scannon; Rodman and Andrew Thornton are close friends like Lewis and Clark; and Rodman possesses in exaggerated form some of Lewis's characteristics. He is deeply melancholic and suicidal, where Lewis was only fitfully so. Although the 'editor' of Rodman's journal claims in a footnote that, unlike Lewis, he never exaggerates facts, he admits that Rodman's account is coloured by 'the sombre hue of his own spirit'.[13]

It is often suggested that 'The Journal of Julius Rodman' is incomplete. It was published in six instalments in *Burton's Magazine* in 1840 and was never included by Poe in any selection of his work, perhaps indicating his dissatisfaction with it. On the other hand, an unconcluded narrative, as we have seen with *Pym*, is not necessarily a sign of Poe's dissatisfaction. The text, moreover, breaks off at an interesting moment. As one critic remarks, the narrative ends at the point where the Rodman Expedition would have taken a different route from Lewis and Clark. The end, moreover, occurs just after Rodman has experienced 'wild and savage pleasure' from combat with bears at such close quarters that he felt their 'hot and horribly fetid breath' on his face.[14] Poe, it is clear, had developed a number of the nuances of the Biddle edition to emphasise themes of savagism and doubling.

Whether or not Poe was unhappy with 'The Journal of Julius Rodman', his long-term interest in Lewis and Clark is indicated by four other tales. 'The Gold Bug' (1843) in part concerns an expedition in search of an Eldorado, Captain Kidd's treasure. The leader, William Legrand, is 'well-educated, with unusual powers of mind, but infected with misanthropy, and subject to perverse moods of alternate enthusiasm and melancholy'. On the expedition he is accompanied (in addition to the narrator) by his Black servant, Jupiter, and – again – a large and affectionate Newfoundland dog. These reassorted members of the Lewis and Clark Expedition travel 'in a northwesterly direction, through a tract of country excessively wild and desolate, where no trace of a human footstep was to be seen'. The terrain they venture into, with its soft crags and ravines, resembles the Breaks of the Missouri.

'The Landscape Garden' (1842) focusses on the promoter of the Lewis and Clark Expedition. Once again, a similarity of names is suggestive. Ellison, the protagonist of the tale, could partly be based on Jefferson. Ellison inherits forty-five million dollars. With this fortune, three times the sum Jefferson paid for Louisiana, he decides to create a landscape garden which will rival the paintings of Claude, and which will reflect 'the Almighty Design' in features such as '*strangeness*, vastness, definitiveness, and magnificence'. 'The Domain of Arnheim' (1847) extends 'The Landscape Garden' into American terrain. It adopts some of the images of the 1831 poem 'The City in the Sea' and strips them of their apocalyptic overtones. Ellison now attempts to find the perfect site for his landscape-gardening enthusiasm. In his search he does not send an amanuensis but goes west himself. He discovers there that nature conforms with Jefferson's ordering principles in 'a weird symmetry, a thrilling uniformity, a wizard propriety'. As his boat approaches Paradise, it descends faster and faster 'into a vast ampitheatre' which contains a strange and highly-coloured landscape, with purple mountains, golden and crimson birds, meadows of painted flowers, and an amazing, Arabian–Gothic construction suspended in mid-air. Western American space here is filled with some of Poe's most exotic motifs.[15]

'The Domain of Arnheim', as befits Poe's final 'Biddle' tale, took Lewis and Clark to an extreme resembling that of 'Hans Pfaall'. The earliest one used the explorers for more sombre purposes. That tale, of course, is *Pym*. It is here that the relationship of western and polar travel, suggested in the review of Reynolds's *Address*, achieves its perfect fusion. Indeed, the review could be regarded as a Prologue to *Pym*, for it appeared in the same issue of the *Southern Literary Messenger* as the first instalment of the tale. In view of the emphasis Poe gave to Jefferson's instructions to Lewis, it is appropriate that the first reference in *Pym* to Lewis and Clark begins in a library. The hold of the whaler in which Pym is hidden is, fortunately, well stocked with books, 'chiefly books of voyages and travels'. Pym pulls down the Biddle edition from this Jeffersonian collection, and browses.

Eventually he falls asleep. When he wakes up he is cramped, breathless and inordinately hungry. He assumes he has slept for a very long time, but has no way of checking because he is trapped. His disorientation continues into his next sleep, when he dreams of a terrifying landscape:

> Every species of calamity and horror befell me. Among other miseries, I was smothered to death between huge pillows, by demons of the most ghastly and ferocious aspect. Immense serpents held me in their embrace, and looked earnestly in my face with their fearfully shining eyes. Then deserts, limitless, and of the most forlorn and awe-inspiring character, spread themselves out before me. Immensely tall trunks of trees, gray and leafless, rose up in endless succession as far as the eye could reach. Their roots were concealed in wide-spreading morasses, whose dreary water lay intensely black, still, and altogether terrible, beneath. And the strange trees seemed endowed with a human vitality, and, waving to and fro their skeleton arms, were crying to the silent waters for mercy, in the shrill and piercing accents of the most acute agony and despair.

Suddenly there is a transformation which affects both the terrain and its inhabitants. The scene changes to the Sahara Desert, and Pym is attacked by a lion. The lion is Tiger, the dog.

Using the Biddle edition as a springboard, the dream runs together a number of popular images of the West. It does this by adapting the mutable landscape of Clara Wieland's dream and the spatial disorientation of Edgar Huntly's waking nightmare in the pit. Per Kalm's 'fascinating' snakes emerge out of a Wieland nightmare only to dissolve into a horrific Great American Desert. The 'hot breath' and 'white ghastly fangs' of the lion turn into the caresses of Tiger. They recall the closeness of both Edgar and the panther, and Lewis and the bear. This particular conflation of two of Brown's novels with the Biddle edition results in a potent form of dream-saturated natural description which plays an important role in the text. As in *Wieland*, the dream is predictive. The image of the black waters anticipates the blackness of the Tsalalians who, as their name suggests, are a transformation of the Sioux Indians which Lewis and Clark feared so much. The episode with Tiger provides yet another motif of doubling and savagism, anticipating the fight between Dirk Peters and the bear (which I will discuss in a moment) – and, of course, the encounter with the bears which closes 'The Journal of Julius Rodman'.[16]

The allusions to the Biddle edition and the West continue throughout *Pym*. Tiger is yet another Newfoundland dog. The Black servant this time is the whaler's villainous Black cook. When the crew of the whaler land on Kerguelen's Island on the way south to Tsalal, they encounter a rectangular method of settlement recommended to frontiersmen by the *Historical Account of Bouquet's Expedition*, and reaching its fullest expression in the Jeffersonian grid. But – and here again is the double irony – the settlement is undertaken by albatrosses and penguins in symbiotic relationship, and it is on 'one of the most dreary and utterly barren countries in the world'.

Kerguelen's Island cannot compete with Tsalal, which is unlike anything 'hitherto visited by civilized men' (p. 193). Yet here is another irony; a terrain such as this has been visited before. Edgar Huntly describes one that is remarkably similar near Norwalk, Connecticut, and Lewis tried to write about one at the Breaks of the Missouri. Even the chasms had appeared before. They are drawn by Pym in a way which makes them resemble Egyptian hieroglyphics. Certainly, they provide further evidence that Poe's interest in the origin of languages matched Noah Webster's in passion. But they also resemble Jefferson's 'Eye-draught of Madison's cave' in *Notes on the State of Virginia*. At this stage, it seems that there is an aboriginal relationship between the world and the word in Tsalal and, by extension, in America. Poe would later reconstruct this episode from *Pym* in 'The Gold Bug', both in its terrain and its concerns over the origin of language.[17]

Poe's most significant debt to Lewis and Clark, however, is the grizzly bear. Its first appearance is as a wig on the naked head of Dirk Peters, the son of a fur-trader and 'an Indian squaw of the tribe of Upsarokas, who live among the fastnesses of the Black Hills near the source of the Missouri'. Exploring an ice-floe in one of the whaler's boats, Pym, the mate and Peters meet the grizzly's cousin, 'a gigantic creature of the race of the Arctic bear, but far exceeding in size the largest of these animals'. They shoot it several times, but despite its wounds the beast swims over and attacks the boat. The bear is perfectly white and has huge blood-red eyes. Peters kills it by leaping onto its back and plunging a knife into its neck. The bear falls and rolls over the half-breed as it dies (pp. 84–85, 184–185).

The fight, with its hints at the primal intimacy of love and death, brings to a climax the motifs of doubling and savagism. Such motifs had appeared briefly in ursine contexts in two earlier English texts. One, the 1783 poem *The Progress of Refinement*, was the work of the future Poet Laureate Henry James Pye. Its argument relies on the environmentalist debate initiated by Montesquieu; and it asserts that:

> in the sad extremes of polar frost,
> The sacred beam of human reason lost,
> Man scarcely rises from the shaggy brood
> That prowl insatiate o'er the icy flood.

The second is Robert Bage's popular novel *Hermsprong*, first published in 1796 and reprinted in Philadelphia in 1803. The eponymous hero has been raised amongst Indians in the western wilderness of America. He relates a tale of lands even further west surrounding 'a large lake called the White Bear' and the subject of territorial dispute between generations of bears and men. Both sides agree to peace talks, but they are forestalled by a figure 'of vast dimensions' which rises from the lake:

> viewed from one side, it seemed to be a bear; on the other, it seemed to be a man. The white bear part of this awful figure waved its paw in the air to command silence, then said, with a terrific voice. . .

The tale breaks off here, to point the moral that, however incredible, the traditions of alternative cultures must be respected.[18]

These two moments, universalist and pluralist, polar and western, are echoed in *Pym*. (Indeed, as we shall see in a moment, the episode in *Hermsprong* reappears at the close of Poe's tale.) *Pym* fleshes out fully the hints of consanguinity between bears and humans which appear momentarily in the two English texts. It does so partly by a transformation of Edgar Huntly and the panther in the pit; and partly by reference to the Biddle edition. The fight with the bear is reminiscent of several recounted in the latter text, and it occurs just before Pym and his party meet a landscape which contains the prickly pear that was such an obstacle to the Lewis and Clark Expedition.

This second conflation of *Edgar Huntly* and the Biddle edition (with a little English help) seems to have made an impression on later accounts of fights with bears. Faulkner's 'The Bear', published in the *Saturday Evening Post* in 1942, owes a clear debt to *Pym* with its half-breed characters, the huge dog called Lion, and Old Ben the great bear. It may also draw on *Pym* through an intermediate source. In 1934 the *Saturday Evening Post* published a tale apparently told to the folklorist J. Frank Dobie by a half-breed called 'Nat Straw, the last of the Grizzly hunters'. Straw had been cornered by a grizzly which he was trapping. He slipped into a fissure in the canyon wall too narrow to admit the bear who, standing on his hind legs, pawed into the opening. According to Dobie, Straw recalled that 'his bloody jaws, under beady bloodshot eyes, were so close to me that when he tossed and breathed, the red foam covered my own face'. Eventually the bear tired and Straw was able to shoot it, but not before he had time to imagine a slow death, and remember having read 'The Pit and the Pendulum'.[19] And *The Narrative of Arthur Gordon Pym* perhaps?

The fight with the bear is a pivotal moment in *Pym*, resonating through its closing pages. The next day, Pym and his companions encounter the carcass of 'a singular-looking land animal'. It partly resembles a dog, but is only three feet long and six inches tall. It has very short legs, perfectly white silky fur, and scarlet teeth and claws. When the Tsalalians see the carcass, they panic and run away, shouting the word 'Tekeli-li'. This is the last word that the Tsalalian hostage murmurs before he lapses into catatonia and dies; and the word screamed by the 'gigantic and pallidly white birds' as the boat rushes into 'the embraces' of the cataract (pp. 188–189, 218–219, 239).

It is at this point that many of the themes that I have described in earlier chapters coalesce. In echoes of the books of Daniel and Revelations as well as of *Edgar Huntly*, *Symzonia*, *Hermsprong*, and the Biddle edition of Lewis and Clark, Pym and Dirk Peters reach the ultimate American landscape. It encapsulates images as different as Hesiod's whirlpools, Buffon's feminine landscape, and Jefferson's paths. It is a world turned upside down, the very reverse of the hopes of the Revolutionary ideologues; yet a scene so impressive that it will be repeated in doomed settings as diverse as Ambrose Bierce's West, William Faulkner's South, and even Conrad's *Heart of Darkness*. The landscape is so dangerous that it must be guarded by a figure which seems to be human and yet resembles a huge, upright bear. It is so alien that, whereas the landscape of Tsalal could be drawn in terms of an aboriginal language, this one passes beyond language altogether. It recalls the savage landscapes of Morse, Webster, Rush and Brackenridge; but is now so unstable that its outlines can be discerned only momentarily before it vanishes. It caused the hesitations in the texts of Crèvecœur, Dwight and Jefferson. It fractured Meriwether Lewis's journal, and the form of *Edgar Huntly*. It appeared, briefly and decisively, when Lewis died. It will reappear in the evanescent paradisal visions of *Moby Dick*, *The Blithedale Romance* and *The Great Gatsby*. Here it is captured by Poe for a fleeting moment before it escapes once more, out of the text. There can be nothing more to say as the whiteness of the beast in the landscape becomes transfigured into the blankness of the inexpressible:

> And now we rushed into the embraces of the cataract, where a chasm threw itself open to receive us. But there arose in our pathway a shrouded human figure, very far larger than any dweller among men. And the hue of the skin of the figure was of the perfect whiteness of the snow.

The construction and reconstruction of the Lewis and Clark Journals

There were at least nine journalists on the Lewis and Clark Expedition. The writers and locations of the journals are:

Captain Meriwether Lewis ⎱ ⎰American Philosophical Society,
⎱ Philadelphia
Captain William Clark ⎰ ⎱Missouri Historical Society, St Louis
Sergeant Charles Floyd   State Historical Society, Madison, Wisconsin

Sergeant John Ordway   American Philosophical Society
Sergeant Patrick Gass   MS missing, lost after publication
Sergeant Nathaniel Pryor   MS missing
Private Joseph Whitehouse   Original MS and an extended paraphrase at Newberry Library, Chicago
Private George Shannon   MS missing
Private Robert Frazier   MS missing

The journals were scattered, and it is only in this century that their locations have become generally known. Until now the editing of the journals has been piecemeal.

The following is the publication history of the journals:

1807   McKeehan's edition of Gass
1814   Biddle edition
1893   Coues's reprint of Biddle, with considerable commentary[1]
1904   Thwaïtes' *Original Journals*
1916   Quaife's edition of Ordway's journal and Lewis's 'Ohio' journal
1964   Osgood's edition of Clark's 'Field Notes'[2]
1972   Cutright's report on Whitehouse's journal and the paraphrase.[3]

Coues provided a detailed physical description of the journals that were available to him. It is reprinted in Thwaites, VII, 411–423. A new edition of all the journals is under preparation at the Center for Great Plains

Studies of the University of Nebraska-Lincoln. To date (1988) the first two volumes have been published, the first being an Atlas and the second containing the journals up to 24 August 1804.[4]

The Osgood edition confirmed what had earlier been suspected, that the captains wrote field notes as and when they could, enlarging and polishing when transferring them to their notebook journals. On completion the notebook journals were sealed in tins. I examined the journals held by the American Philosophical and Missouri Historical Societies. The fine condition of the notebooks clearly shows that they were carefully protected during the course of the Expedition. They present a marked contrast to the poor condition of the field notes and some other fragments.[5] On a number of occasions the field notes were lost. Sergeant Ordway noted, for instance, one such mishap:

> Capt Clarks notes of 2 days blew overboard this morning in the storm, and he
> was much put to it to Recolect the courses &.C.   (Quaife, 97)

The extant records show that the journalists took their writing very seriously. Sergeant Ordway kept a record for every one of the 863 days of the Expedition. William Clark was almost as conscientious. His only omission was while he was away from Fort Mandan on a ten-day hunting trip; and when he returned he made a summary of the intervening period.[6]

In contrast, there are three major gaps in Meriwether Lewis's journals. The record is as follows:

Quaife 31–76	'Ohio journal', complete 30 August to 28 November 1803.	
Thwaites, I	Fragments only until 7 April 1805.	Gap 1
Thwaites, I, 283 to III, 43	Complete, 7 April to 25 August 1805.	
Thwaites, III	No journals 27 August to 31 December 1805, save for three short periods.	Gap 2
Thwaites, III, 301 to V, 244	Complete, 1 January to 12 August 1806, when Lewis wounded. Nothing thereafter.	Gap 3

The reason for the third gap is obvious. It is possible, too, to explain the first gap in Lewis's journals. On 28 November he handed over command of the boat to Clark and travelled by land to St Louis. There was therefore no reason to continue journalising. Clark maintained a record almost continuously from 28 November 1803 onwards. The existing fragments in Lewis's writing until April 1805 suggest that he maintained a journal after the Expedition left St Louis on 14 May 1804. But any journal has been lost. On 1 April 1805 Clark sent a letter to Jefferson from

Fort Mandan (via the returning support group) enclosing his notes. A draft of that letter said that Lewis 'has not Leasure to Send . . . a correct Coppy journal of our proceedings' (Jackson, I, 226). On 14 May 1805, exactly one year after they had left St Louis, a sudden squall hit one of the boats. It almost sank, and a number of stores and papers were lost (Thwaites, II, 34–6). It is possible that the journals which Lewis had not the leisure to send from Fort Mandan were destroyed in this accident.[7]

The evidence regarding the second gap suggests not that the journals were lost, but rather that Lewis failed to keep a journal for most of the period 27 August to 31 December 1805. There are four reasons:

1   The entry for 26 August breaks off in mid-sentence and mid-page. Clearly, Lewis intended (as in the preceding days) to record Clark's activities, but no draft remains. Nor do any drafts exist for the three-month period to 31 December 1805, with the exception of 29 November to 1 December, when Lewis was away from the main party. The type of paper used, handwriting and style used for these three days confirm Clark's added remark that these were 'rough notes' (Codex Ia, p. 10).

2   Journals also exist for the periods 9–10 and 18–22 September 1805. The paper used here (Codices Fc and Fd) was from a notebook of the kind normally used for final journals. The handwriting and style also suggest that these (unlike Codex Fa, which contains drafts for 1–4 August 1805) are the polished versions. The type of paper initially suggests that a notebook may have been broken up or simply fallen apart, and therefore there may have been other journal entries which have disappeared. This is unlikely, however, because each remaining fragment begins with the opening date of the period at the top of the page, whilst the other dates simply follow the preceding entry.

3   Similarly, when Lewis recommences regular journalising he begins a new notebook (Codex J) with the place and date, 'Fort Clatsop [1 January] 1806'. Clark began neither 1805 nor 1806 with a new notebook. They would have been too valuable to have wasted space.

4   The suggestion that Lewis made sporadic attempts to write but failed to maintain a regular journal is further supported by Codex Fe, Lewis's weather diary for April to September 1805. While the tables are complete for the period, there are remarks for 7 and 21 August only in the last two months. In this respect, too, it seemed that Lewis failed to continue records. There exists no weather diary written by him for the period October to December 1805.

The reason for Lewis's lapse is suggested in chapter 6.

Notes

PROLOGUE   AN AMERICA OF THE IMAGINATION

1 Conrad Aiken, 'A Letter from Li Po', *Collected Poems*, 913. A word about quotations. In many cases the spelling and punctuation of the writers examined is unusual by modern standards. I have taken care to be faithful to the text while keeping editorial notes to a minimum. Marks such as [*sic*] would become intrusive if used frequently, and I have employed them only where the sense of the passage is unclear. In just one instance has a spelling been modernised: the occasional eighteenth-century habit (to which Jefferson was particularly prone) of using 'it's' as a possessive. To modern eyes it looks like a crass error; and this is why it has been altered.

2 Carl Ortwin Sauer, 'The morphology of landscape', reprinted in *Land and Life*, ed. John Leighly, 315–350. J. Wreford Watson, *Mental Images and Geographical Reality in the Settlement of North America*, 9. Watson's emphases. Other texts I have drawn on are Ralph H. Brown, *Historical Geography of the United States*; John R. Stilgoe, *Common Landscape of America, 1580 to 1845*; Yi-Fu Tuan, *Topophilia*; John K. Wright, *Human Nature in Geography*; and the essays of John B. Jackson and David Lowenthal listed in the Bibliography. Of more general use are Jay Appleton, *The Experience of Landscape*; Peter Gould and Rodney White, *Mental Maps*; and *Man, Space, and Environment*, ed. Paul Ward English and Robert C. Mayfield. A recent survey of the field is Peirce Lewis, 'Learning from looking: geographic and other writing about the American cultural landscape'.

3 Henry James, *What Maisie Knew*, 49. 'Landscape', *OED*. For a discussion of the meanings of the word, see John B. Jackson, 'The meanings of landscape', and *Discovering the Vernacular Landscape*, 3–8.

4 Benjamin Lee Whorf, 'Science and linguistics', reprinted in *Language, Thought, and Reality*, ed. John B. Carroll, 213. Discussions of the basis and context of Whorfian linguistics are given by Garrett Hardin, 'The threat of clarity'; Peter C. Rollins, 'The Whorf hypothesis as a critique of western science and technology'; and George Steiner, 'Whorf, Chomsky and the student of literature', reprinted in *On Difficulty*, 137–163, and integrated into *After Babel*, 73–109.

5 Barbara Maria Stafford, *Voyage into Substance: Art, Science, Nature, and the Illustrated Travel Account, 1760–1840*, 306–313. Hans Aarsleff, *The Study of Language in England, 1780–1860*, 5.

6 See Richard Poirier, *A World Elsewhere: The Place of Style in American Literature*, particularly Ch. 1; and Tony Tanner, *City of Words: American Fiction 1950–1970*,

281

particularly the Introduction and appendices. More than any other secondary texts, these two provided the inspiration for this book.

7 This view of factual writing leans towards Hayden White's theories of historical narrative as expounded in *Metahistory* and subsequent works. Recent discussions of White's theories are to be found in Dominick LaCapra, *History and Criticism*, Ch. 1; and Alan Munslow, 'The historical text as literary artefact', which applies them to the Frontier Thesis.

8 Friedrich Waismann, 'Analytic-synthetic', 10. A suggestive and more extended discussion of this subject is given by Wayne Franklin, 'Speaking and touching: the problem of inexpressibility in American travel books', reprinted in *America: Travel and Exploration*, ed. Steven E. Kagle, 18–38. An analysis of some of the descriptive strategies employed is to be found in Robert C. Bredeson, 'Landscape description in nineteenth-century American travel literature', and Franklin, *Discoverers, Explorers, Settlers*; while examples of the fracture of one descriptive strategy are given by I. S. MacLaren, 'The limits of the picturesque in British North America'.

9 Hesiod, 'Works and Days', ll. 166–173, *The Remains of Hesiod*, trans. Elton, 22–23. William H. Tillinghast, 'The geographical knowledge of the ancients'. G. A. Wood, 'Ancient and medieval conceptions of Terra Australis'. Dallas Pratt, 'Discovery of a world: early maps showing America'. Daniel Boorstin, *The Discoverers*, Ch. 13. Terry G. Jordan, *The European Culture Area*, 2–4. John Noble Wilford, *The Mapmakers*, 25, 34–36. Loren Baritz, 'The idea of the west', 618–629.

10 Boorstin, *The Exploring Spirit*, 3. Christopher Columbus, *Select Documents Illustrating the Four Voyages of Columbus*, ed. Cecil Jane, II, 4, 28–38. Samuel Eliot Morison, *Christopher Columbus*, 92–95, 556–557. Leonardo Olschki, 'What Columbus saw on landing in the West Indies', 647. Boorstin, *The Discoverers*, chs. 30–32. Tzvetan Todorov, *The Conquest of America*, 16, 23, 31.

11 J. H. Elliott, *The Old World and the New*, 40, 28–29. Thomas Goldstein, 'Geography in fifteenth-century Florence'. On the importance of the Waldseemüller maps, see *The Voyages of Giovanni da Verrazzano*, ed. Lawrence P. Wroth, 49; and Boorstin, *The Discoverers*, 252–254.

12 Edmundo O'Gorman, *The Invention of America*, 73, 124. W.E. Washburn, 'The meaning of "discovery" in the fifteenth and sixteenth centuries', 20–21. See also Washburn, 'Review of German Arciniegas, *Amerigo and the New World*'; and Washburn and Arciniegas, 'Letters to the Editor, *William and Mary Quarterly*'. An exposition of O'Gorman's theories is given by Edwin C. Rozwenc, 'Edmundo O'Gorman and the idea of America'.

13 Columbus, *Select Documents*, ed. Jane, II, 9. Amerigo Vespucci, *The First Four Voyages*, 6, 34. On Columbus see Morison, *Columbus*, 384–385, 547–548, 554. On Vespucci see Boorstin, *The Discoverers*, Ch. 33.

14 Francis Bacon, *Novum Organum* LXXII, *The Philosophical Works*, ed. John M. Robertson, 276. John Locke, *Second Treatise on Civil Government*, S.49, *Social Contract: Essays by Locke, Hume, Rousseau*, ed. Sir Ernest Barker, 29. See also Basil Willey, *The Seventeenth-Century Background*, chs. 1–3; and Lewis Mumford, *The Golden Day*, 6–11.

15 Jefferson, letter 21 March 1801 to Priestley, *The Writings*, ed. A. A. Lipscomb and A. E. Bergh x, 229; also in *The Portable Thomas Jefferson*, ed. Merrill D. Peterson, 484. Montaigne, 'Of Cannibals', *The Essays*, trans. Charles Cotton, 133–134. Shakespeare, *The Tempest* II, i, 150–172. Margaret T. Hodgen, 'Montaigne and Shakespeare again'. For discussions of the 'American' nature of *The Tempest*, see Leo Marx, *The Machine in the Garden*, Ch. 2; and Bryan Jay Wolf, *Romantic Re-Vision*, 24–28. James, *Hawthorne*, 55. Terence Martin, 'The negative character in American fiction' and 'The negative structures of American literature'.

16 Claude Lévi-Strauss, *Tristes Tropiques*, 95. Ralph Waldo Emerson, 'The Poet', *Selected Essays*, ed. Larzer Ziff, 281. E. M. Forster, 'The United States' (1947), *Two Cheers for Democracy*, 339. Peter Conrad, *Imagining America*, and Christopher Mulvey, *Anglo-American Landscapes*, Part II, discuss the varied British responses to America.

17 Charles Olson, *Call Me Ishmael* (1947), 15. Louis Legrand Noble, *The Life and Works of Thomas Cole*, 219. See also Thomas Cole, 'Essay on American scenery', 11; James T. Flexner, *That Wilder Image*, 40; and Barbara Novak, *Nature and Culture*, 149–153.

18 Henry Adams, *The Education of Henry Adams*, 12. D. H. Lawrence, *Studies in Classic American Literature*, 61, 169. Lévi-Strauss, *Tristes Tropiques*, 493. Todorov, *The Conquest of America*, 49–50, 247–249.

19 Wolf, *Romantic Re-Vision*, 3–4, 138. Herman Melville, 'Bartleby', *Billy Budd, Sailor and Other Stories*, ed. Harold Beaver, 67–68. Laurence Sterne, *Tristram Shandy*, Vol. V, Ch. 3, 351.

20 An introduction to such images is provided by Malcolm Bradbury, 'Dangerous pilgrimages: transatlantic images in fiction (I)'; R. R. Cawley, *Unpathed Waters*; Marcus Cunliffe, 'Europe and America'; Elliott, *The Old World and the New*, chs. 1–2; Robert B. Heilman, *America in English Fiction*, 10–29; Howard Mumford Jones, *O Strange New World*, chs. 1–2; Marx, *The Machine in the Garden*; Charles L. Sanford, *The Quest for Paradise*; John Seelye, *Prophetic Waters*; Henry Nash Smith, *Virgin Land*, Book 3; Howard Temperley, 'Anglo-American images', *Contrast and Connection*, ed. H. C. Allen and Roger Thompson, 321–345; Louis B. Wright, *The Dream of Prosperity in Colonial America*; and finally Mary Sayre Haverstock, *An American Bestiary*, and Hugh Honour, *The New Golden Land*, both superbly illustrated.

21 Drayton, 'To the Virginian Voyage', *The Literature of America: Colonial Period*, ed. Larzer Ziff, 22. Thomas More, *Utopia*, trans. and introd. Paul Turner, 38–39.

22 George Sandys, *Ovid's Metamorphosis Englished*, 273. Sandys' emphasis. For an appropriate discussion of this text, see Richard Beale Davis, 'America in George Sandys' "Ovid"'. Joseph Hall, *The Discovery of a New World (Mundus Alter et Idem)*, trans. John Healey, 17.

23 Columbus, *Select Documents*, ed. Jane, I, 12. Cawley, *Unpathed Waters*, 102. Sandys, *Ovid's Metamorphosis Englished*, 79. Sandys' emphasis. See also Davis, 'America in Sandys' "Ovid"', 300–304; Lee T. Pearcy, *Mediated Muse: English Translations of Ovid, 1560–1700*, Ch. 3; and Rudolf Wittkower, 'Marvels of the east: a study of the history of monsters'.

24 Tom Stoppard, *Dirty Linen*, 60–65.

25 Sydney Smith, 'Review of Adam Seybert, *Statistical Annals of the United States of America*', 79. Samuel Miller, *A Brief Retrospect of the Eighteenth Century* II, 404–410, 171–179. Miller's emphasis. Gilbert Chinard, 'Progress and perfectibility in Samuel Miller's intellectual history', analyses the *Brief Retrospect*. Accounts of the pressures operating on American literature are to be found in Maurice J. Bennett, 'A portrait of the artist in eighteenth-century America: Charles Brockden Brown's *Memoirs of Stephen Calvert*'; Marcus Cunliffe, '"They will *all* speak English": some cultural consequences of independence', *Peace and the Peacemakers*, ed. Ronald Hoffman and Peter J. Albert, 132–159; Lawrence J. Friedman, *Inventors of the Promised Land*; Terence Martin, *The Instructed Vision: Scottish Common Sense Philosophy and the Origins of American Fiction*; Russell Blaine Nye, *The Cultural Life of the New Nation*, Ch. 11; G. Harrison Orians, 'Censure of American fiction in American romances and magazines, 1789–1810'; Lewis P. Simpson, 'The symbolism of literary alienation in the revolutionary age', *The Brazen Face of History*, 23–45; and Benjamin T. Spencer, *The Quest for Nationality: An American Literary Campaign*, Ch. 2. An alternative view is given by Robert B. Winans, 'The growth of a novel-reading public in late-eighteenth-century America'.

26 Sacvan Bercovitch, 'How the Puritans won the American revolution'. Emerson, 'The American Scholar', *Selected Essays*, ed. Ziff, 83, 104. F. O. Matthiessen, *American Renaissance*, vi–vii. On the attitudes of American visitors to the Old World, see Benjamin Lease, *Anglo-American Encounters: England and the Rise of American Literature*; Joy S. Kasson, *Artistic Voyagers*; and Christpher Mulvey, *Anglo-American Landscapes*, Part I. Recent distinguished reconsiderations of the American Renaissance are provided by Larzer Ziff, *Literary Democracy: The Declaration of Cultural Independence in America*; Robert Clark, *History, Ideology and Myth in American Fiction, 1823–52*; and John P. McWilliams, Jr, *Hawthorne, Melville, and the American Character*.

27 Frederick Jackson Turner, *The Significance of the Frontier in American History*, ed. Harold P. Simonson, 51. Matthiessen, *American Renaissance*, ix. John Jay Chapman, *Emerson and Other Essays*, 113.

28 Excellent guides to the Revolutionary generation are to be found in A. Owen Aldridge, *Early American Literature*, Part II; Emory Elliott, *Revolutionary Writers*; Joseph J. Ellis, *After the Revolution; American Literature, 1764–1789: The Revolutionary Years*, and *Major Writers of Early American Literature*, both ed. Everett Emerson; Stephen Fender, *American Literature in Context I: 1620–1830*, parts II and III; Lewis Leary, *Soundings*; and Kenneth Silverman, *A Cultural History of the American Revolution*. William L. Hedges thoughtfully discusses the dialectical, questioning structure of the writing of the period in 'Toward a theory of American literature, 1765–1800'; 'The myth of the Republic and the theory of American literature'; and 'The Old World yet: writers and writing in Post-Revolutionary America'.

Recent and interesting accounts of the links between Revolutionary culture and later forms are provided by Michael Davitt Bell, *The Development of American Romance: the Sacrifice of Relation*; Robert A. Ferguson, *Law and Letters in American Culture*; and Donald Ringe, *American Gothic: Imagination and Reason in Nineteenth-Century Fiction*.

Edwin Fussell, *Frontier: American Literature and the American West* and Nash Smith, *Virgin Land*, remain valuable applications of the Turner Thesis to American culture. Recent environmentalist investigations into American literature and culture include Leonard Lutwack, *The Role of Place in Literature*; Roderick Nash, *Wilderness and the American Mind*; William Spengemann, *The Adventurous Muse: The Poetics of American Fiction, 1789–1900*; Cecilia Tichi, *New World, New Earth: Environmental Reform in American Literature from the Puritans through Whitman*; and Albert J. Von Frank, *The Sacred Game: Provincialism and Frontier Consciousness in American Literature, 1630–1860*. William Cronon, *Changes in the Land: Indians, Colonists, and the Ecology of New England* is particularly valuable because it applies a broad range of techniques to analyse a closely focussed topic.

29 Anon., 'Review of *Poems on Several Occasions*', *Gentleman's Magazine* 56 (December 1786), 1064–1065. William Carlos Williams, *In the American Grain*, 122, 219. Williams's emphasis. (Copyright 1933 by William Carlos Williams. Reprinted by permission of New Directions Publishing Corporation and Carcanet Press.)

30 Moses Coit Tyler, *A History of American Literature, 1607–1765*, 7. *Literary History of the United States*, ed. Robert E. Spiller *et al.*, xix. Recent discussions of the problems confronting early American literary history are to be found in Carl R. Kropf, 'The nationalistic criticism of early American literature'; and Von Frank, *The Sacred Game*, 1–10.

31 Donald Davie, 'American literature: the canon', *Trying to Explain*, 189–190. Lawrence Buell, 'New views of American narrative'. Nina Baym, 'Melodramas of beset manhood: how theories of American fiction exclude women authors'. Jane Tompkins, *Sensational Designs: The Cultural Work of American Fiction, 1790–1860* particularly Ch. 7. Further discussions are to be found in Ferguson, *Law and Letters*,

'Prologue to Part I'; William L. Hedges, 'Review of Alan Axelrod, *Charles Brockden Brown*'; Frank Kermode, *Forms of Attention*; LaCapra, *History and Criticism*, chs. 4 and 5; and Lillian S. Robinson, 'Treason our text: feminist challenges to the literary canon'. Annette Kolodny, *The Land Before Her: Fantasy and Experience of the American Frontiers, 1630–1860*, explores women's private responses to new lands.

1 THE TRIUMPH OF REDCOATISM

1 Harold Rosenberg, 'Parable of American painting', *The Tradition of the New*, 13–15. Philip Rahv, 'Paleface and Redskin', *Literature and the Sixth Sense*, 1–6. J. F. C. Fuller, *The Conduct of War, 1789–1961*, Ch. 1, provides an introduction to the concept of limited warfare. The most comprehensive account of Braddock's defeat is given in Paul E. Kopperman, *Braddock at the Monongahela*. Brief accounts appear in Howard H. Peckham, *The Colonial Wars, 1689–1762*, 143–8; R. Ernest Dupuy and Trevor N. Dupuy, *Military Heritage of America*, 76–77; and Russell F. Weigley, *History of the United States Army*, 19–24. See also Stanley Pargellis, 'Braddock's defeat', which attributes the disaster not to the hallucination of displaced terrain but rather to Braddock's incompetence. Benjamin Franklin reports Braddock's last words and provides a personal reminiscence of the campaign in his *Autobiography*, 151–154, while Oliver Goldsmith, *A History of England* II, 85–87, gives a good contemporary account of the campaign. Stephen S. Webb, 'Army and empire: English garrison government in Britain and America, 1569 to 1763', shows that militarism was an integral part of Anglo-American colonial relations.

2 Captain John Underhill, *News from America*, 10–11, 9, 15. On the Pequot War see Alden T. Vaughan, *New England Frontier*, Ch. 5; and on Underhill see Richard Slotkin, *Regeneration Through Violence*, 69–78. For other images of Indians as devils and beasts, see Peter N. Carroll, *Puritanism and the Wilderness*, 76–77; Seelye, *Prophetic Waters*, 220, 244, 289; and Cronon, *Changes in the Land*, 56. Nash, *Wilderness and the American Mind*, 1–41, provides the sources and setting of pejorative attitudes to the wilderness.

3 See Peter Paret, 'Colonial experience and European military reform at the end of the eighteenth century', and, particularly, Peter E. Russell, 'Redcoats in the wilderness: British officers and irregular warfare in Europe and America, 1740 to 1760'.

4 See Weigley, *History of the US Army*, 23–27; Edward E. Curtis, *The Organization of the British Army in the American Revolution*, 19–21; Stanley Pargellis, *Lord Loudoun in North America*, 299–306; Daniel Boorstin, 'A nation of minutemen', *The Americans: The Colonial Experience*, 383–384; Peckham, *The Colonial Wars*, 153; John Shy, *Toward Lexington*, 98, 173–176; Louis Morton, 'The end of formalized warfare'; Felix Reichmann, 'The Pennsylvania Rifle: a social interpretation of changing military techniques'; and Eric Robson, 'British light infantry in the eighteenth century: the effect of American conditions'.

5 [William Smith], *An Historical Account of the Expedition Against the Ohio Indians in the Year 1764 under the Command of Henry Bouquet*, 44. The identity of the author, who was the first Provost of the University of Pennsylvania, was established in Francis Parkman's 1868 edition, xv. Further references to this important book appear in chapters 4, 5 and 6 above. For an account of the Expedition's leader, see E. Douglas Branch, 'Henry Bouquet, professional soldier'; J. C. Reeve, 'Henry Bouquet'; and Shy, *Toward Lexington*, 137.

6 Unidentified Redcoat letters, *American Archives; Fourth Series*, ed. Peter Force, II, 440–441; Force's emphasis. William Duff, letter 13 June 1775 to William Rose, Duff Family Correspondence, Aberdeen University Archives, MS 2226/96/9. Other Redcoat accounts of Lexington and Concord are provided by John Barker, *The*

British in Boston, 31–37; and *Letters of Hugh Earl Percy*, ed. Charles K. Bolton, 49–53. Christopher Ward, *The War of the Revolution* I, 43–51, gives a fine summary of 'one of the strangest battles in the war'. See Shy, *Toward Lexington*, 127–129; and Charles Royster, *A Revolutionary People at War*, 33–34 for British fear of the woods; and *The Lost War*, ed. Marion Balderston, 135, for annoyance at a terrain which allowed the Americans to escape. See also John William Ward, *Andrew Jackson*, 13–29 and *passim*, for the development of the myth of the rifleman after the Battle of New Orleans (1815).

7 *Letters of Brunswick and Hessian Officers*, trans. William L. Stone, 79. Chatham, speech 20 November 1777, in William Cobbett, *The Parliamentary History of England* XIX, 364, 369, 372. See also Piers Mackesy, *The War for America*, 78, 517–518, and 'What the British Army learnt', *Arms and Independence*, ed. Ronald Hoffman and Peter J. Albert, 191–215; Robson, 'British Light Infantry'; Reichmann, 'The Pennsylvania rifle', 10–11; Samuel F. Scott, 'Military nationalism in Europe in the aftermath of the American Revolution', *Peace and the Peacemakers*, ed. Hoffman and Albert, 160–189; and Bernard W. Sheehan, 'Ignoble savagism and the American Revolution', *Legacies of the American Revolution*, ed. Larry R. Gerlach *et al.*, 152–157.

8 Burke's speech of 6 February 1778 is paraphrased in Cobbett, *Parliamentary History*, XIX, 694–699. Cobbett omits the parody, which is reported by Horace Walpole in his letter 12 February 1778 to the Rev. William Mason, *Letters* VII, 29–30. Another version, differing in detail, is in Horace Walpole's *Journal of the Reign of King George the Third* II, 193–194. There were several more parodies. See James Clinton Gaston, *An Anthology of Poems Dealing with the American Revolution*, 339–340, 363. Francis Hudleston, *Gentleman Johnny Burgoyne*, and Richard J. Hargrove, *General John Burgoyne*, generally provide good introductions to a complex man who was probably more skilled as a playwright than as a commanding officer. The text of the Proclamation is in *The Spirit of 'Seventy-Six: The Story of the American Revolution as Told by Participants*, ed. Henry Steele Commager and Richard B. Morris, I, 544–548.

9 Francis Hopkinson, 'An Answer to General Burgoyne's Proclamation', *Miscellaneous Essays and Occasional Writings*, 147. Hopkinson's emphasis.

10 Chatham, speech in the Lords 30 May 1777, Cobbett, *Parliamentary History* XIX, 317. Paret, 'Colonial experience', 51–53; Weigley, *History of the US Army*, 63–68; Marcus Cunliffe, *George Washington, Man and Monument*, 110–111, and *Soldiers and Civilians*, 148–149; and the essays by Don Higginbotham and Robert K. Wright, Jr in *Arms and Independence*, ed. Hoffman and Albert, 1–24, 50–74. On the limited war mentality, see Reginald C. Stuart, *Citizens in Arms*, chs. 1 and 2. On the development of professionalism in the Continental Army, and the crucial role of von Steuben, see Royster, *A Revolutionary People*, 12, 70–71, 83, 144, 180, 213–235, 331. Also see Royster p. 117 on the deep-rooted American desire to hold fixed positions; and Shy, *A People Numerous and Armed*, 103 on the way that British tactics at Bunker Hill were governed by their need to win a conventional battle. For an account of General Charles Lee, one of the few Revolutionary leaders after 1775 to propose methods of warfare suited to Americans and the terrain, see Shy, 'American strategy: Charles Lee and the radical alternative', *A People*, particularly 154–155.

11 Washington, 'General Orders' 27 September 1781, in *Writings*, ed. John C. Fitzpatrick XXIII, 147. Contemporary accounts of the surrender may be found in James Thacher, *Military Journal*, 344–348; and Abbé Robin, *New Travels Through North-America*, 64–65. Good modern summaries of the battle and surrender are provided by Douglas S. Freeman, *George Washington* V, 384–390, and Ward, *The War* II, 894–895, while Burke Davis, *The Campaign that Won America* deals with the battle and its background at length.

12 Chatham, speech 30 May 1777, Cobbett, *Parliamentary History* XIX, 319. Examples of

the detailed information given to Pitt about an American terrain that was impregnable to all save Indians are to be found in letters from General John Forbes, 17 June, 10 July and 20 October 1758, *Correspondence of William Pitt*, ed. Gertrude S. Kimball, I, 279, 294–295, 373.

13 John Trevor, letter 16 April 1782 to Charles Fox, Shelburne Papers, Vol. 34, No. 2, William L. Clements Library, University of Michigan. (I am grateful to Galen R. Wilson, Manuscript Curator at the Clements Library, for checking this reference for me.) Yet another irony was that, in the earlier stages of the war both Tom Paine and a British pamphleteer had come to the same conclusion. See Royster, *A Revolutionary People*, 115–116.

14 The tradition of 'The World Turned Upside Down' can be traced back to Alexander Garden, *Anecdotes of the Revolutionary War*, 2 Ser., 17–18, but not further. See also Freeman, *George Washington* v, 388, and *The Spirit of 'Seventy-Six*, ed. Commager and Morris, II, 1,245–1,248.

15 *The Spirit of 'Seventy-Six*, ed. Commager and Morris, II, 1,246. David Kunzle, 'World upside down' and 'Bruegel's proverb painting and the world upside down' provide a broad summary of the visual image. Christopher Hill, *The World Turned Upside Down* discusses the various contexts of the phrase during the English Civil War, and A. L. Morton, *The World of the Ranters*, 36 gives an extract from a ballad of that title. Another version is printed in *Cavalier and Puritan: Ballads and Broadsides*, ed. Hyder E. Rollins, 160–162. James Fenimore Cooper refers to the Jacobite song in his historical novel *Wyandotté*, 221, 381. 'Goody Bull' first appeared in the *London Chronicle*, 11 March 1766, 236, and was quickly reprinted in the *Gentleman's Magazine*, 36 (March 1766), 140–141. It will also be found in Gaston, *An Anthology*, 119–120, and (in expurgated form) in Frank Moore, *Songs and Ballads of the American Revolution*, 33–35. A version dating from the 1870s is to be found in *A Touch on the Times: Songs of Social Change*, ed. Roy Palmer, 321–323.

16 See, for instance, Walpole, letter 7 September 1775 to Sir Horace Mann, *Letters* VI, 250. Further evidence of the complexity of British attitudes is conveyed by Dora Mae Clark, *British Opinion and the American Revolution*; Fred J. Hinkhouse, *The Preliminaries of the American Revolution as seen in the English Press*; Heilman, *America in English Fiction, 1760–1800*; Gaston, *An Anthology*; and John Sainsbury, 'The pro-Americans of London'.

17 Examples of British superciliousness may be found in *Boswell's Life of Johnson*, ed. George Birkbeck Hill, I, 367; and John Bowater, letter 4 April 1777 in *The Lost War*, ed. Balderston, 122. Others are reported in Clark, *British Opinion*, 241, 260; Hinkhouse, *The Preliminaries*, 84, 114, 149, 183, 189; Heilman, *America in English Fiction*, 157; Carl Bridenbaugh, *The Spirit of '76*, 62, 93; and Ralph N. Miller, 'American nationalism as a theory of nature', 81–83.

18 Luttrell, speech 23 January 1775, Cobbett, *Parliamentary History* XVIII, 175–176. Further information on Luttrell appears in Sir Lewis Namier and John Brooke, *The House of Commons, 1754–1790* III, 67–68. After it was apparent that the Americans preferred the alternative, Luttrell rejoined the navy, commanding in 1779 the squadron that captured Omoa in the Gulf of Honduras. Henry Ellis, former Governor of Georgia, was even more familiar with the Colonies, yet shared Luttrell's belief in American inferiority. See Shy, *A People*, 43.

19 See, for instance, W. G. Evelyn, *Memoirs and Letters*, 27, 51. Further examples appear in Kopperman, *Braddock*, 15; Royster, *A Revolutionary People*, 10, 36; Alan Rogers, *Empire and Liberty*, Ch. 6; James K. Martin and Mark E. Lender, *A Respectable Army*, 19, 52; and Shy, *Toward Lexington*, 93, 100, 278, 411, and *A People*, 31–32, 43.

20 Franklin, letter 19 August 1784 to William Strahan, *The Writings of Benjamin Franklin*, ed. Albert H. Smyth, IX, 261. Franklin emphasises the Yankee's lack of

boldness because it was a cliché at the time. The proposed mass castration first prompted a response from Franklin in 'A Method of Humbling Rebellious American Vassals', 21 May 1774, *The Papers of Benjamin Franklin*, ed. William B. Wilcox, XXI, 220–223. For further information on Clarke see *Benjamin Franklin's Letters to the Press*, ed. Verner W. Crane, 262–264; and *Papers* XIV, 323. Horace Walpole (in *Letters* VI, 467), on learning in 1777 of Burgoyne's latest pomposity, recalled that others had earlier boasted 'that five thousand men would overrun all America'.

Franklin, 'An Open Letter to Lord North', 5 April 1774, *Papers* XXI, 185. Other examples of Franklin's responses are to be found in *Papers* XII, 406–407, 413–416; and XXI, 482–485.

21 'Airs, Waters, Places', *Hippocratic Writings*, ed. G. E. R. Lloyd, 161, 165–167. Montesquieu, *The Spirit of Laws*, Book 18, chs. 7 and 9, Vol. I, 300–301. See also Genevieve Miller, '"Airs, Waters, and Places" in history'. In this and the succeeding paragraphs I have drawn upon: Antonello Gerbi, *The Dispute of the New World*; Clarence Glacken, *Traces on the Rhodian Shore*; Gilbert Chinard, 'Eighteenth-century theories of America as a human habitat'; *Was America A Mistake?*, ed. Henry Steele Commager and Elmo Giordanetti; and Durand Echeverria, *Mirage in the West*, Ch. 1.

22 Anon., *The Project*, 1, 7, 9. Author's emphases. On the popularity and influence of Montesquieu generally, see F. T. H. Fletcher, *Montesquieu and English Politics*, Section A.

23 Anon., *Otaheite*, 5–6. Max Nordau, *Degeneration*, 560. Montaigne, 'Of Cannibals', *Essays*, 131–140. On the Great Chain of Being and its metamorphoses, see Arthur O. Lovejoy, *The Great Chain of Being*, particularly chs. 6–9; *The Wild Man Within*, ed. Edward Dudley and Maximillian Novak; Todorov, *The Conquest of America*, 154–156, 179–180; and Bernard Smith, *European Vision and the South Pacific 1768–1850*, 6–7. Smith provides fascinating material on antipodal inversion, on the origin of which see Franz Cumont, *After Life in Roman Paganism*, 79–81. On the various attitudes to the sun, see Karen Ordahl Kupperman, 'Fear of hot climates in the Anglo-American colonial experience', 217–220.

24 Edward Tyson, *Orang-Outang*, iii. Denis Diderot, 'Suite de l'Entretien', *Oeuvres Complètes* II, 190. Lord Monboddo, *Origin and Progress of Language* I, 174–176, 207, 248, 272, 289. See also Frank A. Beach, 'The descent of instinct'; Robert Wokler, 'Tyson and Buffon on the orang-utan'; Boorstin, *The Discoverers*, Ch. 58; Smith, *European Vision*, 70–73; Winthrop D. Jordan, *White Over Black*, 234–239; *A Hotbed of Genius: The Scottish Enlightenment*, ed. David Daiches *et al.*, 19–21; Bernard W. Sheehan, *Seeds of Extinction: Jeffersonian Philanthropy and the American Indian*, Ch. 1; Gary Wills, *Inventing America*, 218–223; Aarsleff, *The Study of Language in England*, 36–42; and Barbara Harrisson, *Orang-Utan*, 10–16, which gives a reproduction of a charming 1714 illustration.

25 Thomas Burnet, *The Theory of the Earth*, Book 1, Ch. 5, 64, Ch. 6, 68 and Ch. 9, 117, 123; Book 2, Ch. 11, 325. Marjorie Nicolson, *Mountain Gloom and Mountain Glory: The Development of the Aesthetics of the Infinite*. Christopher Thacker, *The Wildness Pleases*, 145–151, and 'The volcano: culmination of the landscape garden', *British and American Gardens in the Eighteenth Century*, ed. Robert P. MacCubbin and Peter Martin, 74–83. See also H. V. S. Ogden, 'Thomas Burnet's *Telluris Theoria Sacra* and mountain scenery'; E. G. R. Taylor, 'The English worldmakers of the seventeenth century and their influence on the earth sciences'; Boorstin, *The Discoverers*, 92; and Don Cameron Allen, *The Legend of Noah*, Ch. 5. Daniel Defoe, *Robinson Crusoe*, 78, 96–97, 102–103. See also J. Paul Hunter, *The Reluctant Pilgrim*, 151–154, 161–162. John Wesley, Sermon LVII, 'The Cause and Cure of Earthquakes', *Sermons on Several Occasions* II, 35; *Serious Thoughts Occasioned by the late Earthquake at Lisbon*. T. D.

Kendrick, *The Lisbon Earthquake*, chs. 1 and 8. Stafford, *Voyage into Substance*, 249–264. Keith Thomas, *Religion and the Decline of Magic*, 109–110.

26 Le Comte de Buffon, *Natural History* v, 136, 130, 135, 139. Plinius Secundus, *The History of the World*, Book 5, Ch. 17, Tome I, 101. On Buffon's reputation, see Otis E. Fellows and Stephen F. Milliken, *Buffon*, 15–16, 55–56; and for an extended discussion of female metaphors of the terrain in American letters, see Annette Kolodny, *The Lay of the Land*.

27 Peter [Per] Kalm, *Travels into North America* I, 102–104, 319; II, 189, 203–207. See also Brooke Hindle, *The Pursuit of Science in Revolutionary America*, 34–35; Chinard, 'Eighteenth century theories', 32–33; Echeverria, *Mirage in the West*, 8–9; and David Scofield Wilson, *In the Presence of Nature*, 131. Wilson, 40, 56, 148, 222 gives evidence that snakes, particularly rattlesnakes, were a source of great interest, and taletelling. On the reception of Kalm's *Travels* see the anonymous review in the *Monthly Review* 45 (September 1771), 209–220; and for an example of its influence see Gottfried Achenwall, 'Achenwall's observations on North America, 1767', trans. J. G. Rosengarten.

28 Cornelius de Pauw, *Recherches Philosophiques sur les Américains* I, 4–7, 19, 35. Accurate translations, from which the quotations have been taken, are to be found in *Broken Image: Foreign Critiques of America*, ed. Gerald E. Stearn, 3–13; and *Was America a Mistake?*, ed. Commager and Giordannetti, 85–102. Anonymous reviews of the *Recherches* may be found in the *Monthly Review* 42 (1770), Appendix, 515–536; *The Scots Magazine* 31 (September 1770), 485–491 and (October 1770), 551–557. For the supposed origin of syphilis, see Morison, *Christopher Columbus*, 359; Alfred W. Crosby, *The Columbian Exchange*, 122–164; C.-E. A. Winslow, 'The drama of syphilis', and *The Conquest of Epidemic Disease*, 124–131. For information on de Pauw, see Henry W. Church, 'Corneille de Pauw, and the controversy over his *Recherches Philosophiques sur les Américains*'; on his influence, on Kant amongst others, see Gerbi, *The Dispute, passim*.

29 Raynal, *The Sentiments of a Foreigner on the Disputes of Great-Britain with America; A Philosophical and Political History* . . . IV, Book 17, 184; Book 18, 387–391. See also Echeverria, *Mirage in the West*, 33; and Gerbi, *The Dispute*, 45–50. On the popularity and influence of Raynal, see the 1782 edition of the *Philosophical and Political History* I, v; Anon., Review of the second edition, *Monthly Review* 55 (November 1776), 402; and Dallas D. Irvine, 'The Abbé Raynal and British humanitarianism'.

30 Heilman, *America in English Fiction*, 184, 337–339. Anon., *The Genius of Britain, to General Howe*, 6–7. See also Miller, 'American nationalism', 78–81.

31 Goldsmith, 1760 essay reprinted as Letter xvII in *The Citizen of the World; or Letters from a Chinese Philosopher, Residing in London, to his Friends in the East, Works* II, 73; 'The Effect which Climates have upon Men, and other Animals' (1760), *Works* III, 112–114; *The Traveller, Works* IV, 268; *A History of England* II, 86.

32 'Preface' to R. Brookes, *A New and Accurate System of Natural History* (1763–64), *Works* v, 245–246; *A History of the Earth, and Animated Nature* II, 322–323, IV, 231; *The Deserted Village, Works* IV, 300–301. *Critical Review* 38 (8, 11/1770), rpt. *Goldsmith: The Critical Heritage*, ed. G. S. Rousseau, 135–152. See also Winifred Lynskey, 'The scientific sources of Goldsmith's *Animated Nature*'; and John Robert Moore, 'Goldsmith's degenerate song-birds'.

33 William Robertson, *The History of America*, 10th edn, I, 14–21, 87, 3, 7–9. Edward Gibbon, *Letters* II, 153. See also Gerbi, *The Dispute*, 158–159. Other images of the vastness of America may be found, for instance, in Walpole, *Letters* VI, 129, 203, 253; and Edmund Burke, speeches in the Commons 22 March 1775 and 7 March 1783, Cobbett, *Parliamentary History* XVIII, 489–490 and XXIII, 613. Chapter 4 continues the discussion about the size of the new British territory.

34 Anon., letter 28 April 1775, *American Archives; Fourth Series,* ed. Force, II, 440. Anon. Hessian Officers, letters 18 January 1778 and 16 January 1779, *Letters of Brunswick and Hessian Officers,* 215–216, 219, 237. Major John Bowater, letter 17 November 1777, *The Lost War,* ed. Marion Balderston, 147.

35 Smith, 'Review of Seybert, *Statistical Annals'.* Lease, *Anglo-American Encounters,* 7–9 and *passim,* traces the culture, from Washington Irving to Mark Twain, that grew around the irritant planted by Smith.

36 Franklin, 'A Traveller' (1765), *Papers,* ed. Labaree, XII, 134–135. See also *Benjamin Franklin's Letters to the Press,* ed. Crane, 32–35.

37 See, for instance, Thomas Jefferson's long letter of 7 June 1785 to le Marquis de Chastellux, which attacks Buffon, Raynal, Robertson and de Pauw, but says little about American terrain. *The Papers of Thomas Jefferson,* ed. Julian P. Boyd, VIII, 184–186. Hereafter cited as *Papers.* See also Chinard, 'Eighteenth-century theories', 39ff.

38 Richard Alsop, 'Preface' to Juan Ignacio Molina, *The Geographical, Natural and Civil History of Chili,* xii.

39 Henry F. May, *The Englightenment in America.* Jay Fliegelman, *Prodigals and Pilgrims: The American revolution against patriarchal authority, 1750–1800,* Part I, 'The Ideological Inheritance'. Henry Steele Commager, *Jefferson, Nationalism, and the Enlightenment.* Garry Wills, *Cincinnatus: George Washington and the Enlightenment,* 195–198. Hindle, *The Pursuit of Science,* 18, 58. Seelye, *Prophetic Waters,* 3–4 and *passim,* identifies the continuities to be found in Virginian and New England perceptions of the terrain, and traces them to their British roots. On *translatio emperii* see Ellis, *After the Revolution,* Ch. 1.

40 Thomas Sprat, *History of the Royal Society,* 383–385. Sprat's emphases. George Berkeley, 'Verses on the Prospect of Planting Arts and Learning in America', *Works* VII, 369–373.

41 On the convention in which the poem is located, see Rexmond C. Cochrane, 'Bishop Berkeley and the progress of arts and learning'. On its influence see Walpole, *Letters* VI, 153, 237; Ellis, *After the Revolution,* 6–8; Emory Elliott, *Revolutionary Writers,* 29; Sacvan Bercovitch, *The American Jeremiad,* 110–115; Aldridge, *Early American Literature,* Ch. 6; and Merle Curti, *The Roots of American Loyalty,* 6.

42 Nathaniel Ames, *An Astronomical Diary: or, An Almanack for the Year of our Lord Christ 1758,* [15–16]. Similar rhetoric may be found in 'The Address of America's Genius' and 'A Prophesy of the Future Glory of America', *Royal American Magazine* I, No. 1 (January 1774), 10–11, 31. On Ames and his almanac, see Marion B. Stowell, 'The influence of Nathaniel Ames on the literary taste of his time'.

43 Ezra Stiles, *A Discourse on the Christian Union,* 55, 109, 120–122. On the demography of Franklin and Stiles see Ellis, *After the Revolution,* 13–19; Edmund S. Morgan, *The Gentle Puritan,* 139–142; and James H. Cassedy, *Demography in Early America.* On the legacy of Puritan rhetoric see Bercovitch, *The American Jeremiad,* 93–131, and Tichi, *New World,* 70–71, 77–84, 94–95. Some later nineteenth-century examples may be found in R. Lawson-Peebles, 'Henry George the prophet', 48–50.

44 Anon., *Private Letters from an American in England in his Friends in America,* 'Advertisement', 25–26, 121–122, 139, 158. Review of *Private Letters, Monthly Review* 41 (July 1769), 68. Catherine S. Crary, 'The humble immigrant and the American Dream'. May, *The Enlightenment,* 34–35. Hindle, *The Pursuit of Science,* 74–79, 105–106, 168–172, 190–215, 337–338. Dirk J. Struik, *Yankee Science in the Making,* Part I. John C. Greene, *American Science in the Age of Jefferson,* 5–6. Nye, *Cultural Life of the New Nation,* chs. 3 and 4. Bridenbaugh, *The Spirit of '76,* chs. 3 and 4. Chester E. Eisenger, 'Land and loyalty', 164–165. Wilson, *In the Presence of Nature,* 30. On the idea of the American empire, see William Appleman Williams, 'The age of

mercantilism', 420–421; and Richard W. Van Alstyne, *The Rising American Empire*, Ch. 1.

45 Sprat, *History of the Royal Society*, 385. Ezra Stiles, *The United States Elevated to Glory and Honor* (1783), in *The Pulpit of the American Revolution*, ed. John W. Thornton, 440–441, 460. For examples of a rhetoric similar to Stiles', see Friedman, *Inventors of the Promised Land*, 6–8; Royster, *A Revolutionary People*, Ch.4; Aldridge, *Early American Literature*, Ch. 7; and Bridenbaugh, *The Spirit of '76*, 135–137.

46 George Grieve, translator's footnote to le Marquis de Chastellux, *Travels in North-America* I, 329. On the impact of *Common Sense*, see Moses Coit Tyler, *The Literary History of the American Revolution* I, 468–474; Fender, *American Literature in Context* I, 92–93; Eric Foner, *Tom Paine and Revolutionary America*, 71–87; Aldridge, *Early American Literature*, 142–143; and Isaac Kramnick, 'Editor's introduction' to Thomas Paine, *Common Sense*, 8–9.

47 Paine, *Common Sense*, 120, 107–108, 84–85, 118. On the idea of the asylum see Curti, *The Roots of American Loyalty*, 68–71; and Robert Ernst, 'The asylum of the oppressed'.

48 Paine, *Rights of Man*, ed. Henry Collins, 181–182; 'Six Letters to Rhode Island' (1783) and 'An Act for Incorporating the American Philosophical Society' (1780), both in *Complete Writings*, ed. Philip Foner, II, 347, 39. See also Aldridge, *Early American Literature*, 197–198; Leo Marx, *The American Revolution and the American Landscape*, 7–9; and Jack P. Greene, 'Paine, America, and the "modernization" of political consciousness'.

49 John Filson, *The Discovery and Settlement of Kentucke*, 108. John Walton, *John Filson of Kentucke*, 66 and *passim*. Slotkin, *Regeneration*, 268–316.

50 Gilbert Imlay, *A Topographical Description*, 28–29. For information on Imlay, see Oliver F. Emerson, 'Notes on Gilbert Imlay'; Ralph L. Rusk, 'The adventures of Gilbert Imlay'; and Slotkin, *Regeneration*, 316–320. On the comparison of republics, see Mumford Jones, *O Strange New World*, Ch. 7, 'Roman virtue'.

51 Letters 21 May 1787 to William Short and 2 September 1785 to le Marquis de Chastellux, *Papers* XI, 372 and VIII, 467–469.

52 Anon., 'The Power of Civilization and Freedom: A Poem', *Universal Asylum and Columbian Magazine* 5 (December 1790), 407–408.

53 John R. Howe, *The Changing Political Thought of John Adams*, 28–58, 88–89, 98–99. Royster, *A Revolutionary People*, *passim*. See also John T. Agresto, 'Liberty, virtue and republicanism'; Gordon S. Wood, *The Creation of the American Republic*, 65–70; and J. G. A. Pocock, *The Machiavellian Moment*, Ch. 15.

54 William Currie, *An Historical Account of the Climates and Diseases of the United States of America*, 2, 91, 398, 404–409. On Barlow see Kenneth Ray Ball, *A Great Society: The Social and Political Thought of Joel Barlow*; Robert D. Richardson, 'The Enlightenment view of myth and Joel Barlow's *Vision of Columbus*'; Elliott, *Revolutionary Writers*, Ch. 3; and Tichi, *New World*, Ch. 4. On land transformation and its effects, see Michael Kammen, *Season of Youth*, 99–100; Chinard, 'Eighteenth-century theories', 46, 50–51, and 'The American Philosophical Society and the early history of forestry in America'; Harry Hayden Clark, 'The influence of science on American ideas, from 1775 to 1809', 334–339; Hindle, *The Pursuit of Science*, chs. 12, 16, 17; John B. Jackson, *The Necessity for Ruins and Other Essays*, 48; Cronon, *Changes in the Land*, Ch. 6; and Tichi, *New World*, 89–94. On the vastness of America see Curti, *The Roots of American Loyalty*, 4, 32–35, 40–42.

55 Thomas Bond, *Anniversary Oration, Delivered May 21st . . . 1782*, 23–29.

56 Jeremy Belknap, *The History of New Hampshire* (2nd edn) III, 172. See also Sidney Kaplan, '*The History of New-Hampshire*: Jeremy Belknap as literary crftsman'; and

Hindle, *The Pursuit of Science*, 317–319. A general guide to the environmentalism of the state histories is to be found in Miller, 'American nationalism', 86–95; Lester H. Cohen, *The Revolutionary Histories*, 122–125; and Arthur H. Shaffer, *The Politics of History*, Ch. 4.

57 Samuel Williams, *The Natural and Civil History of Vermont*, 76–77, 80, vii. David Ramsay, *Sketch of the Soil, Climate, Weather and Diseases of South-Carolina*, 5, 8–9, 11–12. James Sullivan, *History of the District of Maine*, 7–8, 396.

58 Hugh Williamson, 'An Attempt to account for the Change of Climate which has been observed in the Middle Colonies of North-America'; *Observations on the Climate in Different Parts of America*, 2, 30, 173–174, 179–180; *The History of North Carolina* II, 183. See also Chinard, 'Eighteenth-century theories', 45; and Miller, 'American nationalism', 86–88.

59 Marx, 'Pastoral ideals and city troubles', 255–256.

60 The following provide good analyses of the temper of the times: Agresto, 'Liberty'; Bercovitch, *The American Jeremiad*, 132–141, and 'How the Puritans won the American Revolution'; Richard Buel, Jr, *Securing the Revolution*; Richard L. Bushman, 'Freedom and prosperity in the American Revolution', in *Legacies*, ed. Gerlach, 70–83; Cohen, *Revolutionary Histories*, 185–188, 192–198; Ellis, *After the Revolution*, 30–38; Fliegelman, *Prodigals and Pilgrims*, Ch. 8; Friedman, *Inventors of the Promised Land*, Ch. 1; Richard Hofstadter, *The Idea of a Party System*; Howe, *The Changing Political Thought of John Adams*, chs. 4–8, and 'Republican thought and the political violence of the 1790s'; Stow Persons, 'The cyclical theory of history in eighteenth-century America'; Pocock, *The Machiavellian Moment*, Ch. 15; Marshall Smelser, 'The Federal period as an age of passion'; and Wood, *The Creation of the American Republic* and 'Rhetoric and reality in the American Revolution'.

61 Wood, 'Conspiracy and the paranoid style'. For details of the conspiracy theories that informed American politics in the second half of the eighteenth century, see Cohen, *The Revolutionary Histories*, 146–160; J. Wendell Knox, *Conspiracy in American Politics, 1787–1815; The Fear of Conspiracy*, ed. David Brion Davis, 'Introduction' and 1–65; and *Conspiracy: The Fear of Subversion in American History*, ed. Richard O. Curry and Thomas M. Brown, 1–41.

62 *Acts and Proceedings of the General Assembly of the Presbyterian Church in the United States of America*, 17 May 1798, quoted in Vernon Stauffer, *New England and the Bavarian Illuminati*, 100.

63 Paine, 'Letter to George Washington' (1795), *Complete Writings* II, 707. Joyce Appleby, 'America as a model for the radical French reformers of 1789', 267–268. Sung Bok Kim, 'The American Revolution and the modern world', in *Legacies*, ed. Garlach, 228–235. *Gazette of the United States* No. 41 (2 September 1789), 164. 'On the American and French Revolutions', *American Museum* VII (1790), Appendix I, 44. Detailed accounts of American attitudes to the French Revolution are provided by Charles D. Hazen, *Contemporary American Opinion of the French Revolution*; Lance Banning, *The Jeffersonian Persuasion*, Ch. 8; Fliegelman, *Prodigals and Pilgrims*, 248–254; Richard J. Moss, 'The American response to the French Revolution, 1789–1801'; Ann Butler Lever, '*Vox Populi, Vox Dei*: New England and the French Revolution, 1787–1801'; Gary B. Nash, 'The American clergy and the French Revolution'; *Federalists, Republicans and Foreign Entanglements, 1789–1815*, ed. Robert McColley; and Stauffer, *New England and the Bavarian Illuminati*.

64 See William Dunlap, *Diary* I, 176 (entry for 30 November 1797); Noah Webster, *A Compendious Dictionary of the English Language*, 167; Nash, 'The American clergy', 402–404; Knox, *Conspiracy*, 31–33, 36–43; Eugene P. Link, *The Democratic-Republican Societies*; Curti, *The Roots of American Loyalty*, 52–53; Charles Warren, *Jacobin and*

Junto, 50–55; and the two articles by Marshall Smelser entitled 'The Jacobin phrenzy'.

65 Madame d'Houdetot, letter to Jefferson 3 September 1790 in Jefferson, *Papers* XVII, 486. For an example of the American fear of vulnerability, see John Wells, *An Oration . . . on the Fourth of July, 1798*, 16.

66 *The Political Green-House, for the Year 1798* in Richard Alsop, *The Echo*, 246–248. Similar images are to be found in many of the sermons of the time, like Samuel Blair's *A Discourse . . .* 20–21. Robert Burns, 'The Cotter's Saturday Night' (1786), *Poems and Selected Letters*, 107.

67 Fisher Ames, 'Laocoon No. 1' (1799), *Works* II, 111–113. Gibbon, *Letters* III, 325. On Ames, see Winfred Bernhard, *Fisher Ames* and Elisha P. Douglass, 'Fisher Ames, spokesman for New England Federalism'.

68 Odell, 'Ode for the New Year' (1780) in *The Loyal Verses of Joseph Stansbury and Doctor Jonathan Odell*, ed. Winthrop Sargent, 59; 'The American Times' (1780) in *The World Turned Upside Down: Prose and Poetry of the American Revolution*, ed. James H. Pickering, 225; 'Inscription for a curious Chamber-Stove' (1777) in Sargent, 6. For further information on Odell, see James McLachlan, *Princetonians, 1748–1768*, 109–112; and Cynthia Dubin Edelberg, 'The shaping of a political poet'. Similar if less acerbic examples may be found in Thomas Brewer Vincent, 'Keeping the faith: the poetic development of Jacob Bailey, loyalist', and Eisenger, 'Land and loyalty', 168–169. A general introduction to the work of the loyalists is given by Charles E. Modlin, 'The Loyalists' reply', *American Literature, 1764–1789*, ed. Everett Emerson, 59–71.

2 A REPUBLIC OF DREAMS

1 *Curti, The Roots of American Loyalty*, 124–125.

2 Benjamin Rush, letter 25 May 1786 to Richard Price, *Letters of Benjamin Rush*, ed. Lyman H. Butterfield, I, 388. Henceforth cited as *Letters*. Rush, 'Address to the People of the United States', *The American Museum* I, No. 1 (January 1787), 8. Rush's emphases.

3 Adams to Morse 29 November 1815. The letter more frequently quoted, in which Adams uses the identical phrase, is 26 November 1815 to Thomas McKean. John Adams, *Works of John Adams* X, 182, 180.

4 Jedidiah Morse, *The American Geography* (1789), vii. Curti, *The Growth of American Thought*, 143. Interpretations of Morse's life and work are provided by Ralph H. Brown, 'The American geographies of Jedidiah Morse'; James F. Chamberlain, 'Early American geographies'; James K. Morse, *Jedidiah Morse: A Champion of New England Orthodoxy*; Sidney E. Morse, *Memorabilia in the Life of Jedidiah Morse*; William B. Sprague, *The Life of Jedidiah Morse*; John C. Greene, *American Science in the Age of Jefferson*, Ch. 8; and Tichi, *New World*, 106–113.

5 Elijah Parish, *A New System of Modern Geography*, iii. Morse, letter 11 April 1784 to his father. MS, Morse Family Papers, Box 1, YU.

6 Morse, *An Appeal to the Publick on the Controversy*, vi; *The American Geography* (1792), 383. On Morse's tendency to New-Englandise America, see Tichi, *New World*, 108–109, and Cassedy, *Demography*, 233.

7 St George Tucker, *A Letter, To the Rev. Jedediah [sic] Morse*, 8. See also Ralph H. Brown, 'St George Tucker *versus* Jedidiah Morse on the subject of Williamsburg', 490–91; and 'The American geographies', 198–199.

8 Morse, letter 27 May 1794 to Ebeling. MS, Morse Family Papers, Box 1, YU. Morse's emphases.

9 Morse, *The American Geography* (1789), vi. Morse, copy letter 18 January 1788 to Belknap. MS, Morse Family Papers, Box 1, YU. Morse's emphases.

10 Belknap, copy letter 28 July 1786 to Morse. Belknap repeated the warning in his letters of 16 June 1788 and 17 February 1789. MSS, Morse Family Papers, Boxes 1 and 21, YU.

11 Mitchill, letter 4 July 1789 to Morse, 'Letters of American physicians and surgeons', ed. Victor H. Paltsits, 550. Wolcott, letter 6 May 1792 to Morse, *Memoirs of the Administrations of Washington and John Adams*, ed. George Gibbs, I, 76. Brown, 'The American geographies', 176.

12 Robert Boyle, 'General Heads for a Natural History of a Countrey', 186–189. J. K. Wright, 'Some British "grandfathers" of American geography', 147–160.

13 Ebeling, unidentified press cutting dated Boston 26 May 1794 criticising Morse's *Geography* and used by Morse as an introduction in his letter of 27 May. Ebeling, copy letter 1 September 1811 to Morse. MSS, Morse Family Papers, Boxes 1 and 21, YU. Morse, 'Population', *The American Geography* (1792), 68. Brown, 'The American geographies', 181.

14 Morse, letter 27 May 1794 to Ebeling, MS, Morse Family Papers, Box 1, YU. Lever, '*Vox Populi*', 87–88. Nash, 'American clergy and the French Revolution', 393–399.

15 Morse, MS notes, 'Mr Cabot's and Genl Knox's Statemt. of Volney's conversation', dated 22 December 1798. Morse Papers Box 1, NYPL. Lever, '*Vox Populi*', 74–76. Morse had earlier attacked Volney in his *Sermon Preached . . . November 29th 1798*, 21–22. See Chapter 7 for discussion of Brown's translation of Volney.

16 John Robison, *Proofs of a Conspiracy*. 1977 Catalogue, Western Islands publishers, in my possession. James Billington, *Fire in the Minds of Men: Origins of the Revolutionary Faith*, 93–105. Buel, *Securing the Revolution*, 170–173. Stauffer, *New England and the Bavarian Illuminati*. On the occult tradition of which the Illuminati were a part, see Frances Yates, *The Rosicrucian Enlightenment*.

17 Morse, *A Sermon Delivered . . . May 9th 1798*. Alan Briceland, 'The Philadelphia Aurora, the New England Illuminati, and the election of 1800'. Stauffer, *New England and the Bavarian Illuminati*, 103–141. Sprague, *Life of Morse*, 230–240. Knox, *Conspiracy*, 115–121. Wood, 'Conspiracy and the paranoid style', 433–435.

18 Rodgers, letter 25 August 1798 to Morse. Abbott, letter 9 December 1798 to Morse. MSS, Morse Papers, Box 1, NYPL. Ebeling, letters 20 March and 2 September 1799 to Morse. Morse, copy letter 5 March 1801 to Ebeling and letter 17 April 1801 to Dwight. MSS, Morse Family Papers, Box 1, YU. See also Henry A. Pochmann, *German Culture in America*, 54.

19 Morse, copy letter to Ebeling 5 March 1801. MS, Morse Family Papers, Box 1, YU.

20 Morse, *A Sermon Preached . . . November 29th 1798*, 14–15, 20–23 (Morse's emphases); *American Universal Geography* (1812), I, v.

21 Morse, *American Universal Geography* (1812), I, iii. The correspondence with Webster begins on 13 September 1793 and ends 22 January 1797. MSS, Webster Papers Boxes 1 and 2, NYPL; Morse Papers Box 1, NYPL; Morse Family Papers Box 1, YU; MSS Dept, University of Virginia.

22 Morse, *American Universal Geography* (1812), I, 100. Mitchill, letter 23 April 1803 to Webster. MS, Webster Papers Box 3, NYPL.

23 Morse, 'Preface' and 'Fredonia', *Gazetteer* (1810), n.p. Arthur Campbell, letter to Morse 20 November 1806, introducing Ordway. MS, Morse Papers Box 1, NYPL. See also Greene, *American Science*, 213–215.

24 Morse, *Annals of the American Revolution*. James K. Morse, *Jedidiah Morse*, 158–161. On the alternative names for the United States, see Frank Luther Mott, *A History of American Magazines* I, 464–465; and David Simpson, *The Politics of American English, 1776–1850*, 41. There are, I believe, Fredonias in Arizona, Arkansas, Iowa, Kansas,

Kentucky, New York, North Dakota, Pennsylvania and, appropriately, in Colombia. See Robert Sklar, *Movie-Made America*, 182, 184 for a brief but apposite analysis of *Duck Soup*.

25 Witherspoon, 'The Druid', Nos. 5, 6 and 7, *Pennsylvania Journal and Weekly Advertiser* 9, 16, 23 and 30 May 1781.

26 Adams, letter 5 September 1780 to the President of Congress, *Works* VII, 249–250. For a similar example, see 'To the Literati of America', *Royal American Magazine* I, No. 1 (January 1774), 6–7. See Chastellux, *Travels* II, 499 on the proposal to speak Hebrew. H. L. Mencken, *The American Language*, 88–89 summarises the truth and rumour of the whole affair. See Chapter 3 for a discussion of Brackenridge.

27 In the discussion of Webster I have drawn on Gary Coll, 'Noah Webster: journalist'; Joseph J. Ellis, *After the Revolution*, Ch. 6; Emily E. F. Ford, *Notes on the Life of Noah Webster*; Richard M. Rollins, *The Long Journey of Noah Webster*; Ervin C. Shoemaker, *Noah Webster: Pioneer of Learning*; David Simpson, *The Politics of American English*; Harry R. Warfel, *Noah Webster: Schoolmaster to America*; Dennis E. Baron, *Grammar and Good Taste*, particularly 41–67, 132–139; *The Beginnings of American English*, ed. Mitford M. Mathews; Mencken, *The American Language*; and Thomas Pyles, *Words and Ways of American English*.

28 Webster, *A Grammatical Institute* Part I, 13–15. Webster's emphases. Henceforth this work will be cited by its commonly accepted name, the *Speller*. Webster, letter 6 January 1783 to John Canfield, *Letters*, ed. Harry Warfel, 4. Webster's emphases. Ford, *Notes* II, 334–337. Warfel, *Webster*, Ch. 18.

29 Webster, 'Remarks on the Manners, Government and Debt of the United States', in *A Collection of Essays and Fugitiv [sic] Writings*, 91. Webster's emphasis. See also Kemp Malone, 'A linguistic patriot'.

30 Webster, 'Preface', *An American Dictionary of the English Language*, n.p.; *Dissertations on the English Language*, 22; *Speller* (1783), 3. Webster would repeat his belief in neologism in his 1817 pamphlet, *Letter to John Pickering*, 7–8.

31 Webster, *Dissertations*, 58–59, 177; 'The State of English Philology', *A Collection of Papers on Political, Literary and Moral Subjects* (1843). Webster differed from many of his contemporaries in dismissing the English philologists; see Friedman, *Inventors of the Promised Land*, 9, 35; and Baron, *Grammar and Good Taste*, 46.

32 Webster, *Dissertations*, iii; letter 10 July 1796 to Volney, MS, Webster Papers Box 1, NYPL. Webster's emphases. See also Cassedy, *Demography*, 297–304.

33 Webster, *Sketches*, 44; *Miscellaneous Papers, On Political and Commercial Subjects*, vii; letter 24 July 1787 to Morse, Morse Family Papers Box 1, YU. Ford, *Notes* II, 35, 44–48. May, *Enlightenment*, 193. Rollins, *Webster*, Ch. 7. Coll, 'Webster', 174.

34 Webster, letter 15 December 1800 to Rush, *Letters*, 228; *Poems by Noah Webster*, ed. Ruth F. and Harry R. Warfel, 12. Webster's emphasis.

35 Webster, 'Reflections on Federalism, & Presidents Washington & Adams', MS Webster Papers Box 8, NYPL; letter 20 November 1837, in Ford, *Notes* II, 353. See also letter from Oliver Wolcott 10 August 1793 to Webster in Wolcott, *Memoirs* I, 103–104; and Rollins, *Webster*, 76–77.

36 Webster, *Observations on Language and on the Errors of Class-Books*, 32 (Webster's emphasis); 'The Times, No. III', *American Minerva* I, No. 107, 10 April 1794; letter 29 April 1836, quoted in Warfel, *Webster*, 425.

37 Webster, *Observations on Language*, 12; *Speller*, 7th edn (1793), 74. Rollins, *Webster*, deals at length with Webster's authoritarianism. Lloyd George Becker, 'Language and landscape', 73–82 discusses landscape imagery in the *Speller*.

38 Webster, 'Preface', *American Dictionary*, n.p.

39 Sterling Andrus Leonard, *The Doctrine of Correctness in English Usage, 1700–1800*, 135. Aarsleff, *The Study of Language*, 3–43.

40 Webster, *Observations*, 7; letter 24 January 1807 to Morse, and Manuscript Lecture, 'A Discourse pronounced before the Connecticut Academy of Arts and Sciences', 1808, MSS Webster Papers Boxes 1 and 7, NYPL. Charlton Laird, 'Etymology, Anglo-Saxon, and Noah Webster'. Aarsleff, *The Study of Language*, Ch. 4. Baron, *Grammar and Good Taste*, 50.

41 Edward Wagenknecht, 'The man behind the Dictionary', 247.

42 Webster, 'Intelligence', *Monthly Anthology and Boston Review* 7 (1809), 208; *Dissertations*, 25–27.

43 Leonard, *The Doctrine*, 42–43, 75.

44 Kemp Malone, 'Benjamin Franklin on spelling reform'. Raoul N. Smith, 'The philosophical alphabet of Jonathan Fisher'. James Carrol, *An American Criterion of the English Language*. Leonard, *The Doctrine*, 238. Baron, *Grammar and Good Taste*, 68–98.

45 Webster, *A Collection of Papers on Political, Literary and Moral Subjects*, 289; letter 22 June 1841 to Queen Victoria, and A. Stevenson, letter 12 August 1841 to Lord Melbourne, MSS Webster Papers, Boxes 1 and 6, NYPL. Friedman, *Inventors*, 37–38.

46 Poe, 'Fifty Suggestions', *Graham's Magazine* (June 1849), *Essays and Reviews*, 1307. Jefferson, letter 27 January 1821 to William S. Cardell. Microfilm, Jefferson Papers, Library of Congress, Reel 88, fo. 39,187. See also Allen Walker Read, 'American projects for an academy to regulate speech', 1161–1162, and 'The membership of proposed American academies', 146–148; Baron, *Grammar and Good Taste*, 101–102, 109–110; and E. H. Criswell, *Lewis and Clark: Linguistic Pioneers*.

47 Rush, 'Eulogium' to Rittenhouse, in *Essays, Literary, Moral and Philosophical*, 370–371; *Benjamin Rush's Lectures on the Mind*, ed. Eric T. Carlson *et al.*, 169–171. Michel Foucault, *Madness and Civilization*. Susan Sontag, *Illness as Metaphor*. George Rosen, 'Noah Webster – historical epidemiologist', 99. George E. Bates, 'Seventeenth- and eighteenth-century American science: a different perspective', 187–190. In the discussion that follows I have also drawn on Daniel Boorstin, 'New World medicine', in *The Americans: The Colonial Experience*, 235–270; C. Helen Brock, 'Scotland and American medicine', in William R. Brock, *Scotus Americanus*, 114–126; René Dubos, *The Dreams of Reason*, Ch. 4, 'Medical utopias'; Michel Foucault, *The Birth of the Clinic*; Lester H. King, *The Medical World of the Eighteenth Century*; Richard H. Shryock, *Medicine and Society in America, 1660–1860*; and C.-E. A. Winslow, *The Conquest of Epidemic Disease*, Ch. 11.

48 Rush, 'To His Fellow Countrymen: On Patriotism', 20 October 1773; letter 12 January 1778 to Patrick Henry; *Letters* I, 83, 182. Other sources of Rush's life and work that I have used are: *The Autobiography of Benjamin Rush*, ed. George W. Corner; Carl Binger, *Revolutionary Doctor: Benjamin Rush*; Lyman H. Butterfield, 'The reputation of Benjamin Rush'; Donald J. d'Elia, 'Dr Benjamin Rush and the American medical revolution'; Nathan G. Goodman, *Benjamin Rush, Physician and Citizen*; David F. Hawke, *Benjamin Rush, Revolutionary Gadfly*; Joseph McFarland, 'The epidemic of yellow fever in Philadelphia in 1793 and its influence upon Dr Benjamin Rush'; and I. Woodbridge Riley, 'Benjamin Rush as materialist and realist'.

49 Rush, letters 5 December 1783 to Dr Charles Nisbet and 17 July 1809 to James Cheetham, *Letters* I, 316, II, 1,007; *Autobiography*, 113–115.

50 Rush, letter 16 November 1776 to John Morgan, and 'Observations on the Federal Procession in Philadelphia 9 July 1788', *Letters* I, 29, 475; *Medical Inquiries and Observations* (1789), 227; 'An account of the influence of military and political events of the American revolution upon the human body', *Medical Inquiries and Observations* (1805), I, 279–294.

51 Rush, *Sixteen Introductory Lectures*, 13; *Benjamin Rush's Lectures on the Mind*, 171. Hindle, *The Pursuit of Science*, 300–301.

52 'Airs, Waters, Places', *Hippocratic Writings*, ed. G. E. R. Lloyd. Genevieve Miller, ' "Airs, Waters, and Places" in history'. Rush, *Autobiography*, Appendix I, 'Rush's medical theories'.

53 Thomas Sydenham, *Works*, ed. Benjamin Rush, xxiv–xxvi, xxix. See also Foucault, *Birth of the Clinic*, 7. On Sydenham see Winslow, *The Conquest of Epidemic Disease*, Ch. 9; and Kenneth Dewhurst, *Dr Thomas Sydenham*.

54 Rush, 'Dedication' to his edition of Sydenham, *Works*, iv–v, vii; *Sixteen Introductory Lectures*, 16, 164, 286, 357, 361–362; *An Account of the Bilious remitting Yellow Fever*, 337; letter 18 January 1793 to Elizabeth Graeme Ferguson?, *Letters* II, 627; 'Appendix', *Medical Inquiries* (1789), 260. Ramsay, 'Dedication' of *A Review of the Improvement, Progress, and State of Medicine in the XVIIIth Century*. See also James H. Cassedy, 'Meteorology and medicine in colonial America', 194–195, and *Demography*, Ch. 11.

55 Rush, *Sixteen Introductory Lectures*, 86–87; *An Inquiry into the Influence of Physical Causes upon the Moral Faculty* (1786), in *Medical Inquiries* (1805), II, 24–57; 'A Moral and Physical Thermometer' (1789), *Letters* I, opp. 512.

56 Rush, *An Inquiry, Medical Inquiries* (1805), II, 24; *Benjamin Rush's Lectures on the Mind*, 161–163; letter 4 February 1797 to Jefferson, *Letters* II, 785.

57 Rush, letter 9 February 1802 to Lyman Spalding; 'To American Farmers About to Settle in New Parts of the United States' (March 1789); *Letters* II, 843, I, 505. Rush's frontier theory first appeared in a 1786 article, 'An account of the Progress of Population, Agriculture, Manners, and Government in Pennsylvania', reprinted in his 1798 *Essays*, 213–225.

58 Rush, letters 25 May 1786 to Richard Price; 29 October 1788 'To Friends of the Federal University: A Plan for a Federal University'; 4 May 1784 to William Linn (Rush's emphasis); and 22 August 1800 to Jefferson; *Letters* I, 388, 491–494, 333, II, 820. Rush, *Sixteen Introductory Lectures*, 99.

59 Rush, letter 22 December 1784 to William Cullen, *Letters* I, 347; 'Dr Benjamin Rush's journal of a trip to Carlisle in 1784', ed. Lyman H. Butterfield, 450–451; 'An account of the manners of German Inhabitants of Pennsylvania', *Essays*, 226–248; 'An Account of the Climate of Pennsylvania', *Medical Inquiries* (1805), I, 75, 78, 108–109. Ramsay, *A Sketch of the Soil*, 21. Belknap, *History of New Hampshire* III, 172.

60 Rush, letter 6 October 1800 to Jefferson, *Letters* II, 824. William Cowper, *The Task* I, 749, in *Poetical Works*, ed. H. S. Milford, 145. Cobbett, *Cobbett's Weekly Register* 45, No. 8 (22 February 1823), 480–481. Cobbett uses the image throughout his *Rural Rides* (1830).

61 Rush, letter 15 June 1789 to John Adams; 'Information to Europeans Who are Disposed to Migrate to the United States', 16 April 1790; letter 21 June 1792 to Jeremy Belknap; 'Observations on the Federal Procession in Philadelphia, 9 July 1788'; *Letters* I, 516, 560, 620, 470–477.

62 Rush, letter 25 November 1806 to Adams, *Letters* II, 934. Sontag, *Illness as Metaphor*, 81 and *passim*. Gazette of the United States No. 41 (2 September 1789), 164, and Ames, 'Laocoon No. 1' (1799), *Works* II, 111–113. Wolcott, letter 22 June 1794 to Morse; MS, Morse Papers Box 1, NYPL. Lathrop, *National Happiness*, 10.

63 Rush, letter 25 November 1793 to William Kidd, *Letters* II, 764. John Duffy, *Epidemics in Colonial America*, 138–163, 239. John B. Blake, 'Yellow fever in eighteenth-century America'.

64 Rush, letter 15 September 1798 to William Marshall, *Letters* II, 806–807. Rodgers, letter 3 October 1798 to Morse, MS Morse Papers, Beinecke Library, YU; Rodgers' emphasis.

65 Rush, *An Inquiry, Medical Inquiries* (1805), II, 31–32. Wesley, Sermon XCIII, 'On Dress', *Sermons* ii, 421. Owsei Temkin, 'An historical analysis of the concept of

infection'. Michael Durey, *The Return of the Plague*, 190. Asa Briggs, 'Cholera and society', 81–82. For American religious responses to cholera, see Charles E. Rosenberg, *The Cholera Years*, chs. 2 and 7.

66 Rush, 'Account of Vices Peculiar to Indians', *Essays*, 257–262; *Benjamin Rush's Lectures on the Mind*, 155; letter 18 April 1806 to John Coakley Lettsom, *Letters* II, 917. On Webster and 'demoralization' see Rollins, *Webster*, 80; and Ellis, *After the Revolution*, 163. On Rush's attitude to Indians see Roy Harvey Pearce, *Savagism and Civilization*, 152–153, and particularly Sydney J. Krause's 'Historical essay' to Charles Brockden Brown, *Edgar Huntly*, 360–364, which gives another context for Rush's influence on Brown. For his part, Rush thought that Brown had a 'masterly pen'; see letter 19 October 1803 to Thomas Eddy, *Letters* II, 874. The details of the 1793 epidemic have been drawn from Mathew Carey, *A Short Account of the Malignant Fever*, 23–26, 40, 93. This graphic account was first published in November 1793 and by January 1794 had gone through four editions. It still provides gripping reading. It can be supplemented by two other first-hand accounts: Oliver Wolcott's *Memoirs* I, 108–113, and Charles Caldwell's *Autobiography*, Ch. 5. See also J. H. Powell, *Bring Out Your Dead: The Great Plague of Yellow Fever in Philadelphia in 1793*; John K. Alexander, 'The city of brotherly fear: the poor in late-eighteenth-century Philadelphia'; and Joann Peck Krieg, 'Charles Brockden Brown and the empire of romance', Ch. 3.

67 William Currie, *A Description of the Malignant, Infectious Fever*, 7; *An Impartial Review of Dr Rush's Late Publication . . . in which his opinion is shown to be erroneous; The importation of the disease established; and the wholesomeness of the city vindicated*, 14. Alfred Stillé, *Elements of General Pathology*, 100–101. Blake, 'Yellow fever', 678–679. William H. McNeill, *Plagues and Peoples*, 244–245.

68 Walpole, letter 5 July 1740 to H. S. Conway, *Letters* I, 50. Martin, letters 20 January and 15 October 1832 to Webster; MSS, Webster Papers Box 5, NYPL. Rosen, 'Noah Webster', 108–112. Stillé, *Elements of General Pathology*, 95–100. Temkin, 'An historical analysis', 134–137.

69 Alsop, *The Political Green-House, for the Year 1798*, in *The Echo*, 243. Alsop's emphasis.

70 Sydenham, *Works*, ed. Rush, 4. Stillé, *Elements of General Pathology*, 101. Rush, 'Facts, Intending to prove the Yellow Fever not to be Contagious', *Medical Inquiries* (1805), IV, 226–271.

71 Caldwell, *Autobiography*, 185–186. Another version is given in William Cobbett, *Porcupine's Works* VII, 234.

72 Rush, 'A Defence of Blood-Letting', *Medical Inquiries* (1805), IV, 359; *Medical Inquiries* (1796), IV, 255–256. The millennial remarks do not appear in the 1789 and 1794 editions of the essay.

73 Rush, letters 25 August and 13 September 1793 to Julia Rush, *Letters* II, 640, 663; *An Account of the Bilious remitting Yellow Fever*, 104, 107–109, 341.

74 Devèze, *An Enquiry*, title page and 50. Rush, 'A Defence of Blood-Letting', *Medical Inquiries* (1805), IV, 334–361.

75 Currie, *An Impartial Review*, 10; *An Historical Account of the Climates and Diseases of the United States of America*, 404–409. Rush, letter 24 October 1793 to Julia Rush, *Letters* II, 725.

76 Cobbett, *Porcupine's Works* VII, 254. See also 'the Cobbett–Rush Feud', Appendix III, *Letters* II, 1,213–1,218; and *Autobiography*, 95–105.

77 Samuel Hodgdon, letter 17 August 1797 and Elias Boudinot, letter 4 September 1797, both to Timothy Pickering; Rush, letter 11 October 1797 to John Dickinson; all in *Letters* II, 791fn3, 1,209, 793. William Smith, letter 25 February 1798 to Oliver Wolcott in Wolcott, *Memoirs* II, 55.

78 Rush, letter 2 October 1810 to John Adams, *Letters* II, 1,067–1,068. See also James S. Young, *The Washington Community*, Ch. 1.

79 Rush, letters 16? October 1797 to Rodgers, 23 January 1807 and 8 July 1812 to John Adams; *Letters* II, 794, 936, 1148.
80 Rush, letter 10 June 1806 to John Adams, *Letters* II, 919. Cowper, *The Task* II, 1–5, *Works*, 146.

3 DREARY WASTES AND AWFUL SOLITUDE

1 The major biography is still Julia P. Mitchell's 1916 *St Jean de Crèvecœur* and the most extensive critique is provided by Thomas Philbrick, *St John de Crèvecœur*. I have made use of three unpublished dissertations: Doreen Saar, 'Crèvecœur's lucubration on the meaning of America'; A. D. Pol, 'The idea of moral landscape', Ch. 2; and Margaret M. Nettles, 'The land, the self, and the word', Ch. 3. I have also consulted Bernard Chevignard, 'St John de Crèvecœur in the looking glass'; Marcus Cunliffe, 'Crèvecœur revisited'; Fender, *American Literature in Context* I, Ch. 7; John Hales, 'The landscape of tragedy: Crèvecœur's "Susquehanna"'; Myra Jehlen, 'J. Hector St John Crèvecœur: a monarcho-anarchist in Revolutionary America'; Marx, *The Machine in the Garden*, 107–116; A. W. Plumstead, 'Hector St John de Crèvecœur', *American Literature*, 1764–1789, ed. Everett Emerson, 213–231; Elayne Antler Rapping, 'Theory and experience in Crèvecœur's America'; Slotkin, *Regeneration*, 259–267; and Roger B. Stein, *Susquehanna: Images of the Settled Landscape*, 23–26.
2 Crèvecœur, *Letters from an American Farmer and Sketches of Eighteenth-Century America*, ed. Albert E. Stone, 81–82. Further references are to this edition and will usually be given parenthetically. Washington, letter 19 June 1788 to Richard Henderson, *Writings* XXIX, 522.
3 Crèvecœur, *Letters*, 69–70. Chester E. Eisenger, 'Land and loyalty', 175. See Fliegelman, *Prodigals and Pilgrims*, 31–32, 62–63, and 180–182 on Crèvecœur's Lockeian environmentalism; and Novak, *Nature and Culture*, 105, which shows how Crèvecœur's organicism was developed in the nineteenth century into a positive nationalism.
4 Crèvecœur, *Letters*, 57, 68–69. See Saar, 'Crèvecœur's lucubration', Ch. 3 for a detailed comparison with Defoe.
5 On Crèvecœur and the middle landscape, see Marx, *The Machine in the Garden*, 107–116; and Tichi, *New World*, 99–106. On Crèvecœur's last book, see Percy G. Adams, 'The historical value of Crèvecœur's *Voyage dans la haute Pensylvanie et dans New York*'. On the narrative complexity of the *Letters* see Philbrick, *Crèvecœur*, Ch. 3; James C. Mohr, 'Calculated disillusionment'; Jean F. Béranger, 'The desire of communication'; Mary E. Rucker, 'Crèvecœur's *Letters* and Enlightenment doctrine'; and Robert P. Winston, '"Strange order of things!": the journey to chaos in *Letters from An American Farmer*'.
6 Genesis chs. 6 and 7. Roger B. Stein has written widely and with much insight on the importance of the seascape in American culture. See the bibliography for a listing of his work which I have used generally in this study. Of particular relevance at this point are *Seascape and the American Imagination*, 2; and 'Copley's *Watson and the Shark* and aesthetics in the 1770s', 117–119.
7 Crèvecœur, *Letters*, 189, 191, 193, 199. On the relationship between Crèvecœur and Bartram, see Chevignard, 'Crèvecœur', 181–182, and Saar, 'Crèvecœur's lucubration', 150–151.
8 Crèvecœur, *Letters*, 227. For some details of the Revolution as a savage civil war, see Royster, *A Revolutionary People*, 277–278. On contemporary sentimental images of the Indians, see Herbert Ross Brown, *The Sentimental Novel in America*, 140–142.
9 Crèvecœur, *Letters*, 393, 414–415, 478–479. The influence of Rosa and Claude will be discussed in chapters 4 to 7.

10 'The Rising Glory of America', in Philip Freneau, *Poems Written and Published during the American Revolutionary War* I, 75, 78. Henceforth cited as *Poems* (1809). In this discussion of Freneau I have used two major biographies, Lewis Leary, *That Rascal Freneau* and Jacob Axelrad, *Philip Freneau*. The most extensive examination of the poetry is Richard C. Vitzthum's fine *Land and Sea: The Lyric Poetry of Philip Freneau*. Briefer but discriminating assessments of the writer are to be found in Elliott, *Revolutionary Writers*, Ch. 4; Fender, *American Literature in Context* I, Ch. 8; and Lewis Leary, 'Philip Freneau: a reassessment', *Soundings*, 131–160.

11 Abbé Robin, *New Travels Through North-America*, trans. Freneau, [2]. Freneau, *The Poems of Philip Freneau*, ed. Fred Lewis Pattee, I, 82 reprints the 1772 version of 'The Rising Glory', from which the quotation is taken. The other versions, which differ only in punctuation, are in *Poems, Written Chiefly During the Late War*, 58 (hereafter cited as *Poems* (1786)) and *Poems on Several Occasions*, 46 (hereafter cited as *Poems* (1795)). Vitzthum, *Land and Sea*, 162–163 talks briefly of their textual history.

12 Brackenridge and Freneau, *Father Bombo's Pilgrimage to Mecca*. Martha Pike Conant, *The Oriental Tale in England in the Eighteenth Century*. Johnson, *A Voyage to Abyssinia*, ed. Joel J. Gold.

13 Freneau, *The American Village*, 7. Goldsmith, *The Deserted Village, Works* IV, 300–301. William L. Andrews, 'Goldsmith and Freneau in "The American Village"' provides a detailed comparison of the two poems.

14 Freneau, letter 22 November 1772 to Madison, *The Papers of James Madison*, ed. William T. Hutchinson and William M. E. Rachal, I, 78.

15 Freneau, 'The Power of Fancy', *Poems* (1786), 23–27. See Fender, *American Literature in Context* I, 152 and James Engell, *The Creative Imagination*, 194–196 for further discussions of this poem.

16 Freneau, 'MacSwiggen; A Satire', *Poems* (1786), 95–100. Freneau, manuscript notes in his copy of *Miscellanies for Sentimentalists* (Philadelphia, 1778), Special Collections, Alexander Library, Rutgers University. I am grateful to Edward Skipworth of the Alexander Library for providing a photocopy of this item.

17 Freneau, 'The Beauties of Santa Cruz', *Poems* (1786), 133–150; 'Account of the Island of Santa Cruz', *United States Magazine* I (February 1779), 83. See also Axelrad, *Freneau*, 78–84; Vitzthum, *Land and Sea*, 35–37, 77–81; Jane Donahue Eberwein, 'Freneau's "The Beauties of Santa Cruz"'; and Elliott, *Revolutionary Writers*, 139–140. Another example of the rhetoric of inexpressibility may be found in the first sonnet of Sir Philip Sidney's *Astrophel and Stella* (1591).

18 Freneau, 'George the Third's Soliloquy', *The Poems of Philip Freneau*, ed. Pattee, II, 3–6; 'The House of Night', *Poems* (1786), 101–123. Once again, the poem is altered from its 1779 version. In the first stanza quoted above 'howling dogs' and 'roving wolves' are ousted by 'roaring wolves' and 'roving bears' in 1779. The 1786 version has been used, but differs little from the earlier version for purposes of this analysis. The Pattee edition, I, 212–239 gives details of the variations. Defoe, *Robinson Crusoe*, 292–296. On the significance of the episode of the wolves in *Robinson Crusoe*, see Hunter, *The Reluctant Pilgrim*, 191–199. For further analyses of Freneau's two poems, see Vitzthum, *Land and Sea*, 73–77; Lewis Leary, 'The dream visions of Philip Freneau'; Matthiessen, *American Renaissance*, 202; G. Ferris Cronkhite, 'Freneau's "The House of Night"'; and Elliott, *Revolutionary Writers*, 140–142.

19 Freneau, 'The British Prison Ship', *Poems* (1786), 186–206. Axelrad, *Freneau*, 108–110. See however Mary Weatherspoon Bowden, 'In search of Freneau's prison ships', which questions if the poet was ever imprisoned.

20 Freneau, 'The Hurricane', *Poems* (1795), 270–271. For further discussions of this poem see Elliott, *Revolutionary Writers*, 162–164 and Vitzthum, *Land and Sea*, 59–63. See also Stein, 'Seascape and the American imagination: the Puritan seventeenth century', 30–31, and 'Pulled out of the bay: American fiction in the eighteenth century', 21–22.

21 Freneau, 'Light, Summer Reading', *The Miscellaneous Works* (1788), 251–269. The Sangrado poems are 'Sangrado's Expedition', *Poems* (1795), 321–322; 'Sangrado's Flight', *Poems* (1809), II, 288; and 'On the Free Use of the Lancet', *A Collection of Poems on American Affairs and a Variety of Other Subjects Chiefly Moral and Political* I, 146. This edition is hereafter cited as *Poems* (1815).

22 Reprinted as 'Prologue' in *Poems* (1786), 235.

23 Freneau, 'The Pilgrim, No. VIII', *The Freeman's Journal*, No. 38 (9 January 1782), 1.

24 Freneau, 'Pictures of Columbus', *Miscellaneous Works* (1788), 1–30. Freneau's emphases. Carol A. Kyle, 'That poet Freneau: a study of the imagistic success of *The Pictures of Columbus*', gives a sensitive reading of the poem. Vitzthum, *Land and Sea*, 111 discusses its date. See Stein, *Seascape*, 52–55, for a brief illustrated discussion of later uses of Columbus as a historical hedge against nihilism in the American seascape.

25 'Science', *Poems* (1809), I, 262.; 'The Great Western Canal', *The Last Poems of Philip Freneau*, ed. Leary, 21–24. See Ball, *A Great Society*, 171–175, 201–226, 275–278 for Barlow's interest in roads and canals. See my Chapter 5 for a discussion of Jefferson's advocacy of public works.

26 Between 1791 and 1793 Freneau edited the Jefferson-sponsored *National Gazette*, becoming the first effective crusading newspaperman in America. Again, see my Chapter 5 for this aspect of Jefferson's thinking.

27 Freneau, 'On American Antiquity' and 'Pennsylvania', *Poems* (1795), 17–18, 376.

28 Freneau, 'Reflections on the Constitution; or Frame of Nature', *Poems* (1809), I, 262–263.

29 'Ode written on a Remote Perspective View of Princeton College', *The Last Poems of Philip Freneau*, ed. Leary, 99–102. Freneau's emphases. Pope's use of the telescope to order chaos is to be found, *inter alia*, in 'The Essay on Man', I, 289 and IV, 49.

30 Brackenridge, 'Preface', *United States Magazine* I (January 1779), 3. Brackenridge's emphasis. A modernised version is given in *A Hugh Henry Brackenridge Reader*, ed. Daniel Marder, 70. The standard appreciations of Brackenridge's life and work are by Claude M. Newlin and Daniel Marder. I have also drawn on a Ph.D. dissertation, William E. Vincent's 'Hugh Henry Brackenridge: frontier commentator'. Good analyses of Brackenridge's work are to be found in Ellis, *After the Revolution*, Ch. 4; Leary, *Soundings*, 161–174; Simpson, *Politics of American English*, 113–118; Von Frank, *The Sacred Game*, 44–49; and, particularly, Elliott, *Revolutionary Writers*, Ch. 5.

31 Brackenridge, 'The Cave of Vanhest', *United States Magazine* I (January 1779), 14–15; (March 1779), 110; (April 1779), 150; and (July 1779), 311–312. The tale is reprinted, with a number of omissions, in the *Brackenridge Reader*, ed. Marder, 78–92. See Ellis, *After the Revolution*, 86, for Brackenridge on the British.

32 *United States Magazine* I (December 1779), 483.

33 Brackenridge, article in the *Tree of Liberty* 13 September 1800, quoted in Newlin, *Brackenridge*, 220.

34 See Michael T. Gilmore, 'Eighteenth-century oppositional ideology and Hugh Henry Brackenridge's *Modern Chivalry*'. On the Whiskey Rebellion, see *The Whiskey Rebellion: Past and Present Perspectives*, ed. Steven R. Boyd; Thomas P. Slaughter, *The Whiskey Rebellion*; Knox, *Conspiracy*, 44–64; and Ellis, *After the Revolution*, 102–108.

35 Brackenridge, 'Thoughts on the Present Indian War' and 'Thoughts on the Excise Law' (both 1792), *Incidents of the Insurrection*, ed. Daniel Marder, 42, 50–51.

36 Brackenridge, *Incidents of the Insurrection*, 134–136, 130. For Brackenridge's earlier view of the French Revolution, see 'Louis Capet Lost His Caput' and 'To the President of the United States' (both 1793) also in *Incidents*, 52–55. Marder, *Brackenridge*, 105–115 gives a thoughtful discussion of the *Incidents*.

37 Wendy Martin, 'On the road with the philosopher and the profiteer' and Amberys R.

Whittle, '*Modern Chivalry*: the frontier as crucible' ably isolate some of the reasons for the complexity of the book. William L. Nance. 'Satiric elements in Brackenridge's *Modern Chivalry*' indicates its generic background while Mary Mattfield's fine '*Modern Chivalry*: the form' shows at length how its generic form is modified into something distinctively American. A Ph.D. dissertation, John F. Engell, 'Brackenridge, Brown, Cooper, and the roots of the American novel', chs. 2 and 3 locates its place at the head of American fiction. Elliott, *Revolutionary Writers*, 181–217, provides a skilful discussion of the complexity of the text.

38 Brackenridge, *Modern Chivalry*, 6, 89. Further references to this text will be given parenthetically. On Brackenridge's debt to Cervantes see, for instance, Joseph J. Harkey, 'The Don Quixote of the frontier'. On his use of cultural relativity, see Martin, 'On the road', 248–252.

39 For further discussions of the significance of the cave, see Martin, 'On the road', 251–252; and Elliott, *Revolutionary Writers*, 200. Elliott, 185–197, rightly distinguishes the narrator from Farrago but gives an analysis of Farrago's character that is more pejorative than mine.

40 Wendy Martin, 'The rogue and the rational man: Hugh Henry Brackenridge's study of a con man in *Modern Chivalry*'. Robert Munford, *The Candidates; or, the Humours of a Virginia Election*, 246. See also Rodney M. Baine, *Robert Munford, America's First Comic Dramatist*; Robert A. Ferguson, *Law and Letters in American Culture*, 115–118, 122; and Gordon S. Wood, 'Rhetoric and reality in the American Revolution', 28, and *The Creation of the American Republic*, Ch. 7, 'The worthy against the licentious'.

41 See Elliott, *Revolutionary Writers*, 201, and Martin, 'On the road', 245–253 on the linked themes of madness and the alienated artist in *Modern Chivalry*. See Chapter 7 above and Paul Scott Steinberg, 'On the brink of the precipice', chs. 2 and 3 on the relation of madness and bestiality in the work of Brockden Brown.

42 Other examples of anti-Irish feeling are to be found in Alsop, *The Echo*, 242, 249; and Peter K. McCarter, 'Mother Carey's Jacobin chickens'. Although McCarter does not make the connection, it is fairly clear that 'Mother Carey' is a thinly-veiled insult against Mathew Carey, author of *A Short Account of the Malignant Fever* of 1793, publisher in that same year of the American edition of Crèvecœur's *Letters*, and a leading figure in the Irish community in Philadelphia during the years that Brackenridge lived there. For the background to anti-Irish sentiments, see Edward C. Carter II, 'A "wild Irishman" under every Federalist's bed'; Link, *Republican-Democratic Societies*, 82–83; and Knox, *Conspiracy*, 122–127. McCarter, 'Mother Carey's Jacobin chickens' is also a good example of the beast-fable. For more details of its usage in Brackenridge's novel, see Mattfield, '*Modern Chivalry*: the form', 22–23; and Lucille M. Schultz, 'Uncovering the significance of the animal imagery in *Modern Chivalry*'.

43 Brackenridge, 'The Trial of Mamachtaga' (1785) and 'Thoughts on the Present Indian War' (1792), both in *Incidents of the Insurrection*, ed. Marder, 25–34, 38–39; *Narratives of the Late Expedition Against the Indians*, 32. See also Marder, *Brackenridge*, 99–105.

44 Henry Fielding, *Tom Jones*, 52. Farrago's assertion that there should be 'no commixture of name' anticipates John Quincy Adams's contempt over the suggested renaming of the Columbia River, discussed in Chapter 6. See Mattfield, *Modern Chivalry*: the form', 310–311, for a further comparison with Fielding; and Martin, 'On the road', 247–248, 252–256 for a discussion of the open-ended structure of the novel and of the various hedges against chaos.

45 Brackenridge, *Law Miscellanies*, iii, 576–579. Ferguson, *Law and Letters*, 119–128, is a good discussion of the intimate relation of Brackenridge's two callings.

4 THE NATURAL LIMIT OF A REPUBLIC

1 William Petty, 'Political Arithmetick', Ch. 5, in *Economic Writings*, ed. Charles H. Hull, I, 300–302. Goldsmith, *The Citizen of the World* I, 61; *A History of England* II, 121–122. Hinkhouse, *The Preliminaries of the American Revolution*, 42–43, 105, 174. Clark, *British Opinion*, 127, 181.

2 [Egremont], 'Hints Relative to the Division and Government of the Conquered and Newly Acquired Countries of America', ed. Verner W. Crane, 371. J. Leitch Wright, *Britain and the American Frontier, 1783–1815*, 2–3. An earlier, less sophisticated version of the proposal is to be found in Thomas C. Barrow, 'A project for imperial reform'; and the Royal Proclamation is reprinted in *Sources and Documents Illustrating the American Revolution*, 1–4. Samuel Eliot Morison's 'Introduction' to *Sources and Documents*, xvii–xxxii, provides a succinct summary of 'The Western Problem'. See also Max Farrand, 'The Indian boundary line'; R. A. Humphries, 'Lord Shelburne and the Proclamation of 1763'; Clarence W. Alvord, *The Mississippi Valley in British Politics* I, 160–179, 198–203, 286; Thomas P. Abernethy, *Western Lands and the American Revolution*, chs. 1–4; John Richard Alden, *General Gage in America*, Ch. 8; Jack M. Sosin, *Whitehall and the Wilderness*, particularly 56–61; and Shy, *A People*, Ch. 3.

3 Webster, *Sketches of American Policy*, 25–29. See also Ellis, *After the Revolution*, 179–180, 195; J. G. A. Pocock, *The Machiavellian Moment*, 532–544; Arthur E. Bestor, 'Patent-office models of the good society', 514; and George Rosen, 'Noah Webster – historical epidemiologist', 101–102.

4 Rev. James Smith, 'Tours into Kentucky and the Northwest Territory: Three Journals', ed. and introd. Josiah Morrow, 390. Henry Nash Smith in *Virgin Land*, Book 3, talks generally about such images and at page 193 quotes another segment of Smith's journal. Michael Kammen, *A Season of Youth*, 96–102, discusses the 'peace and plenty' iconography of the period. See also Marx, *The Machine in the Garden*, particularly Ch. 3.

5 Walpole, *On Modern Gardening*, ed. W. S. Lewis, 43–44. See also Christopher Hussey, *English Gardens and Landscapes 1700–1750*; *The Genius of the Place: The English Landscape Garden 1620–1820*, ed. John Dixon Hunt and Peter Willis; David C. Streatfield and Alastair M. Duckworth, *Landscape in the Gardens and the Literature of Eighteenth-Century England*; Paul Shepard, *Man in the Landscape*, Ch. 3; and Keith Thomas, *Man and the Natural World*.

6 Montesquieu, *The Spirit of Laws*, Book 7, Ch. 16, Vol. I, 123. For evidence of the influence of Montesquieu in this respect, see Wood, *The Creation of the American Republic*, 356, 499–502; Henry S. Commager, *Jefferson, Nationalism, and the Enlightenment*, 175–176; and Paul Spurlin, *Montesquieu in America*, chs. 6 and 7. See also F. T. H. Fletcher, *Montesquieu and English Politics*, Ch. 11.

7 Rufus King, letter 3 September 1786 to Jonathan Jackson, in *Letters to Members of the Continental Congress*, ed. Edmund C. Burnett VIII, 458. Similar sentiments may be found in the same volume at pp. 376, 380, and 440. See also Peter S. Onuf, 'Liberty, development, and union: visions of the West in the 1780s'; Abernethy, *Western Lands*, chs. 22–23; and Agresto, 'Liberty, virtue and republicanism', 479.

8 *The Records of the Federal Convention*, ed. Max Farrand, I, 533, 583; I, 579; and II, 454. See also Rush Welter, 'The frontier West as image of American society'.

9 Coxe, 'Address to the Honourable the Members of the Convention of Virginia', *American Museum* 3, No. 5 (May 1788), 426–433. Madison, 'The Federalist No. XIV', (30 November 1787), in *The Federalist*, 62–63. For similar, later images of the unity of American nature, see Curti, *The Roots of American Loyalty*, 42–44.

10 [James Winthrop], 'Agrippa IV', *Massachusetts Gazette* 3 December 1787, reprinted in *Essays on the Constitution of the United States*, ed. Paul Leicester Ford, 64–65.

11 Rush, 'An Address to the People of the United States', *American Museum* I (1787), 8–11; 'Information to Europeans Who Are Disposed to Migrate to the United States', 16 April 1790; and letter to David Hosack 25 December 1812; *Letters*, ed. Butterfield, I, 563 and II, 1162. Benjamin Smith Barton, *New Views of the Origin of the Tribes and Nations of America*, v. For an example of the Puritan fear of degeneration, see the discussions of Thomas Morton of Merrymount in Seelye, *Prophetic Waters*, 166–174, and Slotkin, *Regeneration*, 58–65.

12 Anon., 'Plan for Revolution in Louisiana', from Les Archives des Affaires Etrangères, reprinted in the *Annual Report of the American Historical Association for the Year 1896*, 951. My translation. An inadequate translation is to be found in *Federalists, Republicans, and Foreign Entanglements*, ed. Robert McColley, 17.

13 See Abernethy, *Western Lands*, passim; Wright, *Britain and the American Frontier*, 7–8, 132–143; Donald Barr Chidsey, *Louisiana Purchase*, passim; *The Political Correspondence and Political Papers of Aaron Burr*, ed. Mary-Jo Kline and Joanne Wood Ryan II, 919–925, 973–986; and Knox, *Conspiracy*, chs. 3, 5–7.

14 On Revolutionary savagism, see Royster, *A Revolutionary People*, 111–112, 277–278; and Sheehan, 'Ignoble savagism', in *Legacies*, ed. Garlach, 162–177. Important discussions of the place of frontier violence in American culture are contained in Arthur K. Moore, *The Frontier Mind*; Slotkin, *Regeneration*; and W. Eugene Hollon, *Frontier Violence*.

15 On the anxious quest for cohesion after the Revolution, see Kammen, *People of Youth*, 16–18. For a thoughtful discussion of the gap between Enlightenment theory and frontier actuality, see Lester H. Cohen, 'Eden's constitution: the paradisiacal dream and Enlightenment values in late eighteenth-century literature of the American frontier'.

16 Timothy Dwight, 'The Flourishing Village', ll.1–18, from *Greenfield Hill*, in *The Major Poems*, introd. William J. McTaggart and William K. Bottorff, 397. Further references to this text will be given parenthetically, citing line and page numbers. A contemporary poem revealing similar political views is 'The American Farmer', *American Museum* VII, Appendix I (January–June 1790), 38–39. In this discussion of Dwight I have drawn on Robert D. Arner, 'The Connecticut Wits', *American Literature*, ed. Emerson, 240–245; Chester E. Eisenger, 'Land and loyalty'; Elliott, *Revolutionary Writers*, Ch. 2; John Griffith, '*The Columbiad* and *Greenfield Hill*: history, poetry, and ideology in the late eighteenth century'; Leon Howard, *The Connecticut Wits*; Kenneth Silverman, *Timothy Dwight*; Slotkin, *Regeneration*, 338–342; Tichi, *New World*, 89–94; and Von Frank, *The Sacred Game*, 49–60.

17 On Dwight's role in the development of the typology of mission see Bercovitch, *The American Jeremiad*, 128–130; and Elliott, *Revolutionary Writers*, 79–82.

18 William Gilpin, *An Essay on Prints*, 57–58. Walpole, letter 28 September 1739 to Richard West, *Letters* I, 26. Thomson, 'The Castle of Indolence', Canto I, Stanza XXXVIII, *Complete Poetical Works*, 265. On Claude, see Marcel Rothlisberger, *Claude Lorrain*. On Rosa, see John Sunderland, 'The legend and influence of Salvator Rosa in England in the eighteenth century'; P. A. Tomory, *Salvator Rosa: His Etchings and Engravings after his Work*; and Richard W. Wallace, *The Etchings of Salvator Rosa*. On eighteenth-century landscape aesthetics and the influence of Italian painting, see Elizabeth Manwaring, *Italian Landscape in Eighteenth-Century England*; Christopher Hussey, *The Picturesque*; Walter John Hipple, *The Beautiful, The Sublime and The Picturesque in Eighteenth-Century British Aesthetic Theory*; John Dixon Hunt, *The Figure in the Landscape*; Martin Price, 'The Picturesque moment'; Shepard, *Man in the Landscape*, chs. 4–5; George B. Parks, 'The turn to the Romantic in the travel

literature of the eighteenth century'; J. R. Watson, *Picturesque Landscape and English Romantic Poetry*, 11–49; John Barrell, *The Idea of Landscape and the Sense of Place 1730–1840*, Ch. 1; Christopher Thacker, *The Wildness Pleases*; Stein, *Susquehanna*, Ch. 4; and a Ph.D. dissertation, Beth Lynne Lueck, 'The Sublime and the Picturesque in American landscape description', chs. 1 and 2. Smith, *European Vision and the South Pacific*, 23, 46, 197–200, shows the influence of Italian painting on antipodean landscape aesthetics.

19 Dwight, *Travels in New-England and New-York* II, 128. Further references to this text will normally be given parenthetically, citing volume and page numbers. See John F. Sears, 'Timothy Dwight and the American Landscape' for a further account of the *Travels* and a useful comparison with Thomas Cole and William Bartram.

20 Dwight also published, in 1811, *A Statistical Account of Connecticut*. Silverman, *Dwight*, 116–121 discusses at greater length Dwight's use of fact to refute the Philosophes. See Chapter 5 above for an analysis of Jefferson's *Notes*.

21 For more detailed accounts of Dwight's attitudes to Allen and the frontier see Silverman, *Dwight*, 130–132; and Vincent Freimarck, 'Timothy Dwight's Brief Lives in *Travels in New York and New England*'. The influence of Allen is described in John McWilliams, 'The faces of Ethan Allen'; Nash, 'American clergy and the French Revolution', 400–404; and Darline Shapiro, 'Ethan Allen: philosopher–theologian to a generation of American Revolutionaries'. On the transformations of the Burkean Sublime, see Thomas Weiskel, *The Romantic Sublime*; Wolf, *Romantic Re-Vision*, particularly Part III; and Novak, *Nature and Culture*, Ch. 3.

22 Imlay, *A Topographical Description*, 116. For Morse see John L. Allen, 'Geographical knowledge and American images of the Louisiana Territory', 158, 162, 166–167.

23 Brown, *An Address to the Government of the United States, on the Cession of Louisiana to the French*, 15–16. This text will be discussed further in Chapter 7. Jefferson, letter 12 August 1803 to Breckinridge, *The Writings*, ed. Lipscomb and Bergh, x, 408. The letter can also be found in *The Portable Jefferson*, ed. Peterson, 495–496. Jefferson, 'Description of Louisiana', 344.

24 Jefferson, 'Description', 345–346, 350. By 'desert', Jefferson means unoccupied territory. New York *Evening Post* No. 632, 28 November 1803. See also Dumas Malone, *Jefferson and His Time* IV, 340–342.

25 Thomas Hutchins, *A Historical Narrative and Topographical Description of Lousiana and West-Florida*, 92–93, 29. Vilemont, letter 3 July 1802 to a French Minister, in *Before Lewis and Clark: Documents Illustrating the History of the Missouri, 1785–1804*, ed. Abraham P. Nasatir, II, 699. A sketch of Hutchins's life is to be found in his *A Topographical Description of Virginia, Pennsylvania, Maryland, and North Carolina*, ed. Frederick C. Hicks, 8–48. See also Hindle, *The Pursuit of Science*, 318–319. John L. Allen, *Passage Through the Garden* and Donald Jackson, *Thomas Jefferson and the Stony Mountains* discuss at length Jefferson's imagery of the West.

26 Jefferson, *Notes on the State of Virginia*, ed. William Peden, 63, 102; letter 27 May 1813 to Adams, *The Writings*, ed. Lipscomb and Bergh, XIII, 246–249. James Adair, *The History of the American Indians*. Anon., 'Extract from Campbell's Lives of the Admirals', *The Scots Magazine* 32 (July 1770), 360. John Campbell's four-volume *Lives of the Admirals* was first published from 1742 to 1744. Jean Bossu, *Travels through that part of North America formerly called Louisiana*. Monboddo, *Of the Origin and Progress of Language* I, 409. See also Don Cameron Allen, *The Legend of Noah*, 120–132; Ralph N. Miller, 'American nationalism', 83–84; John Walton, *John Filson*, 37–38; A. P. Nasatir, 'John Evans, explorer and surveyor'; David Williams, 'John Evans' strange journey'; and Gwyn Williams, 'John Evans's mission to the Madogwys', *The Search for Beulah Land* and *Madoc*.

27 Buffon, *Natural History* VI, 1. Williamson, *Observations on the Climate*, 78–82. *Royal*

American Magazine I, No. 9 (September 1774), 350. Smith, 'Tours into Kentucky', ed. Morrow, 383. On the general interest in mammoths see Haverstock, *An American Bestiary*, 52–54. On Bartram see David S. Wilson, *In the Presence of Nature*, 94. On Charles Willson Peale see Charles Coleman Sellers, *Mr Peale's Museum*, Ch. 5; and Clive Bush, *The Dream of Reason*, 80–83, both of which reproduce Peale's painting of the disinterment of bones later exhibited at his Museum. Peale also painted Jefferson's portrait.

28 Jefferson, *Notes*, ed. Peden, 43–58; 'A Memoir of the Discovery of certain Bones of a Quadruped of the Clawed Kind in the Western Parts of Virginia', 250–252. The correspondence with George Rogers Clark is in *Papers* VI, 139, 159–160. Letters about William Clark's find are in *The Writings*, ed. Lipscomb and Bergh, XI, 403–405. Other letters reflecting Jefferson's interest are in *Papers* VI, 204 and 206; and IX, 260. Material on the megalonyx is in *Papers* XIV, xxv–xxxiv and 501–505. See also Davis, *Intellectual Life*, 190–191; David D. Gillette, 'Thomas Jefferson's pursuit of illusory fauna'; John C. Greene, *American Science*, 44, 282–284, 288–291; and George Gaylord Simpson, 'The beginnings of vertebrate palaeontology in North America'.

29 Rush, draft letter 25 September 1812 to David Hosack, *Letters*, ed. Butterfield, II, 1163. Important discussions of the Northwest Passage are to be found in Allen, *Passage*; Bernard DeVoto, *Westward the Course of Empire*, 55–60, 243–252, 277–285; Seelye, *Prophetic Waters*, 29–34 and *passim*; Smith, *Virgin Land*, Prologue and Book 1; and Glyndwr Williams, *The British Search for the Northwest Passage in the Eighteenth Century*.

30 Franklin, 'Benjamin Franklin defends Northwest Passage navigation', introd. Bertha Solis-Cohen, 25, 32. Smith, *Virgin Land*, 15. See also Henry R. Wagner, 'Apocryphal voyages to the North-West coast of America'; and Percy G. Adams, *Travelers and Travel Liars*, 64–74, and 'Benjamin Franklin's defense of the de Fonte Hoax'.

31 Carver, *Three Years' Travels through the Interior Parts of North America*, 121, 541; *The Journals of Jonathan Carver*, ed. John Parker. On Carver see Wilson, *In the Presence of Nature*, Ch. 3. Truteau's account of his journey is available in *Before Lewis and Clark*, ed. Nasatir, I, 97–98 and II, 377. On Truteau, see Annie Louise Abel, 'Trudeau's [*sic*] description of the Upper Missouri'; and Allen, *Passage*, 42–43. Alexander Mackenzie, *Voyages from Montreal . . . to the Frozen and Pacific Oceans*. On Mackenzie, see Allen, *Passage*, 120; Jackson, *Thomas Jefferson and the Stony Mountains*, 94–95; and I. S. MacLaren, 'Alexander Mackenzie and the landscapes of commerce'.

32 Good accounts are in Merrill D. Peterson, *Thomas Jefferson and the New Nation*, 745–789; Malone, *Jefferson*, IV, chs. 14–16; and Irving Brant, *James Madison, Secretary of State*, chs. 10 and 11.

33 White, speech 2 November 1803 reported in *Debates and Proceedings of the Congress of the United States*, 8 Cong., 1 Sess., Cols. 33–34. Further references to this text will be given parenthetically, identifying Congress, Session and Column numbers. The background to the Purchase is provided by Curtis Manning Geer, *The Louisiana Purchase and the Westward Movement*, and Alexander DeConde, *This Affair of Louisiana*. Everett Somerville Brown, *Constitutional History of the Louisiana Purchase* is more closely focussed, while *Louisiana under the Rule of Spain, France, and the United States, 1785–1807*, ed. James Alexander Robertson, makes available a valuable collection of documents. Jerry W. Knudson, 'Newspaper reaction to the Louisiana Purchase'; and Allen, 'Geographical knowledge' deal with the debate in the Press.

34 Plumer, notes on the Bill for the Government of Louisiana, January–February 1804, in Brown, *Constitutional History*, 'Appendix', 212–215, 225, 229. Morris, letter 25 November 1803 to Henry W. Livingston, *The Diary and Letters of Gouverneur Morris*, ed. Anne Cary Morris, II, 441–442. See also Geer, *Louisiana Purchase*, 208–214, and Malone, *Jefferson* IV, chs. 17–19.

35 'Fabricius', *Columbian Centinel* 39, Nos. 2,015–2,019, 13, 16, 20, 23 and 27 July 1803. 'Fabricius's' emphasis.

36 Alsop, *Sketches of the Times, for the Year 1803*, in *The Echo*, 307. For other attacks on Jefferson see *The Echo*, 166–184; and Linda K. Kerber, *Federalists in Dissent*, Ch. 3. Ames, letter 3 October 1803 to Christopher Gore, *Works* I, 323–324. See also *Works* I, 328–332. Charles Warren, *Jacobin and Junto*, 162 reprints the claim of Nathaniel Ames Jr that Fisher wrote the 'Fabricius' articles. They are not, however, included in the 1809 or 1854 editions of Fisher's works; and Winfred Bernhard, *Fisher Ames*, makes no mention of them. The accusation may simply derive from the political animus between the brothers. Morris, *Diary* I, 359–360.

37 'Watty Watersnake', letter reprinted in the *National Intelligencer* III, No. 457, 26 September 1803. Ellicott, *The Journal of Andrew Ellicott*, v, 25. Yrujo, letter 3 August 1803 to Don Pedro Cevallos y Guerra, in *Louisiana*, ed. Robertson, II, 75.

38 W.M.P., *A Poem on the Acquisition of Louisiana* (1804), quoted in Allen, 'Geographical knowledge', 152–153. Allen, 'Geographical knowledge' and DeConde, *This Affair*, 180, 186, comment on the popular approval of the Purchase. See Chapter 6 for further reference to 'the Great American Desert'.

39 Alliot, 'Historical and Political Reflections on Louisiana', *Louisiana*, ed. Robertson, 146–147, 139, 35. For further brief details on Alliot see Frank Monaghan, *French Travellers in the United States*, 98.

40 Ramsay, *Oration*, 12, 4, 19–22. For St George Tucker, writing under the pseudonym of 'Sylvestris', see Brown, *Constitutional History*, 37.

41 Prior to the Purchase the US comprised 892,135 square miles. The Purchase added another 924,279. See Frank Bond, *Historical Sketch of 'Louisiana' and the Louisiana Purchase*, 13.

42 Jefferson, letter 12 August 1803 to Breckinridge, in *Writings*, ed. Lipscomb and Bergh, x, 409–411, and in *The Portable Jefferson*, 495–497. Zadoc Cramer, *The Navigator*, 7th edn (1811), 254–255. See Chapter 6 for a further discussion of Cramer.

5 THOMAS JEFFERSON

1 Letter 3 August 1771 to Skipwith in Jefferson, *The Papers*, ed. Boyd, I, 76–81. Further references to this edition will in this chapter be given parenthetically, indicating the editor, volume and page numbers. Twenty-one volumes of the edition had been published by 1983 (the last being an Index), making available Jefferson's papers up to 4 August 1791. Various editions have been used for later materials. The most extensive biography of Jefferson is Dumas Malone's six-volume *Jefferson and his Time*. I have also consulted three shorter biographies: Gilbert Chinard, *Thomas Jefferson: The Apostle of Americanism*; Merill D. Peterson, *Thomas Jefferson and the New Nation*; and Fawn Brodie, *Thomas Jefferson: An Intimate History*. Garry Wills's splendidly pugnacious *Inventing America: Jefferson's Declaration of Independence* supplies many of the contexts of Jefferson's thought, and provides a useful balance to the more speculative elements of Fawn Brodie's biography.

2 *The Cyclopaedia of Names*, ed. Benjamin E. Smith, 871. Chastellux, *Travels in North-America*, ed. Howard C. Rice, II, 390–391.

3 La Rochefoucault-Liancourt, *Travels through the United States* II, 81, 71.

4 12 October 1786; Boyd, x, 447. For a later account of the prospect which both shares Jefferson's enthusiasm and provides a description that is still accurate today, see William Wirt, 'Eulogy on Jefferson', given in the House of Representatives 19 October 1826 and reprinted in Jefferson, *The Writings*, ed. Lipscomb and Bergh, xiii, xlv–xlvi. This edition will hereafter be cited as Lipscomb–Bergh.

5 'An American', *American Husbandry* (1775), 157–158. See Jefferson's letter to Washington from Paris, 14 November 1786. An aristocratic government renders life a 'curse' for the French, even when they possess 'the finest soil, the finest climate, the most compact state' (Boyd, x, 532–533). The wrong political system is incapable of creating a proper relation to the environment.

6 'Hints to Americans Travelling in Europe', Boyd, xiii, 268. Frederick D. Nichols and Ralph E. Griswold, *Thomas Jefferson, Landscape Architect*, 15, 38–75, 161.

7 Letter 21 March 1801 to Priestley, Lipscomb–Bergh, x, 229, and in *The Portable Jefferson*, 484. 'First Inaugural Address', 4 March 1801, Lipscomb-Bergh, iii, 319–320. Henry Adams, *History of the United States of America during the Administrations of Jefferson and Madison*, 26. The imagistic opposition of stormy seas subsiding under the rule of reason was commonplace in the later eighteenth century. See Stein, 'Pulled out of the bay', 16–22.

8 Letter 12 August 1801 to James Madison, *The Writings*, ed. P. L. Ford, viii, 80. Letter 27 January 1821 to William S. Cardell, Microfilm, Jefferson Papers, Library of Congress, Reel 88, fo. 39,187. Jefferson makes similar remarks in his letter 16 August 1813 to John Waldo, Lipscomb–Bergh, xiii, 338–347. The essay on Anglo-Saxon is to be found in Lipscomb–Bergh, xviii, 361–411. See also Albert C. Baugh, 'Thomas Jefferson, linguistic liberal', and Chapter 2 above for discussions of Jefferson's linguistics.

9 For evidence of Jefferson's interest, see letter 8 May 1786 to David Ross (Boyd, ix, 473), and his 1806 proposals with Albert Gallatin for a National Pike (Malone, *Jefferson* v, 553–560).

10 Eleanor D. Berman, *Thomas Jefferson Among the Arts*, 200. Brodie, *Jefferson*, 22. Wills, *Inventing America*, 118–121 disputes Brodie's findings, yet agrees that 'observation and accounting was a constant discipline with him'. Letter 14 November 1825 to Ellen Randolph Coolidge, Lipscomb–Bergh, xviii, 348; and in *The Family Letters of Thomas Jefferson*, ed. Edwin Morris Betts and James Adam Bear, 461. Shakespeare, *The Tempest* iv, i, 146–163. Mathew Carey used the same phrase less hyperbolically when surveying the carnage wrought by the 1793 Philadelphia plague. Carey, *A Short Account*, 11.

11 *Thomas Jefferson's Farm Book* and *Thomas Jefferson's Garden Book*, both ed. Edwin Morris Betts. Richard Beale Davis, *Intellectual Life in Jefferson's Virginia*, 90–91. Arthur E. Bestor, David C. Mearns and Jonathan Daniels, *Three Presidents and their Books*, 2–23. E. Millicent Sowerby, *Catalogue of the Library of Thomas Jefferson*. This invaluable text, based on Jefferson's own catalogues, has been used extensively. Henceforth references will be given parenthetically, citing the surname, volume and page numbers.

12 Colin Clair, *A Chronology of Printing*, 80. Davis, *Intellectual Life*, 9, 71; *A Colonial Southern Bookshelf*, 9, 22, 124. Berman, *Jefferson Among the Arts*, 250. *Jefferson's Ideas on a University Library*, ed. Elizabeth Cometti, 7–8.

13 *Jefferson's Garden Book*, ed. Betts, 111. The 'Memorandum' will also be found in Lipscomb–Bergh, xvii, 236–244. On Jefferson's tours generally, see Edward Dumbauld, *Thomas Jefferson, American Tourist*, chs. 4–6; and on his English tour see Dumbauld, 'Jefferson and Adams' English garden tour', *Jefferson and the Arts: an Extended View*, ed. William Howard Adams, 137–157.

14 Kames, *Elements of Criticism* ii, 439. *Jefferson's Garden Book*, ed. Betts, 112; also in Lipscomb–Bergh, xvii, 238–239. On Jefferson's garden aesthetics, see Berman, *Jefferson Among the Arts*, Ch. 8; Nichols and Griswold, *Jefferson, Landscape Architect*, Ch. 4; and William L. Beiswanger, 'The temple in the garden: Thomas Jefferson's vision of the Monticello landscape', *British and American Gardens in the Eighteenth Century*, ed. MacCubbin and Martin, 170–185.

15 In the 'Hints' he commanded American travellers to 'fall down and worship the site' but in the next sentence made clear what precisely should be worshipped: 'This road is probably the greatest work of this kind which ever was executed either in antient or modern times' (Boyd, XIII, 272).

16 George G. Shackelford, 'Thomas Jefferson and the fine arts of Northern Italy', 16–17. See also Boyd, XIII, 276; and Shackelford, 'A peep into Elysium', *Jefferson and the Arts*, ed. Adams, 237–269.

17 Jefferson, 'Notes of a Tour through Holland and the Rhine Valley'; Boyd, XIII, 8–33. The quotation is from page 23. He uses the same technique to describe Vaucluse itself in the 'Hints', Boyd, XIII, 267.

18 Davis, *Intellectual Life*, 219; Fiske Kimball, 'Jefferson and the arts'; Shackelford, 'A peep into Elysium', 237–242; Frank Weitenkampf, 'Early American landscape prints'; Joseph Allard, 'West, Copley and eighteenth-century American provincialism'; Stein, 'Copley's *Watson and the Shark* and aesthetics in the 1770s'; and Dennis Berthold, 'Charles Brockden Brown, *Edgar Huntly*, and the origins of the American Picturesque', 63–64. On American colonial indebtedness to British portrait mezzotints, see Waldron P. Belknap, *American Colonial Painting*, 273–277 and *passim*.

19 Kames, *Elements of Criticism* II, 427. See Wills, *Inventing America*, 201–205 for Jefferson's youthful admiration of Kames, and 268–271 on the influence of Burke. [Thomas Whately], *Observations on Modern Gardening*, I.

20 Sowerby, IV, 385–392. See, for instance, Richardson, *An Essay on the Theory of Painting*, 206: 'Salvator Rosa's landscapes are Great, as those of Claude Lorrain are Delicate'.

21 Wirt, 'Eulogy on Jefferson', Lipscomb–Bergh, XIII, xlvii; Berman, *Jefferson Among the Arts*, Ch. 5; Davis, *Intellectual Life*, 227–228; Marie Kimball, *Jefferson, The Scene of Europe, 1784–1789*, 114–120, 323–327, and 'Jefferson's works of art at Monticello'; and Harold E. Dickson, 'Jefferson as art collector', *Jefferson and the Arts*, ed. Adams, 105–132.

22 Davis, *Intellectual Life*, 227-229. Dwight, *Travels* II, 462. Chastellux, *Travels* I, 226. Wirt, 'Eulogy on Jefferson', Lipscomb–Bergh, XIII, xlix. For Washington's interest in Claude see James T. Flexner, 'George Washington as an art collector'.

23 Written in Jefferson's copy of the *Virginia Almanac for 1771; The Writings*, ed. Ford, I, 391–392.

24 Letters 5 December 1801 to the Rev. Isaac Story, and 14 March 1818 to Nathaniel Burwell; Lipscomb–Bergh, X, 298–300; XV, 165–168. Hogarth, *Analysis of Beauty*, 86. Letter 13 June 1814 to Thomas Law, Lipscomb–Bergh, XIV, 140, 143; and in *The Portable Jefferson*, 544. Jefferson's emphasis. He also praises Kames in the letter. On the Scottish Common Sense background to Jefferson's rejection of the imagination see Terence Martin, *The Instructed Vision*.

25 It takes up the major part of Query IV and occurs at pp. 19–20 of the edition by William Peden. This is the edition used here. Future references will be in parentheses, giving the editor's surname and the page numbers. Howard Mumford Jones, *O Strange New World*, 358–359, quoted and discussed the passage, omitting only the long final sentence that I have included. In addition to Mumford Jones and Wills, *Inventing America*, illuminating discussions of Jefferson's *Notes* are to be found in Ferguson, *Law and Letters*, 34–58; Franklin, *Discoverers, Explorers, Settlers*, 26–28; Harold Hellenbrand, 'Roads to happiness: rhetorical and philosophical designs in Jefferson's *Notes on the State of Virginia*'; Clayton W. Lewis, 'Style in Jefferson's *Notes on the State of Virginia*'; Marx, *The Machine in the Garden*, 117–141; Floyd Ogburn, Jr, 'Structure and meaning in Thomas Jefferson's *Notes on the State of Virginia*'; and Pol, 'The idea of moral landscape', Ch. I.

26 Sowerby, I, 299. See also Wills, *Inventing America*, 265–267.

27 It is at Peden, 24–25 as amended by Peden, 263–264. For brief discussions of some Americans who have found the Sublime oppressive, see Shephard, *Man in the Landscape*, 175–176; Mary E. Woolley, 'The development of the love of romantic scenery in America'; E. S. Perry, 'Time and the land', 365; and David Lowenthal, 'The American scene', 63.

28 Wills, *Inventing America*, 259–272. Stein, *Susquehanna*, 56 and 134fn14, briefly indicates the widespread influence of Jefferson's description. Jefferson would again reveal his interest in the use of water-power at another Sublime setting, when he wrote to William Short on 21 May 1787 of Petrarch's chateau at Vaucluse. At the foot of the rock gushed a stream 'sufficient to turn 300 mills'. Boyd, XI, 372.

29 Wills, *Inventing America*, 260.

30 Francis William [*sic*] Gilmer, 'On the Geological Formation of the Natural Bridge in Virginia'. Peterson, *Jefferson*, 953. See also Richard Beale Davis, 'The Abbé Correa in America'.

31 Chastellux, *Travels* II, 392. Ferguson, *Law and Letters*, 40–50. On Jefferson's enthusiasm for Ossian see Wills, *Inventing America*, 183; Frederic I. Carpenter, 'The vogue for Ossian in America', 405–410; and Gilbert Chinard, 'Jefferson and Ossian'. The letters that Chinard reproduces may now be found in Boyd, I, 96–97, 100–102.

32 Locke, *An Essay Concerning the True Original, Extent and End of Civil Government* S.49, in *Social Contract*, introd. Sir Ernest Barker, 29. See Wills, *Inventing America*, 93–110 for further evidence of Jefferson's admiration of Rittenhouse; and 169–175, 181–183 for a balanced assessment of the influence of Locke.

33 Peden, 38–42, 66–70, 50–52, 162–163. In Chapter 1 we saw Jefferson, in his letter of 2 September 1785 to Chastellux, divide the inhabitants of the Northern and Southern States along the lines proposed by Hippocrates and revived by Montesquieu (Boyd, VIII, 468–469). On the influence of Linnaeus's *Systema Naturae* (1735) in America, see Philip Marshall Hicks, 'The development of the natural history essay in American literature', Ch. 2; and Novak, *Nature and Culture*, 104–105.

34 Letter 14 May 1809 to Horatio Spafford, Lipscomb–Bergh, XII, 280–281. As we saw in Chapter 2, Volney excited strong sensations in Jedidiah Morse.

35 Letter 10 December 1814 to John Melish, Lipscomb–Bergh, XIV, 220–221; and in Peden, xxi.

36 William D. Pattison, *Beginnings of the American Rectangular Land Survey System*, 60–63. In the following discussion I have also used Hildegard Binder Johnson, *The Orderly Landscape*, and *Order Upon the Land*; Amelia Clewley Ford, 'Colonial precedents of our national land system as it existed in 1800'; John R. Stilgoe, *Common Landscape of America*, 87–88, 93–106; and John Noble Wilford, *The Mapmakers*.

37 Evans, *Geographical . . . Analysis of a General Map of the Middle British Colonies in America*, 5–6. See also Stein, *Susquehanna*, 19–20; and Walter Klinefelter, 'Lewis Evans and his maps'. On the early American use of the grid see Pattison, *Beginnings*, 60–63, 169; Ford, 'Colonial precedents', 9–11, 19–22; and Johnson, *Order Upon the Land*, 33–35.

38 [William Smith], *Historical Account of Bouquet's Expedition Against the Ohio Indians*, 51, 61. Cunliffe, *The Nation Takes Shape*, 74.

39 Boyd, VI, 582–615. See also Wills, *Inventing America*, 146–147; Pattison, *Beginnings*, 15–16; and *The American Territorial System*, ed. John P. Bloom, 13–55. The text of the Plan, together with Jefferson's map, is also in *The Portable Jefferson*, 254–258.

40 'Report of a Committee to Establish a Land Office', Boyd, VII, 140–148. The 1785 Ordinance is reprinted in *Documents of American History*, ed. Henry Steele Commager, 123–124. See also Pattison, *Beginnings*, 86–104. Hugh Williamson, a member of Jefferson's committee, claimed authorship of the grid. He had attended university at Utrecht and perhaps had been impressed by the Dutch grid. He would

later write the *History of North Carolina*. See Johnson, *Order Upon the Land*, 42, and Chapter 1 above.

41 The Northwest Ordinance is in *Documents*, ed. Commager, 128–132. See also Robert R. Berkhofer, 'The republican origins of the American territorial system', and 'Jefferson, the Ordinance of 1784, and the origins of the American territorial system'; and Jack E. Eblen, 'Origins of the United States colonial system: the Ordinance of 1787'.

42 Octavius Pickering, *Life of Timothy Pickering* I, 506–507. Spaight, letter 5 June to Richard Caswell, *Letters to Members of the Continental Congress*, ed. Edmund C. Burnett, VIII, 135. Washington, letters 22 August 1785 to Grayson and 14 December 1784 to Richard Henry Lee, *Writings*, ed. Fitzpatrick XXVIII, 234, 12. See Seelye, *Prophetic Waters*, 146, 203 on the use of frames in Puritan thought. See also Stilgoe, *Common Landscape*, 103–106; and Johnson, *Order Upon the Land*, 47–48. Johnson *passim*, explores the costs and benefits of the grid.

43 Hutchins, letter 17 September 1785 to the President of Congress, *Papers of the Continental Congress*, Microcopy 247, Roll 74, Item 60, fos. 191–192. Pattison, *Beginnings*, 120–121, 166. The quotation, from the report of the boundary commissioners, appears on page 121. See also Pattison, 'The survey of the Seven Ranges'.

44 Johnson, *The Orderly Landscape*, 15. For examples of the development of the grid in modern art, see *Grids: Format and Image in 20th Century Art*, introd. Rosalind Krauss. On Mondrian see Johnson, *Order Upon the Land*, 232; Robert Hughes, *The Shock of the New*, 200–207; and Peter Conrad, *The Art of the City*, 120–121.

45 Hutchins, letter 5 March 1788 to the Committee of Congress, quoted in Pattison, *Beginnings*, 230.

46 Kames, *Elements of Criticism* II, 439. Shepard, *Man in the Landscape*, 234.

47 Ledyard, *A Journal of Captain Cook's Last Voyage to the Pacific Ocean*, 86, 90; letter 19 March 1787 to Jefferson, in *John Ledyard's Journey Through Russia and Siberia*, ed. Stephen D. Watrous, 122, and in Boyd, XI, 217. Freneau would later collaborate with Ledyard's brother Isaac on a biography about the 'American Traveller', as Ledyard was known. The project was abandoned in 1798. See Helen Augur, *Passage to Glory: John Ledyard's America*, 139, 288.

48 Jefferson, letter 20 September 1787 to Charles Thomson, *Ledyard's Journey*, ed. Watrous, 135, and in Boyd, XII, 160. Anon., 'To the Memory of the celebrated American traveller Ledyard', *American Museum* 12, Part II, Appendix I (June–December 1792), 23–24. Sanford Bederman, *The Ethnographical Contributions of John Ledyard*. A discerning and sympathetic appraisal of Ledyard's writings is to be found in Donald Davie, 'John Ledyard: the American Traveler and his sentimental journeys'.

49 Allen, *Passage*, 65–67. *Jefferson and Southwestern Exploration*, ed. Dan L. Flores, 6. Jefferson's instructions to Michaux are given in *Letters of the Lewis and Clark Expedition*, ed. Donald Jackson, II, 669–672. This invaluable collection of documents will hereafter normally be cited parenthetically, giving the editor's surname, volume and page numbers.

50 Donald Jackson, 'Jefferson, Meriwether Lewis, and the reduction of the United States Army'. In the succeeding paragraphs and the next chapter I have used Allen, *Passage*; Jackson, *Jefferson and the Stony Mountains*; John Bakeless, *Lewis and Clark: Partners in Discovery*; Pol, 'The idea of moral landscape', Ch. 4; and DeVoto, *Westward the Course of Empire*. A recent narrative account of the Expedition is given by David Freeman Hawke, *Those Tremendous Mountains*.

51 Roy M. Chatters, 'The enigmatic Lewis and Clark air gun'.

52 Jefferson, letter 28 February 1803 to Benjamin Rush, Jackson, I, 18. Sowerby, III,

159–351. The importance of Jefferson's library in shaping the image of the West that he and Lewis shared is discussed generally in Jackson, *Jefferson and the Stony Mountains*, chs. 5 and 6; and Allen, *Passage*, chs. 1 to 4.

53 Sowerby, III, 237. Donald Jackson, 'Some books carried by Lewis and Clark'. Paul Russell Cutright, 'Lewis and Clark and Du Pratz'. Jefferson passed to Lewis information from Jean-Baptiste Truteau, James Mackay and John Evans. See Chapter 4 above and Allen, *Passage*, 139–140 and *passim*.

54 Le Page du Pratz, *The History of Louisiana*, 301. Sandys, letter 8 April 1623, quoted in Richard Beale Davis, *George Sandys*, 156. See my Prologue for another of Sandys' reports of America. Jefferson, 'Message to Congress', 18 January 1803, Jackson, I, 12.

55 Allen, *Passage*, 121–122; and Jackson, *Jefferson and the Stony Mountains*, 37, 90. Jefferson's letter of 13 November 1787 to Le Roy (Boyd, X, 528) gives a cross-section drawing of the American continent which further suggests his belief in its symmetry.

56 Pratz, *History of Louisiana*, 136.

57 John B. Jackson, *The Necessity for Ruins*, 46–47. Boorstin, *The Discoverers*, chs. 54–56. Donald Jackson, 'Some books carried by Lewis and Clark'.

58 Jefferson, letter 28 February 1803 to Caspar Wistar, Jackson, I, 18. The letter resembles in some of its phrases that of the same date sent to Benjamin Rush, and already mentioned.

59 Gwyn A. Williams, 'John Evans's mission to the Madogwys', 598. Nasatir, 'John Evans, explorer and surveyor', 441–447. Jackson, II, 669–672.

60 Jackson, I, 62, 64–65. Jefferson's instructions to the Freeman-Custis Red River Expedition of 1806 are in identical terms. The books taken on the Expedition included Linnaeus and Le Page du Pratz. See *Jefferson and Southwestern Exploration*, ed. Flores, 321, 65.

6 THE LEWIS AND CLARK EXPEDITION

1 MS Journals of Lewis and Clark, APS, Codex A, p. 4. The most complete edition of the Journals so far is the *Original Journals of the Lewis and Clark Expedition*, ed. Reuben Gold Thwaites. The phrase quoted is at I, 16–17. Thwaites was, however, not always accurate in transcribing spelling and punctuation. Future references will usually be given parenthetically and, when taken direct from the MS, will give both the MS and the Thwaites volume and page numbers. A number of journals have come to light since Thwaites. They will be identified in due course and are discussed in the Appendix. As I mentioned in the first footnote of the Prologue, I have kept editorial intrusion to a minimum. Interpolations have been made only where misinterpretation would otherwise be likely.

2 'First Inaugural Address', 4 March 1801, Lipscomb–Bergh, III, 320; and in *The Portable Jefferson*, 292.

3 Columbus, *Select Documents*, ed. Jane, I, 6. Lucian, 'The True History', Book 2, *Satirical Sketches*, trans. and introd. Paul Turner, 278. I am grateful to Dr Nicola Mackie of the University of Aberdeen for providing this reference. Bradstreet, 'Contemplations', Stanza 26. Keats, 'Ode on a Nightingale'. Le Page du Pratz, *History of Louisiana*, 281. Jefferson, letters 21 June 1785 to Abigail Adams and 21 May 1787 to Martha Jefferson and William Short; Boyd, VIII, 241 and XI, 369–370, 372. Thwaites, I, 38–39. See also Jones, *O Strange New World*, 14–15; Gerbi, *Dispute of the New World*, 161–163, 375–377, 429–430; and A. Lincoln, 'Jefferson the scientist'. Allen, *Passage*, Ch. 4 deals with the images of the West shared by Jefferson, Lewis and Clark.

4 Jared Sparks, 'Riley's narrative', 390. Berchtold, *Essay to Direct and Extend the Inquiries*

of Patriotic Travellers I, 19–20, 43. Similarly, Samuel Johnson attacks the traveller who 'defers the description to a time of more leisure'. *A Journey to the Western Islands*, ed. R. W. Chapman, 133. For discussions of travel literature, see Charles L. Batten, *Pleasurable Instruction*; Stafford, *Voyage into Substance*; Lawrence Buell, *Literary Transcendentalism*, Ch. 7; Parks, 'The turn to the Romantic in the travel literature of the eighteenth century'; J. C. Greene, 'Science and the public in the age of Jefferson'; and Martin J. S. Rudwick, 'The emergence of a visual language for geological science'.

5 [William Smith], *Historical Account of Bouquet's Expedition*. Thomas Hutchins, 'A Journal of a March from Fort Pitt to Venango, and from thence to Presqu'Isle'; *A Topographical Description of Virginia, Pennsylvania, Maryland, and North Carolina*; and *A Historical Narrative and Topographical Description of Louisiana and West-Florida*. Ellicott, *The Journal of Andrew Ellicott*. Carver, *Three Years' Travels*. Mackenzie, *Voyages from Montreal*. Sowerby, I, 219; IV, 182, 223, 248, 249. On the formats of travel literature see Batten, *Pleasurable Instruction*, 36. On Carver, see *The Journals*, ed. Parker, 27–30; and Wilson, *In the Presence of Nature*, Ch. 3. On Mackenzie, see I. S. MacLaren, 'Alexander Mackenzie and the landscapes of commerce'; W. Kaye Lamb, 'Introduction' to *The Journals and Letters of Alexander Mackenzie*; and Franz Montgomery, 'Alexander Mackenzie's literary assistant'.

6 MS, Missouri Historical Society.

7 *The Journals of Captain Meriwether Lewis and Sergeant John Ordway*, ed. Milo M. Quaife, 33. Further references will usually be given parenthetically, giving the editor's surname and the page number.

8 Thwaites, VII, 150–151. H. M. Brackenridge, *Views of Louisiana*, 183.

9 Thwaites, I, 119. Steven Kagle, 'Unaccustomed earth', *America: Travel and Exploration*, ed. Kagle, 4–5.

10 Rush, letter 22 August 1800 to Jefferson, *Letters* II, 820. See also Chapter 2 above. E. H. Criswell, *Lewis and Clark: Linguistic Pioneers*, cxix–ccvii. Todorov, *The Conquest*, 27–28, discusses the relation of nomination and possession during Columbus's expeditions. Seelye, *Prophetic Waters*, 135, briefly refers to Puritan name-giving, while Stephen Fender, *Plotting the Golden West*, 67–68, 79–80, notes that the forty-niners went through a process of naming as a stay against chaos.

11 Mackenzie, *Voyages*, 267. I am grateful to Professor I. S. MacLaren for drawing my attention to this allusion.

12 *Audubon and his Travels*, ed. Maria R. Audubon, I, 460. Maximilian, Prince of Wied, *Travels*, in *Early Western Travels*, ed. R. G. Thwaites, XXII, 244. For a good account of the sheer power of the Missouri, see Hiram Chittenden, *History of Early Steamboat Navigation of the Missouri River* I, 74–81.

13 Sowerby, IV, 367–376. For further information on Jefferson's interest in architecture, see William B. O'Neal, *Jefferson's Fine Arts Library* and Fiske Kimball, *Thomas Jefferson, Architect*. When Henry Marie Brackenridge saw the Missouri Breaks some six years later, he described them in similar terms. See Brackenridge, *Views of Louisiana*, 31. It would become commonplace later in the century to compare this terrain with dead cities. See Paul Shepard, 'Dead cities in the American West' and Yi-Fu Tuan, 'Mountains, ruins and the sentiment of melancholy'.

14 Gass, *A Journal of the Voyages and Travels of a Corps of Discovery*, 125. Unfortunately, the original journal is lost, and the only available text has been 'polished' by the editor. Further references to the text will usually be given parenthetically, giving the Sergeant's name and the page number.

15 Shakespeare, *The Winter's Tale* III, iii, 58. Defoe, *Robinson Crusoe*, 288–296. 'Lord' George Sanger, *Seventy Years a Showman*, 115–117. Richard Ormond, *Sir Edwin Landseer*, 205–209. See also *The Wild Man Within*, ed. Dudley and Novak, 186–194.

16 For a brief guide to Amerindian bear mythology, see the *Standard Dictionary of Folklore, Mythology and Legend*, ed. Maria Leach, 124, 126–128. Recent bear rituals in some subpolar islands are described in Joseph M. Kitagana, 'Ainu bear festival'.

17 Kalm, *Travels into North America* I, 116–117. See Chapter 1 above for other tales by Kalm. John Bartram, the teller in this instance, was more circumspect when talking to Iwan Al-z, the Russian visitor in Letter XI of Crèvecœur's *Letters*. See Chapter 3. John Bartram's son William would later assert that bears ate both fruit and flesh, but that he 'could never learn a well attested instance of their attacking mankind'. *Travels of William Bartram*, 232. Jefferson owned a copy (Sowerby, IV, 208). Le Page du Pratz, *History of Louisiana*, 248–262. This text was published in English in London in 1763 and would therefore have been available to Forster.

18 Sowerby, III, 237; IV, 206. Mackenzie, *Voyages*, 160, 164. Jackson, I, 295–296; II, 440. Jackson, *Jefferson and the Stony Mountains*, 187–189, 260. Sellers, *Mr Peale's Museum*, 206–209. Grizzly-lore may be found in *Man Meets Grizzly: Encounters in the Wild from Lewis and Clark to Modern Times*, ed. F. M. Young and Coralie Beyers; John C. Ewers, 'The awesome bear in Plains Indian art'; Andy Russell, *Grizzly Country*; and William H. Wright, *The Grizzly Bear*.

19 Gass, 289. Codex E, p. 78; Thwaites, II, 156–157. Brackenridge, *Views of Louisiana*, 55–56. Brackenridge's emphasis. From William Byrd's *History of the Dividing Line* (1728; first published 1841) to John Irving's *The Hotel New Hampshire* (1981) the bear has exerted a potent influence on American writing. For a discussion of some elements of that influence, see Clive Bush, *The Dream of Reason*, 293–296, and Seelye, *Prophetic Waters*, 369–370. Many bears are now safely domesticated. Claes Oldenburg has even proposed a giant teddy-bear monument, suitably, for Central Park. In contrast, the potent, at times sexual, threat of the grizzly still haunts us, as in the 1976 film of that name.

20 Thomson, 'Spring' ll.308–318 in *Complete Poetical Works*, 15. Nicolson, *Mountain Gloom and Mountain Glory*, 226–227. Sowerby, IV, 473, 539. Michael Kraus, 'Literary relations', 224. See Smith, *European Vision and the South Pacific*, 175, for the influence of Thomson on Australian landscape description.

21 Thwaites, II, 266, 287–292. For another example of Lewis's depression, see his thirty-first birthday reflections (Codex F, p. 129; Thwaites, II, 368). No such reflections exist for his thirtieth birthday.

22 See Mary E. Woolley, 'The development of the love of Romantic scenery in America', 61–62; and Herbert Ross Brown, *The Sentimental Novel in America*, 133–135.

23 Ruskin, *Seven Lamps of Architecture*, Ch. 6, S.1, in *Ruskin Today*, ed. Kenneth Clark, 96. Wordsworth, *The Prelude* VI, 446–468 in 1805 edition, 517–540 in 1850 edition. For a related discussion of Wordsworth's recollection of the Simplon Pass, see Weiskel, *The Romantic Sublime*, 195–204; while Aldous Huxley, 'Wordsworth in the Tropics', explores the limitations of the poet's topophilia. Occasionally, British travellers in America would become aware of the fragility of the conventions of terrestrial description. See Mulvey, *Anglo-American Landscapes*, chs. 10–12.

24 *Karl Bodmer's America*, ed. David C. Hunt and Marsha V. Gallagher. Remington, *Pony Tracks*, 109–110, and 169. On Bierstadt and the 'Rocky Mountain School' see Flexner, *That Wilder Image*, 293–302; and Novak, *Nature and Culture*, Ch. 7. Patricia Trenton and Peter Hassrick, *The Rocky Mountains*, provides a more detailed and well-illustrated survey of the painters' work. See also Thomas Hornsby Ferril, 'Writing in the Rockies'; and Fender, *Plotting the Golden West*, who at 43–49 recounts John C. Frémont's difficulties describing the Rockies in the early 1840s.

25 Thwaites, III, 301. See the Appendix for a discussion of the gaps in Lewis's journal.

26 See Criswell, *Lewis and Clark: Linguistic Pioneers*, xix–xxiv.

27 William Nichols, 'Lewis and Clark probe the unknown', 94–101. A fuller account of the relations between the Expedition and the Indians is given by James P. Ronda, *Lewis and Clark Among the Indians.*

28 The account by James Neelly, the Indian agent, is given in a letter of 18 October 1809 to Jefferson, in Jackson, II, 467–468. Alexander Wilson's account is in *The Port Folio* 7 (1811), 34–47. The debate over the death of Lewis is summarised in Jackson, II, 574–575, 747–749; Jackson, *Jefferson and the Stony Mountains*, 272, 291fn11; and in Howard I. Kushner, 'The suicide of Meriwether Lewis: a psychoanalytic inquiry', which also provides a fresh interpretation.

29 'Intelligence', *Monthly Anthology and Boston Review* 8 (April 1810), 283.

30 Jared Sparks, *The Life of John Ledyard*, 323; Augur, *Passage to Glory*, 282–283; *John Ledyard's Journey*, ed. Watrous, 202; David Williams, 'John Evans' strange journey', 527–528.

31 Wilson, *The Port Folio*, 7 (1811), 38. Wilson's emphases. The phrase 'so hard to die', first noticed by Bakeless, *Lewis and Clark*, 419, would provide a less striking coincidence, and may not have been emphasised by Wilson, had it been in regular use at the time. A search through Webster's *Dictionary*, Craigie's *Dictionary of American English*, Mathews's *Dictionary of Americanisms* and Partridge's *Dictionary of Slang* reveals that the term 'hard' was in use in the sense of 'tough' or 'difficult'. No reference was found to the usage 'hard to die'.

32 Barlow to Jefferson 13 January 1807, Jackson, I, 361–362. Barlow, 'On the Discoveries of Captain Lewis', *The National Intelligencer* 7, No. 976 (16 January 1807). Barlow's emphases.

33 Brown, *Constitutional History of the Louisiana Purchase*, 45. [John Quincy Adams], 'On the Discoveries of Captain Lewis', *The Monthly Anthology and Boston Review* 4 (March 1807), 143–144. The author is identified in M. A. DeWolfe Howe, 'The capture of some fugitive verses'. See also Alsop, *The Echo*, 178, 320 for another attack on the poor prairie-dog.

34 *The Journals of Zebulon Montgomery Pike*, ed. Donald Jackson, II, 27–28. Pike's account was first published in 1810.

35 Donald Jackson, 'Some advice for the next editor of Lewis and Clark', 52; 'The race to publish Lewis and Clark', 163–164, 174. Letter from Arthur Campbell to Jedidiah Morse introducing Ordway 20 November 1806. Box 1, Morse Papers, NYPL.

36 Lewis, letter 14 March 1807 in *The National Intelligencer*; McKeehan, letter 7 April 1807 in the Pittsburgh *Gazette*. Both are reprinted in Jackson, II, 385–386, 399–408. Jackson, II, 391 provides a few facts about McKeehan. Brigham, *History and Bibliography of American Newspapers* II, 1449, lists him as the printer of the *Natchez Gazette* (1811–1813) and the New Orleans *Louisiana Gazette* (1813–1814).

37 Gass, 87, 92, 106–109, 168, 137. Pike, *The Journals*, 27, compares the plains to 'the sandy deserts of Africa', as does Brackenridge, *Views of Louisiana*, 28–29, which acknowledges Pike. Together, the three texts provided evidence before the publication of the Biddle edition that parts of Louisiana were not a Garden. On the myth of the 'Great American Desert', see G. Malcolm Lewis, 'Changing emphases in the description of the Great American Plains area'; 'Early American explorations and the Cis-Rocky American Desert'; and 'Three centuries of desert concepts in the Cis-Rocky Mountain West'. Also see Ralph C. Morris, 'The notion of the Great American Desert east of the Rockies'; and two articles by Martyn J. Bowden: 'The Great American Desert and the American Frontier', and 'The perception of the western interior of the United States'.

38 'Meriwether Lewis', *The Travels of Lewis and Clarke*, 14. There may have been as

many as eight or nine spurious editions, and reprints were still appearing some thirty years later. Details are given in *History of the Expedition under the Command of Lewis and Clark*, ed. Elliott Coues, I, cxi–cxvii; and Paul R. Cutright, *A History of the Lewis and Clark Journals*, Ch. 3.

39 'Meriwether Lewis', *The Travels of Lewis and Clarke*, 14–21, vii. 'Intelligence', *The Monthly Anthology and Boston Review* 8 (February 1810), 143. William Fisher, *An Interesting Account of the Travels of Captains Lewis and Clarke*, 13. Fisher's emphases.

40 Jefferson, letter to Alexander von Humboldt 6 December 1813, Jackson, II, 596. Paul Allen [and Nicholas Biddle] (eds.), *History of the Expedition under the Command of Captains Lewis and Clark* I, 37. In future this text will usually be cited parenthetically, giving Biddle's name, the volume and page numbers. For further discussions of the Biddle edition see Cutright, *History of the Lewis and Clark Journals*, Ch. 5; and Robert E. Lee, *From West to East*, 32.

41 Anon., 'Original Review of Lewis and Clarke's Travels', *Analectic Magazine* 5 (February 1815), 127–149 and (March 1815), 210–234. Anon., 'Life of Captain Lewis and Review of *History of the Expedition...*', *Western Gleaner* I (April 1814), 293, 296–297 and (May 1814), 350–365, 370–375.

42 Peden, 20, 262–263. Lewis and Clark did not carry a barometer with them and therefore could not measure elevation with any accuracy. (Jackson, *Jefferson and the Stony Mountains*, 289.) But even without instruments the greater height of the Rockies must have been apparent. Morse, *The American Gazetteer* (1810), n.p., entries under 'Louisiana' and 'Rocky Mountains'. In the sixth (1812) edition of *The American Universal Geography* (I, 135) Morse admits that he does not know if the height of the Rockies has been ascertained. See Chamberlain, 'Early American geographies', 24; and Allen, 'Geographical knowledge', 167 on the prevailing ignorance about the Rockies.

43 Cramer, *The Navigator*, 7th edn (1811), 245–246, 254–268; 10th edn (1818), 283–284, 290–296; 12th edn (1824), 256–257, 263–267; 'Advertisement' to those editions. Brackenridge, *Views of Louisiana*, 4–5 remarks that great portions of Louisiana still 'remain an entire blank on the map'. On *The Navigator*, see Richard A. Bartlett, *The New Country*, 145–146.

44 E. Soteris Muszynska-Wallace, 'The sources of *The Prairie*'. John R. Milton, *The Novel of the American West*, 70–72.

7 CHARLES BROCKDEN BROWN

1 Charles Brockden Brown, untitled poem written September 1794 and included in a letter dated 4 October 1794 to Debby Ferris. MS, Special Collections Dept., Hawthorne–Longfellow Library, Bowdoin College. (Quotations from this Collection are made by kind permission of the Librarian, Bowdoin College.) The poem was first published in a slightly altered form and with the title 'Devotion: An Epistle' in Brown's *The American Register* 3 (1808), 567–578, and reprinted in David Lee Clark, *Charles Brockden Brown: Pioneer Voice of America*, 319–329.

2 Earlom, *Liber Veritatis; or A Collection of Prints, after the Original Designs of Claude le Lorrain*. 'Landscape with Apollo and the Muses' is II, 126, first published 1 January 1776. I am grateful to Professor David Irwin of the University of Aberdeen for drawing my attention to this text. Other paintings by Claude which contain similar elements are to be found in Rothlisberger, *Claude Lorrain* II, figs. 26, 123, 207, 296, 314 and 315.

The standard biographies of Brown are Harry R. Warfel, *Charles Brockden Brown:*

American Gothic Novelist, and Donald Ringe, *Charles Brockden Brown*. Two early biographies are useful for preserving much of Brown's writing to which access would otherwise be difficult or impossible. They are by William Dunlap, the painter and playwright who was a friend of Brown; and Paul Allen, the final editor of the 'Biddle Edition' of Lewis and Clark. The body of criticism of Brown's works is substantial and growing, fortunately in sophistication as well as size. I have drawn generally on Norman S. Grabo, *The Coincidental Art of Charles Brockden Brown*; Bell, *The Development of American Romance*, Ch. 3; Ringe, *American Gothic*, Ch. 3; Elliott, *Revolutionary Writers*, Ch. 6; Tompkins, *Sensational Designs*, chs. 2 and 3; and particularly Alan Axelrod, *Charles Brockden Brown: An American Tale*. The footnotes below will indicate the more immediately relevant of the many articles written about Brown's work.

A standard 'Bicentennial Edition' of Brown's work is being issued. Four volumes have appeared so far: *Wieland* (with its companion-piece, the *Memoirs of Carwin*), *Ormond*, *Arthur Mervyn*, and *Edgar Huntly*. They are the texts used here, and they will be cited parenthetically, quoting initial letters (*W*, *O*, *AM*, and *EH*) and page numbers. Various editions have had to be used for the other texts; reference will be made to them in due course.

3 Brown, undated letter (but from internal evidence clearly 1792) to Joseph Bringhurst. MS, Bowdoin College. A helpful 'Annotated Census' of most of Brown's letters has been published by Charles E. Bennett. The letter quoted is Census No. 20. Bennett's Census number will henceforth be given after the date of the letter. Warfel, *Brown*, 29 shows Brown referring to the law as 'rubbish' on two occasions. He would also use the term in *Ormond*. For an interesting discussion of Brown's ambivalent attitudes to his twin professions see Ferguson, *Law and Letters*, Ch. 5.

4 Fielding, *Joseph Andrews*, 139. Letters 30 May and ? May 1792. MSS Bowdoin College; Bennett Census 23 and 18.

5 Undated letters (but clearly 1792). MSS Bowdoin College; Bennett Census 19 and 20. Letter 19 was printed in David Lee Clark, 'Unpublished letters of Charles Brockden Brown and W. W. Wilkins', 88–91. The 'death' of Brown's bride occurs in a letter dated 9 August 1792; Bennett Census 30.

6 Letters May 1792, undated (1792) and June 1793 (?). MSS Bowdoin College; Bennett Census 18, 20 and 45.

7 Letter 5 May 1792. MS Bowdoin College; Bennett Census 12. Other letters which talk of suicide are Bennett Census 5, 7, 13 and 14. Axelrod, *Brown*, xviii–xx and *passim*, develops with much insight, and at greater length than I can, the relation of terrain and psychology in Brown's thought.

8 Letter 16 August 1793. 'The Story of Cooke', in letter 29 July 1793. MSS Bowdoin College; Bennett Census 49, 48. 'Cooke' is dated 1788 by Bennett, 'The Charles Brockden Brown Canon', 245.

9 'The Story of Julius' is in a letter dated 20 May 1792. MS Bowdoin College; Bennett Census 21. It has been printed in Herbert Brown, 'Charles Brockden Brown's "The Story of Julius": Rousseau and Richardson "improved"', 38–50. The quotation is from pages 43–44.

10 For a further examination of Brown's indebtedness to Burke and Gilpin, see Kenneth Bernard, 'Charles Brockden Brown and the Sublime', and Dennis Berthold, 'Charles Brockden Brown, *Edgar Huntly*, and the origins of the American Picturesque'.

11 Brown, 'Sky-Walk', in *The Rhapsodist, And Other Uncollected Writings*, ed. Harry R. Warfel, 135–141. The quotation is from page 135. Bennett, 'The Charles Brockden Brown Canon', 190–194; and Sidney J. Krause, 'Historical essay', *EH*, 303–317, discuss the date of 'Sky-Walk' and its relation to *Edgar Huntly*. See my Chapter 2 for

Jedidiah Morse, and the close of Chapter 6 for the review of *Poems on Several Occasions*.

12 Brown, 'Signior Adini', in Dunlap, *Life of Charles Brockden Brown* II, 140–169. It will also be found in Allen, *The Life of Charles Brockden Brown*, ed. Charles E. Bennett, 359–387. James Fenimore Cooper would later take up Adini's hint. In *The Crater* (1847) Cooper's protagonist leaves America to create a utopia on a volcanic Pacific island. Unfortunately, the utopia is fragile. It exists only until it is invaded by a minister, a lawyer and a journalist, whereupon Cooper has his island collapse into the ocean.

13 Discussions of Brown's thinking on psychology tend to operate on polarised models of mind as mechanism or mind as organism. The models are too simple for the complexity of Brown's thought and the discussions are, to a greater or lesser extent, reductive. See Arthur G. Kimball, *Rational Fictions*, and three doctoral dissertations: Harvey M. Craft, 'The opposition of mechanistic and organic thought in the major novels'; Jane T. Flanders, 'Charles Brockden Brown and William Godwin: parallels and divergencies'; and Beverly Rose Voloshin, 'The Lockean tradition in the Gothic fiction of Brown, Poe and Melville'. Another doctoral dissertation, Paul Scott Steinberg, 'On the brink of the precipice: madness in the writings of Charles Brockden Brown', is more sophisticated if rather too schematic.

14 Brown, 'Memoirs of Stephen Calvert', first published serially in the *Monthly Magazine*, 1799–1800 and reprinted in *Carwin the Biloquist, and Other American Tales and Pieces* II, 158. Maurice J. Bennett, in 'A portrait of the artist in eighteenth-century America: Charles Brockden Brown's *Memoirs of Stephen Calvert*', argues the centrality of this text, not only to Brown's work but to the question of the relation of art and politics in Revolutionary America. See also Hans Borchers's Introduction to the modern edition of the *Memoirs*.

15 Peckham, 'Toward a Theory of Romanticism', 15, 20–21. M. H. Abrams, *The Mirror and the Lamp: Romantic Theory and the Critical Tradition*, 54–58. R. P. Adams, 'Romanticism and the American Renaissance', 430.

16 Donald Ringe points out that the conflict of appearance and reality is central to *Wieland*. See Ringe, 'Charles Brockden Brown', in *Major Writers of Early American Literature*, ed. Everett Emerson, 275. This is certainly true, as it is for all of Brown's 'major' fiction; but finally there is no way of telling one from the other. Brown's fictions end not with a clear resolution but rather with a suspension of the problems they address. Recently, critics have begun to deal with the narrative complexity of *Wieland* and the unreliability, even schizophrenia, of its narrator. See Grabo, *Coincidental Art*, Ch. 1; Fliegelman, *Prodigals and Pilgrims*, 237–241; Ketterer, *New Worlds for Old*, Ch. 7; James D. Wallace, *Early Cooper and his Audience*, Ch. 2; James R. Russo, '"The chimeras of the brain": Clara's narrative in *Wieland*'; Cynthia S. Jordan, 'On rereading *Wieland*: "the folly of precipitate conclusions"'; and Edwin Sill Fussell, '*Wieland*: a literary and historical reading'.

17 See, for instance, the second stanza of George Herbert's 'Sinnes Round':

> My words take fire from my inflamed thoughts,
> Which spit it forth like the Sicilian hill.
>
> Herbert, *The English Poems*, ed C. A. Patrides, 134.

18 Cogswell's poem includes the following stanza:

> No folly lures his feet from virtue's way,
> No gay delusion leads his feet astray,
> But every eye with rapture sees the youth
> Opposing vice, and zealous for the truth.

See Smith, *Diary of Elihu Hubbard Smith*, ed. James E. Cronin, 5. On the friendship between Brown and Smith see Cronin, 'Elihu Hubbard Smith and the New York

Friendly Club, 1795–1798'; and Charles E. Bennett, 'A poetical correspondence among Elihu Hubbard Smith, Joseph Bringhurst, Jr, and Charles Brockden Brown in *The Gazette of the United States'*. Joann Peck Krieg's Ph.D. dissertation, 'Charles Brockden Brown and the empire of romance', discusses Brown's fictional career as a dialogue with Smith.

19 Desmond King-Hele, *Doctor of Revolution: The Life and Genius of Erasmus Darwin*, 146, 174, 261, 339–340. E. H. Smith, 'Epistle to the author of the Botanic Garden', n.p. See also Smith, *Diary*, 74, 236, 461. Warfel, *Brown*, 76, 107.

20 Undated letter (1792). MS Bowdoin College; Bennett Census 20. 'Devotion'; MS Bowdoin College; rpt. Clark, *Brown*, 323. Axelrod, *Brown*, 31–33, 43, 163 comments on the significance of 'Devotion' and in his Ch. 3 develops the point in relation to *Wieland*.

21 See Herbert Ross Brown, *The Sentimental Novel in America*, 135–137 on the popularity of the image of the summer-house retreat. The original translator of Chastellux, *Travels in North-America* I, 325–326, noted that the 'beautiful banks of the Schuylkill' were a popular site for 'elegant country houses'. Indeed, Jefferson would build one there in 1806.

22 La Rochefoucault-Liancourt, *Travels* II, 71. Richard Bridgman, in 'Jefferson's farmer before Jefferson', 575, has noticed that this description of Wieland Junior contains an echo of John Dickinson, *Letters from a Farmer in Pennsylvania* (1768). He concludes that Brown's view of farming is superficial. The remarks of la Rochefoucault-Liancourt suggest that if the view was superficial it was one that was shared by the principal apologist for agrarianism.

23 Brown writes, for instance: 'I am conscious . . . that this form of composition may be regarded by you with indifference or contempt . . . I need not say that my own opinions are different.' The letter, with Jefferson's response, is printed in William Peden, 'Thomas Jefferson and Charles Brockden Brown', 63–68. Charles C. Cole, 'Brockden Brown and the Jefferson Administration' gives plentiful evidence of Brown's later dislike of Jefferson, while Cronin, 'Smith and the New York Friendly Club', 474, notes that Brown's earlier intellectual circle, including Smith, was Federalist 'almost without exception'. Tompkins, *Sensational Designs*, 91–92, from analyses of *Wieland* and *Arthur Mervyn* that are different from mine, also thinks that Brown was a Federalist. On Brown's enthusiasm for architectural drawing – one interest he *did* share with Jefferson, no matter how he treated it fictionally – see Axelrod, *Brown*, 66, 100–104.

24 For a discussion of *Ormond* as a feminist text, see Donald Ringe, *Charles Brockden Brown*, 50. James R. Russo, 'The tangled web of deception and imposture in Charles Brockden Brown's *Ormond*', deals with the text as an unreliable narrative on the theme of deceit anticipating Melville's *The Confidence Man*.

25 *O*, 5, 29, 20. See Eleanor Tilton's fascinating detective work on the possible sources of Brown's allusion to Fuseli in her 'In the labyrinth of Charles Brockden Brown's prose: the Bicentennial Edition', 201–204. The choice of Fuseli as Dudley's teacher at first sight seems odd, given Dudley's enthusiasm for the Picturesque. It is probably accounted for by Brown's interest in psychology, and almost certainly by the fact that Fuseli engraved the frontispiece for Part I of Darwin's *The Botanic Garden*.

26 Brown's friend and future biographer, William Dunlap, met Jedidiah Morse on several occasions in 1797 and 1798. Dunlap noted on 10 April 1798 that he had learnt from Morse 'the State of our politics'. On 14 September Dunlap read the draft of Brown's *Memoirs of Carwin* and noted that 'he has taken up the schemes of the Illuminati'. Dunlap, *Diary* I, 240, 338–339. Robert S. Levine, 'Villainy and the fear of conspiracy in Charles Brockden Brown's *Ormond*'; Ringe, *American Gothic*, 38–40; and Axelrod, *Brown*, 120–125, provide accounts of Brown's interest in the Illuminati;

while Wood, 'Conspiracy and the paranoid style', 436–437, gives an astute analysis of Brown's insight into the reasons for the scare. Krieg, 'Brown', 94, remarks Brown's tendency to play with names, and notes that Orme is an anagram of More.

27 James, *The Ambassadors*, 348–349. Burke, *A Philosophical Enquiry*, ed. J. T. Boulton, 58.

28 Alsop, *Political Greenhouse, for the Year 1798*, in *The Echo*, 243–244. Brown's letter 4 October 1794 is signed 'Charles B. Brown, Author of Arthur Myrven, etc'. MS, Bowdoin College. Norman S. Grabo's 'Historical introduction' in *AM*, 449, discusses Brown's presence in Philadelphia, while Ferguson, *Law and Letters*, 142–147, and Axelrod, *Brown*, 44–45, 116–118, 156–158, detail his complex response to the plague. Krieg, 'Brown', chs. 3 and 4, also gives an interesting discussion of the impact on Brown of the plague and Smith's death. There are some similarities between Dr Stevens, the principal narrator of *Arthur Mervyn*, and Benjamin Rush. See Chapter 2 above and William L. Hedges, 'Benjamin Rush, Charles Brockden Brown, and the plague year' for a summary of the events of 1793 and their effect on both men.

29 Elliott, *Revolutionary Writers*, 247, notes the influence of *Tom Jones* on *Arthur Mervyn*. Bernard Harrison, *Henry Fielding's Tom Jones: The Novelist as Moral Philosopher*, particularly chs. 2, 5 and 6, illuminates the thought of Brown as well as that of his mentor.

30 Carey, *A Short Account*, 5th edn, 39–41, first published in November 1793.

31 The fifth edition of Carey, *A Short Account*, 25, returns the compliment of Brown's use of his text by recommending *Arthur Mervyn* for its 'vivid and terrifying picture ... of the horrors of that period'. Among those deeply affected by it were the Shelleys. See E. Sickels, 'Shelley and Charles Brockden Brown', and Joel Porte, 'In the hands of an angry God: religious terror in Gothic Fiction', 50–52.

32 Grabo, 'Historical essay', *AM*, 462 and *The Coincidental Art*, 105–106. Elliott, *Revolutionary Writers*, 237–240. Patrick Brancaccio, 'Studied ambiguities: *Arthur Mervyn* and the problem of the unreliable narrator' gives a detailed analysis of the subject.

33 Peterson, *Jefferson*, 625–651. Elliott, *Revolutionary Writers*, 244, 298fn21. Cole, 'Brockden Brown and the Jefferson Administration'.

34 For the sources of *Edgar Huntly* see: Sidney J. Krause, 'Historical essay', *EH*; Steinberg, 'On the brink', particularly chs. 1 and 6; Krieg, 'Brown', 182–202; Roy Harvey Pearce, 'The significances of the Captivity Narrative', 14–15; Oral S. Coad, 'The Gothic element in American Literature before 1835', 81; Arthur G. Kimball, 'Savages and Savagism: Brockden Brown's dramatic irony', particularly 220–221; Slotkin, *Regeneration*, 382–390; Paul Witherington, 'Image and idea in *Wieland* and *Edgar Huntly*'; Leslie Fiedler, *Love and Death in the American Novel*, 147–151; and Philip Russell Hughes, 'Archetypal patterns in *Edgar Huntly*'. On doubling, see Fiedler, 149; Krause, 'Historical essay', 303, 317–330; and Grabo, *The Coincidental Art*, 160–185. A most sensitive discussion of the way in which Brown fractures the conventions of the Gothic, and thereby anticipates Ortega y Gasset's awareness of the extrinsicality of the natural world, and even the urban claustrophobia of Baudelaire and Rilke, is provided by George Toles in 'Charting the hidden landscape: *Edgar Huntly*'. See also Berthold, 'Brown'; and Lueck, 'The Sublime and Picturesque', whose Ch. 3 discusses *Edgar Huntly* as a sustained attack on the aesthetics of William Gilpin.

35 See, for instance, Witherington, 'Image and idea', 22–23; Grabo, *The Coincidental Art*, 56; and Krieg, 'Brown', 192–195.

36 Robert A. Aubin, 'Grottoes, geology and the Gothic revival'; Yi-Fu Tuan, 'Mountains, ruins and the sentiment of melancholy'.

37 Kimball, 'Savages and Savagism', 221.

38 Amy Tucker, in her Ph.D. dissertation, 'America's Gothic landscape', 65, has also noticed the hiatus, and comes to the same conclusion.

39 James Fenimore Cooper, 'Preface', *The Spy* (1821), 1.

40 Axelrod, *Brown*, shares this opinion of Ch. 16. He treats Edgar in the pit as the central motif of Brown's fiction and shows how it relates to other stages in the writer's career.

41 The passage is also notable for a strange coincidence. Meriwether Lewis remarked that he would prefer to fight Indians than bears. The bear that prompted the preference was shot twice. Lewis himself was shot twice. Both Lewis and the bear died slowly. Here, some six years before Lewis met the bear and ten before he met his death, Brown erodes the distinction between the Indian and a fierce animal, and has Edgar shoot the 'savage' twice. The bullets only wound him, and Edgar has to despatch him with a bayonet. Both incidents indicate the ease with which the 'civilised' can slide into bestiality in such an environment, and illustrate the fragility of Revolutionary culture. Further discussions of regression in *Edgar Huntly* can be found in Voloshin, 'The Lockean tradition', 131–132; Steinberg, 'On the brink', 49–79; Krieg, 'Brown', 195–197; and Sidney J. Krause, '*Edgar Huntly* and the American nightmare'. Grabo, *The Coincidental Art*, 62–66 is particularly perceptive in this respect. His discussions of the sequential imagery of houses (another anticipation of Henry James), and of the conjunction of man and beast provide further evidence of the belief that American civilisation can easily be inverted into savagism.

42 Grabo, *The Coincidental Art*, 131, 142, suggests that *Clara Howard* and *Jane Talbot* could have been written *before* the major fictions. He admits, however, that this view is speculative. Yet if this were the case, and even if Brown had not altered the manuscript in the intervening period, the fact that the novels were *published* at this stage would still support my point.

43 Brown, *Clara Howard* and *Jane Talbot*, in *Novels* (1887), VI, 382–383, 403; and VII, 229–230, 234, 217.

44 Letter 1 September 1800 to R.P., in Dunlap, *Life* II, 100–102. See also Friedman, *Inventors of the Promised Land*, 90–103; and Elliott, *Revolutionary Writers*, 267–269.

45 'Facts and Calculations Respecting the Population and Territory of the United States of America', *The Weekly Magazine* III, Nos. 28 and 29 (11 and 18 August 1798), 45–50 and 71–75. The quotation is from page 75. Brown's work is reminiscent of the demography of Benjamin Franklin and Ezra Stiles. See Ellis, *After the Revolution*, 13–15.

46 'Thessalonica: A Roman Story', *The Monthly Magazine and American Review* I, No. 2 (May 1799), 99–117. The quotations are from pages 116–117. For further discussion of Brown's authoritarianism, see Inez Adel Martinez, 'Charles Brockden Brown: fictitious historian', particularly chs. 7 and 8.

47 Brown, 'The Editors' [*sic*] Address to the Public', *The Literary Magazine, and American Register* I, No. 1 (1 October 1803), 4. R. W. B. Lewis, *The American Adam*, 90–98. The date of the 'History of the Carrils' is discussed in Bennett, 'The Charles Brockden Brown Canon', 233, and W. B. Berthoff, 'Charles Brockden Brown's historical "Sketches". A consideration'. Brown's non-fictional work in this last period includes: editor, *The Monthly Magazine* from April 1799 to December 1800; author, *An Address . . . on the Cession of Louisiana to the French*, January 1803 (a second edition quickly followed); author, *Monroe's Embassy*, March 1803; editor, *The Literary Magazine*, October 1803 to June 1807; translator, Volney's *View of the Soil . . .* in 1804; author, *The British Treaty*, in 1807; wrote the 'Prospectus' for *A System of General Geography*, also in 1807; editor, *The American Register*, from November 1807 until his death; author, *An Address . . . on the Utility and Justice of Restrictions upon Foreign Commerce* in January 1809.

48 'A Jaunt to Rockaway, in Long-Island', *The Literary Magazine, and American Register* I, No. 1 (October 1803), 10–14.

49 Brown, 'Annals of America', *The American Register* I (1807), 71.

50 Brown noted in January 1805, for instance, that the Expedition had set out and that 'important discoveries' were expected. *The Literary Magazine* III, No. 16 (January 1805), 30.

51 'Specimen of Political Improvement', and 'A Specimen of Agricultural Improvement', *The Literary Magazine* III (February 1805), 124, 88–89.

52 Brown's letter of 24 October 1795 looks forward to a forthcoming lecture by Volney in Philadelphia. MS Bowdoin College; Bennett Census 63.

53 Volney, *A View of the Soil . . .*, trans. Brown, 260n, 225n, 259n, 425n. Further discussion of Brown's translation is given by Cecilia Tichi, 'Charles Brockden Brown, translator'; John C. Greene, *American Science*, 225–227; and Axelrod, *Brown*, 5, 20–22, 157.

54 Brown's 'Preface' to Volney, xxiii.

55 [Brown], *An Address to the Government of the United States, on the Cession of Louisiana to the French*, 39, 52, 56 (Brown's emphases). Axelrod, *Brown*, 3–5, 104, 151, suggests that the *Address* is Brown's most ambitious fiction. Certainly, it is his most extended essay in the imperial ideology, of which the standard treatment is Albert K. Weinberg, *Manifest Destiny*.

56 [Brown], *Monroe's Embassy*, 35; *The British Treaty*, 4, 11, 37, 65; *An Address to the Congress of the United States on the Utility and Justice of Restrictions upon Foreign Commerce*, 89–90 (Brown's emphasis).

57 'Proposal' for *A System of General Geography*, 3, 5. 'Statistical View of the United States of America', *The Literary Magazine* II, No. 9 (July 1804), 179–180.

58 'On a Taste for the Picturesque', *The Monthly Magazine* III, No. 1 (July 1800), 13. Brown's emphasis. The essay was reprinted in *The Literary Magazine* II, No. 9 (June 1804), 163–165. See also Berthold, 'Brown', 65–66.

59 'On the Picturesque' and 'Volcanoes', *The Literary Magazine* VI, No. 34 (July 1806), 8; and III, No. 19 (April 1805), 290–291.

EPILOGUE: EDGAR ALLAN POE

1 Levin, *The Power of Blackness*. Fender, *Plotting the Golden West*. Tanner, *City of Words*, 27, 145 and *passim*. Barth, *Sabbatical*, 18.

2 Krutch, *Edgar Allan Poe: A Study in Genius*, 197, 192. On the French response to Poe, see Patrick F. Quinn, *The French Face of Edgar Poe*; and Barbara Johnson, 'The frame of reference: Poe, Lacan, Derrida'. Vincent Buranelli, *Edgar Allan Poe*, and Julian Symons, *The Tell-Tale Heart*, provide judicious introductions to the arcana of Poe criticism.

3 Williams, 'Edgar Allan Poe', *In the American Grain*, 227–228.

4 Poe, review of *Wyandotté*, *Graham's Magazine*, November 1843; 'Marginalia', *Democratic Review*, December 1844; rpt. *Essays and Reviews*, 480, 1,342. Boyd Carter, 'Poe's debt to Charles Brockden Brown'; Burton R. Pollin, *Discoveries in Poe*, 18; Steinberg, 'On the brink', 296–306; Voloshin, 'The Lockean tradition', chs. 4 and 5. Axelrod, *Brown*, 9–13, 33–50, contains a discussion of Poe's 'reading of Brown' which is relevant to my argument here, and at 182fn10 cites further accounts of the connection between them.

5 Paul Zweig, *The Adventurer*, Ch. 11. William C. Spengemann, *The Adventurous Muse*, 138–150. John T. Irwin, *American Hieroglyphics*, 119–195 and *passim*. Janis P. Stout, *The Journey Narrative in American Literature*, 93–95. Beaver, 'Introduction' to

The Narrative of Arthur Gordon Pym, 27–28. Further references to this text will usually be given parenthetically. I have also drawn extensively on Edwin Fussell, *Frontier: American Literature and the American West*, Ch. 3; Kent Ljungquist, *The Grand and the Fair: Poe's Landscape Aesthetics and Pictorial Techniques*; and Douglas Tallack, 'Language and form in nineteenth century American short fiction', Ch. 1; and to a lesser extent on Sharon Furrow, 'Psyche and setting: Poe's Picturesque landscapes'; David Halliburton, *Edgar Allan Poe: A Phenomenological View*, 257–277; Jeffrey A. Hess, 'Sources and aesthetics of Poe's landscape fiction'; Lueck 'The Sublime and Picturesque', Ch. 6; Burton Pollin, 'Poe's *Pym* and contemporary reviewers'; Barton Levi St Armand, 'The dragon and the uroboros: themes of metamorphosis in *Arthur Gordon Pym*'; Judith L. Sutherland, *The Problematic Fictions of Poe, James, and Hawthorne*, Ch. 1; Tucker, *America's Gothic Landscape*, Ch. 3; and Richard Wilbur, 'The house of Poe'.

6 'The Murders in the Rue Morgue', *Collected Works*, ed. Thomas O. Mabbott, II, 558. See also Fussell, *Frontier*, 173.

7 Fussell, *Frontier*, 150. On the elder Symmes and the Miami Purchase see Symmes, *The Correspondence of John Cleves Symmes*, ed. Beverley W. Bond; C. H. Winfield, 'The life and public services of John Cleves Symmes'; and Pattison, *Beginnings of the American Rectangular Land Survey System*, 180–184. On the younger Symmes see Harold Beaver's 'Introduction' to *Pym*, 10–14; John Wells Peck, 'Symmes' theory'; William Stanton, *The Great Exploring Expedition of 1838–1842*, 8–17; and J. O. Bailey, *Pilgrims Through Space and Time*, 40–41.

8 'Seaborn', *Symzonia*, 14, 27, 99. Burnet, *The Theory of the Earth*, Book 1, ch. 5, 57–58, 64.

9 Poe, 'Daniel Defoe', *Southern Literary Messenger*, January 1836. Poe runs off another list of travel texts in his review of John L. Stevens, *Incidents of Travel in Egypt, New York Review*, October 1837. Both reviews are reprinted in *Essays and Reviews*, 201, 923–924. The *Southern Literary Messenger* published much travel material; see Mott, *A History of American Magazines* I, 632. For Brown's interest in Defoe, see '*Robinson Crusoe*', *Literary Magazine and American Register* I, No. 5 (February 1804), 324. I. S. MacLaren has written several absorbing articles on Arctic travel accounts. A fuller listing is given in the bibliography; I note here only those articles concerning explorers mentioned by Poe: '"... where nothing moves and nothing changes": The second Arctic expedition of John Ross (1829–1833)'; 'Retaining captaincy of the soul: response to nature in the first Franklin expedition'; and 'The aesthetic mapping of nature in the second Franklin expedition'. Another text which provides an extremely suggestive context for *Pym* is Bernard Smith, *European Vision and the South Pacific*.

10 Poe, 'MS. Found in a Bottle' and 'The Unparalleled Adventure of one Hans Pfaall', *The Science Fiction of Edgar Allan Poe*, ed. Harold Beaver, 10–11, 45–47; articles in the *Southern Literary Messenger*, August 1836 and January 1837, and *Graham's Magazine*, September 1843, reprinted in *Essays and Reviews*, 1,227–1,252. Burnet, *The Theory of the Earth*, Book 1, Ch. 9, 83. See my Prologue for a discussion of Hesiod. For further information on Poe's interest in Symmes, Reynolds, Burnet and Hesiod, see Arthur H. Quinn, *Edgar Allan Poe*, 640; Robert F. Almy, 'J. N. Reynolds: a brief biography, with particular reference to Poe and Symmes'; J. O. Bailey, *Pilgrims*, 42–44, and 'Sources for Poe's *Arthur Gordon Pym*, "Hans Pfaal", and other pieces'; Robert L. Rhea, 'Some observations on Poe's origins'; and Ljungquist, *The Grand and the Fair*, 15–17, 65–66.

11 In Chapter 16 Poe uses some 700 words from a 1,500-word passage written by Reynolds. He also refers to Reynolds by name in the same chapter (page 177), borrows the name Augustus Barnard for Pym's companion, and gives Symmes's

name to one of the hands aboard the whaler. Of course, Poe also uses Symmes's theory of a temperate zone within the polar ice-ring. See Almy, 'Reynolds'; and Rhea, 'Some observations'.

12 Poe, reviews of Irving's *Astoria* and Reynolds's *Address, Southern Literary Messenger*, January 1837; 'The Poetic Principle', *Sartain's Union Magazine*, October 1850; review of Hawthorne's tales, *Godey's Lady's Book*, November 1847; review of George Jones, *Ancient America, Aristidean*, March 1845; all rpt. *Essays and Reviews*, 618–619, 1,241, 1,246–1,247, 72, 584, 642–647. For details of Poe's use of Morrell and *The Mariner's Chronicle*, see D. M. McKeithan, 'Two sources of Poe's *Narrative of Arthur Gordon Pym*'.

13 Poe, 'The Journal of Julius Rodman', *The Complete Works*, ed. James A. Harrison, IV, 41–42, 36. On Poe's indebtedness to the Biddle edition, see Polly Pearl Crawford, 'Lewis and Clark's *Expedition* as a source for Poe's "Journal of Julius Rodman"'; and Irwin, *American Hieroglyphics*, 74–75.

14 Poe, 'Rodman', 99–100. Criswell, *Lewis and Clark: Linguistic Pioneers*, 99. On the apparent flaws in 'Rodman', see Irwin, *American Hieroglyphics*, 75–78; Ljungquist, *The Grand and the Fair*, 10–14, 44–46; and Fussell, *Frontier*, 155–162.

15 Poe, 'The Gold Bug', 'The Landscape Garden', 'The City in the Sea', and 'The Domain of Arnheim', *Collected Works*, ed. Mabbott, III, 807, 817; II, 711, Poe's emphasis; I, 196–204; and III, 1,279, 1,282–1,283.

16 Poe, *Pym*, 61–66. This sequence also draws on his 1835 tale 'Berenice', which is set in a library. In its turn, it may have influenced Emily Brontë's *Wuthering Heights*. Lockwood's nightmare in Chapter 3 begins with a reference to a text and moves through multiple dreams, finally modulating into a frozen waking state.

17 Irwin, *American Hieroglyphics*, 74–75, 165–174 and *passim*. Stafford, *Voyage into Substance*, 306. Brown, *Edgar Huntly*, 22. 'Biddle', *History* I, 208. Jefferson, *Notes on the State of Virginia*, ed. Peden, 23. For an interesting and relevant discussion of 'The Gold Bug', see Tallack, 'Language and form', Ch. 3.

18 Pye, *The Process of Refinement*, 71. See also Smith, *European Vision*, 67. Bage, *Hermsprong*, 168–169.

19 Dobie, 'Nat Straw, the last of the Grizzly hunters', *Saturday Evening Post* 1934; rpt. *Man Meets Grizzly*, ed. Young and Beyers, 224–227.

APPENDIX   THE LEWIS AND CLARK
JOURNALS

1 *History of the Expedition under the Command of Lewis and Clark*, ed. Elliott Coues.
2 *The Field Notes of Captain William Clark*, ed. Ernest S. Osgood.
3 Paul R. Cutright, *A History of the Lewis and Clark Journals*, Appendix A.
4 *The Journals of the Lewis and Clark Expedition*, ed. Gary E. Moulton, II, 8–35 contains a detailed discussion of the journal-keeping methods of Lewis and Clark.
5 *The Field Notes*, ed. Osgood, xv.
6 Cutright, *A History*, 9–10.
7 Jackson, *Jefferson and the Stony Mountains*, 192–195, 201–202 comes to the same conclusion.

Works consulted

PRIMARY SOURCES

MANUSCRIPTS

Brown, Charles Brockden. Manuscript Letters and Poems. Special Collections Department, Hawthorne–Longfellow Library, Bowdoin College, Brunswick, Maine.

Clark, William. Notebooks, Journals, Account Books, Miscellaneous Letters and Papers, 1789–1825. Missouri Historical Society, St Louis.

Manuscript Journals of the Lewis and Clark Expedition, American Philosophical Society (APS), Philadelphia, Call No. 917.3/L.58.

Typed Copies of Journals and Notebooks, 1795–1797, held by Indiana Historical Society. Missouri Historical Society, St Louis.

Duff Family Correspondence, University of Aberdeen Archives, MS 2,226, University of Aberdeen, Scotland.

Jefferson, Thomas. Microfilm of Jefferson Papers, Library of Congress, Washington, DC.

Lewis, Meriwether. Manuscript Journals of Lewis and Clark Expedition, American Philosophical Society, Philadelphia, Call No. 917.3/L.58.

Morse, Jedidiah. Morse Family Papers. 32 boxes of MSS. Historical MSS Collection, Yale University Library (YU), New Haven.

2 boxes of Letters and Miscellaneous Papers, Manuscript Division, New York Public Library (NYPL), New York.

Webster, Noah. Noah Webster Papers. 8 boxes of Letters and Miscellaneous Papers. Manuscript Division, New York Public Library, New York.

Manuscript Letters to Jedidiah Morse, MSS Dept., University of Virginia, Charlottesville, Access Nos. 7,895 and 7,610.

NEWSPAPERS

The American Minerva. New York, 1794.

The American Museum, or Repository of Ancient and Modern Fugitive Pieces, Prose and Poetical. Philadelphia, 1787–1792.

The American Register; or, General Repository of History, Politics and Science. Philadelphia, 1806–1810.
The American Review and Literary Journal. Philadelphia, 1801–1802.
The Analectic Magazine and Naval Chronicle. Philadelphia, 1815–1816.
Cobbett's Weekly Register. London, 1823.
The Columbian Centinel and Massachusetts Federalist. Boston, 1803.
Evening Post. New York, 1803.
The Gazette of the United States. Philadelphia, 1789.
The Gentleman's Magazine. London, 1766, 1786.
The Independent Chronicle. Boston, 1803.
The Literary Magazine and American Register. Philadelphia, 1803–1807.
The Monthly Anthology and Boston Review. Boston, 1807–1810.
The Monthly Magazine, and American Review. Philadelphia, 1799–1800.
The Monthly Review. London, 1769–1776.
The National Intelligencer and Washington Advertiser. Washington, DC, 1803–1807.
The Pennsylvania Journal and the Weekly Advertiser. Philadelphia, 1781.
The Port Folio. Philadelphia, 1801–1810.
The Royal American Magazine, or Universal Repository of Instruction and Amusement. Boston, 1774–1775.
The Scots Magazine. Edinburgh, 1770.
The United States Magazine. Philadelphia, 1779.
The Universal Asylum and Columbian Magazine. Philadelphia, 1790.
The Weekly Magazine of Original Essays, Fugitive Pieces, and Interesting Intelligence. Philadelphia, 1798.
The Western Gleaner. Pittsburgh, 1814.

BOOKS, ARTICLES, ETC.

Achenwall, Gottfried. 'Achenwall's Observations on North America, 1767', trans. J. G. Rosengarten, *The Pennsylvania Magazine of History and Biography* 27, No. 1 (1903), 1–19.
Adair, James. *The History of the American Indians . . .* London: Edward and Charles Dilly, 1775.
Adams, Henry. *The Education of Henry Adams.* New York: Random House, 1931.
Adams, John. *The Works of John Adams,* ed. Charles Francis Adams. 10 vols. Boston: Little, Brown, 1856.
   Papers of John Adams, ed. Robert J. Taylor. 4 vols. to date. Cambridge, MA: Harvard University Press, 1977– .
Aiken, Conrad. *Collected Poems.* 2nd edn. New York: Oxford University Press, 1970.
Alsop, Richard, *The Echo, with other Poems.* New York: Printed at the Porcupine Press by Pasquin Petronius, 1807.
   'Preface' to Juan Ignacio Molina, *The Geographical, Natural and Civil History of Chili.* 2 vols. Middletown, CT: I. Riley, 1808.
'An American', *American Husbandry.* 1775; rpt. ed. Harry J. Carman. New York: Columbia University Press, 1939.
American Archives, ed. Peter Force. 4 Ser., Vol. II. Washington, DC: M. St Clair Clarke and Peter Force, 1839.
Ames, Fisher, *Works.* Boston: T. B. Wait and Co., 1809.
   The Works of Fisher Ames, ed. Seth Ames. 2 vols. Boston: Little, Brown, 1854.
Ames, Nathaniel. *An Astronomical Diary: or, An Almanack for the Year of our Lord Christ 1758.* Boston: Printed by J. Draper, n.d.

Anon., *The Genius of Britain, to General Howe, the Night before the Battle at Long-Island. An Ode*. London: John Sewell, 1776.

Anon., *Otaheite: A Poem*. London: Printed for the Author, 1774.

Anon., 'Plan for Revolution in Louisiana'. 1792: rpt. *Annual Report of the American Historical Association for the Year 1896*, 945–953.

Anon., *Private Letters from An American in England to his Friends in America*. London: J. Almon, 1769.

Anon., *The Project. A Poem Dedicated to Dean Tucker*. 3rd edn. London: T. Becket, 1778.

Audubon, John James. *Audubon and His Journals*, ed. Maria R. Audubon, with Zoological and Other Notes by Elliott Coues. 1897; rpt. New York: Dover, 1960.

Austin, Moses. 'Memorandum of M. Austin's journey ... 1796–1797', *American Historical Review* 5 (April 1900), 518–452.

Bacon, Francis. *The Philosophical Works*, ed. John M. Robertson. London: George Routledge and Sons, 1905.

Bage, Robert. *Hermsprong; or, Man As He Is Not*. 1796; rpt. ed. Peter Faulkner. Oxford University Press, 1985.

Barker, John. *The British in Boston, Being the Diary of Lieutenant John Barker of the King's Own Regiment from 15 November 1774 to 31 May 1776*, ed. Elizabeth Ellery Dana. Cambridge, MA: Harvard University Press, 1924.

Barth, John. *Sabbatical*. 1982; rpt. London: Granada, 1984.

Barton, Benjamin Smith. *New Views of the Origin of Tribes and Nations of America*. 1798; rpt. Millwood, NY: Kraus Reprint Co., 1976.

Bartram, William. *Travels*, ed. Mark Van Doren. 1928; rpt. New York: Dover, 1955.

Before Lewis and Clark: Documents Illustrating the History of the Missouri, 1785–1804, ed. Abraham P. Nasatir. 2 vols. St Louis: St Louis Historical Documents Foundation, 1952.

The Beginnings of American English, ed. Mitford McLeod Mathews. 1931; rpt. University of Chicago Press, 1963.

Belknap, Jeremy. *The History of New Hampshire*. 2nd edn. 3 vols. Boston: Bradford and Read, 1813.

Berchtold, Count Leopold. *Essay to Direct and Extend the Inquiries of Patriotic Travellers ...* 2 vols. London: Printed for the Author, 1789.

Berkeley, George. *The Works of George Berkeley Bishop of Cloyne*, ed. A. A. Luce. 9 vols. London: Thomas Nelson and Sons, 1955.

Blair, Samuel. *A Discourse Given May 9 1798 at the First Presbyterian Church, Philadelphia*. Philadelphia: James Watters, 1798.

Blanchard, Claude. *Journal*, trans. William Duane, ed. Thomas Balch. Albany, NY: J. Munsell, 1876.

Bond, Thomas, *Anniversary Oration, Delivered May 21st, before the American Philosophical Society, Held in Philadelphia, for the Promotion of Useful Knowledge; For the Year 1782*. Philadelphia: J. Dunlap, 1782.

Bossu, Jean Bernard, *Travels through that part of North America formerly called Louisiana*, trans. John Reinhold Forster. 2 vols. London: T. Davies, 1771.

Boswell, James. *Boswell's Life of Johnson*, ed. George Birbeck Hill and L. F. Powell. 6 vols. Oxford: Clarendon Press, 1934–1950.

Boyle, Robert. 'General Heads for a Natural History of a Countrey', *Philosophical Transactions of the Royal Society*, ed. Charles Hutton, 1665–1666; rpt. New York: Johnson Reprint Corp., 1963, I, 186–189.

Brackenridge, Henry Marie. *Views of Louisiana: Together with a Journal of a Voyage Up the Missouri River, in 1811*. Pittsburgh: Cramer, Spear and Eichbaum, 1811.

Brackenridge, Hugh Henry. *A Hugh Henry Brackenridge Reader, 1770–1815*, ed. Daniel Marder. Pittsburgh: University of Pittsburgh Press, 1970.

Incidents of the Insurrection, ed. Daniel Marder. New Haven: College and University Press, 1972.

Law Miscellanies . . . 1814; rpt. New York: Arno Press, 1972.

Modern Chivalry, ed. Claude M. Newlin. 1937; rpt. New York: Hafner Publishing, 1968.

Narratives of a Late Expedition Against the Indians. 1783; rpt. New York: Garland Publishing, 1978.

Brackenridge, Hugh Henry and Philip Freneau, *Father Bombo's Pilgrimage to Mecca*, ed. Michael Davitt Bell. Princeton University Library, 1975.

Broken Image: Foreign Critiques of America, ed. Gerald Emanuel Stern. New York: Random House, 1972.

Brown, Charles Brockden. *An Address to the Congress of the United States on the Utility and Justice of Restrictions upon Foreign Commerce*. Philadelphia: C. and A. Conrad, 1809.

An Address to the Government of the United States, on the Cession of Louisiana to the French . . . 2nd edn. Philadelphia: John Conrad and Co., 1803.

Arthur Mervyn; or, Memoirs of the Year 1793, First and Second Parts, ed. Sydney J. Krause *et al.* Bicentennial Edition, Vol. III. Kent State University Press, 1980.

The British Treaty. [Philadelphia]: n.p., n.d. [1807].

Carwin, The Biloquist, and Other American Tales and Pieces. 3 vols. London: Henry Colburn and Co., 1822.

Clara Howard; or, The Enthusiasm of Love. Novels, Vol. VII (with *Ormond*). Philadelphia: David McKay, 1887.

Edgar Huntly; or, Memoirs of a Sleep-Walker, ed. Sydney J. Krause *et al.* Bicentennial Edition, Vol. IV. Kent State University Press, 1984.

Jane Talbot. Novels, Vol. V. Philadelphia: David McKay, 1887.

Memoirs of Stephen Calvert, ed. and introd. Hans Borchers. Frankfurt am Main: Peter Lang, 1978.

Monroe's Embassy, or The Conduct of the Government, in Relation to our Claims to the Navigation of the Mississippi. Philadelphia: John Conrad, 1803.

Ormond; or, The Secret Witness, ed. Sydney J. Krause *et al.* Bicentennial Edition, Vol. II. Kent State University Press, 1982.

'Prospectus' for *A System of General Geography* . . . [Philadelphia]: n.p., n.d. [1807].

The Rhapsodist and Other Uncollected Writings, ed. Harry R. Warfel. New York: Scholars' Facsimiles and Reprints, 1943.

Wieland; or, The Transformation. An American Tale, ed. Sydney J. Krause *et al.* Bicentennial Edition, Vol. I. Kent State University Press, 1977.

Buffon, Georges Louis Le Clerc, Comte de. *Natural History, General and Particular*, trans. William Smellie. 2nd edn. 9 vols. Edinburgh: William Creech, 1780–1785.

Burke, Edmund. *A Philosophical Enquiry into the Origin of our Ideas of the Sublime and Beautiful*, ed. J. T. Boulton. London: Routledge and Kegan Paul, 1958.

Burnet, Thomas. *The Theory of the Earth*. 3rd edn. London: Walter Ketilby, 1697.

Burns, Robert. *Poems and Selected Letters*, ed. David Daiches. London: Collins, 1959.

Burr, Aaron. *The Political Correspondence and Public Papers*, ed. Mary-Jo Kline and Joanne Wood Ryan. 2 vols. Princeton University Press, 1983.

Caldwell, Charles. *Autobiography*, ed. Harriot W. Warner. Philadelphia: Lippincott, Grambo and Co., 1855.

Carey, Mathew. *A Short Account of the Malignant Fever, Lately Prevalent in Philadelphia*. 4th edn. Philadelphia: Printed for the Author, 1794.

A Short Account of the Malignant Fever, Prevalent in the Year 1793, in the City of Philadelphia. 5th edn. In *Miscellaneous Essays*. Philadelphia: Carey and Hart, 1830.

Carrol, James. *An American Criterion of the English Language*. 1795; rpt. Menston, Yorks.: Scholar Press, 1970.

Carver, Jonathan. *The Journals of Jonathan Carver and Related Documents*, ed. John Parker. Minneapolis: Minnesota Historical Society, 1976.

Three Years' Travels through the Interior Parts of North America, in the Years 1766, 1767, and 1768. London: Printed for the Author, 1778.

Cavalier and Puritan: Ballads and Broadsides, ed. Hyder E. Rollins. New York University Press, 1923.

Chastellux, Marquis de. *Travels in North America in the Years 1780, 1781, and 1782*, trans. and ed. Howard C. Rice, Jr. 2 vols. Chapel Hill: University of North Carolina Press, 1963.

Clark, William. *The Field Notes of Captain William Clark, 1803–1805*, ed. Ernest S. Osgood. New Haven: Yale University Press, 1964.

Westward with Dragoons: The Journal of William Clark on his Expedition to Establish Fort Osage, August 25 to September 22, 1808, ed. Kate L. Gregg. Fulton, MO: Ovid Bell Press, 1937.

Cobbett, William. *The Parliamentary History of England*. 36 vols. London: Longman, Hurst, Rees, Orme and Brown, 1806–1820.

Porcupine's Works . . . Exhibiting a Faithful Picture of the United States of America. 12 vols. London: Cobbett and Morgan, 1801.

Cole, Thomas. 'Essay on American Scenery', *American Monthly Magazine*, New Series, 1 (January 1836), 1–12.

Columbus, Christopher. *Select Documents Illustrating the Four Voyages of Columbus*, trans. and ed. Cecil Jane. 2 vols. London: Hakluyt Society, 1930, 1932.

The Connecticut Wits, ed. Vernon L. Parrington. 1925; rpt. with a new Foreword by Kenneth Silverman, New York: Thomas Y. Crowell Co., 1969.

Cooper, James Fenimore. *Gleanings in Europe: England*, ed. Donald A. Ringe *et al.* Albany: State University of New York Press, 1982.

The Last of the Mohicans: A Narrative of 1757, ed. James Franklin Beard. Albany: State University of New York Press, 1983.

The Spy, ed. J. E. Morpurgo. London: Oxford University Press, 1968.

Wyandotté, or The Hutted Knoll. A Tale, ed. Thomas and Marianne Philbrick. Albany: State University of New York Press, 1982.

Cowper, William. *Poetical Works*, ed. H. S. Milford. 4th edn. London: Oxford University Press, 1934.

Cramer, Zadoc. *The Navigator*. 7th edn. Pittsburgh: Cramer, Spear and Eichbaum, 1811.

The Navigator. 10th edn. Pittsburgh: Cramer and Spear, 1818.

The Navigator. 12th edn. Pittsburgh: Cramer and Spear, 1824.

Crèvecœur, Hector St John de. *Letters from an American Farmer and Sketches of Eighteenth-Century America*, ed. Albert E. Stone. Harmondsworth, Middx.: Penguin, 1982.

Currie, William, *A Description of the Malignant Fever Prevailing at Present in Philadelphia*. Philadelphia: T. Dobson, 1793.

An Historical Account of the Climates and Diseases of the United States of America . . . Collected Principally from Personal Observation and the Communications of Physicians of Talents and Experience, Residing in the Several States. Philadelphia: T. Dobson, 1792.

An Impartial Review of Dr. Rush's Late Publication . . . Philadelphia: T. Dobson, 1794.

The Debates and Proceedings of the Congress of the United States. 42 vols. Washington: Gales and Seaton, 1834–1856.

Defoe, Daniel. *The Life and Adventures of Robinson Crusoe*, ed. Angus Ross. Harmondsworth, Middx.: Penguin, 1965.

Devèze, Jean. *An Inquiry Into, and Observations Upon the Causes and Effects of the Epidemic Disease which Raged in Philadelphia from the Month of August till towards the Middle of December, 1793*. Philadelphia: Parent, 1794.

Diderot, Denis. 'Suite de l'Entretien', *Oeuvres Complètes* II, 190. 1875; rpt. Nendeln: Kraus Reprint, 1966.

Documents in American History, ed. Henry S. Commager. 5th edn. New York: Appleton–Century–Crofts, 1949.

Donne, John. *The Complete English Poems*, ed. A. J. Smith. Harmondsworth, Middx.: Penguin, 1971.

Dunlap, William. *Dairy*, ed. Dorothy C. Barck. 3 vols. New York, NY: New York Historical Society, 1930.

Dwight, Timothy. *The Duty of Americans, at the Present Crisis*. New Haven: Thomas and Samuel Green, 1798.

The Major Poems, introd. William J. McTaggart and William K. Bottorff. Gainesville, FL: Scholars' Facsimiles and Reprints, 1969.

Travels in New-England and New-York. 4 vols. 1821–1822; rpt. London: William Baynes and Son, 1823.

Earlom, Richard. *Liber Veritatis; or A Collection of Prints, after the Original Drawings of Claude le Lorrain*. 3 vols. London: Boydell and Co., 1777–1819.

[Egremont, Earl of]. 'Hints Relative to the Division and Government of the Conquered and Newly Acquired Countries in America', ed. Verner W. Crane, *Mississippi Valley Historical Review* 8, No. 4 (March 1922), 366–373.

Eliot, Jared. *Essays upon Field Husbandry and Other Papers 1748–1762*, ed. Harry J. Carman and Rexford G. Tugwell. Columbia University Studies in the History of American Agriculture, Vol. 1. New York: Columbia University Press, 1934.

Ellicott, Andrew. *The Journal of Andrew Ellicott . . . for Determining the Boundary between the United States and the Possessions of his Most Catholic Majesty in America*. Philadelphia: Thomas Dobson, 1803.

Emerson, Ralph Waldo. *Select Essays*, ed. Larzer Ziff. Harmondsworth, Middx.: Penguin, 1982.

Essays on the Constitution of the United States, Published During its Discussion by the People, 1787–1788, ed. Paul Leicester Ford. Brooklyn, NY: Historical Printing Club, 1892.

Evans, Lewis. *Geographical, Historical, Political, Philosophical and Mechanical Essays, the First Containing an Analysis of a General Map of the Middle British Colonies in America*. Philadelphia: Printed by B. Franklin and D. Hall, 1755.

Evelyn, W. G. *Memoir and Letters of Captain W. Glanville Evelyn, of the 4th Regiment, ('King's Own') from North America, 1774–1776*, ed. G. D. Scull. Oxford: James Parker, 1879.

The Fear of Conspiracy: Images of Un-American Subversion from the Revolution to the Present, ed. David Brion Davis. Ithaca, NY: Cornell University Press, 1971.

Federalists, Republicans, and Foreign Entanglements, 1789–1815, ed. Robert McColley. Englewood Cliffs, NJ: Prentice–Hall, 1969.

Fielding, Henry. *The History of Tom Jones, A Foundling*, ed. R. P. C. Mutter. Harmondsworth, Middx.: Penguin, 1966.

Joseph Andrews, ed. A. R. Humphreys. London: Dent, 1973.

Filson, John. *The Discovery and Settlement of Kentucke*. 1784; rpt. Ann Arbor, MI: University Microfilms, 1966.

Fisher, William. *An Interesting Account of the Voyages and Travels of Captains Lewis and Clarke*. Baltimore: P. Mauro, 1813.

Forster, E. M. *Two Cheers for Democracy*. 1951; rpt. ed. Oliver Stallybrass. Harmondsworth, Middx.: Penguin, 1976.

Franklin, Benjamin. *The Autobiography and Other Writings*, ed. L. Jesse Lemisch. New York: Signet, 1961.

Benjamin Franklin's Letters to the Press, ed. Verner W. Crane. Chapel Hill: University of North Carolina Press, 1950.

'Benjamin Franklin defends Northwest Passage navigation', introd. Bertha Solis-Cohen, *Princeton University Library Chronicle* 19, No. 1 (1957–1958), 15–34.

Papers, ed. Leonard W. Labaree and William B. Willcox. 24 vols. to date. New Haven: Yale University Press, 1960–1984.

The Writings, ed. Albert Henry Smyth. 12 vols. New York: Macmillan, 1906.

Freneau, Philip, *The American Village, A Poem. To Which Are Added, Several other Original Pieces in Verse*. 1782; rpt. New York: Burt Franklin, 1968.

A Collection of Poems on American Affairs and a Variety of Other Subjects Chiefly Moral and Political. 1815; rpt. 2 vols. in 1, Delmar, NY: Scholars' Facsimiles and Reprints, 1976.

The Last Poems, ed. Lewis Leary. 1945; rpt. Westport, CT: Greenwood Press, 1970.

The Miscellaneous Works, Containing His Essays, and Additional Poems. 1788; rpt. Delmar, NY: Scholars' Facsimiles and Reprints, 1975.

'The Pilgrim, No. VIII', *The Freeman's Journal; or, the North American Intelligencer* No. 38 (9 January 1782), [1].

The Poems of Philip Freneau, ed. Fred. Lewis Pattee. 3 vols. Princeton, NJ: Princeton University Library, 1902.

Poems, Written Chiefly During the Late War. 1786; rpt. Delmar, NY: Scholars' Facsimiles and Reprints, 1975.

Poems Written and Published During the Revolutionary War. 1809; rpt. 2 vols in 1, Delmar, NY: Scholars' Facsimiles and Reprints, 1976.

Poems Written Between the Years 1768 and 1794. 1795; rpt. Delmar, NY: Scholars' Facsimiles and Reprints, 1976.

Garden, Alexander. *Anecdotes of the Revolutionary War*. 2 Ser. Charleston, SC: A. E. Miller, 1828.

Gass, Patrick. *A Journal of the Voyages and Travels of a Corps of Discovery*, ed. David McKeehan. 1807; rpt. Minneapolis: Ross and Haines, 1958.

Gibbon, Edward. *The Letters*, ed. J. E. Norton. 3 vols. London: Cassell, 1956.

Gilmer, Francis William [Walker]. 'On the Geological Formation of the Natural Bridge in Virginia', *Transactions of the American Philosophical Society*, New Series, 1 (1818), 187–192.

Gilpin, William. *An Essay on Prints*. 5th edn. London: T. Cadell Jr. and W. Davies, 1802.

[Goldsmith, Oliver]. *The Citizen of the World; or Letters from a Chinese Philosopher Residing in London to his Friends in the East*. London: Printed for the Author, 1762.

Goldsmith, Oliver, *Collected Works*, ed. Arthur Friedman. 6 vols. Oxford University Press, 1966.

A History of the Earth, and Animated Nature. 8 vols. London: J. Nourse, 1774.

A History of England, in a Series of Letters from a Nobleman to his Son. A New Edition, continued to the Peace of 1802. 2 vols. London: F. and C. Rivington *et al.*, 1803.

[Oliver] *Goldsmith: The Critical Heritage*, ed. G. S. Rousseau. London: Routledge and Kegan Paul, 1974.

Hall, Joseph, *The Discovery of a New World (Mundus Alter et Idem)*, trans. John Healey. 1609; rpt. Cambridge, MA: Harvard University Press, 1937.

Hamilton, Alexander, James Madison and John Jay, *The Federalist; or, The New Constitution*, introd. W. R. Brock. London: Dent, 1970.

Herbert, George. *The English Poems*, ed. C. A. Patrides. London: Dent, 1974.

Hesiod. *The Remains of Hesiod*, trans. Charles A. Elton. 2nd edn. London: Baldwin, Cradock and Joy, 1815.

Hinde, T. S. 'Letter on Welsh Indians', *American Pioneer* 1, No. 11 (November 1842), 373–374.

Hippocratic Writings, ed. G. E. R. Lloyd. Harmondsworth, Middx.: Penguin, 1978.

Hogarth, William. *The Analysis of Beauty*, ed. Joseph Burke. Oxford University Press, 1955.

Hopkinson, Francis. 'An Answer to General Burgoyne's Proclamation', *Miscellaneous Essays and Occasional Writings*. Philadelphia: T. Dobson, 1792, 146–150.

Hutchins, Thomas. *A Historical Narrative and Topographical Description of Louisiana and West-Florida*. Philadelphia: Printed for the Author, 1784.

'A Journal of a March from Fort Pitt to Venango, and from thence to Presqu'Isle', *Pennsylvania Magazine of History and Biography* 2 (1878), 149–153.

A Topographical Description of Virginia, Pennsylvania, Maryland, and North Carolina. 1778; rpt. ed. Frederick Charles Hicks. Cleveland, OH: The Burrows Bros. Co., 1904.

Imlay, Gilbert. *A Topographical Description of the Western Territory of North America*. London: J. Debrett, 1792.

James, Henry. *Hawthorne*, ed. Tony Tanner. London: Macmillan, 1967.

The Ambassadors. 1903; rpt. Harmondsworth, Middx.: Penguin, 1973.

What Maisie Knew. 1897; rpt. Harmondsworth, Middx.: Penguin, 1985.

Jefferson, Thomas. *The Complete Jefferson, Containing His Major Writings, Published and Unpublished, Except his Letters*, ed. Saul K. Padover. 1943; rpt. Freeport, NY: Books for Libraries Press, 1969.

'Description of Louisiana, Communicated to Congress, on the 14th of November 1803', *American State Papers* Class X, Vol. XXII, Miscellaneous vol. I, 344–356. Washington: Gales and Seaton, 1834.

The Family Letters of Thomas Jefferson, ed. Edwin Morris Betts and James Adam Bear Jr. Columbia: University of Missouri Press, 1966.

Jefferson's Ideas On a University Library: Letters from the Founder of the University of Virginia to a Boston Bookseller, ed. Elizabeth Cometti. Charlottesville: University of Virginia, 1950.

'A Memoir on the Discovery of certain Bones of a Quadruped of the Clawed Kind in the Western Parts of Virginia', *Transactions of the American Philosophical Society* 4 (1799), 246–260.

Notes on the State of Virginia, ed. William Peden. 1954; rpt. New York: Norton, 1972.

The Papers of Thomas Jefferson, ed. Julian P. Boyd. 21 vols. to date. Princeton University Press, 1950–1983.

The Portable Thomas Jefferson, ed. Merrill D. Peterson. Harmondsworth, Middx.: Penguin, 1977.

Thomas Jefferson's Farm Book, ed. Edwin Morris Betts. Princeton University Press, 1953.

Thomas Jefferson's Garden Book, ed. Edwin Morris Betts. Philadelphia: American Philosophical Society, 1944.

The Writings of Thomas Jefferson, ed. Paul Leicester Ford. 10 vols. New York: G. P. Putnam's Sons, 1893–1899.

The Writings of Thomas Jefferson, ed. Andrew A. Lipscomb and Albert Ellery Bergh. 20 vols. Washington, DC: Thomas Jefferson Memorial Association, 1903.

The Writings of Thomas Jefferson, ed. H. A. Washington. 9 vols. New York: Riker, Thorne and Co., 1853–1854.

Jefferson and Southwestern Exploration: The Freeman and Custis Accounts of the Red River Expedition of 1806, ed. Dan L. Flores. Norman: University of Oklahoma Press, 1984.

Johnson, Samuel. *A Journal to the Western Isles of Scotland*, ed. R. W. Chapman. Oxford University Press, 1924.

A Voyage to Abyssinia, ed. Joel J. Gold. Vol. XV of *The Works of Samuel Johnson*. New Haven: Yale University Press, 1985.

Kaims [Kames], Henry Home, Lord, *Elements of Criticism*. 3rd edn. 2 vols. London: A. Millar, 1765.

Kalm, Peter [Per]. *Travels into North America*, trans. John Reinhold Forster. 3 vols. Warrington: William Eyres, 1770.

Karl Bodmer's America, ed. David C. Hunt and Marsha V. Gallagher. Omaha: Joslyn Art Museum and University of Nebraska Press, 1984.

La Rochefoucault-Liancourt, François Alexandre Frédéric de. *Travels through the United States of North America, the Country of the Iroquois, and Upper Canada in the Years 1795, 1796 and 1797*, trans. H. Neuman. 2 vols. London: R. Phillips, 1799.

Lathrop, Joseph. *National Happiness, Illustrated in a Sermon, Delivered at West Springfield, on the Nineteenth of February, 1795*. Springfield, MA: J. W. Hooker and F. Stebbins, 1795.

Lawrence, D. H. *Studies in Classic American Literature*. 1924; rpt. Harmondsworth, Middx.: Penguin, 1971.

Ledyard, John. *John Ledyard's Journey Through Russia and Siberia, 1787–88*, ed. Stephen D. Watrous. Madison: University of Wisconsin Press, 1966.

   A Journal of Captain Cook's Last Voyage to the Pacific Ocean. 1783; rpt. Chicago: Quadrangle Press, 1963.

Le Page du Pratz, Antoine Simon. *History of Louisiana*. 2nd edn., English translation, 1774; rpt. ed. Joseph G. Treigle Jr. Baton Rouge: Louisiana State University Press, 1976.

'Letters of American physicians and surgeons', ed. Victor H. Paltsits, *Bulletin of the New York Public Library* 23, No. 9 (September 1918), 547–554.

Letters of Brunswick and Hessian Officers During the American Revolution, trans. William L. Stone. New York: Da Capo Press, 1970.

Letters to Members of the Continental Congress, ed. Edmund C. Burnett. 8 vols. Washington, DC: Carnegie Institution, 1936.

'Lewis, Meriwether'. *The Travels of Lewis and Clarke*. Philadelphia: Hubbard Lester, 1809.

   Travels of Lewis and Clarke. London: Longman, Hurst, Rees and Orme, 1809.

Lewis, Meriwether and William Clark, *History of the Expedition under the Command of Captains Lewis and Clark*, ed. Paul Allen [and Nicholas Biddle]. 1814; rpt. 2 vols. in 3, New York: New Amsterdam Book Co., 1902.

   History of the Expedition under the Command of Lewis and Clark, ed. Elliott Coues. 4 vols. New York: Francis P. Harper, 1893.

   Journals of the Lewis and Clark Expedition, ed. Gary E. Moulton. 2 vols. to date. Lincoln: University of Nebraska Press, 1983–.

   Letters of the Lewis and Clark Expedition, with Related Documents, 1783–1854, ed. Donald Jackson. 2nd edn., 2 vols. Urbana: University of Illinois Press, 1978.

   Original Journals of the Lewis and Clark Expedition, 1804–1806, ed. Reuben Gold Thwaites. 7 vols. plus Atlas. New York: Dodd, Mead and Co., 1904.

Lewis, Meriwether and John Ordway. *The Journals of Captain Meriwether Lewis and Sergeant John Ordway*, ed. Milo M. Quaife. Madison: Collections of the State Historical Society of Wisconsin, Vol. XXII, 1916.

The Literature of America: Colonial Period, ed. Larzer Ziff. New York: McGraw–Hill, 1970.

The Lost War: Letters from British Officers During the American Revolution, ed. Marion Balderston and David Syrett. New York: Horizon Press, 1975.

Louisiana Under the Rule of Spain, France, and the United States, 1785–1807, ed. James Alexander Robertson. 2 vols. Cleveland, OH: Arthur H. Clark Co., 1911.

The Loyal Verses of Joseph Stansbury and Doctor Jonathan Odell, ed. Winthrop Sargent. Albany, NY: J. Munsell, 1860.

The Loyalist Poetry of the Revolution, ed. Winthrop Sargent. Philadelphia: Collins, 1857.

Lucian. *Satirical Sketches*, trans. and ed. Paul Turner. Harmondsworth, Middx.: Penguin, 1961.

M'Kay [Mackay], James. 'Extract from the Manuscript of James M'Kay', *The Medical Repository*, Hexade II, 4 (1807), 27–36.

Mackay, James. 'Extracts from Capt. Mackay's Journal – and Others.', ed. Milo M. Quaife, *Proceedings of the State Historical Society for Wisconsin*, 63rd Annual Meeting, 1915, 186–210.

Mackenzie, Alexander. *The Letters and Journals of Alexander Mackenzie*, ed. W. Kaye Lamb. Cambridge University Press, 1970.

Voyages from Montreal, on the River St Lawrence, through the Continent of North America, to the Frozen and Pacific Oceans; in the Years 1789 and 1793 . . . London: T. Cadell, Jr and W. Davies, 1801.

Madison, James. *The Papers*, ed. William T. Hutchinson and William M. E. Rachal. 14 vols. to date. University of Chicago Press, 1962–1983.

Man Meets Grizzly: Encounters in the Wild from Lewis and Clark to Modern Times, ed. F. M. Young and Coralie Beyers. Boston: Houghton Mifflin, 1980.

Maximilian, Prince of Wied. *Travels in the Interior of North America*, trans. H. Evans Lloyd. 1843; rpt. in *Early Western Travels, 1748–1846*, ed. Reuben Gold Thwaites, Vol. xxii. Cleveland, OH: Arthur H. Clark Co., 1906.

Melville, Herman. *Billy Budd, Sailor and Other Stories*, ed. Harold Beaver. Harmondsworth, Middx.: Penguin, 1967.

Miller, Samuel. *A Brief Retrospect of the Eighteenth Century*. 2 vols. 1803; rpt. New York: Burt Franklin, 1970.

Monboddo, James Burnet, Lord. *Of the Origin and Progress of Language*. 6 vols. Edinburgh: A. Kincaid and W. Creech, 1773–1792.

Montaigne, Michel, Seigneur de. *The Essays*, trans. Charles Cotton. 3rd edn. 1700; rpt. London: Alex Murray and Son, 1870.

Montesquieu, Charles de Secondat, Baron de. *The Spirit of Laws*. 2 vols. Aberdeen: Francis Douglass and William Murray, 1756.

More, Thomas. *Utopia*, trans. and ed. Paul Turner. Harmondsworth, Middx.: Penguin, 1965.

Morris, Gouverneur. *The Diary and Letters*, ed. Anne Cary Morris. 2 vols. New York: Charles Scribner's Sons, 1888.

Morse, Jedidiah. *The American Gazetteer* . . . 2nd edn. Boston: Thomas and Andrews, 1804.

The American Gazetteer . . . 3rd edn. Boston: Thomas and Andrews, 1810.

The American Geography; or, a View of the Present Situation of the United States of America. Elizabeth-Town, NJ: Printed by Shepard Kollock, 1789.

The American Geography. 2nd edn. London: John Stockdale, 1792.

The American Universal Geography. 2nd edn, 2 vols. Boston: Young and Thomas and Andrews, 1793.

The American Universal Geography. 3rd edn, 2 vols. Boston: Isaiah Thomas and Ebenezer T. Andrews, 1796.

The American Universal Geography. 6th edn. Boston: Thomas and Andrews, 1812.

An appeal to the publick on the controversy respecting the revolution in Harvard College . . . Charlestown, MA: Printed for the Author, 1814.

Annals of the American Revolution. Hartford, CT: n.p., 1824.

A Sermon Delivered on May 9th 1798 . . . Boston: Samuel Hall, 1798.

A Sermon Preached at Charlestown, November 29th 1798, on the Annual Thanksgiving. Boston: Samuel Hall, 1798.

Munford, Robert. *The Candidates; or, the Humours of a Virginia Election*. 1770; rpt. *William and Mary Quarterly*, 3 Ser., 5 (April 1948), 227–257.

The New World: The First Pictures of America, ed. Stefan Lorant. New York: Duell, Sloan and Pearce, 1946.

Paine, Thomas. *Common Sense*, ed. Isaac Kramnick. Harmondsworth, Middx.: Penguin, 1976.

Complete Writings, ed. Philip Foner. 2 vols. New York: Citadel Press, 1945.

Rights of Man, ed. Henry Collins. Harmondsworth, Middx.: Penguin, 1969.

Papers of the Continental Congress, 1774–1789. Washington, DC: National Archives, 1959.

Parish, Elijah. *A New System of Modern Geography*. 2nd edn. Newburyport, MA: E. Little and Co., 1812.

P[auw], [Cornelius de]. *Recherches Philosophiques sur les Américains*. 3 vols. Berlin: n.p., 1771.

Percy, Hugh, Duke of Northumberland. *Letters of Hugh Earl Percy from Boston and New York, 1774–1776*, ed. Charles Knowles Bolton. Boston: Goodspeed, 1902.

Petty, Sir William, *The Economic Writings*, ed. Charles H. Hull. Cambridge University Press, 1899.

Pike, Zebulon. *The Journals of Zebulon Montgomery Pike, with Letters and Related Documents*, ed. Donald Jackson. 2 vols. Norman: University of Oklahoma Press, 1966.

Plinius, Secondus. *The History of the World*, trans. Philemon Holland. London: Printed by Adam Filip, 1601.

Poe, Edgar Allan. *Collected Works*, ed. Thomas Ollive Mabbott. 3 vols. to date. Cambridge, MA: Harvard University Press, 1969–1978.

Essays and Reviews, ed. G. R. Thompson. New York: The Library of America, 1984.

'The Journal of Julius Rodman', *The Complete Works*, ed. James P. Harrison, IV, 9–101. New York: Thomas Y. Crowell, 1902.

The Science Fiction of Edgar Allan Poe, ed. Harold Beaver. Harmondsworth, Middx.: Penguin, 1976.

Selected Writings, ed. David Galloway. Harmondsworth, Middx.: Penguin, 1967.

The Poets of Connecticut, with Biographical Sketches, ed. Charles W. Everest. Hartford, CT: Case, Tiffany and Burnham, 1843.

Pye, Henry James. *The Progress of Refinement*. Oxford: Clarendon Press, 1783.

Ramsay, David. *An Oration, on the Cession of Louisiana, to the United States, Delivered on the 12th May, 1804*. Charleston, SC: Printed by W. P. Young, 1804.

A Review of the Improvement, Progress, and State of Medicine in the XVIIIth Century. Charleston, SC: n.p., 1800.

A Sketch of the Soil, Climate, Weather and Diseases of South-Carolina. Charleston, SC: Printed by W. P. Young, 1796.

Raynal, Guillaume, l'Abbé. *A Philosophical and Political History of the Settlements and Trade of the Europeans in the East and West Indies*, trans. J. Justamond. 4 vols. London: T. Cadell, 1776.

A Philosophical and Political History of the Settlements and Trade of the Europeans in the East and West Indies. A New Translation. 6 vols. Edinburgh: W. Gordon *et al.*, 1782.

The Sentiments of a Foreigner on the Disputes of Great-Britain with America, translated from the French. Philadelphia: James Humphries, 1775.

The Records of the Federal Convention of 1787, ed. Max Farrand. Revised edn, 4 vols. New Haven: Yale University Press, 1937.

Remington, Frederic. *Pony Tracks*. 1895; rpt. Norman: University of Oklahoma Press, 1977.

Richardson, Jonathan. *An Essay on the Theory of Painting*. 1725; rpt. Menston, Yorks.: Scolar Press, 1971.

Robertson, William. *The History of America*. 4 vols. London: W. Strahan, T. Cadell and J. Balfour, 1777.

The History of America. 10th edn, in which is included the Posthumous Volume. 4 vols. London: A. Strahan, T. Cadell and W. Davies, 1803.

Robin, Abbé. *New Travels Through North-America*, trans. Philip Freneau. 1783; rpt. New York: Arno Press, 1969.

Robison, John. *Proofs of a Conspiracy Against All the Religions and Governments of Europe*. 1789; rpt. Belmont, MA: Western Islands, 1967.

Rush, Benjamin, *An Account of the Bilious remitting Yellow Fever as it appeared in the City of Philadelphia in the year 1793*. 2nd edn. Philadelphia: Thomas Dobson, 1794.

The Autobiography of Benjamin Rush, ed. George W. Corner. 1948; rpt. Westport, CT: Greenwood Press, 1970.

Benjamin Rush's Lectures on the Mind, ed. Eric T. Carlson, Jefferey L. Wollock and Patricia S. Noel. Philadelphia: American Philosophical Society, 1981.

'Benjamin Rush's journal of a trip to Carlisle in 1784', ed. L. H. Butterfield, *Pennsylvania Magazine of History and Biography* 74, No. 4 (October 1960), 443–456.

'Dr Rush to Governor Henry on the Declaration of Independence and the Virginia Constitution', ed. L. H. Butterfield, *Proceedings of the American Philosophical Society* 95, No. 3 (June 1951), 250–253.

Essays, Literary, Moral and Philosophical. Philadelphia: Printed by Thomas and Samuel F. Bradford, 1798.

The Letters of Benjamin Rush, ed. Lyman H. Butterfield. 2 vols. Princeton University Press, 1951.

Medical Inquiries and Observations. 2nd London edn. London: C. Dilly, 1789.

Medical Inquiries and Observations. 2nd American edn. 2 vols. Philadelphia: Thomas Dobson, 1794.

Medical Inquiries and Observations. 1st complete edn. 5 vols. Philadelphia: Thomas Dobson, 1794–1798.

Medical Inquiries and Observations. 2nd complete edn. 4 vols. Philadelphia: J. Conrad and Co., 1805.

Sixteen Introductory Lectures. 2nd edn. Philadelphia: Bradford and Inskeep, 1811.

Ruskin, John. *Ruskin Today*, ed. Kenneth Clark. Harmondsworth, Middx.: Penguin, 1967.

Sandys, George. *Ovid's Metamorphosis Englished, Mythologiz'd And Represented in Figures*. London: Andrew Hebb, 1640.

Sanger, 'Lord' George. *Seventy Years a Showman*, introd. Kenneth Grahame. London: Dent, 1927.

Seaborn, Captain Adam [John Cleves Symmes], *Symzonia: A Voyage of Discovery*. 1820; rpt. Gainesville, FL: Scholars' Facsimiles and Reprints, 1965.

Smith, Elihu Hubbard, *The Diary*, ed. James E. Cronin. Philadelphia: American Philosophical Society, 1973.

'Epistle to the author of the Botanic Garden', in Erasmus Darwin, *The Botanic Garden*. 2 vols in 1. New York: T. and J. Swords, 1798.

Smith, Revd. James. 'Tours into Kentucky and the Northwest Territory. Three journals by the Revd. James Smith of Powhatan County, Va.', ed. Josiah Morrow, *Ohio Archaeological and Historical Quarterly* 16 (1907), 348–401.

Smith, Sydney. 'Review of Adam Seybert, *Statistical Annals of the United States of America*', *Edinburgh Review* 33 (January 1820), 69–80.

[Smith, William]. *An Historical Account of the Expedition against the Ohio Indians in the year 1764 under the command of Henry Bouquet . . .* 1765; rpt. London: T. Jefferies, 1766.

Historical Account of Bouquet's Expedition Against the Ohio Indians, ed. Francis Parkman. Cincinnati, OH: Robert Clarke and Co., 1868.

Social Contract: Essays by Locke, Hume, Rousseau, introd. Sir Ernest Barker. Oxford University Press, 1971.

Songs and Ballads of the American Revolution, ed. Frank Moore. New York: Appleton, 1856.

Sources and Documents Illustrating the American Revolution 1764–1788 and the Formation of the Federal Constitution, ed. S. E. Morison. 2nd edn. Oxford: Clarendon Press, 1929.

The Spirit of 'Seventy-Six: The Story of the American Revolution as Told by Participants, ed. Henry Steele Commager and Richard B. Morris. 2 vols. New York: Bobbs–Merrill, 1958.

Sprat, Thomas, *The History of the Royal Society*, ed. Jackson I. Cope and Harold Whitmore Jones. London: Routledge and Kegan Paul, 1959.

Sterne, Laurence. *The Life and Opinions of Tristram Shandy, Gentleman*, ed. Graham Petrie. Harmondsworth, Middx.: Penguin, 1967.

Stiles, Ezra. *A Discourse on the Christian Union*. Boston: Edes and Gill, 1761.

The United States Elevated to Glory and Honor: An Election Sermon Preached May 8, 1783 in *The Pulpit of the American Revolution*, ed. John W. Thornton. 1860; rpt. New York: Burt Franklin, 1970.

Stillé, Alfred. *Elements of General Pathology*. Philadelphia: Lindsay and Blakiston, 1848.

Stoppard, Tom. *Dirty Linen and New-Found-Land*. London: Faber and Faber, 1976.

Sullivan, James. *History of the District of Maine*. Boston: I. Thomas and E. T. Andrews, 1795.

Sydenham, Thomas. *The Works of Thomas Sydenham, M. D., on Acute and Chronic Diseases*, ed. Benjamin Rush. Philadelphia: Benjamin and Thomas Kite, 1809.

Symmes, John Cleves. *The Correspondence of John Cleves Symmes, Founder of the Miami Purchase*, ed. Beverley W. Bond. New York: Macmillan, 1926.

Thacher, James. *Military Journal During the American Revolutionary War, from 1775 to 1783*. Boston: Richardson and Lord, 1823.

Thomson, James. *Complete Poetical Works*, ed. J. Logie Robertson. London: Oxford University Press, 1908.

A Touch on the Times: Songs of Social Change, ed. Roy Palmer. Harmondsworth, Middx.: Penguin, 1974.

[Tucker, St George]. *A Letter to the Rev. Jedediah [sic] Morse, A. M.* 1795; rpt. *William and Mary Quarterly* 1 Ser., 2 (1892), 181–197.

Tyson, Edward. *Orang-Outang, sive Homo Sylvestris: or, the Anatomy of a Pygmie.* 1699; rpt. ed. Ashley Montagu, London: Dawsons of Pall Mall, 1966.

Underhill, Captain John. *News from America; or, A New and Experimentall Discoverie of New England.* 1638; rpt. Boston: Collections of the Massachusetts Historical Society, 3 Ser., 6 (1837), 1–28.

Verrazzano, Giovanni da. *The Voyages of Giovanni da Verrazzano, 1524–1528*, ed. Lawrence C. Wroth. New Haven: Yale University Press, 1970.

Vespucci, Amerigo. *The First Four Voyages.* 1505–1506; rpt. and trans. London: Bernard Quaritch, 1893.

Volney, C. F. [Le Comte de Volney]. *A View of the Soil and Climate of the United States of America*, trans. with occasional remarks by C. B. Brown. 1804; rpt. New York: Hafner Publishing, 1968.

Walpole, Horace. *Journal of the Reign of King George the Third, from the Year 1771 to 1783*, ed. John Doran. 2 vols. London: Richard Bentley, 1859.

The Letters of Horace Walpole, Fourth Earl of Orford, ed. Peter Cunningham. London: Richard Bentley, 1891.

On Modern Gardening, ed. W. S. Lewis. New York: Young Books, 1931.

Was America A Mistake?: An Eighteenth-Century Controversy, ed. Henry Steele Commager and Elmo Giordannetti. Columbia: University of South Carolina Press, 1968.

Washington, George. *The Writings*, ed. John C. Fitzpatrick. 39 vols. Washington, DC: US Government Printing Office, 1931–1944.

Webster, Noah. *An American Dictionary of the English Language.* 1828; rpt. New York: Johnson Reprint Corp., 1970.

The American Spelling Book. 7th edn. Boston: Thomas and Andrews, 1793.

A Collection of Essays and Fugitiv [sic] Writings on Moral, Historical, Political and Literary Subjects. Boston: I. Thomas and E. T. Andrews, 1790.

A Collection of Papers on Political, Literary and Moral Subjects. New York: Webster and Clark, 1843.

A Compendious Dictionary of the English Language. New Haven: Increase Cooke and Co., 1806.

Dissertations on the English Language. 1789; rpt. Gainesville, FL: Scholars' Facsimiles and Reprints, 1951.

A Grammatical Institute of the English Language, Part I. 1783; rpt. Menston, Yorks.: Scolar Press, 1968.

A Grammatical Institute of the English Language, Part II. 1784; rpt. Menston, Yorks.: Scolar Press, 1968.

Letter to John Pickering, on the subject of his Vocabulary; or, Collection of words and phrases, supposed to be peculiar to the United States of America. Boston: West and Richardson, 1817.

The Letters, ed. Harry R. Warfel. New York: Library Publishers, 1953.

Miscellaneous Papers, on Political, and Commercial Subjects. New York: Printed by B. Belden and Co., 1802.

Observations on Languages and on the Errors of Class-Books; addressed to members of the New York Lyceum. Also, Observations on Commerce, addressed to Members of the Mercantile Library Association, in New York. New Haven: Printed by S. Babcock, 1838.

Poems, ed. Ruth Farquhar Warfel and Harry Redcay Warfel. College Park, MD: Harruth Lefraw, 1936.

Sketches of American Policy. 1785; rpt. New York: Scholars' Facsimiles and Reprints, 1937.

Wells, John. *An Oration . . . on the Fourth of July, 1798 . . . Before the Young Men of the City of New-York*. New York: M'Lean and Lang, 1798.

Wesley, John. *Serious Thoughts occasioned by the late Earthquake at Lisbon*. 2nd edn. Bristol: Printed by E. Farley, 1755.

Sermons on Several Occasions. 2 vols. London: J. Kershaw, 1825.

Williams, Samuel. *The Natural and Civil History of Vermont*. Walpole, NH: Isaiah Thomas and David Carlisle, 1794.

Williams, William Carlos. *In the American Grain*. 1925; rpt. Harmondsworth, Middx.: Penguin, 1971.

Williamson, Hugh. 'An Attempt to account for the Change of Climate which has been observed in the Middle Colonies of North America', *Transactions of the American Philosophical Society* I (1769–1770), 272–280.

The History of North Carolina. 2 vols. Philadelphia: Thomas Dobson, 1812.

Observations on the Climate in Different Parts of America . . . Being an Introductory Discourse to the History of North Carolina. New York: T. and J. Swords, 1811.

Wolcott, Oliver. *Memoirs of the Administrations of Washington and John Adams*, ed. George Gibbs. New York: Printed by William van Norden, 1846.

The World Turned Upside Down: Prose and Poetry of the American Revolution, ed. James H. Pickering. London: Kennikat Press, 1975.

SECONDARY SOURCES

Aarsleff, Hans. *The Study of Language in England, 1780–1860*. Princeton University Press, 1967.

Abel, Annie Heloise. 'Trudeau's description of the Upper Missouri', *Missouri Valley Historical Review* 8 Nos. 1–2 (June–September 1921) 149–179.

Abernethy, Thomas P. *Western Lands and the American Revolution*. 1937; rpt. New York: Russell and Russell, 1959.

Abrams, M. H. *The Mirror and the Lamp: Romantic Theory and the Critical Tradition*. 1953; rpt. New York: Norton, 1969.

Abrams, Rochonne. 'The colonial childhood of Meriwether Lewis', *Bulletin, Missouri Historical Society* 34 No. 4 Part 1 (July 1978) 218–227.

Adams, Henry. *History of the United States of America during the Administrations of Jefferson and Madison*, abridged and introd. George Dangerfield and Otey M. Scruggs. Englewood Cliffs NJ: Prentice–Hall, 1963.

Adams, Percy G. 'Benjamin Franklin's defense of the de Fonte hoax', *Princeton University Library Chronicle* 22 No. 3 (Spring 1961) 133–141.

'The historical value of Crèvecoeur's *Voyage dans la haute Pensylvanie et dans New York'*, *American Literature* 25 No. 2 (May 1953) 155–168.

Travelers and Travel Liars, 1660–1800. Berkeley: University of California Press, 1962.

Adams, Richard P. 'Romanticism and the American Renaissance', *American Literature* 23 No. 4 (January 1952) 419–432.

Agresto, John T. 'Liberty, virtue and republicanism: 1776–1787', *Review of Politics* 39 No. 4 (October 1977) 473–504.

Alden, John Richard. *The American Revolution, 1775–1783.* New York: Harper and Row, 1954.

General Gage in America. Baton Rouge: Louisiana State University Press, 1948.

Aldridge, A. Owen. *Early American Literature: A Comparatist Approach.* Princeton University Press, 1982.

Alexander, John K. 'The city of brotherly fear: the poor in late-eighteenth-century Philadelphia', *Cities in American History*, ed. Kenneth Jackson and Stanley Schultz. New York: Knopf, 1972, 79–97.

Allard, Joseph. 'West, Copley and eighteenth-century American provincialism', *Journal of American Studies* 17 No. 3 (December 1982) 391–416.

Allen, Don Cameron. *The Legend of Noah: Renaissance Rationalism in Art, Science, and Letters.* Urbana: University of Illinois Press, 1949.

Allen, Gay Wilson. 'The influence of space on the American literary imagination', *Essays in Honor of Jay B. Hubbell*, ed. Clarence Gohdes, Durham, NC: Duke University Press, 1967, 329–342.

Allen, John L. 'An analysis of the exploratory process', *Geographical Review* 62 (1972) 13–39.

'Geographical conceptions of the Trans-Missouri West, 1673–1806: an historical geosophy'. Unpublished Ph.D. dissertation, Clark University, 1969.

'Geographical knowledge and American images of the Louisiana Territory', *Western Historical Quarterly* 2 No. 2 (April 1971) 151–170.

Passage Through the Garden: Lewis and Clark and the Image of the American Northwest. Urbana: University of Illinois Press, 1975.

'Pyramidal height of land: a persistent myth in the exploration of Western Anglo-America', *International Geography* 2 (1972) 395–396.

Allen, Paul. *The Life of Charles Brockden Brown*, ed. Charles Bennett. Delmar, NY: Scholars' Facsimiles and Reprints, 1975.

Almy, Robert F. 'J. N. Reynolds, Poe and Symmes', *Colophon* New Series, 2 (1937) 227–245.

Alvord, Clarence W. *The Mississippi Valley in British Politics.* 2 vols. Cleveland, OH: Arthur H. Clark Co., 1917.

America: Travel and Exploration, ed. Steven E. Kagle. Bowling Green, OH: Bowling Green State University Popular Press, 1979.

American Literature, 1764–1789: The Revolutionary Years, ed. Everett Emerson. Madison: University of Wisconsin Press, 1977.

The American Territorial System, ed. John Porter Bloom. Athens: Ohio University Press, 1973.

The American Writer and the European Tradition, ed. Margaret Denny and William H. Gilman. Minneapolis: University of Minnesota Press, 1950.

Andrews, William L. 'Goldsmith and Freneau in "The American Village"', *Early American Literature* 5 No. 2 (Fall 1970) 14–23a.

Appleby, Joyce. 'America as a model for the radical French reformers of 1789', *William and Mary Quarterly* 3 Ser., 28 No. 2 (April 1971) 267–286.

Appleton, Jay. *The Experience of Landscape*. London: John Wiley and Sons, 1975.

Arms and Independence: The Military Character of the American Revolution, ed. Ronald Hoffman and Peter J. Albert. Charlottesville, VA: University Press of Virginia, 1984.

Aubin, Robert A. 'Grottoes, geology, and the Gothic revival', *Studies in Philology* 31 No. 3 (July 1934) 408–416.

Augur, Helen. *Passage to Glory: John Ledyard's America*. Garden City, NY: Doubleday, 1946.

Axelrad, Jacob. *Philip Freneau, Champion of Democracy*. Austin: University of Texas Press, 1967.

Axelrod, Alan. *Charles Brockden Brown: An American Tale*. Austin: University of Texas Press, 1983.

Bailey, J. O. *Pilgrims Through Time and Space: Trends and Patterns in Scientific and Utopian Fiction*. 1947; rpt. Westport, CT: Greenwood Press, 1972.

'Sources for Poe's *Arthur Gordon Pym*, "Hans Pfaall", and other pieces', *PMLA* 57 No. 2 (June 1942) 513–535.

Bailyn, Bernard. 'Political experience and Enlightenment ideas in eighteenth-century America', *American Historical Review* 67 No. 2 (January 1962) 339–351.

Baine, Rodney M. *Robert Munford, America's First Comic Dramatist*. Athens: University of Georgia Press, 1967.

Bakeless, John. *Lewis and Clark: Partners in Discovery*. New York: William Morrow and Co., 1947.

'Lewis and Clark's background for exploration', *Washington Academy of Sciences Journal* 44 No. 11 (November 1954) 334–338.

Ball, K. R. 'A great society: the social and political thought of Joel Barlow'. Unpublished Ph.D. dissertation, University of Wisconsin, 1967.

Banning, Lance. *The Jeffersonian Persuasion: Evolution of a Party Ideology*. Ithaca, NY: Cornell University Press, 1978.

Baritz, Loren. 'The idea of the West', *American Historical Review* 66 (April 1961) 618–640.

Baron, Dennis E. *Grammar and Good Taste: Reforming the American Language*. New Haven: Yale University Press, 1982.

Barrell, John. *The Idea of Landscape and the Sense of Place 1730–1840: An Approach to the Poetry of John Clare*. Cambridge University Press, 1972.

Barrow, Thomas C. 'A project for imperial reform: "Hints Respecting the Settlement for our American Provinces", 1763', *William and Mary Quarterly* 3 Ser., 24 No. 1 (January 1967) 108–126.

Bartlett, Richard A. *The New Country: A Social History of the American Frontier, 1776–1890*. New York: Oxford University Press, 1974.

Bates, George E. 'Seventeenth- and eighteenth-century science: a different perspective', *Eighteenth-Century Studies* 9 No. 2 (Winter 1975–76) 178–192.

Batten, Jr, Charles L. *Pleasurable Instruction: Form and Convention in Eighteenth Century Travel Literature*. Berkeley: University of California Press, 1978.

Baugh, Albert C. 'Thomas Jefferson, linguistic liberal', *Studies for William A. Read*, ed. Nathaniel H. Caffee and Thomas A. Kirby. Baton Rouge: Louisiana State University Press, 1940, 88–108.

Baym, Nina. 'Melodramas of beset manhood: how theories of American fiction exclude women authors', *American Quarterly* 33 (1981) 123–139.

Beach, Frank A. 'The descent of instinct', *Instinct: An Enduring Problem in Psychology*, ed.

Robert C. Birney and Richard C. Teevan. New York: Van Nostrand Reinhold, 1961, 165–180.

Becker, Lloyd George. 'Language and landscape: essays on the American search for self-definition'. Unpublished Ph.D. dissertation, State University of New York, Buffalo, 1980.

Bederman, Sanford H. *The Ethnological Contributions of John Ledyard*. Atlanta: Georgia State College, Research Paper No. 4, July 1964.

Beidler, Philip D. 'Franklin's and Crèvecœur's "Literary" Americans', *Early American Literature* 13 No. 1 (Spring 1978) 50–63.

Belknap, Waldron P. *American Colonial Painting*. Cambridge, MA: Harvard University Press, 1959.

Bell, Michael Davitt. *The Development of American Romance: The Sacrifice of Relation*. University of Chicago Press, 1980.

Bennett, Charles E. 'The Charles Brockden Brown canon'. Unpublished Ph.D. dissertation, University of North Carolina, 1974.

'The letters of Charles Brockden Brown: an annotated census', *Resources for American Literary Studies* 6 (Autumn 1976) 164–190.

'A poetical correspondence among Elihu Hubbard Smith, Joseph Bringhurst Jr, and Charles Brockden Brown in *The Gazette of the United States*', *Early American Literature* 12 No. 3 (Winter 1977/78) 277–285.

Bennett, Maurice J. 'A portrait of the artist in eighteenth-century America: Charles Brockden Brown's *Memoirs of Stephen Calvert*', *William and Mary Quarterly* 3 Ser., 39 No. 3 (July 1982) 492–507.

Béranger, Jean F. 'The desire for communication: narrator and narratee in *Letters from an American Farmer*', *Early American Literature* 12 No. 1 (Spring 1977) 73–85.

Bercovitch, Sacvan, *The American Jeremiad*. Madison: University of Wisconsin Press, 1978.

'How the Puritans won the American Revolution', *Massachusetts Review* 17 (1976) 597–630.

Berkhofer, Robert R. 'Jefferson, the Ordinance of 1784, and the origins of the American territorial system', *William and Mary Quarterly* 3 Ser., 29 No. 2 (April 1972) 231–262.

'The republican origins of the American territorial system', *The West of the American People*, ed. Allan G. Bogue, Thomas D. Phillips and James E. Wright. Itasca, IL: F. E. Peacock Publishers, 1970, 152–160.

'Space, time, culture and the new frontier', *Agricultural History* 38 (January 1964) 21–33.

Berman, Eleanor D. *Thomas Jefferson Among the Arts*. New York: The Philosophical Library, 1947.

Bernard, Kenneth. '*Arthur Mervyn*: the ordeal of innocence', *Texas Studies in Literature and Language* 6 No. 4 (Winter 1965) 441–459.

'Charles Brockden Brown and the Sublime', *The Personalist* 45 (1964) 235–249.

Bernhard, Winfred. *Fisher Ames. Federalist and Statesman, 1758–1808*. Chapel Hill: University of North Carolina Press, 1965.

Berthoff, Warner. 'Adventures of a young man: an approach to Charles Brockden Brown', *American Quarterly* 9 (1957) 421–434.

'Brockden Brown: the politics of a man of letters', *The Serif* 3 (December 1966) 3–11.

'Charles Brockden Brown's historical "Sketches": a consideration', *American Literature* 28 No. 2 (May 1956) 147–154.

'A lesson on concealment: Charles Brockden Brown's method in fiction', *Philological Quarterly* 37 (1958) 45–57.

Berthold, Dennis. 'Charles Brockden Brown, *Edgar Huntly*, and the origins of the

American Picturesque', *William and Mary Quarterly* 3 Ser., 41 No. 1 (January 1984) 62–84.

Bestor, Arthur E. 'Patent-office models of the good society: some relationships between social reform and westward expansion', *American Historical Review* 58 No. 3 (April 1953) 505–526.

Bestor, Arthur E., David C. Mearns and Jonathan Daniels. *Three Presidents and their Books*. Urbana: University of Illinois Press, 1962.

Billington, James H. *Fire in the Minds of Men: Origins of the Revolutionary Faith*. New York: Basic Books, 1980.

Binger, Carl. *Revolutionary Doctor: Benjamin Rush, 1746–1813*. New York: W. W. Norton, 1966.

Blake, John B. 'Yellow fever in eighteenth-century America', *Bulletin of the New York Academy of Medicine* 44 (June 1968) 673–686.

Bond, Frank. *Historical Sketch of 'Louisiana' and the Louisiana Purchase*. Washington: Government Printing Office, 1912.

Boorstin, Daniel J. *The Americans: The Colonial Experience*. 1958; rpt. Harmondsworth, Middx.: Penguin, 1965.

  The Discoverers. 1983; rpt. Harmondsworth, Middx.: Penguin, 1986.

  The Exploring Spirit. London: BBC, 1976.

  The Lost World of Thomas Jefferson. 1948; rpt. Boston: Beacon Press, 1960.

Bourne, E. G. 'The travels of Jonathan Carver', *American Historical Review* 11 No. 2 (January 1906) 287–302.

Bowden, Martyn J. 'The Great American Desert and the American frontier, 1800–1882: popular images of the plains', *Anonymous Americans: Explorations in Nineteenth-Century Social History*, ed. Tamara K. Hareven. Englewood Cliffs, NJ: Prentice–Hall, 1971, 48–79.

  'The perception of the western interior of the United States, 1830–1870', *Proceedings of the Association of American Geographers* 1 (1969) 16–21.

Bowden, Mary Weatherspoon. 'In search of Freneau's prison ships', *Early American Literature* 14 No. 2 (Fall 1979) 174–192.

Bowman, Isaiah. 'Geography in the creative experience', *Geographical Review* 28 No. 1 (January 1938) 1–9.

Boynton, Percy H. *The Rediscovery of the Frontier*. 1931; rpt. New York: Greenwood Press, 1968.

Bradbury, Malcolm. 'Dangerous pilgrimages: transatlantic images in fiction (I)', *Encounter* 47 No. 6 (December 1976) 56–67.

Bradsher, Earl M. 'The rise of nationalism in American Literature', *Studies for William A. Read*, ed. Nathaniel M. Caffee and Thomas A. Kirby. Baton Rouge: Louisiana State University Press, 1940, 269–287.

Brancaccio, Patrick. 'Studied ambiguities: *Arthur Mervyn* and the problem of the unreliable narrator', *American Literature* 42 (1970) 18–27.

Branch, E. Douglas. 'Henry Bouquet, professional soldier', *Pennsylvania Magazine of History and Biography* 62 (1938) 41–51.

Brant, Irving. *James Madison, Secretary of State 1800–1809*. New York: The Bobbs–Merrill Co., 1953.

Brebner, John Bartlett. *The Explorers of North America, 1492–1806*. 1933; rpt. New York: Meridian Books, 1964.

Bredeson, Robert C. 'Landscape description in nineteenth-century American travel literature', *American Quarterly* 20 No. 1 (Spring 1968), 86–94.

Breen, T. H. *Puritans and Adventurers: Change and Persistence in Early America*. New York: Oxford University Press, 1980.

Briceland, A. 'The Philadelphia Aurora, the New England Illuminati, and the election of 1800', *The Pennsylvania Magazine of History and Biography* 100 No.1 (January 1976) 3–36.

Bridenbaugh, Carl. *The Spirit of '76: The Growth of American Patriotism before Independence, 1607–1776*. New York: Oxford University Press, 1975.

Bridgman, Richard. 'Jefferson's farmer before Jefferson', *American Quarterly* 14 No. 4 (Winter 1962) 567–577.

Briggs, Asa. 'Cholera and society', *Past and Present* No. 19 (April 1961) 76–96.

Brigham, Clarence S. *History and Bibliography of American Newspapers 1690–1820*. 2 vols. 1947; rpt. Westport, CT: Greenwood Press, 1975.

Bristed, Charles Astor. 'The English language in America', *Cambridge Essays Contributed by Members of the University*. London: John W. Parke and Sons, 1855, 57–78.

British and American Gardens in the Eighteenth Century, ed. Robert P. MacCubbin and Peter Martin. Williamsburg, VA: Colonial Williamsburg Foundation, 1984.

Brock, C. Helen. 'Scotland and American medicine', in William R. Brock, *Scotus Americanus: A summary of the sources for links between Scotland and America in the Eighteenth Century*. Edinburgh University Press, 1982, 114–127.

Brodie, Faun. *Thomas Jefferson: An Intimate History*. New York: W. W. Norton, 1974.

Brown, Alexander D. 'The mysterious death of a hero', *American History Illustrated* 5 No. 9 (March 1971) 18–27.

Brown, Everett Somerville. *Constitutional History of the Louisiana Purchase*. Berkeley: University of California Press, 1920.

Brown, Herbert Ross. *The Sentimental Novel in America, 1789–1860*. Durham, NC: Duke University Press, 1940.

Brown, Ralph H. 'The American geographies of Jedidiah Morse', *Annals of the Association of American Geographers* 31 No. 3 (March 1941) 145–217.

   Historical Geography of the United States. New York: Harcourt, Brace and World, 1948.

   'St George Tucker versus Jedidiah Morse on the subject of Williamsburg', *William and Mary Quarterly* 2 Ser., 20 No. 1 (October 1940) 487–491.

Brown, Roland W. 'Jefferson's contribution to palaeontology', *Journal of the Washington Academy of Sciences* 33 No. 9 (September 1943) 257–259.

Buel, Jr, Richard. *Securing the Revolution. Ideology in American Politics, 1789–1815*. Ithaca, NY: Cornell University Press, 1972.

Buell, Lawrence. *Literary Transcendentalism: Style and Vision in the American Renaissance*. Ithaca, NY: Cornell University Press, 1973.

   'New views of American narrative: a review essay', *Texas Studies in Literature and Language* 19 No. 2 (Summer 1977) 234–246.

Buranelli, Vincent. *Edgar Allan Poe*. 2nd edn. Indianapolis: Bobbs–Merrill, 1977.

Bush, Clive. *The Dream of Reason: American Consciousness and Cultural Achievement from Independence to the Civil War*. London: Edward Arnold, 1977.

Butterfield, Lyman H. 'The reputation of Benjamin Rush', *Pennsylvania History* 17 No. 1 (January 1950) 3–22.

Cairns, William B. *British Criticism of American Writing, 1783–1815*. Madison: University of Wisconsin Studies 1, 1918.

Cappon, Lester J. 'American historical editors before Jared Sparks', *William and Mary Quarterly* 3 Ser., 30 (July 1973) 375–400.

   'Who is the author of *History of the Expedition under the Command of Captains Lewis and Clark* (1814)?' *William and Mary Quarterly* 3 Ser., 19 No. 2 (April 1962) 257–268.

Carpenter, F. I. 'The vogue of Ossian in America', *American Literature* 2 (1930) 405–417.

Carroll, Peter N. *Puritanism and the Wilderness*. London: Columbia University Press, 1966.

Carter, Boyd. 'Poe's debt to Charles Brockden Brown', *Prairie Schooner* 27 (Summer 1953) 190–196.

Carter II, Edward C. 'A "wild Irishman" under every Federalist's bed: naturalization in Philadelphia, 1789–1806', *The Pennsylvania Magazine of History and Biography* 94 (July 1970) 331–346.

Cassedy, James H. *Demography in Early America: Beginnings of the Statistical Mind, 1600–1800*. Cambridge, MA: Harvard University Press, 1969.

'Meteorology and medicine in Colonial America: beginnings of the experimental approach', *Journal of the History of Medicine and Allied Sciences* 24 No. 2 (April 1969) 193–204.

Cawley, Robert Ralston. *Unpathed Waters: Studies in the Influence of Voyages on Elizabethan Literature*. 1940; rpt. New York: Octagon, 1967.

Chamberlain, James F. 'Early American geographies', *Yearbook of the Association of Pacific Geographers* 5 (1939) 23–29.

Chapman, John Jay. *Emerson and Other Essays*. New York: Charles Scribner's Sons, 1898.

Chase, Richard. *The American Novel and Its Tradition*. Garden City, NY: Doubleday, 1957.

Chatters, Roy M. 'The enigmatic Lewis and Clark air gun', *The Record*. Friends of the Library, Washington State University, 34 (1973) 50–60.

Chevignard, Bernard. 'St John de Crèvecœur in the looking glass: *Letters from an American Farmer* and the making of a man of letters', *Early American Literature* 19 No. 2 (Fall 1984) 173–190.

Chidsey, Donald Barr. *Louisiana Purchase*. New York: Crown Publishers, 1972.

Chinard, Gilbert. 'The American Philosophical Society and the early history of forestry in America', *Proceedings of the American Philosophical Society* 89 No. 2 (1945) 444–488.

'Eighteenth-century theories on America as a human habitat', *Proceedings of the American Philosophical Society* 91 No. 1 (February 1947) 25–57.

'Progress and perfectibility in Samuel Miller's intellectual history', *Studies in Intellectual History*, ed. George Boas *et al*. Baltimore: John Hopkins University Press, 1953, 94–122.

Thomas Jefferson: Apostle of Americanism. 2nd edn. Boston: Little, Brown, 1939.

Chittenden, Hiram Martin. *History of Early Steamboat Navigation on the Missouri River*. 2 vols. Cleveland, OH: Arthur H. Clark Co., 1903.

Church, Henry Ward. 'Corneille de Pauw, and the controversy over his *Recherches Philosophiques sur les Américains*', *PMLA* 51 No. 1 (March 1936) 178–206.

Clair, Colin. *A Chronology of Printing*. London: Cassell, 1969.

Clark, David Lee. *Charles Brockden Brown: Pioneer Voice of America*. Durham, NC: Duke University Press, 1952.

'Sources of Poe's "The Pit and the Pendulum"', *Modern Language Notes* 44 (June 1929) 349–356.

'Unpublished letters of Charles Brockden Brown and W. W. Wilkins', University of Texas *Studies in English* 27 No. 1 (June 1948) 75–107.

Clark, Dora Mae. *British Opinion and the American Revolution*. 1930; rpt. New York: Russell and Russell, 1966.

Clark, Harry Hayden. 'The influence of science on American ideas, from 1775 to 1809', *Transactions of the Wisconsin Academy of Sciences, Arts and Letters* 35 (1943) 305–349.

Clark, Robert. *History, Ideology and Myth in American Fiction, 1823–52*. London: Macmillan, 1984.

Clarke, Graham. 'Landscape and geography: approaches to English and American poetry with special reference to Charles Olson'. Unpublished Ph.D. dissertation, University of Essex, 1977.

Cleman, John. 'Ambiguous evil: a study of villains and heroes in Charles Brockden Brown's major novels', *Early American Literature* 10 No. 2 (Fall 1975) 190–219.

Coad, Oral S. 'The Gothic element in American Literature before 1835', *Journal of English and Germanic Philology* 24 No. 1 (1925) 72–93.

Cochrane, Rexmond C. 'Bishop Berkeley and the Progress of Arts and Learning: notes on a literary convention', *Huntington Library Quarterly* 17 No. 3 (May 1954) 229–249.

Cohen, Lester H. 'Eden's constitution: the paradisiacal dream and Enlightenment values in late eighteenth-century literature of the American frontier', *Prospects* 3 (1977) 83–109.

The Revolutionary Histories: Contemporary Narratives of the American Revolution. Ithaca, NY: Cornell University Press, 1980.

Cole, Jr, Charles C. 'Brockden Brown and the Jefferson administration', *Pennsylvania Magazine of History and Biography* 72 No. 3 (July 1948) 253–263.

Coll, Gary. 'Noah Webster: journalist'. Unpublished Ph.D. dissertation, Southern Illinois University, 1971.

Commager, Henry Steele. *Jefferson, Nationalism, and the Enlightenment.* New York: George Braziller, 1975.

Conant, Martha Pike. *The Oriental Tale in England in the Eighteenth Century.* New York: Columbia University Press, 1908.

Conrad, Peter. *The Art of the City: Views and Versions of New York.* New York: Oxford University Press, 1984.

Imagining America. London: Routledge and Kegan Paul, 1980.

Conspiracy: The Fear of Subversion in American History, ed. Richard O. Curry and Thomas M. Brown. New York: Holt, Rinehart and Winston, 1972.

Contrast and Connection, Bicentennial Essays in Anglo-American History, ed. H. C. Allen and Roger Thompson. London: G. Bell and Sons, 1976.

Craft, Harvey M. 'The opposition of mechanistic and organic thought in the major novels of Charles Brockden Brown'. Unpublished Ph.D. dissertation, Tulane University, 1964.

Crary, Catherine S. 'The humble immigrant and the American Dream: some case histories, 1746–1776', *Mississippi Valley Historical Review* 46 (June 1959) 46–66.

Crawford, Polly Pearl. 'Lewis and Clark's Expedition as a source of Poe's "Journal of Julius Rodman"', University of Texas *Studies in English* 12 (1932) 158–170.

Criswell, Elijah Harry. *Lewis and Clark: Linguistic Pioneers.* Columbia: University of Missouri Studies 15 No. 2, 1940.

Cronin, James E. 'Elihu Hubbard Smith and the New York Friendly Club', *PMLA* 64 No. 3 (June 1949) 471–479.

Cronkhite, G. Ferris. 'Freneau's "The House of Night"', *Cornell Library Journal* 8 (1969) 3–19.

Cronon, William. *Changes in the Land: Indians, Colonists, and the Ecology of New England.* New York: Hill and Wang, 1983.

Crosby, Jr, Alfred W. *The Columbian Exchange: The Biological and Cultural Consequences of 1492.* Westport, CT: Greenwood Press, 1972.

Culmsee, Carleton F. *Malign Nature and the Frontier.* Logan: Utah State Monographs 7 No. 2, 1959.

Cumming, W. P. 'Geographical misconceptions of the South-East in the cartography of the seventeenth and eighteenth centuries', *Journal of Southern History* 4 No. 4 (November 1938) 476–492.

Cumont, Franz. *After Life in Roman Paganism.* New Haven: Yale University Press, 1922.

Cunliffe, Marcus. 'Crèvecœur revisited', *Journal of American Studies* 9 No. 2 (August 1975) 129–144.

'Europe and America', *Encounter* 17 (December 1961) 19–29.

George Washington, Man and Monument. New York: New American Library, 1958.

The Nation Takes Shape: 1789–1837. University of Chicago Press, 1959.

Soldiers and Civilians: the Martial Spirit in America, 1775–1865. London: Eyre and Spottiswoode, 1969.

Curley, Thomas M. *Samuel Johnson and the Age of Travel*. Athens: University of Georgia Press, 1976.

Curti, Merle. *The Growth of American Thought*. 3rd edn. New York: Harper and Row, 1964.

The Roots of American Loyalty. New York: Columbia University Press, 1946.

Curtis, Edward E. *The Organization of the British Army in the American Revolution*. 1926; rpt. New York: AMS Press, 1969.

Cutright, Paul Russell. *A History of the Lewis and Clark Journals*. Norman: University of Oklahoma Press, 1976.

'Jefferson's instructions to Lewis and Clark', *Bulletin of the Missouri Historical Society* 22 No. 3 (April 1966) 302–320.

'Lewis and Clark and Du Pratz', *Bulletin of the Missouri Historical Society* 21 No. 1 (October 1964) 31–35.

Lewis and Clark: Pioneering Naturalists. Urbana, Ill.: University of Illinois Press, 1969.

Davie, Donald. 'John Ledyard: the American Traveler and his sentimental journeys', *Eighteenth-Century Studies* 4 No. 1 (Fall 1970) 57–70.

Trying to Explain. Manchester: Carcanet New Press, 1980.

Davis, Andrew M. 'The journey of Moncacht-Apé', *Proceedings of the American Antiquarian Society* N. S., 2 (April 1883) 321–348.

Davis, David Brion. 'Some themes of counter-subversion: an analysis of anti-Masonic, anti-Catholic, and anti-Mormon literature', *Mississippi Valley Historical Review* 47 No. 2 (September 1960) 205–224.

Davis, Richard Beale. 'The Abbé Correa in America, 1812–20', *Transactions of the American Philosophical Society* N. S., 45 No. 2 (May 1955) 85–197.

'America in George Sandys' "Ovid" ', *William and Mary Quarterly* 3 Ser., 4 (July 1947) 297–304.

A Colonial Southern Bookshelf: Reading in the Eighteenth Century. Athens: University of Georgia Press, 1979.

George Sandys, Poet-Adventurer. London: The Bodley Head, 1955.

Intellectual Life in Jefferson's Virginia, 1790–1830. Chapel Hill: University of North Carolina Press, 1964.

DeConde, Alexander. *This Affair of Louisiana*. New York: Charles Scribner's Sons, 1976.

Delanglez, Jean. 'The cartography of the Mississippi', *Mid-America* 30 No. 4 (October 1948) 257–284, and 31 No. 1 (January 1949) 29–52.

D'Elia, Donald J. 'Dr Benjamin Rush and the American medical revolution', *Proceedings of the American Philosophical Society* 110 No. 4 (August 1966) 227–234.

DeVoto, Bernard. 'An inference regarding the expedition of Lewis and Clark', *Proceedings of the American Philosophical Society* 99 No. 4 (August 1955) 185–194.

Westward the Course of Empire. London: Eyre and Spottiswoode, 1953.

Dewhurst, Kenneth. *Dr Thomas Sydenham: His Life and Original Writings*. Berkeley: University of California Press, 1966.

Dillon, Richard. *Meriwether Lewis: A Biography*. New York: Coward–McCann, 1965.

'Stephen Long's Great American Desert', *Proceedings of the American Philosophical Society* 111 No. 2 (1967) 93–108.

Dondore, Dorothy Anne. *The Prairie and the Making of Middle America: Four Centuries of Description*. Cedar Rapids, Iowa: Torch Press, 1926.

Douglass, Elisha P. 'Fisher Ames, spokesman for New England Federalism', *Proceedings of the American Philosophical Society* 103 (October 1959) 693–715.

Dubos, René. *The Dreams of Reason: Science and Utopias.* New York: Columbia University Press, 1961.

Duffy, John. 'An account of the epidemic fever in New York from 1791 to 1822', *New York Historical Society Quarterly* 50 No. 4 (October 1966) 332–364.

Epidemics in Colonial America. Baton Rouge: Louisiana State University Press, 1953.

Dumbauld, Edward. *Thomas Jefferson Tourist, Being an Account of His Journeys in the United States of America, England, France, Italy, the Low Countries, and Germany.* Norman: University of Oklahoma Press, 1946.

Dunlap, William. *The Life of Charles Brockden Brown: Together with Selections from the Rarest of his Printed Works, from his Original Letters, and from his Manuscripts Never Before Published.* 2 vols. Philadelphia: James P. Parke, 1815.

Dupuy, R. Ernest and Trevor N. Dupuy, *Military Heritage of America.* London: McGraw Hill, 1956.

Durey, Michael. *The Return of the Plague: British Society and the Cholera 1831–2.* Dublin: Gill and MacMillan, 1979.

Eberwein, Jane Donahue. 'Freneau's "The Beauties of Santa Cruz"', *Early American Literature* 12 No. 3 (Winter 1977/78) 271–276.

Eblen, Jack E. 'Origins of the United States colonial system: the Ordinance of 1787', *Wisconsin Magazine of History* 51 (Summer 1968) 294–314.

Echeverria, Durand. *Mirage in the West: A History of the French Image of American Society to 1815.* Princeton University Press, 1957.

Edelberg, Cynthia Dubin. 'The shaping of a political poet: five newfound verses by Jonathan Odell', *Early American Literature* 18 No. 1 (Spring 1983) 45–70.

Eisenger, Chester E. 'Land and loyalty: literary expressions of agrarian nationalism in the seventeenth and eighteenth centuries', *American Literature* 21 No. 2 (May 1949) 160–178.

Ekirch, Jr, Arthur A. *Man and Nature in America.* New York: Columbia University Press, 1963.

Elliott, Emory. *Revolutionary Writers: Literature and Authority in the New Republic, 1725–1810.* New York: Oxford University Press, 1982.

Elliott, J. H. *The Old World and the New.* Cambridge University Press, 1970.

Ellis, Havelock. *The Dance of Life.* Boston: Houghton Mifflin, 1923.

Ellis, Joseph J. *After the Revolution: Profiles in Early American Culture.* New York: Norton, 1979.

Emerson, Oliver F. 'Notes on Gilbert Imlay, early American writer', *PMLA* 39 No. 2 (June 1924) 406–439.

Engell, James. *The Creative Imagination: Enlightenment to Romanticism.* Cambridge, MA: Harvard University Press, 1981.

Engell, John Frederick. 'Brackenridge, Brown, Cooper and the roots of the American novel'. Unpublished Ph.D. dissertation, University of North Carolina, Chapel Hill, 1982.

Ernst, Robert. 'The asylum of the oppressed', *South Atlantic Quarterly* 40 (January 1941) 1–10.

Ewers, John C. 'The awesome bear in Plains Indian art', *American Indian Art* 7 (Summer 1982) 36–45.

The Eye of Thomas Jefferson, ed. William Howard Adams. Washington, DC: National Gallery of Art, 1976.

Fagin, N. Bryllion. *William Bartram, Interpreter of the American Landscape.* Baltimore: Johns Hopkins University Press, 1933.

Farrand, Max. 'The Indian boundary line', *American Historical Review* 10 No. 4 (July 1905) 782–791.

Federman, Donald. 'The measure of all things: the conflict of art and biology in American natural history writing'. Unpublished Ph.D. dissertation, Syracuse University, 1975.

Fellows, Otis E. and Stephen F. Milliken. *Buffon*. New York: Twayne Publishers, 1972.

Fender, Stephen. *American Literature in Context I, 1620–1830*. London: Methuen, 1983.
  Plotting the Golden West: American Literature and the Rhetoric of the California Trail. Cambridge University Press, 1981.

Ferguson, Robert A. *Law and Letters in American Culture*. Cambridge, MA: Harvard University Press, 1984.

Ferril, Thomas Hornsby. 'Writing in the Rockies', *Rocky Mountain Reader*, ed. Ray B. West. New York: E. P. Dutton & Co., 1946, 395–403.

Fiedler, Leslie A. *Love and Death in the American Novel*. 2nd edn, 1967; rpt. London: Paladin, 1970.

Fisher, Vardis. *Suicide or Murder: The Strange Death of Governor Meriwether Lewis*. Chicago: Swallow Press, 1962.

Flanders, Jane T. 'Charles Brockden Brown and William Godwin: parallels and divergencies'. Unpublished Ph.D. dissertation, University of Wisconsin, 1965.

Fletcher, F. T. H. *Montesquieu and English Politics (1750–1800)*. London: Edward Arnold, 1939.

Flexner, James Thomas. 'George Washington as an art collector', *The American Art Journal* 4 (Spring 1972) 24–35.
  That Wilder Image: The Painting of America's Native School from Thomas Cole to Winslow Homer. Boston: Little, Brown, 1962.

Fliegelman, Jay. *Prodigals and Pilgrims: The American revolution against patriarchal authority, 1750–1800*. Cambridge University Press, 1982.

Foner, Eric. *Tom Paine and Revolutionary America*. New York: Oxford University Press, 1976.

Ford, Amelia Clewley. 'Colonial precedents of our national land system as it existed in 1800', *Bulletin of the University of Wisconsin* No. 352, History Series 2 No. 2 (1910) 321–478.

Ford, Emily Ellsworth Fowler. *Notes on the Life of Noah Webster*. 2 vols. New York: Privately printed, 1912.

Foucault, Michel. *Madness and Civilisation: A History of Insanity in the Age of Reason*. London: Tavistock, 1967.

Franklin, Wayne. *Discoverers, Explorers, Settlers: The Diligent Writers of Early America*. University of Chicago Press, 1979.
  'Speaking and touching: the problem of inexpressibility in American travel books', *Exploration* 4 No. 1 (December 1976) 1–14.

Fraser, Leon. 'English opinion of the American Constitution and Government'. Unpublished Ph.D. dissertation, Columbia University, 1915.

Freeman, Douglas Southall. *George Washington: A Biography*. 7 vols. London: Eyre and Spottiswoode, 1948–1957.

Freimarck, Vincent. 'Timothy Dwight's Brief Lives in *Travels in New England and New York*', *Early American Literature* 8 No. 1 (Spring 1973) 44–58.

Friedman, Lawrence J. *Inventors of the Promised Land*. New York: Knopf, 1975.

Friis, Herman R. 'Cartographic and geographic activities of the Lewis and Clark Expedition', *Journal of the Washington Academy of Sciences* 44 No. 11 (November 1954) 338–351.

Fuller, J. F. C. *The Conduct of War, 1789–1961*. 1961; rpt. London: Methuen, 1972.

Furrow, Sharon. 'Psyche and setting: Poe's picturesque landscapes', *Criticism* 15 (1972) 16–27.

Fussell, Edwin. *Frontier: American Literature and the American West.* Princeton University Press, 1965.

'*Wieland*: a literary and historical reading', *Early American Literature* 18 No. 2 (Fall 1983) 171–186.

Fussell, Paul. *The Rhetorical World of Augustan Humanism.* Oxford: Clarendon Press, 1965.

Galinsky, Hans. 'Exploring the "exploration report", and its image of the overseas world: Spanish, French, and English variants of a common form type in early American Literature', *Early American Literature* 12 No. 1 (Spring 1977) 5–24.

Garrow, Scott. 'Character transformation in *Wieland*', *Southern Quarterly* 4 (April 1964) 308–318.

Gaston, James Clinton. 'An anthology of poems dealing with the American Revolution taken from prominent London magazines and newspapers, 1763–1783'. Unpublished Ph.D. dissertation, University of Oklahoma, 1975.

Geer, Curtis Manning. *The Louisiana Purchase and the Westward Movement.* Philadelphia: G. Barrie and Sons, 1904.

The Genius of the Place: The English Landscape Garden 1620–1820, ed. John Dixon Hunt and Peter Willis. London: Paul Elek, 1975.

Geographies of the Mind: Essays in Historical Geosophy in Honor of John Kirtland Wright, ed. David Lowenthal and Martyn J. Bowden. New York: Oxford University Press, 1976.

Gerbi, Antonello. *The Dispute of the New World: The History of a Polemic, 1750–1900.* Revised edn, trans. Jeremy Moyle. Pittsburgh: University of Pittsburgh Press, 1973.

Gillette, David D. 'Thomas Jefferson's pursuit of illusory fauna', *Frontiers* 40 (Spring 1976) 16–21.

Gilmore, Michael T. 'Eighteenth-century oppositional ideology and Hugh Henry Brackenridge's *Modern Chivalry*', *Early American Literature* 13 No. 2 (Fall 1978) 181–192.

Glacken, Clarence. *Traces on the Rhodian Shore: Nature and Culture in Western Thought from Ancient Times to the End of the Eighteenth Century.* Berkeley: University of California Press, 1967.

Goldstein, Thomas. 'Geography in fifteenth-century Florence', *Merchants and Scholars: Essays in the History of Exploration and Trade*, ed. John Parker. Minneapolis: University of Minnesota Press, 1965, 9–32.

Goodman, Nathan G. *Benjamin Rush, Physician and Citizen, 1746–1813.* Philadelphia: University of Pennsylvania Press, 1934.

Gould, Peter and Rodney White. *Mental Maps.* Harmondsworth, Middx: Penguin, 1974.

Grabo, Norman S. *The Coincidental Art of Charles Brockden Brown.* Chapel Hill: University of North Carolina Press, 1981.

Green, Martin. 'The God that neglected to come: American Literature, 1780–1820', *American Literature to 1900*, ed. Marcus Cunliffe, 1973; rpt. London: Sphere Books, 1975, 72–105.

Greene, Jack P. 'Paine, America, and the "modernization" of political consciousness', *Political Science Quarterly* 93 No. 1 (Spring 1978) 73–92.

Greene, John C. *American Science in the Age of Jefferson.* Ames: Iowa State University Press, 1984.

'Science and the public in the age of Jefferson', *Isis* 49 No. 1 (March 1958) 13–28.

Grids: Format and Image in 20th Century Art, introd. Rosalind Krauss. New York: Pace Gallery, 1980.

Griffith, John. '*The Columbiad* and *Greenfield Hill*: history, poetry and ideology in the late eighteenth century', *Early American Literature* 10 No. 3 (Winter 1975/76) 235–250.

Griswold, A. Whitney. 'The agrarian democracy of Thomas Jefferson', *American Political Science Review* 40 No. 4 (August 1946) 657–681.

Guinness, Ralph B. 'The purpose of the Lewis and Clark Expedition', *Mississippi Valley Historical Review* 20 No. 1 (June 1933) 90–100.

Hales, John. 'The landscape of tragedy: Crèvecœur's "Susquehanna"', *Early American Literature* 20 No. 1 (Spring 1985) 39–63.

Halliburton, David. *Edgar Allan Poe: A Phenomenological View*. Princeton University Press, 1973.

Hardin, Garrett. 'The threat of clarity', *American Journal of Psychiatry* 114 No. 5 (November 1957) 392–396.

Hargrove, Jr, Richard J. *General John Burgoyne*. London: Associated University Presses, 1983.

Harkey, Joseph J. 'The *Don Quixote* of the frontier: Brackenridge's *Modern Chivalry*', *Early American Literature* 8 No. 2 (Fall 1973) 193–203.

Harrison, Bernard. *Henry Fielding's Tom Jones: The Novelist as Moral Philosopher*. London: Sussex University Press, 1975.

Harrisson, Barbara. *Orang-Utan*. London: Collins, 1962.

Haverstock, Mary Sayre. *An American Bestiary*. New York: Harry N. Abrams, 1979.

Hawke, David Freeman. *Benjamin Rush, Revolutionary Gadfly*. New York: Bobbs–Merrill, 1971.

  Those Tremendous Mountains: The Story of the Lewis and Clark Expedition. New York: Norton, 1980.

Hazen, Charles D. *Contemporary American Opinion of the French Revolution*. Baltimore: Johns Hopkins University Studies in Historical and Political Science, Extra Volume 16, 1897.

Hedges, William L. 'Benjamin Rush, Charles Brockden Brown, and the plague year', *Early American Literature* 7 No. 3 (Winter 1973) 295–311.

  'Charles Brockden Brown and the culture of contradictions', *Early American Literature* 9 (1974) 107–142.

  'The myth of the Republic and the theory of American Literature', *Prospects: An Annual of American Cultural Studies* 4 (1979) 101–120.

  'The old world yet: writers and writing in post-Revolutionary America', *Early American Literature* 16 No. 1 (Spring 1981) 3–18.

  'Review of Alan Axelrod, *Charles Brockden Brown: An American Tale*', *Early American Literature* 19 No. 1 (Spring 1984) 85–90.

  'Toward a theory of American Literature, 1765–1800', *Early American Literature* 4 No. 1 (Spring 1969) 5–15.

Heilman, Robert B. *America in English Fiction 1760: 1800. The Influences of the American Revolution*. Baton Rouge: Louisiana State University Press, 1937.

Heimert, Alan. 'Puritanism, the wilderness, and the frontier', *New England Quarterly* 26 No. 3 (September 1953) 361–382.

Hellenbrand, Harold. 'Roads to happiness: rhetorical and philosophical designs in Jefferson's *Notes on the State of Virginia*', *Early American Literature* 20 No. 1 (Spring 1985) 3–23.

Hemenway, Robert E. 'Fiction in the age of Jefferson: the early American novel as intellectual document', *Midcontinent American Studies Journal* 9 No. 1 (Spring 1968) 91–102.

Hemphill, W. Edwin. 'The Jeffersonian background of the Louisiana Purchase', *Mississippi Valley Historical Review* 22 No. 2 (September 1935) 177–190.

Hess, Jeffrey A. 'Sources and aesthetics of Poe's landscape fiction', *American Quarterly* 22 No. 2 Part 1 (Summer 1970) 177–189.

Hicks, Philip Marshall. 'The development of the natural history essay in American literature'. Unpublished Ph.D. dissertation, University of Pennsylvania, 1924.

Hill, Christopher. *The World Turned Upside Down: Radical Ideas During the English Revolution*. London: Temple Smith, 1972.

Hindle, Brooke. *The Pursuit of Science in Revolutionary America, 1735–1789*. Chapel Hill: University of North Carolina Press, 1956.

Hinkhouse, Fred J. *The Preliminaries of the American Revolution as Seen in the English Press, 1763–1775*. New York: Columbia University Press, 1926.

Hipple, Jr, Walter John. *The Beautiful, the Sublime, and the Picturesque in Eighteenth-Century British Aesthetic Theory*. Carbondale: Southern Illinois University Press, 1957.

Hodgen, Margaret T. 'Montaigne and Shakespeare again', *Huntington Library Quarterly* 16 (1952) 23–42.

Hofstadter, Richard. *The Idea of a Party System: The Rise of Legitimate Opposition in the United States, 1780–1840*. Berkeley: University of California Press, 1969.

Hollon, W. Eugene. *Frontier Violence: Another Look*. New York: Oxford University Press, 1974.

Holloway, David. *Lewis and Clark and the Crossing of North America*. London: Weidenfeld and Nicolson, 1974.

Honour, Hugh. *New Golden Land: European Images of America from the Discoveries to the Present Time*. New York: Pantheon Books, 1975.

A Hotbed of Genius: The Scottish Enlightenment, 1730–90, ed. David Daiches, Peter Jones and Jean Jones. Edinburgh University Press, 1986.

Howard, Leon. *The Connecticut Wits*. University of Chicago Press, 1943.

Howe, John R. *The Changing Political Thought of John Adams*. Princeton University Press, 1966.

'Republican thought and the political violence of the 1790s', *American Quarterly* 19 No. 2 (Summer 1967) 147–165.

Howe, Mark Anthony DeWolfe. 'The capture of some fugitive verses', *Proceedings of the Massachusetts Historical Society* 43 (1910) 237–241.

Hudleston, Francis J. *Gentleman Johnny Burgoyne*. Indianapolis: Bobbs–Merrill, 1927.

Hughes, Philip Russell. 'Archetypal patterns in *Edgar Huntly*', *Studies in the Novel* 5 (Summer 1973) 176–189.

Hughes, Robert. *The Shock of the New: Art and the Century of Change*. London: BBC, 1980.

Hume, Robert D. 'Charles Brockden Brown and the uses of the Gothic: a re-assessment', *Emerson Society Quarterly* 18 (1972) 10–18.

'Gothic versus Romantic: a revaluation of the Gothic novel', *PMLA* 84 (1969) 282–290.

Humphries, R. A. 'Lord Shelburne and the Proclamation of 1763', *English Historical Review* 49 No. 194 (April 1934) 241–264.

Hunt, John Dixon. *The Figure in the Landscape: Poetry, Painting, and Gardening during the Eighteenth Century*. Baltimore: Johns Hopkins University Press, 1976.

Hunter, J. Paul. *Occasional Form: Henry Fielding and the Chains of Circumstance*. Baltimore: Johns Hopkins University Press, 1975.

The Reluctant Pilgrim: Defoe's Emblematic Quest for Form in 'Robinson Crusoe'. Baltimore: Johns Hopkins University Press, 1966.

Hussey, Christopher. *English Gardens and Landscapes, 1700–1750*. London: Country Life, 1967.

The Picturesque: Studies in a Point of View. 1927; rpt. Hamden, CT: Archon Books, 1967.

Huxley, Aldous. 'Wordsworth in the tropics', *Collected Essays*. London: Chatto and Windus, 1960.

Irwin, John T. *American Hieroglyphics: The Symbol of the Egyptian Hieroglyphics in the American Renaissance*. New Haven: Yale University Press, 1980.

Jackson, Donald. 'Jefferson, Meriwether Lewis, and the reduction of the United States Army', *Proceedings of the American Philosophical Society* 124 (April 1980) 91–96.

'The race to publish Lewis and Clark', *Pennsylvania Magazine of History and Biography* 85 (April 1961) 163–177.

'Some advice for the next editor of Lewis and Clark', *Bulletin of the Missouri Historical Society* 24 No. 1 (October 1967) 52–62.

'Some books carried by Lewis and Clark', *Bulletin of the Missouri Historical Society* 16 No. 1 (October 1959) 3–13.

Thomas Jefferson and the Stony Mountains: Exploring the West from Monticello. Urbana: University of Illinois Press, 1980.

Jackson, John Brinckerhoff. *Discovering the Vernacular Landscape*. New Haven: Yale University Press, 1984.

Landscapes: Selected Writings of J. B. Jackson, ed. Ervin H. Zube. Amherst: University of Massachusetts Press, 1970.

'The meanings of "landscape"', *Kulturgeografi* 88 (1964) 47–50.

The Necessity for Ruins and Other Topics. Amherst: University of Massachusetts Press, 1980.

'The order of a landscape: reason and religion in Newtonian America', *The Interpretation of Ordinary Landscapes*, ed. D. W. Meinig. New York: Oxford University Press, 1979, 153–163.

James, Stuart B. 'Western American space and the human imagination', *Western Humanities Review* 24 (Spring 1970) 147–155.

Jefferson and the Arts: An Extended View, ed. William Howard Adams. Washington, DC: National Gallery of Art, 1976.

Jehlen, Myra. 'J. Hector St John Crèvecœur: a monarcho-anarchist in Revolutionary America', *American Quarterly* 31 (1979) 204–222.

Johnson, Barbara. 'The frame of reference: Poe, Lacan, Derrida', *Yale French Studies* 55–56 (1977) 457–505.

Johnson, Hildegard B. *The Orderly Landscape: Landscape Tastes and the United States Survey*. Minneapolis: James Ford Bell Library, 1977.

Order Upon the Land: The United States Rectangular Land Survey and the Upper Mississippi Country. New York: Oxford University Press, 1976.

Jones, Howard Mumford. 'The colonial impulse: an analysis of the "promotion" literature of colonization', *Proceedings of the American Philosophical Society* 90 No. 2 (May 1946) 131–161.

O Strange New World: American Culture, the Formative Years. New York: Viking Press, 1964.

Jordan, Cynthia S. 'On rereading *Wieland*: "the folly of precipitate conclusions"', *Early American Quarterly* 16 No. 2 (Fall 1981) 154–174.

Jordan, Terry G. *The European Culture Area: A Systematic Geography*. New York: Harper and Row, 1973.

Jordan, Winthrop D. *White Over Black: American Attitudes Toward the Negro, 1550–1812*. 1968; rpt. Harmondsworth. Middx: Pelican, 1969.

Kallen, Horace M. 'The arts and Thomas Jefferson', *Ethics* 53 No. 4 (July 1943) 269–283.

Kammen, Michael, *A Season of Youth: The American Revolution and the Historical Imagination*. New York: Knopf, 1978.

Kaplan, Sidney. '*The History of New Hampshire:* Jeremy Belknap as literary craftsman',

William and Mary Quarterly 3 Ser., 21 No. 1 (January 1964) 18–39.

'An introduction to *Pym*', *Poe: A Collection of Critical Essays*, ed. Robert Regan. Englewood Cliffs, NJ: Prentice–Hall, 1967, 145–163.

Kasson, Joy S. *Artistic Voyagers: Europe and the American Imagination in the Works of Irving, Allston, Cole, Cooper, and Hawthorne.* Westport, CT: Greenwood Press, 1982.

Kellogg, Louise P. 'The mission of Jonathan Carver', *Wisconsin Magazine of History* 12 (1928) 127–145.

Kendrick, T. D. *The Lisbon Earthquake.* London: Methuen, 1956.

Kerber, Linda K. *Federalists in Dissent: Imagery and Ideology in Jeffersonian America.* Ithaca, NY: Cornell University Press, 1970.

Ketterer, David. *New Worlds for Old: The Apocalyptic Imagination, Science Fiction, and American Literature.* Bloomington: Indiana University Press, 1974.

Kimball, Arthur G. *Rational Fictions: A Study of Charles Brockden Brown.* McMinnville, Oregon: Linfield Research Institute, 1968.

'Savages and savagism: Brockden Brown's dramatic irony', *Studies in Romanticism* 6 (1967) 214–225.

Kimball, Fiske. 'Jefferson and the arts', *Proceedings of the American Philosophical Society* 87 No. 3 (July 1943) 238–246.

Thomas Jefferson, Architect, 1916; rpt. introd. Frederick D. Nichols. New York: Da Capo Press, 1968.

Kimball, Marie. 'Jefferson's works of art at Monticello', *Antiques* 59 No. 4 (April 1951) 297–299.

Jefferson, The Scene of Europe. New York: Coward–McCann, 1950.

King, Lester S. *The Medical World of the Eighteenth Century.* University of Chicago Press, 1958.

King-Hele, Desmond. *Doctor of Revolution: The Life and Genius of Erasmus Darwin.* London: Faber and Faber, 1977.

Kitagawa, Joseph M. 'Ainu bear festival', *History of Religions* 1 No. 1 (Summer 1961) 95–151.

Klinefelter, Walter. 'Lewis Evans and his maps', *Transactions of the American Philosophical Society* 61 Part 7 (July 1971) 1–65.

Knox, J. Wendell. *Conspiracy in American Politics, 1787–1815.* 1966; rpt. New York: Arno Press, 1972.

Knudson, Jerry W. 'Newspaper reaction to the Louisiana Purchase', *Missouri Historical Review* 63 No. 2 (January 1969) 182–213.

Kolodny, Annette. *The Land Before Her: Fantasy and Experience of the American Frontiers, 1630–1860.* Chapel Hill: University of North Carolina Press, 1984.

The Lay of the Land: Metaphor as Experience and History in American Life and Letters. Chapel Hill: University of North Carolina Press, 1975.

Kopperman, Paul E. *Braddock at the Monongahela.* Pittsburgh: University of Pittsburgh Press, 1977.

Kraus, Michael. 'America and the utopian ideal in the eighteenth century', *Mississippi Valley Historical Review* 22 No. 4 (March 1936) 486–504.

'Literary relations between Europe and America in the eighteenth century', *William and Mary Quarterly* 3 Ser., 1 No. 3 (July 1944) 210–234.

Krause, Sidney J. '*Edgar Huntly* and the American nightmare', *Studies in the Novel* 13 (Fall 1981) 294–302.

Krieg, Joann Peck. 'Charles Brockden Brown and the empire of romance'. Unpublished Ph. D. dissertation, City University of New York, 1979.

Kropf, Carl R. 'The nationalistic criticism of early American literature', *Early American Literature* 18 No. 1 (Spring 1983) 17–30.

Krutch, Joseph Wood. *Edgar Allan Poe: A Study in Genius.* 1926; rpt. New York: Russell and Russell, 1965.

Kunzle, David. 'Bruegel's proverb painting and the world upside down', *The Art Bulletin* 59 No. 2 (June 1977) 197–202.

    'World upside down: the iconography of a European broadsheet type', *The Reversible World: Symbolic Inversion in Art and Society*, ed. Barbara A. Babcock, Ithaca, NY: Cornell University Press, 1978, 39–94.

Kupperman, Karen Ordahl. 'Fear of hot climates in the Anglo-American colonial experience', *William and Mary Quarterly* 3 Ser., 41 No. 2 (April 1984) 213–240.

Kushner, Howard I. 'The suicide of Meriwether Lewis: a psychoanalytic inquiry', *William and Mary Quarterly* 3 Ser., 38 No. 3 (July 1981) 464–481.

Kyle, Carol A. 'That poet Freneau: a study of the imagistic success of *The Pictures of Columbus*', *Early American Literature* 9 No. 1 (Spring 1974) 62–70.

LaCapra, Dominick. *History and Criticism.* Ithaca, NY: Cornell University Press, 1985.

Laird, Charlton, 'Etymology, Anglo-Saxon, and Noah Webster', *American Speech* 21 No. 1 (February 1946) 3–15.

Langford, Nathaniel Pitt. 'The Louisiana Purchase and preceding Spanish intrigues for the dismemberment of the Union', *Minnesota Historical Society Collections* 9 (1908) 453–508.

Lawson-Peebles, R. 'Henry George the prophet', *Journal of American Studies* 10 No. 1 (April 1976) 37–51.

Leary, Lewis. *Soundings: Some Early American Writers.* Athens: University of Georgia Press, 1975.

    That Rascal Freneau: A Study in Literary Failure. 1942; rpt. New York: Octagon Books, 1971.

    'The dream visions of Philip Freneau', *Early American Literature* 11 No. 2 (Fall 1976) 156–182.

Lease, Benjamin. *Anglo-American Encounters: England and the Rise of American Literature.* Cambridge University Press, 1981.

Lee, Robert Edson. *From West to East: Studies in the Literature of the American West.* Urbana: University of Illinois Press, 1966.

Legacies of the American Revolution, ed. Larry R. Gerlach, James A. Dolph, and Michael L. Nicholls. Salt Lake City: Utah State University Press, 1978.

Lehmann-Hartleben, Karl. 'Thomas Jefferson, archaeologist', *American Journal of Archaeology* 47 No. 2 (April–June 1943) 161–163.

Leonard, Sterling Andrus. *The Doctrine of Correctness in English Usage, 1700–1800.* Madison: University of Wisconsin Studies in Language and Literature No. 25, 1929.

Lever, Ann Butler. '*Vox Populi, Vox Dei*: New England and the French Revolution, 1787–1801'. Unpublished Ph.D. dissertation, University of North Carolina, Chapel Hill, 1972.

Levin, Harry. *The Power of Blackness: Hawthorne, Poe, Melville.* London: Faber and Faber, 1958.

Levine, Robert S. 'Villainy and the fear of conspiracy in Charles Brockden Brown's *Ormond*', *Early American Literature* 15 No. 2 (Fall 1980) 124–140.

Lévi-Strauss, Claude. *Tristes Tropiques*, trans. John and Doreen Weightman. 1973; rpt. Harmondsworth, Middx: Penguin, 1976.

Lewis, Clayton W. 'Style in Jefferson's *Notes on the State of Virginia*', *Southern Quarterly* 14 No. 4 (October 1978) 668–676.

Lewis, G. Malcolm. 'Changing emphases in the description of the great American plains area', *Transactions, Institute of British Geographers* 30 (1962) 75–90.

'Early American explorations and the Cis-Rocky Mountain Desert, 1803–1823', *Great Plains Journal* 5 No. 1 (Fall 1965) 1–11.

'Three centuries of desert concepts in the Cis-Rocky Mountain west', *Journal of the West* 4 No. 3 (July 1965) 457–468.

Lewis, John E. 'A short history of taxonomy from Aristotle to Linnaeus', *Medical Arts and Sciences* 17 (1963) 106–123.

Lewis, Peirce. 'Learning from looking: geographic and other writing about the American cultural landscape', *American Quarterly* 35 (May 1983) 242–261.

Lewis, R. W. B. *The American Adam. Innocence, Tragedy, and Tradition in the Nineteenth Century.* University of Chicago Press, 1955.

Lincoln, A. 'Jefferson and the west', *Pacific Discovery* 17 No. 1 (January–February 1964) 2–9.

'Jefferson the scientist', *Pacific Discovery* 17 No. 4 (July–August 1964) 10–15.

Link, Eugene P. *The Democratic-Republican Societies, 1790–1800.* New York: Columbia University Press, 1942.

Literature as a Mode of Travel, ed. Warner G. Rice. New York: New York Public Library, 1963.

Literary History of the United States, ed. Robert E. Spiller, Willard Thorp, Thomas H. Johnson, Henry Seidel Canby, Richard M. Ludwig, and William L. Gibson. 4th edn, 2 vols. New York: Macmillan, 1974.

Ljungquist, Kent. *The Grand and the Fair: Poe's Landscape Aesthetics and Pictorial Techniques.* Potomac, MD: Scripta Humanistica, 1984.

Lodge, Henry Cabot, *The Life and Letters of George Cabot.* Boston: Little, Brown, 1877.

Loos, John Louis. 'A Biography of William Clark, 1770–1813'. Unpublished Ph.D. dissertation, Washington University, St Louis, 1953.

'William Clark's part in the preparation of the Lewis and Clark Expedition', *Bulletin of the Missouri Historical Society* 10 (1954) 490–511.

Lovejoy, Arthur O. 'Goldsmith and the Chain of Being', *Journal of the History of Ideas* 7 (1946) 91–98.

The Great Chain of Being: A Study in the History of an Idea. 1936; rpt. Cambridge, MA: Harvard University Press, 1964.

Lowenthal, David. 'The American scene', *The Geographical Review* 18 No. 1 (January 1968) 61–68.

'The American way of history', *Columbia University Forum* 9 No. 3 (Summer 1960) 27–32.

'Geography, experience and imagination: toward a geographical epistomology', *Annals of the Association of American Geographers* 51 No. 3 (September 1961) 244–260.

Lucas, Frederick A. 'Thomas Jefferson – palaeontologist', *Natural History* 26 No. 3 (May–June 1926) 328–330.

Lueck, Beth Lynne. 'The Sublime and the Picturesque in American landscape description, 1790–1850'. Unpublished Ph.D. dissertation, University of North Carolina, Chapel Hill, 1983.

Lutwack, Leonard. *The Role of Place in Literature.* Syracuse, NY: Syracuse University Press, 1984.

Lynskey, Winifred. 'The scientific sources of Goldsmith's *Animated Nature*', *Studies in Philology* 40 No. 1 (January 1943) 33–57.

McCarter, Peter Kyle. 'Mother Carey's Jacobin chickens', *Early American Literature* 14 No. 2 (Fall 1979) 163–173.

McDonald, Mary Jane. 'The Lewis and Clark Expedition: the return trip'. Unpublished Ph.D. dissertation, St Louis University, 1970.

McFarland, Joseph. 'The epidemic of Yellow Fever in 1793 and its influence upon Dr Benjamin Rush', *Medical Life* 36 (1929) 465–489.

McKeithan, D. M. 'Two sources of Poe's "Narrative of Arthur Gordon Pym"' University of Texas *Studies in English* 13 (1933) 116–137.

Mackesy, Piers. *The War for America 1775–1783*. London: Longmans, 1964.

McLachlan, James. *Princetonians, 1748–1768: A Biographical Dictionary*. Princeton University Press, 1976.

MacLaren, I. S. 'The aesthetic map of the north, 1845–1859', *Arctic* 38 No. 2 (June 1985) 89–103.

'The aesthetic mapping of nature in the second Franklin Expedition', *Journal of Canadian Studies* 20 No. 1 (Spring 1985) 39–57.

'Alexander Mackenzie and the landscapes of commerce', *Studies in Canadian Literature* 7 No. 2 (1982) 141–150.

'The grandest tour: the aesthetics of landscape in Sir George Back's explorations of the eastern Arctic 1833–1837', *English Studies in Canada* 10 No. 4 (December 1984) 436–456.

'The limits of the Picturesque in British North America', *Journal of Garden History* 5 No. 1 (January–March 1985) 97–111.

'Retaining captaincy of the soul: response to nature in the first Franklin Expedition', *Essays in Canadian Writing* No. 28 (Spring 1984) 57–92.

'Samuel Hearne and the landscapes of discovery', *Canadian Literature* No. 103 (Winter 1984) 27–40.

'". . . where nothing moves and nothing changes": the second Arctic expedition of John Ross (1829–1833)', *Dalhousie Review* 62 (1982) 485–494.

McNeill, William H. *Plagues and Peoples*. 1967; rpt. Harmondsworth, Middx.: Penguin, 1979.

McWilliams, Carey. 'Localism in American criticism', *Southwest Review* 19 No. 4 (July 1934) 410–428.

McWilliams, John. 'The faces of Ethan Allen, 1760–1860', *New England Quarterly* 49 No. 2 (June 1976) 257–282.

Hawthorne, Melville, and the American Character: A looking-glass business. Cambridge University Press, 1984.

Major Writers of Early American Literature, ed. Everett Emerson. Madison: University of Wisconsin Press, 1972.

Malone, Dumas. *Jefferson and his Time*. 6 vols. Boston: Little, Brown, 1948–1981.

Malone, Kemp. 'Benjamin Franklin on spelling reform', *American Speech* 1 No. 2 (October 1925) 96–100.

'A linguistic patriot', *American Speech* 1 No. 1 (1925) 26–31.

Man, Space, and Environment: Concepts in Contemporary Human Geography, ed. Paul Ward English and Robert C. Mayfield. New York: Oxford University Press, 1972.

Manley, Gordon, 'The weather and diseases: some eighteenth-century contributions to observational meteorology', *Notes and Records of the Royal Society* 9 No. 2 (May 1952) 300–307.

Manly, William H. 'The importance of point of view in Brockden Brown's *Wieland*', *American Literature* 35 No. 3 (November 1963) 311–321.

Manwaring, E. W. *Italian Landscape in Eighteenth-Century England*. New York: Oxford University Press, 1925.

Marder, Daniel. *Hugh Henry Brackenridge*. New York: Twayne Publishers, 1967.

Martin, James Kirby and Mark Edward Lender. *A Respectable Army: The Military Origins of the Republic, 1763–1789*. Arlington Heights, IL: Harlan Davidson, 1982.

Martin, Terence. *The Instructed Vision: Scottish Common Sense Philosophy and the Origins of*

American Fiction. Bloomington: University of Indiana Press, 1961.

'The negative character in American fiction', *Toward a New Literary History: Essays in Honor of Arlin Turner*, ed. Louis J. Budd, Edwin H. Cady and Carl L. Anderson. Durham, NC: Duke University Press, 1980, 230–243.

'The negative structures of American Literature', *American Literature* 57 No. 1 (March 1985) 1–22.

Martin, Wendy. 'On the road with the philosopher and the profiteer: a study of Hugh Henry Brackenridge's *Modern Chivalry*', *Eighteenth-Century Studies* 4 No. 3 (Spring 1971) 241–256.

'The rogue and the rational man: Hugh Henry Brackenridge's study of a con man in *Modern Chivalry*', *Early American Literature* 8 No. 2 (Fall 1973) 179–192.

Martinez, Inez Adel. 'Charles Brockden Brown: fictitious historian'. Unpublished Ph.D. dissertation, University of Wisconsin, Madison, 1979.

Marx, Leo. *The American Revolution and the American Landscape*. Washington, DC: American Enterprise Institute for Public Policy Research, 1975.

The Machine in the Garden: Technology and the Pastoral Ideal in America. New York: Oxford University Press, 1964.

'Pastoral ideals and city troubles', *Journal of General Education* 20 (1969) 251–271.

Mattfield, Mary S. '*Modern Chivalry*: the form', *Western Pennsylvania Historical Magazine* 50 (October 1967) 305–326 and 51 (January 1968) 17–29.

Matthiessen, F. O. *American Renaissance: Art and Expression in the Age of Emerson and Whitman*. London: Oxford University Press, 1941.

May, Henry F. *The Enlightenment in America*. New York: Oxford University Press, 1976.

Mencken, H. L. *The American Language: An Inquiry into the Development of English in the United States*. 4th edn. and 2 supplements, abridged with annotations and new material by Raven I. McDavid, Jr. London: Routledge and Kegan Paul, 1963.

Miller, David Cameron. '"Desert places": the meaning of swamp, jungle, and marsh images in nineteenth-century America'. Unpublished Ph.D. dissertation, Brown University, 1982.

Miller, Genevieve. '"Airs, Waters, and Places" in history', *Journal of the History of Medicine and Allied Sciences* 17 No. 1 (January 1962) 129–140.

Miller, Perry. *Errand into the Wilderness*. Cambridge, MA: Harvard University Press, 1956.

'The shaping of the American character', *New England Quarterly* 28 No. 4 (December 1955) 435–454.

Miller, Ralph N. 'American nationalism as a theory of nature', *William and Mary Quarterly* 3 Ser., 12 (1955) 74–95.

Milton, John R. *The Novel of the American West*. Lincoln: University of Nebraska Press, 1980.

Mitchell, Julia P. *St Jean de Crèvecœur*. New York: Columbia University Press, 1916.

Mohr, James C. 'Calculated disillusionment: Crèvecœur's *Letters* reconsidered', *South Atlantic Quarterly* 69 (1970) 354–363.

Monaghan, Frank. *French Travellers in the United States 1765–1932*. New York: Antiquarian Press, 1961.

Monk, Samuel H. *The Sublime: A Study of Critical Theories in XVIII-Century England*. Ann Arbor: University of Michigan Press, 1960.

Montgomery, Franz. 'Alexander Mackenzie's literary assistant', *Canadian Historical Review* 18 No. 3 (September 1937) 301–304.

Moore, Arthur K. *The Frontier Mind: A Cultural Analysis of the Kentucky Frontiersman*. Lexington: University of Kentucky Press, 1957.

Moore, John Robert. 'Goldsmith's degenerate song-birds: an eighteenth-century fallacy in ornithology', *Isis* 34 Part 4 No. 96 (Spring 1943) 324–327.

Morgan, Edmund S. *The Birth of the Republic, 1763–1789*. University of Chicago Press, 1956.

The Gentle Puritan: A Life of Ezra Stiles, 1727–1795. New Haven: Yale University Press, 1962.

Morison, Samuel Eliot. *Christopher Columbus: Admiral of the Ocean Sea*. London: Oxford University Press, 1942.

Morris, Ralph C. 'The notion of a Great American Desert east of the Rockies', *Mississippi Valley Historical Review* 13 No. 2 (September 1926) 190–200.

Morse, James King. *Jedidiah Morse: A Champion of New England Orthodoxy*. New York: Columbia University Press, 1939.

Morse, Sidney E. *Memorabilia in the Life of Jedidiah Morse, D. D.* Boston: Arthur W. Locke, 1867.

Morton, A. L. *The World of the Ranters: Religious Radicalism in the English Revolution*. London: Lawrence and Wishart, 1970.

Morton, Louis, 'The end of formalized warfare', *American Heritage* 6 (August 1955) 12–19, 55.

Moss, Richard J. 'American reactions to the French Revolution, 1789–1801'. Unpublished Ph.D. dissertation, Michigan State University, 1974.

Mott, Frank Luther. *A History of American Magazines*. 5 vols. Cambridge, MA: Harvard University Press, 1957–1968.

Mulvey, Christopher. *Anglo-American Landscapes: A Study of Nineteenth-Century Anglo-American Travel Literature*. Cambridge University Press, 1983.

Mumford, Lewis. *The Golden Day: A Study in American Literature and Culture*. 1957; rpt. New York: Dover Publications, 1968.

Munslow, Alan. 'The historical text as literary artefact: Frederick Jackson Turner and the Frontier Thesis', *Over Here* 5 No. 1 (Spring 1985) 3–16.

Muszynska-Wallace, E. Soteris. 'The sources of *The Prairie*', *American Literature* 21 (May 1949) 191–200.

Nance, William L. 'Satiric elements in Brackenridge's *Modern Chivalry*', *Texas Studies in Literature and Language* 9 (1967–68) 381–389.

Nasatir, A. P. 'John Evans, explorer and surveyor', *Missouri Historical Review* 25 (October 1930–July 1931) 219–239, 432–460, 585–608.

Nash, Gary B. 'The American clergy and the French Revolution', *William and Mary Quarterly* 3 Ser., 22 No. 3 (July 1965) 392–412.

Nash, Roderick. *Wilderness and the American Mind*. New Haven: Yale University Press, 1973.

Nelson, Jr, Lowry. 'Night thoughts on the Gothic Novel', *Yale Review* 52 (December 1962) 236–257.

Nettles, Margaret M. 'The land, the self, and the word: verbal landscapes in William Byrd's *The History of the Dividing Line*, St John de Crèvecœur's *Letters from an American Farmer*, and Washington Irving's *A Tour on the Prairies*'. Unpublished Ph.D. dissertation, University of Georgia, 1983.

Newlin, Claude M. *The Life and Writings of Hugh Henry Brackenridge*. 1932; rpt. Mamaroneck, NY: Paul Appel, 1971.

Newmann, J. H. 'American pronunciation according to Noah Webster'. Unpublished Ph.D. dissertation, Columbia University, 1924.

Nichols, Frederick Doveton and Ralph E. Griswold, *Thomas Jefferson, Landscape Architect*. Charlottesville: University of Virginia Press, 1978.

Nichols, William. 'Lewis and Clark probe the unknown', *American Scholar* 49 (Winter 1979–1980) 94–101.

Nicolson, Marjorie Hope. *Mountain Gloom and Mountain Glory: The Development of the Aesthetics of the Infinite.* Ithaca, NY: Cornell University Press, 1959.
Newton Demands the Muse: Newton's 'Opticks' and the Eighteenth-Century Poets. Princeton University Press, 1946.
Noble, Louis Legrand. *The Life and Works of Thomas Cole*, ed. Elliott S. Vesell. Cambridge, MA: Harvard University Press, 1964.
Nordau, Max. *Degeneration.* London: Heinemann, 1895.
Novak, Barbara. *Nature and Culture: American Landscape and Painting, 1825–1875.* New York: Oxford University Press, 1980.
Nye, Russell Blaine. *The Cultural Life of the New Nation, 1776–1830.* 1960; rpt. New York: Harper and Row, 1963.
'Michel-Guillaume St Jean de Crèvecœur: *Letters from an American Farmer*', *Landmarks in American Writing*, ed. Hennig Cohen. New York: Basic Books, 1969, 33–43.
Ogburn, Jr, Floyd. 'Structure and meaning in Thomas Jefferson's *Notes on the State of Virginia*', *Early American Literature* 15 No. 2 (Fall 1980) 141–150.
Ogden, H. V. S. 'Thomas Burnet's *Telluris Theoria Sacra* and mountain scenery', *English Literary History* 14 No. 2 (June 1947) 139–150.
O'Gorman, Edmundo. *The Invention of America: An Inquiry into the Historical Nature of the New World and the Meaning of its History.* Bloomington: Indiana University Press, 1961.
The Old Northwest in the American Revolution: An Anthology, ed. David Curtis Skaggs. Madison: The State Historical Society of Wisconsin, 1977.
Olschki, Leonardo. 'What Columbus saw on landing in the West Indies', *Proceedings of the American Philosophical Society* 84 (1941) 633–659.
Olson, Charles. *Call Me Ishmael.* 1947; rpt. London: Jonathan Cape, 1967.
O'Neal, William B. *Jefferson's Fine Arts Library. His Selection for the University of Virginia Together with His Own Architectural Books.* Charlottesville: University of Virginia Press, 1976.
Onuf, Peter S. 'Liberty, development, and union: visions of the West in the 1780s', *William and Mary Quarterly* 3 Ser., 43 No. 2 (April 1986) 179–213.
Orians, G. Harrison. 'Censure of American fiction in American Romances and magazines', *PMLA* 52 No. 1 (March 1937) 195–214.
Ormond, Richard. *Sir Edwin Landseer.* London: Thames and Hudson, 1981.
Osborn, Henry F. 'Thomas Jefferson as a palaeontologist', *Science* New Series, 82 No. 2136 (December 1935) 533–538.
Paret, Peter. 'Colonial experience and European military reform at the end of the eighteenth century', *Bulletin of the Institute of Historical Research* 37 (May 1964) 47–59.
Pargellis, Stanley. 'Braddock's defeat', *American Historical Review* 41 (1936) 253–269.
Lord Loudoun in North America. New Haven: Yale University Press, 1933.
Parks, George B. 'The turn to the Romantic in the travel literature of the eighteenth century', *Modern Language Quarterly* 25 (1964) 22–33.
Pattison, William D. *Beginnings of the American Rectangular Land Survey Systems, 1784–1800.* 1957; rpt. New York: Arno Press, 1979.
'The survey of the Seven Ranges', *Ohio Historical Quarterly* 68 (April 1959) 115–140.
Peace and the Peacemakers: The Treaty of 1783, ed. Ronald Hoffman and Peter J. Albert. Charlottesville: University Press of Virginia, 1986.
Pearce, Roy Harvey. *Savagism and Civilization: A Study of the Indian and the American Mind.* Baltimore: Johns Hopkins University Press, 1965.
'The significances of the captivity narrative', *American Literature* 19 No. 1 (March 1947) 1–20.

Pearcy, Lee T. *Mediated Muse: English Translations of Ovid, 1560–1700*. Hamden, CT: Archon Books, 1984.

Peck, John Wells. 'Symmes' theory', *Ohio Archaeological and Historical Quarterly* 18 (1909) 28–42.

Peckham, Howard H. *The Colonial Wars, 1689–1762*. University of Chicago Press, 1964.

Peckham, Morse. 'Towards a theory of Romanticism', *PMLA* 66 No. 2 (March 1951) 5–23.

Peden, William. 'Thomas Jefferson and Charles Brockden Brown', *Maryland Quarterly* 2 (1944) 65–68.

Perry, E. S. 'Time and the land: the work of the American historians during the generation of the American Revolution'. Unpublished Ph.D. dissertation, Selwyn College, Cambridge, 1977.

Persons, Stow. 'The cyclical theory of history in eighteenth-century America', *American Quarterly* 5 (1954) 147–163.

Peterson, Merrill D. *Thomas Jefferson and the New Nation: A Biography*. New York: Oxford University Press, 1970.

Phelps, Dawson. 'The tragic death of Meriwether Lewis', *William and Mary Quarterly* 3 Ser., 13 No. 3 (July 1956) 305–318.

Philbrick, Francis S. *The Rise of the West, 1754–1830*. New York: Harper and Row, 1965.

Philbrick, Thomas. 'Crèvecœur as New Yorker', *Early American Literature* 11 No. 1 (Spring 1976) 22–30.

St John de Crèvecœur. New York: Twayne Publishers, 1970.

Pickering, Octavius. *The Life of Timothy Pickering*. 4 vols. Boston: Little, Brown, 1867.

Plumstead, A. W. 'Crèvecœur: a "man of sorrows" and the American Revolution', *Massachusetts Review* 17 (1976) 286–301.

Pochmann, Henry A. *German Culture in America: Philosophical and Literary Influences, 1600–1900*. Madison: University of Wisconsin Press, 1961.

Pocock, J. G. A. *The Machiavellian Moment*. Princeton University Press, 1975.

Poirier, Richard. *A World Elsewhere: The Place of Style in American Literature*. New York: Oxford University Press, 1966.

Pol, A. D. 'The idea of moral landscape in selected prose writings of the early American Revolutionary period (1782–1835)'. Unpublished MA dissertation, University of Warwick, 1977.

Pollin, Burton R. *Discoveries in Poe*. Notre Dame, IN: University of Notre Dame Press, 1970.

'Poe and Godwin', *Nineteenth-Century Fiction* 20 (December 1965) 237–253.

'Poe's *Pym* and contemporary reviewers', *Studies in American Fiction* 2 (1974) 37–56.

Porte, Joel. 'In the hands of an angry God: religious terror in Gothic Fiction', *The Gothic Imagination: Essays in Dark Romanticism*, ed. G. R. Thompson. Pullman: Washington State University Press, 1974, 42–64.

Powell, J. H. *Bring Out Your Dead: The Great Plague of Yellow Fever in Philadelphia in 1793*. Philadelphia: University of Pennsylvania Press, 1949.

Pratt, Dallas. 'Discovery of a world: early maps showing America', *Antiques* 96 (December 1969) 900–906 and 97 (January 1970) 128–134.

Price, Martin. 'The Picturesque moment', *From Sensibility to Romanticism: Essays Presented to Frederick A. Pottle*, ed. Frederick W. Hilles and Harold Bloom. New York: Oxford University Press, 1965, 259–292.

Pyles, Thomas. *Words and Ways of American English*. 1952; rpt. London: Andrew Melrose, 1954.

Quinn, Arthur Hobson. *Edgar Allan Poe: A Critical Biography*. 1941; rpt. New York: Cooper Square Publishers, 1969.

Quinn, Patrick F. *The French Face of Edgar Poe*. 1954; rpt. Carbondale: Southern Illinois University Press, 1971.

Rahv, Philip, 'Paleface and Redskin', *Literature and the Sixth Sense*. London: Faber and Faber, 1970, 1–6.

Rainwater, Catherine, 'Poe's landscape tales and the Picturesque tradition', *Southern Literary Journal* 16 (Spring 1984) 30–43.

Rapping, Elayne Antler. 'Theory and experience in Crèvecœur's America', *American Quarterly* 19 (1967) 707–718.

Ray, Verne F. and Nancy Oestreich Lurie. 'The contributions of Lewis and Clark to ethnography', *Journal of the Washington Academy of Sciences* 44 No. 11 (November 1954) 358–370.

Read, Allen Walker. 'American projects for an academy to regulate speech', *PMLA* 51 No. 4 (December 1936) 1,141–1,179.

'British recognition of American speech in the eighteenth century', *Dialect Notes* 6 Part 6 (July 1933) 313–334.

'The comment of British travelers on early American terms relating to agriculture', *Agricultural History* 7 No. 3 (July 1933) 99–109.

'The membership of proposed American academies', *American Literature* 7 (May 1935) 145–165.

Reeve, J. C. 'Henry Bouquet. His Indian campaigns', *Ohio Archaeological and Historical Quarterly* 26 (1917) 489–506.

Reichmann, Felix, 'The Pennsylvania Rifle: a social interpretation of changing military techniques', *Pennsylvania Magazine of History and Biography* 79 (1945) 3–14.

Rhea, Robert Lee. 'Some observations on Poe's origins', University of Texas *Studies in English* 10 (1931) 135–142.

Richardson, Jr., Robert D. 'The Enlightenment view of myth and Joel Barlow's *Vision of Columbus*', *Early American Literature* 13 No. 1 (Spring 1978) 34–44.

Rickett, H. W. 'John Bradbury's exploration in Missouri Territory', *Proceedings of the American Philosophical Society* 94 No. 1 (1950) 59–89.

Riley, I. Woodbridge. 'Benjamin Rush, as materialist and realist', *Johns Hopkins Hospital Bulletin* 18 No. 192 (March 1907) 89–101.

Ringe, Donald. *American Gothic: Imagination and Reason in Nineteenth-Century Fiction*. Lexington: University Press of Kentucky, 1982.

Charles Brockden Brown. New York: Twayne Publishers, 1966.

Robertson, Rev. Charles F. 'The attempts made to separate the West from the American Union', *Missouri Historical Society Collections* 1 No. 10 (1885) 1–60.

'The Louisiana Purchase in its influence upon the American system', *Papers of the American Historical Association* 1 No. 4 (September 1885) 3–42.

Robinson, Lillian S. 'Treason our text: Feminist challenges to the literary canon', *Studies in Women's Literature* 2 No. 1 (Spring 1983) 83–98.

Robson, Eric. 'British light infantry in the eighteenth century: the effect of American conditions', *Army Quarterly* 63 No. 2 (1950) 209–222.

Rogers, Alan. *Empire and Liberty: American Resistance to British Authority, 1755–1763*. Los Angeles: University of California Press, 1974.

Rogers, Colonel H. C. B. *The British Army of the Eighteenth Century*. London: George Allen and Unwin, 1977.

Rohrbough, Malcolm J. *The Land Office Business: The Settlement and Administration of American Public Lands, 1789–1837*. Oxford University Press, 1968.

Rollins, Peter C. 'The Whorf hypothesis as a critique of Western science and technology', *American Quarterly* 24 No. 5 (December 1972) 563–583.

Rollins, Richard M. *The Long Journey of Noah Webster*. Philadelphia: University of Pennsylvania Press, 1980.

Ronda, James P. *Lewis and Clark among the Indians*. Lincoln: University of Nebraska Press, 1984.

Rosen, George. 'Noah Webster – historical epidemiologist', *Journal of the History of Medicine* 20 (1965) 97–114.

Rosenberg, Charles E. *The Cholera Years: The United States in 1832, 1849, and 1866*. University of Chicago Press, 1962.

Rosenberg, Harold. *The Tradition of the New*. 1959: rpt. New York: McGraw–Hill, 1965.

Rothlisberger, Marcel. *Claude Lorrain: The Paintings*. 2 vols. New Haven: Yale University Press, 1961.

Royster, Charles. *A Revolutionary People at War: The Continental Army and American Character, 1775–1783*. Chapel Hill: University of North Carolina Press, 1979.

Rozwenc, Edwin C. 'Edmundo O'Gorman and the idea of America', *American Quarterly* 10 No. 2 (Spring 1958) 99–115.

Rucker, Mary E. 'Crèvecœur's *Letters* and Enlightenment doctrine', *Early American Literature* 13 No. 2 (Fall 1978) 193–212.

Rudd, Velva E. 'Botanical contributions of the Lewis and Clark Expedition', *Washington Academy of Sciences Journal* 44 No. 11 (November 1954) 351–356.

Rudwick, Martin J. S. 'The emergence of a visual language for geological science, 1760–1840', *History of Science* 14 Part 3 No. 25 (September 1976) 149–195.

Rusk, Ralph L. 'The adventures of Gilbert Imlay', *Indiana University Studies* 10 No. 57 (March 1923) 3–26.

Russell, Andy. *Grizzly Country*. London: Jarrolds, 1969.

Russell, Peter E. 'Redcoats in the wilderness: British officers and irregular warfare in Europe and America, 1740 to 1760', *William and Mary Quarterly* 3 Ser., 35 No. 4 (October 1978) 629–652.

Russo, James R. '"The chimeras of the brain": Clara's narration in *Wieland*', *Early American Literature* 16 No. 1 (Spring 1981) 60–88.

'The craft of Charles Brockden Brown's fiction'. Unpublished Ph.D. dissertation, University of Arizona, 1979.

'The tangled web of deception and imposture in Charles Brockden Brown's *Ormond*', *Early American Literature* 14 No. 2 (Fall 1979) 205–227.

Saar, Doreen. 'Crèvecœur's lucubration on the meaning of America: a study of *Letters from an American Farmer*'. Unpublished Ph.D. dissertation, State University of New York, Buffalo, 1983.

Sainsbury, John. 'The pro-Americans of London', *William and Mary Quarterly* 3 Ser., 35 No. 3 (July 1978) 423–454.

Sanford, Charles H. *The Quest for Paradise: Europe and the American Moral Imagination*. Urbana: University of Illinois Press, 1961.

San Juan, Epifanio. 'Spatial orientation in American Romanticism', *East-West Review* 2 (Spring-Summer 1965) 33–55.

Sauer, Carl Ortwin. *Land and Life: A Selection from the Writings of Carl Ortwin Sauer*, ed. John Leighly. Berkeley: University of California Press, 1963.

'The morphology of landscape', *University of California Publications in Geography* 2 (1925) 19–54.

Savage, Jr, Henry. *Discovering America, 1700–1875*. New York: Harper and Row, 1979.

Schultz, Lucille M. 'Uncovering the significance of the animal imagery in *Modern Chivalry*: an application of Scottish Common Sense Realism', *Early American Literature* 14 No. 3 (Winter 1979/80) 306–311.

Sears, John F. 'Timothy Dwight and the American Landscape: the composing eye in Dwight's *Travels in New England and New York*', *Early American Literature* 11 No. 3 (Winter 1975/76) 311–321.

Seelye, John. *Prophetic Waters: The River in Early American Life and Literature*. New York: Oxford University Press, 1977.

Sellers, Charles Coleman. *Mr Peale's Museum: Charles Willson Peale and the First Popular Museum of Natural Science and Art*. New York: W. W. Norton, 1980.

Seltzer, Mark. 'Saying makes it so: language and event in Brown's *Wieland*', *Early American Literature* 13 No. 1 (Spring 1978) 81–91.

Shackleford, George Green. 'Jefferson and the fine arts in northern Italy: "a peep into Elysium"', *America: The Middle Period*, ed. John B. Boles. Charlottesville: University of Virginia Press, 1973, 14–35.

Shaffer, Arthur H. *The Politics of History: Writing the History of the American Revolution, 1783–1815*. Chicago: Precedent Publishing, 1975.

Shapiro, Darline. 'Ethan Allen: philosopher–theologian to a generation of American revolutionaries', *William and Mary Quarterly* 3 Ser., 21 No. 2 (April 1964) 236–255.

Sheehan, Bernard. *Seeds of Extinction: Jeffersonian Philanthropy and the American Indian*. Chapel Hill: University of North Carolina Press, 1973.

Shepard, Paul, 'Dead cities in the American West', *Landscape* 6 (1956/57) 23–28.

Man In the Landscape: A Historic View of the Esthetics of Nature. New York: Knopf, 1967.

Shoemaker, Ervin C. *Noah Webster: Pioneer of Learning*. New York: Columbia University Press, 1936.

Shryock, Richard H. 'The health of the American people: an historical survey', *Proceedings of the American Philosophical Society* 90 No. 4 (September 1946) 251–258.

Medicine and Society in America, 1660–1860. New York University Press, 1960.

Shy, John. *A People Numerous and Armed: Reflections on the Military Struggle for American Independence*. Oxford University Press, 1976.

Toward Lexington: The Role of the British Army in the Coming of the Revolution. Princeton University Press, 1965.

Sickels, Edith. 'Shelley and Charles Brockden Brown', *PMLA* 45 (1930) 1116–1128.

Silverman, Kenneth. *A Cultural History of the American Revolution*. New York: Thomas Y. Crowell Co., 1976.

Timothy Dwight. New York: Twayne, 1969.

Simpson, David. *The Politics of American English, 1776–1850*. New York: Oxford University Press, 1986.

Simpson, George Gaylord. 'The beginnings of vertebrate palaeontology in North America', *Proceedings of the American Philosophical Society* 86 No. 1 (September 1942) 130–188.

Simpson, Lewis P. *The Brazen Face of History: Studies in the Literary Consciousness in America*. Baton Rouge: Louisiana State University Press, 1980.

Sinclair, Andrew. *The Savage: A History of Misunderstanding*. London: Weidenfeld and Nicolson, 1977.

Sklar, Robert. *Movie-Made America: A Cultural History of American Movies*. London: Chappell and Co., 1975.

Slaughter, Thomas P. *Whiskey Rebellion: Frontier Epilogue to the American Revolution*. New York: Oxford University Press, 1986.

Slotkin, Richard. *Regeneration Through Violence: The Mythology of the American Frontier, 1600–1860*. Middletown, CT: Wesleyan University Press, 1973.

Smelser, Marshall. 'The Federal period as an age of passion', *American Quarterly* 10 (1958) 391–419.

'The Jacobin phrenzy: Federalism and the menace of liberty, equality and fraternity', *Review of Politics* 13 No. 4 (October 1951) 457–482.

'The Jacobin phrenzy: the menace of monarchy, plutocracy, and Anglophilia, 1789–1798', *Review of Politics* 21 No. 1 (1959) 239–258.

Smith, Allan Gardner, *The Analysis of Motives: Early American Psychology and Fiction*. Amsterdam: Editions Rodopi, 1980.

Smith, Benjamin E. *The Cyclopaedia of Names*. London: T. Fisher Unwin, 1895.

Smith, Bernard. *European Vision and the South Pacific 1768–1850: A Study in the History of Art and Ideas*. Oxford University Press, 1960.

Smith, Henry Nash. *Virgin Land: The American West as Symbol and Myth*. Cambridge, MA: Harvard University Press, 1950.

Smith, Raoul N. 'The philosophical alphabet of Jonathan Fisher', *American Speech* 50 Nos. 1–2 (Spring–Summer 1975) 36–49.

Sontag, Susan. *Illness as Metaphor*. New York: Farrar, Straus and Giroux, 1978.

Sosin, Jack M. *Whitehall and the Wilderness*. Lincoln: University of Nebraska Press, 1961.

Sowerby, E. Millicent. *Catalogue of the Library of Thomas Jefferson*. 5 vols. Washington, DC: Library of Congress, 1955.

Sparks, Jared. *The Life of Gouverneur Morris, with Selections from his Correspondence and Miscellaneous Papers*. 3 vols. Boston: Gray and Bowen, 1832.

The Life of John Ledyard, the American Traveller. Cambridge, MA: Hilliard and Brown, 1828.

'Riley's narrative', *North American Review* 5 (September 1817) 390.

Spencer, Benjamin T. *The Quest for Nationality: An American Literary Campaign*. Syracuse, NY: Syracuse University Press, 1957.

Spengemann, William C. *The Adventurous Muse: The Poetics of American Fiction, 1789–1900*. New Haven: Yale University Press, 1977.

'Discovering the literature of British America', *Early American Literature* 18 No. 1 (Spring 1983) 3–16.

Spiller, Robert E. 'The cycle and the roots: national identity in American Literature', *Toward a New American Literary History: Essays in Honor of Arlin Turner*, ed. Louis J. Budd, Edwin H. Cady and Carl L. Anderson. Durham, NC: Duke University Press, 1980, 3–18.

Sprague, William B. *The Life of Jedidiah Morse, D. D.* New York: Anson D. F. Randolph and Co., 1874.

Spurlin, Paul. *Montesquieu in America, 1760–1801*. 1940: rpt. New York: Octagon Books, 1969.

Stafford, Barbara Maria. *Voyage into Substance: Art, Science, Nature, and the Illustrated Travel Account, 1760–1840*. Cambridge, MA: MIT Press, 1984.

The Standard Dictionary of Folklore, Mythology and Legend, ed. Maria Leach. London: New English Library, 1972.

Stanton, William. *The Great United States Exploring Expedition of 1838–1842*. Berkeley: University of California Press, 1975.

Starke, Aubrey. 'Poe's friend Reynolds', *American Literature* 11 (1939) 152–159.

St Armand, Barton Levi. 'The dragon and the uroboros: themes of metamorphosis in *Arthur Gordon Pym*', *American Transcendental Quarterly* No. 37 (Winter 1978) 57–71.

Stauffer, Vernon. *New England and the Bavarian Illuminati*. 1918; rpt. New York: Russell and Russell, 1967.

Steffen, Jerome O. *William Clark: Jeffersonian Man on the Frontier*. Norman: University of Oklahoma Press, 1977.

Stein, Roger B. 'Copley's *Watson and the Shark* and aesthetics in the 1770s', *Discoveries and Considerations: Essays on Early American Literature & Aesthetics Presented to Harold Jantz*, ed. Calvin Israel. Albany: State University of New York Press, 1976, 85–130.

'Pulled out of the bay: American fiction in the eighteenth century', *Studies in American Fiction* 2 (1974) 13–36.

Seascape and the American Imagination. New York: Clarkson N. Potter, Inc., 1975.

'Seascape and the American imagination: the Puritan seventeenth century', *Early American Literature* 7 No. 1 (Spring 1972) 17–37.

Susquehanna: Images of the Settled Landscape. Binghamton, NY: Roberson Center for the Arts and Sciences, 1981.

Steinberg, Paul Scott. 'On the brink of the precipice: madness in the writings of Charles Brockden Brown'. Unpublished Ph.D. dissertation, University of California, Berkeley, 1982.

Steiner, George, *After Babel*. Oxford University Press, 1975.

On Difficulty and Other Essays. Oxford University Press, 1978.

'Whorf, Chomsky and the student of literature', *New Literary History* 4 No. 1 (Autumn 1972) 15–34.

Stevenson, Lloyd G. 'Putting disease on the map: the early use of spot maps in the study of Yellow Fever', *Journal of the History of Medicine and Allied Sciences* 20 (1965) 226–261.

Stilgoe, John R. *Common Landscape of America, 1580 to 1845*. New Haven: Yale University Press, 1982.

Stone, Jr, Albert E. 'Crèvecœur's *Letters* and the beginning of American Literature', *Emory University Quarterly* 18 (1962) 197–213.

Storm, Colton. 'Lieutenant Armstrong's expedition to the Missouri River, 1790', *Mid-America* 25 No. 3 (July 1943) 180–188.

Stout, Janis P. *The Journey Narrative in American Literature: Patterns and Departures*. Westport, CT: Greenwood Press, 1983.

Stowell, Marion B. 'The influence of Nathanial Ames on the literary taste of his time', *Early American Literature* 18 No. 2 (Fall 1983) 127–145.

Streatfield, David C. and Alistair M. Duckworth, *Landscape in the Gardens and the Literature of Eighteenth-Century England*. Los Angeles: William Andrews Clark Memorial Library, 1981.

Struik, Dirk J. *Yankee Science in the Making*. Revised edn. New York: Collier Books, 1962.

Stuart, Reginald C. *War and American Thought, From the Revolution to the Monroe Doctrine*. Kent State University Press, 1982.

Surface, George T. 'Thomas Jefferson: a pioneer student of American geography', *Bulletin, American Geographical Society* 41 (1909) 743–750.

Sutherland, J. 'The legend and influence of Salvator Rosa in England in the eighteenth century', *The Burlington Magazine* 115 (December 1973) 785–789.

Sutherland, Judith L. *The Problematic Fictions of Poe, James, and Hawthorne*. Columbia: University of Missouri Press, 1984.

Symons, Julian. *The Tell-Tale Heart: The Life and Works of Edgar Allan Poe*. 1978; rpt. Harmondsworth, Middx.: Penguin, 1981.

Tallack, Douglas. 'Language and form in nineteenth-century American short fiction'. Unpublished D.Phil. dissertation, University of Sussex, 1982.

Tanner, Tony. *City of Words: A Study of American Fiction, 1950–1970*. London: Cape, 1971.

Taylor, E. G. R. 'The English worldmakers of the seventeenth century and their influence on the earth sciences', *Geographical Review* 38 (1948) 104–112.

Taylor, William R. 'A journey into the human mind: motivation in Francis Parkman's *La Salle*', *William and Mary Quarterly* 3 Ser., 19 No. 2 (April 1962) 220–237.

Teggart, Frederick J. 'Notes supplementary to any edition of Lewis and Clark', *Annual Report, American Historical Association* 1 (1908) 185–195.

Temkin, Owsei. 'An historical analysis of the concept of infection', *Studies in Intellectual History*, ed. George Boas *et al*. Baltimore: Johns Hopkins Press, 1953, 123–147.

Thacker, Christopher. *The Wilderness Pleases: The Origins of Romanticism*. London: Croom Helm, 1983.

Thomas, Keith. *Man and the Natural World: Changing Attitudes in England 1500–1800*. London: Allen Lane, 1983.

Religion and the Decline of Magic: Studies in Popular Beliefs in Sixteenth- and Seventeenth-Century England. London: Weidenfeld and Nicolson, 1971.

Thompson, Kenneth. 'Insalubrious California: perception and reality', *Annals of the Association of American Geographers* 59 No. 1 (March 1969) 50–64.

Thwaites, Reuben Gold. 'William Clark: soldier, explorer, statesman', *Missouri Historical Society Collections* 2 No. 7 (October 1906) 1–24.

Tichi, Cecilia. 'Charles Brockden Brown: translator', *American Literature* 44 (1972) 1–12.

New World, New Earth: Environmental Reform in American Literature from the Puritans Through Whitman. New Haven: Yale University Press, 1979.

Tillinghast, William H. 'The geographical knowledge of the Ancients considered in relation to the discovery of America', *Narrative and Critical History of America*, ed. Justin Winsor, 8 vols. Boston: Houghton Mifflin and Co., 1889, I, 1–58.

Tilton, Eleanor M. 'In the labyrinth of Charles Brockden Brown's prose: the Bicentennial Edition', *Early American Literature* 19 No. 2 (Fall 1984) 191–208.

Todorov, Tzvetan. *The Conquest of America: The Question of the Other*, trans. Richard Howard. New York: Harper and Row, 1984.

Toles, George. 'Charting the hidden landscape: *Edgar Huntly*', *Early American Literature* 16 No. 2 (Fall 1981) 133–153.

Tomory, P. A. *Salvator Rosa: His Etchings and Engravings After His Works*. Sarasota, FL: John and Mable Ringling Museum of Art, 1971.

Tompkins, Jane. *Sensational Designs: The Cultural Work of American Fiction, 1790–1860*. New York: Oxford University Press, 1985.

Treat, Payson Jackson. *The National Land System, 1785–1820*. New York: E. B. Treat and Co., 1910.

Trenton, Patricia and Peter Hassrick, *The Rocky Mountains: A Vision for Artists in the Nineteenth Century*. Norman: University of Oklahoma Press, 1983.

Tuan, Yi-Fu. *Landscapes of Fear*. Oxford: Basil Blackwell, 1979.

'Mountains, ruins and the sentiment of melancholy', *Landscape* 14 (1964) 27–30.

Topophilia: A Study of Environmental Perception, Attitudes, and Values. Englewood Cliffs, NJ: Prentice–Hall, 1974.

Tucker, Amy. 'America's Gothic landscape'. Unpublished Ph.D. dissertation, New York University, 1979.

Turner, Frederick Jackson. *The Significance of the Frontier in American History*, ed. Harold P. Simonson. New York: Frederick Ungar Publishing, 1963.

The Significance of Sections in American History. 1932; rpt. Gloucester, MA: Peter Smith, 1959.

Turner, H. Arlin. 'A note on Poe's "Julius Rodman"', *University of Texas Studies in English* 10 (1930) 147–151.

Tyler, Moses Coit. *A History of American Literature, 1607–1765*. 1878; rpt. Ithaca, NY: Cornell University Press, 1949.

The Literary History of the American Revolution, 1763–1783. 2 vols in 1. 1897; rpt. New York: Burt Franklin, 1970.

Van Astyne, R. W. *The Rising American Empire*. 1960; rpt. New York: Norton, 1974.

Vaughan, Alden T. *New England Frontier: Puritans and Indians 1620–1675*. Boston: Little Brown, 1965.

Vincent, Thomas Brewer. 'Keeping the faith: the poetic development of Jacob Bailey, Loyalist', *Early American Literature* 14 No. 1 (Spring 1979) 3–14.

Vincent, William Ellsworth. 'H. H. Brackenridge: frontier commentator'. Unpublished Ph.D. dissertation, University of Maryland, 1974.

Vitzthum, Richard C. *Land and Sea: The Lyric Poetry of Philip Freneau*. Minneapolis: University of Minnesota Press, 1978.

Voloshin, Beverly Rose. 'The Lockean tradition in the Gothic fiction of Brown, Poe and Melville'. Unpublished Ph.D. dissertation, University of California, Berkeley, 1979.

Von Frank, Albert J. *The Sacred Game: Provincialism and Frontier Consciousness in American Literature, 1630–1860*. Cambridge University Press, 1985.

Wagenknecht, Edward. 'The man behind the Dictionary', *Virginia Quarterly Review* 5 (April 1929) 246–256.

Wagner, Henry R. 'Apocryphal voyages to the north-west coast of America', *Proceedings of the American Antiquarian Society* N.S. 41 (1931) 179–234.

Waismann, Friedrich. 'Analytic-synthetic', *Analysis* 13 No. 1 (October 1952) 1–14 and 13 No. 4 (March 1953) 73–89.

Wallace, James D. *Early Cooper and His Audience*. New York: Columbia University Press, 1986.

Wallace, Richard W. *The Etchings of Salvator Rosa*. Princeton University Press, 1979.

Walton, John. *John Filson of Kentucke*. Lexington: University of Kentucky Press, 1956.

Ward, Christopher. *The War of the Revolution*. 2 vols. New York: MacMillan, 1952.

Ward, John William. *Andrew Jackson – Symbol for an Age*. London: Oxford University Press, 1955.

Warfel, Harry R. *Charles Brockden Brown: American Gothic Novelist*. 1949; rpt. New York: Octagon Books, 1974.

   Footnotes to Charles Brockden Brown: American Gothic Novelist. Gainesville: University of Florida Press, 1953.

   Noah Webster – Schoolmaster to America. 1936: rpt. New York: Octagon Books, 1966.

Warren, Charles, *Jacobin and Junto, or Early American Politics as Viewed in the Diary of Dr Nathaniel Ames, 1758–1822*. Cambridge, MA: Harvard University Press, 1931.

Washburn, W. E. 'The meaning of "discovery" in the fifteenth and sixteenth centuries', *American Historical Review* 68 No. 1 (January 1962) 1–21.

   'Review of German Arciniegas, *Amerigo and the New World*', *William and Mary Quarterly* 3 Ser., 13 No. 1 (January 1956) 102–106.

Washburn, W. E. and German Arciniegas, 'Letters to the Editor', *William and Mary Quarterly* 3 Ser., 13 No. 3 (July 1956) 448–453.

Watson, J. R. *Picturesque Landscape and English Romantic Poetry*. London: Hutchinson, 1970.

Watson, J. Wreford. 'Image geography: the myth of America in the American scene', *The Advancement of Science* 27 No. 131 (September 1970) 71–79.

   Mental Images and Geographical Reality in the Settlement of North America. Nottingham: University of Nottingham, 1967.

Wayland, John W. 'The poetical tastes of Thomas Jefferson', *Sewanee Review* 18 (1910) 283–299.

Webb, Stephen Saunders. 'Army and empire: English garrison government in Britain and America, 1569 to 1763', *William and Mary Quarterly* 3 Ser., 34 No. 1 (January 1977) 1–31.

Weigley, Russell F. *History of the United States Army*. New York: Macmillan, 1967.

Weinberg, Albert K. *Manifest Destiny: A Study of Nationalist Expansionism in American History*. 1935; rpt. Chicago: Quadrangle Books, 1963.

Weiskel, Thomas. *The Romantic Sublime: Studies in the Structure and Psychology of Transcendence*. Baltimore: Johns Hopkins University Press, 1976.

Weitenkampf, Frank. 'Early American landscape prints', *Art Quarterly* 8 (1945) 40–68.

Welter, Rush. 'The frontier West as image of American society: conservative attitudes before the Civil war', *Mississippi Valley Historical Review* 46 No. 4 (March 1960) 593–614.

Wheeler, Olin D. *The Trail of Lewis and Clark, 1804–1904*. 2 vols. New York: G. P. Putnam's Sons, 1904.

The Whiskey Rebellion: Past and Present Perspectives, ed. Steven R. Boyd. Westport, CT: Greenwood Press, 1985.

White, Hayden, *Metahistory: The Historical Imagination in Nineteenth-Century Europe.* Baltimore: Johns Hopkins University Press, 1973.

White, Morton and Lucia White, *The Intellectual Versus the City: From Thomas Jefferson to Frank Lloyd Wright.* Cambridge, MA: Harvard University Press, 1962.

Whittle, Amberys R. '*Modern Chivalry:* the Frontier as crucible', *Early American Literature* 6 No. 3 (Winter 1971–72) 263–270.

Whittlesey, Charles. 'Origins of the American system of land surveys', *Association of Engineering Societies Journal* 3 (September 1884) 275–280.

Whorf, Benjamin Lee. *Language, Thought, and Reality: Selected Writings,* ed. John B. Carroll. Cambridge, MA: MIT Press, 1956.

Wickersham, James Pyle. *A History of Education in Pennsylvania.* Lancaster, PA: Inquirer Publishing Co., 1886.

Wilbur, Richard. 'The house of Poe', *Poe: A Collection of Critical Essays,* ed. Robert Regan. Englewood Cliffs, NJ: Prentice–Hall, 1967, 98–120.

The Wild Man Within: An Image of Western Thought from the Renaissance to Romanticism, ed. Edward Dudley and Maximilian E. Novak. Pittsburgh: University of Pittsburgh Press, 1972.

Wilford, John Noble. *The Mapmakers.* London: Junction Books, 1981.

Willey, Basil. *The Seventeenth-Century Background: Studies in the Thought of the Age in Relation to Poetry and Religion.* Harmondsworth, Middx.: Penguin, 1962.

Williams, David. 'John Evans' strange journey', *American Historical Review* 54 (January–April 1949) 277–295, 508–529.

Williams, Glyndwr. *The British Search for the Northwest Passage in the Eighteenth Century.* London: Longmans, 1962.

Williams, Gwyn A. 'John Evans's mission to the Madogwys', *Bulletin of the Board of Celtic Studies* 27 (1978) 569–601.

Madoc: The Making of a Myth. London: Eyre Methuen, 1980.

The Search for Beulah Land: The Welsh and the Atlantic Revolution. London: Croom Helm, 1980.

Williams, Raymond. *Keywords: A Vocabulary of Culture and Society.* London: Fontana, 1976.

Williams, William Appleman. 'The age of mercantilism: an interpretation of American political economy, 1763 to 1828', *William and Mary Quarterly* 3 Ser., 15 No. 4 (October 1958) 419–437.

Wills, Garry. *Cincinnatus: George Washington and the Enlightenment.* Garden City, NY: Doubleday, 1984.

Explaining America: The Federalist. London: The Athlone Press, 1981.

Inventing America: Jefferson's Declaration of Independence. Garden City, NY: Doubleday, 1978.

Wilson, David Scofield. *In the Presence of Nature.* Amherst: University of Massachusetts Press, 1978.

Wiltse, Charles M. *The Jeffersonian Tradition in American Democracy.* New York: Hill and Wang, 1960.

Winans, Robert B. 'The growth of the novel-reading public in late eighteenth-century America', *Early American Literature* 9 No. 3 (Winter 1975) 267–275.

Winfield, C. H. 'Life and public services of John Cleves Symmes', *New Jersey Historical Society Proceedings* Ser. 2, 5 (1877) 22–43.

Winslow, Charles-Edward Amory. *The Conquest of Epidemic Disease. A Chapter in the History of Ideas.* Princeton University Press, 1943.

'The drama of Syphilis', *Journal of Social Hygiene* 23 No. 2 (February 1937) 57–72.

Winston, Robert P. '"Strange order of things!": the journey to chaos in *Letters from an American Farmer*', *Early American Literature* 19 No. 3 (Winter 1984/85) 249–267.

Witherington, Paul. 'Image and idea in *Wieland* and *Edgar Huntly*', *The Serif* 3 No. 4 (December 1966) 19–26.

'Narrative technique in the novels of Charles Brockden Brown'. Unpublished Ph.D. dissertation, University of Texas, 1964.

Wittkower, Rudolf. 'Marvels of the East: a study in the history of monsters', *Journal of the Warburg and Courtauld Institutes* 5 (1942) 159–197.

Wokler, Robert. 'Tyson and Buffon on the orang-utan', *Studies on Voltaire* 155 (1976) 2,301–2,319.

Wolf, Bryan Jay. *Romantic Re-Vision: Culture and Consciousness in Nineteenth-Century American Painting and Literature*. University of Chicago Press, 1982.

Wood, G. A. 'Ancient and Medieval conceptions of Terra Australis', *Journal of the Royal Australian Historical Society* 3 (1916) 455–465.

Wood, Gordon S. 'Conspiracy and the paranoid style: causality and deceit in the eighteenth century', *William and Mary Quarterly* 3 Ser., 39 No. 3 (July 1982) 401–441.

The Creation of the American Republic, 1776–1787. 1969; rpt. New York: W. W. Norton and Co., 1972.

'Rhetoric and reality in the American Revolution', *William and Mary Quarterly* 3 Ser., 23 No. 1 (January 1966) 3–32.

Woolley, Mary E. 'The development of the love of Romantic scenery in America', *American Historical Review* 3 (1897) 56–66.

Wright, Jr., J. Leitch. *Britain and the American Frontier, 1783–1815*. Athens: University of Georgia Press, 1975.

Wright, John Kirtland. *Human Nature in Geography: Fourteen Papers, 1925–1965*. Cambridge, MA: Harvard University Press, 1966.

'Some British "grandfathers" of American geography', *Geographical Essays in Memory of Alan G. Ogilvie*, ed. Ronald Miller and J. W. Watson. London: Nelson, 1959, 144–165.

Wright, Louis B. *The Dream of Prosperity in Colonial America*. New York University Press, 1965.

Wright, William H. *The Grizzly Bear: The Narrative of a Hunter-Journalist*. 1913; rpt. London: University of Nebraska Press, 1977.

Wroth, Lawrence C. 'The early cartography of the Pacific', *Papers of the Bibliographical Society of America* 38 No. 2 (1944) 87–268.

Yates, Frances. *The Rosicrucian Enlightenment*. London: Routledge and Kegan Paul, 1972.

Young, James Sterling. *The Washington Community, 1800–1828*. New York: Columbia University Press, 1966.

Ziff, Larzer. *Literary Democracy: The Declaration of Cultural Independence in America*. 1981; rpt. Harmondsworth, Middx: Penguin, 1982.

'A reading of *Wieland*', *PMLA* 77 (1962) 51–57.

Zink, David D. 'The beauty of the Alps: a study of the Victorian mountain aesthetic'. Unpublished Ph.D. dissertation, University of Colorado, 1962.

Zweig, Paul. *The Adventurer*. Princeton University Press, 1974.

Index

Abbott, Abiel, 70
Adair, James, 153
Adams, Henry, 12–13, 168
Adams, John 2, 54, 57, 64, 70, 73, 90,
    98–99, 107, 153, 159, 170
Adams, John Quincy, 223–224, 229,
    302n44
Addison, Joseph, 77, 138
Agamemnon, 91
agoraphobia, 68, 104, 167, 215, 236, 242
AIDS, 91
Aiken, Conrad, 1
Ailly, Pierre d', 9, 16
Allen, Ethan, 142, 143, 149–151, 160
Allen, Paul, 222, 317n1
Alliot, Paul, 162
Alsop, Richard, 45, 60, 61, 94, 160, 244
American canon, 20
American Philosophical Society, 54, 56,
    87, 128, 130, 155, 180, 181, 189
American Poems, Selected and Original,
    238
Ames, Fisher, 60–61, 90–91, 145,
    160–161, 307n36
Ames, Nathaniel, Sr, 46, 48, 49, 53, 58,
    60, 61
Ames, Nathaniel, Jr, 307n36
amplitude, rhetoric of, 11, 43, 49, 50, 99
Amundsen, Roald, 269
Analectic Magazine, 228
animals, *see under* bears, buffaloes,
    cougars, cows, dogs, elephants,
    jaguars, lions, mammoths,

monkeys, monsters, orang-utans,
    panthers, prairie-dogs, sheep, tigers,
    toads, whales, wolves; *see also* birds,
    insects, snakes
Antarctic, *see* Poles, North and South
Arabian Nights, 111, 271
Arctic, *see* Poles, North and South
Arnold, Benedict, 142
asylum, America as, 49, 51, 53, 54, 57,
    107, 244, 246
Audubon, John James, 204
Austen, Jane, 6

Bacon, Francis, 10, 91, 181
Bage, Robert, *Hermsprong*, 275, 276
Barlow, Joel, 54, 120, 223, 224, 225, 271
Barth, John, *Sabbatical*, 264
Barton, Benjamin Smith 141, 153, 191,
    193, 227
Bartram, John, 105–106, 123, 130, 154,
    209, 314n17
Bartram, William, 130, 305n19
Baudelaire, Charles-Pierre, 320n34
Baym, Nina, 20
bears, images of, 26, 37, 41, 62, 98, 107,
    149, 162, 208–210, 276, 277,
    300n18, 314n19
    grizzly, 209–212, 218–219, 221, 228,
    274, 275, 276, 314n19
    Polar, 209–210, 275
    relation to humans, 33, 102, 120, 129,
    131, 209–211, 272, 274, 321n41
Beautiful, the, 147, 148, 173, 174, 216;

Beautiful, the, (*cont.*)
  see also the Sublime, the
    Picturesque
Beaver, Harold, 265–266
Belknap, Jeremy, 66–67, 89
  History of New Hampshire, 55, 182,
    258
Bellini, Charles, 170, 171, 172
Berchtold, Count Leopold, 197
Bercovitch, Sacvan, 17
Bering Strait, 156, 189
Berkeley, George, Bishop of Cloyne,
    45–47, 53, 56, 85, 102, 110, 146
bestiality, fear of, 28, 33–34, 93, 141,
    143, 263, 264
  and Brackenridge, 123, 129–134, 218
  and Brown, 251, 255
  and Crèvecoeur, 102–103, 107
  and Lewis, 218
  and Poe, 266–267, 272, 275
  and Noah Webster, 79
Bible, King James, references to, 8, 11,
    14, 30, 47, 110, 208, 276
Biddle edition of Lewis and Clark
    Journals, 222, 227–228, 229, 230,
    265, 270, 271, 273, 274, 276, 278
Biddle, Nicholas, 222, 227
Bierce, Ambrose, 276
Bierstadt, Albert, 216
Birch, John, Society, 69
birds, images of, 41–42, 52, 79, 105, 114,
    129–130, 267, 276; *see also* eagles,
    nightingales
bloodletting, 95, 96
Bodin, Jean, 31
Bodmer, Karl, 216
Boil, the Benedictine monk, 39
Bond, Thomas, 54–55, 58, 85, 93, 163
Boone, Daniel, 51
Boorstin, Daniel, 8
Borges, Jorge Luis, 111
Bossu, Jean Bernard, 153
Bouquet, Colonel Henry, 24–25, 28,
    152, 184, 186, 198
Bowater, Major John, 43
Boyd, Julian, 169
Boyle, Robert, 67, 181, 197
Brackenridge, Henry Marie, 200, 212,
    225, 313n13
Brackenridge, Hugh Henry, 2, 62, 73,
    100, 109–111, 122–134, 140, 141,

    142, 143, 216, 218, 249, 266, 277
  Father Bombo's Pilgrimage, 110–113,
    122, 123, 127, 130
  Modern Chivalry, 127–133, 176
  'The Rising Glory of America',
    109–110, 122
  United States Magazine, 113, 122–123,
    125, 129, 131
Braddock, General Edward, 23–25, 27,
    41, 123
Bradstreet, Ann, 196
Bratton, Private William, 211–212
Breckinridge, Senator John, 151–152,
    163–164
Brentano, M. de, 29
Brodie, Fawn, 169, 170
Brontë, Emily, *Wuthering Heights*,
    324n16
Brown, Charles Brockden, 3, 4, 7, 17,
    20, 100, 107, 126, 127, 129, 134,
    151, 222, 230, 231–262, 265, 266,
    269, 270
  Addresses, 259–260
  The American Register, 258–259
  'Annals of America', 256
  Arthur Mervyn, 93, 243–248, 250,
    252–253, 256
  The British Treaty, 259
  Clara Howard, 253–254
  'Devotion', 231, 239, 244
  early letters, 232–234
  Edgar Huntly, 3, 6, 235, 248–252, 254,
    266–267, 274, 276, 277
  'Facts and Calculations', 255
  'History of the Carrils', 257
  Jane Talbot, 253–254, 256
  'A Jaunt to Rockaway', 256
  'Memoirs of Stephen Calvert', 236,
    246
  Monroe's Embassy, 259
  'On a Taste for the Picturesque',
    260–261
  Ormond, 241–243, 260
  'Signior Adini', 235–236, 239, 242,
    248
  'Sky-Walk', 235, 248
  'Story of Cooke', 234
  'The Story of Julius', 234, 254
  System of Geography, 260, 262
  'Thessalonica', 255
  translation of Volney's *A View*, 69,

182, 257–258
Wieland, 176, 236, 237–241, 274
Bryant, William Cullen, 178
Buell, Lawrence, 20
buffaloes, images of, 162, 192, 200, 203, 208
Buffon, Georges Louis Le Clerc, Comte de, 35–41, 52, 55, 56, 76, 149, 154, 163, 181, 212, 249, 276
Bunker Hill, Battle of, 27–28, 286n10
Bunyan, John, *Pilgrim's Progress*, 238
Buonincontri, Lorenzo, 9
Burgoyne, General John, 26–27, 249
Burke, Edmund, 26–27
 Reflections on the Revolution in France, 59
 A Philosophical Enquiry into . . . the Sublime and Beautiful, 146–147, 148, 150, 173, 179, 243
Burnet, Bishop Thomas, *The Theory of the Earth*, 34–35, 55, 58, 94, 208
 and Fisher Ames, 61
 and Dwight, 145, 150
 and Goldsmith, 41
 and Jefferson, 178, 179
 and Lewis, 206, 214
 and Poe, 267, 270
 and *Symzonia*, 268
 and James Thomson, 214
Burns, Robert, 60
Burr, Aaron, 143
Bush Hill, 90, 93, 245
Bushy Run, Battle of, 24–25, 27
Bute, John Stuart, Earl of, 35
Butler, Samuel, *Hudibras*, 209–210
Byrd, William, 314n19
Byron, George Gordon, Lord, 176

Caliban, and Brackenridge, 124, 129; *see also* Shakespeare, *The Tempest*
California, 16, 113, 189, 263
canals, 40, 120, 139; *see also* paths
cannibals and cannibalism, 11, 26, 28, 33–34, 37, 39, 93, 123, 267
Captivity Narrative, 248, 251, 252
Carey, Matthew, 92–93, 109, 245, 302n42, 308n10
Caribbean, 91
Carolina, North and South, 56, 104
Carrol, James, 82
Carter, William, 174

Carver, Jonathan, 67, 156, 191, 198, 226
Cather, Willa, 263
Cervantes, Saevedra Miguel de, 127
Chapman, John Jay, 19
Charles Town, 104
Chastellux, François-Jean, Marquis de, 165–166, 170, 174, 179, 180, 191, 194, 214–215
Chateaubriand, François René, Vicomte de, 130
Chatham, William Pitt, Earl of, 26–29, 32, 35, 287n12
Chaucer, Geoffrey, 175, 176
Chesapeake Bay, 115, 264
cholera, 92; *see also* disease, yellow fever
Clark, George Rogers, 142–143, 154–155, 189–190
Clark, William, 155, 190–193
 at the Great Falls, 207
 attitude to the West 196, 200
 journals of, 195, 197–200, 217, 278–280
 on absence of Shannon, 201, 212
 on death of Floyd, 201
 Poe's interest in, 272
 Yellowstone expedition, 218
Claude-glass, 147, 215–216
Cobbett, William, 90, 96–97
Cogswell, Mason Fitch, 238–239
Cole, Thomas, 12, 178, 215, 305n19
Coleridge, Samuel Taylor, 108, 176, 215
 'Frost at Midnight', 215, 237
Columbia University (King's College), 111
Columbian Centinel, 160
Columbus, Christopher, 8–11, 13, 16, 39, 43, 116–117, 119, 120, 121, 155, 196, 197, 204
 as model for interpreting America, 10, 14, 194, 259
Combe, William, 198
Congreve, William, 175, 176
Connecticut, 137, 146, 233, 235
Connecticut Valley, 148, 150
Connecticut Wits, 60
Conrad, Joseph, *Heart of Darkness*, 276
Constitution, United States, 84–85, 121, 133, 140, 158
Constitutional Convention, 139
Convulsions, terrestrial, 55, 58, 69; *see also* earthquakes, storms, volcanoes

Cook, Captain James, 36, 191, 196, 204, 235, 270
Cooper, James Fenimore, 17, 51, 106, 123, 250
    The Crater, 318n12
    The Prairie, 230
    Wyandotté, 287n15
Copley, John Singleton, 173, 241
Correa de Serra, Abbé Joseph, 180
Corruption, concept of, 57, 79; *see also* Virtue, concept of
Cosway, Maria, 166, 168, 171–177
Cosway, Richard, 166
cougars, images of, 208, 249; *see also* jaguars, lions, panthers, tigers
Cowper, William, 90, 99
cows, images of, 106, 209
Coxe, Tench, 139
Cramer, Zadok, *The Navigator*, 229
Crèvecœur, J. Hector St John de, 2, 17, 62, 100–109, 183, 216, 234, 277
    Letters from an American Farmer, 101–107, 109, 115, 116, 126, 130, 143, 145, 150, 267
    Sketches of Eighteenth-Century America, 107–108
    and Brackenridge, 126, 129, 130, 133
    and Brown, 107
    and Dwight, 149
    and Freneau, 112, 114, 115
    and Morse, 103, 104, 108
    and Rush, 103, 105, 107, 108, 141
    and Webster, 103, 105, 108
cultural anthropology, 5
Cunliffe, Marcus, 184
Currie, William, 54, 96
Curti, Merle, 63

Dante Alighieri, 176
Darwin, Charles, evolution, 33
Darwin, Erasmus, *The Botanic Garden*, 238–239, 248, 319n25
Davie, Donald, 20
Dayton, Jonathan, 158–159
Declaration of Independence, 1, 18, 42, 73, 84, 95, 97, 246
Defoe, Daniel, *Robinson Crusoe*, 35, 55, 102, 112, 115, 209, 269
demography, 47–48
Devèze, Jean, 96
Dickens, Charles, 245

Dickey, James, *Deliverance*, 264
Dickinson College, 88
Dickinson, Emily, 68, 250
Diderot, Denis, 34
disease, contagionist theory of, 93–94
    environmentalist theory of, 93–94
    as metaphor, 58, 78, 108, 265, 267
    as moral retribution, 91–92, 109
    see also cholera, malaria, yellow fever
Divide, the Continental, 213, 217, 228
Dobie, J. Frank, 276
dogs, Newfoundland, 208, 272, 274, 276
Donne, John, 10, 16
double, the, in Brown's work, 248–251
    in Poe's work, 265–266
Drayton, Michael, 'To the Virginian Voyage' 14–15, 110, 114, 118, 124
    Poly-Olbion, 121, 176
Dryden, John, 175, 176
Duck Soup, 73
Duff, William, 25–26
Dunlap, William, 317n1, 319n26
Durand, Asher, 178
Dwight, Timothy, 4, 70, 135, 143–151, 158, 164, 167, 174, 214–215, 216, 238, 251, 257, 277
    The Duty of Americans, 150
    Greenfield Hill, 144–146, 162, 164, 235
    Travels in New-England and New-York, 146–150, 154, 159, 257–258

eagles, images of, 79, 108; *see also*, birds, nightingales
Earlom, Richard, 231
earthquakes, 27, 35, 41, 55, 56, 145; *see also* convulsions, storms, volcanoes
    Lisbon, 35
Ebeling, Christoph, 65–69, 70, 104
Eden, America as, 2, 8–9, 14–15, 51–54, 71, 98–99, 103, 105–106, 112, 145–146, 156, 167, 268, 271; *see also* Elysium, Garden, Paradise, Promised Land
Egremont, George O'Brien Wyndham, Lord 136, 139
Egypt, 214, 226
Eldorado, 272
elephants, 42, 154, 155; *see also* mammoths
Eliot, T. S. 263
Ellicott, Andrew, 161, 198

Elliott, Emory, 246
Ellis, Henry, 287n18
Elton, Charles, 8, 270
Elysium, 8, 15, 171–172, 196; *see also*
  Eden, Garden, Paradise, Promised
  Land
Emerson, Ralph Waldo, 12, 16, 18, 259
English Civil War, 30, 287n15
environmental ideology, European, 8,
  22, 31–44, 51, 88, 275, *passim*
Evans, John, 153–154, 156, 194, 221
Evans, Lewis, *General Map*, 183

'Fabricius', 160–161
Faulkner, William, 'The Bear', 276
Federalist, The, 140
Federalists, 60, 62, 157, 159, 247
Fender, Stephen, 263
Ferguson, Robert, 181
Fielding, Henry, 244, 246, 247
  Joseph Andrews, 233
  Tom Jones, 132
Filson, John, 50–51, 53, 57, 103, 111,
  153
Fisher, Jonathan, 82
Fisher, William, *Travels of Lewis and
  Clarke*, 227
Fitzgerald, F. Scott, 'The Diamond as
  Big as the Ritz', 264
  The Great Gatsby, 277
Flood, The, 34–35, 39, 58, 112, 114,
  120; *see also* Noah
Floyd, Sergeant Charles, 197, 201, 278
Fonte, Admiral Bartholomew de,
  155–156
Forbes, General John, 287n12
Forster, E. M. 12, 16
Forster, John Reinhold, 36, 153, 209,
  314n17
Fort Clatsop, 217, 280
Fort Mandan, 191, 200, 202, 211, 279,
  280
Fort Pickering (Memphis), 220
Foucault, Michel, 84
Franco-British War, 59, 91
Franklin, Benjamin, 17, 45, 47, 67, 77,
  82, 92, 170, 181, 264, 321n45
  and the de Fonte hoax, 155–156, 192
  and Old World attitudes, 31, 44, 62
Franklin, Sir John, 209, 269
Frazier, Private Robert, 225, 278

Fredonia, 72–73, 83, 98, 224, 257
French and Indian War, 23, 35, 41, 43,
  59, 91, 134, 140
French Revolution, 58–61, 68–69, 78,
  90, 91, 92, 93, 126, 151, 160–161
Freneau, Philip, 2, 62, 72, 96, 100,
  109–122, 129, 131, 133, 140, 141,
  167, 187, 192, 215, 234, 236, 251,
  254, 311n47
  'The American Village', 111–112
  'The Beauties of Santa Cruz',
  113–114, 117, 118, 145, 175, 176
  'The British Prison Ship', 116
  Father Bombo's Pilgrimage, 110–113,
  122, 123, 127, 130
  Freeman's Journal, 117, 119, 257
  'George the Third's Soliloquy', 115
  'The House of Night', 115–116
  'The Hurricane', 116, 119, 267
  'Light, Summer Reading', 117
  National Gazette, 125
  'Ode . . . on Princeton College',
  121–122
  'Pictures of Columbus', 119
  'Reflections on the Constitution', 121
  'The Rising Empire', 120–121
  'The Rising Glory of America',
  109–110
  'Science, Favourable to Virtue',
  119–120
Fries's Rebellion, 126
Frontier Thesis, 18–19, 88, 93, 103, 141;
  see also Benjamin Rush, Frederick
  Jackson Turner
Fuseli, Henry, 241, 319n25
Fussell, Edwin, 268

Garden, America as, 125, 137–138, 150,
  152–153, 162, 192–193, 223, 225,
  226, 227, 229, 261; *see also* Eden,
  Paradise, Promised Land
  Lewis and Clark's images of, 200–204,
  206, 208, 213, 214
Gass, Sergeant Patrick, 208, 212,
  225–226, 227, 278
Genêt, Edmond, 59, 69, 78, 93, 142, 190
Genius of Britain, to General Howe, The,
  40, 42, 61
geology, 34–35
George II, King, 77
George III, King, 1, 67, 77, 103, 115

Germans, attitudes to, 89, 93
Gibbon, Edward, 40, 42, 61
Gilmer, Francis Walker, 180
Gilpin, William, 146–147, 148, 179, 215, 261, 320n34
Golden Gate Pass, 216
Goldsmith, Oliver, 40–42, 52, 55, 56, 61, 136, 145, 147, 197, 208
   The Deserted Village, 41–42, 111, 114, 144
Gorge of Saorge, 171–173, 174, 178, 182
Gothic, the, 62, 173, 238, 248, 252, 273
Grabo, Norman, 246
'Great American Desert', 162, 225–226, 273–274
Great Chain of Being, 33–34, 39, 41, 103, 123, 141
Great Falls of the Missouri, 207, 213, 214, 215, 216, 218, 227, 228
grid, the, 4, 120, 183–188; *see also* symmetry, human
Griffin, Thomas, 158–159
Grinder, Mr and Mrs Robert, 219–221
Griswold, Roger, 159
Grotius, Hugo, 23
Guthrie, William, 67, 71

Hall, Bishop Joseph, 15–16, 141, 224
Hamilton, Alexander, 126
Hamilton, William, 90
Hamilton, Sir William, 35
Hannibal, 215
Havana, 16
Hawthorne, Nathaniel, 11, 18, 243, 265
   The Blithedale Romance, 277
   Our Old Home, 18
Heidelberg, 173, 178, 182
Hell, America as, 2, 14–16, 39, 60–62, 105, 117, 208; *see also* Tower of Babel, the, world turned upside down
Heller, Joseph, *Catch-22*, 127, 132, 263
Herbert, George, 91, 318n17
Hesiod, 8, 14–15, 31, 115, 116, 175, 238, 270, 277
Hippocrates, 31, 36, 53, 54, 85–86, 87, 96, 310n33
Hitchcock, Alfred, *North by Northwest*, 187
Hogarth, William, 138, 171, 176, 188, 210

Hopkinson, Francis, 27
Horace, 176
Houdetot, Elisabeth, Comtesse d', 59
Hutchins, Thomas, 152–153, 186–188, 191, 198

Illuminati Scare, the, 68–71, 151, 242, 243, 319n26
Imlay, Gilbert, 51–53, 56–57, 88, 103, 111, 151
Indian tribes, Flathead, 200
   'Israelite', 153, 271
   Natchez, 191
   Shoshone, 217, 218
   Sioux, 202, 274
   see also Welsh Indians
Indians, white attitudes to, 23–26, 28, 33, 36, 40–42, 141; *see also* cannibals, Great Chain of Being
   and Brackenridge, 130–131
   and Brown, 249, 251, 258
   and Crèvecœur, 102, 107
   and Freneau, 120
   and Lewis, 218
   and Rush, 93, 141, 155
inexpressibility, literal, 7, 10, 216
   and Brown, 254–255
   and Dwight, 150, 277
   and Jefferson, 14, 172–173, 181–182, 277
   and Lewis, 214–216
   and Poe, 277
   and Stoppard, 16
inexpressibility, rhetorical, 7, 10, 113–114, 216
   and Freneau, 113
   and Jefferson, 172–173, 179, 214–215
   and Lewis, 214–216
insects, 39, 43, 105, 214; *see also* mosquitoes
Irish, attitudes towards, 89, 93, 130, 136, 234, 248, 249, 302n42
Irving, John, *The Hotel New Hampshire*, 314n19
Irving, Washington, 17, 270–271
Italy, 94, 147, 171–173

Jacobins, 59, 60, 61, 70, 126, 130
jaguars, 43; *see also* cougars, lions, panthers, tigers
James, Henry, 243, 250, 321n41

The Ambassadors, 243
Hawthorne, 11, 12
What Maisie Knew, 4
Jefferson, Thomas, 2–3, 18, 59, 70, 87,
  89, 102, 120, 134, 143, 150,
  151–195, 216, 225, 247
beliefs: geographical symmetry 72,
  192–193, 312n55; the aerial view,
  166–167, 207; novelty, 11, 76, 168;
  language, 83, 168; value of
  roads/canals, 120, 168–169, 172,
  177–179, 205, 309n15; value of
  records 165–169, 194–195
attitude to the West 151–156, 196,
  201, 226
'Description of Louisiana', 152, 157,
  161, 224, 229, 259
Notes on the State of Virginia, 52, 55,
  149, 153, 154–155, 174, 177–183,
  188, 195, 201, 203, 229, 258, 274
Second Annual Message to Congress,
  222, 226
and Monticello, 165–174, 177, 182,
  188–189, 193, 207, 216, 241
library of, 152, 165, 169, 170–174,
  178, 191, 198, 204, 206, 209, 235,
  258
and Europe, 170–174
and the grid, 4, 120, 183–188
views on 'imagination', 175–181, 189,
  190, 195, 204, 220, 235, 241
and Meriwether Lewis, 190–191,
  193–195, 220–221, 271
and the Lewis and Clark Journals,
  194–195, 217, 219, 222, 227
letters: to Breckinridge, 151–152,
  163–164; Maria Cosway, 171–172,
  174, 175; Priestley, 11–14, 167–168;
  Skipwith, 165, 169
Louisiana Purchase, 151–164, 196
sponsors exploration, 188–195
and Land ordinances, 184–185, 188
and the miasmatists, 52–53, 56, 71, 88,
  153, 181–182, 290n37
and the mammoth, 154–155
and nightingales, 52, 197
and Brown, 235, 240, 241, 246, 247,
  248, 252, 253, 255, 256, 258, 259
and Poe, 269, 271, 272–273, 274, 276,
  277
Johnson, Samuel, 77, 111, 313n4

Jones, George, *Ancient America*, 271
Jones, Sir William, 80

Kalm, Per, 36–37, 44, 49, 55, 56, 57,
  153, 191, 209, 274
Kames, Henry Home, Lord, 138, 171,
  173, 188
Kammen, Michael, 54
Keats, John, 196
Kent, William, 138, 193
Kentucky, 50
Kerouac, Jack, *On the Road*, 263
Kidd, Captain William, 272
King, Rufus, 139
King, Stephen, *The Shining*, 264
King Kong, 34
Krutch, Joseph Wood, 264

Lake District, English, 147, 233–234
land clearance, 54, 89, 106, 112
Land Ordinances: 1784, 184–185, 194
  1785, 185–188, 268
  1787, 'Northwest Ordinance', 185
landscape, definition of, 4
landscape gardening, 138, 170–171,
  173–174, 188
Landseer, Sir Edwin, 209–210
language as metaphor, 5–6; *see also*
  linguistics
La Rochefoucault-Liancourt, François
  Alexandre Frédéric de, 166–167,
  179, 191, 240, 319n22
Lathrop, Joseph, 90
Lawrence, D. H., 13
Ledyard, John, 189–191, 204, 221, 256,
  311n47
Le Grand, Joachim, 111
Le Page du Pratz, Antoine, 191–193,
  196, 202, 209, 312n60
Le Roy, Louis, 31
Le Sage, Alain-René, *Gil Blas*, 96, 117
Levin, Harry, 263
Lévi-Strauss, Claude, 11–12, 13
Lewis, Meriwether, 3, 6, 7, 190–230
  and Jefferson, 190–191, 193-195, 199,
  203, 220–221, 271
  appointed to Expedition, 190–191
  education of, 191, 193–194, 217
  attitude to the West, 190, 196–197,
  200–221
  journals of, 194–195, 197–200, 217,

journals of, (*cont.*)
  218, 219, 222, 277–280
  compared with Clark, 199, 217
  collapsible boat 'Experiment', 190,
    192, 212
  and the Rocky Mountains, 192, 205,
    213
  and the Missouri Breaks, 205–206
  and the Great Falls, 214–216
  and bears, 208–212, 218–221, 321n41
  attitude to Indians, 218
  and 'imagination', 195, 204, 206, 208,
    213–214, 220–221
  death of, 220–221
  and Brown, 239, 248, 251–252, 254,
    255, 261
  and James Dickey, 264
  and Symmes, 268
  Poe's interest in, 271–272, 274
Lewis and Clark Expedition, 3, 73, 83,
    134, 154, 155, 190–230, 278
  equipment of, 190, 192, 201, 212–213
  journalistic method, 197–200, 278–279
  Jefferson's instructions to, 194–195
  journey to Fort Mandan, 196,
    199–203
  journey to Fort Clatsop, 203–218
  return journey, 219
  achievement of, 213, 230
  responses to, 222–229
  Biddle edition of journals, 227–228
  Original Journals, 230, 271
  and Brown, 257
  Poe's interest in, 265, 270, 272, 274,
    275, 276
Lewis, R. W. B., 256
Lexington and Concord, Battles of, 25,
    27–28, 48
linguistics, Whorfian, 5
  Websterian, 79–82; *see also* language
    as metaphor, Tower of Babel
Linnaeus, Carl von, 106, 181, 193,
    238–239, 312n60
lions, 24, 26, 98, 107, 109, 274, 276; *see*
    also cougars, jaguars, panthers,
    tigers
Lisbon earthquake, 35
Literary History of the United States, 20
Livingston, Robert, 157
Lobo, Father Jeronimo, 111
Locke, John, 4, 10, 31, 102, 181, 184

Lorrain, Claude, 108, 146–147, 173–174,
    193, 202, 206, 231–233, 235, 236,
    239, 240, 261, 269, 272
  Liber Veritatis, 231
Louis XVI, execution of, 59, 91, 126
Louisiana, 151–164, 190, 191, 200, 213,
    219, 229, 259
Louisiana Purchase, 3, 135, 151,
    156–164, 168, 186, 203, 222, 223,
    224, 272
Louisville, 199
Lowth, Robert, 77
loyalists, 61–62, 79, 82
Lucian, 111, 196
Luttrell, John, 30–31, 287n18
Lyon, Matthew, 'The Beast of
    Vermont', 142–143

McCarthy, Senator Joseph, 70
Mackay, James, 154, 156, 194
McKean, Thomas, 161
McKeehan, David, 225, 278
Mackenzie, Alexander, 156, 191, 198,
    204, 211, 226
McNeal, Private Hugh, 218
Madison, James, 112, 140, 158
Madoc, Prince, 153
malaria, 94; *see also* disease
mammoths, 154–155, 160, 164, 196, 212,
    223; *see also* elephants
Mandeville, Sir John, 16
Marbois, François Barbé de, 181, 182
Mariner's Chronicle, The, 270
Marshall, Moses, 189
Martin, Ennalls, 94
Martin, Terence, 11
Marx Brothers, 73
Marx, Leo, 57
Mason, George, 139, 141
Massachusetts, 149
Matthiessen, F. O. 18–19, 115
Maximilian, Prince of Wied, 204, 216
Melbourne, Lord, 82
Melville, Herman, 12
  'Bartleby', 13
  The Confidence Man, 319n24
  Moby Dick, 277
Mercator system, 185
miasma, 35–43
miasmatist debate, 29–62, 152–155, 212
Michaux, André, 189–190, 194

Miller, Samuel, 17
Milton, John, 110, 146, 150, 175, 176
Mississippi River, 72, 118, 125, 135, 136,
    141, 142, 153, 156, 157, 158, 159,
    160, 161, 184, 224, 253, 259
Missouri Breaks, 205–206, 248, 251, 272,
    274, 313n13
Missouri River, 118, 152, 154, 159, 191,
    194, 200–207, 216, 221–227, 253,
    275
Mitchill, Samuel Latham, 67, 72, 143
Monboddo, James Burnet, Lord, 34,
    123, 153
Moncacht-Apé, 191–193, 203, 213
Mondrian, Piet, 187
Monongahela, or Wilderness, Battle of,
    23–24, 27
monkeys, 33, 38–39, 41, 62, 124, 245;
    see also orang-utans
monsters, 16
Montaigne, Michael, Seigneur de 11, 31,
    33
Montesquieu, Charles de Secondat,
    Baron de 31–33, 35–37, 41, 44, 51,
    52, 56, 80, 81, 102, 127, 138–139,
    140, 142, 143, 150, 152, 158, 160,
    164, 181, 224, 275, 310n33
More, Thomas, 15, 236, 242
Morrell, Captain Benjamin, 270
Morris, Gouverneur, 139, 159–160, 161
Morrison, Toni, *Sula*, 263
Morse, Jedidiah, 2, 62, 63–73, 90, 91,
    100, 216, 262, 277
    and Christian geography, 64–65
    on Williamsburg, 65, 163
    geographical method, 66–67, 71–72
    and geographical symmetry, 72, 192
    British models, 67, 71–72
    and the French Revolution, 68–69
    and the Illuminati Scare, 69–71, 242,
        319n26
    and 'Fredonia', 72–73, 118, 143
    and 'The Great American Desert',
        161–162
    and the Lewis and Clark Expedition,
        73, 225, 229
    and Belknap, 66, 67
    and Brackenridge, 127, 129
    and Brown, 69, 235, 242, 257, 260,
        319n26
    and Crèvecœur, 103, 104, 108

    and Dwight, 70, 150–151
    and Ebeling, 65–70
    and Freneau, 72, 118, 121
    and Jefferson, 68, 70, 71, 72, 181, 183
    and Rush, 70, 85, 92, 98, 99
    and Stiles, 65, 67, 69, 70
    and Webster, 71, 72, 74, 76, 77–78,
        80, 83
mosquitoes, 91, 96, 160, 214; *see also*
    insects
mountains: Allegheny, 72, 139, 151
    Alps, 215
    Appalachian, 46, 118, 136
    Blue Ridge, 165, 173, 177, 179, 182,
        192, 203, 205, 229
    Catskills, 174
    Green, 149–151, 160, 164
    Mont Blanc, 215
    Mount Soracte, 231, 261
    Olympus (Rowandiz), 165–166
    Pyrenees, 115, 209
    'salt', 152, 160, 224, 229, 259
    White, 148, 229; *see also* Rocky
        Mountains
Munford, Robert, *The Candidates*, 128

Nantucket, 103, 105, 267
Napoleon, 146, 157, 163
Natchez Trace, 219–221
National Intelligencer, 161, 225
Natural Bridge, 177, 178–181, 182,
    201
negation, rhetoric of, 11, 13, 16
New Orleans, 142, 157, 161
Newton, Sir Isaac, 121, 131, 181, 239
New York, 233
New York *Evening Post*, 152, 161
Niagara Falls, 27, 44, 177
Nicolson, Marjorie Hope, 35, 214
nightingales, 52, 196–197; *see also* birds,
    eagles
Noah, legend of, 39, 49, 50, 57, 104; *see
    also* Flood
Nordau, Max, 33
Northwest Ordinance, 185; *see also* Land
    Ordinances
Northwest Passage, 152, 155–156, 189,
    192, 203, 209, 253, 254; *see also*
    Passage to India
Norwalk, CT, 6, 235, 248, 274
novelty, rhetoric of, 10–11, 13, 168

Odell, Jonathan, 61–62
Oedipus, 91
O'Gorman, Edmundo, 10
O'Keeffe, Georgia, 264
Oldenberg, Claes, 314n19
Olson, Charles, 12, 263, 271
'On the American and French
    Revolutions', 58
orang-utans, 34, 39, 123, 124, 130, 133,
    266; *see also* monkeys
Ordway, Sergeant John, 73, 200, 204,
    207, 225, 229, 278, 279
Ortega y Gasset, José, 320n34
Orwell, George, *1984*, 79
Ossian, 112, 175, 176, 180
Otaheite, 32–33, 36
Ovid, 15–16

Paine, Tom, 48–50, 53, 58, 158, 287n13
    and John Quincy Adams, 224
    and Brackenridge, 128
    and Crèvecœur, 101, 108
    and Dwight, 145, 146, 149
    and Filson, 51
    and Freneau, 111
    and Hutchins, 152
    and Morse, 68
    and Ramsay, 163
    and Rush, 84, 85, 88, 90
    and Webster, 76
    Age of Reason, The, 59
    Common Sense, 32, 48–50, 53, 57, 59,
        60, 84, 104, 114, 118, 127
    Rights of Man, 50, 56, 59, 129
panthers, 120, 250–251, 266–267, 274; *see
    also* cougars, jaguars, lions, tigers
Paradise, America as, 10, 109–110, 273;
    see also Eden, Elysium, Garden,
    Promised Land
Parish, Elijah, 64, 161–162
Parnassus, 231
Passage to India, 120, 155; *see also*
    Northwest Passage
Pastoral, 89, 112, 118, 138, 208, 244,
    246, 247, 270
Patagonians, 128, 141
paths, images of, 67–68, 120, 168–169,
    172, 178, 205, 238–240, 242–243,
    249, 252, 276, 309n15
Pauw, Cornelius de, 37–45, 49, 50, 52,
    55, 61

Peale, Charles Willson, 154, 174, 211
Peckham, Morse, 237
Penn, William, 184
Pennsylvania, 235
    as golden mean, 53, 56, 71, 88, 121
    University of, 54, 85, 191, 193
Pequot War, 23
perceptual geography, definition of,
    3–4, 64
Petty, Sir William, 135–136, 138
Philadelphia, 89, 111, 117, 184, 211, 228,
    230, 233, 238, 257, 258, 266
    as paradigm of urban life, 53, 92
    Federal Procession in, 84–85
    plagues, 78, 88–98, 208, 257, 258
    as sink of iniquity, 89–90, 128–130
    in *Arthur Mervyn*, 243, 244–245, 246,
        247
Pickering, Timothy, 159, 186
Picturesque, the, 147, 149, 172, 178, 216,
    226, 234, 241, 242, 243, 248,
    260–261, 269, 319n25; *see also* the
    Beautiful, the Sublime
Pike, Zebulon, 224, 225
Pindar, Peter, 8
Pinkerton, John, 71
Piranesi, Giovanni Battista, 206
Pittsburgh, PA, 124, 126, 199, 225, 228
Plato, 9, 15
Pliny (Plinius Secundus), 16, 36
plough, image of, 54
Plumer, William, 159
Poe, Edgar Allan, 20, 82, 115, 134, 230,
    245, 248, 261, 263–277
    'The Domain of Arnheim', 273
    'The Gold Bug', 272, 275
    'The Journal of Julius Rodman', 271,
        274
    'The Landscape Garden', 272–273
    'MS. Found in a Bottle', 270
    'The Murders in the Rue Morgue',
        266
    The Narrative of Arthur Gordon Pym,
        265–277
    'The Pit and the Pendulum', 265, 276
    'Unparalleled Adventure of One Hans
        Pfaall', 270, 273
    and Brown, 265–268
    and *Symzonia*, 268–271
    and the Biddle edition of Lewis and
        Clark, 271–277

Poems on Several Occasions, review of, 19, 235
Poirier, Richard, 6
Poles, North and South, 209, 269–270
Polignac, Cardinal de, 34, 39, 266
Pontiac's War, 25
Pope, Alexander, 122, 138, 171, 175, 176, 206
Poussin, Gaspar, 147, 174, 193
'Power of Civilization and Freedom, The', 53, 54
prairie-dogs, 202, 224
Priestley, Joseph, 11, 68, 167–168, 172, 175
Princeton University, 67, 73, 84, 109, 111, 121–122, 132
Private Letters from an American . . ., 47–48
Project, The, 32
Promised Land, America as, 84–85; *see also* Eden, Elysium, Garden, Paradise
Pryor, Sergeant Nathaniel, 278
Puritan imagery of the terrain, 24, 46, 51, 84, 162, 186
Pye, Henry James, *The Progress of Refinement*, 275

Quincy, Josiah, 159

Rahv, Philip, 23
Ramsay, David, 56, 86, 89, 162–163, 182
Raynal, Guillaume, l'Abbé, 39–40, 42, 44, 55, 76, 89, 101, 181, 212
Redcoatism, 22–62, 98–99, 100, 184, 261, 270
  definition of, 23
Reign of Terror, 59, 69, 78, 79, 107, 108
Remington, Frederic, 216
Revolutionary War, 25–31, 63, 107–108, 115
Reynolds, Jeremiah, 269–271, 273
Reynolds, Sir Joshua, 138
Richardson, Jonathan, 174
Richardson, Samuel, 175, 176, 234
Rilke, Rainer Maria, 320n34
Rip Van Winkle Syndrome, 17–19
Rittenhouse, David, 47, 84, 89, 181, 187
rivers: Columbia, 159, 213, 217, 222, 223, 224, 226
  Connecticut, 233

Delaware, 234
Hudson, 178
Nile, 116, 189, 221, 226
Ohio, 118, 137, 148, 154, 155, 184, 186, 199, 223, 229, 253, 268
Potomac, 98, 177–178, 180–181, 203, 223
Red, 159
Schuylkill, 234, 239, 240, 319n21
Shenandoah, 203
Susquehanna, 108, 227
  see also Mississippi, Missouri
Robertson, William, 43–44, 50, 55, 56
Robin, Abbé, 110
Robison, John, 69–70, 91
Rochambeau, Jean Baptiste Donatien de Vimeur, Comte de 29
Rocky Mountains, 3, 6, 151, 156, 216, 226, 227
  height of, 151, 229
  and Brown, 254
  and Jefferson, 192, 194, 222
  and Stephen King, 264
  and Lewis and Clark Expedition, 3, 192, 194, 203, 205, 213, 215, 216, 217, 218, 223, 252
  and Morse, 72, 151, 229
  and Poe, 271
Rodgers, John, 70, 91, 98
Rogers, Robert, 64
Rogers' Rangers, 24
Romanticism, 176, 215, 237
Rosa, Salvator, 108, 146–147, 173, 174, 206, 213, 214, 215, 227, 233, 236, 248, 261
Rosenberg, Harold, 22–23
Rothko, Mark, 264
Rousseau, Jean-Jacques, 77, 233
Royal American Magazine, 154
Royal American Regiment, 24
Royal Proclamation of 7 October 1763, 136
Rush, Benjamin, 2, 4, 62–64, 70, 84–99, 100
  medical utopianism of, 85–86, 88, 90
  Frontier theory of, 88–89, 93, 103, 140–141, 161
  theory of disease, 86–88, 93–95
  and French Revolution, 90–91
  and Philadelphia plagues, 91–97
  and bloodletting, 95–97

Rush, Benjamin (*cont.*)
    and Washington, DC, 97–98
    and Sydenham, 86–87
    and Paine, 84–85, 90
    and mammoths, 155
    and Indians, 93, 153, 155
    and Brackenridge, 125, 129, 130, 131
    and Brown, 93, 238, 244, 245, 246,
        248, 251, 258, 262, 320n28
    and Crèvecœur, 105, 107, 108
    and Dwight, 145, 149
    and Freneau, 112, 117
    and Jefferson, 155, 167, 191, 202,
        312n58
    and Lewis, 191, 200, 202, 208, 216
    and Poe, 277
    and Webster, 77, 78, 82
Ruskin, John, 215, 237, 249
Rutledge, John, 173

Sainte-Beuve, Charles Augustin, 35
St Louis, 196, 197, 199, 200, 218, 219,
    220, 222, 279, 280
Sandys, George, 15–16, 34, 192, 203
Santo Domingo (Haiti), 91, 93, 159
Sauer, Carl, 3, 5
Scott, General Charles, 198
Scott, Captain Robert Falcon, 269
Scottish Common Sense Philosophy, 17,
    176
Shakespeare, William, 7, 175, 176, 211
    The Tempest, 11, 124, 129, 169
    The Winter's Tale, 209
Shannon, Private George, 201, 212, 278
Shays's Rebellion, 126
sheep, 44, 109
Shelburne, William Petty, Earl of, 136
Siberia, 189, 221, 269
Skipwith, Robert, 165, 169, 170, 171,
    173, 175
slavery, 34, 104, 114, 145, 158–159, 175, 266
Slotkin, Richard, 18
Smith, Elihu Hubbard, 238–239, 244
Smith, Henry Nash, 155
Smith, Rev James, 137–138, 146, 148,
    152, 154
Smith, Senator John, 159
Smith, Sydney, 17, 46
Smith, William, *Historical Account of the
    Expedition . . .*, 25, 28, 152, 184,
    186, 191, 198, 274, 285n5

Smollett, Tobias, 175, 176
snakes, 36–37, 39, 41, 43, 44, 57, 79, 98,
    107, 109, 160, 208, 273, 274,
    289n27
Snodgrass, W. D., 263
Snyder, Gary, 263
Sontag, Susan, 84, 90, 92
Southern Literary Messenger, 270
Sowerby, Mildred, 176
Spaight, Richard, 186
Spain, 125, 157–158, 161
Spectator, The, 171
Sprat, Thomas, 45, 48, 102
Stein, Roger, B., 299n6
Sterne, Laurence, 13, 175, 176, 225
Steuben, General Friedrich Wilhelm
    Augustus von, 27, 286n10
Stevens, Wallace, 263
Stiles, Ezra, 46–49, 50, 61, 65, 67, 69,
    70, 76, 95, 102, 163, 321n45
Stillé, Alfred, 95
Stoppard, Tom, 16
storms and tempests, 42, 55, 115, 226,
    207–208, 214; *see also* convulsions,
    earthquakes, volcanoes
Sublime, the, 147, 148, 150, 173, 174,
    178, 179, 180, 214, 216, 243, 264,
    269; *see also* the Beautiful, the
    Picturesque
Sullivan, James, 56
Swift, Jonathan, *Gulliver's Travels*, 31,
    124
Sydenham, Thomas, 86, 87, 94, 96
Symmes, John Cleves (1742–1814), 268
Symmes, John Cleves (1780–1829), 268
    Symzonia, 265, 268–270, 276
symmetry, geographical, 7–9, 34, 72,
    192–193, 223, 236, 257, 273, 312n55
    human, 40, 101; *see also* grid
Syntax, Doctor, 198
syphilis, 39, 43, 162
system, concept of, 68, 80, 87, 102, 120,
    260

Tanner, Tony, 6, 263
Tarzan, 34
Tatler, The, 171
Taylor, Edward, 46
Tennessee, 219–221
Theocritus, 30
Thomson, Charles, 178

Thomson, James, 89, 175, 176, 214–215, 227
   'The Castle of Indolence', 147
   The Seasons, 214
tigers, 40–43, 79, 109, 120, 212, 249, 266–267, 274; *see also* cougars, jaguars, panthers
toads, 39, 44, 61
Todorov, Tzvetan, 13
Tompkins, Jane, 20
Tower of Babel, images of, 5, 57, 80, 224; *see also* linguistics, Websterian
translatio emperii, 45, 47–48, 67, 77, 85, 99, 101, 110, 112
Travels of Lewis and Clarke, (anon.) 226–227
Treaty of Paris, 1763, 43, 49, 136, 161, 191
Treaty of San Ildefonso, 157
Trumbull, John, 28–29
Tucker, St George, 65, 163
Turner, Frederick Jackson, 18–19, 88; *see also* Frontier Thesis
Twain, Mark, *Huckleberry Finn*, 127, 132, 263
Tyler, Moses Coit, 20
Tyson, Edward, 34, 266

Underhill, Captain John, 23–25

vaccine, 190, 212; *see also* disease
Vanbrugh, Sir John, 175, 176
Vanderlyn, John, 174
Vattel, Emmerich de, 23
Vermont, 135, 142, 149–151
Vernet, Claude Joseph, 261
Vespucci, Amerigo, 9–11, 15, 16
   as model for interpreting America, 10, 14, 194, 259
Vesuvius, 35; *see also* volcanoes
Victoria, Queen, 82
Vilemont, Louis, 153, 157
Virgil, 89, 113
Virginia, 65, 142, 160, 167, 168, 181–183, 190, 207, 266
   University of, 167, 169
Virtue, concept of, 53, 54, 57; *see also* Corruption, concept of
volcanoes, 35, 41, 231, 238, 261; *see also* convulsions, earthquakes, storms
Volney, Constantin François Chassebeuf, Comte de 69, 77, 182, 257–258

Waismann, Friedrich, 7
Waldseemüller, Conrad, 9–10, 15
Walpole, Horace, 46, 94, 138, 147, 174, 288n20
War of 1812, 132, 286n6
Warton, Joseph, 112
Washburn, Wilcomb, 10
Washington, George, 23, 27–28, 45, 50, 58, 78, 84, 97, 101, 108, 117, 142, 159, 174, 186
Washington, DC, 92, 97–98, 167, 219, 220, 221, 223
Watson, James Wreford, 3–4,
'Watty Watersnake of Possum Town', 161
weapons: air gun, 190
   bayonet, 24, 27–28
   musket, 24
   rifle, 24–25
   tomahawk, 249, 251
Webster, Noah, 2, 62, 63–64, 73–83, 100, 137
   American Dictionary, An, 74, 79–80, 81, 82
   Compendious Dictionary, A, 74
   Dissertations on the English Language, 76–77, 81
   Observations on Language, 80
   Sketches of American Policy, 77–78, 137, 138, 146
   Speller, The, 74–77, 79, 81
   and epidemiology, 63, 86, 94
   and the French Revolution, 78–79
   and 'Fredonia', 72, 83
   and John Quincy Adams, 224
   and Brackenridge, 127, 129, 131–132, 133
   and Brown, 251, 256, 262
   and Crèvecœur, 103, 105, 107, 108
   and Dwight, 143, 151
   and Jefferson, 76, 83, 87, 152, 168, 194
   and Morse, 65, 71, 74, 76, 77–78, 80, 83, 92
   and Poe, 82, 274, 277
   and Rush, 77, 78, 82, 84, 85, 95, 98, 99
   and Stiles, 76
Weiskel, Thomas, 150
Welsh Indians, 153–154, 160, 164, 196, 200, 223–224; *see also* Indians, white attitudes to

Wesley, John, 35, 55, 91
West, Benjamin, 173, 241
Western Gleaner, 228
whales, 44
Whately, Thomas, *Observations on Modern Gardening*, 170–171, 172, 173–174, 195, 219
whirlpools, 8, 35, 238, 270, 276
Whiskey Rebellion, 125–127, 129, 157
White, Hayden, 282n7
White, Samuel, 157–158, 161, 162
Whitehouse, Private Joseph, 225, 278
Whitman, Walt, 19, 259
Whorf, Benjamin Lee, 4
Wilbur, Richard, 263
Wilderness, Battle of the, 23–24, 27
Wilkinson, General James, 143
Williams, Samuel, 55–56, 182
Williams, William Carlos, 20, 264–265
Williamsburg, 65, 67, 163
Williamson, Hugh, 56, 89, 154, 182, 258, 311n40
Wills, Garry, 179
Wilson, Alexander, 220–221
Winthrop, James, 140, 141
Wirt, William, 174

Wistar, Caspar, 191, 193, 194
Witherspoon, John, 67, 73, 122
Wolcott, Oliver, 67, 90
Wolf, Bryan Jay, 13, 150
Wollstonecraft, Mary, 51
wolves, 26, 62, 102, 115, 129, 131, 147, 149, 208, 209, 300n18
Wood, Gordon, 57–58
Wordsworth, William, 176, 215
world turned upside down, images of, 15, 29–30, 33, 40, 52, 55, 60–62, 83, 104–105, 114–115, 120, 208, 218–219, 224, 251, 263–264, 270, 276–277
Wren, Sir Christopher, 184

xyz Affair, 59

Yale University, 48, 65, 70, 74, 143, 146, 150
yellow fever, 91–98, 244, 245–246; *see also* cholera, disease, malaria
Yorktown, Battle of, 27–30, 59
Yrujo, Marques de Casa, 161

Zoffany, Johann, 174